The Center for South and Southeast Asia Studies of the University of California is the unifying organization for faculty members and students interested in South and Southeast Asia Studies, bringing together scholars from numerous disciplines. The Center's major aims are the development and support of research and language study. As part of this program the Center sponsors a publication series of books concerned with South and Southeast Asia. Manuscripts are considered from all campuses of the University of California as well as from any other individuals and institutions doing research in these areas.

RECENT PUBLICATIONS OF THE CENTER FOR SOUTH AND SOUTHEAST ASIA STUDIES :

Surinder Mohan Bhardwaj
Hindu Places of Pilgrimage in India : A Study in Cultural Geography

Murray J. Leaf
Information and Behavior in a Sikh Village : Social Organization Reconsidered

Robert Lingat
The Classical Law of India, translated by J. Duncan M. Derrett

Gordon C. Roadarmel
A Death in Delhi : Modern Hindi Short Stories

Elizabeth Whitcombe
Agrarian Conditions in Northern India.
Volume One : The United Provinces under British Rule, 1860–1900

THE LARGE SUTRA ON PERFECT WISDOM

This volume is sponsored by the

CENTER FOR SOUTH AND SOUTHEAST ASIA STUDIES,
University of California, Berkeley

THE LARGE SUTRA ON PERFECT WISDOM

with the divisions of the Abhisamayālaṅkāra

Translated by
EDWARD CONZE

UNIVERSITY OF CALIFORNIA PRESS
BERKELEY, LOS ANGELES, LONDON

University of California Press
Berkeley and Los Angeles, California

University of California Press, Ltd.
London, England

ISBN : 0-520-02240-8

Library of Congress Catalog Card Number : 71-189224

Photosetting by
Thomson Press (India) Limited, New Delhi,
and printed in the United States of America

Contents

Abbreviations

A : *Aṣṭasāhasrikā Prajñāpāramitā*, ed. R. Mitra, 1888
AA : *Abhisamayālaṅkāra*
AAA : *Abhisamayālaṅkārāloka*, ed. U. Wogihara, 1932-1935
Ad : *Aṣṭādaśasāhasrikā Prajñāpāramitā*
AdT : Tibetan translation of *Ad*
AK : *Abhidharmakośa*, trad. de la Vallée-Poussin
A.N. : *Aṅguttara Nikāya*
Asl : *Atthasālinī*
Cpd : *Compendium of Philosophy*, trsl. S. Z. Aung and Mrs. Rhys Davids, 1910
CPD : *Critical Pali Dictionary*
DaBhu : *Daśabhūmika*
Dhs : *Dhammasaṅgaṇi*
Divy : *Divyāvadāna*
D.N. : *Dīgha Nikāya*
DR : Dezhung Rinpoche
E : Edgerton, *Buddhist Hybrid Sanskrit Dictionary*
H : Haribhadra (=*AAA*)
JAOS : Journal of the American Oriental Society
J. As. : *Journal Asiatique*
JRAS : Journal of the Royal Asiatic Society
Ku : Kumārajīva
Lal. V. : *Lalita Vistara*
Madhy-v-t : *Madhyāntavibhāgaṭikā*
Mhv : *Mahāvastu*
Mhvy : *Mahāvyutpatti*
M. N. : *Majjhima Nikāya*
Mpp-s : *Mahāprajñapāramitāśāstra* =*Nag*
MsL : Ms of *P*, Cambridge Add. 1629
MsT : Ms of *P*, Tokyo, No. 234 in Matsunami's Catalogue
MW : Monier Williams
Nag : Nāgārjuna, *Ta chih tu lun*, trsl. E. Lamotte, 1944-1970, *Mpp-s*
Nar : Narthang Kanjur
ND : New Delhi Ms of Large P.P.=Gilgit manuscript
(Ob) (ermiller) : *Analysis of the AA*, 1933-1943
P : *Pañcaviṃśatisāhasrikā Prajñāpāramitā*
PDc : Pali-English Dictionary
P.P. : Perfection of Wisdom
PT : Tibetan translation of *P*
Pts : *Paṭisambhidāmagga*
PTS Dict or PDc : Pali-English Dictionary
R : *Ṛgs*
Rgs : *Ratnaguṇasaṃcayagāthā*

S : *Satasāhasrikā Prajñāpāramitā*
Sapt : *Saptaśatikā Prajñāpāramitā*
SaPu : *Saddharmapuṇḍarīka*
Si : *Śikṣāsamuccaya*
Siddhi : *La Siddhi*, trad. L. de la Vallée-Poussin, 1928-1930
S. N. : *Samyutta Nikāya*
Sn : *Sutta Nipāta*
Sten Konow : *The two first chapters of the Daśasāhasrikā Prajñāpāramitā*. Oslo, 1941
Suv : *Suvikrāntavikrāmiparipṛicha prajñāpāramitā*
T : *Taishō Issaikyō*
Ta : ch. 83 in Narthang III 130a7-147a6
Tb : other text of ch. 83
To : Tohoku Catalogue
Vbh : *Vibhaṅga*
V. M. : *Visuddhimagga*, ed. Mrs. Rhys Davids or ed. Kosambi

Preface

The translation of pages 37 to 430 (*abhisamayas* I-IV) normally follows the version in 25,000 lines which has been adjusted to conform to the divisions of the *Abhisamayālaṅkāra*.[1] In some passages of chapters 1-21 I have, however, translated the version in 100,000 lines,[2] or adopted readings of the version in 18,000 lines,[3] and of those various Chinese translations which seemed to represent an older or more intelligible text. For chapters 22-54 also I have generally followed the revised *Pañcaviṃśatisāhasrika*.[4] But portions of the original, unadjusted version in 25,000 lines,[5] as well as the version in 18,000 lines,[6] which are preserved in Gilgit and Central Asian manuscripts of the sixth or seventh centuries, are the basis of pages 229-239 (*P*), 339-362 (*P*), 363-367 (*Ad*) and 369-395 (*Ad*) of this translation, and I have followed them in those passages which occur in Ms. Stein Ch. 0079a,[7] although I have noted all the variants of *P* insofar as they affect the divisions of the AA.

Pages 431-643 (*abhisamayas* V to VIII, chapters 55-82) translate the Gilgit manuscript of the version in 18,000 lines, and I here simply reproduce, with the kind permission of Prof. G. Tucci, my translation as it first appeared in *Serie Orientale Rome* (1962 and 1974), though I have, where necessary, rearranged the sequence of the text to make it correspond to the divisions of the *Abhisamyālaṅkāra*. In the eighth *abhisamaya*, at VIII 1-3 and VIII 5,2,5-21, this correspondence breaks down altogether and I have therefore given the relevant text from *P* in pages 653-656 as an Appendix. Finally, chapter 83, Maitreya's Chapter, is missing in the Gilgit Ms, but is preserved in the Tibetan *Ad* (*To*. no. 3790), which corresponds almost literally to the Sanskrit text of *P* 578a-583b, which I have edited in 1968 in *Mélanges d'Indianisme à la mémoire de L. Renou*, pp. 233-242.

[1]For the Bibliography see no. 2A of my The Prajñāpāramitā Literature (= *PP*), 1960, p. 42.

[2]*Śatasāhasrikā prajñāpāramitā*, ed. P. Ghosha, 1902-1913; and Ms. Cambridge Add. 1630.

[3]*Aṣṭādaśasāhasrikā prajñāpāramitā*.

[4]i.e. for pages 203-228, 240-338, 367-370, 396-414.

[5]*PP* no. 2, p. 40.

[6]*PP* no. 3, p. 45.

[7]*PP* p. 46, i.e. at *P* 216a-217a, 223a-224a, 226b-228a, 241A-B, 242B-243A, 250b-251a, 256b-257a, 271a-272a, 294a-297a, 302b-304b, 305b-306a, 347, 357a-361b, 363a-364b, 367a-b, 381a-383a, 406b-407b, 408b-409b. Also Sten Konow's Ms (*PP* p. 45) for *P* 221 and *P* 313.

To philological purists, unacquainted with the particular problems of the *Prajñāpāramitā,* my procedure must appear questionable, and they will insist that I should keep the different recensions rigidly apart. There has, for instance, been some criticism of my superimposing the chapter headings of *Ad* on the text of *P,* which has no such headings. What motivated me was the belief that this exceptionally difficult text can be studied much more easily if broken up into relatively short and manageable chapters, and I chose those of *Ad* because *Ad* alone, in its Tibetan version, gives all the headings, whereas *Ś* and the unrevised *P* normally only number the chapters and give the headings just occasionally.[8] If there were even the slightest hope that each of the chief versions, i.e. *S, P* and *Ad,* might be translated in the foreseeable future, I would have stuck strictly to *P*. As it is, there is no such hope. What is needed at present is to make known the contents and message of the *Large Sutra* in its entirety and, aware of the execrable nature of the Nepalese Mss. on which alone the text of *P* can be based, I naturally relied frequently on the older manuscripts, which are more accurate than the often unbelievably careless and corrupt late Nepalese Mss.[9] This translation is a continuation of my work on the *Abhisamayālaṅkāra* (*SOR* vi, 1954), and there seems to me some value in showing how the headings of *AA* fit the text of *P*. This correspondence is, I admit, not always easy to see, particularly where the Path of Vision is concerned, but with some patience everything will become clear.

The most outstanding feature of contemporary *Prajñāpāramitā* studies is the disproportion between the few persons willing to work in this field and the colossal number of documents extant in Sanskrit, Chinese, and Tibetan. Looking ahead to the year 2,000, I would say that further study would have to proceed in three stages:

First, the general outlines of the argumentation of the *Large Sutra* must be determined, irrespective of the different versions and recensions. This is what I am trying to do in this publication, which has achieved its main purpose if it has rendered the course of the argument intelligible. In this context it must be admitted that my treatment of the lengthy repetitions lacks somewhat in consistency, and has been chiefly guided by the desire to cut down their bulk.

Second, the literal meaning of many now obscure passages must be ascertained with the help of the *Ta chih tu lun,*[10] which ought to be translated in its entirety into a European language.

After that is accomplished, it would be necessary and useful to scrutinize

[8]cf. *PP* pp. 47-50.

[9]There is the good news that *abhisamayas* II-IV will soon be published from the Gilgit Ms. by my friend Professor L. Lancaster of the University of California, Berkeley.

[10]*PP* p. 41.

the many versions and recensions of the *Large Sutra,* to note their differences as well as their agreements, and to try to work out their mutual interrelations. To attempt such a detailed study now would be to put the cart before the horse.

At the top of each page I give a page number, marked *P* and the appropriate section of the *Abhisamayālaṅkāra,* marked *AA*. The latter follows the numeration adopted in my English translation of the *AA*. *P* refers first, i.e., up to page 202, to N. Dutt's 1934 edition of *P*, and after that to the pagination of the Ms. Cambridge Add. 1628. I have used this Ms. in all my publications as the standard reference for everything I have said about the unpublished portions of the Large Sutra on Perfect Wisdom, because back in 1947 I thought it to be a particularly good Ms. Further study has revealed substantial omissions; for instance, between P 241 and 254 no fewer than ten and a half leaves are simply left out.[11] In spite of this, it will be better to continue to treat Ms. Cambridge Add. 1628 as a kind of master copy until we can refer to a printed copy of a critical edition of the text.

The translation could not have been accomplished without the help of many institutions and individuals which has been acknowledged with gratitude in the previous editions, i.e. on page v of part I as issued by Luzac & Co. in London in 1961, and on page i of parts II and III as issued in Madison, Wisconsin in 1964, and again in Seattle, Washington in 1966.

OṂ NAMO BHAGAVATYAI ĀRYAPRAJÑĀPĀRAMITĀYAI!

Berkeley, California E. C.

[11]They are: P 240A, B, 242A, B, 243A, B, C, D, E, 253A, B.—This state of affairs has misled N. Dutt and myself (*PP* p. 43) into affirming that 'one can notice some desire to abbreviate the treatment of the merit derived from perfect wisdom to which *A* ch. 3-5 and *S* ch. 17-23 devote a great deal of space'. What we did was to count the pages instead of reading them, and we failed to see that 21 pages in this Ms. were missing in this section.—Further imperfections of MS. Add. 1628 are that *P* 233 is missing, *P* 264 follows after *P* 265 instead of preceding it, *P* 282 is missing, while *P* 283 occurs twice, and *P* 319, also occurring twice, had to be renumbered *P* 319A and 319B.

Chapter Headings of

THE PERFECT WISDOM IN 18,000 LINES

Divisions of the Abhisamayālaṅkāra

INTRODUCTION TO CHAPTERS 1-21

A

A1. The book opens with an account of the *scene and circumstances of the sermon.*

On the first page we have a condensed description of both *Arhats* and *Bodhisattvas.* The contrast between the two goes through the argument of the entire book. The epithets used here are explained in great detail by Nāgārjuna.[1]

The remainder of the description of A1 is designed to establish the authority of the Sutra. A section on "Entrusting"[2] towards the end of the Sutra has the same end in view. In the "Introduction", the preaching of perfect wisdom is credited with three excellencies:

1. It is valid independent of temporal or spatial circumstances, at all times, and throughout the universe. This claim is less presumptuous than it may sound at first sight because the assertions of this book are really no assertions at all and that is why they can endure.

2. It proceeds from the highest level of spirituality, i.e. from the Buddha himself. The Buddha does not teach it in his human body—which could be seen in Magadha about 500 B.C.—but in his glorified "body". The "glorified body" of the Lord is either called here *āsecanaka-ātmabhāva,*[3] i.e. the body which is so beautiful that the beholder can never be satiated with looking at it;[4] or it is call *prakṛty-ātmabhāva,* literally the body which brings out, or corresponds to, his "essential original nature", here rendered as "extraordinary body".[5] "The Buddha always had this body—when he was born, when

[1] *Mpp-s. Le traité etc.* pp. 203-219 and 316-428.

[2] *parīndanā. A* xxxviii 460-464; xxxii 527-529 = *S* L 177a sq = *P* 447a sq.

[3] *P* 11-13, but not in Gilgit MS.

[4] from *SHIC,* to satisfy; or *SIC,* to sprinkle; cf. *CPD,* "unmixed, unadulterated", "with full and unimpaired properties"; or *SIC.,* cs, to saturate.

[5] so Gilgit MS; *P* 10 *ātmabhāvam prākṛitam.* The idea is well brought out by a passage in the Pali *Dīghanikāya* (xviii 17 = xix 16). "When, O Lord, Brahma Sanaṃkumāra appears (*pātu bhavati*) among the Gods of the Thirty-three, he appears after having created (*abhinimmitvā*) a gross (material) body (*olārikam attabhāvam*). For that which is the natural appearance (*pakativaṇṇo*) of Brahmā, that, O Lord, is not sufficiently materialised to impress their vision (*anabhisambhavanīyo... cakkhupathasmin*)."—Instead of "extraordinary" one might have translated "natural", "primary", "original", "real", "usual".

he became a Buddha, when he turned the wheel of dharma. That is why beings can say to themselves, 'What I now see that is truly the Buddha's body'," and thereby those who hesitated so far can be delivered through their faith.[6]

The wonderful qualities of the Buddha and his great wonder-working power are taken as tokens of his capacity to teach the real truth about the actual facts of existence. Power and knowledge go together. Omniscience implies omnipotence and omnipresence. The descriptions wish to magnify the Buddha's stature in the eyes of the reader, and to generate and foster an attitude of pure faith in his authority. At the same time they counteract the notion that the Buddha is a mere man, with a man's imperfections and limitations, and they try to give an idea of his true body and personality which are immense and inconceivable.

3. The teaching has not only an intellectual and spiritual, but also a cosmic significance. The universe vibrates in consonance with it, and gives its consent to its message. A series of cosmic miracles precedes the teaching of this, as of other Mahayana Sutras. We speak of a "miracle" when occult or spiritual forces visibly transform or overlay the natural world in such a way as to produce wonder and awe. The description of A1 is a mythological way of conveying the idea that the spirit is victorious over matter. E. Lamotte has divided the drama of A1 into 10 scenes. The translation follows his division.

A2. Secondly, there is a survey of the *aims* one may have in view *in cultivating perfect wisdom.* The translation follows P, which has carried out extensive rearrangements in the text of S, omitted many passages, and added a few. The purpose was to make this section appear as a teaching about the "thought of enlightenment"—first (P 18-19, 1 a-d) about the thought of enlightenment in general, and secondly (P 19-37, le) about its 22 kinds.

The "thought of enlightenment" is (a) the decision to win full enlightenment, or all-knowledge; (b) the desire for the welfare of others. Emptiness and compassion are its two constituents.[7] It makes one into a Bodhisattva. The term is used twofold[8]: 1. For the initial, first, production of the thought of enlightenment, the "vow"[9]. 2. For the marching towards[10] enlightenment. In the second sense it covers the entire career of a Bodhisattva, and its 22 forms correspond to its stages (cf. III1f), and end in Buddhahood. The 22 kinds of P are also found in Asaṅga's

[6] *Nag.* 518-9.

[7] *śūnyatā-karuṇā-garbha. H.*

[8] *H* 16.

[9] *praṇidhi.*

[10] *prasthāna*=setting out, see CII,4.

Sūtrālaṃkāra (ch. IV. 15-20), although in a different order.

A3. Thirdly, there are various *preliminary instructions*, which aim throughout at contrasting the Bodhisattva-doctrine of the great vehicle with the teachings of the Disciples, and at correcting the views and practices of the Disciples by infusing them with the spirit of emptiness.

In the first pages (A3a), we get a brief statement about the *nature of reality*, and about the *attitude* to be adopted towards it. Things, or "dharmas", are, by their nature, empty; they are really emptiness itself. We cannot "get at" them, but only at their names, which do not really represent them. We therefore should not "review" anything at all, should not "settle down" in anything.

It is noteworthy that the ontology of the Prajñāpāramitā is represented here, and elsewhere (cf. P 39, 99, 150), as a simple continuation, or extension, of the traditional Buddhist doctrine of "not-self" *(an-attā)*. It is supposed to be well known and agreed upon that the "self", and other expressions which imply a "self", such as "being", "living soul", "person", "organism", "individual", "one who feels", "agent", or "thinking subject", etc. are mere words, to which in ultimate reality nothing at all corresponds. What is true of the self is now said to be true also of all other supposed entities which, in their differentiation, are data which somehow imply a separate self, and therefore will be unreal on the level of accomplished self-extinction on which alone the truth becomes discernible.

A3b. It is then said that the wisdom of a Bodhisattva is superior to that of the Arhats, because in his compassion he puts it at the disposal of all beings, so that they may be able to win Nirvana. This superiority is based on the "thought of enlightenment" (see A2), and the 6 perfections (P 41), and it finds an expression in the fact that, as the source of all that is good in the world, the Bodhisattvas are worthy of the gifts of all beings, including the Arhats.

A3c. The preliminary instructions next deal with the *Yoga of perfect wisdom*. The translation is not easy to follow because of the ambiguities of the word *yoga*, and of its derivatives *yukta* and *yojayati*, which are used in many shades of meaning, and have to be rendered by "joins", "join up", "undertaking", "endeavour", "endeavouring", "discipline", and so on.

The argument begins with a reinterpretation of the *four holy Truths* of the sermon at Benares (A-D). The connection is not immediately obvious at first sight, and requires prolonged study to be noticed.[11] Then follows a discourse on the first two "Jewels", i.e. the *Buddha* (E) and the *Dharma* (F). The third, the *Saṃgha*, the Community of Saints, is dealt with in A3d.

[11] *A-C* form the core of the *Heart Sutra*.

A3d. The remaining instructions have in common that they begin with the formula "there are Bodhisattvas, great beings". They deal with the various kinds of Bodhisattvas. First of all (A3dI) they consider the differences which *arise from the circumstances of their rebirth,* and their place on the spiritual ladder. The decisive experience of a Buddhist takes place when he "wins the Path". He then ceases to be a common man, and becomes a "saint", or *ārya.* The classification of the "saintly, or holy persons" (*āryapudgalā*) had, early on, occupied the minds of the scholastics, and this section of the Sutra may usefully be compared with the Pali *Puggalapaññatti,* and with Vasubandhu's *Abhidharmakośa.*

I have not discovered the principle which underlies the classification adopted by S. P read into the text a scheme of 20 different kinds of saints, all of them "irreversible" according to H. But P had to make considerable rearrangements, as well as some additions and omissions. In a general way the types seem arranged, both in S and in P, in an ascending order of worth. The enumeration begins with the "Streamwinner", and ends with the last stage of a Bodhisattva's career, when he has become a Buddha.

This leads to a number of remarks on a variety of *practices,* or endowments, of a Buddha (A3dII), first of all *perfect purity* (1), and *all-knowledge* (2, 3); and then the *five eyes* (4), the *six superknowledges* (5), and the *knowledge of all modes* and *evenmindedness* (6).

The *five eyes,* or kinds of vision (A3dII4) of a Buddha are mentioned quite early on in Buddhist history. The account here agrees in general with the tradition of the older schools. The essential objects of each "eye", are, according to H :1. separate differentiated things; 2. decease and rebirth of beings[12]; 3. all dharmas viewed in direct intuition, without intervention of any discursive thought (*avikalpana*)[13]; 4. the faculty of attainment (*adhigama*) peculiar to different kinds of saints[14]; 5. all dharmas which are fully understood (*abhisambodha*) in all their aspects and modes.[15] The insistence on the nonapprehension of the five "eyes" is the special instruction here.

The list of the *six superknowledges* (A3dII5) likewise belongs to the traditional lore of the Buddhists. The first five describe psychic qualities, the sixth is peculiar to the Buddha. The special instruction consists, according to H, in that they should be seen from the standpoint of the Absolute as "quiescent from the outset".[16]

[12]The heavenly eye sees beings and things which are found in the six places of rebirth.

[13]The wisdom eye knows the true character of dharmas. *Nag.* 439.

[14]The dharma-eye sees by which means (*upāya*) and which teaching (*dharma*) a given person finds the Path. *Nag.* 439.

[15]The Buddha-eye is the direct intuition of all dharmas. *Nag.* 439.

[16]*ādi-śāntatvena-avabodha. H.*

A3dII6. Finally, there is a short discussion of two prerogatives of a Buddha: 1. *The knowledge of all modes,* which does not proceed by opposing one concept to another, and which is not an act of mind, and 2. an *evenmindedness* to which all dharmas are the same, and identical. H treats A3dII6 as a part of A3dII5. In several texts the magical power "without outflows" is equated with evenmindedness.[17]

A4. The preliminary instructions are concluded by an *Interlude,* which falls into three parts: In the second part the great Disciples give their assent to the instructions; they acknowledge the superiority of the perfection of wisdom of the Bodhisattvas, and the Buddha once more (cf. A3b) explains that the Bodhisattvas are the source of all the good there is in the world. The first and third parts deal briefly with the prediction of the future Buddhahood of various members of the assembly. The descriptions follow in general the stereotyped lines laid down in early Mahayana Sutras. They have, however, some special features which also appear in two passages of the *Ashta,*[18] which are later additions. The parallel suggests that this section of the Sutra was composed about the time of the Christian era, i.e. between 50 B.C. and 50 A.D.

B

It is only at this point that the central theme of the Prajñāpāramitā is reached. All the many thousand lines of this Sutra can be summed up in two sentences: 1. One should become a Bodhisattva (a Buddha-to-be), i.e. someone content with nothing less than all-knowledge attained through the perfection of wisdom for the sake of all living beings. 2. There is no such thing as a Bodhisattva, or all-knowledge, or a "being", or the perfection of wisdom, or an attainment. The solution of this dilemma lies in nothing else than the fearless acceptance of both contradictory facts.

The *phases of the extinction of self,* or of anything it may be based on, is the common theme of B. B1 reiterates the teaching of A1, that the doctrine preached here proceeds from the Buddha's might, who ever may give utterance to it. At the beginning of B2 the central theme is then stated. Thereafter, chapter 2 of S (=B2) is an expansion and restatement of the short outline of the teaching in A3a. The Bodhisattva, and all that he is made of, is *a mere word, inaccessible as dharma,* or as factual reality. If B2 were regarded as an attempt at argumentation, it would be unduly prolix. It aims, however at describing a repetitive meditation which is designed to bring about a certain state of mind, and not merely to convince the intellect, but to reform the whole personality.

[17]*Nag.* 330 n. 1.

[18]ch. 19 end, ch. 28 beginning.

B3. Chapter 3 of S begins with some obscure and cryptic remarks about the *degrees of ripeness in insight,* which are difficult to follow because the terminology is unfamiliar, and the argument relies to some extent on a play of words. The passage is, however, important in that it sets the theme for the remainder of B.

B3 contrasts, by a series of allusions, the distinctive attitude of a Bodhisattva with that of a Disciple. When a Disciple practises the meditation on the (16) aspects, or attributes, of the four holy Truths, i.e. impermanence, etc.,[19] he uses it as an antidote to the belief in a separate individual self. With this end in view he "settles down" in the conviction that impermanence, etc., represent actual properties of actual facts (dharmas). The Bodhisattva, on the other hand, contemplates those same aspects as antidotes to a belief in separate dharmas. He can therefore accuse the Disciple of a "craving for separate dharmas" (*dharmatṛishṇā*), "craving" being the very opposite of the emancipation intended by such contemplations.

A Bodhisattva who adopts the Disciples' methods is characterised by "rawness", or "immaturity". The translation is here somewhat unintelligible because the argument relies on contrasting two Sanskrit words, *āmah* and *ny-āmah. Nyāma,* Pali *ni-yāma,* means "the way of salvation", "the certainty of winning salvation by pursuing a certain way". Buddhist etymology derives *nyāma* from *āma,* "raw, crude, immature"—as *nis-āma* "de-rawing, ripening".[20] "Rawness" is identified with the defilements, and the condition of being an ordinary unconverted person.

One distinguishes (at P 182) the distinctive Bodhisattva's "way of salvation" from that of a Disciple[21] and of a Pratyekabuddha.[22] The term *nyāma* denotes that stage at which each type knows for certain that they will, by their own distinctive methods, win the particular kind of salvation of which they are capable, i.e. Arhatship, Pratyekabuddha-enlightenment, full enlightenment. In the case of Bodhisattvas one can also say that they "enter into the fixed condition of a Bodhisattva" (as *nyāma* is translated at P 66). At P 107 the entrance into the *bodhisattva-niyāma* is mentioned together with the entrance into the irreversible stage.

The stage of certainty is preceded by another stage of which it is a characteristic that one can "fall" from it. Traditionally that stage is known as the "Summits". The scholastics of the Sarvāstivādins distin-

[19]For the list see my *Buddhist Meditation,* 1956, pp. 142-146.

[20]Tibetan: *nyāma = skyon med-pa,* absence of fault; *niyāma = ṅes-par'gyur-ba* = fixed determination, what is certain to come about.

[21]Also called *samyaktva-niyāma* in *A* ii 38, as Pali *sammattaniyāma-avakkanti. samyaktva* = Nirvana at *A.K.* vi 181.

[22]so *H* 903, 14 opposes *bodhisattva-nyāma-avakrānti* to *śrāvaka-pratyekabuddhabodhi.* Similarly *P* 21.

guished four stages preceding entrance into the Path by the name of "Aids to penetration" (*nirvedhabhāgīyā*). They bore the names "Heat", "Summits", "Patience", "Supreme mundane dharmas". In the text here they are referred to by the term "wholesome roots". The Aids to penetration are parts of the preparatory path (*prayogamārga*) which leads up to the intuition of the truth (*satya-abhisamaya*) in the Streamwinner, and they have the four Truths in their 16 aspects for object. On the second stage, the "Summits" (*mūrdhan*), one has yet little faith in the three Jewels, and from it one can "fall". The definition of the "Summits" which the Sutra here has in view is given in the *Abhidharmakośa*[23] : "They are called 'Summits' because they are the highest among the unfixed (*a-cala*) wholesome roots, i.e. of those from which one can fall; either one falls back from them, or one goes beyond them into the (next stage of) Patience". The third stage Patience (*kshānti*), seems alluded to in the phrase "adaptable craving for dharmas"[24] in the text. It implies a contrast to "patience conforming to dharmas",[25] which is an attitude to be adopted relative to "deep dharmas," and the descriptions given by Nāgārjuna[26] well tally with the attitude to dharmas enjoined here.

The text therefore envisages here two traditions : The one distinguishes three "clans" (*gotra*) of saints, each with a distinctive aim, programme of practices, and stages of progress. The other distinguishes four preparatory stages in the career of the saints, the "Aids to penetration". The two traditions are combined already in the Abhidharma of the Sarvāstivādins. According to the *Mahāvibhāsha*[27] the Disciples and Pratyekabuddhas can, in the first two preparatory stages, still change their clan, and choose to become Buddhas. But by the time they have reached the stage of "Patience", they are too specialised and fixed to modify (*avivartya*) their approach. Once he has gone to his distinctive stage of "Patience", a Disciple or Pratyekabuddha can no more fall into the bad destinies, i.e. he cannot be reborn in hell, as an animal, or as a ghost. This fact then excludes him from the career of a Bodhisattva who has made a vow to be sometimes reborn in the bad destinies, so as to comfort and convert the damned, the animals and the ghosts. The Sutra here states

[23]VI 164.

[24]*anulomikī dharma-tṛishṇā.*—In *H* to *A* xvi 322 the *bodhisattva-nyāma-avakrānti* is identified with the third *nirvedha-bhāgiya* (esp. *H* 663, 21), in *H* to *A* xvii 331, however, with *duḥkhe dharma-jñāna-kshānti.* In *A.K.* vi 175 one is capable of entering *nyāma* after the fourth stage, *agra-dharma. A* vi 179 sq., *dharma-jñāna-kshānti* follows immediately on *agradharma,* i.e. the *duḥkhe dharma-jñāna-kshānti.* This is entrance into *samyaktva-niyāma,* which makes an *ārya.*—The whole problem of *kshānti* is full of obscurities, which have so far not been cleared up.

[25]*dharma-anulomikī kshānti.*

[26]*Mpp-s* 327, 337, 396.

[27]Lin li-kuan, *L'aide-mémoire de la vraie loi,* 1949, p. 293.—cf. also *A.K.* VI pp. 175-6.

the conditions under which a Bodhisattva falls from his own distinctive path, and those under which he goes along it. So much about B3.

After the Bodhisattva has spent one incalculable aeon in the "instructions",[29] he now enters into the "path of training", the stage of a "beginner".[30] The purpose of the "Aids to penetration" is, as we saw, to bring about a condition which makes the path of vision appear, and which destroys the quality of being an average, unconverted person.[31] Buddhaghosa's *Visuddhimagga* gives a masterly account of the meditations which precede entrance into the Path. As a result of these meditations[32] indifference or repulsion (*pātikulyatā*) to complexes (*sankhārā*), or conditioned events, is established. One wants to be released from them, grasps them in contemplation, sees nothing in them one could seize upon as I or mine, puts away fear or delight, and becomes indifferent (*udāsīno*) and impartial (*majjhato*) to all "complexes", as not really concerning one at all. One turns away from them and views the tranquil Path, Nirvana as calm. All signs which indicate anything conditioned stand out as mere impediments, or obstacles (*palibodha*).[33] One makes Nirvana into the object, which is signless, procedureless, without complexes, the stopping of complexes, by means of a cognition "which passes beyond the kinship and plane of average men, which enters into the kinship and plane of the Ariyas". It is the first turning to, the first laying to heart, the first bringing to mind of Nirvana as object.[34]

We do not, I think, possess a description of the meditational practices associated with the "Aids to penetration" among either Sarvāstivādins or Mādhyamikas. We are much better informed about the interpretation of the Yogācāra School.[35] As interpreted by the Yogācārins, the Aids to penetration aim at first to remove the belief in separate outer *objects,* and the inclination towards them, and thereafter to bring about a concentration in which "the light of the gnosis appears as without the distractions caused by the separate representation of a perceiving *subject*".[36] Although in their details the Yogācāra accounts of the Aids to penetration are heavily coloured by theories which are specific to that school, in a general way the removal of both object and subject can be regarded as the red thread which goes through the argumentation of B4 to B10.

It must still be mentioned that the Aids to penetration arise through

[29]so *H* 36.

[30]*prayoga-mārga* = *adhimukti-caryā-bhūmi* *H* 64. *ādikarmika*. cf. at *P* 154.

[31]*A.K.* VI 167.

[32]*V.M.* 656.

[33]*V.M.* 672.

[34]For similes see *V.M.* 673 sq.

[35]Haribhadra 63-64; *Sūtrālaṃkāra* VI 9; XIV 23-26; *Madhyāntavibhāga* 26-27; *Mahāyānasaṃgraha* III 7, 9, 13. *Siddhi* 575-584, 602-3.

[36]*artha-grāhaka-vikshepa-anābhāso jñānāloka nishpadyate. H* 64.

meditational development,[37] and that they require a state of concentration, or trance. As a matter of fact, the two last Aids to penetration can be accomplished only in the fourth trance (*dhyāna*), which is the necessary prerequisite (*āśraya*) for entry into the path of vision.[38] The Sutra mentions two concentrations, one at P 133 and one at P 142, which occur according to H on the "Summits" and "Supreme dharmas" respectively. The two insights are called "concentrations", because of the peaceful calm which accompanies them.[39]

B4 to 10 gives an ontological analysis of a Bodhisattva on the decisive stages of his career. These stages are not thought to be achieved here, but are described as they are conceived in the course of the meditations preceding the path of vision. The argument refers to the following ten events in a Bodhisattva's career: 1. He gains the thought of enlightenment, P 121-122; 2. becomes irreversible P 107, 117-120, 123, 128; wins 3. perfect wisdom P 123, 136; and 4. the prediction, P 144; 5. he "goes forth" to the knowledge of all modes, P 138, 141; 7. obtains perfect purity, P 138 (cf. A3dII1); 8. gains apparitional rebirth, P 138 (corresponds to the 9th *bhūmi* in P 224); 9. is able to know full enlightenment, P 141; and 10. reaches the knowledge of all modes, P 151-154.

Alternatively chapters 3 to 6 of S may survey four aspects of a Bodhisattva's spiritual life:—

I. The thought of enlightenment, which initiates, accompanies, and concludes it (B4).

II. The perfect wisdom which inspires him, viewed as an object (B5, 6, 6a).

III. His relation to all-knowledge and enlightenment (B7b-8).

IV. That all the constituents of his spiritual life are due to ignorance and are illusory (B9, 10).

I have had great difficulty in unravelling the sequence of the argument, and am not sure that I have always succeeded in doing so.

I. (B4) The idea that the thought of the Absolute, being an absolute thought, is "transparent luminosity" (*pra-bhāsvara*)[40] repeats an old tradition, that "thought in its substance is luminous through and through, but has become defiled by adventitious taints".[41] Such a self-luminous and pure thought is at the heart of all reality. It is the original reality which we have covered up with all sorts of coverings. The dialectics of a thought which is really no thought—a thought, which, as unconditioned, is included neither in mind nor in conciousness, and is without a

[37]*bhāvanā. A.K.* VI 170.

[38]*Siddhi* 583.

[39]*Rgs* I 10. . . *anupādadhi spṛiśati śānti-samādhi śreshṭhām.* 11. *eva-ātma-śānta viharann*. . .

[40]Pali: *pabhassara*; or *paṇḍara* in *Asl.* 140.

[41]*Anguttara Nikāya,* 1, 8-10.

separate object—is here simply asserted. Its logical implications are ignored, but the descriptions of the ways of getting to it occupy the rest of the Sutra. At this point the Sutra is content to state that in his attitude to this thought, as to all data of experience, the Bodhisattva should not "fancy himself". The connotations of the Sanskrit phrase *na manyate* cannot be reproduced by one single English word. *Man-yate* is connected on the one side with *man-as* "mind", and on the other with *māna,* "conceit". In the first sense it can be translated as "to think of or about", "to consider", "to mind (about)", "to put one's mind to", "to have in mind", "to have in view", "to set one's heart on", "to fix the thoughts on", "to wish, or strive", "to care about". In the second sense it means "to be conceited about", "to fancy oneself for".[42] Conceit is due to a false sense of ownership and an insufficient extinction of self. It is discussed more amply in the later parts of the Sutra.[43]

IIa. (B5) The Bodhisattva next considers that from the point of view of ultimate reality all things neither appear nor disappear, and that in consequence they can be neither affirmed nor denied. Furthermore (at I3g), seen from the Absolute all dharmas are unutterable, and verbal fictions are all that we ever operate with.

IIb. (B6a) Because of the emptiness of all entities one should "not stand" in, or on, them, i.e. one should not insist on their reality. "Not to take one's stand" is equated with "not settling down in the fixed conviction" that this is so or so, or with not having a fixed inclination to do, to win or to lose something.[44] The best way of avoiding the fault of "standing" on dharmas is not to bring them in at all,[45] and to refrain from any act of discrimination which may turn to them.[46] The often repeated saying that the Bodhisattva should "stand in perfect wisdom by not taking his stand anywhere" is explained by Asaṅga[47] as the avoidance of five standpoints :

1. He does not take his stand on a belief in a self (see P 132), and thus does not say "I know", "this is my wisdom".

2. He does not take his stand on the conceptions of Bodhisattvas who have not seen the true reality, and thus he does not try to define wisdom in any way.

[42]Also Pali *maññati,* to be proud of, to be conceited, to boast.—*manyanā* = Pali *maññanā,* at *A* xxi 387, 389, and xxix 480.—*H* to *A* xi 235 explains by *utkarsha.* In this sense the term is used at *A* i 5, 8, 13.—Also *P* 84, 121, 145, 171.—Often *manyate* means to "think falsely, fancy", as e.g. in *A* i 24, iv 94, xi 233, and other cases.—At *A* vi 161 "mind" = seize = get at = construct = discriminate = see = review.—*H* to *A* i 5 = *abhiniveśam na kuryād, H* to *A* i 9 = *tattvato na budhyate. H* to *A* i 13 = *savikalpena tattvato'sattvāt.*

[43]*S* ch. 45.

[44]*asthānayogena* = *anabhiniveśayogena H* to *A* i 8 = *S* 582.

[45]*asthānata* = *aniveśataḥ H* to *A* xii 274.

[46]*rūpa-ābhoga-vikalpa.*

[47]*Mahāyānasaṃgraha* 253.

"When you see a thing, it puts you into its bondage;
When you do not see it, then you are free of it."

3. He does not abide in either Samsara or Nirvana, avoiding them both as extremes (*anta*).

4. He rejects the standpoint of the Disciples who are content to cut off their own passions, as well as 5. that of the Disciples who dwell in Final Nirvana to the detriment of the welfare of beings.

"Turning of the mind"[48] is, according to Vasubandhu,[49] the decisive trait of the act of attention which dwells on an object for more than one moment, and the negation of "formative influence" therefore follows directly from that of "standing". In the *Ashta*[50] the Lord is quoted as identifying "formative influence"[51] with "discrimination",[52] and the later Pali tradition counts "formative influence" among the Maras.[53] As a secondary meaning of the term we may mention "accumulation of karma".[54] In its etymological meaning the term means "to bring together", "perform", "prepare", "render effective". In its connotations the term is connected with *saṃskārā,* "impulses", the fourth skandha, which is defined by *abhisaṃskaraṇa* as its mark,[55] and with the will[56] and its creations, and with the conditioned, which is created by it. In B6a "formative influences" are further connected with "taking hold" of something, and he who attempts to take hold of something does not reckon with its essential emptiness.

IIc. (B6b) Further, all "signs" should be avoided. We have to do with a "sign" (*nimitta*) wherever the impression of a stimulus is either taken as an indication that there is something there—as in perception—or as a reason for doing something about something. The taking up of a "sign" is regarded as the salient feature of perception. Innocuous as it may seem, perception as such is an obstacle to salvation in that it is both erroneous and misleading. It is erroneous because the world as perceived is largely a fabrication of our desire for adaptation to it, and covers up the vision of what is really there, i.e. Nirvana, or the succession of ceaselessly changing momentary dharmas. It is misleading because, as the commentators put it, we first "recognize" a set of data as a "man",

[48]*cetasa ābhoga.*

[49]*Triṃśika* 20.

[50]*A* xviii, 346 = *S* ch 41.

[51]*Abhisaṃskāro = citta-ābhoga H.*

[52]*vikalpa = viparyāsa H.*

[53]*Thag-A* II 46, *Ud-A* 216, *V.M.* 211. Five Māras: *khandha-, kilesa-, abhisankhāra-, maccu-, devaputta-, -C.Nidd.* no. 506 *kammābhisankhāravasena paṭisandhiko khandhamāro dhātumāro āyatanamāro.*

[54]as in *A* vii 183.

[55]*saṃkhatam abhisaṃkharonti A.K.* I 29, *S.N.* 87.

[56]*A.K.* iv 169 = *cetayate.*

or a "woman", and then base bad actions on that "recognition". The sign is "defilement", and the Absolute is called the "signless" (*animitta*). It is, indeed, unrecognizable when met.

Śreṇika the Wanderer is, according to Nāgārjuna[57] the Śreṇika Vatsagotra, who in the Pali texts is simply called Vacchagotta. A number of his conversations with the Buddha are recorded. They are scattered through the Pali Canon, but combined into one section in the *Samyuktāgama* of the Sarvāstivādins. The text refers here to a Sutra[58] which, according to Nāgārjuna,[59] discussed "Śrenika the Believer" and at the same time, according to the *Vibhāsha*[60] and Nāgārjuna, preached the emptiness of all dharmas. Since Subhuti's argument is difficult, and since we are inclined to lean on signs, and do not see how we can have faith without a sign, "Subhuti here takes as his witness the Little Vehicle where it speaks of the emptiness of dharmas, How could those who practise the great vehicle not believe in it?"

Śrenika showed "faith", first, in that he believed that the Buddha could help him to find the path,[61] and, second, in that he was willing to accept the Tathagata in spite of the fact that he could not be related to any of the skandhas, i.e. to form, etc. He entered into a "cognition with a limited scope" which, according to Haribhadra means that it was directed to the absence of a self in persons,[62] (and not also in dharmas). Śrenika was concerned to find a true self, in other words, the Tathagata. Nāgārjuna relates that Śrenika originally took the person as one lump, and that therefore the Buddha asked him about its elements. He had also heard people speak of the "I" in two ways, as identical with the five skandhas, and as different from them. The skandhas are multiple, and the I is one—so they cannot be identical. The self would be born and perish as the skandhas do, and it would not be independent of causes and conditions—thus it would not be the true self. Therefore, how can something outside the five skandhas have the character of "I" or "self"? As Nāgārjuna puts it, "Śrenika's second act of faith consisted in that, when he had heard that the Buddha denied the self, and said that from the beginning there was none, he accepted the fact that, because there is no self, the dharmas have no support, and are like a dream, a mirage, nonapprehensible. Having obtained this power of faith, he entered into the true mark of dharmas, and did not mistake form for the Tathagata."

Śreṇika "did not take hold of form, etc." The Buddha asked him:

[57] *Mpp-s,* Lamotte 46 n, 184 n.

[58] i.e. *Samyukta* no. 105 (pp. 31c-32) = *A.N.* IV 395-400—IV 383 (cf. III 99 sq.) + *M.N.* 72, 487, cf. 481.

[59] *Mpp-s* chüan 42, p. 368b; cf. 350a.

[60] p. 3 profound abhidharma (?) = *śūnyatā.*

[61] *Samyuktāgama*: My thought has obtained a pure faith towards the Buddha.

[62] p. 50 *pudgala-nairātmya.*

"Do you regard the Tathagata as form?" "No." "As in form?" "No." "As outside form?" "No." "As the absence of form?" "No." "When, under all these aspects, you do not see the Tathagata, should you doubt, and say: What is there fixed and definite in the Buddhas' doctrine?" "No." Śrenika then won the path, and became an Arhat. This is how Nāgārjuna recounts the Sutra. The *Samyukta-āgama* has some variations. There it is stated expressly that the initial question assumes that the true self is identical with the reality which survives death, and that three answers are possible: 1. The self is eternal, 2. the self is cut off, 3. (the self is) the Tathagata.

IId. (B6c) Perfect wisdom is obviously not a *"something"*. It is neither found nor got at, and one should accept this fact without losing heart.

IIe. (B6a) Nor is perfect wisdom *a property*. When one says that a Bodhisattva has perfect wisdom, "is not lacking in it", one seems to attribute to him a property. Such attribution of properties is quite incompatible with the emptiness of all dharmas.

III. then considers the statements one may make about a Bodhisattva's relations to the knowledge of all modes, or to enlightenment. In each case, such statements must be seen in the light of emptiness, and they really assert or posit nothing at all.

B7b. The Bodhisattva "goes forth" to all-knowledge. That statement must take account of the fact that no dharma is ever "born"—originated into birth-and-death, or "goes forth", escapes from it—since it has no own-being and no nature of its own.

B7c. Skill in means is a well-known condition of winning full enlightenment. It is now defined as the absence of all the false attitudes described in B5-7a.

B7d. The knowledge of all modes is directed to dharmas. Since those dharmas do not in themselves exist, it is without an object, it is a non-dual cognition, i.e. one which differs substantially from the cognitions with which we are familiar.

B8. It is stated that the Buddhas deliver their prophecy of future enlightenment to a Yogin who practises true meditation and whose personality possesses such a constitution, made of form, etc. that the Buddhas can base a prophecy on it. This statement is not, however, really true, because it implies false discriminations.

IV. The analysis is fitly summed up by the conclusion that separate entities do not exist, and are all *ignorance* (B9) and *illusion* (B10). B9 can be regarded as the removal of the false discrimination of an object, and B10 (from 1 3u) that of a subject.

B9a. First of all, the non-existence of separate dharmas, which results from the foregoing analysis, is connected with ignorance. This Sanskrit root VID means both to "know" and to "find", and therefore *a-saṃ-VID-*

yamānā "do not exist", and *a-VID-yā,* "ignorance", are more closely connected in Sanskrit than they are in English. The belief in the existence of dharmas which really do not exist is ignorance. Ignorance is the first link of conditioned coproduction. The doctrine of conditioned coproduction is restated in what follows. The argument is perhaps made more intelligible by a parallel passage in Candrakīrti's *Prasannapadā*[64]: "Because of the apprehension of a self, and of what belongs to a self, beings do not overcome birth-and-death. And why? It is because one reviews self and other, that action-forming forces (*karma-abhisaṃskārā*) come about. The foolish untaught common people who do not know that all dharmas are absolutely, completely nirvanised get at 'self' and other. Having got at that, they settle down in it. They then become greedy, full of hatred and confused. Thereupon they bring about the threefold action—by body, speech, and mind. Discriminating, by superimposition,[65] what does not exist, they say 'I am greedy, full of hatred, confused'."

B9b then infers from this analysis of conditioned coproduction the attitude to be adopted to perfect wisdom, enlightenment.

B9c is absent in S. It is an addition made by P, to bring home the fact that neither must one assume the reality of the objective elements, nor must one believe in the subject as an ultimately real agent that experiences.

B10 considers, finally, the mode of existence of the person who goes to enlightenment and finds that it is nothing but an illusion.

B11, 12. The negative attitude to all the separate data of experience, which has been expounded in B4-10, would have a most demoralising effect on spiritual life if it were not counterbalanced by a positive attitude to other people. While he is still in the initial stages of his training, on the level of a beginner,[66] the Bodhisattva needs some social support, some "sustenance" (*samparigraha H*). In order to stand the Void he must be firmly anchored in society. Those who are engaged in completely isolating themselves from everything, and in purifying themselves of it, are in need of association with spiritual friends (B12) to keep up their morale. If the house is well garnished and cleaned, one must beware lest worse devils enter into it. According to a Tibetan commentary,[67] the two supports mentioned in B11 and 12 are 1. internal, i.e. the cognition which enables one to reject the two extremes of phenomenal existence and of the Hinayanistic Nirvana; 2. external, i.e. the spiritual preceptor and teacher.

B11. First, all *people in general* are one's support in so far as one

[64] xvi, 296.

[65] *so'sat-samāropeṇa vikalpayati.*

[66] *nava-yāna-samprasthita = ādikarmika A* xv, 292.

[67] cf. Obermiller, p. 85

regards their welfare as one's personal responsibility, and "never abandons all beings", as the Sutra says elsewhere.[68] The text here indicates the practice of the six perfections with a thought associated with the knowledge of all modes as the basis for the "skill in means", and the absence of depression and fear as its fruit.

B12. Buddhist texts frequently emphasise the necessity of a *good spiritual friend* (*kalyāṇa-mitra*). It is mentioned in other parts of the Sutra as well,[69] and Śāntideva has collected an instructive number of passages from a variety of texts.[70] The "true friend" is one who helps us to win a better destiny, or the ultimate goal of Buddhahood. The term does not refer so much to good companions as to one's teacher, the spiritual adviser from whom one learns the Dharma, and whom one should revere. He is important as a protector against the forces of evil, personified in Māra—who twist the teaching. In other parts of the Sutra[71] the "deeds of Māra" are enumerated in greater detail than here.

C

C. A new topic is now taken up in chapters 7 to 11 of S: What is a *Bodhisattva?* (CI) What is a *great being?* (CII) What is the *great vehicle?* (CIII).

CI. As to the first, the exact question is: *bodhisattva kaḥ pada-arthaḥ?* literally, "Bodhisattva", "what is the *pada-artha?*" *"Pada-artha"* either means, 1. "meaning (*artha*) of a word" (*pada*), or, 2. that which corresponds to the meaning of a word, i.e. a "thing". The answer is: *"a-pada-arthaḥ bodhisattva-pada-artha"*, literally "nothing is the meaning of the word 'Bodhisattva'". One may also translate: "'Bodhisattva', what entity is that?—The entity 'Bodhisattva' is a nonentity".

The remainder of the chapter is based on a play of words, between *pada-artha* and *padam,* as noted in the translation. It elaborates a famous verse in the *Dhammapada,*[72] which I quote here according to the Sanskrit version of the *Udānavarga.*[73]

"Of those who have no hoard, who have well comprehended food.[74]
Whose range is the Void, is the Signless, is Detachment[75]—
As the track of birds in the sky (space), so is their track[76] hard to follow.

[68] *A* xxvii, 448=*S* ch. 49.

[69] *A* xv, 292=*S* ch. 37; *A* xxii, 396=*S* ch. 45.

[70] *Śikshāsamuccaya* pp. 34-44.

[71] *A* xii=*S* ch. 31-32; *A* xxi=*S* ch. 45.

[72] vv. 92-93.

[73] XXIX, 23-24 in Rockhill; no. 35-42 in *Stzb. Pr. Ak. Wiss.*, 1908, pp. 977-985.

[74] *bhajana*: the necessaries of life.

[75] *vi-veka.*

[76] or: future destiny; *padam,* or *gati.*

Those in whom becoming has dried up, who do not lean on the future,[77]
Whose range is the Void, is the Signless, is Detachment—
As the track of birds in the sky, their track is hard to follow."

The text here inserts a *classification of dharmas,* by way of describing the objective foundation (*ālambanam*) of a Bodhisattva's activity, as a counterpart to CI which, according to Haribhadra, demonstrates the true essential inner nature of a Bodhisattva, the subjective substratum of the properties of a Buddha.[78] In the form of a diagram:

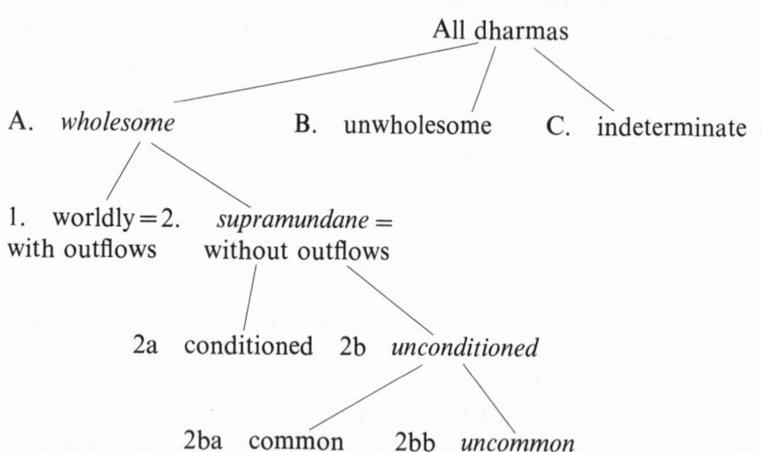

"Indeterminate" dharmas are actions which have no karmic effect, either wholesome or unwholesome. "Wholesome" dharmas should be accepted, "unwholesome" rejected, "indeterminate" ignored. As to the "wholesome", the "worldly" are found in ordinary people, while the "supramundane" are included in the right path of the Saints. Since worldly dharmas are "with outflows", not an antidote to the seizing on self, they should be shunned, just as the "supramundane" should, for the opposite reason, be accepted. The "supramundane" are, when contemplated, either "conditioned" or "unconditioned". "Conditioned" elements relate to the empirical conventional world, are included in the triple universe, and depend on causes and conditions. Haribhadra instances the 37 wings of enlightenment. The "unconditioned" elements relate to ultimate reality, are not included in the triple universe, and do not depend on conditions. Suchness is an example. When developed, supramundane dharmas are either "common" or "uncommon". The "common" manifest themselves in the spiritual stream (*santāna*) of all

[77]are unconcerned about it; *hy apārantaṃ ca nāśritāḥ.*

[78]*pada-artha* = *pratishtha-artha* = *prakṛitisthaṃ gotram* = primordial lineage = *pratipatter ādhāra.*

the Saints, the "uncommon", such as the 10 powers, only in that of the Buddha. Again the latter should be preferred.

CII. Next, the meaning of "great being". Four definitions are given, by the Buddha himself, by Śāriputra, by Subhuti, and by Pūrṇa (CII, 4), CII, 1-3 expound the aim, goal or programme (*samuddeśa*) of Mahayanistic activity. Haribhadra[79] says that CII,1-3 correspond to the three stages of the conquest of a country by a king: he annihilates all hostile forces; takes possession of the ground thus gained; attains a predominant position with regard to other kings.

CII,1. *The Buddha,* the great Compassionate One, sees the greatness of the Bodhisattva in his comprehensive service to others.

CII,2. *Śāriputra*, chief protagonist of Abhidharma-wisdom, characteristically stresses the negative aspects of his greatness, the forsaking of all false views.

CII,3. *Subhuti* sees the greatness of the Bodhisattva in his final positive achievement (*adhigama*), i.e. the thought of enlightenment and of all-knowledge. In his explanation of the Bodhisattva's nonattachment to this thought, Subhuti, in the account given by the *Ashta,*[80] repeats what he had said before (at B4) about the "thought of enlightenment", and it is there, and not in CII,3, either in S or in P, that he makes one of the remarks about which Śāriputra questions him (see ch. 12 n. 3).

CII,4. Pūrṇa, son of Maitrāyaṇī, was "the foremost in explaining the doctrine".[81] With his answer a new argument begins—a description of the various stages of progress (*pratipatti, H*) of the Bodhisattva.

According to Haribhadra, the argument from CII,4 to the end of D is occupied with the four kinds, or stages, of "progress". These correspond, according to Asaṅga,[82] as follows, to the stages of a Bodhisattva's career. The "putting on of the armour" (CII,4), which signifies vigour, and the "setting out"[83] (CII,5-6) correspond to the initial stages of "equipment with merit" and of "action in resolute faith", the "progress in equipment",[84] up to CIII,1e, to the upper part of the "path of training", the first stages of CIII,1f to the "path of vision", the remaining stages of CIII,1f to the "path of development", CIII,2 to both paths, and the "progress in going forth" (CIII,3 and D) has the last three stages of the "path of development" for basis (*adhishṭhāna*).

[79]p. 83.

[80]I 19-20.

[81]*A.N.* I, p. 23.-*Mpp-s* 196 n.

[82]*H* 84.

[83]*samprasthita.*

[84]def. *H* 106, Ob. 184: *samasta-mahāyāna-anushṭhānena sambhriyate samudāgama-bhāvena mahābodhir ebhiḥ.,* bring to full accomplishment the whole of the Mahayanistic Path, representing thus an amassing (of the factors) of the great enlightenment, in the sense of bringing it to full realisation.

CII,4. The first step in the progress is "to put on the great armour". The Bodhisattva is a hero, a warrior, and an "armour" seems appropriate to him. The armour consists in the six perfections, which are again described, first in general, with special stress on the altruism of a Bodhisattva, and then one by one in great detail. Thirty-six varieties are surveyed, 6 groups of 6—each perfection being combined with all the others.

CII,5,6. After that we hear what occurs when the Bodhisattva, next, *sets out*[85] in the great vehicle (CII,5), and, after that when he *mounts on*[86] it (CII,6). To "set out" means to get started. If "mounting on" is a later step, the translation is faulty, and one should render the term by "ascend on". This is suggested by Haribhadra,[87] according to whom the Bodhisattva first "sets out" in the vehicle which represents the factors and results of the path,[88] and then "ascends on" it, or "by means of it", inasmuch as he comes to higher and still higher degrees of perfection.[89]

CII,7. After Pūrṇa had (at CII,4-6) explained the practical task of a Bodhisattva in its three initial stages, Subhuti and the Buddha consider the actual reality which can be attributed to these practical endeavours. They and their objects have only the reality value of a magical illusion, of a magical show, owing to the illusory nature of the "beings" involved.

The ontological analysis now proceeds in three steps:

1. In actual reality, the Bodhisattva is not armed with the great armour, because "to be armed with the great armour" is an attribute, a mark, which may be said to be his own, and the emptiness of all "marks" means that their negation can be attributed to a thing, or a person, with the same justification as their affirmation.

2. One makes practical efforts to bring something about, to "make" something. But there is no maker of anything, nor any power to make, or to put together. This is, in the final analysis, due to their "beyond-end-ness".

3. The practical efforts aim at emancipation, or deliverance. As such they are without a real basis, because one cannot claim that anything, as it exists, is either bound or freed. Candrakīrti[90] defines "bondage" as the defilements, like greed, etc., since they deprive of their autonomy[91] the beings who are bound by them. Because a common man is in their bondage, he cannot rise above the triple world. Freedom

[85]Its mark (*H* 86) is to be *samyak-vyavasthita*, its essence is the attainment of a correct position, and the process of mastering all the properties of a Mahayanistic saint (*samasta-mahāyāna-dharmākramaṇa-svabhāva*).

[86]*samārūḍho*.

[87]*H* 85.

[88]*hetu-phala-ātmaka-dharma*.

[89]*uttarottara-viśesha-adhigamān*.

[90]*Prasannapadā* 290.

[91]*a-sva-tantrī-karaṇe*.

consists in cutting through the bonds of the passions. These passions are essentially ignorance, which again is the result of making distinctions, e.g. between "to be" and "not to be", or between "Nirvana" and "birth-and-death", "emancipation" and "bondage", and so on.[92]

CIII. Next, the argument proceeds to the meaning of the *great vehicle*. The Sutra begins here with five questions asked by Subhūti, as in AI23. The questions are then answered, one by one: the first in CIII, 1 a-e, the second in CIII,1f, and the third to fifth in CIII,2. It must be borne in mind that the Large *Prajñāpāramitā* is an expansion of the *Ashta,* and that CIII,1,a-f are represented there by only three short sentences.

In one of the more systematic parts of the Sutra, the great vehicle is now defined through its *constituents* (CIII,1).

CIII,1a. First, of course, *the six perfections,* which are briefly defined, with special emphasis on the "skill in means", or the help which we owe to others.

CIII,1b. Considering the paramount importance of the idea of emptiness, a list of 20 *kinds of emptiness* is particularly welcome. The term "emptiness" as such is said to mean "neither unmoved nor destroyed". "Unmoved" (*a-kūṭastha*) means that it overtowers (*kūṭa*) all change, is unchangeable in what it is, in its own being, "steadfast as a mountain peak, as a pillar firmly fixed".[93] The opposite would be the change, or destruction, of its own being. Both of these are excluded.

Now, from its beginnings, Buddhism has been taught as the "middle way" between the two heresies of Eternalism and Annihilationism. It is now maintained that to say "a thing is" is equivalent to "it is eternally what it is", "it remains for ever what it is", and that the formula "it is destroyed" is equivalent to saying that "it is not". The whole doctrine of emptiness, as taught here, rests on this equivalence.

"Emptiness" is a word for the identity, or nondifference, of "yes" and "no". It is an antidote to all grasping at false discriminations and conceptions (*vikalpa*), and it is another term for "nonduality". "Yes" and "no" are not reflections of actual fact, but of the attitudes of self-willed individuals.

The general notion of emptiness is then applied to 20 different concepts or categories. Lists of emptinesses were very popular in the Mahayana, and also the Theravādins had one. Outside the Prajñāpāramitā tradition we have a list of 24 in *Paṭisambhidā magga* (*Pts.*) II, 177-184, and of 7 in the *Lankāvatārasūtra* (p. 74). The formulations of the *Pts* provide an instructive contrast to this section of the Sutra. "Empty" is taken there to mean "empty of self, or of anything that would constitute a self—i.e. of permanence, stability, everlastingness, nonliability to reversal". On

[92] see *Prasannapadā* ch. 11, and Schayer's German translation, 98-103.
[93] *D.N.* I 14 and *D.N.-A.* 1, 10.

the whole, three meanings of "empty" can be distinguished in that text:

1. Empty of self;[94]
2. Moving in the direction of Nirvana;[95]
3. Absence of correlative items in each other.[96]

The Prajñāpāramitā list itself, the most authoritative in the Mahayana, may have originally comprised only 16 items, to which at some later date first two,[97] and then two more items were added. Sometimes, however, we meet with lists of 7 and 14.[98] A few of these forms occur independently in other parts of the text.[99]

We possess a number of explanations of the items, which however, vary widely among themselves. The earliest is that of Nāgārjuna (*c.* A.D. 150?), as yet untranslated.[100] The Yogācāra authors, whose writings have come to us, seem to have largely ignored the original intention of the text. We possess a commentary in the *Sandhinirmocana-sūtra* (*c.* 150),[101] in Sthiramati's *Madhyāntavibhāgaṭikā*,[102] *c.* 450, and in Diṅnāga's *Piṇḍārtha*,[103] *c.* 450. The deviation of these authors from the original meaning is due to their desire to find "the real esoteric meaning" of the Sutras.[104] The hints of Haribhadra,[105] *c.* 800, are of great help, although he often seems to do violence to the text by coordinating the 20 forms of emptiness with the ten stages (*bhūmi*) of a Bodhisattva and with the ten kinds of ignorance, which, according to the Yogācāras,[106] are removed on the ten stages. Suzuki's notes[107] should also be consulted.

CIII,1c. The 20 forms of emptiness, which constitute the "equipment with cognition",[108] are followed by a list and short explanation of 112[109] *concentrations,* constituting the "equipment with merit" according to Haribhadra. The Old Wisdom School had known only two kinds of concentrations: either a list of 8, i.e. the 4 trances and the four formless

[94] no. 1, 3, 11-13, 14?

[95] no. 4, 6-10, 16-24.

[96] no. 2, 5, 15.

[97] A number of passages mention only 18 items, e.g. *P* 161; *S* 1374, 15; 1375, 21; 1403.

[98] 7 : *S* I 137. 14: Gilgit *Ad* LXIII, 248b.

[99] e.g. 3, 9, 12, 13, 14, 15, 19.—3 at *P* 134 (cf. *P* 89 and *A* ix 205); 12 at *P* 173-4, 263; *S* 137, 139 (*P* 45), *S* 604, 613, *P* fol. 592a; 13 at *S* 137; 14 at *P* 48, 93, 134, 169, 191, 222, fol. 470, 477b, 523a; *A* vii 171, xvii 331, 15 at *P* 39; 19 at *P* 84, 198, 262, cf. *P* 39, 138, fol. 593b.

[100] *Mpp-s* ch. 48, chüan 31, pp. 285b-296b.

[101] VIII, 29.

[102] pp. 45–63.

[103] vv. 8-18.

[104] *Madhy-v-t.* p. 58 : *sarva-sūtrānta-abhisaṃdhi-vyākaraṇa-artham.*

[105] pp. 95-6.

[106] i.e. *Mahāyānasaṃgraha* ch. 5, 1. *Madhy-v-t.* pp. 101-107. *Siddhi* pp. 639-660.

[107] *Essays* III, 222-228.

[108] *jñāna-sambhāra* H.

[109] The number varies in different documents. The Tibetan translation of S, for instance, gives 162.

trances (see P 210), or a list of 3 concentrations which are identical with the 3 doors to freedom, i.e. the signless, emptiness, and the wishless (see P 208). In the beginnings of the Mahayana it became usual to give names to a manifold variety of concentrated attentions on insights into aspects of the truth, and even to the concomitants of being in a state of concentration. These concentrations, really innumerable, are said to be varieties of the 3 doors to freedom,[110] and they belong to the plane of the 4th trance.[111] Lists of such concentrations seem to have been popular in the first centuries of the Christian era. A few are mentioned in the body of the Sutra, outside this chapter.[112] Others are found in the *Ashta,*[113] the *Saddharmapuṇḍarīka.*[114] *Samādhirājasūtra, Karuṇāpuṇḍarīka*[115] and *Guhyasamāja.*[116]

The terminology used in this context has not yet been scientifically explored. It is obviously esoteric, and requires initiation by a Guru, which in its turn is said to depend on the merit acquired in the past.

CIII,1d. Next comes a survey of 21 *practices,* which constitute the "equipment with the path" according to Haribhadra. Most of them are common to all Buddhist schools. As given here they agree to a large extent with the traditions of both Theravādins and Sarvāstivādins.

CIII,1e. Next, the 43, or 42,[117] *Dhāraṇī-doors.* A *dhāraṇī*—from DHṚI, to carry—is a verbal expression which permits to "bear in mind" a certain truth. It is a help to memory, to prolonged meditation, and, in addition, like a mantra it encloses the magical efficacy of the doctrine, and has power to protect its user from danger. *Mukha* means "door", the entrance to a truth, or to an aspect of reality (*dharma*), or it may mean the "aspect" itself.

In Sanskrit, the vowel A is considered as inseparable from all consonants. A mystical alphabet, the A-RA-PA-CA-NA, became at some unspecified time current in some Buddhist circles.[118] It differs from the regular Sanskrit alphabet by the sequence of the letters, the omission of ṅ and of all (i.e. 12) vowels except A, and the inclusion of 13 double consonants. One of these, the letter YSA = Z, cannot possibly occur in

[110] *Mpp-s.* chüan 28, 268a.

[111] Lamotte, *Mahāyānasaṃgraha* 44.

[112] cf. *Mpp-s* 434, 472.

[113] xxx, 490-494, a later addition.

[114] xxiii, 352-3.

[115] p. 99 (118).

[116] chapter 13.—A list of four is found in Asanga's *Mahāyānasaṃgraha* (xii 3), and in the *Siddhi* (p. 632), as well as in *Dharmasaṃgraha* cxxxvi.

[117] Some sources give 43, others 42 letters, and we cannot at present decide which number was originally intended. See my *The Prajñāpāramita Literature,* 1960, p. 11 n. 16.

[118] Its use seems not to have been confined entirely to the Mahayana, as it is mentioned in the *Dharmaguptavinaya, T* 1428 xix, in connection with the 6th *pācittiya,* as a type of joint collective recital.

Sanskrit words. This fact, together with some other particularities,[119] suggests that it took its present shape in the North West corner of India. With the help of the Chinese and Tibetan translations we can follow the development which this section of the Sutra underwent between A.D. 200 and 900. The letters which comprise the Arapacana have remained substantially the same during that period. But there are great variations in the choice of the words used to illustrate them. In one case Nāgārjuna's commentary indicates that a word had its origin in Southern India.[120] The text of the Nepalese manuscripts of the Sanskrit text, which date from *c.* 1800, is, through the ignorance and carelessness of the scribes, often unsatisfactory. My translation follows in general the Gilgit Ms. of *Ad,* but in a number of cases the Chinese and Tibetan versions. The Arapacana is found also in the *Gaṇḍavyūha,*[121] but there the explanation of the letters is quite different. The use of the Arapacana continues to the present day, and in later literature it is always connected with the Bodhisattva Mañjuśrī.[122] Images of an Arapacana-Mañjuśrī are fairly common.[123]

The idea of connecting the letters of the alphabet with points of the doctrine is at least as old as the *Lalita Vistara,*[124] where, when the Bodhisattva as a child learns the Sanskrit alphabet, the enunciation of each syllable evokes the miraculous sound, or audition, of a corresponding doctrinal term. The principle is the same as in "A for apple, C for Cat." It has been reproduced in English only occasionally, as in B for "bond". The present scheme is in many points dependent on that of the *Lalita Vistara.*

CIII,1f. Next, the 10 *stages* of a holy life. Mystics of all ages have never tired of mapping out the steps of the spiritual ladder. The present arrangement becomes more intelligible when considered as the result of two trends of Buddhist tradition. On the one hand, there was a scheme of the four Paths—Streamwinner, Once-returner, Never-returner and Arhat—elaborated by the Sarvāstivādins into a scheme of 7 stages, also mentioned in this Sutra (P 225, 230). On the other hand, the development of a Jātaka literature focussed attention on the past lives of the

[119]e.g. *shaṅga* for *saṅga* at no. 10 is also found in the Kharoshthī *Dharmapāda, J.As.* IX, xii, 1898, pp. 229 v. 3; 245 v. 37.—YSA was introduced between 100 B.C. and A.D. 100 for foreign words. It is akin to the Z of Iran, and is found also in Khotan and Kucha.

[120]at no. 9, DA—"they do not burn". See my *The Prajñāpāramita Literature,* 1960, p. 11 n. 17.

[121]ch. 45, pp. 448-51. Each letter is called a *prajñāpāramitāmukha.*

[122]e.g. *T* 1171-1174.

[123]B. Bhattacharya, *The Indian Buddhist Iconography,* 1958, 120-121.—Filchner p. 441. Tib. A-ra-ba-rtsi-na, connected with Mañjughosha. Waddell. *Lamaism* 151, *Arapacana dhi* as mantra of Mañjughosha.

[124]ch. 10 pp. 127-128.

Bodhisattva who became later on the Buddha Sākyamuni. Four fixed points stood out in that career: 1. The prediction by Dīpaṅkara; 2. the stage of becoming irreversible; 3. the sojourn in the Tushita heavens, and, of course, 4. the attainment of Buddhahood. When the career of this Bodhisattva was held to be the prototype not only of that of all the Bodhisattvas, but even of everyone who followed the doctrine of the Mahayana, it became natural that one should wish to alter the tradition about the stages of the Path, which had been elaborated on the assumption that Arhatship was the goal. The old scheme was not entirely abandoned, but in some way integrated with the six perfections.

It is likely that originally seven stages only were assumed, and that the number was raised to ten when the decimal system became popular.[125] Since Buddhahood is the goal of a Bodhisattva, the very last stage (10) was obviously that of a Buddha, or Tathāgata. The one before (9) would be that of a Bodhisattva's last birth. Prediction and irreversibility—both linked together—would then go into the 7th and (or) 8th stage. The first stage would be that of the "thought of enlightenment", with which the career of a Bodhisattva properly begins. Another fixed point would be the stage on which the perfection of wisdom in its specific doctrines is fully understood. In this Sutra it is the seventh.[127] The correspondence of stages 2 to 6 with the first five perfections does not appear to me to be clearly marked here, but perhaps it was intended.

The Mahāsaṃghikas worked out a primitive, and rather unsystematic, scheme in the *Mahāvastu*.[128] Later the *Daśabhūmika, c.* A.D. 100, the *Bodhisattvabhūmi, c.* 400, and the *Madhyamakāvatāra, c.* 650, worked out a neater arrangement, which has become classical in Mahayana tradition. Our Sutra stands halfway between the earlier and the final arrangement, and, according to Rahder, it seems to correspond closely to a treatise on the "stages" which is preserved only in the Chinese translation of Fo Nien (383-417).[129]

The text gives, first of all, a simple enumeration of the items. It then repeats them, and adds an explanation to each. The second list often differs verbally from the first, but there are few material discrepancies. In other schemes names are attached to the stages. There are none here.

CIII,3. Next, we hear *why the "great vehicle" is so called.* In this part, the Sutra first simply repeats the answer, or rather the five answers, as found in the *Ashta* (I, 24), and then considers each one of them in detail.

Haribhadra sees here a discussion of "going forth", which was fore-

[125]Har Dayal, *The Bodhisattva doctrine,* 1932, p. 271.

[127]In *Bodhisattva-bhūmi* and *Daśabhūmika* it is, however the 6th.

[128]I, 76 sq.

[129]*T* 309.

shadowed in CIII,2, and which continues until the end of D. "Going forth" (*nir-yāṇa*) may mean also "marching out of", or "issuing from", and there is, of course, in the Sanskrit the connection with "vehicle" (*yāna*). "Progress in going forth" (see at CII,4) brings about, in the end, the attainment of the omniscience of a Buddha.

D

D. We reach now the climax of the argument, i.e. *the dialectics of attainment*. First of all we are assured (D1) that the Bodhisattva reaches his goal, and attains to all-knowledge. I do not understand, however, what contribution the remarks on "expounding the great vehicle in agreement with the perfection of wisdom"—with which chapter 12 of S begins—make to the progress of the argument.

D2. The impossibility of any kind of attainment is then demonstrated in 3 steps. D2a and D2b employ the same literary device as C did. First, Subhūti gives his answers in brief, and then they are amplified bit by bit. It is rather confusing that one of the remarks here attributed to Subhūti (P 250, ch. 20 n. 6) has in fact been made by Śakra in another, later, part of the Sutra.[130]

D2a and 2b both begin with the same statement about what a Bodhisattva should do, i.e. not "approach" (*upaiti=upa-eti*), not "go to", not "move in the direction of" form, and of the other elements which constitute a Bodhisattva as he is when he has attained. The word "approach" seems synonymous with "get at",[131] and even with "obtain".[132] According to Haribhadra[133] one must insert at P 244 after "approach" (cf. ch. 20n. 1): "a Bodhisattva as something that should be attained, and that in its own-being consists of form, etc. Because that Bodhisattva, who should be attained, does not exist".[134] He does not approach the condition of a being who is perfectly identified with enlightenment. The remainder of both D2a and 2b is occupied with the ontological reasons for this practical attitude.

D2a. First of all, nothing is *really ever brought forth*. The translation here makes clumsy reading, because the words *abhi-nir-vṛitti, abhi-nir-vṛitta* (*abhinibbatta* in Pali) can, as far as I can see, not be rendered by

[130] i.e. A ii 47=*P* f. 219.

[131] cf. *A* xxvi 439: *yaś ca-atyanta-vivikta dharmo na so'stīti vā nāstīti vā upaiti* ("is got at", "is applicable").

[132] *Rgs* I 22=*labhyate; Rgs* I 23=*upalabhyate. H* 114 *upaiti=pratipadyate,* "go to, arrive at, obtain, gain, receive, perceive, ascertain, consider"; ibd. the synonym *upagacchati=svikaroti,* "make his own", "appropriate".

[133] p. 109.

[134] *nopaiti-iti bodhisattvaṃ kaṃcit prāpyaṃ rūpa-ādi-svabhāvam iti śeshaḥ. tasyaiva prāpyasya bodhisattvasya-avidyamānatvād iti bhāvaḥ.*

one single English word. I have translated "is not really a created thing". "Reproduced", or "re-existence", or "is really there" would also have been possible. The idea is akin to "produced", "born", and its negation (*an-abhinirvṛitti*) is explained by Haribhadra as "unborn",[135] or as "without own-being".[136] It has the traditional connotation of "produced in dependence on craving".

D2b. The argument here assumes that what has never been brought forth, is "nonproduction", or "the unproduced". The dialectics of that concept is now investigated, and leads to the *nonduality* of all the features of existence. An attainment obviously requires not only one, but quite a number of dualisms.

D2c. Thirdly,[137] *nonproduction* is brought into direct relation with attainment. The sequence of the argument seems to be fairly clear:

1. Śāriputra points out that, if everything is "unproduced" and if "nonproduction" is equivalent to attainment, then everybody has already attained, without any effort, everything that can be attained. So what is the use of any spiritual striving? One must here bear in mind that the "cognition of nonproduction" is traditionally one of the chief attributes of an Arhat. Originally it meant that an Arhat perceives that unwholesome states will no more be produced in him. In the Mahayana the term acquires an ontological meaning.

2. Subhuti, in reply, points out that
(a) one should not "wish" for any spiritual results, and
(b) that a sense of effort would not help the actual work of a Bodhisattva.

As to (a) one must remember that in Buddhist Sanskrit "to wish" (*icchati*), also "to desire", "to expect", is confused with *eshati,* "to strive", "to seek for", "to search".[138] The connection between (a) and (b) is therefore clearer in Sanskrit than it is in English. The idea itself is similarly expressed in the *Tathāgataguhya*[139]: "There is no production of a Buddha for those who wish for (*icchanti*) the production or stopping of any dharma. Nor do those rise above birth-and-death who search for (*paryeshanti,* desire) a realistic (*bhāvataḥ*) Nirvana".

3. One then discusses the degree of fact there can be in the relation of the production of an attainment to the "unproduced".

4. The argument ends with an indication that all this does not touch ultimate reality and ultimate truth, but is mere conventional talk.

[135] p. 617.

[136] *niḥ-sva-bhāvaḥ,* to A ix, 206.

[137] properly begins at *P* 257=*S* fol. 100a.

[138] To some extent the term was apparently confused even with *ṛicchati=appeti, arpayati* to procure.

[139] *Prasannapadā* 540-541.

D3. The Sutra concludes with a description of the practical attitude which alone can solve the logical difficulties advanced. We should *not lean on anything.*

This is first explained from an ontological angle (D3a), i.e. it is said of dharmas that they do not lean on anything. The nonleaningness is said to be in the nature of things. The term "not-leaning" (*a-niśrita*) can be applied to dharmas (1) either in their relation to our practical demands on them, or (2) in their relation with each other, or (3) it can be applied to persons in their relation to dharmas.[140]

In the first sense, it refers to the "unreliability" of dharmas which give our practical activity nothing to lean upon. As Haribhadra explains, "dharmas, because of the lack of either single or manifold own-being, are unworthy of reliance."[141]

The second meaning is that of "independence" in connection with the analysis of causation. It occurs in such passages as: "That consciousness-element does not lean[142] on the eye-organ, nor has it come from the stimuli, nor does it stand in the middle between them—not within, not without, not between both".[143] Or in the *Vimalakīrtinirdeśa*[144]: "What foundation[145] is there for an imagination of what is unreal (*abhūta-parikalpa*)?"—"The foundation is a perverted (*viparyastā*) perception"—"What is the foundation of that?"—"The fact that it has no support (*a-pratishthānam*)"—"What is the foundation of that?"—"This standing without support, of that there is no foundation at all. For all dharmas are supported (*pratistishṭhita*) on standing without support as their foundation."

In the third meaning, persons, i.e. the Saints and Buddhas, are people who do not lean on anything. Haribhadra[146] explains "not leaning" as "not inclined towards", "not settled down in" (*an-abhinivishta*). This meaning of the term prevails in the Pali Scriptures,[147] where it is connected with the loss of lust and hate,[148] with absence of clinging, grasping and

[140]Sometimes all three meanings are intended, as in *Dharmasangīti* (*Śi* 285, 11): "The teacher of emptiness is not captivated (*saṃhriyate*) by worldly dharmas, because of non-leaningness (*a-niśritatvād*)."

[141]H 123: *a-niśraya-arhatvād. niśraya*=home, to reside in, to dwell in.*āśrayati*=to take refuge in.—Also *A* xxx, 490: *sarva-dharmeshv aniśrita-saṃjñā,* where *H* comments: *māyopama-saṃjñā.*

[142]*niśrito,* is (not) dependent on.

[143]*Pitṛiputrasamāgama, Si* 250, 7.

[144]*Śi,* 264, 4. A more elegant rendering in *Buddhist Texts,* 1954, no 153.

[145]lit. "root", *mūla.*

[146]*H* 123.

[147]cf. *CPD.*

[148]*anissito chetvā sinehadosam, Sn* 66 (*Pj*).

attachment,[149] with independence from the authority and guidance of others,[150] and with absence of wavering.[151] The scholastics of the Abhidhamma defined this state by the freedom from two "supports" (*nissaya*), i.e. craving and false views.[152] Just as in this Sutra the discussion of "approaching" in P 244 sq. leads up to the "nonleaningness" of P 263, so also the Pali texts connect the two ideas.[153]

In addition, the argument here implies a play of words between *ni-śri-ta,* "leaning", and *niḥ-sṛi-ta,* "to find a way out", which is fairly common in Buddhist literature.[154] The connection was probably suggested by the assonance of the words,[155] but, though etymologically false, it is metaphysically and religiously sound. *"Niḥ-saraṇa"* means "escape",[156] issuing from, flight to salvation. The term is analogous to Nirvana, and is closely connected with *nir-yāṇa,* "going forth",[157] a synonym of the Path, which is discussed in this part of the Sutra. At the same time the word *"Niḥśaraṇa"* is loaded with associations with *śaraṇam,* "refuge", which again implies a seeking for support,[158] a place which one can flee to, on which one can rely, or in which one can find a refuge. When it is

[149]*anupādāya anissito kuhiñci Sn* 363 (*Pj*).—*anissito anupādāno Sn* 753.—*anissito viharati na ca kiñciloke upādiyati D.N.* II 292=*M.N.* I 56.—Also *Nd,* and *Pj* to *Sn* 1069 syn. *anallīno,* not clinging, and so in *A* xxi, 393.

[150]*anissito anañña-neyyo Sn* 364. In Prajñāpāramitā=*a-parapraṇeya* in *A* xvii 329, 337, trsl. "others cannot lead him astray".

[151]*anissitassa calitaṃ n'atthi Ud.* 81; *anissito na calati Sn* 752; *Pts.* II 206; *anissitaṃ cittaṃ diṭṭhiyā na iñjati,* quot. *Ud-A* 186, *VM* 386.—Also *Śi* 285, 11 *acalita aniśritatvād.*—Also in A I 31 *dharmatāyāṃś ca na calati,* and in *A* xii 273.

[152]e.g. *Niddesa. Sv* to *D.N.* II 292.

[153]*pubbam antam anissito Sn* 849=*P* 244 sq.—*tesu dhammesu anupāyo anapāyo anissito M.N* III 25, *anupāya,* from *upa-I,* like *upaiti,* means "without going near, without having a propensity for", *anapāyo,* "going away, lapse". Also *Nd.* syn. *an-upa-gata,* as in A I 31.

[154]e.g. *Lankāvatāra* 145: *dvaya-niśrito'yaṃ Mahāmate loko yaduta astitvaniśritaś ca nāstitva-niśritaś ca bhāva-abhāvac-chanda-dṛishṭi-patitaś ca aniḥśaraṇe* (V.R.: *aniḥsṛitasya*) *niḥśaraṇa-buddhiḥ.* "People in the world depend on two things, i.e. on 'it is' and 'it is not'; they fall into views through which they become keen on existence and non-existence. They imagine an escape where there is none."—The beginning is an echo of *S.N.* II 17: *dvaya-nissito...loko yebhuyyena atthitañ ceva natthitañ ca.*—*Nd* gives as synonym of *nissito nikkhanto* from *KRAM,* gone away, departed.

[155]The manuscripts regularly confuse *niśrit(y)a* with *niḥsṛit(y)a,* often written *niḥśrit(y)a* or *niśṛit(y)a.*

[156]so *A* xxiv 421. *Mhv* I 433.—(*Lal. Vist.*) *Śi* 203, 16: *bhava-niḥsaraṇe,* in fleeing from becoming; 205, 12 and 18 speaks of *jarā-n.* and *duḥkha-n.,* fleeing from old age and ill.—*Sūtrālaṃkāra* p. 87: *kleśa-n.,* and *rāgasya-n.,* escape from defilements and greed. *A.N.* I 260 *loke nissaraṇam,* escape from the world. def. *S.N.* III 62, as forsaking of greed etc.—*Śi* 236, 7 *niḥsaraṇam*=*buddhadharmā*=*bodhi*=*mārga.*—cf. *A.K.* III 10,200; VI 239; VII, 32-3, 37; VIII, 140-1.

[157]cf. *H.* 23: *niryāyur*=*niścitya prāpnuyur.*

[158]in *P* 216 *niśraya* is used for "refuge", and *H* 208 connects *śaraṇa* with *āśraya.*—*A* xvii 329 *dharmatām eva pratisarati.*

said that the Disciples "find a way out", it means not only that "they are saved", but also denotes a capacity to make the Dharma prevail in the face of any audience whatsoever.[160]

D3b. The *practical* side of this "nonleaning" is then explained in more detail in relation to the *practice of the six perfections*.[161] The translation follows P, which gives only the first and last perfections in detail. S, on the other hand, treats also the other four perfections in detail, but omits here the detailed account of the perfection of wisdom, which occurs elsewhere. It will be noticed that at this point the Sutra develops more fully the theme which began the discussion at P 17.

D3c. Finally,[162] *the achievement of perfect wisdom, and the dwelling in it*. In P and in S, D3b begins and ends with a reference to the "path of enlightenment" (*bodhi-mārga*), which somewhat obscures the course of the argument. In A I 31, where the whole of D3b is missing, the connection of D3c with D3a is clearer and more explicit. It is there effected by the sentence: "Śāriputra: Which is, in the Bodhisattvas, this perfection of the nonleaning on all dharmas?" to which Subhūti replies: "Just this perfection of wisdom", etc. as D3c.

The reward of accepting these teachings is that the Bodhisattva "dwells in the dwelling of the perfection of wisdom". It is one of the paradoxes of the *Prajñāpāramitā* literature that the relation of "support" which was rejected for the unconverted man in relation to his environment, is now used to describe the relation of the wise to wisdom. The wise "rely on" wisdom, are supported by it.[163] Although they are "unsupported", although they do not "dwell on" anything, do not "stand" anywhere, have no "home" anywhere, yet they "dwell" in perfect wisdom as their "dwelling". The phrase, "he dwells in the dwelling of the perfection of wisdom", occurs frequently in this Sutra, and we have met it before.[164] Haribhadra explains it to mean "the acquisition of wieldiness of thought in the four postures".[165] Wieldiness (Pali: *kammaññattā*) can also be

[160]cf. *Mpp.-s.* 354-6. *H* 123 connects with *parihāra*, the ability to protect, guard or look after.

[161]*S* fol. 137b (35)—140a.

[162]From *S* xiii, 140 (36) to *S* xiii, 144a.

[163]*Rgs* IV 2: *prajñāpāramitā-niśrita buddha-dhātuḥ.*—xii 7, *prajñāpāramitā-niśrita dharma-rājo.*—The Bodhisattvas and Buddhas as *prajñāpāramitām āśritya* in *Hṛidaya*. Synonyms for *āśritya* are *ā-GAM-ya* (in *A*) and *adhishṭhāya* (*A.K.* III 113).—*Śi* 32, 4: *sarvasattvā buddhopaniśraya-vihāriṇo bhavantu*: may all beings come to dwell depending on the Buddhas. —*prajñāpāramitām upaniśritya* in *A* xii 274 (=Pali *upanissāya*, "resorting to" = *ārammaṇam ālambanaṃ karitvā Nd* II 368.—*P* 207: "based upon" *viveka virāga nirodha. Sumaṇgalavilāsinī* 1019 says on that: *viveko virāgo nirodho ti, tīni pi nibbānassa nāmāni. . . Tasmā vivekanissitan ti ādisu ārammaṇa-vasena vā ādhigantabbavasena vā nibbāna-nissitan ti attho.*—*It-A* to *It*. 38: *nibbāna-dhātu nissitena tādinā.*

[164]e.g. *P* 60, where *S* I 266 has—*yogena* for—*vihāreṇa*.

[165]*caturbhir iryāpathaiś citta-karmaṇyatāpādanāt*, *H* 125.

rendered as "adaptability", "readiness for, flexibility", and even by "an active mind". "Wieldiness" is associated with "luminosity of mind",[166] and its opposite is also in the Pali Scriptures a mind that is "cowed", stolid, stiff, rigid, inflexible, and which resists attempts to move it in a certain direction, or to certain actions. To "dwell" is a technical term which is regularly connected with the "four postures",[167] and it seems to indicate a condition, attitude, or state of mind, which is kept up in whatever position the body may find itself. One can therefore render the idea of "dwelling in the dwelling of perfect wisdom" by saying that "he adjusts himself, his whole personality, to perfect wisdom."

In addition, he will "never cease from taking it to heart". Literally, the text says, "he is not lacking in this attention". This attribute is often coupled with the first, because of the assonance of the sounds involved, i.e. *viharaty...vihāreṇa, avirahitaś ca...manasikāreṇa*. "Attention" can also mean "mental activity", "mind-work", "action in the mind" (*manasikāra*). Although a special mental function—the fixation of the mind on an object—it is nevertheless coextensive with all mental activity, and inseparable from it. An act of consciousness requires three conditions: an inward sense organ, an outward sense-object, and an act of attention.[168] The difference between wholesome and unwholesome actions is due to the difference in the quality of the attention, which is either unwise (*ayoniso*),[169] or wise (*yoniso*). The first, in conflict with the truth,[170] turns to "signs"; the second is directed to Nirvana.[171] The Sutra now considers the problem of the mutual relation of these two kinds of attention:

The difficulty which Śāriputra raises in this respect is expressed more clearly in the *Ashta*. It is this: "Attention" is defined as a "turning-towards of a mind-in-action and it makes thought support itself in the object".[172] Attention and perfect wisdom are therefore incompatible and

[166] *A.N.I* 257. cf. *P* 121-2.

[167] e.g. *Asl.* 167, *VM* 145.

[168] *samanvāhāra*. *Prasannapadā* p. 553-5. *M.N.* 28, I. 190 and cy. *Cpd* 282 compares it to a charioteer who harnesses two horses (mind and object) into one pair.

[169] *ye keci bhikkhave akusalā dhammā, subhe te ayoniso-manasikāra-mūlakā*: whatever unwholesome dharmas there are, they are all rooted in unwise attention *S.N.* I 91; *VM* 542.—*D.N.* III 273: *eko dhammo hānabhāgīyo*: *ayoniso-manasikāro. eka dhammo visesa-bhāgīyo, yoniso-manasikāro.*

[170] *sacca-vippaṭikulena Vbh.* 373 = *saccānām anuloma-vasena Vbh-A.*

[171] *dve paccayā ānimittāya cetovimuttiyā samāpattiyā: sabbanimittānān ca amanasikāro, animittāya ca dhātuyā manasikāro.* Two are the conditions of the attainment of the signless deliverance of the heart: nonattention to all signs, attention to the signless element. *M.N.* I 296.

[172] *H* 125: *manaskāraś cetasa ābhoga ālambane citta-dhāraṇa-karmakaḥ.* Vasubandhu, *A.K.* II 154: *ālambane cetasa āvarjanam avadhāraṇam.*—*Vbh.* 373: *cittassa āvaṭṭanā anvaṭṭa-nā ābhogo samannāhāro manasikāro.*

mutually exclusive,[173] and the presence of attention in perfect wisdom would pervert its essential being.[174] One has either mental activity and no wisdom, or wisdom and no mental activity. Because, if one could have both, one and the other, then all beings would, without any effort (cf. P 258), have wisdom, because they all have mental activity. On the other hand, if we may complete the argument with a reflection from Asaṅga[175]: perfect wisdom "is not lack of mental activity because then it would be found in sleep and madness, where one does not think at all, and that cannot be, because then one would without effort arrive at the loss of perverted views". Wise attention is indeed the cause of perfect wisdom.[176]

The answer is that no reality should be considered as identical and as consistent with itself, and that mental activity is in reality no mental activity.[177] The difficulty arises only when one assumes that words refer to real entities. When one does not, all perverted views are avoided,[178] and the problem disappears.

The *Epilogue* requires no comment.

[173]*H* 125 : *paraspara-virodha* : as we saw at B6a.

[174]*H* 125 : *prajñāpāramitā-vihāraś ca tad-viparīta-svabhāva iti.*

[175]*Mahāyānasaṃgraha* VIII, 2, p. 233—cy.

[176]ib, VIII, 4.

[177]*H* 126 : *kim tv amanaskāra eva manaskāro' bhipretaḥ.*

[178]*H* 127 : *aviparyāsa-pravṛittatvād.*

Outline of Chapters 1–21

A. PREFACE
   1. THE SCENE AND CIRCUMSTANCES OF THE SERMON
      Ad-ch. 1
   2. THE AIMS IN CULTIVATING PERFECT WISDOM
      AA I 1. *Ad*-ch. 2
   3. VARIOUS PRELIMINARY INSTRUCTIONS
      AA I 2. *Ad*-ch. 3
      (*a*) Short outline of method of coursing in perfect wisdom. *AA* I 2, 1
      (*b*) Superiority of Bodhisattvas over Disciples
      (*c*) The Yoga of perfect wisdom. *AA* I 2, 2
      (*d*) Varieties of Bodhisattvas
         i. According to the circumstances of their rebirth. *AA* I 2, 3c
         ii. According to their practices
            1. Perfect Purity. *AA* I 2, 4
            2. All-knowledge. *AA* I 2, 5
            3. Cognition of the All-knowing. *AA* I 2, 6
            4. The Five Eyes. *AA* I 2, 7
            5. The Six Superknowledges. *AA* I 2, 8
            6. Emptiness, No-minding and Sameness
   4. INTERLUDE (*Ad*-ch. 4, 5)

B. PHASES OF EXTINCTION OF SELF AND OF ANYTHING IT MAY BE BASED ON
   1. THE TEACHING PROCEEDS FROM THE BUDDHA'S MIGHT
      AA I 2, 9a. *Ad*-ch. 6
   2. THE BODHISATTVA, A MERE WORD, INACCESSIBLE AS DHARMA.
      AA I 2, 9, 1
   3. DEGREES OF RIPENESS IN INSIGHT.
      AA I 2, 10. *Ad*-ch. 7
   4. THOUGHT TRANSPARENTLY LUMINOUS.
      AA I 3d
   5. HOW THE IRREVERSIBLE BODHISATTVA VIEWS THINGS.
      AA I 3f. *Ad*-ch. 8

6. PERFECT WISDOM OPPOSED TO
   (*a*) Formative Influences. *AA* I 3h
   (*b*) The Sign. *AA* I 3i
   (*c*) What Exists. *AA* I 3k
7. THE BODHISATTVA, WISDOM, AND ENLIGHTENMENT
   AA I 31. *Ad*-ch. 9
8. THE BODHISATTVA AND HIS PREDICTION.
   AA I 3p
9. ALL IS IGNORANCE.
   AA I 3s
10. ALL IS ILLUSION.
    AA I 3v. *Ad*-ch. 10
11. TWO FACTORS COUNTERACTING THE DEMORALIZING EFFECT OF THIS TEACHING:
    (*a*) Skill in Means. *AA* I 3w
    (*b*) Good Friends, as contrasted with Bad Friends. *AA* I 3x

C. WHAT TO BECOME

I THE MEANING OF "BODHI-BEING".
AA I 4. *Ad*-ch. 11
CLASSES OF DHARMAS.
AA I 5

II THE MEANING OF "GREAT BEING"
1. A Saviour of Many. *AA* I 6, 1
2. He forsakes all false views. *AA* I 6, 2. *Ad*-ch. 12
3. Unattached to even the highest thought. *AA* I 6, 3
4. Armed with the great armour. *AA* I 7. *Ad*-ch. 13
5. Set out in the great vehicle. *AA* I 8, 1
6. Mounted on the great vehicle. *AA* I 8, 6
7. Emancipation a Mock Show. *AA* I 9, 1. *Ad*-ch. 14

III THE MEANING OF "GREAT VEHICLE"
1. Its Constituents:
   (*a*) Six Perfections. *AA* I 9, 11. *Ad*-ch. 15
   (*b*) 20 Kinds of Emptiness. *AA* I 9, 12
   (*c*) 112 Concentrations. *AA* I 9, 13
   (*d*) 21 Practices. *AA* I 9, 14. *Ad*-ch. 16
   (*e*) 43 Dharani-doors. *AA* I 9, 15
   (*f*) 10 Stages. *AA* I 9, 16. *Ad*-ch. 17
2. Three questions concerning the great vehicle.
   AA I 9, 17. *Ad*-ch. 18
3. Why the "Great Vehicle" is so called. *AA* I 10, 1.
   Ad-ch. 19.

D. ATTAINMENT

1. The Bodhisattva goes forth to attainment. *AA* I 10, 6a. *Ad*-ch. 20
2. Impossibility of Attainment
   (*a*) Nothing is really ever brought forth. *AA* I 10, 6b
   (*b*) Nonduality. *AA* I 10, 6d
   (*c*) Nonproduction. *AA* I 10, 7. *Ad*-ch. 21
3. No Leaning on Anything.—*AA* I 10, 8
   EPILOGUE

In Chapters 1-21 three systems of division were used: (a) the chapters of *Ad,* (b) the divisions of *AA* which are an integral part of *P,* and (c) my own subdivisions, explained in detail in the 'Introductory Remarks'. In the later chapters the third system has been dropped. Whereas I believed to discern an architectonic unity in chapters 1-21, there seems to be no such unity in the remainder of the Sutra.

TRANSLATION OF THE SUTRA

Chapter 1

INTRODUCTION

A. PREFACE.

(1. *The Scene and Circumstances of the Sermon.*)

Thus have I heard at one time. The Lord dwelt at Rajagriha, on the Vulture Peak, together with a large gathering of monks, with 1,250 monks, all of them Arhats—their outflows dried up, undefiled, fully controlled, quite freed in their hearts, well freed and wise, thoroughbreds, great Serpents, their work done, their task accomplished, their burden laid down, their own weal accomplished, with the fetters that bound them to becoming extinguished, their hearts well freed by right understanding, in perfect control of their whole minds—
with 500 nuns, laymen, and laywomen, all of them liberated in this present life—
and with hundreds of thousands of niyutas of kotis of Bodhisattvas—(1) all of whom had acquired the Dharaṇis; (2) dwellers in emptiness, their sphere in the signless, who had not fashioned any desire for the future; (3) who had acquired sameness and patience[1]; (4) who had acquired the Dharaṇi of nonattachment; (5) who had imperishable superknowledges; (6) were of acceptable speech; (7) not tricksters; (8) not chatterers, (9) with thoughts that had left behind all desire for reputation and gain, (10) disinterested demonstrators of the spiritual dharma; (11) ready to accept deep dharmas without reserve; (12) who had obtained the grounds of self-confidence; (13) had transcended Mara's deeds, (14) were free from obstacles caused by their (past) deeds; (15) and skilful in expounding the analysis of investigations into dharma; (16) who had formed their vows incalculable aeons ago; (17) who address others with smiling countenances; (18) without a frown on their faces; (19) skilful in songs, chants and benedictions; (20) with thoughts free from sluggishness;

[1]So Nāgārjuna (pp. 325-7) seems to have understood this attribute. The Bodhisattva has won insight into two kinds of "sameness", i.e. he knows that all beings are the same, and that all dharmas are the same. He also possesses two kinds of "patience",—he is patient towards all beings, and he patiently accepts the Prajñāpāramita teaching about the true nature of all dharmas—The Tibetan seems, however, to interpret as "he acquires the patient acceptance of the sameness of all dharmas".

(21) with their flashes of ideas uninterrupted; (22) endowed with self-confidence when engaged in overpowering endless assemblies; (23) skilled in going forth during endless kotis of aeons; (24) resolutely intent on dharmas which they held to be like an illusion, a mirage, a reflection of the moon in water, a dream, an echo, an apparition, an image in the mirror, a magical creation; (P5) (25) skilful in understanding the destiny of beings, their subtle thoughts, their conduct and intentions;[2] (26) with unobstructed thoughts;[3] (27) endowed with extreme patience; (28) skilful in teaching others how to penetrate to the true character of reality; (29) acquiring through their vows and their setting-out the endless harmonies of all the Buddha-fields; (30) always face to face with the concentrated recollection of the Buddhas of countless world systems; (31) skilful in soliciting[4] innumerable Buddhas; (32) skilful in appeasing the various views, biases, prepossessions, and defilements; (33) and in producing a hundred thousand concentrations and in playing with them. They are the Bodhisattva Bhadrapāla, the great being; the Bodhisattvas Ratnākara, Sārthavāha, Naradatta, Varuṇadatta, Śubhagupta, Indradatta, Uttaramati, Viśeshamati, Vardhamānamati, Amoghadarśin, Susamprasthita, Suvikrāntavikrāmin, Nityodyukta, Anikshiptadhura, Sūryagarbha, Anupamacintin, Avalokiteśvara, Mahāsthāmaprāpta, Mañjuśrī, Vajramati, Ratnamudrāhasta, Nityokshiptahasta and Maitreya the Bodhisattva, the great being, at the head of many hundred thousands of niyutas of kotis of Bodhisattvas.

(I) Thereupon the Lord, having himself arranged the Lion Seat, sat down with his legs crossed; holding his body erect, intent on fixing his mindfulness, he entered into the concentration—"King of Concentrations" by name—in which all concentrations are included, comprehended, and come to meet.

Thereupon the Lord, mindful and self-possessed, emerging from this concentration, (P6) surveyed with the Heavenly Eye the entire world system. His whole body became radiant. From the wheels with a thousand spokes (imprinted) on the soles of his feet issued 60 hundred thousand niyutas of kotis of rays, and so from his ten toes, and similarly from his ankles, legs, knees, thighs, hips and navel, from his two sides, and from the sign "Śrīvatsa"[5] on his chest, a mark of the Superman. Similarly from his ten fingers, his two arms, his two shoulders, from his neck,

[2]So I understand after the Tibetan of *S*. But Nāgārjuna (pp. 389-90): "Knowing the course of the thought and conduct of beings, they are skilful in saving them through their subtle wisdom".

[3]Or, alternatively, "their thought is free from hostility". See also *Nag* 391-4.

[4]"Soliciting", or "invitation", *adhyeshaṇā*: This means that one asks the Buddhas (1) to preach the Dharma, (2) to postpone their entry into Nirvana, so that they may stay in the world and save beings. For the details see *Nag*. 415-422.

[5]i.e. the Svastika.

his forty teeth, his two nostrils, ears and eyes, from the hair-tuft in the middle between his eye-brows, and from the cowl on the top of his head. And through these rays this great trichiliocosm[6] was illumined and lit up. And in the East world systems as numerous as the sands of the Ganges were, by this great illumination of rays, lit up and became illumined. So in the South, the West, the North, the North-East, the South-East, the South-West, the North-West, below and above. And the beings who were lit up and illumined by this great illumination of rays, they all became fixed on[7] the utmost, right and perfect enlightenment. (P7)

(II) Thereupon all the Lord's hairpores became radiant, and from each single pore issued 60 hundred thousand of niyutas of kotis of rays through which this great trichiliocosm was illumined and lit up. And in the East world systems as numerous as the sands of the Ganges were, by this great illumination of rays, lit up and illumined. And so in the other nine directions. And the beings, who were lit up and illumined by this great illumination of rays, they all became fixed on the utmost, right and perfect enlightenment.

(III) Thereupon the Lord again, with the natural splendour of the Buddhas, the Lords, illumined the great trichiliocosm. And so on, *up to*: In all the ten directions, in each single direction, world systems as numerous as the sands of the Ganges were illumined by His splendour. And the beings who were touched by this splendour, they were all fixed on the utmost, right and perfect enlightenment.

(IV) Thereupon the Lord on that occasion put out his tongue. With it he covered the great trichiliocosm[8] and many hundreds of thousands of niyutas of kotis of rays issued from it. From each one of these rays there arose lotuses, made of the finest precious stones, of golden colour, and with thousands of petals; and on those lotuses there were, seated and standing, Buddha-frames[9] demonstrating dharma, i.e. this very demonstration of dharma associated with the six perfections. They went in all the ten directions to countless world systems in each direction (P 8), and demonstrated dharma to beings, i.e. this very demonstration of dharma associated with the six perfections. And the beings who heard this demonstration of dharma, they became fixed on the utmost, right and perfect enlightenment.

[6]See my *Buddhist Wisdom Books,* 1958, p. 40.

[7]=definitely oriented towards. "Intent on", "focused on", "set on" might be more elegant renderings.

[8]The Buddha's tongue symbolizes his veracity, or the truth of what he says. In the Rig Veda already Agni's tongue, the priestly voice, "touches heaven". S. Thomas Acquinas has a similar idea when he says: "The tongue of an angel is called metaphorically the angel's power, whereby he manifests his mental concepts. Since the intellectual operations of an angel have no reference to here and now, in angelic speech distance is no impediment".

[9]A "Buddha-frame" is the figure of a Buddha, magically conjured up by the real Buddha.

(V) Thereupon the Lord, seated on that very Lion Seat, entered into the concentration called "The Lion's Play". With his supernatural power he shook this great trichiliocosm in six ways—it moved, moved back, trembled, trembled from one end to another, tossed, tossed along. At the sides it rose up, in the middle it sank down; in the middle it rose up, at the sides it sank down; it became soft and pliable, and all beings came to be at ease.

Thereupon, at that moment, minute and second, in this great trichiliocosm the hells, and the animal world, and the world of Yama,[10] they all were abolished and became empty, and all the places of untoward rebirth disappeared. And the beings who had deceased in these destinies—i.e. the hells, the animal births, and the world of Yama—they all, through their very joy and rejoicing, were reborn among men, and also among the six kinds of gods (of the realm of sense desire). (P 9)

Thereupon these men and gods, through the very might of the Lord recalled their former lives. In their great joy and rejoicing they then approached the Lord, saluted his feet with their heads, raised their folded hands to the Lord and paid homage to him. And so in each one of the ten directions, in world systems countless as the sands of the Ganges, all the hells, animal births, and worlds of Yama were abolished and became empty, and all untoward moments[11] disappeared. And the beings who deceased in these three destinies, they all, through their very joy and rejoicing, were reborn among men, and also among the six kinds of gods (of the realm of sense desire). And those who were thus reborn among gods and men, through the might of the Lord, recalled their former lives. They then, in their great joy and rejoicing, went each to his own Buddha-field and approached the presence of the Buddha, the Lord who had arisen therein, saluted his feet, and they all raised their folded hands and paid homage to the Lord.

Thereupon in this great trichiliocosm the beings who were born blind saw forms with their eyes; the deaf heard sounds with their ears; the insane regained their mindfulness; those with distracted thoughts became one-pointed in their thoughts. The hungry were fed, the thirsty found their thirst stilled, the sick were healed and the cripples made whole. Those with unwholesome deeds of body, word and mind, and with unwholesome livelihood gave up their unwholesome habits. (P 10) All beings considered each other as one considers one's mother, father, brother, sister, friends, companions, kinsmen, and relations; and they tended the ten wholesome paths of action. Guarding their chastity,[12]

[10]Yama is the Judge of the Dead, and the king of the underworld.

[11]Or: places of unpropitious rebirth. If a man is born at an "untoward moment", it is the concentration of the misfortunes which result from the bad deeds of his past.

[12]*brahmacaryā*.

pure, they lived in the odour of sanctity. And all beings, possessed of all happiness, acquired the ease which a monk feels when immersed in the third Trance.[13] And at that very time they were endowed with such wisdom that the Buddhas and Lords in other Buddha-fields cried out: "Good is self-discipline! Good is quietude! Good is self-mastery! Good is it to have observed the practice of the religious life![12] Good is the nonharming of living beings!"

(VI) Thereupon the Lord, seated on this very Lion Seat, overtowered this great trichiliocosm. There the Tathagata stood in all his glory, shone forth, gleamed and shed light, surpassing with his splendour, lustre, brilliancy, and beauty world systems as numerous as the sands of the Ganges in each of the ten directions. He did so in the same way in which Sumeru, king of mountains, overtowering all mountains, stands, shines forth, gleams, and sheds light, surpassing them with its splendour, lustre, brilliancy, and beauty.

(VII) Thereupon the Lord exhibited His own natural body in this great trichiliocosm. The gods of the world of sense desire and of the world of form, in this great trichiliocosm (P 11), saw that glorified body of the Tathagata. They took celestial flowers, incense, perfume, garlands, ointments, powders, robes, parasols, flags, banners, and streamers; they took celestial lotuses—blue lotuses, night lotuses, water lilies, white lotuses—they took Keśara flowers and Tamāla leaves; and they approached with them the glorified body of the Tathagata. Likewise the human beings in this great trichiliocosm took land and water flowers and approached the Tathagata's glorified body. Both gods and men then strewed these flowers, etc., over the body of the Tathagata. By the sustaining power of the Buddha all these flowers, etc., formed high in the firmament one single pointed tower, which had the dimensions of the great trichiliocosm. And from this tower the celestial flowers and silken tassels hung down and were suspended, and they made this great trichiliocosm look very beautiful. And because the brightly shining golden colour of the Lord streamed forth in the ten directions, in each direction countless world systems were (P 12) lit up and illumined. In this great trichiliocosm, and in all the world systems, the same thought occurred to each one of these gods and men: "It is for me that the Tathagata, seated there, demonstrates Dharma".

(VIII) Thereupon the Lord, seated on this very Lion Throne, smiled once again. Through the illumination from that smile this great trichiliocosm, and the innumerable world systems in the ten directions, were lit up. And all the beings in this great trichiliocosm saw the Buddhas, the Lords, and their assemblies of disciples in countless world systems in the East. And conversely, all the beings in countless world systems in the

[13]See my *Buddhist Meditation*, 1956, p. 117.

East saw this Sahā world system,[14] and Śākyamuni, the Tathagata, together with his community of monks.

(IX) In the East, beyond countless world systems, at the very limit of these world systems, there is a world system called Ratnavatī.[15] In it the Tathagata Ratnākara[15] stands, holds and maintains himself.[16] He demonstrates to the Bodhisattvas this very perfection of wisdom as the Dharma. Now, in that world system a Bodhisattva, a great being, called Samantaraśmi[17] saw this great illumination, and this great shaking of the earth, and this glorified body of the Lord, and he approached the Lord Ratnākara, the Tathagata, saluted his feet with his head, and said to him: "What is the cause, O Lord, (P 13) what is the reason for this great illumination being manifested in the world, and for this great shaking of the earth, and for the exhibition of the glorified body of that Tathagata?"

The Tathagata Ratnākara replied: "There is, O son of good family, from here in the Western direction, beyond countless world systems, a world system called Sahā. There the Tathagata Śākyamuni stands, holds, and maintains himself. He reveals the perfection of wisdom to the Bodhisattvas, the great beings. This is his doing."

Samantaraśmi replied: "I will go to that Sahā world system, to see, salute, and honour that Tathagata Śākyamuni, and those Bodhisattvas, great beings, for the most part candidates to Buddhahood, who have acquired the Dharanis, are skilful in the consummation of the concentrations, and have reached the highest control over all the concentrations."

Ratnākara said: "Go then, you son of good family, for the right time has come."

Thereupon the Tathagata Ratnākara gave to the Bodhisattva Samantaraśmi lotuses made of manifold jewels, shining like gold, each with thousands of petals. "These lotuses, O son of good family, scatter over the Tathagata Śākyamuni! And say to him: 'The Lord Ratnākara hopes that the Lord Śākyamuni is well and free from sickness, alert and buoyant, strong, happy and comfortable. And these lotuses have been sent to the Lord by this Lord Ratnākara, the Tathagata'! Act with full self-possession in that Buddha-field! For the Bodhisattvas who are reborn in that Sahā world system are difficult to deal with." (P 14)

Thereupon the Bodhisattva Samantaraśmi took from the Tathagata Ratnākara those lotuses made of manifold jewels, shining like gold, each with a thousand petals. He was surrounded and accompanied by

[14]This is the name of the world in which we live.

[15]"Thick with Jewels", "Jewel mine".

[16]This is a cryptic phrase for describing a Buddha's presence in this, or any other, world system.

[17]"Rays-all-round".

many hundreds of thousands of niyutas of kotis of Bodhisattvas, both householders and recluses, and by young men and women. And before they left they honoured, worshipped, and revered the Buddhas and Lords in the world-systems of the East.

(X) With the flowers, etc., he reached the Sahā world system, approached the Tathagata Śākyamuni, saluted the Lord's feet with his head, and stood on one side. The Bodhisattva Samantaraśmi then said to the Lord Śākyamuni: "The Lord Ratnākara hopes that the Lord Śākyamuni is well and free from sickness, alert and buoyant, strong, happy and comfortable. It is the Tathagata Ratnākara who has despatched to the Lord these lotuses made of manifold jewels, shining like gold, with thousands of petals."

Thereupon the Lord Śākyamuni, the Tathagata took up these lotuses, and threw them in the Eastern direction into countless world systems, which were lit up by these lotuses. Buddha-frames were seated on those lotuses. In those Buddha-fields they demonstrated dharma, i.e. this very demonstration of dharma associated with the perfection of wisdom. And the beings who heard that dharma became fixed on the utmost, right and perfect enlightenment.

Thereupon those Bodhisattvas, both the householders and recluses, and the young men and women who had come from that world system Ratnāvatī with Samantaraśmi, the Bodhisattva, the great being, each one by virtue of his own wholesome roots[18] revered, respected, honoured and worshipped the Lord Śākyamuni, and sat down on one side.

So far about the East (P 15). From all the ten directions Bodhisattvas came to the Lord Śākyamuni. The same scene took place, but the names of the world system, the Tathagata, and the Bodhisattva differ in each case. They are: for the South Sarvaśokāpagato, Aśokaśrī, and Vigatāśoko respectively; for the West Upaśānta, Ratnārcis, Cāritramati; for the North Jayā, Jayendra, Jayadatta; (P 16) for the North-East Samādhyalaṅkritā, Samādhihastyuttaraśrī, Vijayavikrāmin; for the South-East Bodhimaṇḍalākārasurucirā, Padmottaraśrī, Padmahasta; for the South-West Vigatarajaḥsancayā, Sūryamaṇḍalaprabhāsottamaśrī, Sūryaprabhāsa; for the North-West Vaśībhūtā, Ekacchattra, Ratnottama; (P 17) for the region below Padmā, Padmaśrī, Padmottara; and for the region above Nandā, Nandaśrī, Nandadatta.

Thereupon at that moment, minute and second, this great trichiliocosm became composed of[19] the seven precious substances,[20] and was over-

[18]I.e. the merits they had acquired in the past enabled them to perform this act of reverence. Without them they would neither have seen the Buddha, nor felt the urge to worship Him.

[19] =was changed into.

[20]See my *Buddhist Wisdom Books,* 1958, p. 40.

strewn with flowers. Bundles of silken tassels were affixed to it, and it was adorned with Kalpa trees[21]—manifoldly ornamented with branches bending down with fruits—with trees with flowers and fruits, with perfumes and garlands. Just like the world system Padmāvatī, the Buddha-field of the Tathagata Samantakusuma, where Mañjuśrī the Crown Prince resides, and the Bodhisattva Susthitamati, and other very powerful Bodhisattvas.

[21]This seems to refer to the fabulous trees of Indra's paradise, which are said to grant all wishes.

CHAPTER 2

THE THOUGHT OF ENLIGHTENMENT

(2. *The Aims in Cultivating Perfect Wisdom.*)

I. THE KNOWLEDGE OF ALL MODES.

I 1. The Varieties of the Thought of Enlightenment.

I 1a. THE THOUGHT OF ENLIGHTENMENT CONNECTED WITH THE DESIRE FOR FULL ENLIGHTENMENT, IN GENERAL

When *the Lord* saw that the whole universe, with the world of the gods, the world of Mara, the world of Brahmā, with its śramaṇas and brāhmaṇas, had assembled, and also the Bodhisattvas who would one day reach the state of a Buddha, he said to the Ven. Śāriputra : A Bodhisattva, a great being who wants to fully know all dharmas (P 18) in all their modes[1] should make endeavours in the perfection of wisdom.

I 1b. THE THOUGHT OF ENLIGHTENMENT, CONNECTED WITH THE DESIRE FOR FULL ENLIGHTENMENT, IN DETAIL.

Śāriputra: How then should he make endeavours in the perfection of wisdom?

The Lord: Here, Śāriputra, a Bodhisattva, a great being, having stood in the perfection of wisdom, by way of not taking his stand on it, should perfect the perfection of giving, by way of seeing that no renunciation has taken place, since gift, giver, and recipient have not been apprehended. He should perfect himself in the perfection of morality, through not transgressing into either offence or nonoffence. He should perfect the perfection of patience and remain imperturbable. He should perfect the perfection of vigour, and remain indefatigable in his physical and mental vigour. He should perfect the perfection of meditation, and derive no enjoyment (from transic meditation). He should perfect the perfection of wisdom, on account of the fact that he apprehends neither wisdom nor stupidity.[2]

[1]or "aspects". See also *Nag*. 640-2.

[2]This definition of the six perfections is so important that it is repeated at *P* 26 and 89. Nearly the whole second volume of E. Lamotte's translation of *Mpp-s* (pp. 650-1013) is devoted to its elucidation.

I 1c. THE THOUGHT OF ENLIGHTENMENT, WHICH HAS THE WELFARE OF OTHERS FOR ITS OBJECT, IN GENERAL.

Moreover, a Bodhisattva, a great being who wants to lead to Nirvana, into the realm of Nirvana which leaves nothing behind, all the beings who are in each of the ten quarters, in world systems as numerous as the sands of the Ganges—he should train in Perfect Wisdom.

I 1d. THE THOUGHT OF ENLIGHTENMENT, WHICH HAS THE WELFARE OF OTHERS FOR ITS OBJECT, IN DETAIL.

Likewise a Bodhisattva, a great being should train himself in perfect wisdom if he desires to establish niggardly beings in giving, the immoral in morality, those abounding in ill will in patience, the slothful in vigour, those with distracted thoughts in concentrated meditation (P 19) and the stupid in the achievement of wisdom.

I 1e. THE 22 VARIETIES OF THE THOUGHT OF ENLIGHTENMENT.

I 1e,1. ASSOCIATED WITH DETERMINATION, AND LIKE THE EARTH.

Moreover, a Bodhisattva, a great being who wants to know fully all dharmas in all their modes should stand in Perfect Wisdom.

I 1e,2. ASSOCIATED WITH EARNEST INTENTION, AND LIKE BRIGHT GOLD.

Thus the Bodhisattva, the great being should here, having stood in the perfection of wisdom, by way of not taking his stand on it, perfect the perfection of giving, on account of the nonapprehension of gift, giver, and recipient. And so with the perfection of morality . . . perfection of wisdom, on account of the nonapprehension of either wisdom or stupidity (see I,1b).

I 1e,3. ASSOCIATED WITH RESOLUTE INTENTION, AND LIKE THE NEW MOON.

Thus having stood in the perfection of wisdom, a Bodhisattva, a great being should fulfil the four stations of mindfulness; the four right efforts; the four bases of psychic power; the five dominants; the five powers; the seven limbs of enlightenment; the eightfold Path. He should develop the emptiness concentration, the signless concentration, the wishless concentration. So he should develop the four trances, the four Unlimited, the four formless attainments, the eight deliverances, the nine attainments of successive stations, and the nine unlovely perceptions. Which nine? i.e. the perception of a swollen corpse, a worm-eaten corpse, a festering corpse, a bloody corpse (P 20), a blueish corpse, a corpse being devoured, a scattered corpse, a burned corpse, a corpse of only bones. He should develop the perception of revulsion from food. He should develop the recollection of the Buddha, of the Dharma, of the

Saṃgha, of morality, of renunciation, of the Gods, of breathing, of agitation, of death, of what belongs to the body; the perception of impermanence, of ill, of not-self, unloveliness, death, lack of delight in anything in the world, distrust for every thing in the world; the cognition of ill, origination, stopping, path; the cognition of extinction, of nonproduction, the cognition of dharma, the subsequent cognition, the cognition conforming to worldly convention, the cognition of mastery, the cognition according to the letter. He should develop the concentration with thoughts adjusted and discursive; the concentration without thoughts adjusted, and with only discursive thoughts; the concentration without either thoughts adjusted or thoughts discursive. He should develop the dominant "I shall come to understand the not yet understood", the dominant of understanding, the dominant of one who has understood. He should develop the stations of mastery, the all-bases, the cognition of the all-knowing, both calming-down and insight, the three knowledges, the four analytical knowledges, the four grounds of self-confidence, (P 21) the five imperishable superknowledges, the six perfections, the seven prizes, the eight discoursings of the Superman, the ten powers of a Tathāgata, the eighteen Buddha-dharmas; the great friendliness, the great compassion, the great pathetic joy, the great evenmindedness.

I 1e,4. Associated with exertion, and like a blazing fire.

A Bodhisattva, a great being who wants fully to know the cognition of the All-knowing, which is furnished with the best of all modes, should develop the perfection of wisdom.[3] A Bodhisattva, a great being who wants to fulfil the knowledge of the paths, to reach the knowledge of all modes, to fulfil the cognition of the thoughts and doings of all beings, to tear out the defilements and all the residues relating to them, should make efforts in the perfection of wisdom. Thus should a Bodhisattva, a great being be trained in perfect wisdom. Likewise he should train in perfect wisdom if he wants to enter into the fixed condition of a Bodhisattva, to pass beyond the level of a Disciple or Pratyekabuddha, to stand on the irreversible stage, completely to pass beyond the stage of a Crown Prince, to attain the six superknowledges, to become aware of the restless thoughts and doings of all beings, to surpass the cognition of all Disciples and Pratyekabuddhas, to acquire the Dharani-doors and the concentration-doors,

I 1e,5. Associated with the perfection of giving, and like a great treasury.

to establish stingy beings in giving, desirous of surpassing the gifts which

[3]The translation here follows *S* 67, instead of *P*. The phrase "furnished with the best of all modes" is explained in *Śikshāsamuccaya,* p. 272.

are given by all the Disciples and Pratyekabuddhas by means of one single production of a thought associated with Rejoicing,[4] (P 22)

I 1e,6. Associated with the perfection of morality, and like a jewel mine.

to establish the immoral in morality,

I 1e,7. Associated with the perfection of patience, and like the great ocean.

those with angry thoughts in patience,

I 1e,8. Associated with the perfection of vigour, and like a thunderbolt.

the slothful in vigour,

I 1e,9. Associated with the perfection of meditation, and like a mountain.

those with distracted thoughts in trance,

I 1e,10. Associated with the perfection of wisdom, and like a remedy.

and the stupid in wisdom.

I 1e,11. Associated with skill in means, and like a teacher.

A Bodhisattva, a great being who wants to make by skilful conversion[5] one single production of thought, directed to the knowledge of all modes, into an immeasurable and incalculable one, should also train in perfect wisdom. Having given but a little gift, having guarded but a little morality, having developed but a little patience, having exerted but a little vigour, having entered trance but a little, having developed wisdom but a little, a Bodhisattva, a great being, who wants by skilful conversion to make (this small amount) for all beings on account of the knowledge of all modes[6] into an immeasurable and incalculable one, should train in perfect wisdom.

(1) Moreover, a Bodhisattva, a great being who wants to course in the perfection of giving, should train in perfect wisdom; and so (2)—(6) with the other five perfections.

A Bodhisattva, a great being should train in perfect wisdom if he

[4]For a description of Rejoicing see *A* chapter 6.

[5]Or "dedication", "transformation". See *A* ch. 6.

[6]The meritorious actions enumerated above are dedicated to the aim of making all beings win the knowledge of all modes. If directed to this purpose, they automatically become infinitely more effective, because more and more selfless.

wants (7), for the sake of all (P 23) beings, patiently to endure the sufferings of the hells, of animal births, and the world of Yama; (8) out of regard for beings to renounce (the merit gained from) morality, though it had been piled up for hundreds of aeons; (9) to be reborn in the family of the Buddha; (10) to achieve the eighty minor characteristics and (11) the thirty-two marks of a Superman;

I 1e,12. ASSOCIATED WITH THE VOW, AND LIKE A WISHING JEWEL.

(12) to achieve the body of a Buddha; (13) to step on to the stage of a Crown Prince; (14) never to be without the Buddhas and Bodhisattvas.

Moreover, a Bodhisattva, a great being, should train in perfect wisdom if he wants (15) with one single voice to instruct countless world systems in each one of the ten directions; (16) to ensure the unbroken tradition of the Triple Jewel; (17) to foster in himself all the wholesome roots which will enable him to respect, honour, revere, and worship the Tathagatas.

I 1e,13. ASSOCIATED WITH THE POWERS, AND LIKE THE SUN.

Moreover, a Bodhisattva, a great being should train in perfect wisdom if he wants (18) to fulfil the wishes of all beings for food, drink, garments, perfumes, garlands, flowers, incense, medicinal powders, ointments, beds, seats, houses, money, grain, ornaments, jewels, gems, pearls, lapis lazuli, shells, quartz, coral, gold, silver, groves, kingdoms, etc.; (P 24) to establish in the six perfections all beings in the world which has as its highest (development) the Dharma-element, and the space element as its terminus (limit)[7]; (20) to make one single production of a skilful thought unfailing until the time when full enlightenment is reached on the terrace of enlightenment; (21) to be praised by the Buddhas and Lords in the ten directions;

I 1e,14. ASSOCIATED WITH COGNITION, AND LIKE A SWEET SONG.

(22) to be trained in the eighteen kinds of emptiness, i.e. the emptiness of the subject, etc.; (23) to look through to the Suchness of all dharmas, (24) to the Suchness of the Dharma-element, etc. to; (25) the Suchness of all reality limits;[8] (P 25), (26) to cognize in the great trichiliocosm the atomic entities[9] of earth, water, fire, and air.

(27) Moreover, a Bodhisattva, a great being, when coursing in perfect wisdom, knows that a gift thus[10] given is fruitful. When he has thus

[7]This somewhat obscure phrase also occurs at *P* 87, *S* 1444.

[8]*S*. "the reality-limits of all dharmas".

[9]This means the atoms of which all material things are composed.

[10]i.e. in the spirit of perfect wisdom, or, as at (28), "with skill in means". "Fruit" means "reward".

given a gift, he is reborn in good families, i.e. among warriors, brahmins or householders; or among various kinds of gods. Such a gift is also conducive to the acquisition of the first trance, and so on to the eighth trance, to the acquisition of the thirty-seven dharmas which act as wings to enlightenment, of the fruit of a Streamwinner, etc. to: the acquisition of Pratyekabuddhahood, of full Buddhahood.

Moreover, (28) a Bodhisattva, a great being who courses in perfect wisdom, should know that a gift thus given with skill in means fulfils the perfection of giving. And so with the other five perfections. (P 26)

Śāriputra: How is the perfection of giving fulfilled by a Bodhisattva, a great being who gives a gift, and how the other five perfections?

The Lord: The perfection of giving is fulfilled when gift, giver, and receiver are not taken as a basis; the perfection of morality through not transgressing into either offence or nonoffence; the perfection of patience through imperturbability; the perfection of vigour through indefatigability of body and mind; the perfection of meditation by the absence of distractions and representations; the perfection of wisdom by wisely knowing all dharmas without looking for definite facts. In this way are the six perfections fulfilled by a Bodhisattva, a great being who gives a gift. In the same way are all the six perfections fulfilled in the perfection of morality, etc. to the perfection of wisdom. (P 27)

I 1e,15. ASSOCIATED WITH THE SUPERKNOWLEDGES, AND LIKE A GREAT KING.

Moreover, a Bodhisattva, a great being should train in perfect wisdom if he wants (29) to transcend, through the production of one single thought, countless world systems in each of the ten directions; (30) to lift, with the fine point of the tip of a hair split a hundredfold, all the watery element in the great trichiliocosm, that there is in the great oceans, in rivers great and small, in ponds and pools, without, however, wanting to hurt the beings inhabiting it; (31) to blow out with one mighty breath from his mouth the fires in the great trichiliocosm which is all aflame with the universal conflagration raging at the end of an aeon;[11] (32) to cover with the tip of the joint of one single finger the all-shaking whirlwind which, when it proceeds, shakes, disperses, and reduces to dust the entire earth and all the mountains, beginning with Sumeru, the great Sumeru, the mountain rings, the great mountain rings; (P 28) (33) to irradiate during one single session of cross-legged meditation the entire space-element in the great trichiliocosm; (34) after he has, with one single hair, tied up and uplifted the mountains in the great trichiliocosm, i.e. Sumeru, the great Sumeru, the mountain rings, the great mountain rings, etc.,

[11]Three catastrophes, due to water, fire, and wind, mark the end of a "great aeon". See *A.K.* III 184, 215.

to hurl them forth beyond countless world systems.

Moreover, (35) a Bodhisattva, a great being should train in perfect wisdom if he wants, in each of the ten directions, in all Buddha-fields, to see the Buddhas and Lords with the heavenly eye; to hear their demonstration of Dharma with the heavenly ear; to know the thoughts and doings of all beings, to remember their former lives, to call forth the superknowledge of the cognition of the extinction of the outflows, and to realize the Reality limit.

I 1e,16. Associated with the equipment with cognition and merit, and like a storehouse of jewelry.

Moreover, a Bodhisattva, a great being should train in perfect wisdom if he wants (36) to present with one single almsbowl all the Buddhas and Lords, together with their congregations of disciples, as many as there are in the world systems countless as the sands of the Ganges, in each single direction; and equally so a Bodhisattva, a great being who wants to honour respect, revere, and worship those Tathagatas with showers of flowers, incense, perfumes, garlands, unguents, aromatic powders, strips of cloth, parasols, flags and streamers. Moreover a Bodhisattva, a great being should train in perfect wisdom if he wants (37) to establish all beings in countless world systems, in each one of the ten directions, in the five portions[12] of the Dharma, i.e. in morality, concentration, wisdom, liberation, the vision and cognition of liberation; in the fruit of a Streamwinner, etc. to : in Pratyekabuddha-enlightenment, etc., to : in the realm of Nirvana which leaves nothing behind. (P 29)

I 1e,17. Associated with the wings of enlightenment, and like a highway.

Moreover, a Bodhisattva, a great being should train in perfect wisdom if he wants (38) to gain the Buddha-qualities of the past, future, and present Buddhas and Lords; (39) to go beyond (the contrast of) conditioned and unconditioned dharmas; (40) to look through to the Suchness of all dharmas, past, future, and present, and to reach the nonproduction limit;

I 1e,18. Associated with calming-down and insight, and like a chariot

(41) to win precedence over all Disciples and Pratyekabuddhas; (42) to become an attendant of the Buddhas and Lords; (43) to belong to the intimate retinue of the Buddhas and Lords; (44) to have a great retinue, and to acquire a retinue of Bodhisattvas; and (45) to purify the donations made by others. Moreover, a Bodhisattva, a great being should train in

[12]Or "constituents", *skandha*.

perfect wisdom if he wants (46) to suppress all thought of meanness; (47) to prevent all thought of immorality and (48) of ill will from ever recurring; (49) to abandon all thought of indolence; (50) to prevent all distracted thoughts and (51) all stupid thoughts from ever recurring.

Moreover, a Bodhisattva, a great being should train in perfect wisdom if he wants to establish all beings (52) in the foundation of meritorious work consisting in giving, (53) in the foundation of meritorious work consisting in morality (P 30); (54) in the foundation of meritorious work consisting in meditional development; (55) in the foundation of meritorious work connected with the service; (56) in the foundation of meritorious work derived from material gifts given in faith to the Tathagata.[13]

Moreover, a Bodhisattva, a great being should train in perfect wisdom if he wants (57) to produce the five eyes, i.e. the fleshly eye, the heavenly eye, the wisdom eye, the Dharma-eye, the Buddha-eye; (58) to see, in each of the ten directions, with the heavenly eye the Buddhas and Lords, countless like the sands of the Ganges; to hear, with the heavenly ear, the dharmas which those Buddhas and Lords teach; to comprehend, with his heart, as it really is, the thought of those Buddhas and Lords; to recall the Bodhisattvahood, connected with their previous lives, of those Buddhas and Lords; and to see the display of their wonderworking power.

Moreover, a Bodhisattva, a great being should train in perfect wisdom if he wants (59) to keep in mind, until he fully awakens to enlightenment, by the assumption of the power of unbroken memory, all the dharmas which the Buddhas, the Lords teach in all the ten directions in all the world systems, after he has heard them; (60) to see the Buddha-fields of the past Buddhas and Lords, of the future Buddhas and Lords (P 31), and of those Buddhas and Lords who just now in the world, in all the ten directions, stand, hold, and maintain themselves;

I 1e,19. Associated with the inspiration of the dharanis, and like unto a fountain.

(61) to learn whatever has been taught, or is being taught, or will be taught, by the Buddhas, the Lords in the ten directions—i.e. the Discourses, Discourses in Prose and Verse Mingled, Predictions, Verses, Summaries, Origins, Thus-was-said, Birth Stories, Expanded Texts, Marvels, Tales, Expositions, and what has not been heard by the Disciples—to bear it in mind, to preach it, to progress to its Thusness,[14] and to illuminate it in detail for others.

[13]This list of five *puṇyakriyāvastūni* differs at (55) from that in *Mhvy.* 1699-1703. The "service" is understood to be rendered to the Buddha, or to monks and holy men.

[14]The word *tathatva* occurs often in these Sutras, but to my knowledge it is nowhere explained either in the text or the commentaries. The Tibetan equivalent is the same as that for *tathatā*, "Suchness". The phrase probably means, "to arrive at an understanding of what it really means".

I 1e,20. ASSOCIATED WITH THE BESTOWAL OF DHARMA AND LIKE A DELIGHTFUL SOUND.

Moreover, a Bodhisattva, a great being should train in perfect wisdom if he wants (62) to illuminate, in each one of the ten directions, in world systems countless like the sands of the Ganges, all the regions of darkness which the light of sun and moon cannot reach; (63) to proclaim, in each of the ten directions, in countless world systems, the message of the Buddha, of the Dharma, of the Saṃgha, to all the beings who are reborn in the various Buddha-fields, and to establish all those beings in right view. (P 32)

I 1e,21. ASSOCIATED WITH THE PATH OF THE ONE VEHICLE, AND LIKE A RIVER IN FULL SPATE.

Moreover, a Bodhisattva, a great being should train in perfect wisdom if he wishes (64) that all the beings who are blind, in each one of the ten directions, in countless world systems, should, by his might, see forms with their eyes; that the deaf should hear sounds with their ears; the insane regain their mindfulness, the naked obtain clothes, and the hungry be fed; that those beings who were reborn in the states of woe should be freed from all the states of woe and acquire human bodies; that he will help to establish the immoral in morality, the unconcentrated in concentration, the stupid in wisdom, those unliberated in liberation, those who have no vision and cognition of liberation in the vision and cognition of liberation,[15] those who do not see the Truths in the fruit of a Streamwinner, etc., *to*: in the enlightenment of a Pratyekabuddha, in the utmost, right and perfect enlightenment.

I 1e,22. ASSOCIATED WITH THE DHARMA-BODY, AND LIKE A GREAT RAIN CLOUD.

Moreover, a Bodhisattva, a great being should train in perfect wisdom if he wants to (65) train himself in the bearing[16] of a Tathagata. (P 33) Moreover, a Bodhisattva, a great being who courses in perfect wisdom, should consider (*a*) "Where then will I (immediately before my Parinirvana) cast back the elephant look?"[17] He should consider that he should

[15]This again is the list of the five "portions" of the Dharma; see note 12.

[16]*īryāpatha,* lit. "postures", a term pregnant with meaning and not yet fully explored. *S* 110 explains to some extent by adding: "if he wants to train in the purity of the conduct and practices of a Tathagata, in the perfect purity of His deeds of body, speech and mind, which are always preceded and controlled by His cognition".

[17]See my *Buddhist Scriptures,* 1959, p. 60.—This refers to the occasion when the Buddha cast a last look at Vaiśalī before he left that city to go to his Parinirvana. On that occasion He turned round his entire body, as an elephant does when he gazes at something, for the bones in a Buddha's neck are more firmly fixed than those of ordinary men. Hence one speaks of an "elephant look". cf. also *Mil.* 398: "As the elephant turns his whole body when he looks, always looking straight before him, not glancing round this way or that, just so should the Yogin, etc."

train in perfect wisdom, (*b*) so that, his feet may glide at least four inches above the ground; (*c*) so that, surrounded by all the gods, revered by many hundreds of thousands of niyutas of kotis of gods, he may approach the foot of the tree of enlightenment; (*d*) so that those same gods may spread out a carpet at the root of the tree of enlightenment; (*e*) so that, when he has fully known the utmost, right, and perfect enlightenment—whether he walks, stands, sits, or lies down—that spot of earth may become Adamantine;[18] (*f*) so that he may know full enlightenment on the very day that he leaves home, and on that very same day turn the wheel of Dharma; (P 34) so that, when he turns the wheel of Dharma, countless beings purify the dispassionate unstained Dharma-eye in regard to dharmas, are freed from the outflows without further clinging, and become irreversible from full enlightenment; (*g*) so that he may have a community of disciples that can neither be measured nor calculated—countless beings, through one single demonstration of Dharma, becoming austere and solitary Arhats,[19] or Bodhisattvas, great beings who are irreversible from the utmost, right, and perfect enlightenment; so that he may have a community of Bodhisattvas that can neither be measured nor calculated, so that the measure of his life span may be measureless, and he may achieve a measureless splendour; (*h*) so that, when he has known full enlightenment, in his Buddha-field there may be no occasions whatsoever for greed, hate, and delusion; (*i*) so that, when he has known full enlightenment, beings become endowed with such a wisdom that the Buddhas and Lords in other Buddha-fields will be moved to breathe forth this shout of triumph: "Good is quietude! Good is self-discipline! Good is self-mastery! Good is it to have observed the practice of the religious life! Good is the nonharming of all living beings!"; (*k*) so that, when he has passed away into Nirvana, there may be no disappearance of the true Dharma, and so that, when they merely hear his name, the beings in the world systems countless as the sands of the Ganges, in the ten directions, will become fixed on the utmost, right, and perfect enlightenment. (P 35).

At that time, when a Bodhisattva, a great being who courses in perfect wisdom, brings forth these virtuous qualities, the four Great Kings in the great trichiliocosm reflect as follows: "We will give the four bowls to this Bodhisattva, this great being, as the Great Kings of the past

[18]Ordinary earth or rock cannot possibly support a fully enlightened Buddha at the time of his enlightenment. In consequence, the "terrace of enlightenment", i.e. the place where he sits, etc., when becoming enlightened, must be made of the indestructible substance known as *vajra*.

[19]The translation here follows *S* against *P*. "Austere and solitary" renders *ekāsanika*, taking the word to refer to hermits who avoid society, in contrast to Bodhisattvas who live in it. Normally it is a technical term for one of the 12 "austere practices", and refers to someone who eats his meal in one sitting.

have done to the Tathagatas of the past".[20] And the Gods of the Thirty-Three are enraptured, the Yama gods, the Tushita gods, the Nirmanarata gods, and the Parinirmitavasavartin gods are delighted, and decide to arrange for service to that Bodhisattva, that great being. The hosts of the Asuras are derided, and the heavenly hosts in the great trichiliocosm wax strong and rejoice. And the higher gods decide to invite[21] this one, when he has been fully enlightened, to turn the wheel of Dharma.

At the time when a Bodhisattva, a great being who courses in perfect wisdom, grows in the six perfections, at that time the sons and daughters of good family who belong to the Bodhisattva vehicle become enraptured and will want to become his mother and father, his wife and sons, his kinsmen and relations. The gods, right up to the Akanishtha gods, are enraptured, (P 36) because the Bodhisattva shuns sexual intercourse. From the first thought of enlightenment onwards the Bodhisattva is chaste. He is not conjoined with fettering dharmas. He reflects that "one who is not chaste, who pursues sensuous pleasures, he causes an obstacle to rebirth even in the Brahma world, how much more then to supreme enlightenment". Therefore a Bodhisattva, chaste, not unchaste, should, having left his home, know full enlightenment.

Śāriputra: Does then the Bodhisattva in all circumstances have parents, wives, sons, paternal and maternal relatives?

The Lord: Some Bodhisattvas do. Some of them, from the first thought of enlightenment onwards, take chastity upon themselves, and, course in the course of a Bodhisattva always as Crown Princes until they know full enlightment. Some Bodhisattvas taste the five sense qualities through their skill in means, and afterwards leave home and know full enlightenment. Just as a clever (P 37) magician or magician's apprentice, well trained in magical illusions, would conjure up the five sense qualities, delight in them, play with them, minister to them. What do you think, Śāriputra, would that magician, or magician's apprentice, have actually tasted and relished those five sense qualities?

Śāriputra: No, O Lord!

The Lord: Just so do Bodhisattvas, through their skill in means, taste the five kinds of sense qualities, for the sake of maturing beings, but without being stained by those sense qualities. Sense desires are disparaged by the Bodhisattva with the words: "All ablaze are sense desires, disgusting, murderous, inimical!" It is in such a spirit that a Bodhisattva, for the sake of maturing beings, lays hold of the five sense qualities.

[20]For the story of the four bowls see my *Buddhist Scriptures*, 1959, pp. 52-3.

[21]Or "solicit", as in ch. 1 note 4.

Chapter 3

OBSERVATIONS

(3. *Various preliminary instructions*:
(*a*) *Short outline of method of coursing in perfect wisdom.*)

I 2. Instructions.

I 2,1. Instructions About the Progress.[1]

Śāriputra:[2] How then should the Bodhisattva, the great being, course in perfect wisdom?

The Lord: Here[3] the Bodhisattva, the great being, coursing in the perfection of wisdom, truly a Bodhisattva, does not review[4] a Bodhisattva, nor the word "Bodhisattva", nor the course of a Bodhisattva, (nor the perfection of wisdom, nor the word "perfection of wisdom". He does not review that "he courses", nor that "he does not course"). He does not review form, feeling, perception, formative forces, or consciousness. (P38) And why? Because the Bodhisattva, the great being, is actually empty of the own-being of a Bodhisattva, and because perfect wisdom is by its own-being empty. And why? That is its essential original nature. (For it is not through emptiness that form, etc. is empty.) Nor is emptiness other than form, etc.

[1]*H* comments: In progressing in the acquisition of the virtuous qualities which characterize the 22 forms of the thought of enlightenment, one must train oneself in such a way that one deviates from neither conventional nor ultimate truth, and that one employs the method of the nonapprehension of separate entities. This method, peculiar to Bodhisattvas, is not shared by the Disciples.

[2]The "Instructions" are addressed to Śāriputra, who was the unexcelled protagonist of Abhidharma wisdom. Highly skilled in manipulating a multiplicity of dharmas, he felt slightly out of his depth when confronted with the Prajñāpāramitā doctrine which admits no distinction between dharmas. Śāriputra being the interlocutor here, the "Instructions" are held to be of a fairly elementary nature.

[3]This passage, *P* 38-39, became for the Yogācārins the basis of their doctrine of the 10 "discriminations", and of the 10 "antidotes" to them, which are said to be enumerated here. In my *The Prajñāpāramitā Literature*, 1960, pp. 98-100 I have collected a number of different versions of this section from various recensions. The additions in brackets are from *S* I 118-120.

[4]"Sees repeatedly." Most people do not review "Bodhisattva", etc., for they have no idea what it is. But theirs is not the supreme wisdom. The Sūtra assumes that we have done a lot of "reviewing" in the Abhidharma sense, and now tells us to cease doing so. But it does not tell us to stop doing something which we have never started to do.

And why? The very form, etc., is emptiness, the very emptiness is form, etc. And why? Because "Bodhisattva", "perfect wisdom", "form", etc. are mere words. Because form, etc., are like an illusion. Illusions and mere words do not stand at any point or spot; they are not, do not come into being, are false to behold. For of what the own-being is seen to be an illusion, of that there is no production or stopping, no defilement or purification. Thus a Bodhisattva, a great being who courses in the perfection of wisdom, also does not review the production (of any dharma); nor its stopping (or abiding, its decrease or increase), defilement or purification. (He does not review form, etc., nor "enlightenment", nor what is called an "enlightenment-being".) And why? Because words are artificial. People have constructed a counter-dharma.[5] They express it conventionally by means of an adventitious designation (which is imagined and unreal, and they settle down in that conventional expression). A Bodhisattva, a great being who courses in perfect wisdom, does not review (that which is said to correspond to) all those words, (does not get at them). Not reviewing them, (not getting at them, he does not mind them), does not settle down in them.[3]

Furthermore, a Bodhisattva, a great being who courses in the perfection of wisdom, does not consider[6] the fact that these are mere words, i.e. this "Bodhisattva", this "enlightenment", this "Buddha", (P39) this "perfection of wisdom", this "coursing in the perfection of wisdom", this "form", etc. Just as one speaks of a "self", and yet no self is got at, and no being, soul, personality, person, individual, or man, etc., on account of unascertainable emptiness.[7] And why? Because there a Bodhisattva does also not review that by means of which he would settle down. Coursing thus, a Bodhisattva, a great being courses in perfect wisdom.

((*b*) *Superiority of Bodhisattvas over Disciples.*)

If this Continent of Jambudvipa were filled with monks similar in worth to Śāriputra and Maudgalyāyana—like a thicket of reeds, bamboos, or sugar cane, of tall grass,[8] or rice, or sesamum plants—their

[5]*prati-dharma.* This means something which looks like a reality, but is in fact the very opposite of one. Words mislead, and far from expressing the reality of what they refer to, they in fact run counter to it. The passage may, however, be corrupt, and *S* as well as *S*-Tib. differ.

[6]lit. investigate.

[7]no. 15 of *P* 197. Where there is no self, there can be no actual progress to Nirvana. To speak of "spiritual progress" usually smuggles in a "self" or a "being", limits the field of the progress, and assumes that this person progresses, and that person does not. It is difficult to have progress without one who progresses, or to speak of "progress" when one cannot locate it anywhere.

[8]lit. the Saccharum Sara reed.

wisdom does not approach the wisdom of a Bodhisattva who courses in perfect wisdom by one hundredth part, nor by one thousandth part, nor by a 100,000th part; it does not bear number, nor fraction, nor counting, nor similarity, nor comparison, nor resemblance. To such an extent does the wisdom of a Bodhisattva, who, coursing in perfect wisdom, develops it for one day only, surpass the wisdom of all the Disciples and Pratyekabuddhas. And why? Because that wisdom of a Bodhisattva, a great being is concerned with (winning) Nirvana for all beings. And that would hold true even if not only Jambudvipa, but if the great trichiliocosm, or even if all the countless world systems in each of the ten directions were filled with monks similar in worth to Śāriputra and Maudgalyāyana. (P40)

Śāriputra: The wisdom of Streamwinners, the wisdom of Once-Returners, Never-Returners, Arhats and Pratyekabuddhas, the wisdom of a Bodhisattva, the wisdom of a Tathagata—all these kinds of wisdom are not differentiated, they are isolated, unproduced, without own-being and empty. But no distinction or difference can be got at of that which is not broken apart, which is isolated, unproduced, without own-being and empty. How then does the wisdom which a Bodhisattva has developed for one day only, that wisdom of one who is coursing in perfect wisdom, surpass the wisdom of all the Disciples and Pratyekabuddhas?

The Lord: When you consider, Sariputra, the task of a Bodhisattva, a great being who courses in perfect wisdom, for which the wisdom, developed for one day only, has been set up and furnished with the best of all modes[9]; the task of one who courses in all-knowledge and works for the welfare of all beings (in the sense that he has resolved that) "once having fully understood all dharmas in all their modes, one should lead all beings to Nirvana";—is that also the task for which the wisdom of all the Disciples and Pratyekabuddhas has been set up?

Śāriputra: No indeed, O Lord.

The Lord: What do you think, Sariputra, does it occur to any of the Disciples and Pratyekabuddhas that "after we have known full enlightenment, we should lead all beings to Nirvana, into the realm of Nirvana which leaves nothing behind"?

Śāriputra: No, indeed, O Lord.

The Lord: One should therefore know that this wisdom of the Disciples and Pratyekabuddhas bears no comparison to the wisdom of a Bodhisattva even though developed for one day only. What do you think, Sariputra, does it occur to any of the Disciples and Pratyekabuddhas that "after I have practised the six perfections, matured beings, purified the Buddha-field, perfected the ten powers of a Tathagata, his four grounds of self-confidence, the four analytical knowledges and the eighteen special dharmas of a Buddha, having known full enlightenment

[9]See note 3, chapter 2.

(P41) I shall lead countless beings to Nirvana"?

Śāriputra: No, O Lord.

The Lord: But such are the intentions of a Bodhisattva. A glowworm, being a mere insect, does not think that its light could illuminate the Continent of Jambudvipa, or shine over it. Just so the Disciples and Pratyekabuddhas do not think, not even one of them, that they should, after winning full enlightenment, lead all beings to Nirvana. But the sun, when it has risen, sheds its light over the whole of Jambudvipa. Just so a Bodhisattva, after he has accomplished the practices which end in full enlightenment, leads countless beings to Nirvana.

Śāriputra: How does a Bodhisattva, a great being, after he has stepped above the level of all the Disciples and Pratyekabuddhas, reach the irreversible level, and purify the path to enlightenment?

The Lord: Here a Bodhisattva, a great being steps above the level of a Disciple and Pratyekabuddha, reaches the irreversible level and purifies the path to enlightenment, because from the first thought of enlightenment onwards he courses in the six perfections, taking his stand on empty, signless, and wishless dharmas.

Śāriputra: On which level does a Bodhisattva, a great being, become constantly and always worthy of the donations of all the Disciples and Pratyekabuddhas? (P42)

The Lord: He is constantly and always worthy of them during the period which begins with the first thought of enlightenment and ends with his arrival on the terrace of enlightenment, during which period a Bodhisattva, a great being courses in the six perfections. And why? Because it is thanks to the Bodhisattva, the great being, that all the wholesome dharmas are manifested in the world, i.e. the ten wholesome paths of action, the five moral rules, the eight Uposatha vows, the four trances, the four Unlimited, the four formless attainments, the five superknowledges, the four applications of mindfulness, the four right efforts, the four bases of psychic power, the five cardinal virtues, the five powers, the seven limbs of enlightenment, the eightfold path; the four grounds of self-confidence, the four analytical knowledges, the six perfections, the ten powers of a Tathagata, the eighteen special Buddha-dharmas. It is a result of the manifestation of these wholesome dharmas in the world that good families are conceived, i.e. nobles, brahmins and well-to-do householders; that the gods are conceived, from the four Great Kings *to*: (P43) the Gods of the sphere of neither perception nor non-perception; and that Streamwinners arise in the world, etc. *to*: Arhats, Pratyekabuddhas, Bodhisattvas and Tathagatas.

Śāriputra: Does then a Bodhisattva, a great being, cleanse the donations he receives, or does he not?

The Lord: He does not cleanse them, because the donations of a

Bodhisattva, a great being, are just absolutely pure. And why? A donor is the Bodhisattva, the great being. Of what is he a donor? Of wholesome dharmas, i.e. of the ten wholesome paths of action *to* the eighteen special Buddha-dharmas.

((*c*) *The Yoga of Perfect Wisdom.*)

I 2,2. INSTRUCTIONS ABOUT THE TRUTHS.[10]

I 2,2a. INSTRUCTION ABOUT THE TRUTH OF ILL.[11]

Śāriputra: How is a Bodhisattva, a great being who is joining (exerting) himself, to be called "joined to perfect wisdom"?

The Lord: (AI) Here, Sariputra, a Bodhisattva, a great being, who is joined to the emptiness of form is to be called "joined". And so if he is joined to the emptiness of feeling, etc.; (P44) of the eye *to* mind, of sight-objects *to* mind-objects, of eye-element, sight-object-element; eye-consciousness-element, etc. *to*: mind-consciousness-element; of suffering, origination, stopping, path; and of ignorance, etc. *to*: decay and death. (II) Joined to the emptiness of all dharmas[12] is he to be called "joined". Of whichever conditioned and unconditioned dharmas he may have formed a notion, joined to the emptiness of all those dharmas is he to be called "joined". Moreover, Sariputra, a Bodhisattva, a great being, who courses in perfect wisdom, should be called "joined" if he is joined to the emptiness of the essential original nature.[13] It is thus, Sariputra, that the Bodhisattva, the great being who courses in perfect wisdom is, when joined to these seven[14] emptinesses, to be called "joined". It is thus, Sariputra, that he who courses in perfect wisdom by means of these seven emptinesses should, because of that, not even be called "joined" or "unjoined". (III) And why? Because there he does not review form, etc., as "joined", or as "unjoined".

I 2,2b. INSTRUCTIONS ABOUT THE TRUTH OF ORIGINATION.[15]

(BI) He does not (P45) review form, etc., as either subject to production,

[10]In *AA* I2,2a-c the translation follows *S* i 136-141, which is fuller than the corresponding text of *P*.

[11]The reader will do well to consult *Prasannapadā* XII on *duḥkha*, if possible in Schayer's translation. It is also useful to compare the exact wording of the four holy Truths, e.g. in my *Buddhism*, 1951, p. 43.

[12]no. 13 at *P* 197.

[13]no. 12 at *P* 197.

[14]"seven" in *S* and *S*-Tib; "ten" in Gilgit *P*; "all" in *P*. The seven emptinesses are probably: 1, form, etc.; 2, eye, etc.; 3, sight-objects, etc.; 4, sight consciousness, etc.; 5, suffering etc.; 6, ignorance, etc.; 7, all dharmas.

[15]Here one should compare *Prasannapadā* XIV on the impossibility of a cooperation (*samsarga*) between distinct entities, on the ground that they have no independent existence.

or as subject to stopping. (II) He does not review form, etc., as either subject to defilement, or as subject to purification. (III) He does not review form as connecting with feeling; feeling as connecting with form; feeling as connecting with perception; perception as connecting with feeling; perception as connecting with impulses; impulses as connecting with perception; impulses as connecting with consciousness; consciousness as connecting with impulses. And why? Because no dharma connects with any other dharma, nor does it disconnect; it is not joined nor disjoined—on account of the emptiness of their essential original nature.[16] (IV) That which is emptiness, that is not form, etc. (V) Because the emptiness of form does not molest[17], the emptiness of feeling does not feel, the emptiness of perception does not perceive, the emptiness of impulses does not put together, the emptiness of consciousness is not aware. (P46) (VI) And why? Form is not one thing, and emptiness another; emptiness is not one thing, and form another. The very form is emptiness, the very emptiness is form. *And so for* feeling, etc.

I 2,2c. INSTRUCTIONS ABOUT THE TRUTH OF STOPPING.

(CI) And that emptiness, that is neither produced nor stopped, is neither defiled nor purified, does not decrease or increase; and that which is neither produced nor stopped, neither defiled nor purified, neither decreased nor increased, that is not past, future, or present. (II) There is no form in it, no feeling, etc.; no eye, etc. *to*: no mind; no form, etc, *to*: no mind-objects; no eye-element, etc. *to*: no mind-consciousness-element; no ignorance, no stopping of ignorance, etc. *to* : (P47) no decay and death, no stopping of decay and death; no suffering and no comprehension of suffering; no origination and no forsaking of origination; no stopping and no realization of stopping; no path and no development of the path; no attainment, and no reunion; no Streamwinner, and no fruit of a Streamwinner; etc. *to*: no Bodhisattva, and no knowledge of the modes of the path; no Buddha, and no enlightenment. (III) It is in this sense, Sariputra, that a Bodhisattva, a great being who courses in perfect wisdom, is to be called "joined".

Also *Dharmasangīti* in *Śi* 263 sq. : "No dharma is ever produced or stopped. In actual fact the eye does not make contact with form, the ear with sounds, etc. Because there can be no union between them, and the eye cannot intimately unite with form, etc., and therefore cannot come into contact (or : collide) with it. There can be no contact (*raṇa*, also : collision, strife, contamination!) with a dharma which is single, and has no second. All dharmas, in fact, are single, they do not cognize or discern one another, they cannot be construed or deconstrued, do not combine or dissolve, cannot grow or diminish".

[16]*S*-Tib. seems to understand this sentence quite differently.

[17]This is a play on words : *rūpam* (form) *rūpayati* (molests). On the face of it that seems to mean that "form has no figure" (cf. *P Dc* s.v.), but *S*-Tib. has *thogs-par byed-pa*, "strike, run against, impede". In *A.K.* I 24, 45 *rūpam* is derived from *rūpyate,* "breaks up" (*rūmpere*), "changes in form", "is brittle", and that is the meaning of *rūpaṇa* (*'jig-pa*) at *P* 197.

I 2,2d. INSTRUCTIONS ABOUT THE TRUTH OF THE PATH.[18]

(DI) One who courses in perfect wisdom does not review himself as "joined" to the perfection of giving, nor as "not joined" to it. *And so with the other perfections*, with form (P48), etc., *to*: the cognition of the All-knowing. Also by this method should it be known that a Bodhisattva, a great being, who has been thus joined to perfect wisdom, is to be called "joined". (II) Moreover, a Bodhisattva, a great being who courses in perfect wisdom, does not join emptiness with emptiness, nor is emptiness a matter for joining; he does not join the signless with the signless, nor is the signless a matter for joining; he does not join the wishless with the wishless, nor is the wishless a matter for joining. And why? Because emptiness is not a matter for joining, or disjoining. When he thus joins himself a Bodhisattva, a great being, is to be called "joined, joined to perfect wisdom". (III) Moreover, a Bodhisattva, a great being who courses in perfect wisdom, plunges into the own-mark emptiness of dharmas. But when he does so, he does not join with form, etc., nor disjoins (himself) from it. He does not join with form, etc. at the beginning or at the end, or in the present. He truly does not review the beginning, end, or present. When he thus joins himself, a Bodhisattva, a great being, is to be called "joined, joined to perfect wisdom". (P49) (IV) Moreover, a Bodhisattva, a great being who courses in perfect wisdom, does not join the beginning with the end, nor the end with the beginning, nor the present with the beginning or end, nor the end with the beginning or present, nor the beginning with the end or the present. And that is on account of the emptiness of the (three) periods of time. When he thus joins himself, a Bodhisattva, a great being, is to be called "joined, joined to perfect wisdom".

I 2,3. INSTRUCTIONS ABOUT THE THREE TREASURES.

I 2,3a. INSTRUCTIONS ABOUT THE TREASURE OF THE BUDDHA.

(E) Moreover, a Bodhisattva, a great being who courses in perfect wisdom, is "bound" thereby to join himself thus that he does not join the knowledge of all modes to the past, the future, or the present. He just does not review the past, future, or present; how can he join the knowledge of all modes to them? When he thus joins himself, a Bodhisattva is to be called "joined, joined to perfect wisdom". (P50) Moreover, a

[18]Obermiller well sums up I2, 2d after *H*: A Bodhisattva cannot be really endowed with the six perfections, nor can he be devoid of them. The emptiness of his internal constituents, which make up his "person", has, from the standpoint of the Absolute, no real relation to the emptiness of his external environment, which constitutes the sphere of his action; at the same time such a relation cannot be entirely absent, because otherwise there could be no skill in means and no spiritual progress.—It is noteworthy that the eight steps of the "holy Path", i.e. right views, etc., are nowhere even alluded to.

Bodhisattva, a great being who courses in perfect wisdom, does not join form, or any other dharma, to the knowledge of all modes. Form, or any other dharma, he just does not review. When he thus joins himself, a Bodhisattva is to be called "joined, joined to perfect wisdom". Moreover, a Bodhisattva, a great being who courses in perfect wisdom does not join the perfection of giving, or any other wholesome dharma,[19] to the knowledge of all modes. The very perfection of giving, or any other wholesome dharma, he does not review. When he thus joins himself, a Bodhisattva is to be called "joined, joined to perfect wisdom". (P51) Moreover, a Bodhisattva, a great being does not join the Buddha to the knowledge of all modes; the very Buddha he does not review; nor does he join the knowledge of all modes to the Buddha; the very knowledge of all modes he does not review. He does not join enlightenment to the knowledge of all modes; the very enlightenment he does not review. Nor does he join the knowledge of all modes to enlightenment; the very knowledge of all modes he does not review. And why? The very Buddha is the knowledge of all modes, the very knowledge of all modes is the Buddha. The very enlightenment is the knowledge of all modes, the very knowledge of all modes is enlightenment. When he thus joins himself a Bodhisattva is to be called "joined, joined to perfect wisdom".

I 2,3b. INSTRUCTIONS ABOUT THE TREASURE OF THE DHARMA.

(F) Moreover, a Bodhisattva, a great being who courses in perfect wisdom, does not join up with the conviction that "form is a positive existent", or that "form is not a positive existent"; that "form is permanent or impermanent"; that "form is ease or suffering"; (P52) that "form is the self, or not the self"; that "form is calm or uncalm". *And so for* the other skandhas. He does not join up with the conviction that "form is empty or not empty", that "form is with sign, or signless", that "form is with wish, or wishless". And so for the other skandhas. One who courses thus does not approach the ideas that "he courses", "he does not course", "he both courses and does not course", "he neither courses nor does he not course". A Bodhisattva, a great being, who courses thus, is to be called "joined to perfect wisdom". (P53)

Moreover, a Bodhisattva, a great being, who courses in perfect wisdom, does not course in perfect wisdom for the sake of the perfection of giving, or any other perfection, nor for the sake of the irreversible stage, nor for the purpose of maturing beings or of purifying the Buddha-field, nor for the sake of the ten powers of a Tathagata, etc. *to*: the Buddha-dharmas; nor for the sake of the emptiness of the subject, etc.; nor for the sake of Suchness, of the realm of Dharma, of the reality limit, etc. And why? Because a Bodhisattva, a great being, who courses in perfect

[19]The usual list up to the 18 Buddhadharmas.

wisdom, does not review the differentiation of any dharma whatsoever. A Bodhisattva, a great being, who courses thus, is to be called "joined to perfect wisdom". He does not course in perfect wisdom for the sake of the heavenly eye, or the heavenly ear, or the cognition of others' thoughts, or the recollection of former lives, or for the sake of wonderworking powers. And why? Because there one who courses in perfect wisdom (P54) does not even review the perfection of wisdom; how then (could he review) a Bodhisattva, or how could he apprehend all the superknowledges in all their modes? It is thus that a Bodhisattva, a great being who courses in perfect wisdom, is to be called "joined".

Moreover, it does not occur to a Bodhisattva, a great being who courses in perfect wisdom, that "I know with the heavenly eye the decease and rebirth of beings in world systems as numerous as the sands of the Ganges in each one of the ten directions; with the heavenly ear I hear their sounds; I know their very thoughts; having also recollected their former lives, and having travelled (to them) with the help of my wonderworking powers, I will demonstrate Dharma (to them)" (P55). It is thus that a Bodhisattva, a great being who courses in perfect wisdom and leads countless beings to Nirvana, is to be called "joined".

In this way Mara, the Evil One, does not get a chance to harm the Bodhisattva, the great being who courses in perfect wisdom. And all the other worldly defilements he may still have will burst asunder. And this Bodhisattva will be protected by the Buddhas, the Lords who, in all the ten directions, stand, hold, and maintain themselves in world systems as numerous as the sands of the river Ganges, and demonstrate Dharma; and also by their Disciples, and also by Pratyekabuddhas, and by the gods, from the Four Great Kings to the Highest Gods. And they will see to it that that Bodhisattva will meet with no impediments at all. If he has any physical defect it will completely cease in this very life. And why? Because he radiates friendliness over all beings. (P56)

Moreover, a Bodhisattva a great being who courses in perfect wisdom, comes with little trouble face to face with the Dharani-doors and the concentration-doors. Wherever he is reborn, he pleases the Tathagatas and is not deprived anywhere of the Buddhas, the Lords, until he has known full enlightenment. It is thus that a Bodhisattva, a great being, who courses in perfect wisdom, is to be called "joined".

Moreover, it does not occur to a Bodhisattva, a great being who courses in perfect wisdom that "there is some dharma which is conjoined with or disjoined from (other) dharmas". Nor does he wish that "he might more quickly fully know the Realm of Dharma, or not fully know it at all". (P57) And why? Because the Realm of Dharma is not fully known by means of the Realm of Dharma. It is thus that a Bodhisattva, a great being who courses in perfect wisdom, is to be called "joined". Moreover, a Bodhisattva, a great being who courses in perfect wisdom, does not review anything as separate from the Realm of Dharma, or distinguish any dharma from the Realm of Dharma. It also does not occur to him that "this Realm of Dharma has been penetrated",[20] or "this Realm of Dharma has not been penetrated". For he does not review any dharma by means of which he could penetrate to that Realm of Dharma. Because he does not join up the Realm of Dharma with the idea that it is empty, or with the idea that it is not empty. It is thus that a Bodhisattva, a great being, who courses in perfect wisdom, is to be called "joined".

Moreover, a Bodhisattva, a great being, who courses in perfect wisdom, does not join up the eye-element, or any of the 18 elements with emptiness; nor does he join up emptiness with the eye-element (P58), or any of the 18 elements.[21] And why? This is the foremost "undertaking" of the Bodhisattva, i.e. the endeavour about emptiness. When he courses in emptiness, a Bodhisattva does not fall on the level of a Disciple or Pratyekabuddha, but purifies the Buddha-field, matures beings, and quickly knows full enlightenment. Among the "endeavours" of a Bodhisattva the "endeavour" about the perfection of wisdom is declared to be the highest, the best, the choicest, the most excellent, the utmost, the unsurpassed, the peerless, the unequalled, the most sublime. And why? There is nothing above (P59) that "endeavour", i.e. above the "endeavour" about perfect wisdom, about emptiness, the signless, the wishless. A Bodhisattva who is "endeavouring" (joining himself) thus, should be borne in mind as predicted (to Buddhahood), as one who has come near the prediction. He will work the welfare of countless beings, but it will not occur to him that "the Buddhas, the Lords will predict me; I have come near the prediction; I will purify the Buddha-field; I will mature beings; I will, after I have known full enlightenment, turn the wheel of Dharma". And why? Because he does not set apart the Realm of Dharma, nor does he review any dharma as other than the Realm of Dharma, e.g., him who would course in perfect wisdom, or who would be predicted by the Buddhas, the Lords, to full enlightenment. And why? Because no perception of a being is produced in a Bodhisattva, a great being who courses in perfect wisdom. And why? Because absolutely no being is produced or stopped, since a being has the nature of nonproduction and of nonstopping And that of which there is neither production nor stopping, how will that course in perfect wisdom? Thus coursing, a

[20]"Realm of Dharma", *dharmadhātu*, "element of Dharma" is a Mahayana word for the Absolute. To "penetrate" to it means that the thick membrane of ignorance must first be pierced. In order to see the Dharmadhātu one must have the equivalent of an operation for cataract of the eyes.

[21]One cannot join any of the 18 elements to emptiness because one has not got the eye-element here and emptiness there. In fact, the eye-element is indissolubly identical with emptiness.

Bodhisattva courses in perfect wisdom through the fact of the non-production of a being, of the emptiness of a being, of the inaccessibility of a being, of the isolatedness of a being. It is thus that one abides in the foremost "endeavour" of the Bodhisattvas, the great beings, i.e. in the "discipline" in emptiness, which has surpassed all other "disciplines". (P60) For a Bodhisattva, a great being who courses in this "discipline", aspires to the great friendliness, and he does not produce a thought of meanness, or of immorality, ill will, sloth, distraughtness, or stupidity.

((*d*) *Varieties of Bodhisattvas*:

I. According to the Circumstances of their Rebirth.)[22]

I 2,3c. INSTRUCTIONS ABOUT THE TREASURE OF THE SAMGHA.

I 2,3c. A. THE EIGHTH LOWEST BODHISATTVA. (= CANDIDATE FOR STREAM-WINNERSHIP)

Śāriputra: The Bodhisattva, the great being who dwells in this dwelling of perfect wisdom, deceased where, is he reborn here, or deceased here, where will he be reborn?

The Lord: The Bodhisattva, the great being who dwells in this dwelling

[22]The classification of the Saints given here presents many difficulties. It is not at all easy to grasp the scheme of *AA*, which is taken straight from *A.K.* VI pp. 193-240. In addition its relation to the text of the Sutra is sometimes rather obscure. The reader will also do well to refresh his memory of the stages of the Path, as well as of the 28 classes of gods (*see* the Numerical Lists), for, as he will see, a Bodhisattva, once he has reached a certain stage of perfection, ceases to live on earth and dwells for long periods among the *devas*.

A few remarks are necessary on the method of classification adopted here. The scheme concerns "all the holy irreversible Bodhisattvas (see I2, 3c, c) who are still in training" (H), but the mahayanistic Arhat is omitted from the list, because he belongs to the Treasure of the Buddha (I2,3a). The 20 types are subdivisions of the traditionally well-known "holy persons". The text of *P* gives 24 headings, of which A, B, C and D represent four of these "holy persons", i.e. I, IV, VI, and VII. In the Numerical Lists I have tried to clarify the situation by a diagram. Some light is also thrown on the subject by the comments of *AAA* (35-36, Ob. 51-56), which I reproduce here in a none too elegant English translation:

"The following varieties of the Congregation of the Bodhisattvas are here considered:

I. *The Candidate for the first Fruit.* He has realized the first 15 moments of the Path of Vision, and may be either 1, a *Faith-follower*, if of feeble intellectual faculties, or 2, a *Dharma-follower*, if of acute intellectural faculties and capable of an intuition of the Truth.

II. *The Streamwinner*, who through the 16th thought moment on the Path of Vision has turned away from the passion that is peculiar to the world of sense desire.

III. *The Candidate for the Second Fruit*, who has attained this state through the removal of five varieties of defilement peculiar to the world of sense desire. Depending on whether his intellectual faculties are more dull or more acute, he may be 3, *one who attains the fruit by faith*, or 4, *one who attains it by correct views*. Another variety of the same are the saints who, abiding on the Path of Development, have removed the defiling forces up of perfect wisdom, deceased in this world, he is reborn here in this very Buddha-field, or, deceased in other Buddha-fields, or among the Tushita Gods, he is reborn here.

I 2,3c,1. THE BODHISATTVA AS FAITH-FOLLOWER.

Among these a Bodhisattva, a great being who, deceased among men, is reborn among them, has dull[23] faculties—except when he is irreversible—he does not immediately make "endeavours" about perfect wisdom, and does not come face to face with the Dharani-doors or the concentradition-doors. If again, Sariputra, you say, "the Bodhisattva, the great

to the 4th degree. Owing to this they secure a succession of rebirths in either a 6, *godly* or 5, *human* form.

IV. The *Once-Returner* has forsaken 6 forms of defilement peculiar to the world of sense-desire. One variety of IV is 7, *the saint with one single interval,* for whom one single birth among the gods is to be undergone before he attains Arhatship.

V. The *Candidate for the third Fruit* has removed 7 or 8 forms of defilement belonging to the world of sense-desire. He may attain this position either by faith or by correct views, as at I and III.

VI. The *Never-Returner* has removed all 9 forms of defilement belonging to the world of sense-desire. He can be of five kinds, as follows: (A) 8. *The saint who attains Nirvana in an intermediary state of existence,* between the world of sense desire and that of pure form. He has forsaken the fetters which bind him to a future rebirth in the world of form, but not those which lead to his reproduction in the existence intermediary between this sphere and that of sense-desire. Whilst he is reproducing himself there, he comes face to face with the Path and thereby reaches the end of Ill. (B) 9. *The saint who attains Nirvana as soon as he has been reborn,* and since he has not forsaken either of these two kinds of fetters, reaches the end of Ill after having been reborn in the sphere of pure form. (C) 10. the saint who, born in the world of pure form, wins Nirvana *with great effort,* and (D) 11. the reverse of him, the saint who wins it *without effort.* (E) The fifth variety of Never-returners are those who rise up to the highest regions of the phenomenal world to attain Nirvana there. They again are of two kinds: (x) 12. *the saint who has gone up to the Akanishta gods* to win Nirvana there, and (xx) 16. *the saint who has gone up to the highest sphere of phenomenal existence.* (Ex) No. 12 is of three kinds: (Ex 1) 13. *The one who moves along by leaps,* who from the lowest heaven of the world of pure form jumps straight to the highest, i.e. to the Akanishta heavens: (Ex 2) 14. the *"Half-Precipitant",* who from the Brahmaic worlds rises higher up, living among the Gods of the Pure Abode. Having passed through some of the intermediate worlds, he finally enters the Akanishta heaven in two leaps. (Ex 3) 15. the saint who, having *deceased in all stations* on his way through the heavens of pure form up to the Akanishta heaven, has lived on each of these stations and deceased in each one of them. (E xx) No. 16, who 17, is *devoid of greed* for the world of pure form, is of two kinds, i.e. 18. *the saint who has won peace in this very life,* and wins Nirvana in the highest of the immaterial spheres, and 19. *the saint who has witnessed cessation with his body.*

VII. The *Candidate for Arhatship* has removed 8 of the forms of defilement peculiar to the culminating point of phenomenal existence and applies his energy to the removal of the 9th form.

VIII. The *Arhat*—20. The *Pratyekabuddha* who acts on the basis of the Disciple Code, and comes face to face with his own Path at the time when no Buddha arises in the world".

[23]or: slow, weak, sluggish.

being who makes this 'endeavour' about perfect wisdom, when he is deceased here, where will he be reborn?" When he is deceased in this Buddha-field here (P61), he will then pass on from Buddha-field to Buddha-field. In each Buddha-field he will please the Buddhas, the Lords, and nowhere will he be without them.

I 2,3c,2. THE BODHISATTVA AS DHARMA-FOLLOWER.

Moreover, another Bodhisattva, one who is deceased in other Buddha-fields and reborn here, has keen faculties. He quickly makes this "endeavour" about perfect wisdom. When he has passed through this present birth, he will still remain face to face with these very deep dharmas and will continue to make endeavours about perfect wisdom. In whichever Buddha-field he may be reborn, there he will please the Tathagatas. Moreover, the Bodhisattva, who, deceased among the Tushita gods, is reborn here, also has sharper faculties, and comes face to face with the six perfections of which he never loses sight, and with all the Dharani-doors and concentration-doors.

I 2,3c,3. THE CANDIDATE TO THE SECOND AND THIRD FRUIT WHO IS INTENT ON FAITH.

There are Bodhisattvas who course in perfect wisdom, working and exerting themselves in order to mature beings, and who through the power of skill in means realize the fruit of a Streamwinner. And yet they do not fancy themselves for being Streamwinners.

There are Bodhisattvas who without being skilful in means, accomplish the four trances and course in the perfections. Through their acquisitions of trance they are reborn among the Longlived gods. If, after they have deceased there, they are reborn among men or gods, they will please the Buddhas, the Lords. (P62) Their faculties also will be dull and not keen.

There are Bodhisattvas who both enter into the trances and course in perfect wisdom. But, owing to their lack of skill in means, they, having abandoned the trances, are reborn in the world of sense desire. Their faculties also are dull and not keen.

I 2,3c,4. THE CANDIDATE TO THE SECOND AND THIRD FRUIT WHO HAS ATTAINED CORRECT VIEWS.

There are Bodhisattvas who, after they have produced the four trances, enter into the four Unlimited, the four formless attainments, the applications of mindfulness, the right efforts, the bases of psychic power, the (five) dominants, the (five) powers, the (seven) limbs of enlightenment, the Paths. Greatly compassionate, they are reborn through skill in means, and not through the influence of the trances, Unlimited, or formless attainments. And they are reborn where they can please the

Tathagatas. Since they do not lack dwelling in the perfection of wisdom, they will know full enlightenment in this very Bhadrakalpa.

I 2,3c,B. The once-returner.

There are Bodhisattvas, bound to one more birth who, coursing in perfect wisdom with skill in means, enter into and develop the four trances, the four Unlimited, the four formless attainments, the applications of mindfulness, right efforts, bases of psychic power, the dominants, powers, limbs of enlightenment and Paths. They enter into the concentration on Emptiness, on the Signless, on the Wishless (P63). But it is not through the influence of the trances, etc. that they are reborn. When they have, face to face, pleased the Buddhas, the Lords, and (for a long time) have led a holy life under them, they are again reborn among the Tushita gods, where they remain until the end of their lifespan. Thereafter, with non-defective sense-organs, mindful and self-possessed, surrounded and accompanied by hundreds of thousands of niyutas of kotis of gods, having here[24] exhibited a rebirth, they know full enlightenment in various Buddha-fields.

I 2,3c,C. The never-returner.

There are Bodhisattvas who are recipients of the six superknowledges, and who are not reborn in the world of sensedesire, or the world of form, or the formless world; but they pass on from Buddha-field to Buddha-field, honouring, respecting, revering and worshipping the Tathagatas.

There are Bodhisattvas, recipients of the six superknowledges, who, playing with these superknowledges, pass on from Buddha-field to Buddha-field; in those Buddha-fields one has not even a conception of the vehicle of the Disciples and Pratyekabuddhas, and in them the lifespan (of beings) is measureless. (P64)

There are Bodhisattvas, recipients of the six superknowledges, who pass on from world system to world system. They go to where the message of Buddha, Dharma, and Samgha is unknown and abiding there they make beings hear the message of Buddha, Dharma, and Samgha, speaking in praise of the Triple Jewel. As a result of this message of Buddha, Dharma, and Samgha, those beings, when they have deceased from there, are reborn where there are Buddhas and Lords.

I 2,3c,5. Those who are reborn successively in the families of men.

There are Bodhisattvas who, having produced the four trances, enter into the four holy Unlimited, and the four formless attainments. And yet, endowed with skill in means, having turned away from (the reward which follows the) concentrations and attainments, they are reborn in

[24]among the gods, or in this world of ours? *ici-bas* (Lamotte).

the world of sense desire, are reborn in good families, i.e. among nobles, brahmins and well-to-do householders, for the sake of maturing beings.

I 2,3c,6. THOSE WHO ARE REBORN SUCCESSIVELY IN THE FAMILIES OF GODS.

There are Bodhisattvas who enter into the four trances, the four Unlimited, and the four formless attainments. Through the power of their skill in means, and not through the influence of the trances, the Unlimited or the attainments, they are reborn among the Gods of the Plane of Sense Desire (P65). Abiding among them, they mature beings, purify the Buddha-fields, and please the Buddhas, the Lords.

There are Bodhisattvas who, deceased among those gods, are, through their skill in means, reborn in the Brahma-world, *up to* the Highest Gods. Therein they become Brahma gods or Mahabrahma gods. They abide in those realms of Brahma, and then pass on from Buddha-field to Buddha-field, and entreat the Tathagatas who are in those Buddha-fields to turn the wheel of Dharma.

I 2,3c,7. THOSE WITH ONE SINGLE INTERVAL (OF REBIRTH AMONG THE GODS).

There are Bodhisattvas who are recipients of the four trances, etc. to : of the eighteen special Buddhadharmas, and who course in compliance with them. They are recipients of the four Holy Truths and yet they do not penetrate them. And these Bodhisattvas should be known as bound to one more birth.

I 2,3c,8. THOSE WHO ATTAIN NIRVANA IN AN INTERMEDIATE STATE.

There are Bodhisattvas who from the production of the first thought of enlightenment onwards become recipients of the four trances, the four Unlimited, and the four formless attainments. They develop the applications of mindfulness, the right efforts, the bases of psychic power, the dominants, the powers, the limbs of enlightenment, and the Paths. They acquire the (ten) powers (of a Tathagata), the grounds of self-confidence, the analytical knowledges and the (18) special Buddhadharmas. (P66) Through skill in means they are reborn among the gods of Brahma's group, etc. up *to* : the Highest Gods. When they have known full enlightenment, they work for the weal of beings.

I 2,3c,9. THOSE WHO ATTAIN NIRVANA AS SOON AS THEY HAVE BEEN REBORN (IN THE SPHERE OF PURE FORM).

There are Bodhisattvas who, simply through the production of the first thought of enlightenment, fully know full enlightenment, turn the wheel of Dharma, and, having worked the weal of countless beings, enter into the realm of Nirvana which leaves nothing behind. Their good

Dharma abides for an aeon, or more, after their attainment of final Nirvana.

I 2,3c,10. THOSE WHO ATTAIN WITH GREAT EFFORT.

There are Bodhisattvas who, coursing in the six perfections, pass on from world system to world system and there establish beings in enlightenment. Always energetic they never, for the sake of beings, speak an unprofitable word. Always energetic for the sake of beings, they pass on from one Buddha-field to another. Also those Bodhisattvas know full enlightenment in various Buddha-fields, during incalculable, immeasurable aeons, for the sake of beings.

I 2,3c,11. THOSE WHO ATTAIN NIRVANA WITHOUT EFFORT.

There are Bodhisattvas who, simply through the first production of the thought of enlightenment, enter into the fixed condition of a Bodhisattva, or abide on the irreversible state, or procure all the Buddhadharmas. (P67)

There are Bodhisattvas, who, from the production of the first thought of enlightenment onwards, make endeavours about perfect wisdom. Together with hundreds of thousands of niyutas of kotis of Bodhisattvas they pass from one Buddha-field to another, always purifying their own Buddha-field; and in various Buddha-fields they know full enlightenment.

I 2,3c,12. THOSE WHO HAVE GONE TO THE HIGHEST GODS TO WIN NIRVANA THERE.

There are Bodhisattvas who, coursing in the six perfections, have become Universal Monarchs. Having taken the perfection of giving for their guide they will provide all beings with everything that brings ease—food to the hungry, drink to the thirsty. They will provide perfumes, garlands, ointments, medicinal powders, incense, beds, seats, asylum, homes, money, grain, jewels, pearls, gold, silver, coral, ornaments, and the means of life—until, having established beings in the ten ways of wholesome action, they are reborn among the gods of Brahma's group, etc. *to* : up to the Highest Gods, and know full enlightenment in the various Buddha-fields.

I 2,3c,13. THOSE WHO MOVE ALONG BY LEAPS.

There are Bodhisattvas who, having accomplished the four trances, are, when the trances have faded away, in consequence of the first trance reborn among the gods of Brahma's group. Having again accomplished the trances, having been reborn among the Highest Gods, they know full enlightenment in the various Buddha-fields. (P68)

I 2,3c,14. THE HALF-PRECIPITANT.

There are Bodhisattvas who, deceased from the Brahma-world, are reborn among the Gods of the Pure Abode. Having jumped over one or two classes of the Gods of the Pure Abode, they are reborn among the Highest Gods, and then know full enlightenment in the various Buddha-fields.

I 2,3c,15. THOSE WHO, ON THEIR WAY THROUGH THE HEAVENS OF FORM, HAVE DECEASED IN ALL STATIONS.

There are Bodhisattvas who have conjured up a body like that of a Tathagata, purified the Tushita-realm, been reborn among the gods of Brahma's group, etc. *up to*: the Highest Gods, and who, through their skill in means, demonstrate Dharma to beings in the hells, in the animal world, and in the world of Yama.

There are Bodhisattvas who have stood in the six perfections, conjured up a body such as that of a Tathagata, visited countless Buddha-fields and world-systems in all the ten directions, in each single direction, and there demonstrate Dharma to beings, honour the Tathagatas, perfect the Buddha-fields, and hear the Dharma. Having created for those Buddha-fields illusory magical creations,[24a] they perfect the best, the most distinguished, the utmost Buddha-fields. (P69) And, bound to one more birth, these Bodhisattvas, reborn in those Buddha-fields, know full enlightenment in the various Buddha-fields.

I 2,3c,16. THOSE WHO HAVE GONE UP TO THE HIGHEST SPHERE OF PHENOMENAL EXISTENCE.

There are Bodhisattvas who, in consequence of the trances and formless attainments, are reborn among the gods of Brahma's group, etc. *up to*: the Śubhakritsna Gods. Thereafter they are reborn in the station of endless space, etc. *up to*: in the summit of existence. Then they are reborn in various Buddha-fields.

I 2,3c,17. THOSE WHO HAVE FORSAKEN THE GREED FOR THE WORLD OF FORM.

There are Bodhisattvas, recipients of the trances and formless attainments, who are reborn in the station of endless space, etc. *to*: in the summit of existence. Then they are reborn in various Buddha-fields.

I 2,3c,18. THOSE WHO ATTAIN NIRVANA IN THIS VERY LIFE.

There are Bodhisattvas who, coursing in the six perfections, their bodies adorned with the 32 marks of the Superman, become endowed

[24a]The text is here corrupt. *S* i 277 and *P*-Tib. differ. Tib., like one of Dutt's MSS, read "signs" instead of "illusory magical creations".

with the most excellent perfectly pure organs, and who therefore become dear and pleasant to the manyfolk. And the beings who see those Bodhisattvas, do, through just that serene faith in their hearts, gradually attain full Nirvana through the three vehicles. It is thus that a Bodhisattva should train himself in the perfect purity of body, speech and mind.

There are Bodhisattvas who, coursing in the six perfections, acquire refined organs, but do not therefore (P70) exalt themselves or deprecate others.

There are Bodhisattvas who, from the first production of the thought of enlightenment onwards, have stood in the six perfections and are never reborn anywhere in the states of woe even before they have reached the irreversible stage.

There are Bodhisattvas who, from the first production of the thought of enlightenment onwards, never abandon the ten ways of wholesome action until they have reached the irreversible stage.

There are Bodhisattvas who, after they have stood in the perfection of giving, have become Universal Monarchs and, having given gifts to beings, establish them in the 10 ways of wholesome action.

There are Bodhisattvas who, having stood in the perfection of giving, etc., gain many hundreds, many hundreds of thousands of world-wide kingdoms. Having stood therein, they please hundreds of thousands of niyutas of kotis of Buddhas, honour, respect, revere and worship those Buddhas and Lords, and thereafter win full enlightenment.

I 2,3c,19. THOSE WHO HAVE WITNESSED (CESSATION) WITH THEIR BODY.

There are Bodhisattvas who, coursing in perfect wisdom, recipients of the four trances and the four formless attainments, enter, playing with them, into the first trance. Emerged therefrom, they enter into the attainment of (the trance of) Cessation. And so with the second trance, etc. *to* : the fourth formless attainment. (P71) It is thus that these Bodhisattvas, coursing in perfect wisdom, endowed with skill in means, having entered on the concentration which jumps at will from one station to any other,[24b] know full enlightenment in the various Buddha-fields.

I 2,3c,D. THE CANDIDATE TO ARHATSHIP.

There are Bodhisattvas who, having stood in the six perfections, illuminate beings with the Buddhadharma. Neither are they themselves lacking in the splendour of the Buddhadharma, even before they know full enlightenment.

I 2,3c,20. THE PRATYEKABUDDHA.

There are Bodhisattvas who, in Buddha-less world-systems where

[24b] This concentration is described in detail at *AA* V 24-25, and in *Ad* ch. 62.

there are no Disciples, fully know the Pratyekabuddha-enlightenment. Having matured, through skill in means many hundreds of thousands of niyutas of kotis of living beings in the three vehicles, they know full enlightenment.

I 2,3c,a. THE FRUITS WHICH CAN BE OBTAINED ON THE PATH OF THE DISCIPLE AND PRATYEKABUDDHA.

There are Bodhisattvas who are recipients of the applications of mindfulness, the right efforts, the bases of psychic power, the dominants, the powers, the limbs of enlightenment and the Path, recipients of the ten powers, the grounds of self-confidence, the analytical knowledges, and the 18 special Buddhadharmas, but they do not attain the fruit of a Streamwinner, etc. *to*: (P72) the fruit of an Arhat, or Pratyekabuddhahood. Coursing in perfect wisdom they show, through their skill in means, the eightfold path to all beings, and thereby make them attain the fruit of a Streamwinner, etc. *to*: Pratyekabuddha-enlightenment. They themselves do not realize (these), but they establish others in them.

I 2,3c,b. THE ESTABLISHMENT OF OTHERS IN THE DHARMA ONE DOES NOT ONESELF OBTAIN.

The Bodhisattva, the great being patiently accepts the cognition which leads to the attainment of the fruit of all the Disciples and Pratyekabuddhas.[25]

I 2,3c,c. ELUCIDATION OF THE COMMUNITY OF IRREVERSIBLE BODHISATTVAS.

Those Bodhisattvas who dwell in this perfection of wisdom should be known as irreversible.

There are Bodhisattvas who, having stood in the six perfections, purify the Tushita-realm. These Bodhisattvas should surely be known as living in the "Auspicious Acon". Those, Sariputra, are irreversible Bodhisattvas who thus rise up to the Buddhadharmas.

(*II. According to their practices.* 1. *Perfect Purity.*)

Therefore then, Sariputra, a Bodhisattva who courses in perfect wisdom, should give no occasion for faulty deeds of body, speech or mind, and he should train in view of the perfect purity of the deeds of body, speech, and mind. (P73)

I 2,4. INSTRUCTIONS ABOUT NONATTACHMENT.

Śāriputra: What is a faulty deed of body, speech, and mind?

[25]So *S* i 274. *P* I do not understand, and *P*-Tib. differs from it. There is a parallel in *Ad* ch. 69, f. 261a (see my Rome edition).

The Lord: Here is occurs to a Bodhisattva to ask "what is the body by which deeds of the body could be undertaken, what the voice by which deeds of speech could be undertaken, what the mind by which deeds of mind could be undertaken?" Thus investigating, he gets at body, speech, or mind. For a Bodhisattva such an undertaking of deeds of body, speech, and mind is faulty. Furthermore, a Bodhisattva who courses in perfect wisdom does not get at[26] such a kind of body, speech or mind, by which he would produce a thought of meanness, immorality, ill will, sloth, distraction, or stupidity. It is impossible, it cannot be, that a Bodhisattva who courses in perfect wisdom, could produce wickedness[27] of body, speech, or mind. That is quite impossible. And why? Because a Bodhisattva, who courses in the six perfections, cleanses away the wickedness of body, speech, and mind.

Śāriputra: How then does he cleanse away that wickedness?

The Lord: When he does not get at body, speech, or mind. (P74) If, moreover, a Bodhisattva, on account of the first thought of enlightenment, complies with the ten ways of wholesome action, produces no Disciple-thought or Pratyekabuddha-thought, but constantly and always sets up a thought of great compassion for all beings, it is then that I say that a Bodhisattva's wickedness of body, speech, and mind is perfectly purified. There are Bodhisattvas, great beings, who, coursing in perfect wisdom, and purifying the path to enlightenment, course in the perfection of giving, etc. *to*: in the perfection of wisdom.

Śāriputra: What is a Bodhisattva's path to enlightenment?

The Lord: When a Bodhisattva, who courses in perfect wisdom, does not get at body, speech, or mind, at any of the six perfections, at the idea of Disciple, Pratyekabuddha, Bodhisattva, or Buddha, then that is a Bodhisattva's path to enlightenment, i.e. the nonapprehension of all dharmas. The Bodhisattva who walks by that path and courses in the six perfections, cannot possibly be crushed.[28]

I 2,5. Instructions about persistent indefatigability.

(2. *All-knowledge*.)

Śāriputra: Coursing how do Bodhisattvas become uncrushable?

The Lord: When a Bodhisattva, who courses in the six perfections, does not put his mind to form (P75), etc. *to*: to the utmost, right and

[26]or: does not take notice of, does not apprehend. 1, they do not, objectively speaking, exist; 2. they are completely unimportant in any case.

[27]*daushṭulya,* may either mean "depravity" in a general sense; or, more specifically, lewdness, or luxurious living (H).

[28]for the simple reason that he is not there, and no one can find him.

perfect enlightenment, it is then that he grows in the six perfections and that he cannot be crushed by anything. There are Bodhisattvas, great beings, who, having stood in perfect wisdom, fulfil all-knowledge. All doors to the places of woe are closed to those who are endowed with that knowledge, they do not, among men, experience the misfortunes of poverty[29] (P76) and they do not take hold of such a personality by which they would become blameworthy in the world with its gods.

I 2,6. INSTRUCTIONS ABOUT THE FULL ACCEPTANCE[30] OF THE MAHAYANISTIC PATH.

(3. *Cognition of the all-knowing.*)

Śāriputra: What is, on the part of a Bodhisattva, the cognition of the all-knowing?

The Lord: Endowed with that cognition a Bodhisattva sees, in each of the ten directions, Tathagatas as many as the sands of the river Ganges, hears their demonstration of Dharma, honours their Community, and sees the purity of their Buddha-fields. But Bodhisattvas who are endowed with that cognition have no notion of a Buddha, or of enlightenment, or of Disciples or Pratyekabuddhas, or of self or other, or of a Buddha-field. A Bodhisattva who is endowed with that cognition courses in each one of the six perfections, but he does not get at any of them. He develops the applications of mindfulness, etc. *to*: the Buddhadharmas, but he does not get at any of them. Endowed with this cognition a Bodhisattva fulfils all Buddhadharmas, but he does not put his mind to any of them. (P77)

I 2,7. INSTRUCTIONS ABOUT THE FIVE ORGANS OF VISION.

(4. *The five Eyes.*)

There are Bodhisattvas who acquire and cleanse the Five Eyes. Which five? The fleshly eye, the heavenly eye, the wisdom eye, the Dharma-eye, the Buddha-eye.

Śāriputra: What is a Bodhisattva's perfectly pure Fleshly Eye?

The Lord: There is the fleshly eye of a Bodhisattva which sees for hundred miles, for two hundred miles, across Jambudvipa, a four con-

[29]Bodhisattvas are usually reborn in well-to-do families. Poverty is a punishment for meanness, or lack of generosity, in a past life. Wealth is a reward for generosity, but unless wisely used it may undo much of the good accumulated in past lives. The Scriptures often refer to practitioners of the Dharma as "sons and daughters of good family".

[30]or : indispensible factors for mastering.

tinent world-system, a world system consisting of 1,000 worlds, a world-system consisting of 1,000,000 worlds, a world-system consisting of 1,000,000,000 worlds. This is a Bodhisattva's perfectly pure Fleshly Eye.

Śāriputra: What is a Bodhisattva's perfectly pure Heavenly Eye?

The Lord: A Bodhisattva wisely knows[31] the Heavenly Eye of the gods, beginning with the Four Great Kings; (P78) but the gods do not wisely know a Bodhisattva's Heavenly Eye. With his perfectly pure Heavenly Eye he wisely knows, as it really is, the decease and rebirth of all beings in the world systems numerous as the sands of the river Ganges, in each of the ten directions. This is a Bodhisattva's perfectly pure Heavenly Eye.

Śāriputra: What is a Bodhisattva's perfectly pure Wisdom Eye?[32]

The Lord: A Bodhisattva who is endowed with that Wisdom Eye does not wisely know any dharma—be it conditioned or unconditioned, wholesome or unwholesome, faulty or faultless, with or without outflows, defiled or undefiled, worldly or supramundane.[33] With that Wisdom Eye he does not see any dharma, or hear, know, or discern one.[34] This is the perfectly pure Wisdom Eye of a Bodhisattva. (P79)

Śāriputra: What is a Bodhisattva's perfectly pure Dharma-Eye?"[35]

The Lord: Here a Bodhisattva knows, by means of the Dharma-Eye, that "this person is a Faith-follower, that person a Dharma-follower. This person is a dweller in Emptiness, that person a dweller in the Signless, that person a dweller in the Wishless. The five cardinal virtues will arise in this person by means of the emptiness-door to deliverance, in that person by means of the signless door to deliverance, in that person by means of the whishless door to deliverance. By means of the five cardinal virtues this one gazes upon the unimpeded concentration.[36] By means of the unimpeded concentration he will produce the vision and cognition of emancipation. By means of the vision and cognition of emancipation he will forsake three fetters, i.e. the view of individuality, the contagion of mere rule and ritual, and doubt. He then is the person who is called a Streamwinner. After he has acquired the path of development, he attenuates sensuous greed and ill will. He is then the person who is called a Once-Returner. Through making just this path of development preponderant and developing it, he will come

[31] =knows by virtue of his wisdom.

[32] Acc. to *Mpp-s* 439, the wisdom eye knows the true mark (*satyalakshaṇa*) of all dharmas.

[33] Then follow two words I have omitted as duplicating "defiled or undefiled".

[34] However, before he can cease to know them, he must first have known them exactly.

[35] Acc. to *Mpp-s* 439 the Dharma-eye sees persons, and knows by which means or device, or through which teaching (*dharma*) they will find the Path. It differentiates between individual types, and is akin to what Christians call "the gift of spiritual discernment".

[36] See the scheme of the Path in the Numerical Lists. It takes place immediately one enters the Path of Development.

to the forsaking of sensuous greed and of ill will. He is then the person who is called a Never-Returner. Through making just this path of development preponderant and developing it, he will forsake greed for the world of form, greed for the formless world, ignorance, conceit and excitedness.[37] He is then the person who is called an Arhat". This is the perfectly pure Dharma-Eye of the Bodhisattva, the great being. (P80) Moreover, a Bodhisattva knows wisely that "whatever is doomed to originate, all that is also doomed to stop".[38] Coursing in perfect wisdom, he attains the five cardinal virtues. This is the perfectly pure Dharma-Eye of a Bodhisattva.

Moreover, a Bodhisattva knows that this Bodhisattva, who has had his first thought of enlightenment, who courses in the perfection of giving or in the perfection of morality, thereby acquires the virtues of Faith and Vigour; that, endowed with skill in means he acquires a personality at will,[39] and becomes firmly based on his wholesome roots. This Bodhisattva will be reborn among brahmins, that one among nobles, that one among wealthy householders, and that one among the gods. He knows that, having abided among them, he will mature beings, present them with everything that makes for happiness and purify the Buddha-field, and that he will please the Tathagatas, honour, respect and revere them and will not fall on the level of a Disciple or the level of a Pratyekabuddha. He knows that this Bodhisattva will not turn back until he has known full enlightenment. This is the Bodhisattva's perfectly pure Dharma-Eye. (P81)

Moreover, a Bodhisattva knows that "these Bodhisattvas have been predicted to full enlightenment, and those have not. These Bodhisattvas are irreversible, and those are not. These Bodhisattvas are in full possession of their superknowledges, and those are not. This Bodhisattva, in full possession of his superknowledges, goes, in each of the ten directions, to world-systems numberless as the sands of the Ganges, and there he honours, respects, reveres and worships the Tathagatas; that Bodhisattva, not in full possession of the superknowledges, does not go to numberless Buddha-fields, and does not there honour, respect, revere and worship the Tathagatas. This Bodhisattva will become a recipient of the superknowledges, that one will not. This Bodhisattva

[37]According to *V. M.* 469 and Vasubandhu's *Trimśikā* p. 31 this is clearly the meaning of *auddhatya,* and the alternative suggestions of Edgerton and others must be rejected. It is the attitude of a man who loses his peace of mind by getting quite excited over what he is doing; "full of himself", he dwells in his mind on how well things have been going for him, and on how well he is doing for himself.

[38]This is an echo of the first Sermon of Benares, *S. N.*, V 423—"doomed to", *dharmin,* elsewhere translated as "subject to". Whatever has the dharmic nature of originating has the dharmic nature of stopping.

[39]Cf. *P* 187 and stage VIII B4, at *P* 224.

will have a perfectly pure Buddha-field, that one will not. This Bodhisattva has matured beings, that one has not. The Buddhas and Lords praise this Bodhisattva; that one they do not praise. These Bodhisattvas will stand near the Buddhas, the Lords; those will not. This Bodhisattva will have a limited lifespan; that one an unlimited one. This Bodhisattva will have a limited congregation, that one an unlimited one. This Bodhisattva, after he has known full enlightenment, will have a congregation of Bodhisattvas; that one will not. (P82) This Bodhisattva will practise austerities; that one will not. This Bodhisattva is in his last rebirth; that one is not. This Bodhisattva will sit on the terrace of enlightenment; that one will not. This Bodhisattva will have a Mara; that one will not". This is the perfectly pure Dharma-Eye of a Bodhisattva.

Śāriputra: What is a Bodhisattva's perfectly pure Buddha-Eye?

The Lord: The Bodhisattva, when immediately after[40] the thought of enlightenment he has, with a wisdom conjoined with one single thought-moment, entered on the adamantine concentration,[41] reaches the knowledge of all modes. He is endowed with the ten powers of a Tathagata, the four grounds of self-confidence, the four analytical knowledges, the 18 special Buddhadharmas, the great friendliness, the great compassion, the great sympathetic joy, the great evenmindedness, and the unhindered deliverance of a Buddha. And that Eye of the Bodhisattva does not meet with anything that is not seen, heard, known or discerned—in all its modes. That is the Bodhisattva's perfect Buddha-Eye.

It is thus that a Bodhisattva who wants to cleanse the five Eyes should make endeavours about the six perfections. And why? Because in the six perfections all wholesome dharmas are contained, all Disciple-dharmas, (P83) all Pratyekabuddha-dharmas, and all Bodhisattva-dharmas. When those who speak the Truth have spoken of "that which comprehends all wholesome dharmas", they have spoken of the perfection of wisdom. For perfect wisdom is the genetrix of all the perfections, and also of those five Eyes of a Bodhisattva. Having trained themselves in those five Eyes of a Bodhisattva, the Bodhisattvas know full enlightenment.

(5. *The six superknowledges.*)

I 2,8. INSTRUCTIONS ABOUT THE SIX SUPERKNOWLEDGES.[42]

The Bodhisattva, the great being who courses in this perfection of wisdom, develops the perfection of superknowledge. (1) He experiences

[40]This is not clear to me. *P* has *bodhicitta-anantaram*; *S* reads: *anuttaram?*

[41]See the scheme of the Path in the Numerical Lists.

[42]For further details see my *Buddhist Scriptures,* 1959, pp. 121-133.—Of the six superknowledges, five are occult, and the sixth spiritual.

psychic power in its various aspects. He shakes this very earth. Having been one, he becomes manifold; having been manifold, he becomes one. He can make himself visible or invisible. Right through a wall, a rampart, or a hill, he glides unhindered, as though through empty space. Cross-legged he floats along, like a bird on the wing. He plunges into the earth and shoots up again, as if in water. He walks on water[43] without sinking into it, as if on solid ground. With his body he emits smoke and flames of fire, like a great mass of fire, and at the same time releases streams of cold water, like a great raincloud. (P84) Even the sun and the moon, powerful and mighty though they be, he touches and strokes with his hands. Even as far as the Brahma world he has power over his body.—But he does not fancy himself for that psychic power. For he does not get at that psychic power, which would allow him to mind (it)—on account of the emptiness, the isolatedness, the inapprehensibility of its own-being. He does not, apart from his attention to the state of all-knowledge, produce a will for psychic power, nor a will for calling forth psychic power. It is thus that a Bodhisattva who courses in perfect wisdom calls forth the cognition of the realisation of the superknowledge of psychic power.

(2) With the heavenly ear-element, perfectly pure and surpassing that of man, he hears sounds, celestial as well as human.—But he does not, by means of that heavenly ear, fancy that he hears sounds. For he does not get at that sound, because its ownbeing is empty, isolated, cannot be apprehended. Outside his attention to the knowledge of all modes he does not produce a will for the heavenly ear. It is thus that a Bodhisattva who courses in perfect wisdom calls forth the cognition of the realisation of the superknowledge of the heavenly ear. (P85)

(3) With his heart he wisely knows, as it really is, the thought of other beings and persons. He wisely knows, as it really is, a greedy thought as a "greedy thought", a greedless thought as a "greedless thought"; a thought with hate as a "thought with hate", a thought without hate as a "thought without hate"; deluded thought as "deluded thought", undeluded thought as "undeluded thought"; thought with craving as "thought with craving", thought without craving as "thought without craving"; thought with grasping as "thought with grasping", thought without grasping as "thought without grasping"; composed thought as "composed thought", disturbed thought as "disturbed thought"; limited thought as "limited thought", extensive thought as "extensive thought", lofty thought as "lofty thought"; concentrated thought as "concentrated thought", unconcentrated thought as "unconcentrated thought"; detached thought as "detached thought", undetached thought as "undetached thought"; thought with outflows as "thought with

[43]cf. Norman Brown, *Indian and Christian miracles of walking on the water*, 1928.

outflows", thought without outflows as "thought without outflows"; thought with blemish as "thought with blemish", thought without blemish as "thought without blemish"; thought with something above it as "thought with something above it", thought with nothing above it as "thought with nothing above it".—But he does not, because of that, fancy himself. Because that thought is no-thought, on account of its unthinkability. He does not imagine that he knows wisely. And that very thought he does not get at, on account of the emptiness, isolatedness, and inapprehensibility of its own-being. He does not, apart from his attention to the knowledge of all modes, produce a will for the cognition of others' thoughts. It is thus that the Bodhisattva who courses in perfect wisdom calls forth the cognition of the realisation of the superknowledge of the thoughts and actions of all beings. (P86)

(4) With the cognition of the recollection of his past lives he remembers one birth, two births, three births, up to one hundred thousand births. He also remembers one thought, etc. up to one hundred thoughts; one day up to one hundred days; one month up to one hundred months; one year up to one hundred years; one aeon up to one hundred aeons, many hundreds of aeons, many hundreds of thousands of aeons, many hundreds of thousands of niyutas of kotis of aeons; up to the limit of the beginning he remembers. "There I was, that was my name, that was my family, that was my caste, such was my food, such was the length of my life, such was the extent of my lifespan. Deceased from there I was reborn here; deceased from here I was reborn there." It is thus that he recollects his various previous lives with all their modes, details and occasions.—But he does not fancy himself for that superknowledge of the recollection of his former lives. Because that cognition is a non-cognition, on account of its unthinkability. He does not imagine that he knows wisely. And that very thought he does not get at, on account of the emptiness, isolatedness and inapprehensibility of its own-being. (P87) He does not, outside his attention to the knowledge of all modes, produce a will for the knowledge of his past lives. It is thus that the Bodhisattva who courses in perfect wisdom calls forth the cognition of the realization of the superknowledge of the recollection of his former lives.

(5) With the heavenly eye, pure and surpassing that of men, he sees beings, as they die and arise (again). He wisely knows that "those beings, whether beautiful or ugly, low or exalted, undergo a happy or wretched destiny according to karma. Here are the beings who are endowed with good conduct of body, speech and mind, who have not reviled the holy men, who have right views, and who, with this good conduct of body, speech and mind for cause, are reborn in a happy place, in Heaven (among the gods). There, on the other hand, are the beings who are

endowed with bad conduct of body, speech and mind, who have reviled the holy men, who have wrong views, and who, because they have acquired the karma of evil views, are reborn, upon the breaking up of the body, after death, in the states of woe, in a wretched destiny, in great distress, in the hells." It is thus that he wisely knows with the heavenly eye, pure and surpassing that of men, as it really is, the decease and rebirth of beings in the six places of rebirth—in the universe in all the ten directions, in all the world-systems, with the Dharma-element as the highest (development), and the space-element as the terminus. But he does not fancy himself for that. For this eye is no eye, on account of its unthinkability. (P88) He does not fancy himself for the fact that he sees. That very eye he does not get at, on account of the emptiness, isolatedness and inapprehensibility of its ownbeing. He does not, apart from his attention to the knowledge of all modes, produce a will for the heavenly eye. It is thus that the Bodhisattva who courses in perfect wisdom calls forth the superknowledge of the heavenly eye.

(6) He calls forth the supercognition of the realisation of nonproduction, but he does not fall on the level of Disciple or Pratyekabuddha. Nor does he see any dharma which knows full enlightenment.[44] He does not put his mind to the wholesomeness of the achievement of the cognition of the superknowledge of the realisation of the extinction of the outflows. For that cognition is a noncognition, on account of its unthinkability. He does not put his mind to the fact that he knows wisely. It is thus that the Bodhisattva, who courses in perfect wisdom, calls forth the cognition of the realisation of the superknowledge of the extinction of the outflows. (P89)

It is thus again that the six superknowledges of the Bodhisattva, who courses in perfect wisdom, are fulfilled and purified. These superknowledges, when perfectly pure, procure the knowledge of all modes.

(6. *Emptiness, No-minding and Sameness.*)

There are Bodhisattvas, great beings who, coursing in perfect wisdom, and having stood in the perfection of giving, cleanse the roadway to the knowledge of all modes because by means of absolute emptiness they have grasped at nothing at all. There are others who, having stood in the perfection of morality, cleanse it on account of committing no offence. Others, having stood in the perfection of patience, cleanse it on account of their imperturbability. Others, having stood in the perfection of vigour, cleanse it on account of the indefatigability of their bodily and mental vigour. Others, having stood in the perfection of concen-

[44] So *S. P*: Nor does he strive for any dharma except for "I will awake to full enlightenment".

tration, cleanse it on account of the undistracted state of their thought. Others, having stood in the perfection of wisdom, cleanse it on account of their having expelled all stupid thoughts. It is thus that the Bodhisattvas who course in perfect wisdom, having stood in the six perfections, cleanse the roadway to the knowledge of all modes, on account of absolute emptiness.

A gift is conceived on account of taking; morality on account of immorality; patience on account of impatience; vigour on account of sloth; concentration on account of lack of concentration; wisdom on account of stupidity.[45]

The Bodhisattva does not put his mind to such ideas as "I have crossed over", or "I have not crossed over";[46] giver or no giver; one of good conduct, one of bad conduct; one who has achieved patience, one who is angry;[47] one who exerts vigour, one who is slothful; (P90) one who is concentrated, one who is not concentrated; one who is wise, one who is stupid; "I am abused", "I am praised", "I am treated with respect", "I am not treated with respect". And why? Because nonproduction does not put its mind to such ideas. And why? Because the perfection of wisdom cuts off all mindings.

All the virtuous qualities which come to a Bodhisattva who courses in perfect wisdom are not found in the Disciples and Pratyekabuddhas. Perfecting these virtuous qualities, he matures beings, purifies the Buddha-field, and reaches the knowledge of all modes.

A Bodhisattva, Sariputra, who courses in perfect wisdom, produces an even state of mind towards all beings. As a result he acquires insight into the sameness of all dharmas, and learns to establish all beings in this insight. In this very life he becomes dear and pleasing to the Buddhas, the Lords, and to all Bodhisattvas, Disciples and Pratyekabuddhas. Wherever he may be reborn he will never again see unpleasant forms with his eyes, nor hear unpleasant sounds with his ears (P91), nor smell unpleasant smells with his nose, nor taste unpleasant tastes with his tongue, nor feel unpleasant sensations with his body, nor become aware of unpleasant dharmas with his mind. Nor does he fail of full enlightenment.

Interlude.

When this exposition of perfect wisdom was being expounded, three hundred nuns, wearing their religious garments in a proper and correct manner,[47] made offerings to the Lord, and raised their thoughts to the utmost, right and perfect enlightenment. Thereupon the Lord smiled

[45]Virtues are nothing in themselves. They are merely antidotes to undesirable stages.
[46]The translation here follows *S*.
[47]In *P* this passage is not quite clear. For the Tibetan see BLSOAS xxv, 377.

on that occasion. The Venerable *Ānanda* rose from his seat, put his upper robe over one shoulder, placed his right knee on the earth, stretched forth his folded hands towards the Lord, and said to the Lord: "What is the cause, what the reason, for the manifestation of this smile? It is not without cause, not without reason, that the Buddhas, the Lords, manifest. a smile".

The Lord: These three hundred nuns will, Ānanda, appear in the world in the sixty-first aeon from now as Tathagatas by the name of Mahāketu. Having deceased there in the Starlike aeon, they will be reborn in the Buddha-field of Akshobhya, the Tathagata. And sixty thousand gods, matured through this demonstration of Dharma (P92), will win final Nirvana in the presence of Maitreya, the Tathagata.

Thereupon, through the might of the Lord, the four assemblies of the Lord Śākyamuni saw, in each one of the ten directions, a thousand Buddhas, all visible from the circle of the assembly, and they also saw the splendid glory of their Buddha-fields. In this Sahā world-system they cannot see a glory as splendid as that of the Buddha-fields of those Buddhas and Lords in the ten directions. Ten thousand living creatures from the circle of the assembly of the Lord Śākyamuni thereupon made the vow: "We shall bring about enough merit to be reborn in those Buddha-fields!"

Thereupon the Lord, seeing the resolution of those sons of good family, smiled on that occasion.

Ānanda: What is the cause, what the reason for the manifestation of a smile?

The Lord: Do you see, Ānanda, those ten thousand living creatures?

Ānanda: I do, O Lord.

The Lord: These ten thousand living creatures, deceased here, will be reborn in the ten directions in one thousand Buddha-fields, and nowhere will they be deprived of the Tathagatas. Afterwards they will appear in the world as Tathagatas, Vyūharājā by name. (P93)

Chapter 4

EQUAL TO THE UNEQUALLED

Thereupon the Ven. Śāriputra, the Ven Mahāmaudgalyāyana, the Ven. Subhūti, the Ven. Mahākāśyapa, and many other well-known monks and Bodhisattvas, nuns, laymen and laywomen spoke thus to the Lord:

This perfection of wisdom is a great perfection of the Bodhisattvas, the foremost perfection, the most distinguished perfection, the most excellent perfection, the supreme perfection, the highest perfection, the unequalled perfection, a perfection like space, a perfection with an emptiness of own-marks, a perfection endowed with all qualities, an uncrushable perfection. For the Bodhisattvas, who course in this perfection of wisdom, have given a gift which equals the unequalled, and they have fulfilled the perfection of giving which equals the unequalled. They have acquired a personality which equals the unequalled. They will become recipients of the dharma which equals the unequalled, i.e. of the utmost, right, and perfect enlightenment. They have guarded a morality which equals the unequalled, developed a patience which equals the unequalled, exerted a vigour which equals the unequalled (P94), brought forth a concentration which equals the unequalled, and developed a wisdom which equals the unequalled. Coursing in just this perfection of wisdom You, O Lord, have become a recipient of a form which equals the unequalled, of feelings, perceptions, impulses and consciousness which equal the unequalled. You have known an unequalled full enlightenment, you have turned the unequalled wheel of Dharma. Likewise the past, future, and present Buddhas and Lords, coursing in just this perfection of wisdom, have known full enlightenment, will know it, do know it. Therefore a Bodhisattva who wants to go to what is the Beyond of all dharmas, should make endeavours in the perfection of wisdom. By the world with its gods, men, and Asuras, should homage be paid to those Bodhisattvas, those great beings, who course in this perfection of wisdom!

Thereupon *the Lord* said to these many Disciples and Bodhisattvas: So it is, sons of good family, so it is. The world with its gods, men, and Asuras should pay homage to those Bodhisattvas, those great beings, who course in the perfection of wisdom. And why? Because it is thanks to the Bodhisattvas that there takes place in the world the manifestation of the world of men, of the world of gods, of good families, i.e. of nobles, brahmins and well-to-do householders; of Universal-Monarchs, of the various classes of gods; (P95) of Streamwinners, Once-Returners, Never-Returners, Arhats, Pratyekabuddhas, Bodhisattvas and Tathagatas. It is thanks to the Bodhisattvas that there takes place in the world the manifestation of the Triple Jewel. And wherever there appear in the world the worldly means of life—food, drink, clothes, dwelling places, medicinal appliances for sickness, gems, pearls, lapis lazuli, conch shells, camphor, coral, gold and silver, etc. *to*: all that bestows ease in the realms of gods and men, and the ease of Nirvana—that everywhere is due to the Bodhisattvas. And why? Because the Bodhisattva, coursing on his course, enjoins the six perfections on beings—causes gifts to be given and morality to be undertaken, establishes them in patience and enjoins vigour, establishes them in trance and enjoins wisdom. And it is thanks to the Bodhisattva that anyone ever courses in the perfection of wisdom. In that way does the Bodhisattva practice for the benefit and ease of all beings.

CHAPTER 5

THE TONGUE

Thereupon the Lord on that occasion put out his tongue, and with it He covered this great trichiliocosm. Lights of many different colours issued from that tongue, and darted in all the ten directions to world-systems countless as the sands of the Ganges, and caused a great illumination. (P96) In all the ten directions, in Buddha-fields countless as the sands of the Ganges, countless Bodhisattvas who had seen this glorious splendour questioned the Buddhas, the Lords, each one in their own Buddha-field: "Whose is this might through which this splendour and illumination are shown forth?"

The Buddhas and Lords replied: "In the Sahā world-system, in the West, etc. *to*: below, there stands, holds and maintains himself a Tathagata called Śākyamuni. As a result of his putting out his tongue the world-systems countless as the sands of the Ganges have in all directions everywhere been irradiated with illumination, so as to help the Perfection of Wisdom to be demonstrated and revealed to the Bodhisattvas, the great beings".

The Bodhisattvas then said to the Tathagatas: "We will go to that Sahā world system, in order to see, salute, and honour that Lord Śākyamini, the Tathagata and the Bodhisattvas assembled from the ten directions, and to listen to that Perfection of Wisdom".

The Buddhas, the Lords replied: "Go then, sons of good family, as you see fit".

Those Bodhisattvas, those great beings, from all the ten directions, having taken flowers, incense, perfumes, garlands, unguents, powders, robes, parasols, flags, banners and streamers, having taken jewels, gold, silver and flower-buds, approached the Lord Śākyamuni with the music of tūryas and cymbals. And the various classes of gods (P97) having taken heavenly flowers, incense, perfumes, garlands, unguents, powders, robes, parasols, flags, banners, blue lotuses, night lotuses, white lotuses, Mandarava flowers, Keśara flowers and Tamāla leaves, also approached the Lord. The Bodhisattvas and gods scattered those flowers, etc. over the Tathagata. Thereupon those flowers, etc., rose into the intermediate space, and above this great trichiliocosm a pointed Tower of flowers shaped itself, with four pillars, quadrangular, well proportioned, enjoyable, pleasing to the mind.

Hundreds of thousands of niyutas of kotis of living creatures from that assembly thereupon rose from their seats, put their upper robes over one shoulder, placed their right knees on the earth, stretched forth their folded hands to the Lord, and said to the Lord:

"We, O Lord, will in a future period become recipients of such dharmas as the Tathagata is a recipient of, and thus will we foster the community of the disciples and thus will we demonstrate Dharma to the assembly, just as now the Tathagata, the Lord demonstrates Dharma here".

The Lord then knew the resolution of those sons of good family, he knew their patient acceptance of the nonproduction of all dharmas, of their nonstopping, of their not being brought about, of their non-manifestation—and He smiled. Various-coloured rays issued from his mouth, circulated round the whole world, and then returned to the Lord, and disappeared in his head.

The Venerable Ānanda thereupon rose from his seat (P98), put his upper robe over one shoulder, placed his right knee on the earth, stretched forth his folded hands towards the Lord, and said to the Lord: "What is the cause, what the reason for the manifestation of a smile?"

The Lord replied: "These hundreds of thousands of niyutas of kotis of living creatures will, after sixty-eight kotis of aeons, appear in the world as Tathagatas, Bodhyangapushpa by name, in the Pushpākara aeon".

Chapter 6

SUBHUTI

B. PHASES OF THE EXTINCTION OF SELF.

(1. *The teaching proceeds from the Buddha's might.*)

I 2,9. Instructions about the path of vision.

I 2,9a. Survey of the instructions about the path of vision.

**The Lord*: Make it clear then, Subhuti, regarding[1] the perfection of wisdom of the Bodhisattvas, the great beings, how the Bodhisattvas, the great beings, may go forth to the perfection of wisdom!

Thereupon *those Bodhisattvas, great beings, those great Disciples and those gods* thought to themselves: Will the Ven. Subhuti expound perfect wisdom to the Bodhisattvas by exerting his own power of revealing wisdom, or through the Buddha's might?

The Venerable *Subhuti,* who knew, through the Buddha's might, that those Bodhisattvas, Great Disciples, and Gods were in such wise discoursing in their hearts, said to the Ven. Sariputra: Whatever, Sariputra, the Lord's Disciples teach, demonstrate, and expound, all that is to be known as the Tathagata's work. And why? Because in the demonstration of dharma, as demonstrated by the Tathagata, they train themselves, and they realize its true nature.[2] (P99) After they have realized its true nature, whatever they may teach, demonstrate and expound, all that does not contradict the true nature of dharma. It is just the Tathagata who, by skilful means, will expound (through the Disciples) the perfection of wisdom to the Bodhisattvas, the great beings. (Without inspiration from Him) it is outside the province of all the Disciples and Pratyekabuddhas to expound the perfection of wisdom to the Bodhisattvas, the great beings.

[1]*ārabhya*. The exact force of this "preposition" at this point, which coincides with the beginning of the argument in *A*, has puzzled me for a long time. It may also mean "starting from".

[2]*dharmatā*. The teachings of the Buddha have become an object of spiritual realization (*adhigama, H*) in Disciples like Subhuti, who are not Bodhisattvas, and who can therefore, anomalous as it may seem, appear to teach Bodhisattvas who are their spiritual superiors in the Mahayana hierarchy. In fact they are just the mouth-pieces of the Buddha, channels through which the Dharma flows into this world.

(2. *The Bodhisattva, a mere word, inacessible as dharma.*)

I 2,9,1. ACCEPTANCE OF COGNITION OF DHARMA IN SUFFERING.

Subhuti: One speaks, O Lord, of "Bodhisattvas". What dharma does this word "Bodhisattva" denote? I do not see that dharma "Bodhisattva". Since I do not see a Bodhisattva and fail to apprehend a Perfection of Wisdom, which Bodhisattva shall I instruct in which perfection of wisdom?*

The Lord: "Perfect Wisdom" and "Bodhisattva", mere words are these. And the reality which corresponds to the word "Bodhisattva" cannot be apprehended, either inwardly, or outwardly, or between the two. Just as one speaks of a "being" although no being can be apprehended in actual reality; and that word "being" is a mere concept, a conceptual dharma and has the status of a concept.

I 2,9,2. COGNITION OF DHARMA IN SUFFERING.

Except in so far as it is conventionally expressed by means of a mere conventional term, there is no production or stopping of this conceptual dharma. And the same holds good of such terms as "self", "soul", "personality", etc. *to*: "one who sees". (P100) In the same way, that which corresponds in reality to such words as "perfect wisdom" or "Bodhisattva", that is a mere conceptual dharma which is neither produced nor stopped, except for its conventional expression by means of a mere conventional term. Such ideas as "this is inward form, etc." merely refer to conceptual dharmas, and of these conceptual dharmas there is no production or stopping, except in so far as they are conventionally expressed by means of mere conceptual terms. (P101) And what holds good of the skandhas, that is also true of the 18 elements. On the subject-side[3] this body is conventionally called a "body" and also the head, neck, belly, muscles, shoulders, arms, hands, ribs, hips, thighs, legs, and feet are conventionally expressed in those terms; but they are only conceptual dharmas, and of these conceptual dharmas there is no production or stopping, except in so far as they are conventionally expressed by means of mere conceptual terms. On the object-side, such things as a bunch of grass, a branch, a leaf, a petal, etc., are conventionally expressed by manifold designations; but of those words there is no production or

[3]This is a somewhat clumsy attempt to render *ādhyātmikam*, which elsewhere occurs as "inwardly", and is contrasted with "outwardly", or here "on the subject-side", Abhidharmic exercises deal with the distribution of the contents of experience between those facts and events which are "interior to a person" and those which are "exterior to a person". The "person", though implied, must, however, never be mentioned, and so a certain amount of circumlocution is unavoidable. In this example the surface of the skin is taken as the dividing line between "inward" and "outward", but that is not necessarily always the case.

stopping, except in so far as they are conventionally expressed by means of mere conventional terms, and the reality corresponding to those words cannot be apprehended inwardly, outwardly, or between the two. Just so "perfect wisdom" and "Bodhisattva" are mere conceptual dharmas, and there is no production or stopping of them except in so far as they are conventionally expressed by means of mere conventional terms. It is thus that a Bodhisattva should train in perfect wisdom.

Just as a dream, an echo, a mirage, a reflected image, a mock show, a magical creation of the Tathagata, are all conceptual dharmas, and of these conceptual dharmas there is no production or stopping, except in so far as they are conventionally expressed by means of mere conceptual terms, just so "perfect wisdom" and "Bodhisattva" are mere conceptual dharmas, and they are neither produced nor stopped, except in so far as they are conventionally expressed by means of mere conceptual terms. (P102) It is thus that a Bodhisattva, who courses in perfect wisdom, should train in (the insight that) words and conventional terms are but concepts, and that also the instructions and dharmas are but concepts.

I 2,9,3. ACCEPTANCE OF SUBSEQUENT COGNITION OF DHARMA IN SUFFERING.

Therefore a Bodhisattva, who courses in perfect wisdom, does not review that "form", etc. as permanent or impermanent, ease or ill, self or not-self, calm or uncalm, empty or not empty, sign or signless, wish or wishless, conditioned or unconditioned, produced or unproduced, stopped or not stopped, isolated or not isolated, wholesome or unwholesome, faulty or faultless, with or without outflows, defiled or undefiled, worldly or supramundane, defilement or purification, Samsara or Nirvana. (P103) (P104) And the same consideration applies to the 18 elements, and to the feelings of ease, etc., which are produced from contact between eye, form, and eye-consciousness as their condition. *And so for* the other senses. (P105)

I 2,9,4. SUBSEQUENT COGNITION OF SUFFERING.

And why? Because a Bodhisattva, though he courses in perfect wisdom, does not see the perfection of wisdom or the word "perfection of wisdom", the Bodhisattva or the word "Bodhisattva", in either the conditioned or the unconditioned element. For a Bodhisattva who courses in perfect wisdom does not construct or discriminate all these dharmas. Having stood in the undiscriminated dharma, he develops the applications of mindfulness. Coursing in perfect wisdom, he reviews neither the perfection of wisdom nor the word "perfection of wisdom", neither a Bodhisattva nor the word "Bodhisattva". Thus he develops the right efforts, etc. *to*: the Buddhadharmas. And yet, except through his attention to the knowledge of all modes, he reviews neither the perfection of wisdom nor the word "perfection of wisdom", neither a Bodhisattva nor the word "Bodhisattva", neither the Buddha nor the word "Buddha".

I 2,9,5. ACCEPTANCE OF COGNITION OF DHARMA IN ORIGINATION.

For that Bodhisattva who courses in perfect wisdom penetrates to the dharmic mark of dharmas which is neither defiled nor purified. It is thus that a Bodhisattva who courses in perfect wisdom should learn to recognise the concept of dharma as a word and as a conventional term.

I 2,9,6. COGNITION OF DHARMA IN ORIGINATION.

He then will not settle down in form, or in any of the other skandhas. (P106)

I 2,9,7. ACCEPTANCE OF SUBSEQUENT COGNITION OF DHARMA IN ORIGINATION.

Not in any of the perfections, not in their name or their mark, not in the body of a Bodhisattva,[4] nor in any of the Five Eyes, or the superknowledges, or the 18 kinds of emptiness; (P107) not in Suchness, the Reality limit, or the Element of Dharma; not in the maturing of beings, the purification of the Buddha-field, or in skill in means. And why? Because he who could settle down, or whereby or wherein he could settle down, all these dharmas do not exist.

I 2,9,8. SUBSEQUENT COGNITION OF ORIGINATION.

It is thus that a Bodhisattva, who courses in perfect wisdom, not having settled down in all-dharmas, grows in the perfection of giving, and the other perfections. He enters into the Bodhisattva's special way of salvation,

I 2,9,9. ACCEPTANCE OF COGNITION OF DHARMA IN STOPPING.

and into the irreversible stage.

I 2,9,10. COGNITION OF DHARMA IN STOPPING.

Coursing thus, a Bodhisattva fulfils the superknowledges, and then passes on from Buddha-field to Buddha-field, matures beings, and honours, respects and reveres the Buddhas, the Lords; and by means of that wholesome root he is reborn near those Buddhas and Lords, he hears the Dharma (from them) and never again forgets it until he reaches the seat of enlightenment; he will acquire the Dharani-doors and the concentration-doors.[5] It is thus that a Bodhisattva who courses in perfect

[4]So Gilgit-*P* f. 45a. *S* ii 380 *bodhikāye, P kāye.*

[5]The Dhāraṇīs (*P*212) will help him to remember the teaching, and the concentrations enable him to contemplate it with inward calm.

wisdom should learn to recognise the concept of a dharma as a word and as a conventional term. (P108)

I 2,9,11. Acceptance of subsequent cognition in stopping.

What do you think, Subhuti—one speaks of a "Bodhisattva". Is a Bodhisattva form, or is he other than form? Is he in form, or is form in him, or is he without form? (P109) *And the same questions can be asked* about the Bodhisattva's relation to the other skandhas, to the 18 elements, the 6 physical elements, and the 12 links.

Subhuti: "No, O Lord", *is the answer in every case*. (P110)

I 2,9,12. Subsequent cognition of stopping.

The Lord: What do you think, Subhuti, is the Suchness of form, etc., the Bodhisattva, or is the Bodhisattva other than the Suchness of form, etc.? Is the skandha-Suchness the Bodhisattva, or is the Bodhisattva other than the skandha-Suchness? (P111) Moreover, Subhuti, for what reason do you say that "form, etc., is not the Bodhisattva", and that "the Suchness of form, etc., is not the Bodhisattva"? (P112)

Subhuti: Absolutely a Bodhi-being does not exist, is not got at. Then how can a Bodhisattva be form, or anything else, *until we come to*: decay and death? And further, how then can that Suchness of his form, etc., be got at? That is not possible. (P113)

The Lord: Well said, Subhuti. Just so should a Bodhisattva be trained through the nonapprehension of a being in the nonapprehension of the perfection of wisdom.

I 2,9,13. Acceptance of cognition of dharma in the path.

What do you think, Subhuti, does the word "Bodhisattva" denote form, etc.?

Subhuti: No indeed, O Lord.

The Lord: What do you think, Subhuti, does that word "Bodhisattva" denote the permanence of form, etc., or its impermanence, its ease or ill, etc. *to*: its emptiness or nonemptiness, etc.?

Subhuti: No indeed, O Lord.

The Lord: For what reason do you say that? (P114)

Subhuti: Absolutely form, etc., does not exist and is not got at, and so also permanence, etc. How then could the word "Bodhisattva" denote form, etc., or the permanence of form etc., or its impermanence, etc.?

The Lord: Well said, Subhuti. It is thus that a Bodhisattva, who courses in perfect wisdom, and who does not apprehend anything that is denoted by the words form, etc., or permanence, etc., should train in the perfection of wisdom. (P115)

I 2,9,14. Cognition of dharma in the path.

As you said, Subhuti, "I do not see (when reviewing it) that dharma 'Bodhisattva'". For a dharma cannot review the Dharma-element,[6] nor can the Dharma-element review a dharma.

I 2,9,15. Acceptance of subsequent cognition of the path.

The element of form, etc., does not review the Dharma-element, and vice versa. And equally so for the element of feeling, etc.

I 2,9,16. Subsequent cognition of the path.

The conditioned element does not review the unconditioned element, and vice versa.

I 2,10. Instructions about the path of development.

The Unconditioned cannot be made known[7] through the exclusion of the conditioned, nor the conditioned through the exclusion of the Unconditioned.

A Bodhisattva, who courses in perfect wisdom, does not review any dharma. In consequence he does not tremble, is not frightened, nor terrified. No dharma can cow his mind, and he knows to regrets. And why? Because this Bodhisattva who courses in perfect wisdom does not review form, etc., nor the links, nor greed, hate or delusion, nor self, a being, a soul, etc. (P116)

Subhuti: For what reason does the thought of a Bodhisattva not become cowed, or stolid?

The Lord: Because he does not apprehend or review the dharmas which constitute thought and its concomitants.[8]

Subhuti: How is it that his mind does not tremble?

The Lord: He does not get at mind or mind-element and does not review them. It is thus that a Bodhisattva, through the nonapprehension of all dharmas should course in perfect wisdom. If the Bodhisattva, the great being, who follows the perfection of wisdom, does not apprehend that perfection of wisdom, nor a Bodhisattva, nor the word "Bodhisattva" —then this is truly his instruction and admonition in the perfection of wisdom.

[6]At this point one must clearly distinguish between the "dharma-element" in the Hinayana sense, where "dharma" means the objects of the sixth sense-organ, i.e. mind, and the "Dharma-element" in the Mahayana sense, where "Dharma" means Truth, ultimate and absolute Reality.

[7]or: conceived separately from.

[8]Thought, *citta*, refers to the mind-organ and the six kinds of consciousness. For *Dhs* 1189-90 the *cetasikā* are the skandhas of feeling, perception and impulses, whereas for the Sarvāstivādins, the "concomitants" of thought are 46 mental factors "associated with" consciousness, either invariably or only occasionally.

Chapter 7

ENTRANCE INTO THE CERTAINTY OF SALVATION

(3. *Degrees of Ripeness of insight.*)

Subhuti: A Bodhisattva should train in perfect wisdom if he wants to fulfil the six perfections, to comprehend form, etc. (P117), to forsake greed, hate, and delusion, the fetters, unwholesome tendencies and obsessions, the yokes, the four floods, the four bonds, the four graspings, the four perverted views; to forsake the ten unwholesome ways of acting and to fulfil the ten wholesome ways of acting (P118), etc. *to*: if he wants to fulfil the 18 special Buddha-dharmas, to win the concentrations and to fulfil the intentions of all beings. When he has fulfilled all these wholesome roots, he will as a result not fall into the states of woe, is not reborn in low-class families (P119), does not abide on the level of a Disciple or Pratyekabuddha. In addition such a Bodhisattva does not fall from the Summits.[1]

Śāriputra: How does a Bodhisattva fall from the Summits?

Subhuti: When he courses without skill in means in the six perfections. One speaks of the Rawness of a Bodhisattva if, having entered on the concentrations of Emptiness, the Signless, and the Wishless, he does not fall on the level of a Disciple or a Pratyekabuddha, but, being unskilled in means, also does not enter into a Bodhisattva's (distinctive) Way of Salvation.

Śāriputra: For what reason is that called a Bodhisattva's "Rawness"?

Subhuti: A Bodhisattva's craving for (separate) dharmas is called "Rawness".

I 3. The Aids to Penetration.

I 3a. Weak heat with regard to the truth of ill.[1]

Śāriputra: What is the craving for (separate) dharmas?

Subhuti: Here a Bodhisattva, who courses in perfect wisdom, settles down in the idea that "form, etc., is impermanent", insists on it and holds it to be true. This is called the Rawness of Adaptable Craving for separate dharmas on the part of a Bodhisattva. And the same holds

[1]For the sake of simplicity I read *mūrdhānam*, although most documents seem to have something like *mū(r)dhāmam*. See Edgerton s.v.

[1]In I 3a-c the translation follows *S* iii 486-490.

good when he settles down in such ideas as "form, etc., is ill, not self, empty, signless, wishless".

I 3b. WEAK HEAT WITH REGARD TO THE TRUTH OF ORIGINATION.

Or in: "This form, etc., should be forsaken, by him form, etc., should be forsaken". (P120) "This ill should be comprehended, by him ill should be comprehended." "This origination should be forsaken, by him origination should be forsaken."

I 3c. WEAK HEAT WITH REGARD TO THE TRUTH OF STOPPING.

"This stopping should be realised, by him stopping should be realised." "This path should be developed, by him the path should be developed." "This is defilement, this purification." "These dharmas should be tended, those should not be tended." "Here a Bodhisattva should course, there he should not course." "This is the path of a Bodhisattva, that is not." "This is the training of a Bodhisattva, that is not." "This is a Bodhisattva's perfection of giving, etc., that is not." That is the Ripening[2] of the Bodhisattva, the great being. If a Bodhisattva, who courses in perfect wisdom, settles down in these dharmas, insists on them, holds them to be truly real, that is the Rawness of his acting in conformity with the craving[3] for separate dharmas.

Śāriputra: What is the Ripening of a Bodhisattva?

Subhuti: Here a Bodhisattva, who courses in perfect wisdom, does not review the subjective-objective emptiness in the subjective emptiness,[4] nor the subjective in the objective, nor the subjective-objective in the objective, nor the objective in the subjective, nor the emptiness of emptiness in the subjective emptiness, (P121) and so on for all the kinds of emptiness. It is thus that a Bodhisattva, who courses in perfect wisdom, enters into the Ripening of a Bodhisattva.

I 3d. WEAK HEAT WITH REGARD TO THE TRUTH OF THE PATH.

(4. *Thought transparently luminous.*)

A Bodhisattva, who courses in perfect wisdom, should train himself to cognize form, etc., to develop the limbs of enlightenment, etc., and to cognize the 18 Buddhadharmas. But he should not fancy himself for any of this. *It is thus that a Bodhisattva, who courses in perfect wisdom, should cognize his thought of enlightenment, should cognize his even

[2]lit. De-rawing, *ny-āma*; also: his specific way of winning salvation.

[3]*ānulomikī*, very often used in connection with "Patience", as the "patient acceptance" which conforms, or adapts itself to, the actual nature of dharmas.

[4]see *P* 195 no. 1 sqq.

thought,[5] should cognize his exalted thought, but should not, because of that, fancy himself. And why? Because that thought is a nonthought, since in its essential original nature it is transparently luminous.[6]*

Śāriputra: What is the transparent luminosity of thought?

Subhuti: It is a thought which is neither conjoined with greed, nor disjoined from it (P122), which is neither conjoined with hate, delusion, obsessions, coverings, unwholesome tendencies, fetters, or what makes for views, nor disjoined from these.

**Śāriputra*: That thought which is a nonthought, is that something which is?

Subhuti: Does there exist, or can one apprehend, in this state of absence of thought either a "there is" or a "there is not?"

Śāriputra: No, not that.

Subhuti: Was it then a suitable question when the Ven. Śāriputra asked whether that thought which is a nonthought is something which is?

Śāriputra: What then is this state of absence of thought?

Subhuti: It is without modification or discrimination. It is the true nature of all dharmas.[7] This is called the unthinkable[8] No-thoughthood.*

Śāriputra: And just as that no-thoughthood is without modification or discrimination, in the same way also form, and all dharmas up to enlightenment, are without modification or discrimination?

Subhuti: So it is, Sariputra.

**Śāriputra*: Well said, well said, Subhuti, for you are the Lord's legitimate son, born from his mouth, a child of the Dharma (P123),

[5]*S*: "unequalled thought", which seems more suitable. The Bodhisattva is a being who has formed the "thought of enlightenment" and that, as stated expressly in *A* i 5, is the thought which is here referred to. A fine description of the attributes of the *bodhicitta* can be found in the *Nairātmyaparipṛcchā*. It ends with the verse:

"Not subject to modifications, essentially inactive, unoccupied, unfettered,
Immaterial, like unto the firmament, these are the marks of the thought of enlightenment.
It has transcended spiritual development, lies outside the range of the outsiders,
And its nature is that of Perfect Wisdom.
Incomparable, nonappearing, invisible and quite calm
Perfectly pure and insubstantial, these are the marks of the thought of enlightenment".

[6]*prabhāsvara*. *Samādhirājā* xxii 14: "Issued from so much merit, the Buddha's body is pure and transparently luminous", and xxii 27: "When it is no longer eager for name-and-form, then thought becomes transparently luminous"—The "thought which is no-thought" is what we would call the "Spirit". It is easy to see that it is no thought, more difficult to understand how it resembles thought sufficiently to be called "thought", and still more difficult to grasp how its two contradictory attributes are combined in a dialectical unity. It is "Pure Thought", a "mere shine", without an object, and yet it somehow differs from the Thought of Aristotle's Unmoved Mover who contemplates his own Thought.

[7]*dharmatā*, "Dharmahood". *S* and Gilgit-*P* have "Suchness" instead.

[8]in *S* and Gilgit-*P*, but not in *P* or *A*.

conjured up by the Dharma, an heir to the Dharma, not an heir according to the flesh, an immediate eyewitness of these dharmas.[9] Your exposition is that of the one whom the Lord has declared to be the foremost of the Disciples who dwell in Peace.[10] Thus, as you say, Subhuti, should a Bodhisattva train in perfect wisdom. This is the reason[11] why a Bodhisattva should be considered as incapable of turning away from full enlightenment, and be known as one who is not lacking in perfect wisdom.

I 3e. THE DISTINCTIVE CAUSALITY FOR ALL (the vehicles and degrees).[12]

Whether he wants to train on the level of a Disciple, a Pratyekabuddha or a Buddha—a Bodhisattva should listen to this Perfection of Wisdom, learn it, bear it in mind, recite, study, and wisely consider it. And why? Because here in this Perfection of Wisdom are expounded in detail the three careers in which the Bodhisattvas, the great beings, as well as the Disciples and Pratyekabuddhas should train.[13]*

[9]"an immediate eye witness of these dharmas", literally: "the dharmas are directly before his eyes, and he witnesses them with his body" (personally, in the flesh). In *V. M.* 659-60 the "bodily witness" is one of the seven kinds of "holy persons" who have all achieved the "cognition of evenmindedness as regards conditioned things".

[10]See my *Buddhist Wisdom Books,* 1958, p. 45.

[11]i.e., because he does not pride himself on his thought of enlightenment, *H* 41.

[12]This cryptic phrase means: All the degrees of the Aids to Penetration act as a "cause" (*hetu*) which brings about the attainment, on the Mahayanistic Path of Vision, of the specific spiritual realization which is characteristic of the persons who follow any of the three vehicles (see *H* 43, *AA* i 27, *my* translation p. 41, *Ob.* p. 62).

[13]The translation follows Gilgit *P* 53a.

CHAPTER 8

ŚRENIKA THE WANDERER

(5. *How the irreversible Bodhisattva views things.*)

I 3f. THE OBJECT, ASPECT, AND DISTINCTION FOR MEDIUM HEAT.[1]

**Subhuti*: I who do not find or apprehend anything to correspond to the words "Bodhisattva" and "perfect wisdom"—which Bodhisattva should I then instruct and admonish in which perfect wisdom? (P124) It would surely be regrettable if I, unable to get at the arising and passing away of any dharma, should merely in words cause a Bodhisattva and a perfection of wisdom to arrive and to pass away. Moreover, what is thus designated is not continuous nor discontinuous, and it has no stability anywhere.[2] And why? Because of the fact that it does not exist (apart from ignorance). That is why it is not continuous or discontinuous, and has no stability anywhere.* I do not get at the arising and (P125) passing away of form, etc., nor do I see it when reviewing. And so for the other dharmas (P126) up *to*: the Suchness of all dharmas. To what then could that word "Bodhisattva refer? And what is thus designated is not continuous or discontinuous, it has no stability anywhere. Because, apart from ignorance, it does not exist.

I 3g. THE OBJECT, ASPECT, AND DISTINCTION FOR STRONG HEAT.

Moreover, the reality corresponding to "Bodhisattva" taken as a conventional term for a dharma, as a concept of a dharma, cannot be expressed by anything, from form to (P127) the Buddhadharmas. (The reality corresponding to) a dream cannot be expressed by anything, nor that of an illusion, an echo, a mirage, the reflection of the moon in the water, or a magical creation of the Tathagata. (The reality corresponding to) space, earth, and the other physical elements, to Suchness, No-falsehood, unaltered Suchness, Dharma-Suchness, Dharma-element, the Constant Sequence of Dharma, the Reality limit, the perfection

[1]The translation of I3f-h follows *S* iv 504-613.

[2]*na sthitam,* it has no lasting continuous existence (H). *na visthitam,* it is likewise untrue to say that there are breaks or interruptions in its continuous existence, that it does not remain the same, is dissimilar to itself at different times. *na-adhisthitam,* nor is there a constant factor which, standing above all changes, overtowering and outlasting them, sustains it as a durable substance or invariable essence. An alternative translation would be: "It is not self-identical or disparate, and it does not remain substantially the same".

of giving and the other perfections, to morality, concentration, wisdom, emancipation, the vision and cognition of emancipation, to the Streamwinner, etc. *to*: to the Fully Enlightened One, cannot be expressed by anything, be it wholesome or unwholesome, faulty or faultless, permanent or impermanent, ease or ill, self or not self, calm or uncalm, isolated or not isolated, existent or nonexistent. For this reason I say that "it would surely be regrettable if I, unable either to apprehend or review the arising and passing away of any dharma, would bring about (only) the designation of something, i.e., of "Bodhisattva" and "perfect Wisdom"." Moreover that designation is not continuous or discontinuous, and it has no stability anywhere. And why? Because of the fact that it has no existence (apart from ignorance).

If, when this perfection of wisdom is thus being taught and explained through these modes, tokens and signs, the thought of a Bodhisattva does not become cowed, stolid or regretful, and his mind does not tremble, is not frightened or terrified (P128), then certainly that Bodhisattva, that great being, should be known as standing on the level of an irreversible Bodhisattva—by way of not taking his stand anywhere.

I 3h. THE OBJECT, ASPECT, AND DISTINCTION FOR LOW SUMMITS.

(6. *Perfect wisdom opposed to*:

(*a*) *Formative Influences*.)

*Moreover, a Bodhisattva who courses in perfect wisdom should not stand in form, etc. *to*: in decay and death. *And why? Because form is empty of form. What is the emptiness of form, that is not form; nor is emptiness other than form; the very form is emptiness and the very emptiness is form. And so for the other skandhas. By this method a Bodhisattva who courses in perfect wisdom should not stand in form, etc. *to*: consciousness. And the same method should be applied to the other dharmas, (P129, 130) from the eye to the six perfections and the eighteen Buddhadharmas, to the syllables, to single utterances, double utterances, and separate utterances,[3] (P131) to the superknowledges, all concentrations, and all Dharani-doors; to the conviction that "form, etc. is permanent or impermanent, ease or ill, self or not self, calm or not calm, empty or not empty, sign or signless, wish or wishless, isolated or not isolated" (P132); to Suchness, the true nature of Dharma, the Realm of Dharma, the Fixed Sequence of Dharma and the Reality limit.

*If a Bodhisattva who courses in perfect wisdom stands in form, etc.

[3]The exact meaning of these terms is not clear to me.

with a mind devoid of skill in means and prone to I-making and Mine-making, then he courses in the formative influence of form, etc. and not in perfect wisdom. And why? Because, while coursing in formative influences, a Bodhisattva cannot gain perfect wisdom, nor make endeavours about, or fulfil it. When he does not fulfil perfect wisdom, he cannot go forth to the knowledge of all modes. And why? Because form cannot be appropriated. But the nonappropriation of form is not form, on account of the emptiness of its essential original nature. And that applies to all dharmas, including perfect wisdom itself. It is thus that a Bodhisattva, who courses in perfect wisdom, should investigate all dharmas as empty in their essential original nature. (P133) He should survey them in such a way that there is no mental apperception of any dharma. This is the concentration circle of the Bodhisattva which is called "The nonappropriation of all dharmas"—vast, noble and fixed on infinitude, to which all Disciples and Pratyekabuddhas have no claim, and in which they have no share.[4] Dwelling in this concentration circle, a Bodhisattva will go forth to the knowledge of all modes. But also that knowledge of all modes cannot be appropriated, on account of the emptiness of the subject, and all the other kinds of emptiness.

I 3i. THE OBJECT, ASPECT, AND DISTINCTION FOR MEDIUM SUMMITS.

(6. *Perfect wisdom opposed to*:
(*b*) *the Sign*.)

And why? Because the knowledge of all modes should not be seized through a sign; for sign is defilement.* What again is "sign"? Form, etc. *to*: the Reality limit are "signs", and they all are called "defilement".* If, again, perfect wisdom could be seized through a sign, then Śrenika the Wanderer would not have gained faith in this our religion and in the cognition of the All-knowing.* "Faith" here means the believing in perfect wisdom, the trusting confidence, the resoluteness, the deliberation, the weighing up, the testing—and that in the absence of any sign. Thus should ((perfect wisdom)) be taken up through the signless. (P134) *When Śrenika the Wanderer had faith in that cognition of the All-knowing, he entered as a Faith-follower on a cognition with a limited scope. Having entered on it, he did not take hold of form, or any other skandha.* And why? Since all dharmas are empty of their own marks, there was no dharma which he could take hold of, on account of his non-attention to a sign. And why? For he did not review that cognition

[4]The name of the *samādhi* can also be interpreted as "that which cannot be appropriated, or seized upon, by any dharma" (H49). It is as "vast" as the Realm of Dharma; the "infinitude" is that of the number of beings whose welfare is promoted by this trance.

as due to an attainment and reunion which is inward, or outward, or both inward and outward, or elsewhere. And why? For he did not review that dharma which he could have known wisely, or by which he could have known wisely.* And why? He did not review that cognition as inside form, or as outside form, or as both inside and outside form, or as something other than form, on account of subjective-objective emptiness.

According to this Scripture passage, Śrenika the Wanderer, after he had resolutely believed in the cognition of the All-knowing, entered as a Faith-follower on a cognition with a limited scope, and then made the true dharmic nature of the cognition of the All-knowing into his standard, by way of his nonapprehension of all dharmas. Putting his trust in his faith, he took hold of no dharma whatsoever, on account of his nonattention to all signs. He also apprehended no dharma which he might take hold of, or which he might set free, on account of the fact that no dharma can be appropriated or abandoned. (P135) He did not even care about Nirvana. And why? The nonappropriation and the nonabandonment of all dharmas, that is Perfect Wisdom.

This is also of a Bodhisattva the perfection of wisdom, which has gone to a Beyond which is no Beyond,[5] that he does not take hold of form and the other skandhas, because no dharma has been appropriated. Nor does he enter final Nirvana prematurely, i.e. before he has fulfilled the Vows, etc. *to*: the powers of a Tathagata, the four grounds of self-confidence, the four analytical knowledges and the eighteen special Buddhadharmas. And why? Because all the dharmas, including the Buddhadharmas, are no dharmas. In fact they are neither dharmas nor no-dharmas. This is the perfection of wisdom of a Bodhisattva who has not appropriated any dharma whatsoever.

I 3k. Object, aspect, and distinction of high summits.

(6. *Perfect wisdom opposed to*:
(*c*) *What Exists.*)

Moreover, a Bodhisattva who courses in perfect wisdom should investigate what this perfection of wisdom is and whose, how, and whereby it is. If again a Bodhisattva who courses in perfect wisdom meditates on perfect wisdom as a dharma which does not exist and which cannot be apprehended, then he courses (not?) in perfect wisdom.

Śāriputra: Which are the dharmas that do not exist and that cannot be apprehended? (P136)

[5]*prajñāpāramitā apārapāragamanatāmupādāya*; *pha-rol ma mchis-pa'i pha-rol-tu phyin-pas.*

Subhuti: The perfection of wisdom, and the other perfections, the emptinesses, skandhas, Suchness, etc.—on account of the 18 kinds of emptiness. And if the thought of a Bodhisattva who courses in perfect wisdom and investigates and meditates in such a way does not become cowed or stolid, does not tremble, is not frightened or terrified, then that Bodhisattva should be known as not lacking in perfect wisdom.

I 3l. OBJECT, ASPECT, AND DISTINCTION FOR WEAK PATIENCE.
(7. *The Bodhisattva, wisdom, and enlightenment.*)

(*a*) *Śāriputra*: For what reason should a Bodhisattva be known as not lacking in perfect wisdom?

Subhuti: Form, etc., is lacking in the own-being of form, etc.

Śāriputra: What then is the own-being of form, etc.? (P137)

Subhuti: Nonpositivity is the own-being of form, etc. By this method one should know that form, etc., is lacking in the own-being of form, etc. Moreover, form, etc. does not possess the mark of form, etc. The mark does not possess the own-being of a mark, and the own-being does not possess the mark of (being) own-being.

(*b*) *Śāriputra*: A Bodhisattva who trains in this will go forth to the knowledge of all modes?

I 3m. OBJECT, ASPECT, AND DISTINCTION FOR MEDIUM PATIENCE.

Subhuti: He will. And why? Because all dharmas are unborn (P138) and do not go forth.

Śāriputra: For what reason are all dharmas unborn and do not go forth?

Subhuti: Form is empty of the own-being of form; one cannot apprehend any birth or going-forth with regard to it. And so for all dharmas, *up to*: the Reality limit. It is thus that a Bodhisattva, who courses in perfect wisdom, comes near to the knowledge of all modes. To the extent that he comes near it, he obtains the perfect purity of body, thought and marks. To the extent that he obtains the perfect purity of body, thought and marks, he produces no thought accompanied by greed, hate, or delusion, or by conceit, cupidity, or bad views. Owing to the nonproduction of such thoughts he is never again reborn in the belly of a mother, but constantly and always he is reborn apparitionally.[6] From Buddha-field he passes on to Buddha-field, honours the Buddhas, the Lords, matures beings and purifies the Buddha-field. Until the time that he knows full enlightenment he is never again deprived of those Buddhas and Lords. It is thus, Sariputra, that a Bodhisattva comes near to full enlightenment.*

[6]see my *Buddhist Wisdom Books*, 1958, p. 25.—This occurs on the 9th Stage, see *P* 224.

Chapter 9

THE SIGN

I 3n. Object, aspect, and distinction for strong patience.

*(*c*) If, O Lord, a Bodhisattva, who is unskilled in means, coursing in perfect wisdom courses in form, etc., or in any idea about form, etc. being permanent or impermanent, etc., then he courses, in a sign, (P139) and not in perfect wisdom. If a Bodhisattva, who is unskilled in means, coursing in perfect wisdom thinks that "I course in perfect wisdom", then he courses in a basis,[1] then he courses in a sign; and likewise when it occurs to him that "he who courses thus, courses in perfect wisdom and develops it". This should be known as a Bodhisattva's lack of skill in means.*

Śāriputra: For what reason should that be known as a Bodhisattva's lack of skill in means?

Subhuti: Because such a Bodhisattva, when coursing in perfect wisdom, insists on form, etc., perceives it, is intent on it, and in consequence he courses in the formative influence of form, etc. I know that he is not released from birth, decay and death, sorrow, sickness, lamentation, pain, sadness and despair, that he is not released from the great suffering. (P140) And if a Bodhisattva is unable even to realize the level of a Disciple or Pratyekabuddha, how much less can he know full enlightenment! That is impossible. It is thus that a Bodhisattva, who courses in perfect wisdom, should be known as unskilled in means.

Śāriputra: What should be known as his skill in means?

Subhuti: A Bodhisattva, who courses in perfect wisdom, does not insist on form, etc., does not perceive it, is not intent on it. He does not course in form, etc., nor in the sign of form, etc., nor in the conviction that "form, etc., is permanent, etc." (P141) And why? For what is the emptiness of form, not that is form; and no other than form is emptiness, no other than emptiness is form, etc. It is thus that a Bodhisattva should be known as having skill in means. A Bodhisattva, who courses thus in perfect wisdom, is able to know full enlightenment.

*Furthermore, a Bodhisattva does not course in perfect wisdom if he approaches any dharma, or does not approach it, or both approaches and does not approach it, or neither approaches nor does not approach it.

[1]*upalambhe*, also "false idea", "what is falsely considered as an ascertained fact".

Śāriputra: For what reason does a Bodhisattva, who courses in perfect wisdom, not approach (any dharma)?

Subhuti: Because the own-being of perfect wisdom cannot be apprehended. And why? Because perfect wisdom has nonexistence for own-being. In this way a Bodhisattva does not approach the idea that "I course in perfect wisdom", or the idea that "I do not course in it", or "I course and I do not course", or "I neither course nor do I not course". And why? For he has approached all dharmas as having nonexistence for their own-being, and has not appropriated them. If the thought of a Bodhisattva, who is thus coursing in perfect wisdom, does not become cowed or stolid, does not tremble, is not frightened or terrified, then it should be known that that Bodhisattva is near to the knowledge of all modes. (P142)

I 3o. OBJECT, ASPECT, AND DISTINCTION FOR WEAK HIGHEST MUNDANE DHARMAS.

(*d*) That knowledge of all modes, again, is not two nor divided, on account of all dharmas having conexistence for their own-being. This is the concentrated insight of the Bodhisattva which is called "nongenesis of the own-being of all dharmas"—vast, noble, and fixed on infinitude, to which no Disciple or Pratyekabuddha can lay claim. When he dwells in this concentrated insight, a Bodhisattva will quickly win full enlightenment.*

Śāriputra: Dwelling in which concentrations will a Bodhisattva quickly know full enlightenment?

Subhuti: gives a list of Concentrations (P143) (P144), as at CIII,lc (=P198–203).

I 3p. OBJECT, ASPECT, AND DISTINCTION FOR MEDIUM HIGHEST MUNDANE DHARMAS.

(8. *The Bodhisattva and his prediction.*)

*This Bodhisattva has surely been predicted by the Tathagatas of the past. Also those Tathagatas who just now stand, hold, and maintain themselves in this world, they also predict (the enlightenment of) such a Bodhisattva, such a great being.

One who dwells in these concentrations does not, however, review them. He does not think with regard to any concentration, "I am concentrated", "I will enter into concentration", "I have entered into concentration", "I am entering into concentration". All these discriminations the Bodhisattva does not have, does not get at.*

I 3q. OBJECT, ASPECT, AND DISTINCTION OF STRONG HIGHEST MUNDANE DHARMAS.

(P145) *Śāriputra*: Is then a Bodhisattva, who has stood in these concentrations, predestined (to enlightenment) by the Tathagatas?

Subhuti: No indeed, Sariputra. And why? Because perfect wisdom is not one thing, concentration another, and the Bodhisattva another. The Bodhisattva is precisely the concentration, the concentration is precisely the Bodhisattva. And both Bodhisattva and concentration are (identical with) perfect wisdom.

**Śāriputra*: If concentration is not one thing and the Bodhisattva another, and if the concentration is precisely the Bodhisattva and the Bodhisattva precisely the concentration—on account of the sameness of all dharmas—is it then possible to show forth any of these concentrations?

Subhuti: Indeed not.

Śāriputra: Again, does that son of good family preceive any of these concentrations?

Subhuti: No, Sariputra.

Śāriputra: How is it that he does not perceive?

Subhuti: Since he does not discriminate it.

Śāriputra: How does he not discriminate it?

Subhuti: Because no dharma has existence. It is in this way that a Bodhisattva does not perceive any of these concentrations.

Śāriputra: How is it that he does not perceive it?

Subhuti: Because of the nondiscrimination of any of these concentrations.

I 3r. THE CONNECTION WITH THE DISCRIMINATIONS IN GENERAL.

The Lord: Well said, Subhuti, well said, you whom I have declared to be the foremost of those who dwell in Peace. It is in such a way that a Bodhisattva should train in the perfection of wisdom, and in the other perfections, (P146) in the 37 dharmas which act as wings to enlightenment, etc. *to*: in the 18 special dharmas of a Buddha.

Śāriputra: When he trains thus, a Bodhisattva trains in perfect wisdom?

The Lord: So he does, and that because he does not apprehend it as a basis.*

Śāriputra: What does he not apprehend?

The Lord: He does not apprehend a self, or a being, etc. *to*: one who sees; the skandhas, the elements, suffering, origination, stopping, the Path, the triple world, the Unlimited, the trances, the formless attainments, the pillars of mindfulness, etc. *to*: the Buddhadharmas, the Streamwinner, etc. *to*: the Buddha—and all that on account of (the) absolute purity (of these dharmas).

Śāriputra: What then is that purity?

The Lord: The Unproduced, the Unmanifested, the Unascertainable, the Ineffective[2]—that is called "purity".

I 3s. THE FIRST DISCRIMINATION OF THE OBJECT (cr. to Heat).

I 3s,1. THE DISCRIMINATION OF IGNORANCE.

(9. *All is ignorance.*)[3]

(*a*) **Śāriputra*: When he thus trains, which dharmas does a Bodhisattva train himself in?

The Lord: He does not train (P147) in any dharma at all. And why? Because these dharmas do not exist in such a way as the foolish common people are wont to suppose.

Śāriputra: How then do they not exist?

The Lord: They do not exist in such a way as the foolish common people are wont to suppose.

Śāriputra: How then do they exist?

The Lord: As they do not exist, so they exist. And therefore, since they do not exist except for ignorance, they are called (the result of) ignorance.

I 3s,2. THE DISCRIMINATION OF THE SKANDHAS, FORM, ETC.

Śāriputra: For what reason is that which does not exist except for ignorance called (the result of) ignorance?

The Lord: Form, etc., do not exist, on account of the 18 kinds of emptiness.

I 3s,3. THE DISCRIMINATION OF SETTLING DOWN IN NAME AND FORM.

But foolish people have settled down in ignorance and craving. They have constructed (dharmas out of their) ignorance and craving, have settled down (in these results of) of ignorance and craving, have become attached to the two extremes (of existence and nonexistence), and both

[2]*anabhisamskāra*, an almost untranslatable term. At *P* 149 it is rendered as the "Uneffected". *A.K.* III 191 explains as "effortless", without a special act of attention (*anābhogena*), but *H* 603 as "like the firmament it is selfluminous throughout in its essential nature".

[3]*Pras.* xvi 296 gives an interesting parallel to I 3s. "Beings cannot transcend Samsara because they base themselves on ideas about a self and what belongs to a self. For if someone reviews self and other, then his karma-formations are activated. A foolish, untaught common person, who does not wisely know that absolutely all dharmas are completely nirvanized, apprehends self and other. He then settles down in this apprehension, and in consequence he becomes greedy, filled with hate, and confused, with the result that he brings about the triple activity by body, speech and mind. Superimposing his discrimination over that which does not exist, he imagines 'I am greedy, I hate, I am confused'," I 3s obviously deals with some of the chief links of conditioned coproduction.

extremes they do not know or see. After they have constructed those dharmas which yet do not exist, they have settled down in name-and-form, etc. *to*: in the Buddhadharmas.

I 3s,4. THE DISCRIMINATION OF ATTACHMENT TO THE TWO EXTREMES.

After they have settled down in dharmas, they construct the two extremes which yet do not exist, and as a result they neither know nor see. What do they neither know nor see? Form, etc. *to*: the Buddhadharmas. (P148) For that reason they come to be styled "fools".

I 3s,5. THE DISCRIMINATION OF THE NONCOGNITION OF DEFILEMENT AND PURIFICATION.

Conditioned by ignorance and craving they neither know nor see (that) "form is defiled", or that "form is purified". They will not go forth. Wherefrom will they not go forth? From the triple world, and from the dharmas of a Disciple or Pratyekabuddha.

I 3s,6. THE DISCRIMINATION OF THE NONESTABLISHMENT IN THE HOLY PATH.

They have no faith. What do they have no faith in? In the doctrine that form is empty of form, etc. *to*: that enlightenment is empty of enlightenment. They do not stand firmly. What do they not stand firmly in? In the perfection of giving, etc. *to*: in the Buddhadharmas. For these reasons are they called "fools". They have settled down. What have they settled down in? In form, etc. *to*: enlightenment.

(*b*) *Śāriputra*: When he trains thus, is a Bodhisattva trained in perfect wisdom, and will he go forth to the knowledge of all modes?

The Lord: A Bodhisattva who trains thus is not trained in perfect wisdom, and will not go forth to the knowledge of all modes.* Here, Sariputra, a Bodhisattva, unskilled in means, constructs the perfection of wisdom, and settles down in it. He constructs the other perfections, all dharmas, and the knowledge of all modes. In that case a Bodhisattva is not trained in perfect wisdom, and will not go forth to the knowledge of all modes.

Śāriputra: A Bodhisattva, who is trained thus, is not trained in perfect wisdom, and will not go forth to the knowledge of all modes?

The Lord: So it is, Śāriputra. (P149)

I 3s,7. THE DISCRIMINATION OF THE BASIS.

Śāriputra: How then must a Bodhisattva train in perfect wisdom, so that as a result he goes forth to the knowledge of all modes?

The Lord: When a Bodhisattva, who courses in perfect wisdom, neither apprehends nor reviews Perfect Wisdom, when he thus courses and trains in perfect wisdom, then he will go forth to the knowledge of all modes, in consequence of his nonapprehension. In the same spirit he should course in the other perfections, and he should also neither apprehend or review enlightenment, nor the knowledge of all modes.

I 3s,8. THE DISCRIMINATION OF THE SELF, ETC.

Śāriputra: In consequence of the nonapprehension of what (does he achieve this result)?

The Lord : He does not apprehend or review a self, on account of its absolute purity.

I 3s,9. THE DISCRIMINATION OF PURITY IN RELATION TO PRODUCTION, ETC.

And the Unproduced, the Unmanifested, the Uneffected—that is purity.

I 3t. THE SECOND DISCRIMINATION OF THE OBJECT, REFERRING TO THE ANTIDOTES (cr. to Summits).

I 3t,1. CONCERNING THE HEAPS AS ENTITIES.

(*c*) One who is unskilled in means constructs[4] form, etc. *to* : consciousness;

I 3t,2. CONCERNING THE SENSE FIELDS AS ENTITIES.

eye, etc. *to* : mind; form, etc. *to* : dharmas;

I 3t,3. CONCERNING THE ELEMENTS AS ENTITIES.

eye-element, form-element, eye-consciousness-element; etc. *to* : mind-element, mind-objects-element, mind-consciousness-element;

I 3t,4. CONCERNING (THE LINKS OF) COPRODUCTION AS ENTITIES.

ignorance, etc. *to*: decay and death;

I 3t,5. CONCERNING EMPTINESS AS AN ENTITY.

the 18 kinds of emptiness;

I 3t,6. CONCERNING THE PERFECTIONS AS ENTITIES.

the six perfections;

I 3t,7. CONCERNING THE PATH OF VISION.

the 37 dharmas which are the wings to enlightenment;

I 3t,8. CONCERNING THE PATH OF DEVELOPMENT.

the trances, superknowledges, Unlimited, formless attainments;

[4]or "imagines".

I 3t,9. CONCERNING THE PATH OF THE ADEPTS.
the 10 powers of a Tathagata, etc. *to* : the knowledge of all modes. (P150)

I 3u. THE FIRST DISCRIMINATION OF THE SUBJECT, REFERRING TO IT AS A SUBSTANTIAL ENTITY (cr. to Patience).

I 3u,1. CONCERNING THE SELF AS AN INDEPENDENT REALITY.

(The Bodhisattva) does not get at a self, or a being, a soul, a person, a personality, an individual, a man, a youth, one who does, one who knows, one who sees. And why? Because, absolutely, a self does not exist and cannot be apprehended.

I 3u,2. CONCERNING THE SELF AS A UNITY.

He also does not get at form, etc. *to* : consciousness;

I 3u,3. CONCERNING THE SELF AS A CAUSE.
eye, etc. *to* : mind; form, etc. *to* : dharmas;

I 3u,4. CONCERNING THE SELF AS A SPECTATOR.
eye, form, eye-consciousness, etc.;

I 3u,5. CONCERNING THE SELF AS THE RECEPTACLE OF THE DEFILEMENTS.
conditioned coproduction;

I 3u,6. CONCERNING THE SELF AS THE RECEPTACLE OF DISPASSION.
the formless attainments;

I 3u,7. CONCERNING THE SELF AS THE RECEPTACLE OF THE PATH OF VISION.
the holy truths;

I 3u,8. CONCERNING THE SELF AS THE RECEPTACLE OF THE PATH OF DEVELOPMENT.
the eight deliverances, the attainment of the nine successive stations;

I 3u,9. CONCERNING THE SELF AS THE FOUNDATION OF THE STATE OF ONE WHO HAS ATTAINED THE FINAL GOAL.
the ten powers, etc. *to* : the knowledge of all modes. How does he not get at them? Through their connection with selfhood. And why? On account of the absolute purity of self.

Chapter 10

LIKE ILLUSION

(10. *All is illusion.*)

I 3v. The second discrimination of the subject, referring to it as a normal entity (cr. to the Highest Dharmas).

I 3v,1. The concept of the skandhas.

**Subhuti*: If, O Lord, someone should ask—will this illusory man go forth to the knowledge of all modes, will he reach the knowledge of all modes after he has trained in perfect wisdom (P151) and in the other wholesome practices, up to the knowledge of all modes—how should one explain it?

The Lord: I will ask you a counterquestion which you may answer as best you can. What do you think, Subhuti, is form, etc., one thing and illusion another?

Subhuti: No, O Lord.*

I 3v,2. The concept of the sense fields.

The Lord: And does that hold good not only for the skandhas, but also for the sense fields,

I 3v,3. The concept of the elements.

the elements, the six kinds of contact, the eighteen kinds of feeling, the six physical elements, (P152)

I 3v,4. The concept of conditioned coproduction.

the links of conditioned coproduction,

I 3v,5. The concept of purification.

the 37 wings of enlightenment,

I 3v,6. The concept of the path of vision.

the concentrations on Emptiness, the Signless, and the Wishless,

I 3v,7. The concept of the path of development.

the trances and the formless attainments,

I 3v,8. THE CONCEPT OF THE DISTINCTIVE PATH.
the 18 kinds of emptiness,

I 3v,9. THE CONCEPT OF THE PATH OF THE ADEPTS.
the ten powers, the 18 special dharmas of a Buddha, and enlightenmtent itself? (P153)

Subhuti: Yes, it does, O Lord. *Illusion is not one thing and form another. But the very form is illusion, the very illusion is form. And so for all other dharmas.*

The Lord: What do you think, Subhuti, is there a production or stopping of illusion?

Subhuti: No, Lord.

The Lord: Is there a defilement or purification of illusion?

Subhuti: No, Lord.

The Lord: What do you think, Subhuti, that which is without production or stopping, without defilement or purification, can that train itself in perfect wisdom or in the other perfections, and can that go forth to all-knowledge, can that reach the knowledge of all modes?

Subhuti: No, Lord.

**The Lord*: What do you think, Subhuti, is that notion "Bodhisattva", that denomination, that concept, that conventional expression—in the five grasping skandhas?

Subhuti: No, Lord.*

The Lord: What do you think, Subhuti, can one through what is merely a notion, denomination, concept, conventional expression, apprehend the production or stopping, the defilement or purification of the five grasping skandhas?

Subhuti: No, Lord.

The Lord: What do you think, Subhuti, could someone, after he has trained in perfect wisdom, go forth to the knowledge of all modes, if he had no notion, denomination, concept, conventional expression, name or verbal concept; no body, speech, or mind, and no deeds of body, speech or mind; no production or stopping, no defilement or purification?

Subhuti: No, Lord.

The Lord: It is thus that a Bodhisattva, after he has trained in perfect wisdom, goes forth to the knowledge of all modes in consequence of the fact that there is nothing that could be apprehended.

**Subhuti*: Therefore a Bodhisattva, who trains in perfect wisdom, should train himself for full enlightenment just like an illusory man. And why? Because he, or rather the five grasping skandhas, should be known as just like an illusory man.*

The Lord: What do you think, Subhuti, do the five grasping skandhas after they have trained in perfect wisdom, go forth to the knowledge of all modes?

Subhuti: No, Lord. And why? (P154) Because the own-being of the five grasping skandhas is nonexistent. The five skandhas are similar to a dream. A dream cannot be apprehended, because its own-being does not exist, and in the same way the five skandhas cannot be apprehended, because of the nonexistence of their own-being.

The Lord: What do you think, Subhuti, could the five skandhas, after they have trained in perfect wisdom, go forth to the knowledge of all modes, if they were similar to an echo, to an apparition, to a magical creation, to an image of the moon reflected in the water?

Subhuti: No, Lord. And why? For the own-being of an echo, of an apparition, of a magical creation, of a reflected image, is nonexistent, and just so the five skandhas can, because of the nonexistence of their own-being, not be apprehended. And form is like an illusion, and so the other skandhas, and likewise all dharmas. If, when this is being taught, a Bodhisattva does not become cowed or stolid, has no regrets, does not tremble, is not frightened or terrified, then one should know that he will go forth to all-knowledge, and will reach the knowledge of all modes.

I 3w. Skill in means, the first assistance.

(11a. *Skill in means.*)

**Subhuti*: Will not Bodhisattvas, who have newly set out in the vehicle, become cowed, stolid and regretful when they hear this exposition, will they not tremble, be frightened, be terrified?

The Lord: They will tremble, etc., if, newly set out in the vehicle, they course in perfect wisdom while still unskilled in means, or if they have not got into the hands of a good spiritual friend.*

Subhuti: What is of a Bodhisattva, who courses in perfect wisdom, the skill in means which allows him not to be afraid?

The Lord: Here a Bodhisattva, by means of a thought associated with the knowledge of all modes, contemplates form as impermanent, ill, etc. *to*: wishless, and so also the other skandhas, and yet he does not apprehend any real fact. (P155) This should be known as the skill in means of a Bodhisattva who courses in perfect wisdom.

Furthermore, a Bodhisattva, through attentions associated with the knowledge of all modes carries out the demonstration of Dharma, without taking anything as a basis. This is his perfection of giving. His perfection of morality consists in the fact that he remains untarnished by those very attentions; his perfection of patience in the ability to endure those very attentions, his willingness to find pleasure in them, his ability to contemplate them; his perfection of vigour in the non-abandonment of those very attentions; his perfection of concentration in that he gives no opportunity to attentions associated with Disciples or Pratyekabuddhas, or to any other unwholesome dharmas. It is thus that a Bodhisattva, who courses in perfect wisdom, will remain unafraid.

Furthermore, a Bodhisattva, who courses in perfect wisdom, contemplates the fact that form, etc., is not empty of the emptiness of form, etc., but that form, etc., is just emptiness, and the very emptiness is just form, etc. This is a Bodhisattva's perfection of wisdom. (P156) It is thus that a Bodhisattva, who courses in perfect wisdom, will remain unafraid.

I 3x. The good spiritual friend, the second assistance.

(11b. *The Good Friend.*)

**Subhuti*: Who then are a Bodhisattva's Good Friends, with whose help, when they have got hold of him, he will remain unafraid on hearing this exposition of perfect wisdom?

The Lord: Here the good friends of a Bodhisattva are those who demonstrate to him the dharma that "form, etc., is impermanent etc.", without taking anything as a basis. He does not, however, dedicate the wholesome roots (which he gains from such teachings) to the level of a Disciple or Pratyekabuddha, but to nothing else than to the knowledge of all modes. These are a Bodhisattva's Good Friends who help him to remain unafraid.* (P157)

Subhuti: How does it come about that a Bodhisattva, who courses in perfect wisdom, becomes unskilled in means, gets into the hands of the Bad Friend, and becomes afraid when he has heard this exposition of the Perfection of Wisdom?

The Lord: Here a Bodhisattva, having left behind the attentions associated with the knowledge of all modes, develops the perfection of wisdom, gets at it, and fancies himself for it. And so for the other perfections. And again a Bodhisattva, who courses in perfect wisdom, leaves behind the attentions associated with the knowledge of all modes, and then he attends to the fact that "form, etc., is empty of a subject" (and so for all the 18 kinds of emptiness), but gets at that emptiness, puts his mind to it, as a result of assuming an objective basis.

Subhuti: How does it come about that a Bodhisattva is being taken hold of by a Bad Friend, and that (P158) in consequence he becomes afraid when he hears this exposition of Perfect Wisdom?

The Lord: Here a Bodhisattva is dissuaded from Perfect Wisdom by such words as, "One should not train in that! This has not been taught by the Tathagatas", "it is mere poetry made by poets, and one should not listen to it, learn or study it, bear it in mind, preach it, attend to it or demonstrate it to others!" This is what Bad Friends do to a Bodhisattva.

Furthermore, someone is a Bad Friend to a Bodhisattva if he does not point out to him the deeds of Mara, does not describe to him the faults of Mara. Here Mara, the Evil One, approaches the Bodhisattva in the guise of a Buddha and dissuades him from the six perfections, with the words: "What for do you, son of good family, develop the perfection of wisdom, and the other perfections?" Or Mara, the Evil One, will, in the guise of the Buddha, expound, reveal, analyse, amplify and illuminate the scriptures associated with the level of a Disciple, i.e. the Discourses, Discourses in Prose and Verse Mingled, Predictions, Verses, Summaries, Origins, Thus-was-said, Birth-Stories, Expanded Texts, Marvels, Tales, and Expositions. Or Mara, the Evil One, may approach the Bodhisattva and say, "You, son of good family, have never had the thought of enlightenment, nor are you irreversible, nor will you be able to know full enlightenment". Or Mara, the Evil One, may approach the Bodhisattva in the guise of the Buddha, and say to him, "The eye (P159), son of good family, the ear, and everything up to the Buddha-dharmas, (all this) is empty of self and of what belongs to a self. What can you possibly do to know full enlightenment?" Or Mara, the Evil One, may approach the Bodhisattva in the guise of a Pratyekabuddha, and say to him, "Empty, O son of good family, is each of the ten directions of Buddhas and Lords, of Bodhisattvas and Disciples, and it contains no Buddha, and no enlightenment, no Bodhisattva and no Disciple". Or Mara, the Evil One, approaches the Bodhisattva in the guise of a Disciple, dissuades him from attentions associated with the knowledge of all modes and instructs and admonishes him in attentions associated with the Disciples and Pratyekabuddhas. Or Mara, the Evil One, may in the guise of his preceptor or teacher dissuade the Bodhisattva from the course of a Bodhisattva and from the attentions associated with the knowledge of all modes. With regard to the applications of mindfulness, the right efforts, etc. *to*: the paths, with regard to the Empty, the Signless, and the Wishless, he will enjoin that, "after you have realised these dharmas, you should realise the level of a Disciple. What is there for you in knowing the utmost, right and perfect enlightenment?" (P160) Or Mara, the Evil One, may approach the Bodhisattva in the guise of his father or mother and say to him, "Come on, son of good family, make efforts to win the realisation of the fruit of a Streamwinner, etc. *to*: the fruit of an Arhat! What is there for you in knowing full enlightenment, if for the sake of it you must, for countless aeons, wander about in Samsara, and experience the cutting off of hands and feet?" Or, finally, Mara the Evil One may approach the Bodhisattva in the guise of a monk, and demonstrate to him that "form is impermanent, ill, not the self", and so for all the dharmas up to the Buddhadharmas, but while assuming an objective basis.

One who does not point out or describe such deeds of Mara, he should be known as a Bad Friend, and, once recognized as such, should be shunned.

CHAPTER 11

SIMILES[1]

C. WHAT TO BECOME:

(I. *The meaning of "Bodhi-being".*)

I 4. The Lineage or the Source of Progress.[2]

I 4a. THE LINEAGE AS SUCH.

**Subhuti*: A Bodhisattva is called a "Bodhisattva". "Bodhisattva", what is meant by that word?

[1]*apatrāpya*, the chapter heading in *AdT*, means "dread of blame", often coupled with *hrī*, "sense of shame". The explanations of Buddhaghosa, *V. M.* 464-5 and Vasubandhu, *Triṃśikā* 26-7, agree on essentials. Motivated either by self-respect, or by fear for one's reputation, one avoids doing that which one ought not to do. It is, however, difficult to see how this can be regarded as a suitable heading for chapter 11. A Central Asian Ms of *Ad* gives *aupamya*, "similes", which seems to fit better, and may at some time have been corrupted into *auttapya*=*apatrāpya*.

[2]I 4 is one of the more unintelligible parts of the Sutra. Since the ostensible meaning is not very satisfactory, it probably hints at some esoteric teaching. *AA* groups I 4-6 as follows: "(The Bodhisattva who proceeds on the mahayanistic path) of progress is thus able to attain the Aids to Penetration (as discussed in I 3) and also the path of vision, and so on. (I 4). His true own-being is the Dharma-element, which is the *foundation* of his activities, which (I 5) he exercises with all dharmas as the *object* of his meditation, and (I 6) with the triple *aim* which constitutes his program" (H16). This arrangement is not altogether implausible, although I am not sure that at I 4 it reflects the intentions of the original authors of the Sutra. According to *AA*, I 4 concerns the "lineage" (*gotra*) of a Bodhisattva, his true nature, which is nothing else but the Realm of Dharma which through progressive purification becomes fit for enlightenment and represents the source or substratum of the dharmas of a Buddha. It is the active element in the Bodhisattva which urges him on to enlightenment and which through cultivation by study, etc., has Buddhahood for its final metamorphosis, I 4, 1-13 follow the order of the Bodhisattva's progress or his process of cognition. This is clear for no. 1-6, 7 and 8 are the results of the two supramundane paths of vision and development, "and resemble the expulsion of thieves and the act of shutting the door behind them", while 9 removes all realistic imputations about this process of producing the antidotes and stopping the points to be shunned. Then at 10 "wisdom and compassion manifest themselves owing to the force of the Bodhisattva's initial vow, his practice of the six perfections and his skill in means, and they are marked by the fact that he does not abide in either Samsara or Nirvana"; 10 leads to 11, i.e. the four Means of Conversion and four Analytical Knowledges, to 12 and to 13 (H76-77). It is quite a problem how the Dharma-element which is common to all can be regarded as the source of a variety of "lineages", and the reader is referred for the answer to *AA* I v. 39, *H* 77 and *Ob.* 92.

The Lord: Nothing real[3] is meant by the word "Bodhisattva".* And why? Unproduced is enlightenment, unproduced is a being,[4] and so there is no trace[5] of enlightenment, or of a being (anywhere). That is why nothing real is meant by the word "enlightenment-being".

What is meant by the word "Bodhisattva",[6] that does not exist, that cannot be apprehended;

I 4,1. AS THE SOURCE OF HEAT.

just as in space the track[5] of a bird[7] does not exist and cannot be apprehended; just as the track of a dream, an illusion, a mirage, an echo, an image, a reflection of the moon in water, a village of the Gandharvas, or a magical creation does not exist and cannot be apprehended; (P161)

I 4,2. AS THE SOURCE OF THE SUMMITS.

just as the track of the Reality limit, of Suchness, No-Falsehood, unaltered Suchness, the Dharma-element, the established order of Dharma, the fixed sequence of Dharma, the Truth, does not exist and cannot be apprehended.

I 4,3. AS THE SOURCE OF PATIENCE.

No entity corresponding to a Bodhisattva[6] who courses in perfect wisdom does exist, or can be got at, any more than there exists or can be got at the track of the form, etc. of an illusory man;

I 4,4. AS THE SOURCE OF HIGHEST MUNDANE DHARMAS.

any more than there exists or can be got at the entity which corresponds to the form, etc., of an illusory man[8] who courses in the 18 kinds of emptiness, in the perfections, in the applications of mindfulness, etc. *to*: in the Buddhadharmas;

[3]*a-pada-artha.*

[4]A "Bodhi-sattva" is an "enlightenment-being".

[5]*padam.*

[6]*bodhisattva-padārtha.*

[7]This is an allusion to *Dhp.* 92, 93, = *Udānavarga* XXIX 23 sq.

"Those who never accumulate,
Those who know what their food implies,
Their range in the Void, in the Signless, detached,
Their track (*padam*) is very hard to trace.
Like that of birds which fly across the sky".

[8]The illusory being who cognizes the nonsubstantiality of the internal elements does not exist as a separate reality. *Ob.*

I 4,5. As THE SOURCE OF THE PATH OF VISION.
any more than there exists or can be got at with regard to the Tathagata an entity which corresponds to his form, etc.; (P162) and any more than there exists or can be got at an entity corresponding to the form, etc., of a Tathagata who courses in all the wings of enlightenment, in the powers, etc. *to*: in the Buddhadharmas. An entity corresponding to the word "Bodhisattva" does not exist, just as no trace of the unconditioned element exists or can be apprehended in the conditioned element, or vice versa;

I 4,6. As THE SOURCE OF THE PATH OF DEVELOPMENT.
just as that which is meant by such words as "Nonproduction, Nonstopping, the Uneffected, the Unmanifested, the Baseless, Nondefilement, Nonpurification" does not exist, and cannot be got at. And why? What is meant by the words "production, stopping, effected, manifested, basis, defilement and purification", that does not exist and cannot be apprehended. No trace of a real entity corresponding to a Bodhisattva exists or can be apprehended, just as no trace of the sign of form, etc., exists, or can be got at, on account of their absolute isolatedness; (P163) just as no trace of the sign of the applications of mindfulness, etc., *to*: of the Buddhadharmas, exists or can be apprehended, on account of their absolute purity; just as in purity no trace of the self, of a being, a soul, etc. *to*: of one who sees, exists or can be apprehended, on account of the fact that the self, and its equivalents, have no real being.

I 4,7. As THE SOURCE OF THE ANTIDOTES.
No trace of a really existing Bodhisattva can be found, just as, when the disk of the sun has risen (above the horizon), no trace of the (preceding) darkness[9] is either found or got at;

I 4,8. As THE SOURCE OF THE FORSAKING OF DETRIMENTAL STATES.
just as, when the universal conflagration at the end of an aeon has burned up everything, no trace of any conditioned thing is either found or got at;

I 4,9. As THE SOURCE OF FORSAKING THE DISCRIMINATION BETWEEN ANTIDOTES AND HARMFUL STATES.
just as, with regard to the Tathagata, no trace of immorality is either found or got at in his morality, no trace of distraction in his concentration, no trace of stupidity in his wisdom, no trace of lack of emancipation in his emancipation, no trace of lack of vision and cognition of emancipation in his vision and cognition of emancipation.

[9]so *S* vii 1253; *P*: "no trace of the light of the sun when it has risen" (?); but cf. I 4, 10.

I 4,10. AS THE SOURCE OF WISDOM AND COMPASSION.

A real entity corresponding to the word "Bodhisattva" does not exist, and cannot be apprehended, just as one cannot find or get at the track of the light of sun and moon; (P164)

I 4,11. AS THE SOURCE OF THE VIRTUES (OF A BODHISATTVA) NOT SHARED WITH THE DISCIPLES.

the track of the splendour of the planets and constellations, of jewels and of lightning flash,[10]

I 4,12. AS THE SOURCE OF THE SUCCESSIVE ACTIONS FOR THE WELFARE OF OTHERS.

of the splendour of the gods, from the Four Great Kings to the Highest Gods, and of the Bodhisattvas,[11]

I 4,13. AS THE SOURCE OF THE ACTION OF THE COGNITION WHICH WORKS WITHOUT ANY EFFORT.

or of the splendour of the Tathagata.

And why? For there, Subhuti, what enlightenment is, what the Bodhisattva is, and what the "tracks"[12] of the Bodhisattva are—all these dharmas are neither conjoined nor disjoined, immaterial, undefinable, nonresisting, with one mark only, i.e. with no mark.

A Bodhisattva should therefore be trained in nonattachment to all dharmas, and in their unreality—in the sense that he does not construct or discriminate them. In addition he should understand all dharmas.

I 5. The Objective Supports.

(*Classes of Dharmas.*)[13]

I 5a. THE OBJECT IN GENERAL.

Subhuti: What are all-dharmas? And how should a Bodhisattva be trained in their unreality? How should he understand all-dharmas?

The Lord: All-dharmas are the following: (1) Wholesome, (2) unwholesome and (3) indeterminate; (4) worldly and (5) supramundane; (6) with outflows and (7) without outflows; (8) conditioned and (9) unconditioned; (10) common and (11) uncommon. These are called the all-dharmas. (P165) A Bodhisattva should be trained in their non-

[10]*P* couples this item with the "Disciples and Pratyekabuddhas" in a way which I do not understand.

[11]so *S*, also *S*-Tib. Probably inadvertently omitted in Dutt's edition of *P*.

[12]*padārtha*.

[13]For a diagram of dharmas see Introduction p. 16.

beingness. These are the all-dharmas which a Bodhisattva should understand:

I 5,1. WORLDLY WHOLESOME DHARMAS.

Wholesome worldly dharmas are: Honouring father and mother, recluses, brahmins, and the elders of the family. The Foundation of Meritorious Work consisting in Giving, in Morality, in (meditational) Development, (the one) connected with the Service, the one derived from material gifts given, in faith, to the Tathagata.[14] The ten wholesome ways of action. The nine worldly perceptions, i.e. the perception of a swollen corpse, a worm-eaten corpse, a festering corpse, a bloody corpse, a discoloured corpse, a mangled corpse, a scattered corpse, the bones, a burned corpse. The four worldly trances, the four holy Unlimited, the four formless attainments, the five superknowledges. The ten worldly Recollections, i.e. the recollection of the Buddha, of the Dharma, of the Samgha, of morality, of renunciation, of gods, of breathing, of what concerns the body, of agitation, of death. These are called "wholesome worldly dharmas".

I 5,2. WORLDLY UNWHOLESOME DHARMAS.

Unwholesome worldly dharmas are: The ten ways of unwholesome actions, i.e. taking life, taking what is not given, sexual misconduct, false speech, slander, harsh speech, frivolous talk, covetousness, ill will and wrong views. Anger, enmity, jealous disparagement, contentiousness, harming, envy, meanness, conceit, false pride.

I 5,3. INDETERMINATE DHARMAS.

Indeterminate dharmas are: Indeterminate deeds of body, speech and mind; the indeterminate four great elements, the indeterminate five dominants, the indeterminate six sensefields, the indeterminate four formless attainments, the indeterminate skandhas, the indeterminate elements, the indeterminate sense fields, and all karma result. (P166)

I 5,4. WORLDLY (WHOLESOME) DHARMAS.

Worldly dharmas are: The five skandhas, the twelve sense fields, the eighteen elements, the ten ways of wholesome action, the four trances, the four holy Unlimited, the four formless attainments, the five superknowledges, and, except for the supramundane dharmas, whatever other worldly dharmas there are.

I 5,5. SUPRAMUNDANE DHARMAS.

Supramundane dharmas are: The four applications of mindfulness,

[14]The same list occurred at *P* 30.

the four right efforts, the four bases of psychic power, the five dominants, the five powers, the seven limbs of enlightenment, the holy eightfold path. The three doors to deliverance, i.e. emptiness, the signless, the wishless. The dominant of "I shall come to understand the not yet understood", the dominant of understanding, the dominant of one who has understood. The concentration with thought adjusted and discursive; the concentration without thought adjusted, and only with thought discursive; the concentration without either thought adjusted or thought discursive. Science,[15] Liberation, Mindfulness, Full awareness, wise attention. The eight deliverances, (P167) the nine attainments of successive stations, the eighteen kinds of emptiness. The ten powers of a Tathagata, (P168) the four grounds of self-confidence, the four analytical knowledges, the great friendliness, the great compassion, the 18 special dharmas of a Buddha.

I 5,6. Dharmas with outflows.

Dharmas with outflows are: The five skandhas, the twelve sense fields, the eighteen elements, the four trances, the four holy Unlimited, the four formless attainments, the five superknowledges.

I 5,7. Dharmas without outflows.

Dharmas without outflows are: The four applications of mindfulness, the four right efforts, the four bases of psychic power, the five dominants, the five powers, the seven limbs of enlightenment, the holy eightfold path. The four holy truths, the four trances, the eight deliverances, the nine attainments of successive stations, the three doors to deliverance, i.e. emptiness, the signless, the wishless. The ten powers of a Tathagata, the four grounds of self-confidence, the four analytical knowledges, the great friendliness, the great compassion, the 18 special dharmas of a Buddha.

I 5,8. Conditioned dharmas.

Conditioned dharmas are: The world of sense desire, the world of form, the formless world. And also any other dharmas that are included in the conditioned element, i.e. the 37 wings of enlightenment, etc.[16]

I 5,9. Unconditioned dharmas.

Unconditioned dharmas are: That of which there is no production, passing away, or alteration. Extinction of greed, hate, and delusion. Suchness, No-falseness, unaltered Suchness, the true nature of Dharma,

[15] *vidyā*, an untranslatable term, sometimes rendered as "lore".

[16] *S* gives here a long list, from the four applications of mindfulness to: all Dharani-doors.

the Dharma-element, the established order of Dharma, the fixed sequence of Dharma, the unthinkable element, the Reality limit.

I 5,10. COMMON DHARMAS.

Common dharmas are: The four trances, the four holy Unlimited, the four formless attainments, the five superknowledges.

I 5,11. UNCOMMON DHARMAS.

Uncommon dharmas are: The four applications of mindfulness, the four right efforts, the four bases of psychic power, the five dominants, the five powers, the seven limbs of enlightenment, the holy eightfold path. The four holy Truths, the four trances, the eight deliverances, the nine attainments of successive stations, the three doors to deliverance, i.e. emptiness, the signless, the wishless, all concentrations and all Dharani-doors. The ten powers of a Tathagata, the four grounds of self-confidence, the four analytical knowledges, the great friendliness, the great compassion and the 18 special dharmas of a Buddha. (P169)

I 5,b. THE OBJECTIVE SUPPORTS OF PROGRESS.

A Bodhisattva, who courses in perfect wisdom, should not become attached to any of these dharmas, which are empty of own-marks. And all dharmas should be understood in accordance with nonduality—on account of their nondiscrimination and their nonconstruction.

I 6. The Program.

I 6,1. THE GREATNESS OF THE ASPIRATION TO RAISE ALL BEINGS TO THE HIGHEST POSSIBLE STATE.

(II. *The meaning of "Great Being".* 1. *A Saviour of Many.*)

**Subhuti*: A Bodhisattva is called a "great being". For what reason is a Bodhisattva called a "great being"?

The Lord: He is called a "great being" because here he will cause a great mass of beings, a great collection of beings, to achieve the highest.*

Subhuti: What is that great mass of beings, that great collection of beings?

The Lord: The term "a great mass and collection of beings" refers to those who have reached the stage of becoming one of the clan, to those who have reached the eighth-lowest stage, to Streamwinners, Once-returners, Never-returners, Arhats, to Pratyekabuddhas, to Bodhisattvas, great beings, who have had the first thought of enlightenment, *until we come to*: to the Bodhisattvas who stand on the irreversible stage.

That is the great mass and collection of beings which a Bodhisattva will cause to achieve the highest. And he will cause them to achieve the highest after he has produced an adamantine thought.[17]

Subhuti: What is the production of an adamantine thought?

The Lord: Here a Bodhisattva, a great being, produces a thought thus: "After I have in the measureless stream of Samsara put on the armour, I should become one who never abandons all beings. Towards all beings should I adopt the same attitude of mind. All beings should I lead to Nirvana, by means of the three vehicles. (P170) And even when I have led all beings to Nirvana, no being at all has been led to Nirvana. And why? I should look through to the nonproduction and nonstopping of all dharmas. With my thought exclusively set on the knowledge of all modes should I course in the six perfections. Everywhere should I train myself to accomplish the penetration into all dharmas. To the consummation of the one principle of all dharmas should I penetrate, etc., *until we come to*: for the sake of the penetration to the consummation of the perfections should I be trained in all dharmas, for the sake of the penetration to the consummation of the Unlimited, the trances, the formless attainments, the superknowledges, of the ten powers, the grounds of self-confidence, the special Buddhadharmas". This is the production of an adamantine thought by the Bodhisattva, the great being. Supported thereon he will cause a great mass and collection of beings to achieve the highest; and that without depending on anything.[18]

Furthermore, a Bodhisattva, a great being produces the thought that "For the sake of as many beings as feel a painful feeling in the hells, among the animals, or in the world of Yama I will feel that (same) painful feeling!" Likewise a Bodhisattva should produce a thought thus: "For the sake of each single being I will experience for hundreds of thousands of niyutas of kotis of aeons the pains of the hells, of the animal world, of the world of Yama, until those beings have won Nirvana in the realm of Nirvana which leaves nothing behind. Through this skill in means will I, for the sake of all beings, experience that pain of the hells, of the animal world, of the world of Yama, until these beings have won Nirvana in the realm of Nirvana which leaves nothing behind. Afterwards I will, for the sake of my own self, know full enlightenment after I have planted wholesome roots for hundreds of thousands of niyutas of kotis of aeons and become equipped for enlightenment with a manifold equipment". This is a Bodhisattva's production of an adamantine thought.

Furthermore, in order to achieve the highest for all beings a Bodhisattva, should constantly have a sublime thought. The sublime state of his thought consists in that, on account of the first thought of enlighten-

[17]*vajropamam cittam.*

[18]*anupalambhayogena.*

ment, in him no thought of greed is produced, nor of hate, delusion or harming, nor a Disciple-thought or Pratyekabuddha-thought. (P171) This is the sublime state of thought of a Bodhisattva by which he will achieve the highest for all beings. But he does not put his mind to that thought. Furthermore, a Bodhisattva should become one whose thought is unshakable. A Bodhisattva's unshakable state of thought consists in his not putting his mind even to the mental activities associated with the knowledge of all modes. Furthermore, a Bodhisattva should become one whose thought is directed towards the benefit and ease of all beings. The stage of thought which is directed towards the benefit and ease of all beings consists in the sheltering of all beings, in not abandoning them. But he does not put his mind to that. It is thus that a Bodhisattva, coursing in perfect wisdom, will achieve the highest for all beings.

Furthermore, a Bodhisattva should have a constant liking for Dharma, a delight in Dharma, fondness for Dharma, devotion to Dharma. What here is Dharma? The unbroken unity of all dharmas. What is the liking for Dharma? The wish, the eagerness for Dharma. What is delight in Dharma? The pleasure in Dharma. What is fondness for Dharma? The appreciation of its qualities. What is devotion to Dharma? The developing, the making much of that Dharma. It is thus that a Bodhisattva, coursing in perfect wisdom, should achieve the highest for all beings, and that without depending on anything.

Moreover, a Bodhisattva who courses in perfect wisdom should achieve the highest for all beings after he has stood in the 18 kinds of emptiness, the 37 wings of enlightenment, the powers, etc. *to* : the Buddha-dharmas, (P172) and in the concentrations, beginning with the adamantine concentration and ending with the concentration which is, like space, unshackled, free and untainted—and all that without depending on anything. Having stood in these dharmas, a Bodhisattva who courses in perfect wisdom should make a great mass and collection of beings achieve the highest. It is for this reason that a Bodhisattva is called a "great being".

Chapter 12

THE FORSAKING OF VIEWS

I 6,2. The greatness of the forsaking.
(2. *He forsakes all false views.*)

**Śāriputra*: It is clear also to me in what sense a Bodhisattva is called a "great being".

The Lord: Make it clear then, Sariputra, what you think now.

Śāriputra: A Bodhisattva is called a "great being" in the sense that he demonstrates Dharma, in consequence of not depending on anything, so that all false views should be forsaken, i.e. the view of self, of a being, of a soul, of a person, etc. *to*: the view of one who sees; the view of annihilation, the view of eternity,* the view which assumes that "there is", the view which assumes that "there is not"; the view of the skandhas, the elements, the sense fields, of conditioned coproduction, of the dharmas which constitute the wings of enlightenment, of the powers, etc. *to*: of the Buddhadharmas; the view which assumes a maturing of beings, the view which assumes a purifying of Buddha-fields, the view of a Bodhisattva, the view of a Buddha, the view which assumes the turning of the wheel of Dharma.

Subhuti: For what reason may the erroneous view of form, and of the other skandhas, occur to a Bodhisattva?[1]

Śāriputra: Here a Bodhisattva, who courses in perfect wisdom, is unskilled in means. Having got at form, he produces a false view about it, in consequence of taking it as a basis. And so for all other dharmas, up to the Buddhadharmas.

I 6,3. The greatness of the achievement.
(3. *Unattached to even the highest thought.*)

**Subhuti*: It is clear also to me in what sense a Bodhisattva is called a "great being".

The Lord: Make it clear then, Subhuti, what you think!

Subhuti: A Bodhisattva is called a "great being", because he remains unattached even to his thought of enlightenment, the thought which

[1]who, according to *Ad*, is engaged in teaching Dharma to beings so that they may forsake their false views.

equals the unequalled, the thought which is not shared by any of the Disciples and Pratyekabuddhas. (P173) And why? Because he remains unattached even to the thought of all-knowledge, which is without outflows and unincluded in the triple world.*

Śāriputra: What then is the thought of a Bodhisattva that equals the unequalled and is not shared by any of the Disciples or Pratyekabuddhas?

Subhuti: Here a Bodhisattva, on account of the production of the first thought of enlightenment, does not review of any dharma the production or stopping, the decrease or increase, the coming or going, the defilement or purification. And where there is neither defilement nor purification, neither coming nor going, neither decrease nor increase, neither production nor stopping, that is not the thought of a Disciple or of a Pratyekabuddha. This is a Bodhisattva's thought which equals the unequalled and is not shared by any of the Disciples or Pratyekabuddhas.

Śāriputra: With regard to what the Ven. Subhuti has said about the Bodhisattva being "unattached even to the thought of all-knowledge, which is without outflows and unincluded in the triple world",[2] surely form, etc., is also unattached, on account of the emptiness of its essential original nature?

Subhuti: So it is, Sariputra.

Śāriputra: When the Ven. Subhuti speaks of "that thought of all-knowledge, without outflows and unincluded"—surely the thought of the foolish common people also (P174) is without outflows and unincluded, on account of the emptiness of its essential original nature, and the same holds good for the thought of all Disciples, Pratyekabuddhas, and fully enlightened Buddhas?

Subhuti: So it is, Ven. Sariputra.

Śāriputra: Form also is without outflows and unincluded, on account of the emptiness of its essential original nature, and so are all other dharmas?

Subhuti: So it is, Ven. Sariputra, as you say.

Śāriputra: When again the Ven. Subhuti has said[3] that "it is because that thought is no-thought that he remains unattached even to that thought", is not also form unattached to no-form, *and so* for all other dharmas?

Subhuti: So it is, Sariputra, as you say. It is thus that a Bodhisattva who courses in perfect wisdom does not because of that (P175) fancy himself for that thought (for enlightenment and all-knowledge), which equals the unequalled, which is not shared by Disciples and Pratyekabuddhas, and he does not settle down in it, in consequence of taking no dharma as his basis.

[2]so *S* vii 1279; *P*: "unattached even to the thought of the Disciples and Pratyekabuddhas".
[3]This saying of Subhuti does not occur in *P*, but in *A* i 19.

CHAPTER 13

THE SIX PERFECTIONS

I 7-10. THE PROGRESS AS SUCH.

(4. *Armed with the great armour.*)

**Purna, son of Maitrayani*: It is clear also to me in what sense a Bodhisattva is called a "great being".

The Lord: Make it clear then, Purna!

Purna: A Bodhisattva is called a "great being", because that being is armed with the great armour, has set out in the great vehicle, has mounted on the great vehicle.

Śāriputra: How great is that which entitles him to be called "armed with the great armour"?*

Purna: Here a Bodhisattva, who courses towards enlightenment, and has stood firmly in the perfection of giving, gives a gift not for the sake of a limited number of beings, but, on the contrary, for the sake of all beings. And in the same spirit he practises the other perfections. A Bodhisattva is not armed with the great armour if he delimits a certain number of beings, and thinks, "so many beings will I lead to Nirvana, so many beings will I not lead to Nirvana; so many beings will I introduce to enlightenment, so many beings will I not introduce to enlightenment!" But on the contrary, it is for the sake of all beings that he is armed with the great armour, and he thinks, "I myself will fulfil the six perfections and also on all beings will I enjoin them". (P176) And the same with the Unlimited, etc. *to*: the Buddhadharmas. By something as great as that is a Bodhisattva, a great being called "armed with the great armour".

I 7. The Progress which Consists in Putting on the Armour.

I 7a. THE SEXTAD CONNECTED WITH THE PERFECTION OF GIVING.

Furthermore, Sariputra, the perfection of giving of a Bodhisattva, who courses in perfect wisdom and gives gifts, consists in that, with attentions associated with the knowledge of all modes, he turns over to full enlightenment that gift which he gives, after he has made that wholesome root (which results from the act of giving) common to all beings. His perfection of morality consists in that, with his whole attention centred on the knowledge of all modes, he shuns the attentions of Disciples and Pratyekabuddhas; his perfection of patience in the enduring of those dharmas, in his willingness to find pleasure in them, in his ability to tolerate them;[1] his perfection of vigour in the indefatigability with which he continues to dedicate his wholesome roots to full enlightenment, after he has made them common to all beings; his perfection of concentration in his one-pointedness of thought when he gives a gift, so that, when he dedicates that wholesome root to enlightenment, after he has made it common to all beings, he gives, through keeping his whole attention centred on the knowledge of all modes, no opportunity to a Disciple-thought or a Pratyekabuddha-thought. (P177) His perfection of wisdom consists in that he sets up the notion that everything is made of illusion,[2] and in that he gets at no giver, recipient, or gift. With his thought associated with the knowledge of all modes, that Bodhisattva does not make these six perfections into a sign, and does not get at them. It is thus that a Bodhisattva, who courses in perfect wisdom, is armed with the great armour.

I 7b. THE SECOND SEXTAD CONNECTED WITH THE PERFECTION OF MORALITY.

Furthermore, a Bodhisattva, who courses in the perfection of morality, gives a gift with attentions associated with the knowledge of all modes, dedicates it to full enlightenment, after he has made (the merit from) that gift common to all beings—and that without taking anything as a basis. This is the perfection of giving of a Bodhisattva who courses in the perfection of morality. With his whole attention centred on the knowledge of all modes, a Bodhisattva does not long for the level of a Disciple or Pratyekabuddha, and much less still for the level of the common people. This is the perfection of morality of a Bodhisattva who courses in the perfection of morality. The enduring of those dharmas, the willingness to find pleasure in them, the ability to tolerate them, that is the perfection of patience of a Bodhisattva who courses in the perfection of morality. The indefatigability and uncowedness with which he continues to dedicate his wholesome roots to full enlightenment, after he has made them common to all beings that is the perfection of vigour of a Bodhisattva who courses in the perfection of morality. The one-pointedness of thought of a Bodhisattva who practises morality, i.e. that he gives, through keeping his whole attention centred on the knowledge of all modes, no opportunity to productions of thought associated with Disciples and Pratyekabuddhas, when he dedicates that wholesome root to full enlightenment, after he has made it common to all beings. He sets

[1]so *S*, *adhivāsanatā*; the term occurs also at *P* 215 and 221. *P*: the "testing" of these dharmas—as for "faith" at *P* 133.

[2]or: "made by illusion", "has the character, or status, of an illusion".

up the notion that everything is made of illusion; he gets at no one who practises morality, and that morality he does not either mind or get at; this is the perfection of wisdom of a Bodhisattva who courses in the perfection of morality. It is thus that a Bodhisattva who courses in the perfection of morality takes hold of the six perfections. It is thus that he comes to be called "armed with the great armour".

I 7c. THE THIRD SEXTAD CONNECTED WITH THE PERFECTION OF PATIENCE.

Furthermore, a Bodhisattva, who courses in the perfection of patience, gives a gift; with his attention centred on the knowledge of all modes, and not associated with Disciples or Pratyekabuddhas, he dedicates that wholesome root to full enlightenment, having made it common to all beings; (P178) this is the perfection of giving of a Bodhisattva who courses in the perfection of patience. The perfection of morality, patience, vigour, and concentration of the Bodhisattva who courses in the perfection of patience, should be understood by analogy with what has been said before. A Bodhisattva, who courses in the perfection of patience, exerts himself through wisdom to procure all Buddhadharmas, and to mature all beings; this is the perfection of wisdom of a Bodhisattva who courses in the perfection of patience.

I 7d. THE FOURTH SEXTAD, CONNECTED WITH THE PERFECTION OF VIGOUR.

By analogy one should understand the six perfections of a Bodhisattva who courses in the perfection of vigour,

I 7e. THE FIFTH SEXTAD, CONNECTED WITH THE PERFECTION OF MEDITATION.

and concentration.

I 7f. THE SIXTH SEXTAD, CONNECTED WITH THE PERFECTION OF WISDOM.

Furthermore, a Bodhisattva, who courses in the perfection of wisdom, gives a gift which is threefold pure[3]; with his attention centred on the knowledge of all modes, he dedicates to full enlightenment that gift which he gives, after he has made that wholesome root common to all beings. This is the perfection of giving of a Bodhisattva who courses in the perfection of wisdom. Similarly should one understand the perfection of morality, patience, vigour, and concentration of a Bodhisattva who courses in perfect wisdom. (P179) With regard to all perfections, and to all dharmas, he sets up the notion that they are an illusion, a dream, a reflected image, an echo, a reflection, a magical creation; with his attention centred on all-knowledge, he dedicates to full enlightenment that wholesome root, after he has made it common to all beings. It is thus that a Bodhisattva, who courses in perfect wisdom, fulfils the perfection of

[3]i.e. uncontaminated by any ideas about giver, gift, or recipient; cf. *P* 264.

wisdom. A Bodhisattva is then called "armed with the great armour". It is thus that a Bodhisattva, having stood firm in each single perfection, fulfils all the six perfections.

I 7g. THE ARMOUR OF THE SKILL IN MEANS.

Furthermore, a Bodhisattva enters into the trances, Unlimited, and formless attainments, but he does not relish them,[4] is not captivated by them, is not reborn on account of them.[5] This, Sariputra, is of a Bodhisattva, a great being, the perfection of wisdom which is associated with skill in means. A Bodhisattva furthermore dwells in the trances and formless attainments by way of the vision of detachment, of emptiness, of the signless, of the wishless, and yet he does not realize the reality limit. This is the great armour of the skill in means of the Bodhisattva who courses in the perfection of wisdom.

I 7h. THE RÉSUMÉ OF THE SEXTAD ON THE ARMOUR.

It is thus that a Bodhisattva is called "armed with the great armour". About this Bodhisattva the Buddhas, the Lords, in the ten directions utter a shout of triumph, proclaim his praise, announce his name, and make the pronouncement that "in this world system that Bodhisattva, that great being is armed with the great armour!" And he matures beings and purifies the Buddha-field. (P180)

I 8. The Progress in Setting Out.

(5. *Set out in the great vehicle.*)

Śāriputra: Through how much does the Bodhisattva become one who has set out in the great vehicle, one who has mounted on the great vehicle?

I 8,1. THE ENTERING ON AND EMERGING FROM THE TRANCES AND FORMLESS ATTAINMENTS.[6]

Purna: Here, coursing in the perfection of giving, a Bodhisattva dwells detached from sense desires, detached from evil and unwholesome dharmas, in the attainment of the first trance, which is with thoughts

[4]Because trances give a kind of superhuman bliss, a Bodhisattva might be tempted into seeking them from spiritual voluptuousness.

[5]The trances correspond to a number of heavens (see: Numerical Lists). To practise trance at a certain stage permits, after death, rebirth in the corresponding heaven. To avail himself of this possibility would for a Bodhisattva mean idle self-indulgence and a mere waste of time.

[6]according to *H*, the Bodhisattva must at this stage first gain some proficiency in transic meditation so that his mind may be brought to a state of complete firmness.

adjusted and discursive, born of detachment, full of rapture and ease. And so for all the four trances, and for the four formless attainments. These are a Bodhisattva's trances and formless attainments. When a Bodhisattva courses in the perfection of giving through these trances and formless attainments, enters into and emerges from them, through the modes, characteristics and signs of space makes these wholesome roots common to all beings, and dedicates them to full enlightenment—then this is a Bodhisattva's perfection of giving. Similarly he acts with regard to the perfections of morality, patience, vigour, and concentration. Moreover, a Bodhisattva, coursing in the perfection of wisdom, enters into the four trances and the four formless attainments. When a Bodhisattva dwells through these trances and attainments in the perfection of wisdom, and, while entering into and emerging from them attends to the modes, characteristics and signs of space, and, coursing in the perfection of wisdom, makes these, and other, wholesome roots common to all beings, through attentions connected with the knowledge of all modes, and dedicates them to full enlightenment—then this is a Bodhisattva's perfection of wisdom. It is thus that a Bodhisattva, who courses in the six perfections, is called "one who has set out in the great vehicle".

I 8,2. THE SIX PERFECTIONS.

Furthermore, it is the perfection of giving of the Bodhisattva if, with his attention centred on the knowledge of all modes, he produces a thought controlled by the great compassion, and thinks, "for the sake of the demolition of the defilements will I demonstrate the trances, Unlimited and formless attainments to all beings".[7] It is his untarnished perfection of morality if, with his attention centred on the knowledge of all modes, he enters into the trances, and, firmly grounded in them, does not give an opportunity (P181) to other productions of thought associated with the Disciples and Pratyekabuddhas. When it occurs to a Bodhisattva who, with his attention centred on the knowledge of all modes, dwells in the trances and formless attainments, that "for the purpose of the extinction of the defilements of all beings will I demonstrate Dharma", then the enduring of those attentions, the willingness to find pleasure in them, to test and understand them, and to meditate on them, that is a Bodhisattva's perfection of patience. It is a Bodhisattva's perfection of vigour that, through his attentions connected with the knowledge of all modes, he dedicates all wholesome roots to full enlightenment, and never relaxes his vigour. It is his perfection of concentration that, through his attentions connected with the knowledge of all modes, he enters into the trances and formless attainments, and yet does not apprehend them. It is his perfection of wisdom that he contemplates the

[7]so *S*; *P* says that he demonstrates "Dharma".

limbs of the trances under the aspects of impermanent, ill, not-self, etc., *to*: wishless, and yet does not apprehend them. This is the great vehicle of the Bodhisattva, the great being.

I 8,3. THE PATH.

Furthermore, this is the great vehicle of a Bodhisattva that, in all their modes, he develops the dharmas which are the 37 wings of enlightenment, the concentrations which are the doors to freedom—Emptiness, the Signless, the Wishless—the (ten) powers, the grounds of self-confidence, and the 18 special dharmas of a Buddha.

I 8,5. THE FOUR UNLIMITED.

Furthermore, a Bodhisattva dwells with a thought connected with friendliness—a thought that is vast, extensive, nondual, unlimited, free from hostility, rivalry, hindrance, or injury to anyone, extends everywhere and is well cultivated; he radiates friendliness in the ten directions of the world which has as its highest (development) the Dharma-element, and the space-element as its terminus. And so with compassion, sympathetic joy, and impartiality. These are called the four Unlimited of the Bodhisattva, the great being. (P182) A Bodhisattva enters the concentration on friendliness, and strives to save all beings. He enters the concentration on compassion, and directs pity and compassion towards beings. He enters the concentration on sympathetic joy, and resolves to make beings rejoice.[8] He enters the concentration on impartiality, and "extends"[9] to beings the extinction of the outflows. This is the perfection of giving of the Bodhisattva who courses in the Unlimited. When a Bodhisattva enters into the modes, characteristics and signs of the trances and Unlimited, and emerges from them, and yet does not dedicate (the resulting merit) to the level of a Disciple or Pratyekabuddha, but to nothing else than the knowledge of all modes—then this is the untarnished perfection of morality of the Bodhisattva who courses in the Unlimited. When he dwells in those trances, Unlimited, and formless attainments free from contamination, and does not long for the two levels of a Disciple or a Pratyekabuddha, but just the knowledge of all modes seems good to him and pleases him—then this is the perfection of patience of the Bodhisattva who courses in the Unlimited. If, through the production of thoughts associated with the knowledge of all modes,

[8]*modayishyāmīti*. It may perhaps also mean, "I will rejoice with them in their rejoicings", or "I will rejoice at all their spiritual achievements". In *S* (*samādhāyisyāmi*) and in *S*-Tib. (which read *mocayishyāmi*), the text is corrupt.

[9]*nirṇāmayati, rab-tu gshol-bar byed de.* At *P* 7 it meant "put out" in connection with the Buddha's tongue. Here it may mean that he "extends to them a thought", or that "he bends, or inclines, his thoughts to them".

he dwells as one who perseveres in forsaking unwholesome and in accomplishing wholesome dharmas—then this is the perfection of vigour of the Bodhisattva who courses in the Unlimited. If, although he enters into those trances, Unlimited, and formless attainments, he does not gain his rebirths through them, does not relish them, is not captivated by them—then this is the perfection of concentration of a Bodhisattva who courses in the Unlimited. If, with his attentions centred on the knowledge of all modes, he enters into the trances, Unlimited and formless attainments and emerges from them, and contemplates them under the aspects of impermanence, ill, not-self, of quietude, emptiness, signlessness and wishlessness, but does not go forward to the way of salvation of the Disciples and Pratyekabuddhas—then this is the perfection of wisdom of a Bodhisattva who courses in the Unlimited. This is the great vehicle of the Bodhisattva, the great being. (P183)

I 8,5. Absence of devotion to a basis.[10]

Furthermore, also this is the great vehicle of the Bodhisattva, the great being: The cognition of the 18 kinds of emptiness, without taking them as basic facts. That, since his thought is undisturbed in all dharmas, his cognition is concentrated.[11] That his cognition does not proceed through "this is permanent", "this is impermanent", "this is ill", etc. *to*: "this is wishless". That his cognition does not proceed in the past, future, or present period; in fact his cognition does not proceed in the three periods, and takes nothing as a basic fact. That his cognition does not proceed in the world of sense desire, in the world of form, in the formless world; in fact he has no cognition of the triple world, and that because nothing can be apprehended in it. That his cognition does not proceed in worldly or supramundane dharmas, in dharmas with or without outflows, in conditioned or unconditioned dharmas; in fact he has no cognition of any of these kinds of dharmas, and that because there is nothing to apprehend. This is the great vehicle of the Bodhisattva, the great being.

I 8,6. The threefold purity.

(6. *Mounted on the great vehicle.*)

Śāriputra: Through how much, Ven. Purna, is a Bodhisattva called

[10] *H* here comments: Thereupon he who acts for the sake of others comes to the insight that the apprehension (of separate entities) is a fetter (which ties to the phenomenal world). He accordingly secures access to the state of transic meditation in which he takes no separate entities as a basis.

[11] The Sanskrit text of *P* and of *S* vii 1328 seems to be corrupt, and I have translated this sentence tentatively after *S*-Tib. In view of note [10] it may perhaps be better to follow *S*-Skr,

"mounted on the great vehicle"?

Purna: Here a Bodhisattva, coursing in perfect wisdom, mounts on the perfection of giving. He does not get at the perfection of giving, or a giver, recipient, or gift—because there is nothing to get at. And so with the perfections of morality, patience, vigour, and concentration. Here a Bodhisattva, coursing in perfect wisdom (P184), mounts on the perfection of wisdom. He does not get at the perfection of wisdom, or a Bodhisattva, or an act of attention—because there is nothing to get at.

I 8,7. THE PROGRAM.

Furthermore, a Bodhisattva is called "mounted on the great vehicle" if, through an unmixed production of the thought of the knowledge of all modes, he develops the 37 wings of enlightenment, etc. *to*: the 18 special Buddhadharmas, with a development in the sense of annihilation[12] and that because there is nothing that can be got at.

Furthermore, a Bodhisattva is called "mounted on the great vehicle" if he perceives that "Bodhi-being" is a mere conventional expression, since no being can be apprehended. In the same way also all dharmas, from form to the Buddha, are mere words, because the reality corresponding to them cannot be apprehended.

I 8,8. THE SIX SUPERKNOWLEDGES.

Furthermore, during the entire period from the first thought of enlightenment up to full enlightenment (P185) he matures beings and passes on from Buddha-field to Buddha-field, after he has perfected his superknowledges. In all Buddha-fields he treats the Buddhas, the Lords with respect, honours, reveres, and worships them. Owing to his suitable worship of those Buddhas and Lords and his manner of showing respect he hears from them the Dharma, i.e. this great vehicle. Having mounted on the Bodhisattva-vehicle, he passes on from Buddha-field to Buddha-field, purifies the Buddha-fields, and matures beings. But he has no perception either of a Buddha-field or of a being. After he has stood on the level of nonduality, he acquires at will a personality which enables him to work for the welfare of beings. And, until he reaches the knowledge of all modes, he is never again lacking in this great vehicle.

I 8,9. THE KNOWLEDGE OF ALL MODES.

After he has reached the knowledge of all modes, he turns the wheel

and to translate, "when it makes no distinctions with regard to dharmas" instead of "undisturbed in all dharmas".

[12]*bhāvanā-vibhāvanā-arthena*. This rather mysterious phrase occurs frequently in the later parts of the Sutra. It may mean that "development", like everything else, is as much its opposite as it is itself, and that therefore it must be taken to mean an "undevelopment". "In the sense that he annihilates the development"?

of Dharma, which cannot be turned by all the Disciples and Pratyekabuddhas, in the world with its gods, Nagas, Yakshas, Gandharvas, Asuras, Garudas, Kinnaras, Mahoragas, and men. In each of the ten directions, in world systems countless like the sands of the Ganges, the Buddhas and Lords declare the fame, proclaim the praise, and reveal the glory of him who has known full enlightenment and they say of him that "in this world system that Bodhisattva, after mounting on the great vehicle, has reached the knowledge of all modes and thereafter turned the wheel of Dharma". It is thus that a Bodhisattva is called "mounted on the great vehicle".

CHAPTER 14

NEITHER BOUND NOR FREED

I 9. The Equipment.

I 9.1. THE EQUIPMENT WITH COMPASSION.

(7. *Emancipation a mock show.*)

Subhuti: Because he is "armed with a great armour" a Bodhisattva is called a "great being". Armed with how much of an armour can he be called "armed with the great armour"?

The Lord: He is armed with the great vehicle, the six perfections, the applications of mindfulness, etc. *to*: the knowledge of all modes. (P186) Armed with a Buddha-frame,[1] he radiates light over the great trichiliocosm and shakes it in six ways. In all infernal becomings he extinguishes the (great) mass of fire, appeases the sufferings of beings in the hells, and places[2] all of them face to face with Nirvana. The Bodhisattva then utters his message and pronounces the words, "Homage to the Tathagata, the Arhat, the Fully Enlightened One!" When they have heard the word "Buddha", the beings in the hells acquire (some) ease. Through that ease and gladness they emerge from their hells, are reborn in a world system in which they see and can please the Buddhas, the Lords, and win rebirth as gods and men. The same applies to the beings in the animal worlds and the world of Yama. It is thus that a Bodhisattva is called "armed with the great armour".

*Just as if a clever magician, or magician's apprentice, were to conjure up at the cross roads, in front of a great crowd of people, the hells, the animal world, and the world of Yama. He would then make these beings hear the message of Buddha, Dharma, and Samgha. Through that message they would emerge from those hells, from that animal world, from that world of Yama, and would be reborn among gods and men. Would then that magician, or magician's apprentice, have made any beings emerge from the hells, from the animal world, from the world of Yama?

[1]i.e. he takes upon himself the body of a Buddha. The term refers either to the Buddha's physical body, or his glorified body, or both.

[2]read *vijñāpya* instead of Dutt's *vijñaya?*

Subhuti: No, O Lord.

The Lord: Even so, after a Bodhisattva has set free beings in countless world systems from these three states of woe, no being at all has been set free. And why? For such is the true nature of dharmas that in fact they are illusory.[3] It is thus that a Bodhisattva, a great being, who has mounted on the great vehicle, is called "armed with the great armour".* (P187)

I 9,2. THE EQUIPMENT WITH THE PERFECTION OF GIVING.

Furthermore, a Bodhisattva, armed with the great armour, stands firm in the perfection of giving. By his magic he conjures up a trichiliocosm made of lapis lazuli, conjures up a display worthy of a Universal Monarch, and gives food to the hungry, gives away garments, vehicles, perfumes, garlands, flowers, incense, ointments, medicinal powders, houses, dwelling places, robes, the necessities of life, medicines, gold, silver, jewels, gems, coral, conch shells, quartz, pearls, etc. He then demonstrates Dharma to those beings, i.e. this very Dharma connected with the six perfections. And, after they have heard this demonstration of Dharma, those beings will never again be lacking in these perfections until they know full enlightenment. It is thus that a Bodhisattva is called "armed with the great armour". It is just as if a clever magician, or magician's apprentice, were to conjure up a great crowd of people, and give food to the hungry, and thing upon thing to those in need of it. What do you think, Subhuti, has this magician, or magician's apprentice given anything to anyone?

Subhuti: No, Lord.

The Lord: Even so should one understand the actions of the Bodhisattva who has stood in the perfection of giving. And why? For such is the true nature of dharmas that in fact they are illusory.

I 9,3. THE EQUIPMENT WITH THE PERFECTION OF MORALITY.

Furthermore, a Bodhisattva stands firm in the perfection of morality. Through his acquisition of the power to be reborn at will he is reborn in the family of a Universal Monarch. He then establishes beings in the ten ways of wholesome action, the four trances, etc. *to*: in the eighteen special Buddhadharmas. And, until they know full enlightenment, these beings will never again be lacking in this demonstration of Dharma.

[3]This is a translation of *dharmatā-eshā dharmāṇāṃ māyā-dharmatām-upādāya*. "This is the dharmic nature of dharmas, when one takes account of (*upādāya* = *gṛhītvā H*, *S*-Tib. *ñe-bar bzuṅ-na*) the fact that illusion is their dharmic nature". Tib: *sgyu-ma'i chos-ñid ñe-bar bzuṅ na, chos rnams-kyi chos-ñid-kyis de-bshin-pa'i phyir te*. The metaphysical subtleties involved can be seen from *H* 88.

(P188) Just as if a magician, or magician's apprentice, had conjured up a great crowd of people and had established them in all these wholesome practices; however many beings he had established in those practices, no being at all would have been established in them. The same is true of the Bodhisattva. And why? For such is the true nature of dharmas, that in fact they are illusory.

I 9,4. THE EQUIPMENT WITH THE PERFECTION OF PATIENCE.

Furthermore, a Bodhisattva stands firm in the perfection of patience. He instigates, exhorts, introduces beings to patience, in the following way: On account of his first production of the thought of enlightenment he puts on the armour thus: "If all beings were to hit me with sticks, clods, fists, or swords, not even one single thought of rage should be produced in me; and also all beings should I introduce to such patience!" Just as if a clever magician, or magician's apprentice, were to conjure up a great crowd of people: if they all hit him with sticks, clods, fists, or swords, nevertheless, he would produce towards them not even a single thought of rage; and if he were to introduce these magically created beings to such patience, no being at all would have been introduced to it, however many he had introduced to it. The same is true of the Bodhisattva. And why? For such is the true nature of dharmas that in fact they are illusory. (P189)

I 9,5. THE EQUIPMENT WITH THE PERFECTION OF VIGOUR.

Furthermore, a Bodhisattva stands firm in the perfection of vigour. He instigates, exhorts, introduces all beings to the perfection of vigour, in the following way: Here a Bodhisattva, through attentions connected with the knowledge of all modes, is supported by physical and mental vigour, and he introduces all beings to physical and mental vigour. But all this is as though done by a magician with regard to illusory beings, as said before.

I 9,6. THE EQUIPMENT WITH THE PERFECTION OF MEDITATION.

Furthermore, a Bodhisattva stands firm in the perfection of concentration. Here a Bodhisattva, having stood in the sameness of all dharmas, does not review the disturbance or nondisturbance of any dharma. It is thus that a Bodhisattva becomes one standing in the perfection of concentration. And he likewise instigates, exhorts and introduces all beings to the perfection of concentration, with the result that never until the time that they know full enlightenment will they ever again lack in the perfection of concentration. But all this is as though done by a magician with regard to illusory beings, as said before.

I 9,7. THE EQUIPMENT WITH THE PERFECTION OF WISDOM.

Furthermore, a Bodhisattva stands firm in the perfection of wisdom. When he courses in the perfection of wisdom (P190), a Bodhisattva does not get at the Not-Beyond or at the Beyond of any dharma whatsoever. It is then that he is one who stands firm in perfect wisdom, and he likewise instigates, exhorts, and introduces all beings thereto. But all this is as though done by a magician with regard to illusory beings, as said before.

I 9,8. THE EQUIPMENT WITH QUIETUDE.

Furthermore, as a Bodhisattva, armed with the great armour, has himself stood in the six perfections, so he instigates, exhorts, and introduces to them as many beings as there are in each one of the ten directions in world systems numerous as the sands of the Ganges. He demonstrates Dharma to them, i.e. this Dharma connected with the six perfections, and they will never again be deprived of the six perfections until the time that they know full enlightenment. But all this is as though done by a magician with regard to illusory beings, as said before. Furthermore, a Bodhisattva, armed with the great armour, dwells with his thought centred on the knowledge of all modes. He gives no room to other productions of thought, like "only so many beings should I establish in the perfections, in the wings of enlightenment, the Buddhadharmas, the fruits of the Path, Pratyekabuddhahood, or all-knowledge". But on the contrary he resolves to establish countless beings in those practices and their fruits. (P191)

I 9,9. THE EQUIPMENT WITH INSIGHT.

But all this is as though done by a magician with regard to illusory beings, as said before.* And why? For such is the true nature of dharmas that in fact they are illusory.

Subhuti: As I understand the meaning of the Lord's teaching, as certainly not armed with an armour should this Bodhisattva, this great being, be known, on account of the emptiness of ownmarks. And why? Because there form is empty of form, and so for all dharmas up to the Buddhadharmas. The Bodhisattva is empty of the Bodhisattva and the armour of the great vehicle is also empty of the armour of the great vehicle. By this method should a Bodhisattva be known as not armed with an armour.

The Lord: So it is, Subhuti, as you say. And why? Because the knowledge of all modes is not made or unmade, but is in fact uneffected.[4]

[4] "not made", because their is no maker; "not unmade", because it cannot be annihilated, since nothing that has not first been made can be destroyed; "uneffected", it has not actually been generated by the conditions which may be thought to bring it about.—cf. S. Augustine: "This wisdom is not made, but it is at present as it has ever been, and so shall ever be" (Conf. 9, 10).

Those beings also, for the sake of whom a Bodhisattva is armed with the great armour, are not made or unmade, but are in fact uneffected.*

Subhuti: For what reason is that so?

The Lord: On account of the impossibility of apprehending a maker. For form, etc., does not make, nor unmake, nor effect (anything). Because absolutely all these dharmas do not exist, are not apprehended. (P192) The same is true of self, being, soul, person, personality, etc. *to*: one who sees; of a dream, an echo, a reflection of the moon in water, a reflected image, a mirage, and an apparition; of the eighteen kinds of emptiness, the thirty-seven wings of enlightenment, etc. *to*: the Buddhadharmas, of Suchness, etc., and of the knowledge of all modes. It is for this reason that the knowledge of all modes is not made or unmade, but in fact uneffected; and so are those (beings) for whose sake a Bodhisattva is armed with the great armour. It is thus that a Bodhisattva is called "armed with the great armour".

I 9,10. THE EQUIPMENT WITH THE COMBINATION OF INSIGHT AND QUIETUDE.

**Subhuti*: As I understand the meaning of the Lord's teaching, form etc., is neither bound nor freed.

Purna: You say, Subhuti, that form, etc., is neither bound nor freed?

Subhuti: So it is, Purna.

Purna: What then is that form, etc., which is neither bound nor freed?

Subhuti: That form, etc., which is like a dream, like an echo, a mock show, a mirage, a reflection of the moon in water, an apparition, that is neither bound nor freed. (P193) Even so form, etc., which is past, future, or present, is neither bound nor freed. And why? Because of the nonbeingness of form, etc. Even so form, etc., whether it be wholesome or unwholesome, defiled or undefiled, tainted or untainted, with or without outflows, worldly or supramundane, defiled or purified, is neither bound nor freed, on account of its nonbeingness, its isolatedness, its quiet calm, its emptiness, signlessness, wishlessness, because it has not been brought together or produced. And that is true of all dharmas.* It is thus that a Bodhisattva, a great being is neither bound nor freed; and neither are the six perfections etc. *to*: the knowledge of all modes. The beings also whom he will lead to Nirvana are neither bound nor freed; and neither are the Buddha-fields which he will purify, the Buddhas, the Lords whom he will honour, the Dharma which he will hear, and the fact that he will never again be deprived of the Buddhas, the Lords, or of the superknowledges, the five Eyes, etc.—also that is neither bound nor freed. Neither bound nor freed, he will produce a knowledge of the modes of the Path which is neither bound nor freed, he will understand a knowledge of all modes which is neither bound nor freed, he will turn a wheel of Dharma which is neither bound nor freed, and he will, through the three vehicles, lead to Nirvana beings who are neither bound nor freed. It is thus that a Bodhisattva, neither bound nor freed by the six perfections, will fully know all dharmas, on account of their nonbeingness, (P194) their isolatedness, etc. *to* : their unproducedness. It is thus that one should know the Bodhisattva's, the great being's, armour of the great vehicle, which is neither bound nor freed.

Chapter 15

THE CONCENTRATIONS

I 9,11. The equipment with skill in means.

III. *The meaning of "great vehicle".* 1. *Its constituents.*

**Subhuti*: What is the great vehicle of the Bodhisattva, the great being? How should a Bodhisattva be known as one who has set out in the great vehicle? Wherefrom will that vehicle go forth? Where will it come to a halt? Who will go forth by means of that great vehicle?*

The Lord: With regard to what you say, "what is the great vehicle of a Bodhisattva?" The six perfections are the great vehicle of a Bodhisattva.

Subhuti: What are a Bodhisattva's six perfections?

The Lord: A Bodhisattva's perfection of giving consists in that, with productions of thought associated with the knowledge of all modes, he gives gifts, i.e. inward and outward things, makes these common to all beings and dedicates them to full enlightenment; and he instigates others also to do likewise; but always without basing himself on anything. The untarnished perfection of morality of a Bodhisattva consists in that[1] he himself undertakes to observe the ten ways of wholesome action and instigates others also thereto, but without basing himself on anything; his perfection of patience in that he himself becomes one who has achieved patience and also instigates others thereto, but without basing himself on anything (P195); his perfection of vigour in that he dwells persistently in the five perfections and instigates others also thereto, but without basing himself on anything; his perfection of concentration in that he himself enters into the trances with skill in means and is not reborn on account of them, that he instigates others also to do likewise, and that he never bases himself on anything. His perfection of wisdom consists in that he does not settle down in any dharma, contemplates the essential original nature of all dharmas, also instigates other beings to the contemplation of all dharmas, but never bases himself on anything. This Subhuti, is the great vehicle of a Bodhisattva, a great being.

[1] *S* adds at each perfection the phrase, "with productions of thought associated with the knowledge of all modes".

I 9,12. THE EQUIPMENT WITH COGNITION.[2]

Moreover, Subhuti, the great vehicle of the Bodhisattva, the great being, that is the emptiness of the subject, etc. *to*: the emptiness of other-being.

1. What is the emptiness of the subject? Dharmas on the subject-side are eye, ear, nose, tongue, body, and mind. Therein the eye is empty of the eye, on account of its being neither unmoved nor destroyed. And why? Because such is its essential nature. And so for the ear, etc. *to*: mind.

2. What is the emptiness of the object? Dharmas on the object-side are forms, sounds, smells, tastes, touch objects, and mind objects. Therein from is empty of form, on account of its being neither unmoved nor destroyed. For such is its essential nature. And so for sounds, etc. *to*: mind objects.

3. What is the emptiness of both subject and object? The six subjective sense fields and the six objective sense fields, these are the inward (=subjective) and outward (=objective) dharmas.[3] How are the subjective empty of the objective dharmas? Eye, ear, nose, tongue, body, and mind are empty of forms, sounds, smells, tastes, touch objects and mind objects. (P196) How are the objective empty of the subjective dharmas? Forms, sounds, smells, tastes, touch objects and mind objects are empty of eye, ear, nose, tongue, body, and mind, on account of their being neither unmoved nor destroyed. For such is their essential nature.

4. What is the emptiness of emptiness? The emptiness of all dharmas is empty of that emptiness,[4] on account of its being neither unmoved nor destroyed. For such is its essential nature.

5. What is the great emptiness? The Eastern direction is empty of the Eastern direction, on account of its being neither unmoved nor destroyed. For such is its essential nature. And so for the other nine directions.[5]

[2]For this extremely difficult and important section of the Sutra I have added a number of notes from *AAA* 95-96, *Ob.* 126 sq., and *Mahāyānasamgraha* (=M-s) ch. 5. 1 and its commentary.

[3]The translation follows *Ad* and *Da*. In this interpretation no. 3 is similar to no. 15 of *Pts*, the *visabhāga-suñña*, according to which "the six inner sense fields are empty of the six outer sense fields, which are unlike them". The Yogācārins understood no. 3 quite differently.

[4]Because it is merely the cognition of the emptiness of all dharmas.—*Pras.* XII: Emptiness is not a property, or universal mark, of entities, because then its substratum would be nonempty, and one would have a fixed conviction (*dṛṣṭi*) about it. In fact it is a mere medicine, a means of escape from all fixed convictions. It is taught so that we may overcome attachment, and it would be a pity if we were to become attached to it. It is not a positive standpoint, but a mere turning away from all views and thought constructions. To treat it as an object, and to oppose it to nonemptiness, is to miss the point.

[5]This refers to the Absolute, *or dharmadhātu,* as all-pervading. No limitations, like "eastern", "western", etc., are admissible for it, but it is omnipresent, since no dharma is not *anātman*.

6. What is the emptiness of ultimate reality? "Ultimate reality" means Nirvana. And that Nirvana is empty of Nirvana,[6] on account of its being neither unmoved nor destroyed. For such is its essential nature.

7. What is conditioned emptiness? "Conditioned" means the world of sense desire, the world of form, the formless world. Therein the world of sense desire is empty of the world of sense desire, on account of its being neither unmoved nor destroyed. For such is its essential nature. And so for the other two worlds.

8. What is unconditioned emptiness? "Unconditioned" means that of which there is no production, no stopping, no stability, no alteration.[7] The Unconditioned is empty of the Unconditioned,[8] on account of its being neither unmoved nor destroyed. For such is its essential nature.

9. What is infinite emptiness? That of which no end is got at, that infinite is empty of the infinite,[9] on account of its being neither unmoved nor destroyed. For such is its essential nature.

10. What is the emptiness without beginning or end?[10] That of which no beginning or end is got at, of that the middle is nonexistent. And that of which neither beginning nor middle nor end is got at, of that there is no coming or going. Beginning, middle, and end are also empty of beginning, middle, and end, on account of their being neither unmoved nor destroyed. For such is their essential nature.

11. What is the emptiness of nonrepudiation?[11] Of that dharma there

[6]No objective entity "Nirvana" exists as such. Nirvana is in fact nothing but the mere disconnection from all phenomenal elements. cf. *A.K.* I 6.—Nirvana is *parama-artha*, both as the ultimate reality and as the supreme goal.

[7]So *P* and *Ad*, *anyathātva*. *S*: *sthiter anyathātva*, "alteration of its stability, or subsistence". The difference reflects the uncertainties of the Abhidharma tradition about the moments through which a dharmic event is bound to pass. A Sutra (cf. *A.N.* i p. 152) speaks of *sthity-anyathātva*; some authorities interpret this as "the difference between preceding and succeeding moments"; others as "decay". See P. S. Jaini in BSOAS, xxii, 1959, pp. 542-547.

[8]The Unproduced, etc., has no correlation with the produced, etc., which is mere sign and concept.—Here the Dharma-element is considered as "unseizable"; one cannot conceive of it as one's own, cannot imprison it, and when one has attained it one cannot say "it is mine".

[9]*Ad*: "That dharma of which absolutely (*atyantato*) no production can be apprehended. And why? Because such is its essential original nature".—*H* "End" (limit, *anta*) means "portioned out". Now between the limits of eternity and annihilation (regarded as two portions) there exists absolutely nothing by which could be established an own-being through the sign of the delimitation of their respective portions (*Obermiller*: which could draw a boundary between them, and thus make them appear as having each its separate essence)—*aty-anta*, "infinite" "beyond end", "beyond limit".

[10]*an-avara-agra*, Pali *anantamagga*, is normally used for Samsāra. Nos. 10 and 11 belong together, in that 10 refers to birth-death, and 11 to Nirvana.—"A first beginning of suffering, i.e. of beings blinded by ignorance and craving, cannot be conceived" (*Divy*. 197); there is no first and no last (*Pras*. xi).

[11]*anavakāra P, S*: *apratikāra Ad.*, which has only: "wherein there is no rejection of any dharma". The term "casting off" (*vikiraṇam*) occurs in the traditional formula of Arhat-

is no repudiation. "Repudiation" means (P197) casting off, spurning, letting go. The nonrepudiation is empty of the nonrepudiation,[12] on account of its being neither unmoved nor destroyed. For such is its essential nature.

12. What is the emptiness of essential nature? The essential (original) nature of all dharmas, be they conditioned or unconditioned, is not made by the Disciples, or by the Pratyekabuddhas, or by the Tathagatas,[13] nor is it removed by them.[13] The essential nature is empty of the essential nature, on account of its being neither unmoved nor destroyed. For such is its essential nature.

13. What is the emptiness of all dharmas? All dharmas means the five skandhas, the twelve sense fields, the six kinds of consciousness, the six kinds of contact, the six kinds of feeling conditioned by contact. Conditioned and unconditioned dharmas, these are called "all-dharmas". Therein all dharmas are empty of all-dharmas, on account of their being neither unmoved nor destroyed. For such is their essential nature.

14. What is the emptiness of own-marks! To be easily broken is the mark of form, experiencing that of feeling, taking up that of perception, together-making that of the formative forces, being aware that of consciousness.[14] (Likewise, suffering is the mark of the skandhas, resemblance to a venomous snake that of the elements, acting as a door of coming into being that of the sense fields; possessing the full complement of conditions that of conditioned coproduction; renunciation that of the perfection of giving, celibacy that of the perfection of morality, unshakability that of the perfection of patience, uncrushability that of the perfection of vigour, comprehension that of the perfection of concentration, nonattachment that of the perfection of wisdom; unshakability is the mark of the four trances, the four Unlimited, the four formless attainments; leading forth that of the thirty seven wings of enlightenment, detachment that of emptiness as a door to deliverance, quiet calm that of the signless as a door to deliverance, removal of suffering that of the wishless as a door to deliverance; delivering that of the deliverances, to be well massed that of the powers, to be well established that of the grounds of selfconfidence, to be indestructible that of the analytical

ship. The dharma which is not repudiated is Nirvana, because in regard to it absolutely nothing needs removing.

[12]*H*: Nonrepudiation must be understood in relation to its opposite, which is "repudiation" as defined in the Sutra. "Casting off" etc. are not real entities, because they are essentially nonactivities, and therefore also the nonrepudiation is no more than a sign and concept.

[13,13]So *P*, but not *S*. In no. 12 the English cannot reproduce the play of words between *prakṛiti* (essential nature), *saṃskṛta* (conditioned), *asaṃskrta* (unconditioned) and *akṛta* (not made).

[14]*P* adds here: "this should be worked out in detail". The following passage in brackets is from *S* corrected after Gilgit *P* 172a.

knowledges, provision of what is beneficial that of the great friendliness, protection that of the great compassion, rejoicing that of the great sympathetic joy, noncommingling that of the great impartiality, to be something to which no one else has a claim is that of the eighteen special Buddhadharmas, and to be "before the eye" is the mark of the cognition of the knowledge of all modes). Whatever the mark of conditioned or of unconditioned dharmas, all these dharmas are empty of their own-marks, on account of their being neither unmoved nor destroyed. For such is their essential nature.

15. What is unascertainable emptiness! Those dharmas which are past, future, and present, are not got at. And why? In a past (dharma) the future (dharmas) cannot be got at: nor in a future the past; nor in a present (dharma) can the past and future (dharmas) be got at: nor in the past and future (dharmas) the present ones. The unascertainable emptiness is the nonapprehension of these, because they are pure from the very beginning, on account of their being neither unmoved nor destroyed. For such is their essential nature.

16. What is the emptiness of the nonexistence of own-being? There is no own-being of a dharma (acting) in causal connection, because of conditioned co-production.[15] The (causal) connection is empty of the (causal) connection, on account of its being neither unmoved nor destroyed. For such is its essential nature.

17. What is the emptiness of existence? "Existence" means the five grasping skandhas. And that existence is empty of existence,[16] on account of its being neither unmoved nor destroyed. For such is its essential nature. (P198)

18. What is the emptiness of nonexistence? "Nonexistence" means the Unconditioned. And that Unconditioned is empty of that Unconditioned,[17] on account of its being neither unmoved nor destroyed. For such is its essential nature.

19. What is the emptiness of own-being? Because own-being is the unpervertedness of essential nature, that is empty of this, on account of its being neither unmoved nor destroyed. For such is its essential nature.

[15]Indeed it has been said, what is a positive existent beyond, or apart from, the full complement of its causes and conditions? Functional interdependence makes it impossible for anything to have an independent existence. On analysis anything and everything is nothing more than a bundle of conditions, and the formula "this being, that is" binds it up inextricably with many factors outside itself.

[16]A "skandha" means a "group, heap, assemblage, conglomeration". But a conglomeration is not a real entity by itself, and can therefore not act as the basis for an existence which bears the mark of grasping.

[17]It is a non-ens, devoid of an essence of its own. Its existence is merely nominal, because it is nothing but the negation of separate entities, which (usually) obstruct and cover it.

And it is not made by cognition and vision.[18] And why? Because this is its essential nature.

20. What is the emptiness of other-being?[19] This true nature of dharmas, which is established whether Tathagatas are produced or not produced, the established order of dharmas, the fixed sequence of Dharma, Suchness, Not-falseness, unaltered Suchness, the Reality limit;[20] the emptiness of this of that, on account of its being neither unmoved nor destroyed. For such is its essential nature. Nor is it made by something else.[21] And why? Because this is its essential nature.

This is called the great vehicle of the Bodhisattva, the great being.

I 9,13. THE EQUIPMENT WITH MERIT.[22]

Moreover, Subhuti, the great vehicle of the Bodhisattva, the great being, i.e. the concentration called "Heroic Valour", etc. *to*: the concentration called "Like space, unshackled, free, and untainted".

1. The concentration called "Heroic Valour": Through that concentration the range of all the concentrations is experienced. 2. The Jewel Seal: Through that concentration all concentrations are sealed. 3. The Lion's Play: As a result of having stood firm in this concentration, one can play with all the concentrations. 4. The Beautiful Moon: As a result of having stood in this concentration one sheds light on all concentrations. 5. The Moon as a Glorious Ensign: This concentration carries the Ensign of all concentrations (as a token of victory).

[18]The own-being which is understood as emptiness exists from the outset and is not the product of the perfection of wisdom, which is the same as the cognition and vision of the Saints. The knowledge and intuition of the Saints only illuminates the ultimately real principle of nonsubstantiality, but does not produce it. Considered as a fact it is therefore empty of itself.—*Pras.* vi 23: "The Buddhas teach that all dharmas, whether inward or outward, have a double nature. The one is that which is conventionally assumed, the other is that which is ultimately real. The second, though it does not exist in itself, is constituted by the fact that it is the range of the cognition of those who see rightly. The first is constituted by the power of the false views of the common people, whose intellectual vision is covered up with the cataract of ignorance".

[19]*para-bhāva*. That which is produced by others. Or, that which differs in relation to another. *Pras.* 260: "Any own-being in relation to another is called 'other-being'". Warmth, for instance, as the own-being of fire, is "other-being" with reference to fluidity, which is the own-being of water.

[20]This formula also occurs in *A.N.* i 285 and very frequently elsewhere. See MCB v 207. The "true nature" (*dharmatā*) of dharmas is the same as conditioned coproduction, which operates quite irrespective of the appearance or nonappearance of the Tathagatas who alone are capable of discovering it.

[21]Indeed it has been said: Human effort that is directed upon Emptiness will have for its result only useless toil.

[22]The translation of this section is purely speculative. I have failed to understand a large number of the technical terms employed here, and just mechanically followed the dictionaries. *S.P.* and *Ad* often differ, and I have generally followed *P*, without, however, marking the occasions where I have adopted the reading of *Ad* or *S*.

6. Exaltation above All Dharmas: As a result of having stood in this concentration one is elevated above all concentrations. (P199) 7. Surveying the Summits:[23] one surveys the Summits of all concentrations. 8. Fixed on the Element of Dharma: one moves towards certainty in one's understanding of the Dharma-element. 9. The Glorious Ensign of Certainty: one carries the Ensign (which indicates) certainty about all concentrations.

10. Like a Thunderbolt;[14] one is not broken by any concentration. 11. Seal of Entrance into (all) Dharmas: one enters into the Seal of (all) dharmas. 12. The Well-established King of Concentrations: one establishes oneself in all concentrations with the definiteness of a king. 13. The Shedding of Rays: one emits the Rays of all concentrations. 14. Array of Power: one brings about the array of the power of all concentrations. 15. Arisen: To one who has stood in this concentration all concentrations rise up together. 16. The definite Entrance into the (Exposition of) Languages: one can enter into the exposition of the language of all concentrations. 17. Entrance into all Synonyms: one can enter into the designations and synonyms of all concentrations. 19. Surveying the Directions: one surveys the Directions of all concentrations. 19. Carrying the Seal: one carries the Seals of all concentrations.

20. Unimpaired: one does not impair any of the concentrations. 21. The Seal of the Ocean of the Meeting of all Dharmas: as a result of his having stood in this concentration all his concentrations assemble and meet. 22. Radiant Ether: one irradiates all concentrations with a radiation like that of ether. 23. Sharp: one kindles all concentrations with flaming glory. 24. Unlimited Illumination: it illuminates the Unlimited. 25. Without Attachments or Coverings: on account of lacking all attachments, it illuminates without covering. 26. Extermination of the Proceeding of all Dharmas: it enterminates the proceeding of all dharmas. (P200) 27. Forsaking Impurity: one forsakes all signs, how much more so the signs of the defilements. 28. Like the Shining Sun: one illuminates all concentrations, warms them, shines upon them. 29. Desirelessness: one does not desire any dharma appertaining to the concentrations.

30. Utterly Homeless: one reviews in no concentration a dharma which is at home there. 31. Free from Thought: in that concentration no thought proceeds, and none of its concomitants. 32. Immaculate Lamp: it acts as an immaculate lamp for all concentrations. 33. Infinite Splendour: it brings about an infinite splendour. 34. Lightbringer: it throws light on all concentrations. 35. All-round Illumination: as soon as this concentration has been acquired, all concentration-doors are illuminated. 36. Pure Core: one reaches the pure sameness of all concentrations.

[23]The explanation of nearly every item is from now on prefaced by the formula "as a result of having stood in this concentration", which I have omitted in the translation.

[24]Adamantine.

37. Immaculate Splendour: one removes the stains from all concentrations and gives them a brilliant appearance. 38. Giving Delight: one experiences the delight of all concentrations. 39. Lightning Flash: all concentrations are set ablaze. 40. Inextinguishable: one reviews of all concentrations neither the extinction nor the nonextinction. 41. Diamond-Circle: one carries the Circles of all concentrations. 42. Extinction Left Behind: one reviews the nonextinction of all concentrations, and views them in such a way that one reviews not even the least dharma. 43. Immovable: one does not waver or vacillate in any of the concentrations, nor does one mind them, or have idle fancies about them. 44. It cannot be overturned: one does not review the overturning of any concentration. 45. Lamp of the Sun: it illuminates all concentration-doors. 46. Immaculate Moon: one disperses the darkness in all concentrations. 47. Bright Appearance: one acquires the four analytical knowledges with regard to all concentrations. (P201) 48. Illuminator: one throws light on all concentration-doors. 49. Mode of the Doer: one brings about the work and performance of all concentrations. 50. The Ensign of Cognition: one reviews the Ensign of the cognition of all concentrations. 51. Like a Thunderbolt: one penetrates all dharmas, and yet does not review that concentration. 52. Stability of Thought: one's thought does not waver, is not diverted or terrified; it never fails, but one remains unaware that "(this is) thought". 53. Illumination All-round: one reviews in all concentrations the all-round illumination. 54. Well Established: one becomes well established in all concentrations. 55. Jewel Cusp: all concentrations appear bright all round, like a jewel cusp. 56. Seal of the Best Dharma: It results in that all concentrations are Sealed, on account of their being Sealed with a Seal from the very beginning. 57. The Sameness of All Dharmas: one does not review any dharma as sundered from sameness. 58. Forsaking Delight: one forsakes the delight in all concentrations, the delight in all dharmas. 59. The Fulness of Ascent to All Dharmas: elevated above all dharmas one is nevertheless saturated with them.

60. Dispersing: one disperses and tears asunder all dharmas through all concentrations. 61. Cleaving the Verbal Expressions of All Dharmas: one cleaves the verbal expressions for all concentrations and dharmas. 62. Identifying the Letter: one understands the fact that all concentrations have the same letter. 63. All Letters Left Behind: one does not even get at one single letter for all concentrations. 64. Cutting off the Objective Support: the objective support of all concentrations is cut off. 65. Without Modification: one does not apprehend the alteration of any dharma. 66. Modeless: one does not apprehend even the specific constitution of any dharma. 67. Nonentrance into Name and Sign: one does not apprehend the name and sign of any concentration. 68. Wandering Without a Home: one does not get a home in any concentration. 69. All Darkness

Left Behind: one removes all darkness from all the concentrations.

70. Possessing a Manner of Acting: one reviews the manner of acting of all concentrations. 71. Unshakable: one reviews all concentrations as unshakable. (P202) 72. Surpassing the Sphere: one transends the sphere of all concentrations. 73. The Accumulation of All Qualities Takes Place: In this concentration one reaches the accumulation of all the qualities of all dharmas and of all concentrations. 74. The Stability of No-Thought: with regard to all concentrations one's thought does not proceed. 75. Sweetly Blooming Purity: one acquires the sweetly blooming purity of all concentrations. 76. In Possession of the Limbs of Enlightenment: one acquires, through all concentrations, the seven limbs of enlightenment. 77. Infinite Inspiration: one acquires in all concentrations a state of infinite inspiration. 78. Equal to the Unequalled: one acquires, through all concentrations, the state where one is equal to the unequalled. 79. Transcending All Dharmas: one transcends everything in the triple world.

80. Accurate Definer: one can delimitate all dharmas and concentrations. 81. Dispersing Uncertainty: one reaches the dispersal of all uncertainty about all concentrations. 82. All Stability Stopped: one does not review the abiding of any dharma. 83. One Single Harmony: one does not review the duality of any dharma. 84. Consummation of the Modes: one does not review the consummation of the modes of all concentrations and dharmas. 85. One Single Mode: one reviews the single mode of all concentrations. 86. Nonrepudiation of the Modes: one reviews (not) the non-duality of all dharmas. 87. The Penetration, which Disperses the Base of All Becoming: one reaches the penetrating cognition of all concentrations; when that has been reached, there is no dharma that has not been pierced. 88. Entrance into the Meaning of Voices and Sounds: one enters into the meaning of the voices and sounds of all concentrations as freed from the letters which constitute speech.

90. Flaming Torch: With its Splendour it illuminates all concentrations, warms them, shines upon them. 91. Purification of Marks: the marks of all concentrations are purified. 92. Undistinguished: one reviews all concentrations as undistinguished. 93. Furnished with the Best of all Modes: To one who has stood in this concentration all concentrations are furnished with the best of all modes. 94. Not Rejoicing in All Ease or Ill: in all concentrations one does not review the ease or the ill. (P203) 95. Bringing About Nonextinction: one does not review the extinction of all concentrations. 96. Wise Knowledge of Dharanis: it results in that one can bear in mind all the Dharanis. 97. Complete Removal of Rightness and Wrongness: one does not review the rightness and wrongness of all concentrations. 98. Appeasing All Obstruction and Stopping: one does not review the obstruction or

stopping of all concentrations. 99. Compliance and Opposition : one does not review the compliance and opposition of all concentrations.

100. Immaculate Glory : one does not get at the glorious circle of all concentrations. 101. Possessing a Core : one does not review the substantiality of all concentrations. 102. The Stainless Full Moon : in this concentration all his concentrations are fully realized, just like the full moon. 103. Great Harmony : all his concentrations are endowed with great harmony. 104. Light bringer in Every Way : it throws light on all concentrations and on all dharmas. 105. Concentration-sameness : in all concentrations one apprehends neither distraughtness nor one-pointedness. 106. Assemblage of all Peace and Refuge : to one who has stood in this concentration, no concentration can cause strife. 107. Pleased with being independent of a Home : in this concentration one does not approach a settling place for all concentrations. 108. Stability of No-thought in Suchness : in this concentration one does not depart from the Suchness of all concentrations. 109. Crushing the Misery of having a Body : it results in that one does not get at a body for all concentrations.

110. Removing the Misery of Speech : it results in that one does not get at the speech-action of all concentrations. 111. Fashioned like the Firmament : it illuminates like the firmament. 112. Like Space, Unshackled, Free and Untainted : here one reaches the state where all dharmas are, like space, unshackled, free and untainted.

This is the great vehicle of the Bodhisattva, the great being, who courses in the perfection of wisdom.

Chapter 16

ENTRANCE INTO THE DHARANI-DOORS

I 9,14. The equipment with the path.[1]

And further, Subhuti, the great vehicle of the Bodhisattva, the great being:

1. *The Four Applications of Mindfulness.* Which four? Mindfulness as to the body, as to the feelings, as to thought, as to dharmas. (P204)

There the Bodhisattva dwells, with regard to the inward body, feelings, etc., in the contemplation of the body, etc. But he does not form any discursive thoughts associated with the body, etc. He is ardent, clearly conscious and mindful, after putting away all worldly covetousness and sadness. And that without taking anything as a basis. And so he dwells with regard to the outer body, to the inner and outer body, to feelings, thought, and dharmas.

(I.A) How does a Bodhisattva dwell with regard to the inward body in the contemplation of the body?

(I.Aa) Here a Bodhisattva knows, when he walks, "I walk", when he stands, "I stand", when he sits, "I sit", when he lies down, "I lie down". In whichever position his body may be placed, whether in a good way or not, he knows that it is in that position. And that through nonapprehension (of anything).

(I.Ab) Further, a Bodhisattva is clearly conscious when going out and coming back, when looking towards and looking away, when bending and stretching (the arms), when carrying his waist-cloth, robe, and almsbowl; when eating, drinking, chewing, and dispelling exhaustion by sleep; when coming and going, standing and sitting, falling asleep and waking up, speaking and keeping silent, and when retiring for meditation. And that through nonapprehension.

(I.Ac) Further, a Bodhisattva who courses in perfect wisdom, and who, mindful, breathes in, knows as it truly is, "mindful I breathe in". And so when he breathes out, when he makes a long inhalation (P205) or a long exhalation, a short inhalation, or a short exhalation. Just as a potter, or potter's apprentice, would whirl round a wheel, and, when making a long whirl, he would know, as it really is "I make a long whirl"; and so also when he makes a short whirl. So also the Bodhisattva. And that through nonapprehension.

[1]The translation generally follows *S*.

(I.Ad) Further, a Bodhisattva, who courses in perfect wisdom, contemplates this very body according to its elements as it really is: there is, in this body, the element of earth, water, fire, and air. Just as a skilful cows' butcher, or cows' butcher's apprentice, having killed a cow with a sharp knife, cuts it into four quarters, and then examines it, as he stands or sits. Just so the Bodhisattva with regard to the four elements. And that through nonapprehension.

(I.Ae) Further, a Bodhisattva, who courses in perfect wisdom, contemplates this very body as it really is, from the sole of the foot upwards, and from the top of the hair downwards, bounded by nails, down, and skin, and filled with manifold impurities. There are in this body: Hairs of the head, hairs of the body, nails, teeth, skin, hide, flesh, tendons, blood, bones, marrow, kidneys, heart, liver, serous membranes, spleen, lungs, intestines, mesentery, stomach, urine, excrement, tears, grease, sweat, spittle, snot, pus, bile, mucus, lymph, fluid of the joints, dirt, brain, oozings of the eye, oozings of the ear. Just as a husbandman has a sack full of all sorts of grain—sesamum, mustard seed, kidney beans, beans, lentils, barley, wheat, rice, husked rice—and a man with eyes (P206) examining them, would know, "This is rice of such a sort, this is sesamum, these are the mustard seeds, etc." Just so the Bodhisattva with regard to the parts of the body. And that through nonapprehension.

(I.B) And how does the Bodhisattva dwell with regard to the outer body?

(I) When he goes to the burial ground, a Bodhisattva sees all sorts of dead bodies thrown in the burial ground, flung in the charnel-field—one day dead, or two days dead, or three days dead, or four days dead, or five days dead—swollen, dark blue, festering, eaten by worms, or mangled. And thus he compares his own body: "This body also is of such a dharmic nature, of such an own-being, and it has not gone beyond this state of affairs". (II) And so he reflects when he sees dead bodies, cast into the burial ground, six nights dead and seven nights dead, being devoured by crows, eagles, and vultures, by jackals, wolves, dogs, or various other kinds of animals; or (III) when he sees those dead bodies flung in the burial ground, mauled, repulsive, foul, and stinking; or (IV) when he sees in the charnel field a chain of bones, smeared with flesh and blood, joined together by tendons; (V) or when he sees those dead bodies, a mere chain of bones, with flesh, blood and tendons all gone (P207); or (VI) when he sees in the charnel field a chain of bones, separated, nor joined together, disjoined, like shells scattered anyhow on the ground; or (VII) when he sees in the charnel field bones scattered in all directions, i.e. here foot bones, there shin bones, there thigh bones, there a hip and pelvis, there the bones of the spine, there the ribs, there the neck bones, there the arm bones, there the skull; or (VIII) when he sees in the charnel field bones, several years old, several hundred years old, dried up by the wind and sunshine, white like conch shells; or (IX) when he sees in the charnel field bones, dark-coloured, black-blue, grey like pigeons, rotten, powdered into the likeness of dust upon the ground, he compares his own body, and thinks that "this body also is of such a dharmic nature, of such an own-being, and it has not got beyond this state of affairs".

(II.) A Bodhisattva dwells with regard to feelings, inward, outward, and both inward and outward, in the contemplation of feelings, ardent, clearly conscious, and mindful, after putting away all worldly covetousness and sadness. And that through nonapprehension.

(III.) Likewise a Bodhisattva dwells in the contemplation of thought.

(IV.) Likewise a Bodhisattva dwells in the contemplation of dharmas.

This also is the great vehicle of the Bodhisattva, the great being.

2. And again, the great vehicle of the Bodhisattva, the great being, i.e. the four *Right Efforts*. They are: Here a Bodhisattva, who courses in perfect wisdom, rouses his will, makes an effort, puts forth vigour, makes his thoughts tense, correctly exerts himself, 1. So as to bring about the (future) nonproduction of evil and unwholesome dharmas, which have not yet been produced; 2. So as to bring about the forsaking of evil and unwholesome dharmas which have been produced; 3. So as to bring about the production of wholesome dharmas which have not yet been produced; 4. So as to bring about the stability, increase, non-disappearance and completion of the wholesome dharmas which have been produced. And that through nonapprehension. This also is the great vehicle.

3. And again, the great vehicle: *The four Bases of Psychic Power*. They are: 1. Here a Bodhisattva, who courses in perfect wisdom, develops the basis of psychic power which is endowed with concentration from desire-to-do, together with the formative forces of effort—based upon detachment, dispassion, and cessation, dedicated to self-surrender. And so with 2, 3, 4, where "desire-to-do" is replaced at 2 by "vigour", at 3 by "thought", at 4 by "exploration". And that through nonapprehension. This also is the great vehicle.

4. And again the great vehicle: (P208) *The five Dominants,* i.e. Faith, Vigour, Mindfulness, Concentration, and Wisdom.

5. And again, the great vehicle: *The five Powers,* i.e. Faith, Vigour, Mindfulness, Concentration, and Wisdom.

6. And again the great vehicle: *The seven Limbs of Enlightenment,* i.e. Mindfulness, Investigation into Dharma, Vigour, Joyous Zest, Tranquillity, Concentration, and Evenmindedness. What is mindfulness as a limb of enlightenment? Here a Bodhisattva, who courses in perfect wisdom, develops the limb of enlightenment that is mindfulness, based

upon detachment, dispassion, and cessation, dedicated to self-surrender. And so for the other six. And that through nonapprehension.

7. And again the great vehicle, i.e. *The Eightfold Path.* It consists of: Right View, right Intention, right Speech, right Conduct, right Livelihood, right Effort, right Mindfulness, right Concentration. What is right View? Here a Bodhisattva, who courses in perfect wisdom, develops Right View as a limb of the Path, based upon detachment, dispassion, and cessation, dedicated to self-surrender. And so for the other seven. And that through nonapprehension.

8. And again the great vehicle: i.e. *The Three Concentrations,* i.e. the emptiness concentration, the signless concentration, the wishless concentration. What is the emptiness concentration? The stability of thought which contemplates all dharmas as empty of own-marks; emptiness as a door to deliverance. And so with the signless and wishless concentration. These three doors to deliverance are the three concentrations. In them one should train. And that through nonapprehension.

9. And again, the great vehicle, i.e. *The Eleven Cognitions.* They are: The cognitions of suffering, origination, stopping, path, of extinction, of nonproduction, of dharma, the subsequent cognition, the cognition conforming to worldly convention, the cognition of mastery, the cognition according to fact.[2] (P209) 1. The cognition of suffering is the cognition of the nonproduction of suffering. 2. The cognition of origination is the cognition of the forsaking of origination. 3. The cognition of stopping is the cognition that ill has been stopped. 4. The cognition of the Path is the cognition of the Holy Eightfold Path. 5. The cognition of extinction is the cognition of the extinction of greed, hate, and delusion. 6. The cognition of nonproduction is the cognition of the nonproduction of the places of rebirth, and of becoming. 7. The cognition of dharma is the cognition which determines the five skandhas as mere artificial constructs.[3] 8. The subsequent cognition is the cognition that the eye, and the other sense fields, as well as the physical elements and links are impermanent, etc. 9. The cognition conforming to worldly convention is the cognition by the heart of the hearts of other beings and persons.

[2]The text of no. 9 has undergone some corruption in the various versions of the *Prajñāpāramitā*, particularly at no. 7 and no. 9-11. At no. 9 *saṃvṛti* is attested by *S, S*-Ti, *Ad* and *Da*, and there is no need to change it into *paracitta*. This cognition can well be called "conventional" because it refers to "beings" who have no more than a conventional existence (cf. *A.K.* VII, 4). The explanation given at no. 10 is that of *P. S* has "cognition of the antidotes", and *S*-Ti "cognition of the path and of purification". So there is substantial, though not verbal, agreement. At no. 11 several sources have *yathāruta,* apparently an old misreading of *yathābhūta*.

[3]In *Ad* probably *kṛtrima,* to which also the *sgyu-mar* of *S*-Ti may correspond, as at *S* i 119. Sanskrit *P* and *S* are both corrupt. The *aparikṣatima* of *S* may have been originally something like *pratikṛti*—"Artificial", or "counterfeit"; see *P* 39.

10. The cognition of mastery is the cognition of the mastery of the path. 11. The cognition according to fact is the Tathagata's cognition of the knowledge of all modes. And that through nonapprehension.

10. And again, the great vehicle, i.e. *Three Dominants*. They are: 1. The faculty "I shall come to understand the not yet understood", 2. The faculty of "understanding", 3. The faculty of "one who has fully understood". 1. The faculty "I shall come to understand the not yet understood" is the virtue of faith, vigour, mindfulness, concentration, and wisdom of those persons who are learners and who have not yet completely mastered these virtues, do not entirely manifest them, and need further disciplining. 2. The faculty of "understanding" is the virtue of faith, vigour, mindfulness, concentration, and wisdom of the persons who are learners and who have mastered them. 3. The faculty of "one who has fully understood" is the virtue of faith, vigour, mindfulness, concentration, and wisdom of the persons who are adepts—of Arhats, Pratyekabuddhas, Bodhisattvas and Tathagatas.—And that through nonapprehension.

11. And again, the great vehicle, i.e. *Three Concentrations*. They are: 1. The concentration with thought applied and discursive; 2. The concentration without thought applied, and with only thought discursive; 3. The concentration without either thought applied or thought discursive: 1. Is identical with the first trance (see no. 13,1). (P210) 2. Is the interval between the first and the second trance. 3. Covers the trances from the second trance to the attainment of the trance of the cessation of perception and feeling. And that through nonapprehension.

12. And again, the great vehicle, i.e. the *Ten Recollections*. They are: The recollection of the Buddha, the Dharma, the Community, of morality, renunciation, the gods, of agitation, of death, of that which concerns the body, of breathing. And that through nonapprehension.

And again, the great vehicle, i.e. 13. the Four Trances, 14. the four Unlimited, 15. the four formless attainments, 16. the eight deliverances, and 17. the nine attainments of successive stations.

13.[4] *The Four Trances*. 1. Here a Bodhisattva, who courses in perfect wisdom, dwells, detached from sense desires, detached from evil and unwholesome dharmas, in the attainment of the first Trance, which is with thoughts applied, and discursive, born of detachment, full of rapture and ease. 2. Through the appeasement of thoughts applied and discursive, through inward serenity, through the unification of his heart, he dwells in the attainment of the second Trance, which is without thoughts applied and discursive, born of concentration, full of rapture and ease. 3. Through distaste for rapture he dwells evenmindedly, mindful, and clearly conscious, and he experiences with the body that ease of which

[4]The detailed description of 13-17 is omitted in *P* and added from *S*.

the Holy Ones declare: "He that is evenminded and mindful dwells at ease"; and thus he dwells in the attainment of the third Trance. 4. From the forsaking of ease, from the forsaking of ill, and from the previous going to rest of gladness and sadness, he dwells in the attainment of the fourth Trance, which is neither painful nor pleasurable, (but) is utter purity of evenmindedness and mindfulness. And that through nonapprehension.

14. *The Four Unlimited*: 1. Here a Bodhisattva, who courses in perfect wisdom, dwells with a thought connected with Friendliness, a thought which is vast, extensive, nondual, unlimited, free from hostility, rivalry, hindrance or injury to anyone. He radiates friendliness in the ten directions of the world, which has as its highest development the Dharma-element, and the space element as its terminus. 2. 3. 4. And similarly with Compassion, Sympathetic Joy, and Impartiality,—and that through nonapprehension.

15. *The four Formless Attainments*: 1. By completely overcoming all perceptions of form, by the going to rest of the perceptions of impact, by not attending to the perceptions of manifoldness, on thinking "Endless Space", he dwells in the attainment of the station of endless space. 2. By completely overcoming the station of endless space, on thinking "Infinite Consciousness", he dwells in the attainment of the station of infinite consciousness. 3. By completely overcoming the station of infinite consciousness, on thinking that "there is not anything", he dwells in the attainment of the station of nothing whatever. 4. By completely overcoming the station of Nothing Whatever, he dwells in the attainment of the station of neither perception nor nonperception. And that through nonapprehension.

16. *The Eight Deliverances*: 1. Having form, he sees forms. 2. Not perceiving inward form he sees outward forms. 3. He becomes resolved on emptiness. 4-7. are identical with the four formless attainments. 8. Through having in every way overcome the station of neither perception nor nonperception, he dwells in the attainment of the trance of the cessation of perception and feeling. And that through nonapprehension.

17. *The Nine Attainments of Successive Stations*: They are: 1-4, the four trances; 5-8, the four formless attainments; 9, the trance of the cessation of perception and feeling.

18. And again, the great vehicle, i.e. the *Ten Powers of a Tathagata*. They are: Here, Subhuti, a Bodhisattva who courses in perfect wisdom, 1. wisely knows, as it really is, what can be as what can be, and what cannot be as what cannot be. 2. He wisely knows, as they really are, the karmic results of past, future, and present actions and undertakings of actions, as to place and cause. 3. He wisely knows, as they really are,

the various elements in the world. 4. He wisely knows, as they really are, the various dispositions of other beings and persons. 5. He wisely knows, as they really are, the higher and lower faculties of other beings and persons. 6. He wisely knows, as it really is, the Way that leads everywhere. 7. He wisely knows, as they really are, the defilement and purification of all trances, deliverances, concentrations, and meditational attainments, as well as the emergence from them. 8. He recollects his various previous lives. 9. With his heavenly eye he knows the decease and rebirth of beings as it really is. 10. Through the extinction of the outflows, he dwells in the attainment of that emancipation of his heart and wisdom, which is without outflows, and which he has, in this very life, well known and realized by himself. He wisely knows that "Birth is exhausted for me; the higher spiritual life has been lived. I have done what had to be done. After this becoming there will be none further". And all that without any apprehension whatever. (P211)

19. And again the great vehicle, i.e. *The Four Grounds of Selfconfidence.* They are : 1. That I who claim to be fully enlightened am not fully enlightened in those dharmas—I see nothing to indicate that anyone, be he recluse, brahmin, god, Mara, or Brahma, or anyone else in the whole world, can with justice make this charge. And, as I see nothing to indicate this, I dwell in the attainment of security, of fearlessness, of self-confidence. I claim my exalted place as leader of the herd, rightly roar the lion's roar in the assembly, and set rolling the sacred wheel which cannot with justice be set rolling by any recluse, brahmin, god, Mara, or Brahma, or anyone else in the world. 2. That I, who claim to have dried up the outflows, have not completely dried them up, that charge is impossible. I see nothing to indicate, etc. as at. 1. 3. That those dharmas which I have described as impediments should have no power to impede him who pursues them, that charge is impossible. I see nothing to indicate, etc. as at 1. 4. That he who progresses on what I have described as the Path, holy and leading to going forth, to the right extinction of ill for him who does so, should not go forth to the right extinction of ill, that charge is impossible. I see nothing to indicate, etc. as at 1. And all that without any apprehension whatever.

20. And again, the great vehicle, i.e. *the Four Analytical Knowledges.* They are the analytical knowledge of the Meaning, of the Dharma, of Languages, of Inspired Speech. Also they should be practised without taking anything as a basis.

21. And again the great vehicle, i.e. *the eighteen special dharmas of a Buddha.* From the night when the Tathagata knows full enlightenment, to the day when he becomes extinct in Nirvana, during all this time the

Tathagata 1. does not trip up,[5] 2. is not rash or noisy in his speech, 3. is never robbed of his mindfulness. 4. He has no perception of difference. 5. His thought is never unconcentrated. (P212) 6. His evenmindedness is not due to lack of consideration. 7. His zeal, 8. vigour. 9. mindfulness, 10. concentration, 11. wisdom and 12. deliverance never fail. 13. All the deeds of his body, 14. voice and 15. mind are preceded by cognition, and continue to conform to cognition. 16. His cognition and vision regarding the past, 17. future and 18. present period of time proceeds unobstructed and freely. And all that without taking anything as a basis.

I 9,15. THE EQUIPMENT WITH THE DHARANIS[6]

And again, Subhuti, the *Dharani-doors* are the great vehicle of the Bodhisattva, the great being. Which are they? The sameness of all letters and syllables, the sameness of all spoken words, the syllable-doors, the syllable-entrances. What then are the syllable-doors, the syllable-entrances?

1. The syllable A is a door to the insight that all dharmas are unproduced from the very beginning (*ādy-anutpannatvād*); 2. RA is a door to the insight that all dharmas are without dirt (*rajas*); 3. PA is a door to the insight that all dharmas have been expounded in the ultimate sense (*paramārtha*); 4. CA is a door to the insight that the decease (*cyavana*) or rebirth of any dharma cannot be apprehended, because all dharmas do not decease, nor are they reborn; 5. NA is a door to the insight that the Names of all dharmas have vanished; the essential nature behind names cannot be gained or lost.

6. The syllable LA indicates that all dharmas have transcended the world (*loka*); because the causes and conditions of the creeping plant (*latā*) of craving have been utterly destroyed; 7. DA is a door to all dharmas because "tamed" and "taming" (*dāntadamatha*) have been circumscribed; 8. BA indicates that the Bonds have departed from all dharmas; 9. ḌA that the tumult (*ḍamara*) of all dharmas has vanished; 10. SHA that no attachment (*shaṅga*) in any dharma is apprehended; they are neither attached nor bound.

11. The syllable VA is a door to all dharmas because the sound of the paths of speech (*vākpathaghosha*) has been quite cut off; 12. TA because all dharmas do not depart from Suchness (*tathatā*); 13. YA because of the nonapprehension of any fact (*yathāvad*); 14. SHṬA because

[5]The *Syādvādamañjarī*, a Jain work, explains on p. 13 the word as follows: "'Trip-up'—they fall from the path of logical reasoning. The meaning is that they become unable to reply. And here by 'tripping' a ridiculousness in the eyes of authoritative people is suggested". "He never makes a false step" is the probable meaning in the Pali texts (CPD).

[6]My translation generally follows the Gilgit *P*, which is our oldest Sanskrit document. It differs in many details from the translation I gave in *SS* no. 127, at a time when I had no access yet to a microfilm of the Gilgit MS.

of the nonapprehension of a support (*shṭambha*); 15. KA because of the nonapprehension of an agent.

16. The syllable SA is a door to all dharmas because of the nonapprehension of sameness (*samatā*); they never stray away from sameness; 17. MA because of the nonapprehension of Mine-making (*mamakāra*): 18. GA because of that of motion (*gamana*)[7]; 19. STHA because of that of subsistence (*sthāna*); 20. JA because of that of birth (*jāti*).

21. The syllable ŚVA is a doorway to all dharmas because of the nonapprehension of a principle of life (*śvāsa*)[8]; 22. DHA because of that of the Realm of Dharma (*dharmadhātu*); 23. ŚA because of that of calming-down (*śamatha*); 24. KHA because of that of the sameness of[9] space (*kha*); 25. KSHA because of that of extinction (*kshaya*).

26. The syllable STA is a door to all dharmas because each dharma is fixed (*stabdha*?) in its place, and never leaves it[10]; 27. JÑĀ because cognition (*jñāna*) cannot be apprehended (P213) 28. RTA because mortality (*mārtya*)[11] cannot be apprehended; 29. HA because a root-cause (*hetu*), and 30. BHA because breaking-up (*bhaṅga*) cannot be apprehended.

31. The syllable CHA is a door to all dharmas because glamour (*chaver apy*); 32. SMA because remembrance (*smaraṇa*); 33. HVA because true appellations (*āhvāna*); 34. TSA because will-power (*utsāha*) cannot be apprehended; 35. BHA because things and persons are not apprehended each as one solid mass (*ghana*).

36. The syllable ṬHA is a door to all dharmas because of the nonapprehension of fabricated appearances (*viṭhapana*); 37. ṆA because strife (*raṇa*) has departed, no one goes or comes, stands, sits or lies down, or makes any discriminations of this kind; 38. PHA because no fruit (*phala*) is apprehended; 39. SKA because no Skandhas are apprehended; 40. YSA because no decay (*ysara* = *jarā*) is apprehended.[12]

41. The syllable ŚCA is a door to all dharmas, because of the nonapprehension of good conduct (*ścaraṇa*)[13]; 42. ṬA because of the nonapprehension of the other shore[14]; 43. ḌHA because of the nonappre-

[7]*gamana* in *S*, *S*-Ti and *P*-Ti. P: *gagana*. Gilgit *P* differs from both, but the microfilm is somewhat illegible here. Perhaps *grahaṇa*, like Mokshala, who says "to seize on dharmas is no way of seeing them".

[8]So *P*, *S*, *S*-Ti.—*P* Gilgit *svāda*? "taste, flavour"?

[9]Gilgit *P* omits "the sameness of".

[10]The explanation is from Mokshala, who had *astitva* or *stabdha*. Also Yüan-tsang agrees to some extent with it.

[11]Mokshala has here *artha*.

[12]This translation is based on *P* and Yüan-tsang, Gilgit *P* however has, "because the letter YSA cannot be apprehended". *Ysāra* is the Saka equivalent of *jarā*.

[13]so *P* and Kumārajīva; *S caryā*, *S*-Ti *spyod-pa*. But P Gilgit: "Because the letter CA cannot be apprehended".

[14]*ṭalo*? After Kumārajīva who says: "the other shore (*ṭalo*=*sthala*?) of dharmas does not exist"—*S*-Ti has *sdug-bsṅal*, usually *duḥkha*.

hension of unsteadiness. In their ultimate and final station dharmas neither decrease nor are they reborn.[15]

No letters or syllables are in conventional use except the foregoing. And why? For no word that is not composed of them is used when anything is conventionally expressed, talked about, pointed out, written about, made manifest or recited. Simply like space should one pursue all dharmas. This, Subhuti, is called the entrance into the door of the Dharanis, the entrance into the exposition of the letters A, etc. Any Bodhisattva who cognizes this skill in the letters A, etc. will not be tied down by any sounds, he will accomplish everything through the sameness of all dharmas, and he will acquire the skill in the cognition of sounds.

Twenty advantages should be expected for a Bodhisattva who, after having heard this Seal of the entrances into the letters A, etc., will learn it, bear it in mind, recite it, study it and methodically demonstrate it to others. Which are the twenty? 1. He will be mindful, clever, intelligent, steadfast, modest, wise, and inspired. 2. He will acquire the Dharani-doors with little trouble. 3. He will not be assailed by doubts. 4. He will have no uncertainties. 5. Soft words do not win him over, harsh words do not upset him, and he will be neither haughty nor dejected. 6. He will act properly in accordance with circumstances. 7. He will be skilled in sounds; 8. in the skandhas, elements, sense fields, Truths, and conditioned coproduction; 9. in the root-cause, in conditions, in the true nature of dharmas; (P214) 10. in the cognition of the higher and lower faculties of others; 11. in the cognition of the thoughts of others; 12. in the cognition of the various kinds of wonderworking powers; 13. in the cognition of the heavenly ear; 14. in the cognition of the recollection of former births; 15. in the cognition of decease and rebirth; 16. in the cognition of the extinction of the outflows; 17. in the exposition of what can be and what cannot be; 18. in going out and coming back; 19. in the postures; and 20. he will also become skilled in sense of shame and dread of blame. These twenty advantages he will acquire.[16]

Also this entrance into the Dharani-door of the letters A, etc. is the great vehicle of the Bodhisattva, the great being, and that also in consequence of taking nothing at all as a basis.

[15]Here the original text cannot easily be reconstituted. My translation is based on *S*. *S*-Ti, Gilgit *P* and Mokshala. "Unsteadiness" occurs only in *S*-Ti as *gYo-ba*, I have collected 14 Sanskrit equivalents for it, but none contains a ḍh. "Ultimate and final station" is *paryanta-niṣṭhā-sthānena*, *mtha' thug-par gnas-par*.

[16]The numbering of the 20 items is my own. The text itself gives no clue as to which items belong together, and which ones are reckoned separately.

CHAPTER 17

THE PREPARATIONS FOR THE STAGES

I 9,16. THE EQUIPMENT WITH THE STAGES.

As Subhuti has said, "How does a Bodhisattva become one who has set out in the great vehicle?" Here, Subhuti, a Bodhisattva, coursing in the six perfections, passes on from stage to stage. How? In the sense that no dharma ever passes on.[1] And why? Because no dharma whatsoever comes or goes, passes on, or comes near. A Bodhisattva does not mind the stages of dharmas, does not reflect on them. He sets to work on each stage, but does not review[2] that stage. Which then are the preparations for the stages on the part of a Bodhisattva?

I. A Bodhisattva, who proceeds on the first stage, should effect ten preparations. They are: 1. Resolute intention, in a spirit of nonapprehension. 2. He should supply (beings) with beneficial things, but without apprehending a sign. 3. The same attitude of mind to all beings, but without apprehending a being. 4. Renunciation, on account of the nonapprehension of giver, gift, and recipient. 5. Tending the good spiritual friends, in nonintimacy with them. 6. Search for the good Dharma, on account of the nonapprehension of all dharmas. 7. Leaving home again and again, on account of the nonapprehension of a home. 8. Longing for the body of a Buddha, without apprehending His marks, minor characteristics, and signs. 9. The unveiling of Dharma, on account of the nonapprehension of a differentiation between dharmas. 10. Truthful speech, on account of the nonapprehension of speech (as a separate reality). (P215)

II. Furthermore, Subhuti, a Bodhisattva who proceeds on the second stage, attends to eight dharmas and progresses in them. They are: 1. Purity of morality. 2. Gratitude and thankfulness. 3. Firm grounding in the power of patience. 4. The experience of joy and zest. 5. (*a*) The nonabandonment of all beings, (*b*) The manifestation of the great compassion. 6. Respect and faith for the instructors. 7. Reverence for the instructors through the fact that he identifies them with the Teacher. 8. Search for the perfections exclusively and entirely.

[1]*Nag*: The Bodhisattva knows that all dharmas, from the very beginning, do not arise or depart, that they are immobile and incapable of transition, because the Dharma-element is eternally stable.

[2]*Nag*: does not seize on its characteristics.

III. Furthermore, on the third stage, one should stand in five dharmas. They are: 1. An insatiable desire to learn much, but without settling down in the words. 2. The disinterested revelation of the gift of Dharma, but without conceit about that. 3. The dedication of the wholesome roots to the purification of the Buddha-field, but without conceit about that. 4. Indefatigability in measureless birth-and-death, but without conceit about that. 5. Establishment in a sense of shame and a dread of blame, but without conceit about that.

IV. Furthermore, on the fourth stage, one should stand in ten dharmas, and not abandon them. They are: 1. Dwelling in the forest. 2. Fewness of wishes. 3. Contentment. 4. The nonabandonment of the austere penance of the ascetic practices. 5. The nonrenunciation of moral training. 6. Loathing of sensuous qualities. 7. Production of a thought connected with disgust. 8. Renunciation of all that is (his). 9. An uncowed attitude of mind. 10. Disregard for all things.

V. Furthermore, on the fifth stage, one should avoid ten dharmas. They are: 1. Intimacy with householders and wandering mendicants. 2. Jealousy about the families of the faithful. 3. The places where one meets society. 4. Exaltation of self. 5. Depreciation of others. 6. The ten ways of unwholesome action. 7. (a) conceit, and (b) arrogance. 8. Perverted views. 9. Doubt. 10. Toleration of greed, hate, and delusion. (P216)

VI.A. Furthermore, on the sixth stage, six dharmas should be fulfilled. They are the six perfections.

VI.B. Another six dharmas should be avoided. They are: 1. Disciple-thought. 2. Pratyekabuddha-thought. 3. Worrying thought. 4. Annoyance about beggars when one sees them. 5. A thought of sadness, in spite of the fact that one must renounce all things. 6. Distraction by beggars.

VII.A. Furthermore, on the seventh stage twenty dharmas do not become. One does not seize on 1. a self, 2. a being, 3. a living soul, 4. a person, 5. annihilationist views, 6. eternalist views, 7. the notion of a sign, 8. views about causes. One does not settle down in 9. the skandhas, 10. the elements, 11. the sense fields, 12. what belongs to the triple world. 13. One does not attempt to do something about what belongs to the triple world, 14. one does not hang on to what belongs to the triple world. One does not settle down in views which 15. regard the Buddha as a refuge, 16. regard the Dharma as a refuge, 17. regard the Saṃgha as a refuge, 18. regard morality as a refuge. There are 19. no contentions about "empty are the dharmas", and 20. no obstructions to emptiness.

VII.B. One who stands on the seventh stage should fulfil twenty dharmas. They are: 1. Penetration into emptiness, 2. realisation of the signless, 3. cognition of the wishless; 4. the threefold perfect purity, 5. pity and compassion for all beings, 6. no contempt for them, 7. a vision of the sameness of all dharmas but without settling down in it, 8. penetration to the really true principle, but no conceit through that, 9. patient acceptance of nonproduction, 10. cognition of nonproduction, 11. exposition of the one single principle, 12. the uprooting of the imagination of all dharmas, 13. turning away from perception and views, 14. turning away from defilement, 15. pacification through calming-down, coupled with skill in insight, 16. a mind completely tamed, 17. the state of thought in which cognition is nowhere obstructed, 18. no ground for fawning, 19. going to the field one wishes to go to, and 20. having stood there in the circle of the Buddha-assembly, exhibiting a body. (P217)

VIII.A. Furthermore, on the eighth stage four dharmas should be fulfilled. They are : 1. entrance into the thought of all beings, 2. playing with the superknowledges, 3. the vision of Buddha-fields, and the creation, in accordance with what one has seen, of those Buddha-fields, and 4. honouring the Buddhas, and the contemplation of the Buddha-body as it really is.

VIII.B. Another four dharmas should be fulfilled on the eighth stage : 1. The cognition of the higher and lower faculties of others, 2. the purification of the Buddha-field, 3. the perpetual attainment of the concentration on (everything) as an illusion, 4. as the wholesome roots of beings reach consummation, so he conjures up a personality, producing a (new) becoming at will.

IX. Furthermore, on the ninth stage twelve dharmas should be fulfilled. They are : 1. The acquisition of infinite resolve : just as he resolves, so he succeeds; 2. the cognition of the speech of gods, Nagas, Yakshas, Gandharvas, Asuras, Garudas, Kinnaras, and Mahoragas. 3. The cognition of the exposition of ready speech. The accomplishment of 4. the descent into the womb, 5. the family, 6. the birth, 7. the clan, 8. the retinue, 9. the manner of birth, 10. leaving home, 11. the miraculous harmony of the tree of enlightenment, 12. the fulfilment of all virtuous qualities.

X. When he proceeds on the tenth stage, a Bodhisattva, a great being is verily to be called a Tathagata.

I

1. The preparation of *resolute intention*[3] consists in that the Bodhi-

[3]*adhyāśaya*. At this point the Bodhisattva has already had his first "thought of enlightenment", and achieved a great deal. *Nag*: He has cut himself off from the world which he detests, and is automatically drawn towards Buddhahood. His five spiritual faculties, faith, etc., are sufficiently matured to enable him to distinguish between what is and what is not conducive to emancipation. Because he has previously had a taste a Perfect Wisdom, he can now proceed with "resolute intention". Enclosed by his former deeds in the dark prison of the twelve sense fields, all that he sees and knows is false. But once he has heard the Perfection of Wisdom being preached, and has appreciated it to some extent, he thinks

sattva procures all wholesome roots, through attentions connected with the knowledge of all modes.[4]

2. He supplies with *beneficial things* in the sense that, for the weal of all beings, he undertakes the search for the cognition of the great vehicle.

3. *The same attitude of mind to all beings*[5] consists in his aspiring for the four Unlimited,[6] i.e. friendliness, compassion, sympathetic joy and impartiality, and that through attentions associated with the knowledge of all modes. (P218)

4. His *renunciation*[7] means that he gives gifts to all beings without discrimination.

5. In *tending the good friends* he knows that his good friends are those who instigate him to the knowledge of all modes. Those friends he tends, he resorts to them, honours and reveres them.

6. He *searches for Dharma,*[8] by means of attentions associated with the knowledge of all modes, and he does not fall on the level of Disciple or Pratyekabuddha.

deeply about omniscience and resolves by all means (*upāya*) to escape from his prison, as the Buddhas and Aryas did before him.—Before I 1 was reached, he had made his Vow to become a Buddha. Now he begins to act on it.—cf. *Si* 284 sq.

[4]*Nag*: (1) As soon as a Bodhisattva produces the thought of enlightenment, he makes the vow, "In a future existence I will be a Buddha". Because it is linked to the vow to become a Buddha, this thought is connected with omniscience. A Bodhisattva of keen faculties, who has accumulated much merit, whose passions are weak and whose past sins are few, obtains "resolute intention" at the very moment of his first thought of enlightenment. (2) The "thought of enlightenment" consists in desiring enlightenment wholeheartedly. The attenuation of worldly thoughts in the course of successive lives constitutes the "attentions, etc." All the qualities which a Bodhisattva acquires no longer contribute to his present or future happiness, longevity or security; they exclusively have all-knowledge in view. Just as a miser for no particular reason refuses to part with even a penny, and economises and accumulates with the sole aim of augmenting his treasure, so the Bodhisattva, whether he has many merits or few, seeks for nothing else than to economise and accumulate them with a view to omniscience.

[5]*Nag*: All people love their friends and hate their enemies; the Bodhisattva, however, treats friend and foe as the same, as identical.

[6]1,3: when he sees beings happy, he exercises Friendliness and Sympathetic Joy, and makes a vow that he will lead all beings to the happiness of Buddhahood. 2. When he sees them unhappy, he exercises Compassion, and makes a vow to remove the unhappiness of all beings. 4. When he sees them neither happy nor unhappy, he produces Impartiality, and makes the vow to induce all beings to renounce all affection and aversion.—"Aspires for" can also mean "achieves".

[7]*Nag*: The giving up of material objects serves to counteract the desire to keep, hoard, and possess them. When practised long enough, it leads on the seventh stage to the second kind of renunciation, which consists in giving up the "bonds" so as to be able to win enlightenment.

[8]*H*: "he searches for Dharma" as an objective support for his activities. *Nag*: "Dharma" here means the holy Scriptures. To "search for Dharma" means to copy, recite, and study them, to meditate on them, and to be willing, if necessary, to sacrifice one's life for them.

7. He *again and again leaves home,* i.e. in all his births he leaves home life,[9] uncontaminated (by other religious systems) he goes out into the religion of the Tathagata, and nothing comes to him in between to hinder him.

8. The preparation of *longing for the body of a Buddha* consists in that, after he has seen a Buddha-frame, he never again becomes lacking in attention to the Buddha,[10] until he becomes one who has reached the knowledge of all modes.

9. The preparation of the *unveiling of Dharma* consists in that the Bodhisattva, whether the Tathagata is still (visibly) present, or whether he has gone into Parinirvana, demonstrates to beings the Dharma—helpful[11] in the beginning, helpful in the middle, helpful at the end, good in sense, well-phrased, perfect, and complete—and in that he reveals the holy life, perfectly pure and highly cleansed—i.e. the Discourses, Discourses in Prose and Verse Mingled, Predictions, Verses, Summaries, Origins, Thus-was-said, Birth Stories, Expanded Texts, Marvels, Tales, and Expositions.

10. His preparation of *truthful speech* consists in that as he speaks so he acts.[12]

II

1. The perfect *purity of morality* consists in the nonattention to Disciple-thoughts and to Pratyekabuddha-thoughts,[13] and in the nonattention

[9]*Nag*: The Bodhisattva knows that home life causes and occasions many sins. "If I remain in the home life, I shall myself be incapable of observing the pure practices; how then can I lead others to practise them? If I follow the rules which govern life in a household, I will need a whip, stick, etc., and will torment beings. On the other hand, if my mode of life conforms to the Good Law, I must violate the rules of life in a household. A choice between the two ways of life is therefore inevitable. If I do not abandon my home now, I will nevertheless be compelled to do so at the time of my death; if I renounce it today on my own, my merit will be great". The Bodhisattva also reflects: "Kings and noblemen, as powerful as the gods, seek for happiness. but never find it. Death brutally takes them away. Today I will, for the sake of beings, leave home life, in order to observe the perfectly pure morality (of a monk), to seek the enlightenment of a Buddha, and to fulfil the causes and conditions of the perfection of morality".

[10]The "longing" results from "resolute intention", and leads to a meeting with the Buddha in each life (*Nag*).

[11]"helpful", also "lovely, beautiful, good".

[12]*Nag*: If he lived as a householder, a Bodhisattva would often have to lie. In the Buddha's Dharma, Truth is held in great honour, and it is through Truth that Nirvana is gained. At this early stage Truth is honoured by "truthful speech", which can be believed and accepted by others, and which does not simulate liberality, morality, and spiritual knowledge.

[13]The Disciples, etc., are condemned for the traces of self-seeking in them.

also to other dharmas which make for bad behaviour, or cause delays on the road to enlightenment.

2. A Bodhisattva's *gratitude and thankfulness* consists in that, (P219) coursing in the Bodhisattva-course, he does not, throughout the round of birth-and-death, forget a small kindly action (done to him), much less a big one.[14]

3. He is *firmly grounded in the power of patience* because his mental attitude to all beings is free from ill will and harming.

4. The *experience of joy and zest*[15] consists in the maturing of all beings.

5. This is the *manifestation of the great compassion* that a Bodhisattva, who courses on the pilgrimage of a Bodhisattva, thinks that "for the sake of the weal of every single being will I roast in the hells for aeons countless as the sands of the Ganges, until that being has been established in the Buddha-cognition".[16] This fortitude, this indefatigability, for

[14]*Nag*: Some people believe that they owe their present enjoyments and advantages to their former merits and say to their benefactors: "I have my own merit; what benefit have you bestowed on me?" To counteract this false view, the Buddha here enjoins them to feel "gratitude". Although beings have in their former lives acquired a right to happiness (*sukha-hetu*), they could not enjoy this happiness if present circumstances, among them the generosity of the benefactors, did not contribute something also. The seed of the corn is in the earth; but without rain it could not germinate. One cannot say that the rain renders it no service on the pretext that it is the seed which produces the corn. Although the benefits which we reap now have been planted by us in the course of our former lives, yet the respectful and affectionate disposition of our benefactors is an integral part of the benefits. In addition, gratitude is a source of great compassion, and opens the door to wholesome actions. A grateful person is loved and esteemed by men, and his reputation spreads far and wide; after his death he is reborn in the heavens, and finally he reaches enlightenment. The ungrateful are, however, reborn as animals. Moreover the Bodhisattva reflects: "If I want to save even those who have done me harm, why not those who have helped me?"

[15]*Nag*: II 4 follows directly on II 1-3. The Bodhisattva sees that morality has won him purity of body and speech, that gratitude and patience have won him purity of thought. So he "feels joy", like a man who has bathed in perfumed water, put on new clothes and now regards himself in a mirror. Just so the Bodhisattva congratulates himself on having won such excellent qualities. "Morality," he says to himself, "is the root of trance and wisdom; since today I possess this pure morality, I will easily be able to gain infinite merit". In addition, established in morality and patience, the Bodhisattva converts beings and causes them to be reborn in the presence of a Buddha of another region, or among the gods and superior men, where they enjoy happiness, Or he causes them to gain one of the three vehicles. That is why he is said to "feel joy".

[16]"manifestation"="presence".—*Nag.* raises an objection: "Since one cannot take upon oneself the punishment due to someone else, why does the Bodhisattva make such a vow?" The Bodhisattva, in his great resoluteness, loves all beings deeply, and if he could possibly do so he would substitute himself for them. Moreover he notices that among men in some sacrifices to the gods substitutes of one person by another are permitted. He then says to himself, "in the hells also there will be substitutions of this kind, and I will take the place of other men". Beings honour and respect the Bodhisattva for his resolution since his profound solicitude for beings surpasses even that of a loving mother.

the sake of even one single being, that is the manifestation of the great compassion.

6. A Bodhisattva's *respect through faith*[17] consists in that, through being always humble,[18] he has an attitude of faith.

7. His *reverence for, and faith in, the instructor* comes from the fact that in his instructors he sees the Teacher.[19]

8. The *search for the perfections exclusively and entirely* is the state of searching for the perfections, without doing anything else.[20]

III

1. The *insatiable desire to learn much*[21] is the insatiableness which thinks that, whatever has been taught by the Buddhas, the Lords, either here in this world system, or in the world all round in the ten directions, all that I will retain in mind.[22]

2. The *distinterested revelation of the gift of Dharma* consists in that a Bodhisattva demonstrates Dharma, and does not expect for himself even enlightenment as a reward for that gift of Dharma.[23]

3. The *dedication of the wholesome roots to the purification of the Buddha-field* is the dedication of the wholesome roots by which, purifying the Buddha-field, he purifies the thought of himself and of others.

4. His *indefatigability in measureless birth-and-death* consists in that, supported by his wholesome roots, he matures beings and purifies the

[17]This refers to faith in the teachers without whom no one could possibly gain enlightenment. *Nag*: To have a proper attitude to the teacher one must discard all conceit and arrogance, and become respectful and docile. The rain of the Dharma is like the rain which falls from the sky; it does not stay on the summits of the mountains, but is bound to flow down to the more low lying country. So, if a man exalts himself, the Dharma and spiritual virtues will remain outside him.

[18]*nihata-māna,* "with his pride slain".

[19]*Nag*: It is not difficult for the Bodhisattva to consider the master of the Law as the Buddha, because, in possession of wisdom, the *guru* can do a Buddha's work.

[20]*P*-Ku and *S* speak of an "energetic search". *Nag*: Singlemindedly the Bodhisattva cultivates the six perfections, which are the cause of a Buddha's enlightenment. So he cannot fail to succeed.

[21]*Nag*: That is an indispensible condition of wisdom, and with its help one can practise the path with discernment, like a man with eyes who travels along without knocking into obstacles all the time.

[22]so *S*.—*Nag*: Just as the great ocean can retain all the water of the ten regions, so the Bodhisattva can receive and retain all the Dharmas preached by all the Buddhas of the ten regions, and that through the force of the *dharani* of memory, of the perfectly pure heavenly ear and of the *dharani* which suppresses forgetfulness.

[23]*Nag*: A Bodhisattva who practises the gift of Dharma expects no profit or fame in this, or any reward in a future life. In the interest of beings he does not even desire for himself the Nirvana of the Little Vehicle. It is only out of his great compassion for living beings that, following the Buddha, he turns the wheel of Dharma.

Buddha-field, but never feels any fatigue, until he has fulfilled all dharmas and the knowledge of all modes.

5. *The establishment in a sense of shame and a dread of blame* means (P220) the shunning of the thought of all Disciples and Pratyekabuddhas.[24]

IV

1. He does not abandon the *dwelling in the forest,* i.e. he transcends the enlightenment of all the Disciples and Pratyekabuddhas.[25]

2. His *fewness of wishes* consists in that he does not wish even for enlightenment.[26]

3. He has *contentment,* in that he does not put his mind even to the knowledge of all modes.[27]

4. He does not abandon the *austere penance of the ascetic practices,* that is his patient acquiescence in the deep dharmas which his meditation discloses to him.[28]

5. His *nonrenunciation of moral training* consists in the nonobservation[29] of all moral duties.

6. The *loathing for sensuous qualities* is the nonproduction of a sensuous thought.

7. The *production of a thought connected with disgust* consists in that he does not turn to[30] any dharma.

8. His *renunciation of all that is his* consists in the absence of seizing on inward and outward dharmas.

[24]*Nag*: II 5 envisages only one of the many kinds of the sense of shame, etc., i.e., the one directed towards the ideas of the Disciplines, etc. Having resolved to save all beings, a Bodhisattva would be ashamed to live for the purpose of avoiding personal pain, as the Disciples do, or to go alone to Nirvana. A man who had prepared a great festival and invited his friends, would cover himself with shame and blame if avariciously he alone would eat, and give no food to his guests.

[25]The connection between the first and the second part of this sentence is rather obscure. To "dwell in the forest" is one of the austerities mentioned in IV4. *Nag*: It consists in removing oneself from the multitude and living in solitude. When the Bodhisattva rejects the ideas of the Disciples, etc., he removes himself from the multitude.

[26]*Nag*: For he realizes that all dharmas are nonexistent and empty.

[27]*Obermiller*: absence of conceit even when he has secured the most sublime objects.

[28]*Nag*: The twelve ascetic practices produce the purity of morality. That in its turn produces *dhyāna*, and that again wisdom. The patient acceptance, in meditation, of dharmas which fail to be produced, is the reward of the ascetic practices, and the two are related like cause and effect.

[29]*apracāra,* also "unostentatious performance".—*Nag*: commenting on a slightly different text, says: One sees neither morality nor immorality, and yet one does not violate morality. Far more important to a Bodhisattva than morality is his entry into Emptiness as a door to deliverance.

[30]*anabhisaṃskāra,* also "loses interest in". *Nag*: As a reward for his disgust for the world he can now enter the Wishless as a door to deliverance.

9. The *uncowed attitude of mind* means that his thought does not get cowed in any of the foundations of conscious life.[31]

10. The *disregard for all things* means the nonattention to all things.

V

1a. He *avoids intimacy with householders,* i.e. he passes on from Buddha-field to Buddha-field, is reborn apparitionally, and appears with the shaven head, yellow robe, and upper garment of a monk.[32]

1b. He *avoids intimacy with*[33] nuns, i.e. he does not stay with a nun even for the time of a finger snap,[34] and yet does not feel troubled on that account.

2. A Bodhisattva *avoids jealousy about the families of the faithful* when he thinks to himself, "I should bestow on beings all that makes them happy. But if those beings are at their ease simply by their own merits, then I should not grudge them that."[35]

3. His *avoidance of the places where one meets society* consists in that a Bodhisattva will not stay with people who talk as the Disciples and Pratyekabuddhas do, and who may give rise to thoughts connected with them.

4. He avoids *self-exaltation* by the nonreviewing of inward dharmas, and, 5. the *depreciation of others* by the nonreviewing of outward dharmas.[36]

[31] *vijñāna-sthiti*. This seems to refer to the objects and sense organs on which the six kinds of consciousness are based.

[32] *Nag*: By avoiding the company of householders a Bodhisattva can accumulate pure qualities. In his solitude he plunges himself into the recollection of the Buddha, transforms his body, betakes himself to the Buddha-fields, leaves home, shaves his head, and puts on the yellow robe. Why? Because he is satisfied with being a wanderer, and detests the company of householders.—Most texts are corrupt here, Yüan-tsang's being probably the best. Instead of "is reborn apparitionally" he has "wherever he is reborn, he always leaves home".

[33] *P* here adds "monks", but not so the other recensions.

[34] *Nag*: Why, if all beings are considered alike, should he not be with a nun? Because a Bodhisattva who has not yet gained the irreversible stage, who has not yet destroyed all the outflows or accumulated all the virtuous qualities, can still be loved and desired by women. He also must avoid the calumnies of other men, for anyone who would calumniate him would go to hell.

[35] This is not very clear. Nor is *Nag*: The Bodhisattva reflects: "I myself have left home, without greed or regret; why should I feel greed and envy for the families of others (*para-kula*)? It is a rule among Bodhisattvas that they want to lead beings to happiness; these persons help me to give happiness to beings, why be jealous of them? The beings who thanks to the merits of their former lives enjoy some power in their present existence, will pay me their homage".

[36] *Nag*: Inward dharmas are the appropriated, outward dharmas the unappropriated skandhas.

6. He should avoid *the ten ways of unwholesome action* because they cause obstacles to a happy destiny, how much more so to the holy Path and to full enlightenment.

7a. He *avoids conceit* (P221) because he does not review any dharma, how much less its superiority which could make him feel conceited.

7b. He *avoids arrogance* because he does not review that entity with regard to which arrogance could arise.

8. He *avoids perverted views* through his nonapprehension of all entities.

9. He *avoids doubt* because he reviews all dharmas free from the doubts engendered by the view of individuality.[37]

10. He avoids the *toleration of greed, hate, and delusion* because he reviews no objective cause for greed, hate, and delusion.

VI.A

The Bodhisattva should fulfil the six perfections. (Because having stood in these six perfections, the Buddhas and Lords, and the Disciples and Pratyekabuddhas, have gone, do go and will go to the other shore of the flood of the fivefold cognizable. What is the fivefold cognizable? The past, the future, the present, the inexpressible, the unconditioned.)[38]

VI.B

1. A Bodhisattva should avoid *Disciple-thought* and 2. *Pratyekabuddha-thought,* because it is not the path to enlightenment.[39]

2. He should not raise a *worrying thought,*[40] because that is not the path to enlightenment.

4. He *should not produce a thought of annoyance when he sees beggars,* because that is not the path to enlightenment.

5. He *does not become sad even when he has renounced all that he had,* because that is not the path to enlightenment.

[37]No. 9 is missing in *S* and *P*-Ku (but see note 41). *H* explains as the avoidance of false opinions, such as the view of individuality. *P*: *sandeha-apagatān, sandeha* may mean "doubt", or "accumulation, the human body".

[38]The passage in brackets is found in *S* and *P*-Ti only.

[39]*Nag*: At this stage, the Bodhisattva contemplates the emptiness of all dharmas. But since he does not yet possess the power of skill in means, he risks falling on the level of a Disciple, etc. To protect him, he is warned against adopting their manner of thinking.

[40]or "a thought of regret". The explanations of *Nag*. and *H*. do not agree. *Nag*: The Bodhisattva loves beings deeply, has a thought of great compassion, and knows the absolute emptiness of all dharmas. When he gives he spares nothing. *H*: a thought afraid of the idea that there is no own-being on which it could base itself.

6. He *should not be distracted by beggars,* because that is not the path to enlightenment.[41]

VII.A

A Bodhisattva *does not seize on*:

1. *a self,* or
2. *a being,* or
3. *a soul,* or
4. *a person,* because, absolutely, they do not exist.
5. He *does not seize on annihilationist views*; for no dharma (P222) is ever annihilated, since all dharmas are absolutely unproduced.
6. He *does not seize on eternalist views,* because a dharma that has not been produced cannot become eternal.
7. He *has no notion of a sign* because, absolutely, defilement does not exist.
8. He *does not form false views about causes,* because he does not review such views.
9. He *does not settle down in skandhas,*
10. *elements,* or
11. *sense-fields,* because through their own-being these dharmas do not exist.
12. He *does not settle down in that which belongs to the triple world,* because the own-being of that which belongs to the triple world does not exist.
13. He *does not attempt to do something about that which belongs to the triple world,* because such an entity cannot be apprehended.
14. He *does not hang on to what belongs to the triple world,* because everything in it is without own-being
15. He *should not take refuge in Buddha,*
16. *Dharma,* and
17. *Samgha,* because it is not from taking refuge in the view of Buddha, Dharma, and Samgha, that there is a vision of Buddha, Dharma, and Samgha.
18. He *should not take refuge in the view of morality,*[42] because perfect

[41]so *P*, and *H* explains that, although poor himself, he should not be inclined to repel those who ask him for gifts. *S*: "From the first thought of enlightenment onwards he should constantly give gifts, and remain unattached in his thought". So also *P*-Ku, which treats this sentence as a corollary to no. 5—*P*-Ku has as no. 6: "Through the power of his virtuous qualities and of his faith he feels no doubt about deep dharmas". *Nag*: He says to himself, "as distinct from all other teachings the wisdom of the Buddhas alone has no faults, and it destroys all vain arguments". He can then, through skill in means, cultivate all good dharmas. That is why he does not doubt.

[42]*Ob.* 169: This refers to the belief that one's moral merit is sufficient for salvation.

purity of morality does not result from taking refuge in the view of morality.

19. There *should be no contentions about emptiness,* because all dharmas are empty through their own-being, and not through emptiness.[43]

20. *No obstruction should be raised to emptiness,* because all dharmas are empty, and emptiness cannot obstruct emptiness.

VII.B

1. *Emptiness should be fulfilled* through the fulfilment of the emptiness of own-marks.

2. *The signless should be realized* through nonattention to all signs.

3. *The wishless is cognized* when his thought is no longer firmly grounded in anything that belongs to the triple world. (P223)

4. *The threefold perfect purity* is the perfect purity of the ten ways of wholesome action.

5. *The fulfilment of pity and compassion for all beings* is achieved by acquiring the great compassion.[44]

6. He *should despise no being,* because his friendliness has become perfect.

7. His *vision of the sameness of all dharmas* consists in that he adds nothing to all dharmas, and subtracts nothing from them.

8. His *penetration to the really true principle* is the nonpenetration of all dharmas.

9. His *patient acceptance of nonproduction* is the patient acceptance of the fact that all dharmas are not produced, stopped, or put together.

10. His *cognition of nonproduction* is the cognition of the nonproduction of name and form.

11. The *exposition of the one single principle* is the habitual absence of all notions of duality.

12. The *uprooting of the imagination*[45] *of all dharmas* is the nondiscrimination of all dharmas.

13. His *turning away from perceptions and views* is the turning away from the perceptions and views of the level of all Disciples and Pratyekabuddhas.

14. His *turning away from the defilements* is the rejection of all the defilements, and of the residues relating to them.[46]

[43]cf. *Madhyamakāvatāra* 118, in the discussion of the *paratantra* of the Yogacarins: "in their system it is through emptiness that all dharmas are empty, and not through their own-being".—cf. *Pras.* 370.

[44]This, according to *Nag.*, is the compassion which has no object. See *Buddhist Texts*, no. 168.

[45]*kalpanā*, their fashioning by thought-constructions.

[46]*Nag*: The Bodhisattva, by the power of his merits and of his morality, has already

15. The *stage where quietude and insight are in equilibrium* is the cognition of the knowledge of all modes.[47]

16. His *mind is completely tamed,* for he feels no delight for the triple world.

17. His *unobstructed cognition* is the acquiring of the Buddha-eye.

18. His *knowledge of withdrawal from affection*[48] is the evenmindedness concerning everything that belongs to the six sense fields.

19. His *going to the field he wishes to go to* consists in that, without his stirring from one single Buddha-field, he appears in all Buddha-fields, and yet has no notion of a Buddha-field.

20. The *exhibiting of a body everywhere* refers to the exhibition of a body in the circle of the assembly.[49]

VIII.A

1. His *entrance into the thoughts and conduct of all beings* consists in that, with one single thought, he cognizes the thoughts and conduct of all beings.[50]

2. He *plays with the superknowledges* in the sense that, playing with them (at will), he can pass from Buddha-field to Buddha-field for a vision of the Buddha, but he does not become one who has a notion of the Buddha.

subdued the gross passions, and practises the path in full security. He is left with only the subtle passions, like craving, conceit, etc. Here he eliminates also them. In addition, the Bodhisattva, making use of true wisdom, sees in all passions their true character (*bhūta-naya*). He is like a man, endowed with the superknowledges, who can transform repulsiveness into loveliness.

[47]*Nag*: In the first three stages insight predominated over quietude, because the Bodhisattva was still incapable of intense concentration. In the next three stages, quietude predominated over insight, and that was the reason why he could not yet reach the definite position (*niyāma*) of a Bodhisattva. Now, however, an equilibrium is reached between quietude and the insight which he turns on the emptiness of beings and of dharmas, and he can securely take up the career of a Bodhisattva. From the seventh stage onwards, the stage from which no reversal is possible, he obtains the knowledge of all modes successively and by degrees.

[48]*anunaya.* With its opposite, *pratigha,* "aversion", it is regarded as an evil that must be overcome. It means that one is "led along" by somebody, "won over" by him.

[49]The personality which he shows at a given time varies with the composition of his audience. With the help of his power of self-transformation he manifests his own body in different ways according to the body-modifications of beings and their dispositions and intentions. In an assembly of Brahmins he looks like a Brahmin, etc. So *Daśabhūmika,* of the 8th *bhūmi* (M).

[50]*Nag*: The Bodhisattva is like a good physician who has learned how to examine his patients, and knows whether they can be cured or not, and whether their cure is far off or near. He can penetrate the thought-currents of all beings, knows which ones are devoid of the conditions of salvation and which ones are ripe for it, and also knows when and by which means or method they will be saved.

3. The *creation of Buddha-fields in accordance with what he has seen*[51] consists in that, after he has occupied in the great trichiliocosm the position of its Ruler, or that of a Universal Monarch,[52] he renounces all world systems and yet does not fancy himself for that. (P224)

4a. He *honours the Buddhas,* i.e. honours the Dharma in order to help all beings.

4b. His *contemplation of the Buddha-body as it really is,* is the contemplation of the Dharma-body as it really is.

VIII.B

1. His *cognition of the higher and lower faculties of others* consists in that, as a result of having stood in the ten powers,[53] he has a wise cognition of the extent to which the dominants of all beings are perfected.

2. He *purifies the Buddha-field* by purifying the thought of all beings.

3a. His *concentration on everything as an illusion* has the result that he does all deeds, and yet no actual performance takes place.[54]

3b. The *perpetual attainment* of this concentration is due to the fact that to the Bodhisattva it comes as a karma result of the good deeds of his past.

4. He *gains a personality at will,* i.e. as the wholesome roots of beings come to completion, so a Bodhisattva takes hold of a personality at will.[55]

[51]i.e. in those other Buddha-fields.

[52]*Nag*: The eighth stage is called "the stage of the Universal Monarch". Just as the precious wheel of a Universal Monarch goes everywhere without meeting with any obstacle, hindrance or foe, just so the Bodhisattva who dwells in this stage causes the jewel of the Law to rain down, satisfies the wishes of beings, and no one can hinder him. He can also seize on the characteristics of the Pure Lands he has seen, and, taking them as his model, perfect his own field.

[53]This cognition is mentioned at *P* 210 as the fifth of the powers of a Tathagata. Through it the Tathagata, and also to a lesser degree the Bodhisattva, knows to what extent a person's spiritual faculties, or organs, are developed, whether they are dull or keen, and which one of them predominates. This knowledge helps him to save beings.

[54]*Nag*: He fills the universe with his magical creations, and there is no beneficial activity which he does not accomplish. "But the thought of the Bodhisattva remains immobile, and he does not seize the marks of his thought."—He never leaves his concentrated trance, indulges in no mental activity whatsoever, and performs all his world-saving actions spontaneously and without any effort, as a kind of magical play.—*H*, however: "a firm stand in the contemplation of the illusory character of every separate entity". *S*: but his mind does not proceed with regard to any dharma.

[55]*saṃcintya.* (1) He has sovereignty in the choice of his rebirth. (2) He is reborn with the set purpose of doing some good in the world, whereas most of us are forced into a definite rebirth by the effect of our former deeds. (3) He adopts a form of existence which is most suitable to serve the needs of living beings.

IX

1. The Bodhisattva's *infinite resolve* consists in that, as a result of having fulfilled the six perfections, whatever he resolves upon that he accomplishes.

2. His *cognition of the speech of all beings* consists in that, through the analytical knowledge of languages, he comprehends the speech of the gods, etc.

3. His *fulfilled ready speech* consists in that, through the analytical knowledge of ready speech, he penetrates to the cognition which enables him always to expound the Dharma effectively.

4. He *accomplishes the descent into the womb* by being, in all births, reborn apparitionally.

5. He *accomplishes the family* by being reborn in good families.

6. He *accomplishes the birth*[56] by being reborn in noble families, or in good brahmin families.

7. He *accomplishes the clan* by being reborn in that clan from which the former Bodhisattvas have come.

8. He *accomplishes the retinue* by being endowed with a retinue of Bodhisattvas,[57] after he has established beings in enlightenment.

9. He *accomplishes the manner of birth*: even when just born, a Bodhisattva irradiates all world systems with his splendour, and shakes them all in six ways. (P225)

10. He *accomplishes the leaving of his home* by leaving home together with many hundreds of thousands of niyutas of kotis of beings.

11. A Bodhisattva's *accomplishment of the miraculous harmony of the Bodhi-tree* consists in that the root of his Bodhi-tree is made of gold, the trunk of Vaidurya, the branches of all kinds of jewels, the leaves of all kinds of previous things, and the fine fragrance of that tree and its radiance irradiate infinite world systems.

12. A Bodhisattva's *accomplishment of the fulfilment of all virtuous qualities* is the perfect purity of his Buddha-field, through the maturity of the beings in it.

X

How should a Bodhisattva, a great being, who has stood on the tenth stage, be called a Tathagata?

[56]or "caste".

[57]*Nag*: All those who surround him are sages and honest people who, from one life to another, have accumulated virtuous qualities. Here the Buddha says that he is surrounded only by Bodhisattvas. But through the wonder-working power of his concentration on skilful means also other men and women are created who appear to surround him.

When in a Bodhisattva the ten perfections, etc. *to* : the eighteen special Buddhadharmas are fulfilled, and when there is the cognition of the knowledge of all modes, and a forsaking of all defilements and of the residues relating to them, and when the great compassion and all Buddhadharmas have been fulfilled—it is then that a Bodhisattva, a great being, after the tenth Bodhisattva-stage, is verily to be called a Tathagata.

Which are the ten stages of a Bodhisattva, a great being? A Bodhisattva, coursing through skill in means in all the perfections, having been trained in the thirty-seven wings of enlightenment, coursing in the Unlimited, the trances, and the formless attainments, coursing in the ten powers of a Tathagata, the analytical knowledges, the eighteen special Buddhadharmas, having passed beyond nine stages, i.e. the stage of bright insight, the stage of becoming one of the clan, the eighth-lowest stage, the stage of vision, the stage of refinement, the stage of turning away from passion, the stage of him who has done, the stage of a Pratyekabuddha, the stage of a Bodhisattva, is established on the Buddha-stage—this is the tenth stage of a Bodhisattva, a great being.

It is thus, Subhuti, that the Bodhisattva, the great being becomes one who has set out in the great vehicle.

CHAPTER 18

GOING FORTH ON THE STAGES OF THE GREAT VEHICLE

I 9,17. THE EQUIPMENT WITH THE ANTIDOTES.

I 9,17a. ANTIDOTE TO THE FIRST DISCRIMINATION OF THE OBJECT ON THE PATH OF VISION.
(2. *Three questions concerning the "great vehicle".*)

As again, Subhuti, you say, "from where will that vehicle go forth?"* It will go forth from what belongs to the triple world. Where the knowledge of all modes is, there it will come to a stand.* And that again in consequence of nonduality. And why? Because those two dharmas, i.e. the great vehicle and the knowledge of all modes, are neither conjoined nor disjoined, immaterial, undefinable, nonresisting, with one mark only, i.e. no mark. And why? Because unmarked dharmas do not go forth, (P226) will not go forth, have not gone forth. To wish for the going forth of unmarked dharmas is like wishing for the going forth of the Dharma-element, of Suchness, the Reality limit, the unthinkable element, the space-element, the forsaking-element, the dispassion-limit, of non-production, stopping, nonexistence, of the emptiness of form, feeling, etc. And why? Because the form-emptiness, etc. will not go forth from what belongs to the triple world, nor will it come to a stand in the knowledge of all modes. And why? Because form is empty of form, etc. To wish for the going forth of unmarked dharmas is like wishing for the going forth of a dream, a mirage, an illusion, an echo, an image, a reflection, a village of the Gandharvas, a magical creation of the Tathagata. And why? Because the own-being of a dream will not go forth from what belongs to the triple world, nor will it come to a stand in the knowledge of all modes. Even so with the own-being of a mirage, etc. (P227) And why? Because the own-being of a dream, etc., is empty of the own-being of a dream, etc.

I 9,17b. ANTIDOTES TO THE SECOND DISCRIMINATION OF THE OBJECT ON THE PATH OF VISION.

The own-being of the perfections, emptiness, applications of mindfulness, etc. *to* : Buddhadharmas,

I 9,17c. ANTIDOTE TO THE FIRST DISCRIMINATION OF THE SUBJECT ON THE PATH OF VISION.

of the fruit of a Streamwinner, etc. *to* : (P228) the knowledge of all modes, is empty of the own-being of the perfections, etc. *to* : the knowledge of all modes.

I 9,17d. ANTIDOTE TO THE SECOND DISCRIMINATION OF THE SUBJECT ON THE PATH OF VISION.

He would wish for the going forth of a word, a sign, an agreed symbol, a conventional expression, a (mere) concept, who would wish for the going forth of unmarked dharmas. And why? Because that which is the own-being of a word, sign, agreed symbol, conventional expression or concept, that will not go forth from what belongs to the triple world, nor will it come to a stand in the knowledge of all modes. And why? Because the own-being of a word, sign, agreed symbol, conventional expression or concept is empty of the own-being of a word, sign, agreed symbol, conventional expression or concept. And the same holds good of Nonproduction, Nonstopping and the Ineffective. It is thus that the great vehicle will not go forth from what belongs to the triple world, and will not come to a stand in the knowledge of all modes. That vehicle has not started off[1] (even).

I 9,17e. ANTIDOTE TO THE FIRST DISCRIMINATION OF THE OBJECT ON THE PATH OF DEVELOPMENT.

As again Subhuti has said, "where will that vehicle stand?" This vehicle will not stand anywhere. (P229) And why? Because all dharmas have no stand. But that vehicle will stand by way of not taking its stand anywhere. Just as the Dharma-element neither stands nor does not stand, just so the great vehicle. Just as nonproduction, nonstopping, nondefilement, nonpurification, and the Uneffected do neither stand nor not stand, just so the great vehicle. For the Dharma-element is empty of the Dharma-element. And why? Because the own-being of the Dharma-element neither stands nor does not stand. And why? Because the own-being of the Dharma-element is empty of the own-being of the Dharma-element. And so likewise with nonproduction, etc. It is thus that this vehicle does not stand anywhere, but it will stand by way of not taking a stand, and in consequence of the fact that it cannot be moved about.[2]

I 9,17f. ANTIDOTE TO THE SECOND DISCRIMINATION OF THE OBJECT ON THE PATH OF DEVELOPMENT.

As Subhuti has said, "who will go forth by means of this vehicle?"*

[1] *acalitam.*

[2] *acālyayogena.*

No one will go forth by means of that vehicle. Because that vehicle, and that by which he would go forth, and he who would go forth, and that from which he would go forth—all these dharmas do not exist. Since all these dharmas do not exist, which dharma could go forth by means of which dharma?* And why? Because a self, a being, etc. *to*: one who sees, is not got at, on account of the fact that a self, etc., are absolutely pure. And similarly with the Dharma-element, the Unproduced, etc., the Uneffected, etc., the skandhas, etc. *to* : the knowledge of all modes; the joyous stage, the immaculate stage, the light-giving stage, the brilliant stage, the stage which is very difficult to conquer, the stage which is face to face, the far-reaching stage, (P230) the immovable stage, the stage of unerringly effective intentions, the stage of the cloud of Dharma;[3] the beginning, the end, and the present; coming, going, and stability; decease and rebirth, decrease and increase—on account of their absolute purity.

Because of the nonapprehension of what is everything not got at? Because of the nonapprehension of the Dharma-element. And why? Because of the nonapprehension of the Dharma-element is the Dharma-element not got at. And so with Nonproduction, etc. *to* : the Uneffected, etc. *to* : Suchness, etc. *to*: the perfections, etc. *to*: the Buddhadharmas.

I 9,17g. THE ANTIDOTE TO THE FIRST DISCRIMINATION OF THE SUBJECT ON THE PATH OF DEVELOPMENT.

The Streamwinner is not got at because of the nonapprehension of a Streamwinner. And why? A Streamwinner cannot be got at on account of this absolute purity. And so with the Once-Returner, etc. *to*: the Tathagata,

I 9,17h. THE ANTIDOTE TO THE SECOND DISCRIMINATION OF THE SUBJECT ON THE PATH OF DEVELOPMENT.

with : the fruit of a Streamwinner, etc. *to*: Buddhahood; the ten stages, from the joyous stage to the stage of the Dharma-cloud, and likewise the ten stages, from the stage of bright insight, the stage of becoming one of the clan, the eighth-lowest stage, etc. *to* : the stage of one who has done, the stage of a Pratyekabuddha, the stage of a Bodhisattva, the stage of a Buddha. It is because of the 18 kinds of emptiness that the stages are not got at, (P231) nor the maturing of beings, nor the purifying of the Buddha-field, nor the five Eyes, etc.

It is thus that a Bodhisattva, a great being, in consequence of taking in all dharmas nothing at all as a basis, will go forth by means of the great vehicle to the knowledge of all modes.

[3]These names of the ten stages of the Mahayana occur only in *P*, and are obviously a later addition. *S* is content to speak of "the first stage, the second stage, etc.", and then gives the Hinayana names of the ten stages.

Chapter 19

SURPASSING

I 10. The Progress which Consists in Going-forth.

(3. *Why the "Great Vehicle" is so called.*)

**Subhuti*: The great vehicle is called a "great vehicle". Surpassing the world with its gods, men, and Asuras, that vehicle will go forth. That is why it is called a "great vehicle". It is like space. As in space, so in this vehicle there is room for countless beings. In this way is this the "great vehicle" of the Bodhisattvas, the great beings. Just as one can see no coming, going or abiding of space, so one cannot get at the coming, going or abiding of this great vehicle. Just as one cannot get at the beginning of space, or its end, or its middle, on account of the sameness of the three periods of time, so also with this great vehicle. That is why one speaks of a "great vehicle".*

The Lord: So it is, Subhuti. This great vehicle of the Bodhisattva, the great being, (P232) consists in the six perfections, in all Dharani-doors, all concentration-doors, the 20 kinds of emptiness, the applications of mindfulness, etc. *to*: the eighteen special Buddhadharmas.

I 10,1. The program of going forth.

I 10,1a. Going forth to the highest possible state.

Śāriputra: When again Subhuti has said, "surpassing the world with its gods, men, and Asuras, that vehicle will go forth", what then is "the world with its gods, men and Asuras"? The world of sense desire, the world of form, the formless world. If the world of sense desire, the world of form, or the formless world were Suchness, Not-falseness, unaltered Suchness, if they were the Unperverted, Truly Real, True Reality, That which is as it really is, the Permanent, Stable, Eternal, Not liable to reversal, existence, and not nonexistence, then that great vehicle would not go forth, after having surpassed the world with its gods, men, and Asuras. But because the world of sense desire, the world of form and the formless world have been constructed by thought, fabricated from fictions and feigned, because they are not as reality really is, but entirely impermanent, unstable, not eternal, liable to reversal, and nonexistence, therefore this great vehicle will go forth, after having surpassed the world with its gods, men, and Asuras. And this holds good not only of the triple world, but the same formula should be applied to the skandhas, the 20 kinds of emptiness, the Dharma-element, Suchness, the Reality limit, the unthinkable element, etc. *to* : (P233) the applications of mindfulness, etc. *to* : the Buddhadharmas,

I 10,1b. THE GOING FORTH WHICH CONSISTS IN FORSAKING.
the stages, the fruits of a holy life, from Streamwinner to Buddha, the world with its gods, men, and Asuras.

I 10,1c. THE GOING FORTH WHICH LEADS TO ACHIEVEMENT.
and the thoughts which a Bodhisattva produces from the first thought of enlightenment up to his arrival at the terrace of enlightenment. If the adamantine cognition were an existent and not nonexistent, then the Bodhisattva would not, having known all defilements and their residues as nonexistent, reach the cognition of the all-knowing which is furnished with the best of all modes; but he reaches it because the adamantine (P234) cognition is nonexistent and not an existent. If the thirty-two marks of a superman which the Tathagata possesses were existents and not nonexistent, then the Tathagata would not outshine the world with its gods, men, and Asuras with his splendour and majesty; but he outshines it because the thirty-two marks are nonexistent and not existents. And the same applies to the light with which he irradiates countless world systems. If the Tathagata's voice, which has sixty special qualities, were an existent and not nonexistent, then the Tathagata would not make his voice resound through countless world systems in the ten directions; but he makes it resound because it is nonexistent and not an existent. If the Tathagata's wheel of Dharma, with its three revolutions and its twelve spokes, were an existent and not nonexistent, then the Tathagata would not have turned this wheel of Dharma which cannot, with justice, be turned by any recluse, brahmin, god, Mara, Brahma, or anyone else in the world; but he has turned it because it is nonexistent and not an existent. If the beings for whose sake the Tathagata has turned the wheel of Dharma were existents and not nonexistent, then surely he would not have led those beings to Nirvana in the realm of Nirvana which leaves nothing behind. But because the beings for whose sake the Tathagata has turned the wheel of Dharma are nonexistent and not existents, therefore beings have been led to Nirvana, are being led to Nirvana, and will be led to Nirvana.

I 10,2. SAMENESS.
Śāriputra: As, Subhuti, you have said, "the same as space is this

vehicle", so it is : the same as space is the great vehicle. For these are the features which they have in common : The ten directions are inconceivable of them. (P235) They are not long or short, round or square, even or uneven; not blue, yellow, red, white, crimson, or crystalline; not past, future, or present. No decrease, increase, or loss can be conceived of them, no defilement or purification, no production, stopping, stability, instability or alteration of stability. They are not wholesome, unwholesome, or indeterminate. They are not seen, heard, known, or discerned. They are not cognizable or uncognizable, not discernable or comprehensible, not to be realised, forsaken or developed, not karma results or or liable to lead to karma results. They are not included in the world of sense desire, the world of form, or the formless world. They are not with or without greed, with or without hate, with or without delusion. In them there is no first thought of enlightenment, no second, etc. *to* : no tenth; none of the stages and none of the fruits. They are not material or immaterial, (P236) definable or undefinable, resisting or nonresisting, conjoined or disjoined; not permanent or impermanent, at ease or ill, self or not-self, lovely or repulsive, empty or not empty, with sign or signless, with wish or wishless, calm or uncalm, isolated or unisolated. And in both of them there is no light or darkness, both cannot be seized or apprehended, and in both of them there is no utterance or nonutterance. In these ways is the great vehicle the same as space.

I 10,3. (THE ACTIVITY FOR) THE WEAL OF BEINGS.

Again, as Subhuti, you have said, "as in space, so in this vehicle there is room for immeasurable, incalculable, and innumerable beings", so it is. And why? Because from the nonbeingness of beings should the nonbeingness of space be knows, and from the nonbeingness of space should the nonbeingness of the great vehicle be known. In this way there is in this great vehicle room for immeasurable, incalculable, and innumerable beings. And why? Because what the beings are, and what space is, and what the great vehicle is—all that is not got at. Moreover, from the nonbeingness of beings should the nonbeingness of space be known; from the nonbeingness of space should the nonbeingness of the great vehicle be known; from the nonbeingness of the great vehicle should the nonbeingness of the immeasurable, the incalculable, the innumerable be known. And why? Because, what the beings are, and what space is, and what the great vehicle is, and what is the immeasurable, the incalculable (P237), the innumerable—all that is not got at. Moreover, from the nonbeingness of beings should the nonbeingness of space be known; from the nonbeingness of space should the nonbeingness of the great vehicle be known; from the nonbeingness of the great vehicle should the nonbeingness of the Unconditioned be known; from the nonbeingness of the

Unconditioned should the nonbeingness of the immeasurable, the incalculable, the innumerable be known; from the nonbeingness of the immeasurable, the incalculable, the innumerable should the nonbeingness of all dharmas be known. And why? Because what the beings are, and what the Tathagata is, and what space is, what the great vehicle is, and what the Unconditioned is, and what is the immeasurable, the incalculable, the innumerable, and what all dharmas are—all these are not got at. Moreover, from the nonbeingness of self and beings should be known the nonbeingness of being, soul, person, personality, individual, man, youth, doer, feeler, begetter, and of one who sees; from their nonbeingness should be known the nonbeingness of the Reality limit and of the unthinkable element; from their nonbeingness should the nonbeingness of the immeasurable, the incalculable, the innumerable be known; from their nonbeingness should the nonbeingness of all dharmas be known. And why? Because none of these is got at. (P238) And the same should be done with the skandhas, etc., the six perfections, the 20 kinds of emptiness, the applications of mindfulness, etc. *to*: the Buddhadharmas, the stages, (P239) fruits, etc. *to*: the knowledge of all modes. Just as in the Nirvana-element there is room for countless beings, so also in this great vehicle. It is in this sense that in this great vehicle, as in space, there is room for immeasurable, incalculable, and innumerable beings.

I 10,4. THE ABSENCE OF EXERTION.

Again, as Subhuti has said, "of this great vehicle no arrival, departure, or abiding can be seen", so it is. And why? Because dharmas do not move about. They do not go anywhere, do not come from anywhere, do not abide anywhere. Because the essential original nature of form, etc., does not come from anywhere, nor go to anywhere, nor abide anywhere. And that is true of all dharmas. (P240)

I 10,5. BEYOND THE EXTREMES.

Again, as Subhuti has said, "of this great vehicle no initial limit is got at, no final limit, no middle, Self-identical in the three periods of time is that great vehicle. That is why it is called the 'great vehicle'," so it is. And why? Because the past period of time is empty of the past period of time, the future empty of the future, the present of the present. The sameness of the three periods of time is empty of the sameness of the three periods of time. The great vehicle is empty of the great vehicle, the Bodhisattva empty of the Bodhisattva. But emptiness is not one, not two, not three, etc. *to*: not ten. That is why owing to the sameness of the three periods of time this vehicle of the Bodhisattva, the great being, is self-identical. But therein one cannot apprehend "the same" or "not the same", greed or dispassion, hate or its absence, delusion or its absence, conceit or its absence, the wholesome or unwholesome, what has outflows or what has none, what has blemishes or what has none, defilement or nondefilement, extinction or nonextinction of defilement, the worldly or the supramundane, defiling or purification, Samsara or Nirvana, permanence or impermanence, ease or ill, self or not self, calm or uncalm, the world of sense desire or the transcending of the world of sense desire, the world of form or its transcending, the formless world or its transcending. And why? Because the own-being of all that cannot be apprehended. Past form, etc., is empty of past form, etc. And so is future, and present form, etc. And why? In emptiness (P241) one cannot get at past, future or present form, etc. The very emptiness, how ever empty, cannot be got at in emptiness, how much less past, future, and present form, etc.! One cannot get at the initial limit of the perfection of giving, etc., nor at its final limit, nor can one get at it in the present, owing to the sameness of the periods of time. Nor can one get at the past, future, or present period of time in the sameness of the periods of time; the very sameness even cannot be got at in the sameness; how again could one, in sameness, get at the past, future, present perfection of giving, etc.? And what is true of the perfections, that holds good also of the applications of mindfulness, (P242) etc. *to*: the Buddhadharmas. Moreover, the common people cannot be got at, in their initial limit, their final limit, or in the present, owing to the sameness of the periods of time. And why? On account of the fact that no beings can be got at. And that is equally true of Disciples, Pratyekabuddhas, Bodhisattvas, and Tathagatas. It is thus that a Bodhisattva, who has stood firm in perfect wisdom and has trained himself in the three periods of time, should fulfil the knowledge of all modes. This is of a Bodhisattva the great vehicle, on account of the sameness of the three periods of time. Having stood firmly therein the Bodhisattva, surpassing the world with its gods, men, and Asuras, will go forth to the knowledge of all modes.

I 10,6. Attainment.

I 10,6a. Going forth to attainment.

D. ATTAINMENT.

(1. *The Bodhisattva goes forth to attainment.*)

Subhuti: Well said, O Lord. Well has the Lord taught this great vehicle of the Bodhisattvas, the great beings. In the past period, the Bodhisattvas, who have trained in this great vehicle, have reached the knowledge of all modes. Future Bodhisattvas also, by training in this great vehicle, will reach the knowledge of all modes. And those Bodhisattvas also who, in this world in all the ten directions, are present in innumerable world systems, they, having trained in this great vehicle, do reach the knowledge of all modes. This therefore is the great vehicle of the Bodhisattvas, the great beings, owing to the fact that they are the same in the three periods of time.

**The Lord*: So it is, Subhuti. Having trained in this great vehicle, past, future, and present Bodhisattvas have reached the knowledge of all modes, will reach it, do reach it.*

Chapter 20

NONDUALITY

**Purna*: This (P243) Elder Subhuti, O Lord, when requested by the Tathagata to speak about perfect wisdom, fancied that the great vehicle was something that could be explained!

Subhuti: I hope, O Lord, I have not transgressed against perfect wisdom when explaining the great vehicle!

The Lord: In agreement with perfect wisdom, you have Subhuti, explained the great vehicle.* And why? Because whatever wholesome dharmas there are that act as wings to enlightenment—be they Disciple-dharmas, Pratyekabuddha-dharmas, Bodhisattva-dharmas or Buddha-dharmas—they are comprehended in Perfect Wisdom and come together therein.

Subhuti: Which are these wholesome dharmas?

The Lord: They are the applications of mindfulness, etc. *to*: the eighteen special Buddha-dharmas, the state of being always mindful and evenminded. They are all comprehended in the perfection of wisdom and come together therein. But what the great vehicle is, what the perfections are, what the applications of mindfulness, etc. *to*: the Buddha-dharmas, what the Dharma-Vinaya made known by the Tathagata, what form, etc., is, (P244) what the Dharma-element, Suchness, the Reality limit, the unthinkable element, and Nirvana—all these dharmas are neither conjoined nor disjoined, they are immaterial, undefinable, nonresisting, with one mark only, i.e. no mark. In this way you describe, Subhuti, the great vehicle in agreement with the perfection of wisdom. And why? Because the great vehicle is not one thing, and the perfection of wisdom another, the perfection of concentration, etc., again another. For the great vehicle and the perfection of wisdom, and the other perfections, are not two nor divided. Nor is the great vehicle one thing, and the applications of mindfulness, etc. *to*: the Buddhadharmas another. In this way you describe, Subhuti, the great vehicle in agreement with the perfection of wisdom.

I 10,6b. Negation of something to be attained.

(2. *Impossibility of Attainment*:

(a) *Nothing is ever really brought forth.*)

**Subhuti*: Furthermore, O Lord, a Bodhisattva (who sets out on his journey) does not approach (the goal of full Bodhisattvahood)[1] from where it begins, nor from where it ends, nor in the middle either. From the boundlessness of form, etc., should the boundlessness of a Bodhisattva be known. A Bodhisattva's form, etc. does not exist, cannot be apprehended. Since in each and every way I do not get at a Bodhisattva, or see him, what Bodhisattva should I instruct and admonish in what perfection of wisdom? (P245) Moreover, this "Bodhisattva" is a mere designation. It is as with the self. Although we speak of a "self", yet absolutely the self is something uncreated.[2] Since therefore all dharmas have no own-being,[3] what is that form which is something uncreated? What is uncreated, that is not form etc. How shall I instruct and admonish a noncreation in a perfect wisdom which is also a noncreation? And yet, one cannot apprehend as other than uncreated (the dharmas of) a Bodhisattva who courses towards enlightenment. If, when this is being expounded, the thought of a Bodhisattva does not become cowed, stolid, or regretful, and if his mind does not tremble, is not frightened, nor terrified, then that Bodhisattva, that great being courses in perfect wisdom.*

Śariputra: For what reason, Ven. Subhuti, do you say that "a Bodhisattva does not approach from the beginning, end, or middle"?

Subhuti: It is because of the nonbeingness, the emptiness, the isolatedness of a being, because of the absence of an own-being in it, that a Bodhisattva does not approach (a Bodhi-being) at the beginning, at the end, or in the middle. And why? Because as a result of the nonbeingness of a being, its emptiness, its isolatedness, and the absence of own-being in it one cannot apprehend its beginning, etc. Nor is the nonbeingness of a being, (P246) its isolatedness, its emptiness, the absence of own-being in it, one thing, and a Bodhisattva another, and beginning, middle, and end again another; for all these are not two nor divided.

[1]*nopaiti*; see Introduction p. 24.—"from where it begins", etc., *pūrva-antato*. Wherever the term *anta*, "end", occurs, a satisfactory English translation is almost impossible. The term is used here for the temporal limits of an event, i.e. the beginning and the end, the initial and the final limit. In addition it means, in a derogatory sense, any "extreme", or any of two correlative terms. It is the task of wisdom to rise above these "extremes", to contact a thing beyond the limits which arbitrarily confine it, and thus to penetrate to the Absolute. In consequence, *aty-anta-tayā* "because of beyond-end-ness" is usually translated as "absolutely". The idea behind all this is that to isolate a thing from the remainder of reality is due to our self-seeking practical purposes, and is aided and abetted by the use of words which make artificial boundaries where there are none in reality itself. Each event is bound up with all others, and temporal and spatial limitations spring only from craving and ignorance.

[2]*anabhinirvṛtta*; see Introduction pp. 24-25. In *Si* 203 it occurs together with "empty of own-marks, not really there, not fully there". According to A.K. iii 123 *abhinirvṛtti* is akin to "production", and due to the "fetters"; cf. A.K. vi 137-8.

[3]*abhāva-svabhāvā*, or "have nonexistence for own-being".

It is because of the nonbeingness of form, etc., its emptiness, its isolatedness, its lack of own-being, that a Bodhisattva does not approach (a Bodhi-being) from either beginning, end, or middle. Because form, etc., cannot be apprehended in nonbeingness, emptiness, isolatedness, or in lack of own-being. Nor is nonbeingness one thing, emptiness another, isolatedness another, lack of own-being another, a Bodhisattva another form, etc., another, beginning, end, and middle another; but all these are not two nor divided.[4] And that should be done for all dharmas. (P247)

I 10,6c. Negation of someone who attains.

Śariputra: As again, Subhuti, you say: for what reason "should the boundlessness of a Bodhisattva be known from the boundlessness of form, etc."?

Subhuti: Form, etc., is the same as space. And why? (P248) Of space one cannot apprehend a beginning, end, or middle, but it is because of its endlessness and boundlessness that one speaks conventionally of "space". Just so one cannot apprehend a beginning, end, or middle of form, etc. And why? On account of the emptiness of form, etc. Of emptiness one cannot apprehend a beginning, end, or middle, and yet one nevertheless speaks conventionally of "emptiness". And so for all dharmas. It is by this method that the boundlessness of a Bodhisattva should be known from the boundlessness of form, etc.

Śariputra: For what reason do you say that "a Bodhisattva's form does not exist, cannot be apprehended"?

Subhuti: Form, etc., is empty of form, etc. And why? Because in emptiness form, etc., as well as the Bodhisattva, does not exist (and cannot be found).[5] And so for all dharmas. (P249) The Disciple is empty of Discipleship, the Pratyekabuddha of Pratyekabuddhahood, the Tathagata of Tathagatahood. And why? For in emptiness the Tathagata does not exist, nor does a Bodhisattva. It is in this way that a Bodhisattva's form, etc., does not exist, cannot be apprehended.

Śariputra: For what reason do you say that "since in each and every way I do not get at a Bodhisattva, or see him, what Bodhisattva should I instruct and admonish in what perfect wisdom"?

Subhuti: In form, form cannot exist or be apprehended. In feeling form cannot exist or be apprehended, nor can feeling in feeling, feeling in form, form and feeling in perception, perception in perception, perception in form, perception in feeling, form in feeling and perception and impulses, impulses in impulses, impulses in form and feeling and perception (P250), consciousness in form and feeling and perception and

[4]Chapter 13 of *S* begins here in Ghosha's edition, but in Gilgit *P* the beginning of ch. 13 on f. 118a coincides more suitably with that of ch. 21 of *Ad.*

[5]*na samvidyate* can have both these meanings.

impulses. And so for the other dharmas. In Bodhisattvahood the Bodhisattva cannot exist or be apprehended, nor can the Tathagata in Tathagatahood, the perfection of wisdom in the perfection of wisdom, the perfection of wisdom in the instruction and admonition, or the instruction and admonition in the perfection of wisdom. It is thus because all dharmas do not exist and are baseless, that the Bodhisattva does not exist and cannot be apprehended.

I 10,6d. NEGATION OF BOTH OBJECT AND SUBJECT OF ATTAINMENT.

Śariputra: For what reason, Subhuti, do you say that "a 'Bodhisattva' is a mere designation"? And why do you say that "the word 'Bodhisattva' has been added on as an adventitious designation"?[6]

Subhuti: Because words do not come from anywhere in the ten directions, nor do they go to anywhere, nor do they stand anywhere. And that holds good of the words applied to all dharmas and also those applied to the Bodhisattvas. For "form", etc., are adventitious designations, and what is a designation that is not actually form, etc. And why? For words are empty of the own-being of words, and what is empty, that is not a word.[7] It is for this reason that the word "Bodhisattva" is said to be a mere designation.[8] (P251)

Śariputra: For what reason, Subhuti, do you say that "although we speak of a 'self', yet absolutely the self is something uncreated"?

Subhuti: Absolutely a self does not exist; how then could its real creation take place? And that is true also of the synonyms of 'self', like being, soul, etc.; and also of form, etc., and all dharmas. (P252)

Śariputra: For what reason has the Ven. Subhuti said that "all dharmas have no own-being"?

Subhuti: Because an own-being acting in casual connection does not exist.

Śariputra: Of what is there no own-being acting in casual connection?

Subhuti: Of form, etc. By this method all dharmas are without own-being. Moreover, Śariputra, all dharmas are impermanent, but not because something has disappeared.[10]

Śariputra: Which are those all-dharmas which are impermanent, but not because something has disappeared?

[6]"added on"="superimposed (on what is really there) as a mere product of social convention", *H*.—"adventitious" also at *P* 38. The word also refers to the arrival of a stranger.

[7]I understand this to mean that it is the "own-being", or function, of a word to express actual facts; this no word ever does. It is an empty sound, and not a "word" (*nāman*) which has any objective significance or ontological bearing.

[8]*nocyate* in Dutt, but *P*-Ti: *ucyate*.

[10]*no kasyacid vigamena*; *vi-gama* literally "departure". The connotations of this term need further exploration, on the basis of *A* xii 261, xviii 341, xxix 479; *R* ii 11; *Su* i 11a-b, vi 66b; *P* 506.

Subhuti: Form, etc., is impermanent, but not because something has disappeared. And why? For what is impermanent that is nonexistence and extinction. Likewise all-dharmas are ill, notself, calm, empty, signless, wishless, but not because something has disappeared; they are wholesome, faultless, without outflows, undefiled, supramundane, nonpurified, unconditioned.[11] And why? Because the Unconditioned is nonexistence and extinction. By this method all dharmas are without own-being, but not by the disappearance of anything. Moreover, Śariputra, all dharmas are neither unmoved nor destroyed.

Śariputra: For what reason? (P253)

Subhuti: Form, etc. is neither unmoved nor destroyed. And why? Such is its essential original nature. The same is true of all that is wholesome or unwholesome, faulty or faultless, with or without outflows, defiled or undefiled, worldly or supramundane, conditioned or unconditioned, defilement or purification, Samsara or Nirvana. By this method all dharmas have no own-being.[12]

Śariputra: For what reason, Subhuti, have you said that "form, etc., is not brought about"?

Subhuti: Form, etc., is not a really created thing. And why? Because there is no agent who could bring them about, nor can such an agent be apprehended.

Śariputra: For what reason, Subhuti, is "that which is uncreated not form, etc."?

Subhuti : Because form, etc., is empty in its essential nature. And what is empty in its essential nature, of that there is no production or passing away, and in consequence also no alteration can be conceived of it. (P254)

Śariputra : For what reason, Subhuti, do you say, "how shall I instruct and admonish a noncreation in a perfect wisdom which is also a noncreation?"

Subhuti : Because, as a noncreation, so is perfect wisdom, and what is perfect wisdom that is a noncreation. Perfect wisdom and a noncreation are therefore not two not divided.

Śariputra : For what reason "can one not apprehend as other than uncreated (the dharmas of) a Bodhisattva who courses towards enlightenment"?

Subhuti : Because a Bodhisattva, who courses in perfect wisdom, does not review a noncreation as one thing, and a Bodhisattva as another. A Bodhisattva and a noncreation are not two nor divided. Nor does he review form, etc. as other than a noncreation. For a noncreation, and form, etc., are not two nor divided.

[11]The grammatical structure of this sentence is not at all clear.

[12]here again *abhāva-svabhāvā*.

Śariputra : For what reason, Ven. Subhuti, do you say that "if when this is being expounded, the thought of a Bodhisattva does not become cowed, stolid, or regretful, and if his mind does not tremble, is not frightened or terrified, then that Bodhisattva courses in perfect wisdom"?

Subhuti: Because there a Bodhisattva reviews all dharmas as without inward striving,[13] as similar to a mock show, a dream, a mirage, an echo, an image, a reflection of the moon in the water, a magical creation, a village of the Gandharvas. (P255)

(2*b*. *Nonduality*.)

At the time when a Bodhisattva, who courses in perfect wisdom investigates those dharmas, at that time he does not approach form, etc., does not grasp at it, does not take his stand on it, does not settle down in it, does not make it known as "form, etc., is that". For a Bodhisattva, who courses in perfect wisdom, does not review form, etc.* And why? Because the nonproduction of form, etc., is not form, etc. Form, etc., and nonproduction are not two nor divided. *What is the nonproduction of the Dharma-element, that is not the Dharma-element. What is the nonproduction of Suchness, the space-element, the Reality limit, the unthinkable element, enlightenment and the knowledge of all modes, that is not Suchness, etc., *to* : not the knowledge of all modes. It is thus that the Dharma-element and nonproduction are not two or divided. It is thus that Suchness, etc. *to*: not the knowledge of all modes and nonproduction are not two or divided. And why? Because nonproduction is not one or two, not many or single.[14] Therefore the nonproduction of the knowledge of all modes is not the knowledge of all modes.* The passing away of form, etc., is not form, etc. It is thus that the skandhas and passing-away are not two or divided.* And why? Because passing-away is not one or two, not many or single. Therefore, what is the passing-away of the five skandhas, that is not the five skandhas. And so far all dharmas. (P256) *Inasmuch as one calls anything "form", etc., one makes a count of what is nondual.*

[13]*nirīha*. Also "inactive", often associated with "empty". *H* to *A* xviii 465 : "An imaginary dharma cannot generate anything, and therefore it is called "inactive, just as space is inactive'".

[14]*pṛthak*, "separate by itself".

Chapter 21

SUBHUTI THE ELDER

I 10,7. The going-forth to the knowledge of all modes.

Śariputra : How, Subhuti, does a Bodhisattva, who courses in perfect wisdom, investigate these dharmas? What is a "Bodhisattva", what "perfect wisdom", what the "investigating"?

Subhuti: You ask, "what is a Bodhisattva?" Just enlightenment is his substance,[1] therefore is he called a "Bodhi-sattva". But though that enlightenment allows him to know the modes of all dharmas, he does not settle down in them. The modes of which dharmas does he know? He knows the modes of form, etc. *to*: Buddhadharmas, but he does not settle down in them.

Śariputra : What are the modes of all dharmas?

Subhuti : Those modes, those characteristics, those signs, by which form, etc., inner and outer dharmas, conditioned and unconditioned dharmas, are made known,[2] those are called the modes of all dharmas.

Again, Śariputra, you ask, "what is perfect wisdom?" (P257) She has abstained, she has caused to abstain.[3] That is why she is called perfect wisdom. From what has she abstained, from what has she caused (others) to abstain? From the skandhas, sense fields, and elements, from conditioned coproduction, from the perfections, the 20 kinds of emptiness, the applications of mindfulness, etc. *to*: from the Buddhadharmas, and all-knowledge.

Again, Śariputra, you ask, "what is the investigating?" Here a Bodhisattva, who courses in perfect wisdom, investigates form, etc., as not permanent or impermanent, not at ease or ill, etc. *to*: not isolated or unisolated. It is thus that a Bodhisattva, who courses in perfect wisdom, investigates all these dharmas.

[1] *bodhir eva sattvas.*

[2] *ākāra*: *ākāryante.* Are "modalized", or "modified" (if that word is taken in a special sense).—"Mode"="attribute". "The attributes which are attributed to."—*ākāra* also "external sign"; therefore *ākārayati* "make known by a sign". The cy to *A.K.* vii 13, and similarly *H* 611, defines *ākāra* as *ālambana-grahaṇa-prakāra,* "the manner in which one takes hold of an object".—The Hindu grammarians, acc. to Renou, distinguish between the *anākṛti* of a conventional term, which is abstract and without form, and the concreteness (*ākṛmant*) of the named thing. In that case, *ākāryate* could be rendered as "invested with concreteness".

[3] *prajñāpāramitā* : *āratā āramitā,* both from ā-RAM. In Pali *ārata*=*virata* (*PDc*). Other fanciful derivations in *Ad* ch. 63, f. 253a-b, but this one is not among them.

Śariputra : For what reason, Subhuti, do you say that "the nonproduction of form, etc., is not form, etc."? (P258)

Subhuti : Form, etc., is empty of form, etc. And that emptiness is neither form, etc., nor production. In this way the nonproduction of form, etc., is not what form, etc., is.

Śariputra : For what reason, Subhuti, do you say that "the passing-away of form, etc., is not form, etc."?

Subhuti : Because these—that passing away, and that form, etc., and the fact of their being undivided—all these dharmas are neither conjoined nor disjoined, they are immaterial, undefinable, nonresisting, with one single mark only, i.e. with no mark.

Śariputra : For what reason, Subhuti, do you say that, "inasmuch as one calls anything form, etc., one makes a count of what is nondual"?

Subhuti: Because nonproduction is not one thing, and form, etc. another. (P259) The very nonproduction is form, etc., the very form, etc., is nonproduction.

(2*c*. *Nonproduction.*)

*At the time, O Lord, when a Bodhisattva who courses in perfect wisdom investigates those dharmas, at that time he reviews the nonproduction of form, etc. *to*: the Buddhadharmas, on account of their absolute purity.

Śariputra : As I understand the meaning of the Ven. Subhuti's teaching, everything from form to the Buddhadharmas is nonproduction. But if that is so, then surely a Disciple has already attained the enlightenment of a Disciple, one who follows the career of a Pratyekabuddha has already attained the enlightenment of a Pratyekabuddha, and a Bodhisattva has already attained the knowledge of all modes. *There will then be no distinction of the five places of rebirth. If all dharmas are nonproduction, a Bodhisattva has already attained the fivefold enlightenment.[4] For what purpose should the Streamwinner (P260) develop the Path for the sake of forsaking the three fetters? Or the Once-returner for the sake of attenuating greed, hate, and delusion? Or the Never-returner for the sake of forsaking the five lower fetters?[5] Or the Arhat for the sake of forsaking the five higher fetters?[6] Or those who belong to the vehicle of the Pratyekabuddhas for the sake of the attainment of the enlightenment of a Pratyekabuddha? For what reason does a Bodhisattva go on

[4]This is an unusual term, and it seems to refer to the subsequent list of five, from Streamwinners to Pratyekabuddhas.

[5]*A.K.* : "lower" what is in relation, or favourable, to the inferior part, i.e. the world of sense desire.

[6]*A.K.* : "higher" or "superior", because one cannot cross the higher spheres (the world of form and formlessness) without having abandoned them.

the difficult pilgrimage, and experience all those sufferings (which he is said to undergo) for the sake of beings? For what reason has the Tathagata known full enlightenment, and turned the wheel of Dharma?

**Subhuti* : I do not wish or look for[7] the attainment of an unproduced dharma, or for reunion with one. I do not look for the Streamwinnership of nonproduction, or for the fruit of a Streamwinner in nonproduction. I do not, on the part of nonproduction, wish or look for any of the spiritual attainments, *up to* the enlightenment of a Pratyekabuddha and Pratyekabuddhahood. I do not look for a Bodhisattva who has gone on the difficult pilgrimage. In any case, a Bodhisattva does not course in the perception of difficulties. And why? Because one who has generated in himself the notion of difficulties is unable to work the weal of countless beings. On the contrary, he forms the notion that all beings are like his parents and children, that they are like himself, and then he is able to work the weal of countless beings. He also thinks that "just as one speaks of a 'self', and yet, absolutely, a self is unproduced, so also all inner and outer dharmas are unproduced". If he forms such a notion, then he will not have a notion of difficulties. And why? Because Bodhisattvas will in each and every way not produce any dharma or apprehend one. I do not look in nonproduction for a Tathagata, not for his turning of the wheel of Dharma. Nor do I look for an unproduced attainment which is being attained by an unproduced dharma.

Śariputra : Is then an unproduced attainment attained through an unproduced dharma, or through a produced dharma? (P261)

Subhuti : I do not look for an unproduced attainment which is being attained through an unproduced dharma, nor for a produced attainment which is being attained through an unproduced dharma.

Śariputra : Do you look for an attainment by an unproduced, or by a produced dharma?

Subhuti : I do not look for either.*

Śariputra : Is there then no attainment, is there no reunion?

Subhuti : There is attainment, there is reunion, but not in ultimate reality.[8] It is through worldly conventional expressions that attainment and reunion are conceived, that Streamwinners, etc. *to* : Buddhas are conceived. But in ultimate reality there is none of all this.

**Śariputra* : Is it intelligible to talk[9] of an "unproduced dharma"?

[7]*icchāmi*. Also "endeavour to obtain, strive, seek for; expect, ask for".—*Tathāgataguhya* in *Pras.* 540-1 : "Those will not become Buddhas who wish for the production or stopping of any dharma. Those will not transcend Samsara who search for a realistic Nirvana. The practitioner of Yoga who progresses correctly does not effect the production or stopping of any dharma. Nor does he wish for the attainment of any dharma, or for reunion with one".

[8]So *S* xiii f. 131a. *P* : as a duality.

[9]*pratibhāti* (*te S*) *mantrayitum* (*A i* 30 *jalpitum*).—cf. *VvA* 78.—I do not really understand

Subhuti : As you say, Śariputra, it is intelligible to talk of an "unproduced dharma", and likewise of "Nonproduction". And why? Because the unproduced dharma, the intelligibility, the talking, and the nongenesis—all these dharmas are neither conjoined nor disjoined, they are immaterial, undefinable, nonresisting, with one mark only, i.e. no mark.

Śariputra : The talking also is nonproduction, and so is the intelligibility, and so is the dharma—and unproduced are those dharmas about which one can talk intelligibly.*

Subhuti : So it is, Śariputra. And why? Because everything from form to the knowledge of all modes is nonproduction. (P262)

Śariputra : So it is. Moreover, as attainment and reunion take place only by way of worldly conventional expression, does also the differentiation of the five destinies take place only by way of worldly conventional expression, and not in ultimate reality?

Subhuti : So it is, Śariputra. And why? Because in ultimate reality there is no karma or karma result, no production or stopping, no defilement or purification.

Śariputra : Furthermore, Subhuti, is an unproduced dharma produced, or is a produced dharma produced?

Subhuti : I do not look for the production of a produced dharma, and I also do not look for the production of an unproduced dharma.

Śāriputra : Of which unproduced dharma do you not look for the production?

Subhuti : I do not wish for the production, which is empty of own-being, of the unproduced dharma of form, etc. *to* : Buddhadharmas. I do not wish even for the production of enlightenment, which is unproduced and empty of own-being.

Śariputra : And again, Subhuti, is production, or nonproduction produced?

Subhuti : Neither. And why? Because those two dharmas, production and nonproduction, are neither conjoined nor disjoined, they are immaterial, undefinable, nonresisting, with one mark only, i.e. with no mark. In this way neither production nor nonproduction is produced. Talk is therefore nonproduction, and so is intelligible speech, and so is a dharma, and also those dharmas are unproduced concerning which one can talk intelligibly. (P263)

**Śariputra* : In the first rank of the preachers of Dharma should the Ven. Subhuti be placed! And why? For from whatever angle he may be questioned, he always finds a way out.

this, nor Subhuti's answer either. In chapter 21 Subhuti and Śāriputra seem to have reached so high a degree of mutual understanding and familiarity, that they intersperse their discourse with a number of private jokes, which we outsiders cannot always share.

(3. *No leaning on anything.*)

(a) Subhuti : This is the true nature of the Tathagata's Disciples that they do not lean on all dharmas. From whatever angle they may be questioned, they always find a way out. And why? Because no dharma ever leans on another.*

Śariputra : In what way do all dharmas not lean on anything?

Subhuti : Form, etc., is empty in its essential original nature. It is not inwardly supported, not outwardly supported, and it cannot be apprehended anywhere between both.[10] In this manner all dharmas do not lean on anything, on account of the emptiness of their essential original nature. It is thus that a Bodhisattva, who courses in the six perfections, should fully cleanse all dharmas, from form *to* the knowledge of all modes.

I 10,8. GOING-FORTH ON THE PATH.

(b) Śariputra : How does a Bodhisattva, who courses in the six perfections, cleanse the path to enlightenment?

Subhuti : There is a wordly perfection of giving, and there is a supramundane perfection of giving.

Śariputra : What is the worldly, and what the supramundane perfection of giving?

I 10,8a. THE WORLDLY PERFECTION OF GIVING.

Subhuti : This is the worldy perfection of giving : Here a Bodhisattva gives, and gives liberally, to recluses, brahmins, the poor, mendicants, travellers, and beggars. (P264) He gives food to those who are hungry, and to those who desire them he gives drinks, vehicles, garments, perfumes, garlands, ointments, flowers, incense, aromatic powders, homes, asylum, shelter, the requirements of life, services, lodgings, and medicines. Likewise he gives his sons, daughters, and wife, kingdoms, as well as his head, limbs, flesh, blood, and marrow to those who desire them. But he renounces all that while leaning on something. It occurs to him, "I give, that one receives, this is the gift. I renounce all that I have without any niggardliness. I act as the Buddha commands. I practise the perfection of giving. I, having made this gift into the common property of all beings, dedicate it to the supreme enlightenment, and that without basing myself on anything. By means of this gift and its fruit, may all beings in this very life be at their ease, and may they without any further clinging enter the final Nirvana!" Tied by three ties he gives a gift. Which three? The notion

[10]*Si* 250 : "That consciousness-element is not supported by the sense faculty, it has not come from the object, and it does not have its place in the middle between them. In fact it is not within, not without, nor between both". For a parallel from *Lalita Vistara* see *Buddhist Texts* no. 149, v. 105.

of self, the notion of others, the notion of a gift. To give a gift tied by these three ties, that is called the worldly perfection of giving, and it is called "worldly" because one does not swerve away from the world, does not depart from it, does not pass beyond it.

I 10,8b. THE SUPRAMUNDANE PERFECTION OF GIVING.

The supramundane perfection of giving, on the other hand, consists in the threefold purity. What is the threefold purity? Here a Bodhisattva gives a gift, and he does not apprehend a self, a recipient, or a gift; also no reward of his giving. He surrenders that gift to all beings, but does not apprehend those beings, or himself either. And, although he dedicates that gift to the supreme enlightenment, he does not apprehend any enlightenment. This is called the supramundane perfection of giving, (P265) and it is called "supramundane" because one swerves away from the world, departs from it, passes beyond it. In the same way should the difference between the worldly and the supramundane perfections of morality, patience, vigour, and concentration be understood.

Śariputra : What is the worldly, and what the supramundane perfection of wisdom?

I 10,8c. THE WORLDLY PERFECTION OF WISDOM.

Subhuti : This is the worldly perfection of wisdom : Here a Bodhisattva gives a gift, leaning on a basis, i.e. he thinks that "I should suppress all niggardly thought in myself". Leaning on the notions of self, being, and gift, he renounces all that he has, all inner and outer things, appropriated and unappropriated, and there is nothing that he does not renounce. And that wholesome root (which results from this act of renunication) he dedicates to the supreme enlightenment, after he has made it common to all beings,—but leaning on a basis.—He tends morality, and is established in the ascetic practices, while leaning on the body, speech, and thought as a basis. While he tends those ten ways of wholesome action, leaning on the views of self, a being and wholesomeness, he dedicates those moralities, made common to all beings, to an enlightenment which he has apprehended, and throughout basing himself on something.—He exalts not himself, nor depreciates others, and endures being ill-treated by all, while leaning on the views of self, a being, and patience. That wholesomeness he dedicates to the supreme enlightenment, after he has made it common to all beings, but leaning on a basis.—He exerts vigour, while apprehending body, thought, the equipment with merit, the equipment with cognition, a self and enlightenment, and he fancies himself for that exertion in vigour. Having made that (merit) common to all beings, he dedicates it to the supreme enlightenment, while basing himself on something.—He develops friendliness, compassion, sympathetic joy, and impartiality. He enters into the trances and attainments and again emerges from them. But he derives relish from them and in consequence fancies himself for them. He makes the wholesome roots common to all beings and dedicates them to enlightenment, but always having some basis in view.—He develops emptiness, and he apprehends that everything from form to the enlightenment of a Buddha is empty, always basing himself on something. Those wholesome roots he makes common to all beings and dedicates them to the supreme enlightenment (P266), but by way of assuming a basis.—He confesses all the evil he has done, by way of assuming a basis, and rejoices at his own merit and that of others. For his own sake and that of others he entreats the Buddhas for instruction, but while basing himself on something. Without skill in means he dedicates the merit (from his confession, rejoicing, and entreaty) to all-knowledge, having first made it common to all beings. This is called the worldly perfection of wisdom.

I 10,8d. THE SUPRAMUNDANE PERFECTION OF WISDOM.

What, on the other hand, is the supramundane perfection of wisdom? Through his nonapprehension of self, beings, gift, or enlightenment, and through the threefold purity, he cleanses the perfection of giving for enlightenment. Through his nonapprenehsion of self, being, morality, or enlightenment he cleanses the perfection of morality for enlightenment; and likewise the perfection of patience by the nonapprehension of self, beings, enduring, and enlightenment; the perfection of vigour by the nonapprehension of self, physical and mental vigour, merit and cognition, and enlightenment; the perfection of concentration by the nonapprehension of self, beings, trances and concentrations and attainments, and enlightenment; the perfection of wisdom by the nonapprehension of self, beings, all-dharmas and enlightenment. He dedicates all wholesome roots to the supreme enlightenment, by means of a dedication which is undifferentiated, supreme, equal to the unequalled, unthinkable, incomparable, and measureless. This is called the supramundane perfection of wisdom.[11]

I 10,8e. CONCLUSION.

Śariputra : What is a Bodhisattva's path to enlightenment? (P267)

Subhuti : The four applications of mindfulness, and so on (all the 21 practices described in AAI9, 14).

**Śariputra*: Of which perfection is that the doing?

Subhuti: Of the perfection of wisdom. For the perfection of wisdom is the genetrix and recipient of all wholesome dharmas, be they the

[11]Here *P*, but not *S*, gives one more definition of "worldly" and "supramundane" which I have omitted because I do not understand it at all.

dharmas of Disciples, Pratyekabuddhas, Bodhisattvas or Buddhas.* After training in perfect wisdom the Tathagatas of the past have known full enlightenment. The Tathagatas of the future will know full enlightenment after training in perfect wisdom. And those Tathagatas who at present in the world in the ten directions stand, hold, and maintain themselves, and demonstrate Dharma, all these also have known full enlightenment after training in just this perfection of wisdom.* If, when this perfection of wisdom is being taught, a Bodhisattva is not perplexed or stupefied, then one should know that he dwells in this dwelling, and that he is not lacking in this attention, i.e. in the attention which does not abandon all beings in order to protect them, and in the attention of the great compassion.

Śariputra : So it is, as you say. Such a Bodhisattva dwells in this dwelling, and is not lacking in this attention.[12] This being so, Ven. Subhuti, all (P268) beings must already be Bodhisattvas. And why? Because all beings are not lacking in attention.

Subhuti : Well said, Sariputra. And yet I must reprove you, for the Ven. Sariputra has grasped the matter correctly only as far as the words are concerned. And why? One should understand that the nonbeingness of attention results from that of beings; that the emptiness of attention, its lack of ownbeing, and its isolatedness result from the emptiness of beings, their lack of own-being, their isolatedness; that acts of attention do not undergo the process which leads to enlightenment in the same way in which beings do not undergo that process. Similarly one should understand that the nonbeingness, emptiness, etc. of attention results from the nonbeingness, emptiness, etc. of form, etc. It is by this method that a Bodhisattva, a great being, should be known as not lacking in this dwelling and in this kind of attention, which is the attention of the great compassion.*[13]

The Lord: Well said, Subhuti, well said. The perfection of wisdom of the Bodhisattvas, the great beings, should be explained as you have, through the might of the Tathagata, expounded it! As you described it, so should a Bodhisattva, a great being course in the perfection of wisdom!

Epilogue.

When this chapter[14] of the Perfection of Wisdom had been taught by the Ven. Subhuti, the great trichiliocosm shook in six ways. And the Lord smiled on that occasion.

Subhuti: What, O Lord, is the cause, what the reason for the manifestation of a smile?

[12]*manasi-kāra*, see Introduction p. 29.

[13]So *S* xiii f. 144a *P* seems to be corrupt here.

[14]or "section", *parivarta*; also "revolution" of the wheel of Dharma. The meaning may be simply that of "exposition" (*nirdeśa*) as at *A* ii 44 according to *H*.

The Lord: Just as in this world system the Tathagata expounds the Perfection of Wisdom, so the Tathagatas in all the ten directions, in incalculable and immeasurable world systems, also teach the Perfection of Wisdom to the Bodhisattvas, the great beings. (P269) When the Ven. Subhuti expounded this Perfection of Wisdom, twelve myriads of gods and men acquired through wisdom the patient acceptance of dharmas which fail to be produced. And when the Buddhas and Lords in the world systems in the ten directions all round taught this Perfection of Wisdom to the Bodhisattvas, the great beings, the hearts of countless beings were raised to full enlightenment.

CHAPTER 22

THE FIRST ŚAKRA CHAPTER

II. THE KNOWLEDGE OF THE PATHS.

II 1. The Eclipsing, etc. The Limbs of the Knowledge of the Paths.

II 1,A. THE ECLIPSING OF THE GODS.

Thereupon all the great kings in this great trichiliocosm were, together with many thousands of gods, present in that assembly. And so was Śakra, Chief of Gods, and so were Yama gods, Tushita gods, Nirmanarati gods, Parinirmitavaśavartins, gods belonging to the retinue of Brahma, etc., *to*: the Mahabrahma gods, and the Parittabha gods in this great trichiliocosm, as well as the many Suddhavasakayika gods were present in that assembly. But the radiance from the bodies of all these gods, a reward for the deeds they had done in the past, did not approach the natural splendour of the Tathagata by one hundredth part, not one thousandth part, etc. *to*:[1] it did not bear number, nor fraction, nor counting, nor similarity, nor comparison, nor resemblance. Compared with the splendour of these gods, the splendour of the Tathagata must be declared to be the best, etc. *to*: supreme and surpassing. Just as compared with the golden Jambu river a reddish ploughed field does not gleam, does not shine, does not appear bright, just so compared with the Tathagata's natural splendour, the splendour of those gods, a reward for the deeds they had done in the past, did not gleam, did not shine, did not appear bright; but the Tathagata's splendour must be declared to be the best, etc.

II 1,1. FITNESS

Śakra : All these gods of this great trichiliocosm, Ven. Subhuti, have assembled here in order to hear from the Ven. Subhuti an explanation of Perfect Wisdom, because they want to hear his exposition of the perfection of wisdom. How, then, Ven. Subhuti, should a Bodhisattva, a great being, stand in the perfection of wisdom, and what is the perfection of wisdom of the Bodhisattva, the great being?

II 1,2. DEFINITION OF THE OBJECT.

Subhuti : Let me then, Kauśika, through the Buddha's might, through

[1]This refers to the more extensive version in 100,000 lines.

the Buddha's sustaining power, explain to you the perfection of wisdom of the Bodhisattvas, the great beings, and how a Bodhisattva, a great being, should stand in perfect wisdom. And those gods who have not yet raised their thought to the supreme enlightenment, they should do so now. But those again who have entered on the certainty of definite salvation (i.e. the Arhats who have reached their last birth and think that they have done with it all), they are unable to raise their thought to the supreme enlightenment. And why? The flood of birth-and-death hems them in.

II 1,3. PERVASION.

And yet I confirm them also, if they also will raise their thought to the supreme enlightenment.

II 1,4. OWN-BEING.

I shall not obstruct them when they adopt this wholesome idea.

II 1,5. ACTIVITY.

For among distinguished dharmas one should uphold the most distinguished ones.

II 2. The Knowledge of the Paths which Consists in the Cognition of the Path of the Disciples.

II 2,1. THE DEFINITION OF THE SIXTEEN ASPECTS BASED ON THE FOUR TRUTHS, AS A PART OF THE PATH OF THE DISCIPLES.

Therein, Kauśika, what is the perfect wisdom of a Bodhisattva, a great being? (II 2, 1A The aspects of the truth of ill.) Here the Bodhisattva, the great being, with his productions of thought associated with all-knowledge, attends to form, as (1) impermanent, (2) ill, (3) not-self, (4) quiet calm; (II 2,1B Aspects of the truth of origination), as (1) a disease, (2) a boil, (3) a thorn, (4) a misfortune; (II 2, 1C. Aspects of the truth of ill and origination, taken separately, so as to arouse aversion) as (1) foreign, (2) by its nature a disturbance; (II 2, 1D, as II 2, 1C, but so as to arouse dispassion) as (1) shaky and (2) brittle; (II 2, 1E, as II 2, 1C, but so as to arouse cessation) as (1) fearful, (2) troublesome, and (3) a calamity; and that without taking them as a basis. And so with feeling, etc. etc. As impermanent, etc. do come about the consciousness which is conditioned by the formative forces, the name-and-form which is conditioned by consciousness, etc. etc. It is thus that the origination of all this great mass of ill takes place, and he attends to that as impermanent ... a calamity, without however taking it as a basis. (II 2,1.F. Aspects of the truth of cessation.) With a production of thought associated with all-knowledge he attends to the stopping of the formative forces which results from the stopping of ignorance, and that as (1) the absence of quiet calm, (2) isolated, (3) empty, signless, wishless, and uneffected. Because of the stopping of the formative forces there is the stopping of consciousness, etc. etc. It is thus that the stopping of this whole mass of ill takes place, and he attends to that as absence of self . . . uneffected, but without taking it as a basis, and with his attentions associated with all-knowledge. (II 2,1G. Aspects of the truth of the Path. (1) the Path, (2) the correct method, (3) progressive activity, (4) that which allows to go forth to deliverance.) Moreover, Kauśika, the Bodhisattva, the great being, with a production of thought associated with all-knowledge develops the applications of mindfulness, but without taking them as a basis. And so on, etc., he develops the Buddhadharmas in the same way; and so likewise he courses in the six perfections. Moreover, Kauśika, the Bodhisattva, the great being who courses in perfect wisdom understands dharmas just with Dharma. When he thus by means of Dharma softens the dharmas, moistens them, perfects, and augments them, he contemplates: without a self are all these dharmas, devoid of a self or anything belonging to a self. And why? For what is, on the part of the Bodhisattva, the great being, the thought of a wholesome root that is not in touch with the thought of enlightenment. What is the thought of dedication that is not in touch with the thought of enlightenment or with the thought of the wholesome root; what is the thought of enlightenment that is not in touch with the thought of dedication. And why? That which is the thought of enlightenment that does not exist in the thought of dedication and cannot be apprehended in it; that which is the thought of dedication that does not exist in the thought of enlightenment and cannot be apprehended in it. This, Kauśika, is the perfection of wisdom of the Bodhisattva, the great being, that he thus contemplates all dharmas and yet he does not settle down in any dharma or apprehends one.

Śakra : How, Ven. Subhuti, is the thought of dedication not in touch with the thought of enlightenment? How is the thought of enlightenment not in touch with the thought of dedication? And how does in the thought of dedication the thought of enlightenment not exist, and cannot be apprehended in it? How does in the thought of enlightenment the thought of dedication not exist, and cannot be apprehended in it?

Subhuti : What is the thought of dedication (or, of turning over) that is no thought, what is the thought of enlightenment, that is no thought. For no-thoughtness is not turned over into no-thoughtness. Thus what is no-thought, that is unthinkable, and what is unthinkable, that is no-thought, and therefore no-thoughtness is not turned over into no-thoughtness. This is the perfection of wisdom of the Bodhisattva, the great being.

II 2,2. THE AIDS TO PENETRATION.

II 2,2,1. HEAT.

The Lord : Well said, Subhuti, well said by you, Subhuti, you who expound the perfection of wisdom to the Bodhisattvas, the great beings, and encourage them.

Subhuti : Grateful should I be, O Lord, not ungrateful. For the Lord, in the past, when he coursed in the course of a Bodhisattva, has in the presence of the Tathagatas of the past been instructed and admonished in the six perfections by the Disciples, they have been shown to him, he has been initiated into them, made to rejoice at them, has been encouraged by them, introduced to them, established in them; and in consequence the Lord has, after he had definitely become a Bodhisattva, trained in the six perfections and fully known the supreme enlightenment. Just so, O Lord, we also should instruct and admonish the Bodhisattvas, the great beings, in the six perfections, should show them to them, encourage and impell them, make them rejoice in them, introduce them to them and establish them in them. And by us also instructed and admonished, etc., the Bodhisattvas, the great beings, will fully know the supreme enlightenment.

Subhuti then said to Śakra: Therefore then, Kauśika, listen and attend well. I will teach you how a Bodhisattva should stand in perfect wisdom, i.e. how he should not stand in it. Form is empty of form; feeling, etc. The Bodhisattva is empty of the Bodhisattva. It is thus that the emptiness of form, and the emptiness of feelings-perception-impulses-and-consciousness, and the emptiness of the Bodhisattva are not two nor divided. It is thus that the Bodhisattva, the great being, should stand in perfect wisdom. Moreover, the eye is empty of the eye, the ear, etc. It is thus that the emptiness of the eye, etc. *to*: the emptiness of the Bodhisattva are not two nor divided. It is thus that the Bodhisattva, the great being should stand in perfect wisdom. And so for the physical elements, the 12 links, the 6 perfections, the 18 kinds of emptiness, the applications of mindfulness, etc. Moreover, concentration is empty of concentration, the dharani-doors are empty of the dharani-doors, the Bodhisattva is empty of the Bodhisattva. It is thus that . . . Moreover, the disciple vehicle is empty of the disciple vehicle, etc. etc.

II 2,2,2. SUMMITS.

Śakra : How then, Ven. Subhuti, should the Bodhisattva, the great being, stand in perfect wisdom?

Subhuti : Here the Bodhisattva should not stand in forms, in feeling, etc. by way of making nothing into a basis. He should not stand in the eye, in sight objects, in sight consciousness, in sight contact, nor in the feeling born from sight contact; and so for the ear, etc. *to*: the Buddha-dharmas. He should not stand in the fruit of a Streamwinner, etc. *to*: in Buddhahood, by way of making nothing into a basis.

II 2,2,3. PATIENCE.

He should not take his stand on the idea that 'form is permanent or impermanent', 'ease etc.' *to*: 'not isolated', 'form is empty or not empty'. So for feeling, etc. for everything up *to*: the knowledge of all modes. He should not take his stand on the notion that the fruit of a Streamwinner, etc. *to*: Buddhahood derives its dignity from the Unconditioned. He should not take his stand on the idea that the Streamwinner, etc. *to*: the Tathagata is worthy of gifts, by way of making nothing into a basis.

II 2,2,4. HIGHEST MUNDANE DHARMAS.

Moreover, the Bodhisattva, the great being, should not stand in the first, etc. *to*: the tenth stage, by way of making it into a basis. He also should not stand in the following ideas: 'having stood in the first thought of enlightenment I shall fulfill the six perfections, etc. *to*: the paths, and I shall enter on the certainty of a Bodhisattva'. 'I shall enter on the certainty of a Bodhisattva, and, having listened to the Buddhas and Lords, so as to see, praise, worship, and honour them and so as to hear the Dharma from them, I shall make progress in fathoming its Thusness and shall demonstrate the Dharma to others'. 'Whichever Buddha-fields of those Buddhas and Lords there may be, I shall perfect them'. 'I shall mature beings for the supreme enlightenment'. 'Having gone to innumerable and incalculable world systems, I shall honour and serve the Tathagatas there and shall worship them with flowers, incense, perfumes, garlands, etc.'. 'Countless beings I shall establish in the supreme enlightenment'. 'The five eyes I shall produce'. 'The fleshly eye, etc. *to*: the Buddha-eye I shall produce'. 'All concentrations I shall perfect'. 'I shall play with whichever concentration I may desire'. 'All dharani-doors I shall perfect'. 'The Unlimited, the trances, the formless attainments I shall accomplish'. 'The ten powers of a Tathagata I shall accomplish, etc. *to*: the 18 special dharmas of a Buddha, the great friendliness, the great compassion'. 'The thirty-two marks of a superman I shall accomplish in my body'. 'The eighty subsidiary marks I shall accomplish'. He should not stand in the idea of faith-follower, dharma-follower, the eighth-lowest saint, or that the streamwinner will be reborn seven times at the most, or of those who are reborn respectively in the families of gods or men, or of those who proceed with a single interval .... He should not stand in the ideas that 'the Streamwinner is no longer doomed to fall into the states of woe', 'as a Once-Returner I will, after I have once more come back into this world, make an end of ill', 'the Never-Returner has progressed to the realization of the fruit of a Never-Returner', 'the Arhat has progressed to the realization of the fruit of an Arhat'. He should not stand in the idea of a 'Pratyekabuddha'. He should not stand in the idea that 'as a Bodhisattva, having transcended the level of the Disciples and the level of the Pratyekabuddhas. I shall stand on the level of a Bodhisattva'. He should not stand in the cognition of the knowledge of the paths, by not making it into a basis. He should not stand in the idea that 'having fully known all dharmas in all their modes, having made an end of all defilements and the residues relating to them, I will, having as a Tathagata, etc. fully known the supreme enlightenment, turn the wheel of Dharma'. 'Having done a Buddha's work, I shall lead countless beings to Nirvana', also therein he should not stand. And also not in the idea that 'having stood in the four roads to psychic power and in the faculties, I shall enter on such a concentration that through it I shall abide for aeons countless as the sands of the Ganges'; 'an unlimited lifespan I shall have'; 'the 32 marks of a superman, each single mark . . .'; 'my single Buddhafield shall be as large as countless world systems, in all the ten directions, taken together'; 'for me the great trichiliocosm will become adamantine', 'from my Bodhi-tree will emanate an odour so powerful (?) that no one will have any more greed, hate, or delusion, and that no one will have a Disciple-thought or a Pratyekabuddha-thought, but all these beings shall be fixed on the supreme enlightenment; and these beings who will smell this odour, they will have no illness whatever'; 'in that Buddhafield even the word 'form' will be unknown, or the words 'feeling', 'perception', 'impulse' or 'consciousness', or the words 'perfection of giving', etc. *to*: 'applications of mindfulness', etc. It is thus, Kauśika, that the Bodhisattva, the great being, should not stand in the perfection of wisdom, by making it into a basis.

Thereupon the Ven. *Śariputra* thought to himself: How then should the Bodhisattva, the great being, stand in perfect wisdom?

Subhuti read his thoughts and said : What do you think, Śariputra, where did the Tathagata stand?

Śariputra : Nowhere did the Tathagata stand, for the mind of the Tathagata, etc., sought no support. He stood neither in the conditioned element, nor in the unconditioned element; and likewise not in the skandhas, etc. *to*: all dharani-doors, not in the Buddhadharmas, and not in all-knowledge.

Subhuti : It is thus that the Bodhisattva, the great being, should stand in perfect wisdom. 'As the Tathagata has not stood in forms, feelings, etc., nor not stood, just so will I stand', so should the Bodhisattva, the great being, stand in the perfection of wisdom by way of not taking his stand anywhere.

II 3. The Knowledge of the Paths which Consists in the Cognition of the Path of the Pratyekabuddhas.

II 3,A. No need to be instructed by others.

Thereupon the thought came to some of the *gods* in that assembly: What the fairies talk and murmur, that we understand though mumbled. What Subhuti has just taught, uttered, demonstrated, expounded about the perfection of wisdom, that we do not understand.

Subhuti : You do not understand, sons of gods, what has been said?

Gods : We do not understand, Ven. Subhuti!

Subhuti: For there, O gods, not even a single letter has been uttered therein. What has not been uttered, that cannot be heard. What has not been heard that cannot be understood. And why? For not in the letters is the perfection of wisdom, and therefore it is not something that can be cognized or heard or demonstrated. Not in the letters is the enlightenment of the Tathagatas, etc. Just as a man who is asleep and has dreams would see the Tathagata, etc. demonstrate Dharma,—what do you think, O gods, would now therein anything be demonstrated, or heard, or understood?

Gods: No, Rev. Subhuti.

Subhuti: Just so, O gods, all dharmas are like a dream, and therein nothing is heard by anyone, or demonstrated, or understood. Just, O gods, as if there were two men who stood in a valley between mountains, and who would shout words in praise of the Buddha, or the Dharma, or the Samgha, if from that there would issue the sound of an echo, what do you think, sons of gods, would now through that echo a second echo-sound be instructed?

Gods: No, Rev. Subhuti.

Subhuti: Just so, O gods, all dharmas are like an echo; therein nothing is seen, or heard, or discerned. Just as clever magician or magician's apprentice would at the crossroads conjure up the Tathagata, and also the four assemblies, and (that Tathagata) would teach the four conjured-up assemblies Dharma, what do you think, O gods, would now thereby be anything be taught, or heard, or discerned?

Gods: No, Rev. Subhuti.

Subhuti: Just so, O gods, all dharmas are like a magical illusion, and nothing is therein demonstrated or discerned.

II 3,B. The depth of cognition.

Thereupon those *gods* thought to themselves: May the holy Subhuti enlarge on the perfection of wisdom! For what he demonstrates that is deeper than the deep, subtler than the subtle.

II 3,1. THE THREEFOLD DISTINCTIVENESS.

II 3,1,1. THE FORSAKING OF THE DISCRIMINATION OF THE OBJECT BY THE PRATYEKABUDDHAS.

Subhuti : For form is neither deep nor subtle; nor is feeling, etc. And why? For the own-being of form is neither deep nor subtle; and so on, up *to* : the knowledge of all modes.

Thereupon those *gods* thought to themselves: Certainly, in this demonstration of dharma, no form is conceived . . . no perfect wisdom, no dharma which acts as wing to enlightenment, etc. *to*: no Buddha-dharmas, no fruit of a Streamwinner, etc. *to*: no enlightenment, and also no letters.

Subhuti: Just so it is, O gods, just so it is. The enlightenment of the Tathagatas cannot be talked about, it is incommunicable. Nothing is thereby demonstrated by anyone, nor heard, nor discerned. Therefore, those who want to stand in the fruit of a Streamwinner, and to realize it, they cannot do so without having resorted to this patience; and so up to Pratyekabuddhahood. It is thus, O gods, that the Bodhisattva, the great being should, beginning with the first thought of enlightenment, stand in the perfection of wisdom without uttering or hearing anything.

CHAPTER 23

HARD TO FATHOM

II 3,1,2. THE NONFORSAKING OF THE DISCRIMINATION OF THE SUBJECT ON THE PART OF THE PRATYEKABUDDHAS.

Thereupon those *gods* thought to themselves: What should one wish those to be like who are worthy to listen to the doctrine from Subhuti the Elder?

Subhuti : Those who learn the doctrine from me one should wish to be like a magical illusion, to be like a magical creation. In consequence they hear just nothing, study nothing, realize nothing.

Gods : Are then these beings like an illusion, are then these dharma-hearers like an illusion? Are these beings like a magical creation, are these dharma-hearers like a magical creation?

Subhuti: So it is, O gods, so it is. Like an illusion are those beings. like an illusion are those dharma-hearers; like a magical creation, etc. Form also is like a dream, like an illusion; feeling etc. *to* : also the Buddha-dharmas, also the fruit of a Streamwinner, etc. *to*: also the Buddha-dharmas, also the fruit of a Streamwinner, etc. *to*: also the Pratyeka-buddha-enlightenment.

Gods: Buddhahood also, you say, Ven. Subhuti, is like a dream, like an illusion. What do you think, is also Nirvana like a dream, like an illusion?

Subhuti : Even Nirvana, I say, is like a dream, like an illusion. If I could cognize any dharma more distinguished than Nirvana, of that also I should say that it is like a dream, like an illusion. And why? Because dream and illusion, on the one side, and Nirvana on the other, are not two nor divided.

II 3,1,3. ITS FOUNDATION (SOURCE).

Thereupon the Ven. Śariputra, the Ven. Mahamaudgalyayana, the Ven. Mahakoshthila, the Ven. Mahakatyayana, the Ven. Purna, son of Maitrayani, the Ven. Mahakasyapa, the many thousands of niyutas of kotis of devas spoke thus to the Ven. Subhuti the Elder: Who will be those who can grasp this perfection of wisdom when it is being explained, since it is so deep, so incomprehensible, so engaged in incomprehensibilities, so subtle, so delicate, so hard to see, so hard to understand, so calm, so sublime, so truly noble, so much something that can be known only by the wise and the discerning?

Thereupon the Ven. *Ānanda* (?) said to those great disciples and to those deities: Irreversible Bodhisattvas, great beings, can grasp it, or persons who have reached sound views, or Arhats in whom the outflows have dried up, who have fulfilled their intentions, who have performed their duties under the Jinas of the past, who have planted wholesome roots under many kotis of Buddhas, or sons and daughters of good family who have been taken hold of by a good friend. But they again will not discriminate that 'form is empty', or that 'emptiness is form'; feeling, etc.; signless, etc.; wishless, etc.; unproduced or unstopped, calm, isolated. And so for the skandhas, etc. to the knowledge of all modes; the conditioned element, the unconditioned element.

Subhuti : There is no one who can grasp this perfection of wisdom, since it is so deep, so incomprehensible, so much something that can be known only by the wise and the discerning. And why? For therein no dharma whatsoever is being taught, indicated, or lit up. Wherein, however, no dharma whatsoever is taught, indicated or lit up, therein no one will be able to grasp anything.

Śariputra : By you, Ven. Subhuti, have in this perfection of wisdom (no?) three vehicles been explained in detail, i.e. no vehicle of the Disciples, no vehicle of the Pratyekabuddhas, no vehicle of the fully enlightened Buddhas. [The assistance of the Bodhisattvas, the great beings, is explained, and the paths of the Bodhisattvas, beginning with the first thought of enlightenment and ending with the tenth thought;] i.e. the perfection of giving, etc. *to*: the applications of mindfulness, etc. *to*: all dharani-doors are explained as the assistance of all the Bodhisattvas, the great beings. It is thus that the Bodhisattva who courses in perfect wisdom is reborn apparitionally; thus, unfailing in his superknowledges, he will pass on from Buddha-field to Buddha-field. And those wholesome roots, by which (?) he will honour etc. the Buddhas, the Lords, they will wax strong in him. And the dharmas which they will hear from those Buddhas and Lords, they will not forget them ever again until they win full enlightenment. And he will be always concentrated, and his thought free from distraction. His inspiration will be unshackled, uninterrupted, concentrated, not joined (?), quite certain, more distinguished and exalted than anything in all the world.

Subhuti : So it is, Ven. Śariputra, so it is. Just so, as you say, in detail are explained in this perfection of wisdom the three vehicles, i.e. the vehicle of the Disciples, the vehicle of the Pratyekabuddhas, the great vehicle; and the assistance of the Bodhisattvas, the great beings, is explained, etc. to the fact that they will have an inspiration which is more distinguished and exalted than anything else in all the world; and that in the sense that nothing is made into a basis. And what should not be made into a basis? A self, a being, etc. *to*: one who sees, form, etc. *to*: all-knowledge.

Śariputra : For what reason are in this perfection of wisdom the three vehicles, and the other topics, explained in detail, in the sense that nothing is made into a basis?

Subhuti : On account of inward emptiness, and the other kinds of emptiness.

CHAPTER 24

INFINITE

Thereupon the thought came to Śakra and to the other *gods* in this great trichiliocosm, up to the Akanishtha gods: Let us then, since Subhuti the Elder preaches this view of Dharma, conjure up flowers and scatter them over the Buddha, the Lord, the congregation of monks and Bodhisattvas, and the perfection of wisdom! Thereupon Śakra and the other gods in this great trichiliocosm conjured up heavenly Mandarava flowers, and scattered them over the Buddha, the Lord, the congregation of monks, Subhuti the Elder, and this perfection of wisdom. And the entire great trichiliocosm was covered with flowers, and high up in the sky a pointed tower was formed, made of flowers, enjoyable, and pleasing.

Thereupon *Subhuti* the Elder thought to himself: Those flowers which now proceed from all the abodes of the gods, I have not seen them before. These flowers which the gods have scattered are magical creations, and have not issued from trees, shrubs, or creepers; these flowers are mind-made, and have not issued from trees, shrubs, or creepers.

Śakra : These flowers, Rev. Subhuti, did not issue forth at all. These flowers have not issued from the mind, and they have also not issued from trees, shrubs, or creepers.

Subhuti : Just as you have said. But then, Kauśika' if they have not issued forth at all, then they are not flowers.

Śakra : Have then only those flowers not issued forth at all, or also form, feeling, etc.?

Subhuti : Not only have these flowers not issued forth. Form also has not issued forth, and that which has not issued forth, that is not form. And so for everything up to the fully enlightened Buddha.

II 3,2. THE AIDS TO PENETRATION ON THE PATH OF THE PRATYEKABUDDHAS.

II 3,2,1. HEAT.

Śakra : Deeply wise, surely, is the holy Subhuti the Elder, in that he does not obstruct the concept, and yet points out the true nature of Dharma.

The Lord : So it is, Śakra, as you say.

Śakra : How then does Subhuti the Elder not obstruct the concept and yet point out the true nature of Dharma?

The Lord : Form, etc., is a mere concept, and what is mere concept that is the true nature of Dharma; that Subhuti the Elder does not obstruct, but he points it out. And why? What is the true nature of Dharma, that cannot be obstructed, and Subhuti the Elder points it out and does not obstruct it.

Subhuti : So it is, Kauśika, so it is. As by the Lord all dharmas have been pointed out as mere concepts, just so should the Bodhisattva, the great being, having known all dharmas as mere concepts, train in perfect wisdom. And why? Because there he does not review the form in which he trains. When he trains thus, the Bodhisattva, the great being, trains in the perfection of giving. And why? Because he does not review the perfection of giving in which he trains. And so for everything else up to all-knowledge.

Śakra : For what reason does a Bodhisattva not review that form, etc. to all-knowledge, in which he trains?

Subhuti : Because there form, etc., is empty of form, etc. And why? Because form-emptiness does not review form, etc., as emptiness. He who trains in this emptiness, he trains in the emptiness of form, etc. *to* : in the immeasurable and incalculable Buddhadharmas, etc. *to* : in the knowledge of all modes, without making any divisions.

II 3,2,2. SUMMITS.

He does not train for the increase of form, etc., nor for its decrease. And who does not train for the increase or decrease of form, etc. he does not train for the appropriation or vanishing of form, etc.

II 3,2,3. STEADFAST PATIENCE.

Śariputra : For what reason does the Bodhisattva not train for the appropriation or vanishing of form, etc.?

Subhuti : Because there is no appropriation of form, etc. And why? Because form, etc. cannot appropriate form, etc. It is thus, Ven. Śariputra, that the Bodhisattva, the great being, trains in all-knowledge for the sake of the nonappropriation of all dharmas, and goes forth to all-knowledge by way of the nonappropriation of all dharmas.

II 3,2,4. HIGHEST MUNDANE DHARMAS.

Śariputra : When he thus trains, how will the Bodhisattva, the great being, when he has trained for the nonappropriation and nonvanishing of all dharmas, go forth to all-knowledge?

Subhuti : Because there the Bodhisattva, the great being, when he courses in perfect wisdom, does not see of form, etc., the production or stopping, nor the taking hold of or letting go, nor the defilement or purification, nor the heaping up or taking away, nor the decrease or increase. And why? Because form, etc. does through its own-being not exist. It is thus that the Bodhisattva, the great being, trains for the sake of the nonproduction, nonstopping, nonappropriation, nonletting-go, nondefilement, nonpurification, nonaccumulation, nontaking-away, nondecrease and nonincrease of all dharmas. When he trains in perfect wisdom, he will go forth to all-knowledge, by way of nontraining, by way of nongoing-forth.

II 4. The Path of Vision and the Great Advantage.[1]

II 4,1. THE GREAT ADVANTAGE, AND, WITH REFERENCE TO THE PATH OF VISION, ACCEPTANCE OF COGNITION OF DHARMA IN SUFFERING.

Śakra : Where, Rev. Śariputra, should one search for perfect wisdom?

Śariputra : The perfection of wisdom should be sought in the exposition of the Ven. Subhuti.

Śakra : Is it, holy Subhuti, through your own might and authority that the holy Śariputra can say that the perfection of wisdom should be sought in the exposition of the Ven. Subhuti?

Subhuti : This might is not mine, Kauśika, this authority is not mine.

Śakra : Whose then is this might, whose is this authority?

Subhuti : It is the Tathagata's might, it is the Tathagata's authority (adhiṣṭhāna). For the Tathagata cannot be apprehended except through the fact that in his true nature he has no fixed residence (niradhiṣṭhāna; or, is without a solid basis), he cannot be apprehended except through Suchness. Without a fixed residence, Chief of Gods, are all dharmas.

Śakra : How, holy Subhuti, when all dharmas are without a fixed residence, do you say that this is the Tathagata's might, his sustaining power (authority)?

Subhuti : So it is. Except through the fact that in his true nature he has no fixed residence; except through his Suchness the Tathagata cannot be apprehended. And yet, the Tathagata is not apprehended in the fact that in his true nature he has no fixed residence, nor can the fact that in his true nature he has no fixed residence be apprehended in the Tathagata, nor can the Suchness be apprehended in him. The Tathagata cannot be apprehended in the Suchness of form, etc. nor can the Suchness of form, etc. be apprehended in the Tathagata; the Tathagata cannot be apprehended in the true nature of form, etc., nor can the true nature of form, etc. be apprehended in the Tathagata. And why? What is the Tathagata, that is not conjoined with the Suchness of form, etc. nor disjoined from it; that is not conjoined with the true nature of form, etc. nor disjoined from it. Nor is it conjoined with anything other than the Suchness of form, etc. or the true nature of form, etc. or disjoined from it.

[1]Here begins the Bodhisattva path.

He who is not conjoined with all these dharmas, or disjoined from them, it is his might, it is his sustaining power, by way of there being no sustaining power. And when, again, Kauśika, you ask, 'where should a Bodhisattva, a great being, search for perfect wisdom?', he should not search for it in form, etc. nor in that which is other than form, etc. And why? Because the perfection of wisdom, and form, and the other skandhas, all these dharmas are not conjoined or disjoined, immaterial, invisible, nonresisting, with one mark only, i.e. no mark. Moreover, the Bodhisattva should not search for perfect wisdom through the knowledge of all modes, nor outside the knowledge of all modes. And why? Because the perfection of wisdom, the knowledge of all modes, and the searching, all these dharmas are not conjoined nor disjoined, invisible, nonresisting, with one mark only, i.e. no mark. And why? Because there form, etc. is not the perfection of wisdom, nor is the perfection of wisdom other than form, etc.; and so for the true nature of form, etc. *to* : the knowledge of all modes, and the Suchness of form, etc. *to* : the knowledge of all modes. And why? Because there all these dharmas do not exist, and cannot be apprehended. Since thus all dharmas do not exist, and cannot be apprehended, therefore the perfection of wisdom is not form, etc. nor outside form, etc.; not the true nature, or Suchness of form, etc. nor outside the true nature and Suchness of form, etc.

II 4,2. Cognition of dharma in suffering.

Śakra : This is, Rev. Subhuti, a great perfection of the Bodhisattvas, the great beings, i.e. the perfection of wisdom, an immeasurable perfection, an unlimited perfection, an infinite perfection. Those who train in it attain the fruits of the holy life, i.e. the streamwinners attain the fruit of a Streamwinner, etc. *to*: the Bodhisattvas, the great beings reach the knowledge of all modes, and they have known, they know, and they will know full enlightenment.

Subhuti : So it is, Kauśika. And why? Through the greatness of form, etc. is this a great perfection of the Bodhisattvas, the great beings. And why? Because of form, etc. no beginning can be apprehended, no end, and no middle. In this way is this a great perfection of the Bodhisattvas, the great beings.

II 4,3. Acceptance of subsequent cognition of dharma in suffering.

Through the immeasurableness of form, etc. is this an immeasurable perfection of the Bodhisattvas, the great beings. And why? Because of form, etc. no measure can be apprehended. Just as no measure can be apprehended of space, so also of form, etc. Through the measurelessness of space is the measurelessness of form, etc. and through the measurelessness of form, etc. is the measurelessness of the perfection of wisdom.

In this way is this an immeasurable perfection of the Bodhisattvas, the great beings.

II 4,4. Subsequent cognition of suffering.

Through the unlimitedness of form, etc. is this an unlimited perfection of the Bodhisattvas, the great beings. Just as no limit can be apprehended of space, so also of form, etc. Through the unlimitedness of space is the unlimitedness of form, etc. and through the unlimitedness of form, etc. is the unlimitedness of the perfection of wisdom.

II 4,5. Acceptance of cognition of dharma in origination.

a. The Negation of Cause : Through the infinitude of form, etc. is this an infinite perfection of the Bodhisattvas, the great beings. Just as no end can be apprehended of space, so also of form, etc. Through the infinitude of space is the infinitude of form, etc. and through the infinitude of form, etc. is the infinitude of the perfection of wisdom. In this way is this an infinite perception of the Bodhisattvas, the great beings, on account of the infinitude of form, etc. to the knowledge of all modes. *b. The Negation of Origination* : Moreover, Kauśika, because of the infinitude of its objective support is this an infinite perception of the Bodhisattvas, the great beings, i.e. the perfection of wisdom.

Śakra : How is that so?

Subhuti: Because of the infinitude of the objective support of the knowledge of all modes is this an infinite perfection of the Bodhisattvas, the great beings, i.e. the perfection of wisdom. *c. The Negation of the Product* : Moreover, Kauśika, because of the infinitude of the Dharma-element as an objective support is this an infinite perfection of the Bodhisattvas, the great beings, i.e. the perfection of wisdom.

Śakra : How is that?

Subhuti : Because the Dharma-element is an infinite objective support. *d. The Negation of Condition* : Moreover, Kauśika, because of the infinitude of Suchness as an objective support is this an infinite perfection of the Bodhisattvas, the great beings, i.e. the perfection of wisdom.

Śakra : How is that?

Subhuti : Because of the infinitude of Suchness is there an infinitude of it as an objective support. It is thus that this is through the infinitude of Suchness as an objective support an infinite perfection of the Bodhisattvas, the great beings, i.e. the perfection of wisdom.[2]

Moreover, Kauśika, because of the infinitude of beings is this an infinite perfection.

Śakra : How is that?

Subhuti : What do you think, Kauśika, what factual entity (dharma) does the word 'being' denote?

Śakra : This word does not denote any factual entity; this word 'being' has been added on as something adventitious, groundless, unfounded on objective fact.

Subhuti : What do you think, Kauśika, has in this perfection of wisdom any being been shown up?

Sakra : No, Ven. Subhuti.

Subhuti : When no being at all has been shown up, there cannot be an infinite number of beings. If the Tathagata, abiding for aeons countless as the sands of the Ganges, would pronounce the word 'being, being', would thereby any being whatsoever be either produced or stopped?

Śakra : No, holy Subhuti. And why? Because a being is perfectly pure from the very start.

Subhuti : In this way should the infinitude of perfect wisdom be known from the infinitude of beings.

CHAPTER 25

THE SECOND ŚAKRA-CHAPTER

Thereupon the *gods* around Indra, Brahma, and Prajapati, and the hosts of men and women around the Rishis shouted forth in triumph: Hail the Dharma! Hail the Dharma! Hail the Dharmahood of Dharma! Beautifully has Subhuti the Elder, through the Tathagata's sustaining power, demonstrated, indicated, clarified, and revealed this. As potential Tathagatas we shall henceforth bear in mind those Bodhisattvas, great beings, who shall not be lacking in this perfection of wisdom. And yet, no dharma at all can be apprehended, no form, etc. *to* knowledge of all modes, how much less can one conceive of a definite distinction between the three vehicles, i.e. the Disciple-vehicle, the Pratyekabuddha-vehicle and the great vehicle.

The Lord : So it is, O Gods, so it is! As you have said. No dharma can be apprehended, and no definite distinction between the three vehicles can be conceived. As a Thathagata should the Bodhisattva, the great being, be borne in mind who will not be lacking in this perfection of wisdom, and does not treat it as a basis. And why? Because in this perfection of wisdom the three vehicles are explained in detail, i.e. the Disciple-vehicle, the Pratyekabuddha-vehicle, and the great vehicle. And yet, the Tathagata cannot be apprehended apart from the six perfections, or the 20 kinds of emptiness or the knowledge of all modes. The Bodhisattvas, the great beings, train in all dharmas, in the perfection of giving, etc. *to*: the knowledge of all modes. And why? That Bodhisattva should be called just a Tathagata, if he courses as one not lacking in the perfection of wisdom. When I, O gods, in the presence of Dipankara, the Tathagata, etc., in the bazaar of Dipavati, the royal city, was not lacking in the perfection of giving, etc., in the applications of mindfulness, etc. *to*: the dharmas of a Buddha, and that without treating them as a basis, then I had this prediction from the Tathagata, etc. : 'You shall, in a future period, in just this great world-system, after incalculable aeons, become a Tathagata, etc. Śakyamuni by name—endowed with knowledge and virtue, Well-Gone, a Worldknower, unsurpassed, a leader of men to be tamed, a teacher of gods and men, a Buddha, a Blessed Lord'.

II 4,7. ACCEPTANCE OF SUBSEQUENT COGNITION OF DHARMA IN ORIGINATION.

The Gods: It is wonderful, O Lord, how much this perfection of wisdom promotes the knowledge of all modes in the Bodhisattvas, the great beings, by way of the nonappropriation and the not-letting-go of form, etc.

Thereupon *the Lord* saw that the four assemblies—the monks, nuns, laymen and laywomen—were assembled and seated, and so were the Bodhisattvas, the great beings, and the four great kings, the deities who belong to the Four Great Kings, and all the others, up to the Akanishtha gods, and that they all were present as attentive eye-witnesses, and he spoke thus to Śakra, Chief of Gods: Those Bodhisattvas, great beings, and those monks, nuns, laymen and laywomen, or those sons and daughters of good family, or those male and female deities who will take up this perfection of wisdom, bear it in mind, preach, study and develop it, explain it to others in detail and wisely attend to it, and also those who will not be lacking in the thought of the knowledge of all modes, Mara and his hosts will be unable to gain entry to them (so as to harm them). And why? Because these sons and daughters of good family will be well sustained by just the emptiness of form, by the emptiness of feelings, perceptions, impulses, and consciousness. And why? Because emptiness cannot gain entry into emptiness, nor the signless into the signless, nor the wishless into the wishless. In this way, to put it briefly, he is well sustained by the emptiness of the skandhas, elements, sense fields, conditioned coproduction, by the emptiness of the perfections, truths, superknowledges, Unlimited, trances and formless attainments, by the emptiness of all emptinesses, all samadhis, all dharani-doors, the pillars of mindfulness, right efforts, roads to psychic power, dominants, powers, limbs of enlightenment, and paths, by the emptiness of the ten powers ... the special Buddhadharmas, and finally by the emptiness of the knowledge of all modes. And why? Because emptiness cannot gain entry into emptiness, nor the signless into the signless, nor the wishless into the wishless. And why? Because there does not exist their own-being, by which they could gain entry, or of which they could gain entry.

II 4,8. SUBSEQUENT COGNITION IN ORIGINATION.

It is therefore certain that neither men nor ghosts can gain entry to those sons and daughters of good family. For these sons and daughters of good family have developed friendliness, compassion, sympathetic joy, and impartiality towards all beings, and that without taking them as a basic fact. And those sons and daughters of good family will also not die an untimely death. And why? Because those sons and daughters of good family have, coursing in the perfection of giving, presented all beings with all the correct serviceable things.

And those deities in this great trichiliocosm, from those who belong to the Four Great Kings, up to the Akaniṣṭha gods, who have raised their thought to full enlightenment, but have not heard this perfection of wisdom, have not taken it up, not borne it in mind, not preached and studied it, those deities should listen to this perfection of wisdom, take it up, bear it in mind, preach and study it, and wisely attend to it, undeprived of the thought of all-knowledge.

II 4,9. ACCEPTANCE OF COGNITION OF DHARMA IN STOPPING.

Moreover, Kauśika, those sons and daughters of good family, who will take up this perfection of wisdom, who bear it in mind . . . and who are undeprived of the thought of the knowledge of all modes, they will certainly have no fear and they will not be stiff with fright—whether they have gone to an empty place, or an open space, or are on a highway. And why? Because they have well developed the emptiness of the subject, without taking it as a basis . . . the emptiness of the non-existence of own-being, without taking it as a basis. Thereupon all the *gods* in this great trichiliocosm said to the Lord: We shall always arrange for the shelter, defense, and protection of those sons and daughters of good family who will take up this perfection of wisdom, etc. and will not be lacking in the dwelling in all-knowledge. And why? Because it is thanks to the Bodhisattva that the hells are cut off, the animal births, the world of Yama, the worlds of the Asuras, and among men poverty, calamities, and misfortunes are cut off.

Thanks to the Bodhisattva there is in the world a manifestation of the ten wholesome karma paths. And so of the four trances . . . Buddhadharmas; of wealthy warrior families, wealthy Brahmin families, the families of wealthy householders; of universal monarchs. In that way, thanks to the Bodhisattva, the gods are conceived; the fruit of a Streamwinner etc.; the maturing of beings; the purification of Buddha-fields; the Tathagatas are conceived in the world, those who turn the wheel of Dharma; the jewel of Buddha, Dharma, and Samgha. It is in this way, O Lord, that I will constantly arrange for the defense of the Bodhisattva, the great being, by the world with its gods, men and Asuras.

The Lord: So it is, Kauśika, so it is, as you say. Thanks to the Bodhisattva, the great being, are all the hells cut off, the animal births, and the world of Yama; etc. *to*: thanks to him there is a manifestation of the Buddha-jewel, the Dharma-jewel, the Samgha-jewel. Therefore then, Kauśika, should the Bodhisattvas, the great beings, be constantly honoured, revered, and worshipped by the world with its gods, men and Asuras, and constantly should their defense and protection be arranged. He would think that I should be revered, honoured, and worshipped, who would think that the Bodhisattva, the great being, should be honoured, revered, and worshipped. Therefore then, Kauśika, should, by the world with its gods, men and Asuras, defense and protection constantly be arranged for the Bodhisattva, the great being.

If, Kauśika, this great trichiliocosm were full of Disciples and Pratyekabuddhas—like a thicket of reeds, sugar cane, rice, or seasamum plants,—and if some son or daughter of good family would, all their lives, honour, revere, and worship them, with all kinds of services,—and if another one would honour, revere, and worship one single Bodhisattva, who had produced the first thought of enlightenment and who were not lacking in the six perfection—then the latter would beget the greater merit. And why? Because it is not thanks to the Disciples and Pratyekabuddhas that Bodhisattvas, great beings, and that Tathagatas are manifested in the world. But it is thanks to the Bodhisattva, the great being, that all Disciples and Pratyekabuddhas are manifested in the world; and so the Tathagatas. Therefore then, Kauśika, the Bodhisattvas, the great beings, should constantly be honoured, revered, and worshipped by the world with its gods, men and Asuras, and defense and protection should always be arranged for them.

Chapter 26

GAINS

II 4,10. Cognition of dharma in stopping.

Śakra: It is wonderful, O Lord, to what an extent the Bodhisattvas, the great beings, who take up this perfection of wisdom, and bear it in mind, acquire good qualities, mature beings, purify the Buddha-field, and pass on from Buddha-field to Buddha-field. When they honour the Buddhas, the Lords, the wholesome roots by which they desire to honour, revere, and worship the Buddhas, the Lords, these wholesome roots flourish. And the Ḍharma which they hear from the Buddhas, the Lords, that they never again forget, until they have known full enlightenment. And they gain the accomplishment of wholesomeness, and that of the retinue, the marks, the halo, the eye, the voice, the concentration, the dharanis. Having through skill in means conjured up for themselves a Buddha-frame, they pass on from Buddha-field to Buddha-field. Where there is no production or manifestation of the Buddhas, the Lords, there they preach in praise of the perfection of giving ... perfection of wisdom; of the 18 kinds of emptiness; of the 4 trances ... the 18 special Buddha-dharmas. And through skill in means they demonstrate Dharma to beings. They discipline beings in the three vehicles, the Disciple-vehicle, the Pratyekabuddha-vehicle, the Buddha-vehicle.

II 4,11. Acceptance of subsequent cognition in stopping.

Thereupon, again, *Śakra* said to the Lord: It is wonderful how, where this deep perfection of wisdom is taken up (gained), all the six perfections have been gained; so with: the pillars of mindfulness ... the 18 special Buddhadharmas, the fruit of a Streamwinner ... Arhatship ... the knowledge of all modes.

The Lord: So it is, Kauśika, so it is. Where the perfection of wisdom has been gained, there all the six perfections are gained; etc. *to*: the knowledge of all modes.

And again, Kauśika, as to the qualities which a son or daughter of good family acquire in this very life, when they take up the perfection of wisdom, bear it in mind, preach, study, and copy it, and wisely attend to it—listen well to them, with well-placed attention, I will teach them to you.

So be it, Lord, replied *Śakra,* Chief of Gods, to the Lord.

The Lord: If any son or daughter of good family who is not a Buddhist, if Mara, or the deities of Mara's host, if a conceited person wants to dissuade the Bodhisattva, the great being, from this perfection of wisdom, wants to contend against it, to quarrel with it, to contradict it, their quarrels, contentions and contradictions that may have been produced, will quickly simply vanish again. Their intentions will not be fulfilled. And why? For there the Bodhisattva, the great being, has coursed for a long time in the perfection of giving ... perfection of wisdom; having forsaken in every way all the inner and outer dharmas through which beings for a long time undertake quarrels, contentions and disputes, (he has established those beings in the perfection of giving); having forsaken the inner and outer dharmas through which beings for a long time undertake immorality, the Bodhisattva, the great being, establishes those beings in morality; having forsaken those inner and outer dharmas through which beings for a long time are driven to wrath, ill will and doing harm, the Bodhisattva establishes those beings in patience; ... sloth ... the perfection of vigour; ... distracted thought ... trance; ... stupidity ... in the great wisdom; that through which beings for a long time wander about in Samsara, i.e. the obsession with affection and aversion, from that the Bodhisattva, the great being, leads those beings away through his skill in means, and he establishes those beings in the four trances, the four Unlimited ... in Arhatship, Pratyekabuddha-enlightenment, the utmost right and perfect enlightenment. These, Kauśika, will be in this very life the qualities and advantages of a Bodhisattva, a great being, who goes on the pilgrimage of a Bodhisattva. And in a future life he will further awake to full enlightenment, and, having turned the wheel of Dharma, and having established beings in accordance with his (initial) vow, he will lead them into the element of Nirvana which leaves nothing behind. These will be in a future life the qualities and advantages of a Bodhisattva, a great being.

II 4,12. Subsequent cognition of stopping.

Moreover, Kauśika, the spot of earth in which the sons and daughters of good family take up this perfection of wisdom, bear it in mind, preach and study it, and wisely attend to it, in that spot of earth the Maras or the divinities of Mara's host, or the wanderers of other sects, or conceited persons cannot cause any disturbance of thought. When there is a quarrel, contention, or contradiction of this perfection of wisdom, ... they will further have other qualities and advantages, i.e. by means of listening to this perfection of wisdom they will, after they have gradually gone forth by means of the three vehicles, make an end of ill.

There is, Kauśika, a herb, Maghi by name. Suppose a viper, famished, desirous of food, searching for food, were to see a creature. Wanting to eat that creature, it would pursue it. But if that creature went to a patch of that herb, then the viper would be turned back by the smell of that herb. And why? Because that herb has such a healing quality that it overpowers that viper's poison. So powerful, Kauśika, is that herb. Just so with any son or daughter of good family who will take up this perfection of wisdom. Those quarrels, contentions, and contradictions which may have arisen, they will, through the piercing flame of the perfection of wisdom, and through its power, quickly be destroyed and appeased. Wherever they will arise, they will quickly vanish again, they will not grow, but will be appeased.

II 4,13. Acceptance of cognition of dharma in the path.

And why? Because the perfection of wisdom appeases all dharmas, and does not increase them. Which dharmas? i.e. greed, hate, delusion, ignorance, the karma formations ... the whole mass of ill; the hindrances, latent biases, the obsessions; the view of a self, the view of a being ...; immorality ...; the notion of permanence ...; the seizing on the perfection of giving ... the seizing on Nirvana.

II 4,14. Cognition of dharma in the path.

And the great kings in this great trichiliocosm, the world guardians, Śakra, Chief of Gods, ... Sahapati up to the Akanishtha gods, they will always arrange for the shelter, defense, and protection of that Bodhisattva, that great being, who will take up, etc. this perfection of wisdom. And so will the Buddhas and Lords who stand, hold, and maintain themselves in the ten directions. And these sons and daughters of good family will not diminish in wholesome dharmas, and they will grow in them, i.e. the six perfections, and that without taking them as a basis; in the emptinesses, etc.

II 4,15. Acceptance of subsequent cognition of the path.

And he will be one of acceptable speech, of measured speech. Wrath and conceit will not overpower him, and he will not be mean .... He himself will be one who abstains from taking life and others also he establishes in abstention from taking life, and he praises the abstaining from taking life, and he praises others also who abstain from taking life, one acquiescent. He himself ... not take what is not given ... (Ad fol. 295) ... one acquiescent. He himself ... the perfection of patience .... He himself stands in the perfection of wisdom and others also he establishes in the perfection of wisdom; he praises ... he will be acquiescent .... He himself enters into all concentrations and others also he will establish in the attainment of all concentrations ... dharanis .... He himself will develop the concentrations of emptiness, the signless, the wishless, and others also he will establish in them. . . knowledge of all modes. . . acquiescent.

II 4,16. Subsequent cognition of the path.

Moreover, Kauśika, the Bodhisattva, the great being, when he courses in the six perfections, whatever gift he gives, that he makes common to all beings and then turns it over to the supreme enlightenment, and that without taking anything as a basis. Whatever morality he guards . . . When he courses thus, there arises in the son or daughter of good family, who courses in the six perfections, this mindful recollection: If I do not give gifts, I shall be reborn in the states of woe, and there will be no maturing of beings (for me), nor a purifying of the Buddha-field, nor will I gain all-knowledge. It occurs to him: If I do not guard morality, there will be for me a rebirth in the three states of woe, and not among men or gods, and neither the maturing of beings nor the purifying of the Buddha-field will be done, and all-knowledge will not be acquired. It occurs to him: If I do not develop patience, my faculties will go to pieces, my face will be (disfigured?), nor will I acquire that perfect form by the mere sight of which, when I course on the course of a Bodhisattva, beings become fixed on supreme enlightenment, nor can I mature beings through my perfect form or purify the Buddha-field, and how much less will I acquire all-knowledge. It occurs to him: When I become lazy and do not develop the path of a Bodhisattva, and do not exert vigour, how can I fulfill the Buddhadharmas, and how can I gain all-knowledge. It occurs to him: If I become one with distracted thoughts, then I cannot train in the achievement of all concentrations, nor can I mature beings, or purify the Buddha-field, how much less can I gain the knowledge of all modes. It occurs to him: If I, weak in wisdom and unskilled in means, having transcended the level of the Disciples and Pratyekabuddhas, having matured beings and having purified the Buddha-field (except to), fully know all-knowledge . . . I would not fulfill the perfection of giving through meanness, the perfection of morality through immorality, the perfection of patience through ill-will, the perfection of vigour through sloth, the perfection of meditation through distraction, the perfection of wisdom through stupidity. And without fulfilling the six perfections I shall not go forth to the knowledge of all modes. It is thus, Kauśika, that that son or daughter of good family acquires qualities and advantages belonging to both this and the next life, if he takes up, etc. this perfection of wisdom and becomes not lacking in the thought of all-knowledge.

II 5. What the Path of Development Does.

II 5,1-2. The activity of being everywhere self-disciplined and humble.

Śakra: It is wonderful how much this perfection of wisdom has been set up for the control and transformation of the Bodhisattvas, the great beings!

The Lord: How does it do so?

Śakra: Here the Bodhisattva, the great being, coursing in the worldly perfection of wisdom, gives gifts to the Buddhas and Lords, to the Pratyekabuddhas, and to the Disciples, and it does not occur to him: I give gifts as a Bodhisattva to the Disciples and Pratyekabuddhas, to those who are miserable, to mendicants, ... and through this lack of skill in means he becomes arrogant. To a Bodhisattva who guards worldly morality it occurs: 'I course in the perfection of morality, I fulfill the perfection of morality', and through that he becomes arrogant. To a Bodhisattva who develops worldly patience it occurs: 'I course in the perfection of patience, I fulfill the perfection of patience,' and through that he becomes arrogant. And so with a Bodhisattva who exerts worldly vigour, who enters on worldly concentration, who develops worldly wisdom. To a Bodhisattva who has stood in the development of the applications of mindfulness it occurs: 'I develop the applications of mindfulness....I shall obtain the knowledge of all modes'. (Not?) coursing in these I-making dharmas, he gives gifts, but he does not apprehend the gift, or the giver, he does not apprehend the recipient, and he does not apprehend that which he bestows. It is thus that the Bodhisattva, the great being who courses in perfect wisdom, has been set up for control and for transformation.

Likewise, when he develops the other five perfections, he does not apprehend anything. The Bodhisattva, the great being who thus courses in perfect wisdom, has been set up for control and transformation.

Chapter 27

THE SHRINE

II 5,3. Victory over the defilements.

Thereupon *the Lord* said to Śakra, Chief of Gods: If, Kauśika, any son or daughter of good family, while he takes up this deep perfection of wisdom, or bears it in mind, preaches it, studies it, spreads it, repeats it, or wisely attends to it, goes right to the front of a battle while it is in progress, and he either lies down, walks, sits, or stands after he has gone into battle; it is then impossible and it cannot be that, while they take up this perfection of wisdom ... wisely attend to it, any arrow, sword or clod will be hurled at that son or daughter of good family; or if these weapons were hurled at them, that they will fall on them, and it is impossible that there will be a check on their life from the attacks of others. And why? Because for a long time they have, coursing in this perfection of wisdom, vanquished the arrows and swords of their own greed, of their own hate, of their own delusion, and also the arrows and swords of the (greed), hate, and delusion of others they have vanquished; they have vanquished the arrows and swords of their own wrong views, obsessions, and evil inclinations, as well as those of others. It is in this way that an arrow or sword aimed at the body of this son or daughter of good family does not actually hit him.

II 5,4. No occasion for attacks from others.

Moreover, Kauśika, if a son or daughter of good family will take up this perfection of wisdom, bear it in mind, preach it, study it, spread it, wisely attend to it, and if he also is not lacking in the thought of all-knowledge, then, if someone would sprinkle him with a drug, or work devil-lore on him, or put him into a firepit, or strike him with a sword, or give him poison, or throw him into the water—all that will not affect him. And why? A great lore is this perfection of wisdom, the utmost lore is this perfection of wisdom. The son or daughter of good family who trains in this lore does not set his heart on disturbing his own peace, nor that of others, nor that of both himself and others.

II 5,5. Right and perfect enlightenment.

And why? He does not make a basis of his self, or of others, or of both himself and others. He does not make a basis of form, feeling, ... consciousness, ... Buddhadharmas, or even the knowledge of all modes. Since he does not apprehend them, he does not set his heart on disturbing his own peace, or that of others, or of both himself and others. He acquires the utmost, right, and perfect enlightenment. He surveys (the thoughts of) all beings. And why? As they trained themselves in this lore, the former Tathagatas have fully known the utmost, right, and perfect enlightenment. And also those Tathagatas who will be in the future period, also they will, training themselves in this lore, fully awake to the utmost, right, and perfect enlightenment. And also those who are just now, in the ten directions, the immeasurable Tathagatas, they also have, by training themselves in this lore, fully known the utmost, right, and perfect enlightenment.

II 5,6. THE WORTHINESS OF BEING WORSHIPPED.

Moreover, Kauśika, where this perfection of wisdom, after it has been written down, has been taken up, etc. there men and ghosts who seek for entry, who search for entry, do not gain entry. And why? Because there, so as to worship the perfection of wisdom, all the gods in the great trichiliocosm arrange shelter, defense, and protection for these sons and daughters of good family who will bear in mind this perfection of wisdom after it has been written down. And those gods will come there to honour, revere, and worship the perfection of wisdom, and, having worshipped it, they will go away again. He who bears in mind and preaches this perfection of wisdom after it has been written down will have these qualities and advantages belonging to this life. Just as those who have gone to the circumference of the terrace of enlightenment, or to its interior, cannot, even with the help of evil animal beings, be hurt or injured by men or ghosts. And why? Because, seated on it, the Tathagatas of the past have known full enlightenment, and so do those of the future and of the present; and after they have known full enlightenment, they establish all beings in ease, fearlessness, freedom from anxiety, lack of fright, nonenemity, inviolability and undisturbed peace, and, having done so, they establish countless beings in heavenly and human benefits, in the fruit of a Streamwinner, etc. And why? Because this perfection of wisdom makes the spot of earth where it is into a true shrine, worthy of being honoured, revered and worshipped, with flowers, incense, etc.

II 6. Resolute Faith.

II 6,1. ONE AIMS AT ONE'S OWN WELFARE.

II 6,1,1. VERY WEAK.

Śakra: Suppose that there are two persons: One of the two, a son or daughter of good family, has written down this perfection of wisdom and made a copy of it, bears it in mind, honours, reveres, adores and worships it with flowers, wreaths, perfumes, unguents, aromatic powders, strips of cloth, parasols, banners, and flags. The other would erect a Stupa for the relics of the Tathagata who has gone to Parinirvana, and look after it, and would honour, etc. it with flowers, etc. Which one of the two would beget a greater heap of merit?

The Lord: I will question you on this point and you may answer to the best of your abilities. What do you think, Kauśika, with regard to that knowledge of all modes which the Tathagata has obtained and to that body which he has brought forth, in which progressive practices did the Tathagata train so that he could obtain the knowledge of all modes and bring forth that personality?

Śakra: It is because the Tathagata has trained in this perfection of wisdom that he has obtained the knowledge of all modes.

The Lord: So it is, Kauśika, so it is. It is through training in the perfection of wisdom that I have obtained the knowledge of all modes. It is not by his acquisition of this body (which is the basis of the relics) that the Tathagata derives his name, but from his having acquired the knowledge of all modes. And this knowledge of all modes has come forth from the perfection of wisdom. Just so this body is the true foundation of the cognition of the knowledge of all modes. And, supported by this foundation has the Tathagata obtained the knowledge of all modes. Thus as the true foundation of that cognition of the knowledge of all modes has this body become a true shrine for all beings, worthy of being revered, adored, worshipped, honoured and saluted respectfully. Just so, when I have gone to Parinirvana, also my relics will be worshipped. The son or daughter of good family who, having written this perfection of wisdom, will take it up, study, and bear it in mind, etc. *to*: honour, revere, adore, and worship it with flowers, etc. he will perform worship to the cognition of the knowledge of all modes. Compared with him who deposits the relics of the Tathagata who has gone to Parinirvana in a Stupa made of the seven precious things, looks after them, honours, etc. them, someone who studies and worships this perfection of wisdom does beget the greater heap of merit. And why? For come forth from it are the five perfections, the various kinds of emptiness, the four applications of mindfulness, etc. *to*: the 18 special Buddhadharmas, all concentrations, all dharanis, the maturing of beings, the accomplishment of the Buddha-field, the Bodhisattva's accomplishments of the family, the body, the enjoyment, the retinue; the great friendliness, the great compassion, the good warrior, Brahmin and householder families, the various kinds of gods, the Streamwinners etc. *to*: the Pratyekabuddhas, the Bodhisattvas, the great beings, the Tathagatas and the knowledge of all modes.

II 6,1,2. MODERATELY WEAK.

Śakra: Those men of Jambudvipa who do not honour, revere, adore, and worship this perfection of wisdom, do they not know that the cult of the perfection of wisdom is greatly profitable?

The Lord: What do you think, Kauśika, how many men of Jambudvipa are endowed with unbroken faith in the Buddha, the Dharma, and the Samgha; how many are free from hesitation about the Buddha, the Dharma, and the Samgha; how many are unquestionably certain about the Buddha, the Dharma, and the Samgha?

Śakra: Only a few.

The Lord: What do you think, Kauśika, how many men of Jambudvipa have acquired the 37 dharmas which act as wings to enlightenment, the three doors to deliverance, etc, *to*: the six super-knowledges; how many have through the forsaking of the three fetters become Streamwinners, etc. *to*: how many have set out for the enlightenment of a Pratyekabuddha or for full enlightenment?

Śakra: Only a few.

The Lord: So it is, Kauśika, so it is. Few are those beings who are endowed with unbroken faith in the Buddha, Dharma, and Samgha; fewer are those who are free from hesitation about the Buddha, Dharma, and Samgha; fewer still those who are unquestionably certain about the Buddha, Dharma, and Samgha. Fewer still those who have acquired the 37 dharmas which act as wings to enlightenment. Fewer and fewer those who are Streamwinners, etc. *to*: those who have set out for full enlightenment, and fewest those who course in enlightenment. And why? Because formerly, when they wandered about in Samsara, they have not seen the Buddha, heard the Dharma, honoured the Samgha; they have given no gifts, failed to guard morality, develop patience, exert vigour, develop the trances or wisdom; they have neither developed nor heard of the perfection of giving, etc. *to*: the knowledge of all modes. It is by this method, Kauśika, that one should know that few are the men of Jambudvipa who are endowed with an unbroken faith in the Buddha, etc. *to*: fewest are those who with earnest intention course in enlightenment. Leaving aside, Kauśika, the human beings, what do you think, how many living beings of Jambudvipa have acquired the 37 dharmas which act as wings to enlightenment, etc. *to*: have set out for the enlightenment of a Pratyekabuddha? How many living beings in Jambudvipa have no hesitations about the supreme enlightenment, or about the Buddha, Dharma, and Samgha; how many honour their parents and the elders of the family, give gifts, guard their morality, observe the Uposatha days; how many perceive that they ought to be agitated about their body, perceive that it is impermanent, that it does not belong to them, that it is unlovely, or perceive that there is nothing to delight in anywhere in the world, and how many have set out for the supreme enlightenment?

Śakra: Very few indeed.

The Lord: So it is, Kauśika, so it is, just as you say. Few are the living beings who have acquired the 37 dharmas which act as wings to enlightenment, etc. *to*: who have set out for the supreme enlightenment. Fewer than these are those who course in the supreme enlightenment. Fewer still than these are those who want to fully know the supreme enlightenment. Here Kauśika, with my unobstructed Buddha-eye I see in all directions in countless world systems innumerable beings who course in the supreme enlightenment; of these perhaps one or two, not lacking in perfect wisdom and skill in means, might be definitely established on the irreversible stage; but many more than two will be definitely established on the level of the Disciples or Pratyekabuddhas. And why? Those who are lazy, of inferior vigour, inferior beings, of inferior resolve and stupid find it hard to come up to the supreme enlightenment.

II 6,1,3. FAIRLY WEAK.

Therefore then, Kauśika, those sons and daughters of good family who have set out for the supreme enlightenment, if they want quickly and easily to know the supreme enlightenment, they should learn this perfection of wisdom, bear it in mind, preach, study, and wisely attend to it; in addition they should honour, revere, and worship it with flowers, etc. And whichever other wholesome dharmas are contained within this perfection of wisdom they also should be learned, etc., i.e. the six perfections, the various kinds of emptiness, etc. *to*: the superknowledges, and all the other immeasurable Buddhadharmas. And why? Because those sons and daughters of good family will cognize that therein the Tathagata has trained in the past when he coursed in the practice of a Bodhisattva, that they also should likewise train in it, and that the perfection of wisdom is the Teacher, and that also the other immeasurable Buddhadharmas are the religion of the Buddhas, the Lords. Training in this perfection of wisdom, etc. *to*: in the knowledge of all modes, the Buddhas and Lords, the Pratyekabuddhas, the Arhats, the Never-Returners, the Once-Returners and the Streamwinners have gone beyond, do go beyond, will go beyond. Therefore then, Kauśika, the sons and daughters of good family should, whether the Tathagata is present or has gone to Parinirvana, run back to just this perfection of wisdom, to the perfection of concentration, etc. *to*: to all knowledge, etc. *to*: to the knowledge of all modes. And why? Just this perfection of wisdom, etc. *to*: just this knowledge of all modes is the support of all Disciples and

Pratyekabuddhas, of the Bodhisattvas, the great beings, and of the world with its gods, men, and Asuras.

II 6,1,4. WEAKLY MEDIUM.

If some son or daughter of good family would build, for the worship of the Tathagata who has disappeared into final Nirvana, a Stupa made of the seven precious things, one hundred miles high and half a mile broad, and would all his life honour, etc. it with flowers, etc. what do you think, Kauśika, would they on the strength of that beget a great heap of merit?

Śakra: They would, O Lord.

The Lord: Greater would be the merit of that son or daughter of good family who, having copied this perfection of wisdom, will learn it, bear it in mind, preach, study, and wisely attend to it, will reveal it to others, will not be without the thought of the knowledge of all modes, and will in addition honour it, revere, and worship it with flowers, etc.

II 6,1,5. MODERATELY MEDIUM.

Leaving aside the Stupa,—if some son or daughter of good family, when the Tathagata has gone to Parinirvana, would fill this Jambudvipa with Stupas made of the seven precious things, hundreds of miles high and half a mile broad, and would honour, etc. them all his life with flowers, etc.—what do you think, Kauśika, would they on the strength of that beget a great deal of merit?

Śakra: They would, O Lord.

The Lord: Greater would be the merit of one who learns the perfection of wisdom (etc. as before).

II 6,1,6. STRONGLY MEDIUM.

And the same holds good if we replace Jambudvipa by this four-continent world system, or

II 6,1,7. WEAKLY STRONG.

by a small chiliocosm, or

II 6,1,8. MEDIUM STRONG.

a medium dichiliocosm, or

II 6,1,9. STRONGLY STRONG.

a great trichiliocosm.

II 6,2. ONE AIMS AT THE WELFARE OF ONESELF AND OF OTHERS.

II 6,2,1. VERY WEAK.

Leaving aside the great trichiliocosm; if each of all the beings in the great trichiliocosm would build Stupas, etc.—greater will be the merit of those who learn the perfection of wisdom.

Śakra: So it is, O Lord. Those who honour, etc. the perfection of wisdom do honour, etc. the past, present, and future Tathagatas. If each one of all the beings in the countless world systems in all the directions would build Stupas, etc. and honour, etc. them for an aeon or for the remainder of an aeon, would they on the strength of that beget a great deal of merit?

The Lord: They would, Kauśika.

Śakra: Greater would be the merit of those who would learn, etc. the perfection of wisdom. And why? Because in this perfection of wisdom are contained all the wholesome dharmas, i.e. the ten wholesome paths of action, etc. *to*: the knowledge of all modes. This is the religion of the Buddhas and Lords; having trained therein, all the Disciples and Pratyekabuddhas, as well as the past, present, and future Buddhas and Lords, have gone to the Beyond of all dharmas, do go to it, will go to it.

Chapter 28

THE PROCLAMATION OF A BODHISATTVA'S QUALITIES

The Lord: So it is, Kauśika, so it is. These sons and daughters of good family will beget a great deal of merit, they will beget a merit which is immeasurable, incalculable, inconceivable, incomparable, illimitable, if, having copied this perfection of wisdom and made it into a book, they will learn and study it, bear it in mind, preach it and wisely attend to it, and if, in addition, they will honour, revere, adore, and worship it with flowers, etc. *to* : flags. And why? Because from the perfection of wisdom has come forth the all-knowledge of the Tathagatas, and from it have come forth the perfection of concentration, etc. *to*: the supreme enlightenment. Therefore the accumulation of merit of the devotee of the perfection of wisdom bears no proportion at all to the former accumulation of merit (born from building Stupas). And why? As long as the perfection of wisdom abides in Jambudvipa, so long there will be no disappearance of the Jewel of the Buddha, Dharma, and Samgha. As long as there will be a manifestation in the world of the ten wholesome paths of action, of the four trances, of the knowledge of all modes, so long there will be a manifestation of good warrior families, etc. *to* : of the fruit of a Streamwinner, etc. *to*: of Arhatship and Pratyekabuddha-enlightenment, and so long will there be a conception of the full attainment of the Bodhisattvas, the great beings, of the utmost Buddha-cognition, the turning of the wheel of the Dharma, the maturing of beings and the perfect purity of the Buddhafield.

II 6,2,2. Moderately weak.

Thereupon in this great trichiliocosm the deities belonging to the Four Great Kings, and the other *gods,* said to Śakra, Chief of Gods: The perfection of wisdom, Sir, should be taken up, etc. And why? When it has been taken up, etc., then all the unwholesome dharmas wane away and the wholesome dharmas go to the fulfillment of their development; the heavenly hosts wax strong, and the hosts of the Asuras wane away. The guide of the Buddha will not be cut off, nor the guide of the Dharma, nor the guide of the Samgha. So that the Triple Jewel should not be interrupted, there takes place in this world a manifestation of all the perfections, of the 37 dharmas which act as wings to enlightenment, of the course of a Bodhisattva and of the Tathagata, the Arhat, the fully Enlightened One.

The Lord: Kauśika, do take up the perfection of wisdom, bear it in mind, preach and study it, and wisely attend to it! And why? If the Asuras form the idea of having a fight with the Gods of the Thirty-three, then, if you, Kauśika, bring to mind this perfection of wisdom, repeat and wisely attend to it, those Asuras will drop that idea again. Nor will the mental processes grow which occur to the male or female deities at the time of their decease, when they see their future rebirth; when you, Kauśika, repeat this perfection of wisdom in front of them, then through that wholesome root and through hearing the perfection of wisdom they are again once more reborn among the gods. And why? So greatly profitable is it to hear the perfection of wisdom! Whichever son or daughter of good family, whichever male or female deity comes to hear of this perfection of wisdom, they will all, through that wholesome root, in due course know full enlightenment. And why? Those, Kauśika, who in the past period were Tathagatas, with their congregations of disciples, they have, by having trained in this perfection of wisdom, won final Nirvana in the realm of Nirvana which leaves nothing behind. And the same holds good of the Tathagatas who, with their congregation of disciples, just now stand, hold, and maintain themselves, in the ten directions, they all have known full enlightenment, because they have trained in just this perfection of wisdom. And why? Because in the perfection of wisdom are contained all the dharmas which act as wings of enlightenment, be they Disciple-dharmas, Pratyekabuddha-dharmas, Bodhisattva-dharmas, or Buddha-dharmas.

Śakra: A great lore is this perfection of wisdom, the utmost lore, the unequalled lore. And why? Because the perfection of wisdom spurns all unwholesome dharmas and bestows all wholesome dharmas.

The Lord: So it is, Kauśika, so it is. A great lore, the utmost lore, the unequalled lore is this perfection of wisdom. And why? Because those who were Tathagatas in the past period, they have, thanks to this lore, fully known the utmost, right, and prefect enlightenment. Those also who will be Tathagatas in a future period, they will, thanks to this lore, fully know the utmost, right, and perfect enlightenment. Those Tathagatas also who stand, hold, and maintain themselves just now in the world systems in the ten directions, they also do, thanks to this lore, fully know the utmost, right, and perfect enlightenment. And why? Because, Kauśika, thanks to this lore the 10 wholesome paths of action are conceived in the world, the four trances, etc. *to*: the knowledge of all modes. Also thanks to the Bodhisattvas the 10 wholesome paths of action are brought about, and so are the four trances, etc. *to*: the knowledge of all modes, and the Streamwinner, etc. *to*: the Tathagatas. Just as, thanks to the disk of the moon all the hosts of the brightly shining stars become manifest and the constellations are conceived, just so, whatever wholesome conduct, whatever right conduct there is, the ten paths of wholesome action, etc. *to*: the knowledge of all modes—when no Tathagatas are produced all that should be known as having issued from the Bodhisattvas, as having been begotten by the Bodhisattvas. And that skill in means of the Bodhisattva, the great being, should be known as issued from the perfection of wisdom. Endowed with this skill in means the Bodhisattva courses in the perfections, the various kinds of emptiness, the applications of mindfulness, etc. *to*: the 18 special Buddhadharmas. He does not fall on the level of the Disciples, does not realize the level of the Pratyekabuddhas, but matures beings and purifies the Buddha-field. And he acquires the accomplishment of long life, of beings, of the Buddha-field and of becoming a Bodhisattva; and he reaches the knowledge of all modes. Moreover, the son or daughter of good family who takes up this perfection of wisdom, etc. *to*: attends to it wisely, becomes endowed with these qualities belonging to this very life.

Śakra: Which are these qualities?

The Lord: He will not die from poison, or sword, from fire or water, etc. *to*: from ... or sickness, except as a punishment for his past deeds. As to the calamities which threaten them from the courts of princes, if a son or daughter of good family approach the princely court while repeating this perfection of wisdom, then no harm can befall them. Kings and king's councellors will decide to greet them with loving words, to converse with them, to be polite and friendly to them. And why? That is the might of the majesty of just this perfection of wisdom! If a son or daughter of good family approach a princely court while repeating this perfection of wisdom, kings and ministers will think that they should address them with loving words, that they should converse with them, and give them a friendly greeting. And why? Because, Kauśika, those sons and daughters of good family have set up towards all beings a thought of friendliness, compassion, sympathetic joy, and impartiality. Endowed with these good qualities relating to this very life will be that son or daughter of good family who will take up this perfection of wisdom, etc. *to*: wisely attend to it.

And, Kauśika, what qualities relating to the next world will he be endowed with? He will never be lacking in the ten paths of wholesome action, the four trances, etc. *to*: the Buddhadharmas. He will never be reborn in the hells, as an animal, or in the world of Yama. He will never be crippled. He will never be reborn in poor families, or in the families of jugglers, refuse workers or 'vultures', except as a result of his vow to mature beings. Constantly and always he will be endowed with the 32 marks of a superman. He will be miraculously reborn in those Buddha-fields where he can be face to face with the Buddhas, the Lords. Never will he be lacking in the superknowledges of a Bodhisattva. He will, as he plans, pass on from Buddha-field to Buddha-field, for the sake of honouring the Buddhas, the Lords, and of hearing the Dharma. Passing on from Buddha-field to Buddha-field he will mature beings and purify the Buddha-field. Therefore then, those sons and daughters of good family who desire this accomplishment of qualities, should take up this perfection of wisdom, study it, recite it, and wisely attend to it, and they should not become lacking in the thought of the knowledge of all modes. They will be endowed with these qualities, belonging to this and the next life, until they will fully know the utmost, right, and perfect enlightenment.

CHAPTER 29

THE HERETICS

Thereupon a hundred wanderers of other sects with hostile intent approached to where the Lord was. And it occurred to *Śakra*: Those hundred wanderers of other sects approach with hostile intent to where the Lord is. What if now as much as I have learned of the perfection of wisdom from the Lord, if I repeat just that, so that those heretical wanderers, when they have approached, do not cause an obstacle to the Lord, and to the perfection of wisdom being preached.

Thereupon Śakra, Chief of Gods, repeated as much of the perfection of wisdom as he had learned. Thereupon those wanderers of other sects, having from afar reverently saluted the Lord, again went away by that path, by that door.

Thereupon it occurred to the Ven. *Śāradvatīputra*: For what reason have those heretical wanderers, after they had from afar reverently saluted the Lord, again gone away by that path, by that door?

The Lord read Śariputra's thoughts and said to him: It is because Śakra, Chief of Gods, has brought to mind this perfection of wisdom. Because, Śariputra, I see not even one single salubrious dharma in those heretical wanderers. They all wanted to approach with hostile intent, with thoughts of enmity. Nor do I see anyone in this world with its gods, Maras, Brahmas, Śramanas and Brahmanas, who, when this perfection of wisdom is being demonstrated, could approach with hostile intent or with thoughts of enmity. That cannot possibly be. And why? Because all the gods in this great trichiliocosm assist this perfection of wisdom, and so do the Disciples, the Pratyekabuddhas, and the Bodhisattvas, the great beings. And why? Because they have all issued from the perfection of wisdom. Moreover, in all the countless world systems in the ten directions all the Buddhas and Lords, together with their congregations of disciples, assist this perfection of wisdom, and so do the Pratyekabuddhas, the Bodhisattvas, and the gods, Nagas, Yakshas, Gandharvas, Asuras, Garudas, Kinnaras, and Mahoragas. And why? Because they all have issued from the perfection of wisdom.

Thereupon it occurred to *Mara, the Evil One*: The four assemblies are seated face to face with the Tathagata, and so are the gods of the realm of sense desire and of the realm of form. In this assembly Bodhisattvas, great beings, are sure to be predicted to full enlightenment. Let me now approach to where the Lord is in order to blind them.

Thereupon Mara, the Evil One, conjured up a fourfold army and wanted to approach where the Lord was.

Thereupon it occurred to *Śakra*, Chief of Gods: Surely, this is Mara, the Evil One, who, having conjured up a fourfold army, wants to approach to where the Lord is. But this array of the fourfold army of Mara, the Evil One, is not such as the array of the fourfold army of King Bimbisāra, or of king Prasenajit, or of the Śakyas or the Licchavis. This fourfold army has been conjured up by Mara, the Evil One. For a long time indeed has Mara, the Evil One, looked for a chance to do harm to the Lord, has intended to hurt beings who exert themselves rightly. I will now bring this perfection of wisdom to mind, recall, and repeat it! Thereupon Śakra, Chief of Gods, called to mind this perfection of wisdom, and repeated it in his memory. Immediately Mara, the Evil One, turned back on the path, on the door (by which he had come).

Thereupon the *Gods* of the Thirty-three etc. *to*: the highest gods in the assembly conjured up heavenly flowers, flew through the air, and scattered and showered them over the Lord. And they spoke these words: For a long time surely has this perfection of wisdom been pursued by the men of Jambudvipa! Certainly, as long as the men of Jambudvipa pursue this perfection of wisdom, for so long in the great trichiliocosm, in the world systems in the ten directions all around, the Tathagata will not disappear, the Dharma will last long, the Jewel of the Samgha will be manifest in the world, and the specific practices of the Bodhisattvas, the great beings, will be conceived! And in whichever part of the world those sons and daughters of good family will bear in mind this perfection of wisdom and make it into a book, there one would expect them to be born of light, protected by saviours, and free from darkness and blindness.

The Lord: So it is, Kauśika, so it is, O deities, so it is. As long as the men of Jambudvipa will pursue this perfection of wisdom, for so long the Tathagata will not disappear, the Dharma will last long and the Jewel of the Samgha will be conceived in the world, etc. *to*: in the great trichiliocosm, in the world systems in the ten directions all around, the Tathagata will not disappear ... free from darkness and blindness. Thereupon those *deities* once more conjured up heavenly Kusuma flowers, scattered them over the Lord, and spoke these words: Mara and his host will have no chance to harm those sons and daughters of good family who take up this perfection of wisdom, etc. *to*: wisely attend to it. We also, O Lord, will constantly and always arrange for the shelter, defense, and protection of this son or daughter of good family! And why? For they will be endowed with no small wholesome root, they have fulfilled their duties under the Jinas of the past, they have honoured many Buddhas, they have been taken hold of by the good spiritual friends. And why? One should search for all-knowledge through the perfection of wisdom, and this perfection of wisdom, in its turn, should be searched for through the perfection of wisdom. And why? Because, O Lord, the perfection of wisdom is not one thing and all-knowledge another; but perfect wisdom and all-knowledge are not two or divided.

The Lord : So it is, Kauśika, so it is. The all-knowledge of the Tathagatas has issued from the perfection of wisdom, and vice versa. And why? For the perfection of wisdom is not one thing, and all-knowledge another; all-knowledge is not one thing, and the perfection of wisdom another; but perfect wisdom and all-knowledge are not two or divided.

Chapter 30

THE ADVANTAGES OF BEARING IN MIND AND OF REVERENCE

II 6,2,3. Fairly weak.

Ānanda : The Lord does not proclaim the name of the perfection of giving, nor of the perfection of morality, patience, vigour, and concentration, but only that of the perfection of wisdom. He does not proclaim the name of everything up to the 18 special Buddhadharmas, but only that of the perfection of wisdom.

The Lord : The perfection of wisdom controls the five perfections etc. *to*: the 18 special Buddhadharmas. What do you think, Ananda, is a giving undedicated to all-knowledge a perfect giving?

Ānanda : No indeed, O Lord.

And so with morality, patience, etc.

Ānanda : How, on the other hand, does a giving dedicated to all-knowledge become a perfect giving? How does wisdom dedicated to all-knowledge get the name of the perfection of wisdom?

The Lord : By way of nonduality, of nonproduction, of nonbasis. The nonproduction and nonbasis of what? By way of the nonduality of the skandhas, etc. *to* : of enlightenment.

Ānanda : How and in what way?

The Lord : For here form is empty of form. And why? Because form and the perfections are not two or divided. And so for feeling, etc. *to*: enlightenment. Therefore, then, Ananda, just the perfection of wisdom controls these five perfections, etc. *to*: she controls the knowledge of all modes. Just as gems, scattered about in the great earth, grow when all conditions are favourable; the great earth is their support, and they grow supported by the great earth; even so, the five perfections grow supported by the perfection of wisdom and so do the four applications of mindfulness, etc. *to* : the knowledge of all modes. Supported by the knowledge of all modes again do the five perfections grow, the applications of mindfulness, etc. *to* : the 18 special Buddhadharmas. Therefore, then, Ananda, the perfection of wisdom is the leader of these five perfections, etc. *to* : of the 18 special Buddhadharmas.

II 6,2,4. Weakly medium.

Śakra : The Tathagata, O Lord, has not yet proclaimed all the qualities of the perfection of wisdom, qualities which a son or daughter of good family acquire when they learn this perfection of wisdom, bear it in mind, preach and study it, and wisely attend to it. By the perfection of wisdom being learned, etc. *to* : wisely attended to, there takes place in the world a manifestation of the 10 wholesome paths of action, etc. *to* : of the Buddha-dharmas, of good warrior families, etc. *to* : of the Tathagatas.

The Lord : These, I say, are not the only qualities gained through the perfection of wisdom. And why? Such sons and daughters of good family will be endowed with an immeasurable mass of morality, and they will not be lacking in the thought of the knowledge of all modes. They will be endowed with an immeasurable mass of concentration, wisdom, emancipation, and vision and cognition of emancipation, if they will take up this perfection of wisdom, study it, bear it in mind, recite it and attend to it wisely, and they will not be lacking in the thought of the knowledge of all modes. As progressing in the direction of the Tathagata should those sons or daughters of good family be known, who will take up, etc. this perfection of wisdom and are not lacking in the thought of the knowledge of all modes. If we compare, Kauśika, the mass of morality, of concentration, of wisdom, the mass of emancipation and the mass of the cognition and vision of emancipation of all Disciples and Pratyekabuddhas with the mass of morality, etc., of these sons or daughters of good family, then that of all Disciples and Pratyekabuddhas does not approach one hundredth part, etc. *to*: it does not bear comparison. And why? Because those whose thought has been set free on the level of the Disciples and Pratyekabuddhas do not understand any dharma. Of the sons and daughters of good family, who, having written this perfection of wisdom, will take it up, etc. *to*: wisely attend to it, and will honour, revere, adore, and worship it with flowers, incense, scents, wreaths, unguents, rags, parasols, banners, bells, and manifold musical instruments, of those sons or daughters of good family I also just so preach the qualities, relating to this and to the next life.

II 6,2,5. MODERATELY MEDIUM.

Śakra : I also, O Lord, will constantly arrange for the shelter, defense, and protection of that son or daughter of good family who will take up this perfection of wisdom, etc. to manifold musical instruments.

The Lord : When again this son or daughter of good family will joyfully approach in order to hear the Dharma, then the gods will think that of that son etc., who demonstrates the Dharma associated with the perfection of wisdom, the readiness of speech should be brought out. But when the dharma-preachers are not willing to gratify them, the gods will think that by means of just that respect for Dharma their readiness of speech should be brought about. Also this quality, belonging to this very life, will that son, etc. gain who will take up this perfection of wisdom, etc. *to*: manifold musical instruments.

And again, Kauśika, that son, etc., who preaches this perfection of wisdom, will not fell any despondency in front of the assemblies, from fear that someone will censure or reprove him. And why? Because this perfection of wisdom will arrange for his shelter, defense, and protection. And why? Because in this perfection of wisdom all dharmas ... — worldly and supramundane, with and without outflows, common and uncommon, wholesome and unwholesome, conditioned and unconditioned, Disciple-dharmas, Pratyekabuddha-dharmas, and Buddha-dharmas. And why? Because this is the statute of all wholesome dharmas. And that son, etc. established in subjective emptiness, etc. does not review, in the perfection of wisdom, the reproving, or him who would reprove, and also that perfection of wisdom he does not review. Thus certainly no one will reprove that son or daughter of good family, because they are upheld by the perfection of wisdom.

And again, Kauśika, the thought of that son or daughter of good family who takes up this perfection of wisdom, etc. *to*: wisely attends to it, will not become cowed or despondent, will not tremble, be frightened, or terrified. And why? Because they do not review an entity which could make them cowed or despondent, frightened or terrified. Those qualities belonging to this very life will those gain who take up this perfection of wisdom, etc. *to*: will attend to it wisely; how much more so if they will, having copied it, honour it, etc. *to*: manifold musical instruments.

II 6,2,6. STRONGLY MEDIUM.

And again, Kauśika, this son, etc. who will take up this perfection of wisdom, etc. *to*: musical instruments, he will be dear to his mother and father, to friends, Shramanas and Brahmanas. And he will also be dear and pleasing to the Buddhas, the Lords in the world systems in the ten directions, to the Bodhisattvas, the great beings, to the Pratyekabuddhas, the Arhats, the Never-returners, the Once-returners and Streamwinners, and to the world with its gods, with its Maras, with its Brahmas, this world with its Shramanas and Brahmanas, with gods, men, and Asuras.

II 6,2,7. WEAKLY STRONG.

His inspiration will be unbroken; unbroken will be to him the perfection of giving, etc. *to*: the perfection of wisdom, the development of the subjective, etc. emptiness, of the four applications of mindfulness, etc. *to*: the Buddhadharmas, of his concentrations, of the dharanis, of the superknowledges; unbroken will be his maturing, the perfect purity of his Buddhafield, etc. *to*: the knowledge of all modes. And he will be competent, in accordance with Dharma to get out of the counterquestions which may be put to him. Also these qualities belonging to this and the next life are acquired by someone who will take up, etc. this perfection of wisdom, and he will not be lacking in the dwelling in the knowledge of all modes when, having copied it out, he will honour it, etc. *to* : and worship it with flowers, etc.

II 6,2,8. MEDIUM STRONG.

Moreover, when a son or daughter of good family has made this perfection of wisdom into a written book, and bears it in mind, recites and studies it, then those among the gods of the Four Great Kings who have set out for full enlightenment will come to that place, will learn this perfection of wisdom, bear it in mind, recite and study it, pay homage to it, salute it respectfully, and then they will depart again. And so will all the gods, up to the Highest Gods. And those Mahabrahma gods who have made a vow to win the supreme enlightenment will come there, learn, study, bear in mind, recite and respectfully salute this perfection of wisdom, and then they will depart again. And so with the gods, from the Gods of the Pure Abode to the Highest Gods. And that son or daughter of good family should wish that all the gods in the world systems in all the ten directions, who have set out for full enlightenment, as well as other gods, Nagas, Yakshas, Gandharvas, Asuras, Garudas, Kinnaras, and Mahoragas should, after having come there and learned, etc. *to* : worshipped this perfection of wisdom, come there again and receive this gift of Dharma. And those gods in all the world systems in all the ten directions who have set out for the supreme enlightenment will come there, will learn this perfection of wisdom, etc. *to* : worship it, and will then depart again. And all these gods will arrange shelter, defense, and protection for that son or daughter of good family. Nor will anyone who looks for entry or seeks for entry gain entry to him, except as a karmic punishment for past deeds. This is another quality which that son or daughter of good family gains in this very life. And why? Because those gods who have set out for the supreme enlightenment will decide to come there, that is to say those gods who have set out for the supreme enlightenment out of concern for the protection of all beings, for their welfare and happiness.

II 6,2,9. STRONGLY STRONG.

Śakra : How, O Lord, can one know that gods from the ten directions have come (to that place) to learn this perfection of wisdom, etc. *to*: worship it?

The Lord : When one perceives a sublime radiance then one should know for certain that very powerful deities have come there to recite this perfection of wisdom, etc. *to*: pay homage to it. And likewise when one smells a superhuman and heavenly odour, not smelled before. Furthermore, clean and pure habits will attract those gods to come to learn, etc. this perfection of wisdom, and will enrapture them. But those deities of minor power, who had before occupied that place, they will decide to leave it, for they cannot endure the majesty and splendour of those very powerful gods. And as often as those very powerful gods approach, so those sons and daughters of good family will be much confirmed in their faith. And in that place one should not form any unclean or impure habits, and it should be adorned with flowers, incense, perfumes, garlands, ointments, aromatic powders, strips of cloth, parasols, banners, and flags; it should be overstrewn with sweet smelling, loose flowers; garlands and bundles of strips should be suspended, and an awning should erected; in many ways therefore should this place be adorned. Moreover, the body of that son or daughter of good family will not get tired. On the contrary it will be at ease and achieve lightness for the sake of the happiness of many people. And that son or daughter of good family will know lightness, flexibility, and ease in both body and thought. At ease he sleeps at night. When intent on this perfection of wisdom he will see no evil dreams. When he sees anything in his dreams, it will be the Tathagatas, their golden coloured bodies embellished with the thirty-two marks of a superman, surrounded by a community of monks and a host of Bodhisattvas, demonstrating Dharma; and he will hear them talking about the six perfections, the 37 wings to enlightenment, etc. *to*: the 18 special dharmas of a Buddha. And he will hear the meaning of those perfections, etc. *to*: of the 18 special dharmas of a Buddha. And he will see the tree of enlightenment, as well as the Bodhisattva as he approaches the terrace of enlightenment, as he fully knows the supreme enlightenment and as thereafter he turns the wheel of Dharma. And he will see countless beings who are delighted by the chorus which chants the Dharma and which proclaims how all-knowledge should be gained, how beings should be matured and how the Buddha-field should be purified. He hears the sound of the voice of innumerable Buddhas, in the East and in the other directions. (He knows that) in this world system under that name this Tathagata, surrounded and accompanied by so many millions of Bodhisattvas and Disciples, demonstrates Dharma. In the East, etc. he will see innumerable Buddhas who enter Parinirvana, and will also see the countless Stupas of those Tathagatas, which contain their relics and are made of many precious things. And he will honour, revere, and worship those Stupas, with flowers, etc. In this way that son or daughter of good family will see auspicious dreams. At ease he will sleep, at ease he will wake up. Even when food is thrown into it, his body will feel light and not at all heavy.

Just as a monk who practices Yoga, who has emerged from trance and who has been replenished by his mental work, has no strong desire for food, so also that son or daughter of good family. And why? Because his body has been nourished with superhuman food. And also the Buddhas and Lords in the ten directions, as well as the gods, Nagas, etc. *to*: Mahoragas will provide his body with food. This is another quality which in this very life a son or daughter of good family will acquire if they learn this perfection of wisdom, etc. *to* : wisely attend to it, and if they are not devoid of the thought of all-knowledge.

II 6,3. ONE AIMS AT THE WELFARE OF OTHERS.

If someone has not learned this perfection of wisdom, etc. *to* : has not wisely attended to it, nor revealed it to others, but has nevertheless copied it out and honours, reveres, and worships the book, with flowers, etc.; and if someone else were to learn this perfection of wisdom, recite and study it, and wisely attend to it, would reveal it to others, and would honour, revere, and worship, with flowers, etc. a written copy of it; then the latter would on that account beget the greater merit. And his merit would be greater also than that of those who would honour, revere, and worship the Tathagatas in all the world systems in all the ten directions all around, together with their communities of Disciples, and furnish them with robes, etc. and who would erect Stupas, made of the seven precious things, for those Tathagatas who have gone to Parinirvana, together with their communities of Disciples, and would honour these Stupas, etc. *to* : worship them with flowers, etc.

Chapter 31

ON RELICS

II 6,3,2. Moderately weak.

The Lord : If, Śakra, on the one hand someone were to present you with this Jambudvipa filled up to the top with relics of the Tathagata and if on the other hand you were presented with a copy of this perfection of wisdom, which one of the two would you take?

Śakra : The perfection of wisdom. And why? It is not, O Lord, that I lack in respect for these relics of the Tathagata, and it is not that I am unwilling to honour, revere, and worship them. But I am fully aware, O Lord, that the relics of the Tathagata have come forth from the perfection of wisdom and that for that reason they are honoured, revered, and worshipped; I am aware that they are saturated with the perfection of wisdom, and for that reason they become an object of worship.

Śariputra : The perfection of wisdom, Kauśika, cannot be seized, it is undefinable and nonreacting, and has one mark only, i.e. no mark. How then can you think that it can be something that should be taken up? And why? For the perfection of wisdom has not been established for the sake of appropriation or nonappropriation, of diminution or growth, of adding something or taking it away, of defilement or purification; it does not bestow the dharmas of a Buddha, nor does it spurn the dharmas of the common people; it does not bestow the dharmas of a Bodhisattva, Pratyekabuddha, or Disciple; it does not bestow the dharmas of learners or of adepts, not the conditioned nor the unconditioned element, nor the various kinds of emptiness, the perfections, the applications of mindfulness, etc. *to* : the Buddhadharmas.

Śakra : So it is, Ven. Śariputra, as you say. The perfection of wisdom is not the donor of the Buddhadharmas, etc. *to* : all-knowledge. And why? Because it is not set up as twofold, but is nondual. And that holds good also of the other perfections.

The Lord : Well said, Kauśika, so it is as you have explained. One would wish for a duality in the Dharma-element if one were to wish for a duality in the perfection of wisdom. And why? Because the Dharma-element and the perfection of wisdom are not two nor divided. And what is true of the Dharma-element, that is true also of Suchness, the Reality limit and the unthinkable element.

Śakra : I pay homage to the perfection of wisdom to which the world with its gods, men, and Asuras pays homage. Having trained in it the Bodhisattva knows full enlightenment. When I am seated on my own godly seat in Sudharmā, the hall of the gods, then the gods who come along to wait on me salute me as I am seated there. But when I am not there on my own lion seat, then the gods salute this, my seat, and go away again. For they recall that seated on this Dharma-seat Śakra, Chief of gods, demonstrates Dharma to the gods of the Thirty-three. Likewise divinities from all the ten directions, as well as gods, Nagas, etc. *to*: Mahoragas will come to the place into which a copy of this perfection of wisdom has been put, and where it is repeated and explained to others, and they will pay homage to that perfection of wisdom and then go away again. For they recall that from it have come forth the Tathagatas, and from it has come everything that brings ease to all beings; they will recall that even the relics of the Tathagata become an object of worship only because they are saturated with the perfection of wisdom; that the perfection of wisdom is the essential practice of a Bodhisattva and the true foundation and cause of the cognition of the all-knowing and that it nourishes it. Therefore, O Lord, presented with the two lots mentioned before, I would choose just the perfection of wisdom. And whenever, having taken up this perfection of wisdom and repeating it with a mind pervaded by Dharma, I pay homage to the perfection of wisdom, I do not perceive a sign which indicates its existence as a stable entity (?). And why? Because the perfection of wisdom is signless, without attributes, is not to be talked about and incommunicable. And so are the other perfections, and so is everything up to all-knowledge. If, O Lord, the perfection of wisdom had signs and attributes, if it could be talked about and communicated, instead of being signless, without attribute, inexpressible and incommunicable, then the Tathagata, having known all dharmas as signless, without attributes, inexpressible, and incommunicable, would not have, after fully knowing the supreme enlightenment, demonstrated to beings a Dharma which is signless, without attribute, inexpressible and incommunicable. But because this perfection of wisdom is signless, without attribute, inexpressible, and incommunicable, therefore the Tathagata, after knowing all dharmas as signless, without attributes, inexpressible, and incommunicable has, after fully knowing the supreme enlightenment, demonstrated the Dharma to beings as signless, without attributes, inexpressible, and incommunicable.

II 6,3,3. FAIRLY WEAK.

Therefore this perfection of wisdom should be honoured and revered by the world with its gods, men and Asuras, and it should be worshipped with flowers, etc. And if someone honours it one should not expect him to be reborn in the hells, among animals or in the world of Yama, nor should one expect him to choose the level of a Disciple or Pratyekabuddha, until he finally wins full enlightenment. And he will never be without a vision of the Tathagatas, and will continuously mature beings and enter into a Buddha-field so as to honour and revere the Tathagatas, and to worship them with flowers, etc.

II 6,3,4. WEAKLY MEDIUM.

Moreover, O Lord, if I had to choose between a copy of the perfection of wisdom on the one side, and even this great trichiliocosm filled to the top with relics of the Tathagata on the other, I would still choose just this perfection of wisdom. And why? Because from it have come forth the relics of the Tathagata, and for that reason are they honoured, revered, and worshipped, and for that reason also the sons and daughters of good family who have honoured, revered, and worshipped it are no more reborn in the great distress of the wretched destinies. But, having experienced the achievements open to gods and men they enter Nirvana in accordance with their original vow, i.e. through the vehicle of the Disciples, or that of the Pratyekabuddhas, or the great vehicle. In fact the vision of the Tathagata and the vision of the perfection of wisdom are of equal value. Because what is the perfection of wisdom and what is the Tathagata that is not two nor divided.

II 6,3,5. MODERATELY MEDIUM.

Moreover there is equal value in the Tathagata, with the help of the triple miracle, demonstrating Dharma, i.e. the twelve-limbed Dharma which consists of Discourses, etc. *to*: Expositions, and in someone demonstrating this perfection of wisdom in detail to others, after he has learned and studied it. And why? Because from this perfection of wisdom has the triple miracle come forth, and so have the Discourses, etc. *to*: Expositions. Moreover, O Lord, there is equal value in the innumerable Buddhas and Lords in countless world systems in all the ten directions demonstrating Dharma, i.e. the Discourses, etc. *to*: Expositions with the help of the triple miracle, and in someone explaining this perfection of wisdom in detail to others, after he has learned it. *For the same reason as before.* Moreover there is equal value in someone honouring, revering, and worshipping all the countless Tathagatas everywhere, and in someone honouring, revering, and worshipping a copy of this perfection of wisdom. And why? Because from this perfection of wisdom have the Tathagatas come forth.

II 6,3,6. STRONGLY MEDIUM.

Moreover, O Lord, the son or daughter of good family who will take up this perfection of wisdom, etc. *to*: who will explain it in detail to others, of him one should not expect that he will be reborn in the hells, among the animals, or in the world of Yama, or that he will operate on the level of a Disciple or a Pratyekabuddha. Because that Bodhisattva is established on the irreversible level. And why? Because one would not expect of someone who, having copied it out, learns this perfection of wisdom, etc. *to*: worships it with flowers, etc. that he would be afraid anywhere. It is as with a man who, greatly frightened, waits on the king. If he manages (by his good service) to placate the king, he will be served upon also by those of whom he was afraid, and will no longer fear them. And why? In the presence of a powerful support there can be no fear. It is just so that the relics of the Tathagata become an object of worship as being saturated with the perfection of wisdom. In this context the perfection of wisdom corresponds to the king. As that man who is supported by the king becomes an object of worship, just so the relics of the Tathagata become objects of worship because saturated with the perfection of wisdom. And also that cognition of the all-knowing should be known as saturated with the perfection of wisdom. Therefore, if confronted with the two lots mentioned above I would choose just this perfection of wisdom. And why? Because from it have come forth the relics of the Tathagata, as well as the 32 marks of a superman, the ten powers of a Tathagata, etc. *to*: the 18 Buddhadharmas, the great friendliness and the great compassion. As they have come forth from it do the five perfections gain the appellation of 'perfection'. And also the all-knowledge of the Tathagata has come forth from it. Wherever in the great trichiliocosm beings take up this perfection of wisdom, etc. *to*: wisely attend to it, there humans and nonhumans who look or seek for entry to them do not gain entry; and all those beings will gradually move towards Parinirvana. So great is the wonder-working power of this perfection of wisdom! And this perfection of wisdom has been set up in this great trichiliocosm so that beings in it might do the work of a Buddha. One should expect a Buddha to appear in that world system in which the perfection of wisdom is observed. It is, O Lord, like a priceless jewel which has the following properties: It prevents men and ghosts from entering the place where it is put. If someone were possessed by a ghost, one has only to introduce this jewel, and that ghost would depart, unable to endure the splendour of that jewel. If someone's body were burning with bile, one would only have to apply this jewel, and the bile will be held back, could not get worse, and will be appeased. And the jewel would have the same effect when applied to a body oppressed by wind, choked with phlegm, or suffering from a disease resulting from a disorder of the humours. At night it would illuminate the scene. In the heat it would spread coolness, in the cold it would spread warmth, and wherever it is placed the temperature will not be too hot or too cold, but just pleasant. Its presence drives vipers, scorpions, and crawling animals from districts which they have infested. If someone were bitten by a viper, he would only have to exhibit that jewel, and at its mere sight that poison would depart. This is the kind of qualities which that jewel would have. If those people who are vexed by various diseases will but place that jewel on their bodies, then all those diseases will be appeased. Placed in water, it dyes that water all through with its own colour. Wrapped in a blue cloth, and thrown into water, it makes the water blue. Equally when wrapped in a yellow cloth, or a red one, or a crimson one, or a crystal-coloured one, or one dyed in various hues. And it would also completely clear up any turbidity there might be in the water. Endowed with such and other qualities that jewel will be.

Ānanda: Is this jewel a heavenly one, or can it be found among the men of Jambudvipa?

Śakra : This is a heavenly jewel. The jewels of the men of Jambudvipa are rather small and coarse, but the heavenly ones are large and fine; they are as full of all possible qualities as the men of Jambudvipa are lacking in them. In fact the jewels of Jambudvipa are infinitely inferior to the heavenly ones. If now that heavenly jewel were placed into a basket, then that basket would still remain an object of longing even after the jewel had been taken out of it, since one would remember that that jewel had been placed into it. Just so, in that place where this perfection of wisdom has been observed, these physical or mental ills and troubles, whether caused by humans or nonhumans, cannot affect the sons and daughters of good family. And 'great jewel' is a synonym for the perfection of wisdom and the cognition of the all-knowing. One cannot enumerate the qualities of the perfection of wisdom, for they are innumerable. Innumerable are the qualities of the other perfections, etc. *to*: the Buddhadharmas, and so are those of the cognition of the all-knowing, of the Realm of Dharma, the fixed sequence of Dharma, of Suchness, of the Reality limit and of the unthinkable element.

These qualities of the cognition of the all-knowing are the reasons why the relics of the Tathagata who has gone to Parinirvana become an object of worship. These relics of the Tathagata are the true repositories of the cognition of the all-knowing, of the forsaking of all the defilements together with their residues, of the ability to always dwell in evenmindedness and of the state of being always mindful, and that is the reason why they become objects of worship.

II 6,3,7. Weakly strong.

Śakra : These relics of the Tathagata, O Lord, are the repository of the precious perfection, of the perfection which is without defilement or purification, without production or stopping, without coming or going. They are the repository of the perfection of Dharmahood, because as pervaded by Dharmahood do they become objects of worship. Moreover, O Lord, if, on the one side not only the great trichiliocosm, but all the countless world systems were filled to the very top with relics of the Tathagata, and if on the other side I were offered a copy of the perfection of wisdom, then of those two I would choose the perfection of wisdom. And why? Because from it have come forth the relics of the Tathagata which become objects of worship only because they are saturated with the perfection of wisdom. If someone honours, reveres, and worships the relics of the Tathagata, then as a result of his wholesome roots he will experience pleasures open to both gods and men, and he will make an end of ill after having experienced pleasures in the families of warriors, Brahmins, and wealthy householders, and among the gods of the Four Great Kings, etc. *to* : the gods who control enjoyments magically created by others. But if someone learns this perfection of wisdom, etc. *to*: wisely attends to it, then he can fulfill the perfection of meditation, etc. *to* : the perfection of giving, the 37 wings which lead to enlightenment, etc. *to* : the 18 special dharmas of a Buddha; he can transcend the levels of a Disciple or Pratyekabuddha, enter on a Bodhisattva's special way of salvation, acquire the superknowledges of a Bodhisattva, pass on from Buddha-field to Buddha-field, and take up at will all kinds of personifications which enable him to mature beings, whether he appears as a world ruler, or as a warrior, Brahmin, or wealthy householder. Therefore, O Lord, it is not that I lack in respect for the relics of the Tathagata, or that I do not want to be involved with them. But obviously it is because of the perfection of wisdom being honoured, revered, and worshipped that the relics of the Tathagata are honoured, revered, and worshipped. Moreover, those who want to see both the Dharma-body and the physical bodies of the Tathagatas who abide in countless world systems in all the ten directions and demonstrate Dharma, should listen to this perfection of wisdom, learn it, etc. *to*: wisely attend to it. If someone wants to see those Tathagatas, he should, coursing in the perfection of wisdom, develop the recollection of the Buddha by way of two kinds of dharmas. Which are the two kinds of dharmas of the Buddhas and Lords? The conditioned and the unconditioned Dharmahood. What then is conditioned Dharmahood? The cognition of the 18 kinds of emptiness, of the 37 dharmas which act as wings to enlightenment, etc. *to* : of the holy Truths, of the Unlimited, etc. *to*: the Buddhadharmas; and also the cognition of the wholesome roots, be they with or without outflows, faulty or faultless, worldly or supramundane, leading to defilement or purification. This is called the conditioned Dharmahood. And what is meant by the unconditioned dharmas? That dharma of which there is no production or stopping, no stability or instability, or alteration, no defilement or purification, no diminution or growth, etc. *to*: of all dharmas the nonexistence of own-being. And what is of all dharmas the nonexistence of own-being? The 18 kinds of emptiness. The fact that all dharmas are empty of essential original nature, have no basis, etc. *to*: are inexpressible and incommunicable, that is called the unconditioned Dharmahood.

II 6,3,8. Medium strong.

The Lord: So it is, Kauśika, so it is. All the Tathagatas owe their enlightenment to this very perfection of wisdom, whether they live in the past, future, or present. All the Disciples and Pratyekabuddhas, past, future, and present, owe their special forms of enlightenment to it, and thanks to it (the other holy men) at all times win the fruit of a Streamwinner, etc. *to*: Arhatship. And why? Because in this perfection of wisdom the three vehicles are explained in detail, but by way of indicating no sign, by way of nonproduction and nonstopping, nondefilement and nonpurification, by way of not affecting anything, not by way of toiling or withdrawing from it, not by way of adding or subtracting anything, not by way of appropriation or nonappropriation—and in any case only by way of worldly convention and not as it is in ultimate reality. And why? Because in the perfection of wisdom one does not conceive of a not-beyond or a beyond, a shore or a gap (between two shores), even or uneven, sign or signless, worldly or supramundane, conditioned or unconditioned, wholesome or unwholesome, past, future, or present. Nor does the perfection of wisdom bestow any dharma, also not the dharmas of Pratyekabuddhas or the dharmas which constitute Arhatship.

II 6,3,9. Strongly strong.

Śakra: A great perfection is this perfection of wisdom! For when the Bodhisattvas course in it, they can wisely know the thoughts and doings of all beings, although they do not apprehend a being, a living soul, a personality, a man, a human, a young man, one who does, one who feels, or one who sees. Nor do they apprehend form, etc. *to*: enlightenment, or one who is enlightened, or the dharmas of a Buddha. For the perfection of wisdom has not been set up by taking anything as a basis. And why? Because that own-being does not exist and cannot be apprehended, nor that by which it could be apprehended, that which could be apprehended or that wherein it would be apprehended.

The Lord: So it is, Kauśika, so it is. In this way the Bodhisattva who courses in the perfection of wisdom by way of taking nothing for a basis does not even apprehend enlightenment, how much less the dharmas of a Buddha-to-be?

Śakra : Does, then, the Bodhisattva course only in the perfection of wisdom, and not in the other perfections?

The Lord : The Bodhisattva courses in all the perfections, and not only in the perfection of wisdom, but without taking anything as a basis. He does not apprehend the perfection of giving, a donor or recipient; not the perfection of morality, nor one of good conduct, nor immorality; not the perfection of patience, nor one who is patient, nor that which has to be endured; not the perfection of vigour, nor that which has to be done, nor body and thought; not the perfection of meditation, nor thought, nor trance; not the perfection of wisdom, nor one who is wise or stupid. But it is the perfection of wisdom which directs and guides the Bodhisattva who gives gifts, guards his morality, develops patience, exerts vigour, enters into trance and has insight into dharmas, though without taking any dharma as a basis, from the skandhas to the Buddhadharmas. The trees of Jambudvipa have different leaves and foliage, different flowers and fruits, different heights, shapes, and circumferences, but with regard to the shadows cast by these trees no distinction or difference can be apprehended; but they are all just called 'shadows'. Just so no distinction or difference can be apprehended between the five perfections, all of them upheld by the perfection of wisdom and dedicated to all-knowledge—because of the absence of a basis.

II 7. Praise, Eulogy and Glorification.

II 7,1. Praise.

II 7,1,1. Very weak.

Śakra: Endowed with great qualities, O Lord, is this perfection of wisdom, she is perfect as in possession of all qualities, endowed with immeasurable, inconceivable, incomparable, infinite and boundless qualities. Let us again consider two people: One has made a copy of this perfection of wisdom and bears it in mind, recites and studies it, also honours, reveres, and worships it, with flowers, etc. and wisely attends to the perfection of wisdom as it has been expounded; the other, having made a copy of this perfection of wisdom, gives it to others; which one of the two begets the greater merit?

The Lord : I will question you on this point and you may answer to the best of your abilities. What do you think, Kauśika, if one person were to honour, revere, and worship, with flowers, etc. the relics of the Tathagata, and if another person were to give to someone else and share with him a relic of the Tathagata only as big as a mustard seed with the result that its recipient would honour, revere, and worship that relic of the Tathagata as big as a mustard seed, which one of the two would beget the greater merit?

Śakra : As I understand the meaning of the Lord's teaching, compared with the one who by himself honours, etc. the relics of the Tathagata, the one who gives to another a Tathagata-relic only as big as a mustard seed will beget the greater merit. When he considers this state of affairs the Tathagata, having entered on the adamantine trance and having made his body also adamantine, generates the relics of a Tathagata out of his great compassion for the world of beings and leaves the Tathagata-relics for those beings who can be disciplined (?). And why? All those who after the Tathagata's Parinirvana worship a relic even as big as a mustard seed produce a wholesome root of which the end cannot be reached until they themselves win Parinirvana.

The Lord : So it is, Kauśika, so it is. The son or daughter of good family who honours, etc., this perfection of wisdom, and gives a copy of it to someone else, begets the greater merit.

II 7,1,2. Moderately weak.

Moreover, someone will beget still greater merit if, having given to others this perfection of wisdom as it has been explained, he will expound it to them. One would expect him to have found the 'teacher', or a succession of preceptors who represent him and who lead a spiritual life. And why? For this very perfection of wisdom should in this context be regarded as the 'teacher', nor is the teacher one thing and the perfection of wisdom another, but just the perfection of wisdom is the teacher and just the teacher is the perfection of wisdom. And why? Because those who have trained in this perfection of wisdom will appear in the world as the Tathagatas of the past, future, and present. And also those Bodhisattvas who, in possession of the superknowledges and leading a spiritual life, have one after the other stood in irreversibility, have fully known the supreme enlightenment while training in this perfection of wisdom. In just this perfection of wisdom have the Disciples trained, and through it the Arhats have attained Arhatship, the Pratyekabuddha the enlightenment of a Pratyekabuddha, and the Bodhisattvas have entered on their special mode of salvation, enter on it, and will enter on it. Therefore, then, someone who wants face to face to honour, etc. the Tathagatas should honour, etc. a copy of this perfection of wisdom. Considering also this state of affairs it occurred to Me when I had known full enlightenment: 'In dependence on which dharma should I now dwell, which dharma should I honour, revere, and worship?' On perceiving that I had attained to the highest prominence (?) in the world with its gods, Brahmas and Maras, with its Shramanas and Brahmanas, it occurred to me: 'I will now honour, revere, and worship that dharma through which I have been full enlightened, and I will dwell in reliance on that dharma'. But that dharma, that is this perfection of wisdom. So I honour, revere, and worship this perfection of wisdom and, having done so, dwell in dependence on it. How can it be that those who want to know full enlightenment should not honour, revere and worship this perfection of wisdom! And why? Because those who belong to the vehicle of the Disciples and Pratyekabuddhas should honour, etc. this perfection of wisdom. And why? From the perfection of wisdom have the Bodhisattvas come forth, from the Bodhisattvas the Tathagatas, from the Tathagatas all the Disciples and Pratyekabuddhas. Therefore then both the followers of the great vehicle and the followers of the Disciple-vehicle should honour, etc. this perfection of wisdom, and, when they have trained in it, they know and will know the utmost, right, and perfect enlightenment.

Chapter 32

THE DISTINCTION OF MERIT

II 7,1,3. Fairly weak.

If someone, Kauśika, had established one single being in the fruit of a Streamwinner, he would thereby beget an infinite merit. But not so if he had established all the beings in Jambudvipa in the ten ways of wholesome action. And why? Because beings established in the ten ways of wholesome action are not liberated from rebirth in the hells, among animals, in the world of Yama, or among the Asuras, whereas those who have been established in the fruit of a Streamwinner are liberated from all such rebirths.

II 7,1,4. Weakly medium.

Compared with establishing all beings of Jambudvipa in the ten ways of wholesome action, someone would beget the greater merit if he were to establish one single being in the fruit of a Once-Returner,

II 7,1,5. Moderately medium.

or in the fruit of a Never-Returner,

II 7,1,6. Strongly medium.

or in Arhatship,

II 7,1,7. Weakly strong.

or in the establishment of a Pratyekabuddha.

II 7,1,8. Medium strong.

And if one person were to establish the beings of Jambudvipa in the fruit of a Streamwinner, and another were to establish one single being in the supreme enlightenment, then the latter would beget the greater merit. And why? Because he is concerned with the noninterruption of the guide of the Buddhas.

II 7,1,9. Strongly strong.

And just so, if one person were to establish all the beings in Jambudvipa in the fruit of a Once-Returner, and another were to establish one single being in the supreme enlightenment, then the latter would beget the greater merit.

II 7,2. EULOGY.

II 7,2,1. VERY WEAK.

And the same applies to the fruit of a Never-Returner,

II 7,2.2. MODERATELY WEAK.

to Arhatship,

II 7,2,3. FAIRLY WEAK.

and to the enlightenment of a Pratyekabuddha. And why? Because the one who establishes even one single being in the supreme enlightenment is concerned with the noninterruption of the guide of the Buddhas. And why? Because from the Bodhisattvas have come forth all the Tathagatas that there are. By this method also one should know that the Bodhisattvas should be worshipped, adored, honoured, and revered, with flowers, etc. *to*: banners, by the world with its gods, Maras, Brahmas, etc. *to*: this world with its Shramanas and Brahmanas.

II 7,2,4. WEAKLY MEDIUM.

Someone who would establish as many beings as there are in Jambudvipa in the ten paths of wholesome action, what do you think, Kauśika, would he on the strength of that beget a great deal of merit?

Śakra: A great deal, O Lord, a great deal, O Sugata!

The Lord: Someone who would give this book on perfect wisdom to someone else, so that he may read, copy, or recite it, would beget a merit greater than that. And why? Because here in this perfection of wisdom are expounded in detail those dharmas without outflows through which those who train themselves therein have entered into the certainty of salvation, do and will enter into it, etc. *to*: through which they have attained Arhatship and the enlightenment of a Pratyekabuddha, do and will attain it; through which the Bodhisattvas, the great beings have entered into a Bodhisattva's way of salvation, do and will enter it, etc. *to*: through which they have fully known the utmost, right, and perfect enlightenment, do and will fully know it. And which, Kauśika, are the dharmas without outflows? They are the 6 perfections, the 37 wings of enlightenment, the 4 Truths, the 18 kinds of emptiness, the 10 powers of a Tathagata, the 4 grounds of self-confidence, the 4 analytical knowledges, the 18 special Buddhadharmas, the great friendliness, the great compassion, the great sympathetic joy, the great impartiality and the infinite Buddhadharmas, and they are all here expounded in detail by the Tathagatas. By this method also, Kauśika, should one know that someone who has copied this book on perfect wisdom, and gives it to someone else, to be read, copied, and recited, would beget the greater merit compared with the one (who establishes the beings of Jambudvipa in the ten paths of wholesome action). And why? Because in this perfection of wisdom are expounded in detail all the dharmas by which good warrior families are conceived, etc. *to*: the gods, etc. *to*: the applications of mindfulness, etc. *to*: the Tathagatas, the Arhats, the fully enlightened Buddhas. Leaving aside, Kauśika, the beings in Jambudvipa; as many beings as there are in a four-continent world system, if someone were to establish them in the ten paths of wholesome action, what do you think, Kauśika, would that person on the strength of that beget much merit?

Śakra: Much, O Lord, much, O Sugata!

The Lord: Compared with him someone would beget the greater merit if he would give this book on perfect wisdom to someone else, to be read, copied, or recited. And why? For the same reason as before. Leaving aside, Kauśika, the beings in a four-continent world system, as many beings as there are in a small chiliocosm, etc. as before. Leaving aside, Kauśika, the small chiliocosm, as many beings as there are in a medium dichiliocosm, if someone were to establish them all in the ten paths of wholesome action, etc. *to*: in Pratyekabuddhahood, what do you think, Kauśika, would that person on the strength of that beget much merit?

Śakra: Much, O Lord, much, O Sugata!

The Lord: Someone else will beget the greater merit if he gives a copy of this perfection of wisdom to someone else who at least reads and recites it. Leaving aside, Kauśika, the beings in a medium dichiliocosm who have been established in everything up to the enlightenment of a Pratyekabuddha, if someone were to establish all the beings in a great trichiliocosm in the ten paths of wholesome action, etc. *to*: in the enlightenment of a Pratyekabuddha, and if someone else were to give a copy of this perfection of wisdom to others, even only for them to read and recite it, then the latter begets the greater merit. Leaving aside the beings in a great trichiliocosm, if someone had established all the beings in the countless world systems in the ten directions, in the ten paths of wholesome action, etc. *to*: in Pratyekabuddhahood, and if someone else were to give a copy of this perfection of wisdom to someone else if only to read and recite it, then the latter would beget the greater merit. And why? Because here in this perfection of wisdom are expounded in detail, etc. *to*: the Tathagatas, the Arhats, the fully enlightened Buddhas. Moreover, Kauśika, if someone were to establish the beings of Jambudvipa in the four trances, the four Unlimited, the four formless attainments or the five superknowledges, would he on the strength of that beget much merit?

Śakra: Much, O Lord, much, O Sugata!

The Lord: Someone else will beget the greater merit if he gives a copy of this perfection of wisdom to some other person, although that person only reads and recites it. And why? Because therein the dharmas without outflows are expounded in detail. Moreover if someone were to take up this perfection of wisdom, bear it in mind, recite and study it, and wisely attend to it, then he will have begotten a greater merit than someone else who had established the beings in world systems of any size in the ten paths of wholesome action, in the trances, Unlimited, and formless attainments. And here the wise attention consists in that one takes up, etc. *to*: wisely attends to this perfection of wisdom without coursing in duality towards enlightenment, and that without coursing in duality towards enlightenment one takes up, etc. *to*: wisely attends to the other perfections, the emptinesses, etc. *to*: the knowledge of all modes.

II 7,2,5. MODERATELY MEDIUM.

Moreover, if someone were to demonstrate the perfection of wisdom in many ways to others, were to explain it in detail, develop it, comment and enlarge on it, and expound its meaning, and if someone else would show the meaning of this perfection of wisdom by way of nonduality, not through duality; not through sign or the signless; not through toiling or the withdrawal from it; not through adding or subtracting anything; not through defilement or purification; not through production or stopping; not through appropriation or nonappropriation; not through stability or instability; not through what is real or unreal; not through junction or nonjunction; with nothing omitted or nonomitted; not through conditions or nonconditions; not through Dharma or non-Dharma, not through Suchness or non-Suchness, not through the Reality limit or the non-Reality-limit; then that son or daughter of good family will beget the greater merit who would explain this perfection of wisdom in detail to others, who would study, demonstrate, and develop it, and who would enlarge on it and would expound its meaning, and his merit will be much greater than that of the one who only for himself takes it up, bears it in mind, recites and studies it, and wisely attends to it.

II 7,2,6. STRONGLY MEDIUM.

Moreover, someone who explains the perfection of wisdom to others will beget a greater merit than someone who only studies it by and for himself.

Śakra: So it is, O Lord, so it is, O Sugata!

The Lord: It is just so that someone should expound the perfection of wisdom, both its meaning and its letters. When he does so, he will be endowed with an immeasurable, incalculable, and infinite heap of merit.

II 7,2,7. WEAKLY STRONG.

If someone would during his entire life honour the countless Tathagatas in each one of the ten directions with what brings them ease, revere, and worship them, with flowers, etc.; and if someone else would demonstrate this perfection of wisdom to others by various methods and in some detail, and would instruct them in its meaning, then the latter begets the greater merit. And why? Because as a result of having trained in this perfection of wisdom do the Tathagatas of the past, future, and present know full enlightenment.

II 7,2,8. MEDIUM STRONG.

Greater still is the merit of someone who for endless kalpas explains the six perfections to others, and that without taking anything as a basis. What then is a basis? When someone gives a gift while taking something as a basis it occurs to him that 'I give a gift, this gift I give. I will abide in giving gifts to others'; but this is not the perfection of giving. Nor is it the perfection of morality to think that 'this is morality, I am moral, those beings I will protect'; nor is it the perfection of patience to think that 'I make an effort to be patient, I endure this because of someone else, I will abide in this patience' . . . Nor is it the perfection of wisdom to think that 'I develop wisdom, this is wisdom, for the sake of those will I abide in this wisdom'. For someone who courses in a basis cannot fulfill any of the perfections.

Śakra: How then must a Bodhisattva course so that he can fulfill the six perfections?

The Lord: Here a Bodhisattva, when he gives a gift, does not apprehend the gift, the donor, or the recipient; this is called the perfection of giving. He does not apprehend morality, those of good conduct, or a being; that is called the perfection of morality. He does not apprehend patience, that which has to be endured, or one who is patient; that is called the perfection of patience. He does not apprehend vigour, body, or thought; that is called the perfection of vigour. He does not apprehend trance, nor one who experiences the trances, nor that which should be experienced in trance; that is called the perfection of meditation. He does not apprehend wisdom, nor one who is wise, nor that which should be known by wisdom; this is called the perfection of wisdom. When a Bodhisattva courses thus he can fulfill the six perfections. It is thus that someone should without basing himself on anything expound the six perfections, complete in meaning and letters. And why? Because in a future period there will arise some sons and daughters of good family who will expound a counterfeit perfection of wisdom. Also for the sake of those who have set out for the supreme enlightenment and who hear this counterfeit perfection of wisdom should this perfection of wisdom be expounded complete in meaning and letters.

Śakra: What is this counterfeit perfection of wisdom?

The Lord: Here some son or daughter of good family may promise to expound this perfection of wisdom, but in fact will expound the counterfeit perfection of wisdom. And what they explain is that form, and everything else, is impermanent, ill, not-self, and repulsive, and that those who will course in this (insight) course in the perfection of wisdom. As a result those to whom this has been explained will strive to win these insights. But in fact a counterfeit of wisdom has been explained and practised.

Moreover, some will expound the perfection of wisdom by saying, 'Come here, you son of good family, and develop the perfection of wisdom and the other perfections! When you do so you will be able to stand on the first, etc. *to*: tenth stage'. But they will develop the perfection of wisdom by way of a sign, by way of a basis through the perception of the knowledge of all modes. This is the counterfeit perfection of wisdom. Moreover, those sons and daughters of good family will explain as follows, 'Come here, you son of good family, develop the perfection of wisdom! When you do so you will transcend the level of the Disciples and Pratyekabuddhas'. This is the counterfeit perfection of wisdom. Moreover, those sons and daughters of good family, when they explain the perfection of wisdom to followers of the great vehicle, will explain as follows: 'Come here, you son of good family, develop the perfection of wisdom! When you do so you will enter on a Bodhisattva's special way of salvation'. This is the counterfeit perfection of wisdom. Moreover, they will explain the perfection of wisdom as follows, 'Come here, you son of good family, develop the perfection of wisdom! When you do so you will acquire the patient acquiescence in dharmas which fail to be produced, and in consequence you will stand in the superknowledges of a Bodhisattva which will enable you to pass on from Buddha-field to Buddha-field, so that you may there honour, revere, and worship the Buddhas, the Lords'. When they explain it like this they explain the counterfeit perfection of wisdom. Moreover, when they explain the perfection of wisdom to followers of the Bodhisattva-vehicle they will explain as follows: 'Whoever takes up the perfection of wisdom, etc. *to*: wisely attends to it, he will beget an infinite heap of merit'. When they explain it like this, they explain a counterfeit perfection of wisdom. Moreover they will say to followers of the Bodhisattva-vehicle, 'Come here, son of good family! Take all the wholesome root of the Tathagatas of the past, future, and present, from the first thought of enlightenment to their entry into Parinirvana in the element of Nirvana which leaves nothing behind, rejoice at it, pile it up into one single heap, and dedicate it to the supreme enlightenment!' When they explain it like this they explain a counterfeit perfection of wisdom.

Śakra: What then do those explain who explain to those who have set out in the Bodhisattva-vehicle a perfection which is not counterfeit?

The Lord: Here the sons and daughters of good family explain to those who have set out in the Bodhisattva-vehicle the perfection of wisdom as follows: 'Come here, son of good family, when you develop the perfection of wisdom you should not look upon form, etc. *to*: all-knowledge as impermanent. And why? Because form is empty of the own-being of form, etc.; what is the own-being of form, etc. that is nonexistence; and what is nonexistence, that is the perfection of wisdom, which does not describe form, etc. as permanent or impermanent. And why? Because even form, etc. does not exist therein, how much less can there be permanence or impermanence'. Furthermore they will say, 'Come here, son of good family, develop the perfection of wisdom, but do not look on any dharma or rely on one! And why? Because in the perfection of wisdom there exists no dharma which should be seen or in which one should seek support. And why? Because all dharmas are empty in their own-being, and a dharma which is empty in its own-being that is nonexistence, and what is nonexistence, that is the perfection of wisdom, which is not of any dharma the toiling or withdrawal from it, the production or stopping, the annihilation or eternity, the single or multiple meaning, the coming or going away'. Therefore, then, one should describe the meaning of the perfection of wisdom in this way. When one explains it in this way one begets a greater merit than the previously described persons.

II 7,2,9. STRONGLY STRONG.

Moreover, Kauśika, if someone were to establish the beings of Jambudvipa in the fruit of a Streamwinner, would be beget much merit?

Śakra: He would, O Lord.

The Lord: A merit greater than this will he beget who explains this perfection of wisdom, complete in meaning and letters, to others by various methods. And in doing so he will say, 'Come here, son of good family! Take up the perfection of wisdom, study it, bear it in mind, recite it, wisely attend to it, and make progress in the perfection of wisdom as it has been expounded!' And why? Because from this perfection of wisdom the Streamwinner and his fruit become manifest. Leaving aside all beings who have been disciplined in the fruit of a Streamwinner in Jambudvipa, or in a four-continent world system, or in a small chiliocosm, or in a medium dichiliocosm, or in a great trichiliocosm; if someone would establish in all the countless world systems in all the ten directions all beings in the fruit of a Streamwinner, would he on the strength of that beget much merit?

Śakra: He would, O Lord!

The Lord: A merit greater than that will he beget who explains this perfection of wisdom to others in detail, complete in meaning and letters, and who says to them, 'Come here, son of good family! Take up the perfection of wisdom, study it, bear it in mind, recite it, wisely attend to it, and make progress in the perfection of wisdom as it has been expounded!' And why? Because from this perfection of wisdom has the Streamwinner become manifest.

II 7,3. GLORIFICATION.

II 7,3,1. VERY WEAK.

Moreover, Kauśika, if someone were to establish all beings in Jambudvipa in the fruit of a Once-Returner,

II 7,3,2. MODERATELY WEAK.

or of a Never-Returner,

II 7,3,3. FAIRLY WEAK.

or in Arhatship, would he on account of that beget much merit?

Śakra: He would, O Lord.

The Lord: A merit greater than that ... And why? Because from this perfection of wisdom have the fruits of a Once-Returner and of a Never-Returner, as well as Arhatship been conceived. Leaving aside the beings of Jambudvipa who have been disciplined in the three higher fruits, if the same were done to all beings in world systems of any size, in all world systems, would one on the strength of that beget a great deal of merit?

Śakra: One would, O Lord.

The Lord: A merit greater than that ... Arhatship been conceived.

II 7,3,4. WEAKLY MEDIUM.

Likewise, if all beings everywhere were established in Pratyekabuddhahood, the merit from the perfection of wisdom would be the greater.

II 7,3,5. MODERATELY MEDIUM.

Moreover, Kauśika, if someone were to instigate all the beings in Jambudvipa to win the supreme enlightenment, would he on the strength of that beget much merit?

Śakra: He would, O Lord.

The Lord: A merit greater than that ... and make progress in the perfection of wisdom as it has been expounded'. And to the extent that you progress in the perfection of wisdom as it has been expounded, to that extent you will become a recipient of all-knowledge. To the extent that all-knowledge matures in you to that extent will the perfection of wisdom more and more move in you towards the fulfillment of development. To the extent that the perfection of wisdom moves in you towards the fulfillment of its development, to that extent you will know the supreme enlightenment. And why? Because from this have come forth all the Bodhisattvas who anywhere have raised their hearts to full enlightenment.

II 7,3,6. STRONGLY MEDIUM.

And so with the beings in a four-continent world system,

II 7,3,7. WEAKLY STRONG.

a small chiliocosm,

II 7,3,8. MEDIUM STRONG.

a medium dichiliocosm, a great trichiliocosm, or all the world systems everywhere.

II 7,3,9. STRONGLY STRONG.

Moreover, if someone were to establish all beings in Jambudvipa, etc. *to*: in all world systems, on the irreversible level, then someone else would beget the greater merit if he were to explain to all these beings this perfection of wisdom, complete in meaning and letters, and if he would say, 'Come here, son of good family, take up this perfection of wisdom, etc. *to*: make progress in the perfection of wisdom as it has been expounded! To the extent that you have made progress in the perfection of wisdom as it has been expounded, to that extent do you, training in the perfection of wisdom, stand in irreversibility, and you will gradually know the supreme enlightenment. When you train in perfect wisdom, then you will be one who obtains the dharmas of all-knowledge; when you obtain the dharmas of all-knowledge, then you will know the supreme enlightenment. Furthermore, if someone were to establish all beings in Jambudvipa, etc. *to*: in all world systems, in irreversibility from the supreme enlightenment, and were to explain to them the perfection of wisdom complete in meaning and letters; and if among them one single one were to say, 'I will quickly fully know the supreme enlightenment!' then to explain to him the perfection of wisdom complete in meaning and letters would beget the greater merit. And why? Because it is to these irreversible Bodhisattvas that the full meaning (?) of the Dharma should be expounded, for they are definitely destined for full enlightenment and bound to end up in it. They pine away to get out of Samsara, but they are quite filled with the great compassion (and therefore will stay in it).

II 7,3,9x. WINDING UP THE TOPIC OF (THE DIVISIONS INTO) WEAK, ETC.

Śakra: To the extent, O Lord, that the Bodhisattva comes nearer to full enlightenment, to that extent he should be instructed and admonished in the six perfections, the 18 kinds of emptiness, the applications of mindfulness, etc. *to* : the 18 special dharmas of a Buddha. Having been helped with robes, almsfood, lodgings, and medicinal appliances for use in sickness, such a Bodhisattva should be helped with both material and spiritual things. For someone who helps with both material and spiritual things begets the greater merit. And why? Because it so happens that that Bodhisattva is instructed and admonished in the six perfections, etc. *to* : in the 18 special dharmas of a Buddha.

Subhuti: Well said, Kauśika, you who fortify those who belong to the Bodhisattva-vehicle. Even so should you act. Those holy Disciples who want to help beings, give help to the Bodhisattvas, the great beings, help them in (their wish for) the supreme enlightenment, and maintain them with both material and spiritual things. And why? For here the congregation of the Lord's Disciples has its origin, as well as the vehicle of the Pratyekabuddhas and the great vehicle. For if the Bodhisattva had not raised his thought to supreme enlightenment, then he would not have trained in the six perfections, etc. *to*: in the 18 special dharmas of a Buddha, and not having trained in those dharmas he would not have fully known the supreme enlightenment, and in consequence there would be no conception of the supreme enlightenment, nor of the enlightenment of a Pratyekabuddha, nor of the enlightenment of a Disciple. But because the Bodhisattva trains himself in the six perfections, etc. and in all dharmas, therefore he fully knows the supreme enlightenment, cuts off in all world systems the hells, the animal births, and the sphere of the ghosts, and there is a manifestation in the world of good warrior families, good Brahmin families, good householder families, of the various kinds of gods, of the perfections, etc. *to*: of all-knowledge, and of the vehicle of the Disciples, the vehicle of the Pratyekabuddhas, and the great vehicle.

CHAPTER 33

ON DEDICATION AND REJOICING

II 8. Turning Over.

II 8,1. TURNING OVER IN ITS DISTINCTIVE (FUNCTION AND MERIT).

Maitreya: When, Rev. Subhuti, we consider a Bodhisattva's meritorious work which is founded on his rejoicing (at the merit of others) and which, having been made common to all beings, has been dedicated to their supreme enlightenment, and that without taking anything as a basis; and if we compare that with the meritorious work of all beings founded on rejoicing, and with the meritorious work founded on giving, on morality, on meditational development on the part of those who have set out in the vehicle of the Disciples or in that of the Pratyekabuddhas; then a Bodhisattva's meritorious work founded on rejoicing which, having been made common to all beings, has been dedicated to their supreme enlightenment, is declared to be the best, the most excellent and sublime, the highest and supreme, with none above it,

II 8,2. THE TURNING OVER UNDER THE ASPECT OF BASELESSNESS.

unequalled, equalling the unequalled. And why? Because the meritorious work founded on giving, morality and meditational development of all those who belong to the vehicle of the Disciples and Pratyekabuddhas aims at the taming of their own self, the appeasing of their own self, the Parinirvana of their own self, and so do their spiritual practices, such as the 37 dharmas which act as wings to enlightenment, etc. *to*: the six superknowledges. But a Bodhisattva's meritorious work founded on rejoicing is dedicated to the supreme enlightenment for the taming of all beings, for their appeasing and Parinirvana. (So far about the function of dedication).

Subhuti: This Bodhisattva considers the Buddhas and Lords, beyond reckoning, innumerable, and measureless, who have won Parinirvana in the countless world systems in the ten directions, in each single direction, and their store of merit, associated with the six perfections, and acquired in the span of time which begins with their first production of the thought of enlightenment, proceeds to the time when they won the supreme enlightenment, goes on until they finally entered Nirvana in the realm of Nirvana which leaves nothing behind, and ends with the vanishing of the good law. He considers the foundation of meritorious work based on giving, morality and meditational development, on the part of those who belong to the vehicles of the Disciples and Pratyekabuddhas. He considers the roots of good, with outflows, of those who are still in training, as well as the roots of good, without outflows, of the adepts. He considers the mass of morality of those Tathagatas, the mass of concentration, the mass of wisdom, the mass of emancipation, and the mass of the vision and cognition of emancipation, as well as their solicitude for beings, their great friendliness and great compassion, as well as the immeasurable and incalculable Buddhadharmas, and also the Dharma which has been demonstrated by those Buddhas and Lords, and the roots of good of those who through this demonstration of Dharma have attained the fruit of a Streamwinner, etc. *to*: the enlightenment of a Pratyekabuddha, or who through it have entered on the Bodhisattva's special way of salvation; and also the wholesome roots which have been planted under those Tathagatas or Arhats who have now entered Parinirvana. (In his meditational development) he piles up all that (mass of merit) and rejoices over it with the most excellent and sublime jubilation, the highest and utmost jubilation, with none above it, unequalled, equalling the unequalled. Having rejoiced he would make the wholesome root associated with the rejoicing common to all beings and dedicate it to their supreme enlightenment, with the words, 'may it feed the supreme enlightenment (of myself and of all beings)!' Now, when a follower of the great vehicle turns over his thought in such a manner, do then those foundations (of merit) and the objects (involved in these contemplations) exist in such a way and are they apprehended in such a way that they would be treated as signs by those sons of good family who belong to the great vehicle?

Maitreya: Those foundations and objects are not apprehended in such a way that they are turned over into the supreme enlightenment after they have been treated as signs.

Subhuti: If he had, on foundations which do not exist and through objects which do not exist, treated as a sign those Buddhas and Lords and their wholesome roots, as well as the Disciples and Pratyekabuddhas, the learners and adepts, and their wholesome roots, all of which he had turned over into the supreme enlightenment by way of a sign, should he not beware of a perversion of perception? Thinking that there is permanence in the impermanent, ease in suffering, what belongs to a self in what does not belong to a self, calm in what is not calm—there must be a perverted perception, perverted thought, perverted view. But is it not so that as the foundations and objects (are nonexistent), so is enlightenment, so is the thought (which is turned over), so are the six perfections, etc. *to*: so is all-knowledge. But if, just as the foundations and objects, so the enlightenment, the thought, form, etc. *to* : the Buddha-dharmas (are nonexistent), then, what is the foundation, what the object, what the enlightenment, what the thought, what the wholesome roots, and what that foundation of meritorious work associated with rejoicing which is turned over into the supreme enlightenment?

Maitreya: If, Rev. Subhuti, the Bodhisattva is one who has coursed in the six perfections, who has honoured many Buddhas, who has planted wholesome roots, who is upheld by good spiritual friends and who trains in dharmas as empty of their own marks, then he is able to turn over into the supreme enlightenment without having made into a sign those foundations and objects, those Buddhas and Lords, those wholesome roots and those foundations of meritorious work associated with rejoicing. But he succeeds in turning over neither by way of duality nor by way of nonduality, not by way of sign nor by way of the signless, not by way of a basis nor by way of a nonbasis, not by way of defilement or by way of purification, not by way of production or by way of stopping. If, however, those Bodhisattvas have not coursed in the six perfections, have not honoured the Buddhas, have not planted wholesome roots, are not upheld by good spiritual friends and have not trained in dharmas as empty of their own marks, then they turn over into the supreme enlightenment while making those foundations and objects into signs, as well as those wholesome roots and those productions of thought associated with rejoicing. But this perfection of wisdom expounded in such a way, should not be taught in front of a Bodhisattva who has newly set out in the vehicle. And so with the other perfections, and the eighteen kinds of emptiness. And why? For he would lose that little faith which is his, that little serenity, affection, and respect which are his. In front of an irreversible Bodhisattva, great being, should this be taught and expounded, and also the other perfections and the eighteen kinds of emptiness. When he has heard it, he will not tremble nor be frightened or terrified—if he is one who has been taken hold of by the good friend. If he is upheld by the good friend, has done his duties under the Jinas of the past, has planted wholesome roots and honoured many Buddhas, then a Bodhisattva can turn over into the supreme enlightenment the foundation of meritorious work associated with rejoicing.

(*Subhuti*): That thought by which one has rejoiced and turned over, that thought is (at the time of turning over) extinct, stopped, departed, reversed, and so are those foundations and objects. What then is the thought associated with rejoicing, what the foundations and objects, and what the wholesome roots, which he turns over into the supreme enlightenment? What is the thought which he turns over, if two thoughts can never meet and if the own-being of a thought cannot possibly be overturned? But if a Bodhisattva, who courses in the perfection of wisdom, cognizes thus, 'nonexistence is the perfection of wisdom, and so are the other perfections, so is form, etc. *to*: the Buddhadharmas', then the Bodhisattva succeeds in turning over into the supreme enlightenment the foundation of meritorious work associated with rejoicing. When he turns over in this way, then it becomes turned over into the supreme enlightenment.

Thereupon *Maitreya,* the Bodhisattva, the great being, said to Subhuti, the Elder: How do, by a son or daughter of good family who has newly set out in the vehicle, these wholesome roots become turned over into full enlightenment? And how do they become turned over after the foundation of meritorious action, which is connected with Rejoicing, has been acquired?

Subhuti: If, Maitreya, a Bodhisattva who, newly set out in the vehicle, courses in perfect wisdom, and grasps this perfection of wisdom without taking it as a basis or without treating it as a sign, then he has much trusting confidence in the perfections, the 18 kinds of emptiness, etc. *to*: the 18 special Buddhadharmas, he has been taken hold of by the good friend—and these his good friends expound to him, according to the meaning and the letter, just this perfection of wisdom and the other perfections, and expound them to him in such a way that he becomes one who is not lacking in the perfection of wisdom, and in all the perfections, etc. *to*: in the 18 special Buddhadharmas—he has entered on the certainty that he will be saved by the special methods of a Bodhisattva, he will expound the deeds of Mara, and, when he has heard the deeds of Mara, there will be in him neither growth nor diminution. And why? Because of these deeds of Mara no own-being is made manifest. And he will never be deprived of the Buddhas the Lords until the time that he enters on a Bodhisattva's special mode of salvation. Thereafter he will plant sufficient wholesome roots to enable him to obtain the Bodhisattva-family, and he will no more be deprived of the Bodhisattva-family until the time that he fully knows the supreme enlightenment. Moreover, a Bodhisattva who has newly set out in the vehicle considers the accumulations of merit of those Buddhas and Lords whose tracks are cut off, whose course is cut off, whose obstacles are cut off, who are guides through (the world of) becoming, whose tears have dried up, whose impediments are all crushed, whose own burdens are laid down, whose own weal has been reached, in whom the fetters of becoming are extinguished, whose thoughts are well freed by right understanding, and who have attained to the highest perfection in the control of their entire hearts, as well as the accumulations of merit of the Tathagatas who abide it countless world systems in all the ten directions and demonstrate Dharma, together with their congregations of Disciples; and also the accumulations of merit of those who have planted wholesome roots under them, or in the good families of warriors, etc. or among the various kinds of gods—all these he piles up, rolls into one lump, and weighs up, and then rejoices over them with the most excellent and sublime jubilation, the highest and utmost jubilation, which has none above it; and, having rejoiced at it, he should turn over into the supreme enlightenment that wholesome root associated with the rejoicing.

II 8,3. THE TURNING OVER MARKED BY THE ABSENCE OF PERVERTED VIEWS.

Maitreya: If, Ven. Subhuti, a Bodhisattva who has newly set out in the vehicle has brought to mind all the wholesome roots of those Buddhas and Lords, together with their congregations of Disciples, and if, after having rejoiced over them with the best, etc. *to*: with the utmost jubilation, he turns them over into the supreme enlightenment, how is it that the Bodhisattva does not have a perverted perception, perverted thought, or a perverted view?

Subhuti: If, Subhuti, the Bodhisattva brings to mind those Buddhas and Lords, together with their congregations of Disciples, then he is not one who perceives a Buddha, or a Disciple, or a wholesome root; but with regard to the thought by which he turns over he becomes in that very thought one who perceives the thought (only); when he turns over in this way, the Bodhisattva has no perverted perception, thought, or view. But if the Bodhisattva, having brought to mind those Buddhas and Lords and those wholesome roots, makes them into a sign, and, having made them into a sign, turns them over into the supreme enlightenment, then this turning over amounts to a perverted perception, thought, and view. If again a Bodhisattva wisely knows those Buddhas and Lords, and those wholesome roots, and the thought by which he brings them to mind as 'just extinct, extinct'; and if he reflects that what is extinct that cannot be turned over, and that this (extinction) is the very dharmic nature of the thought by which he turns over, as well as of that which he turns over and of that into which he turns over. If he turns over in this way, then he turns over evenly and not unevently, not wrongly. It is thus that a Bodhisattva should turn over. The Bodhisattva considers (the accumulation of merit) of the past, future, and present Buddhas and Lords, from their first production of the thought of enlightenment up to their Parinirvana and further up to the vanishing of the good Dharma, as well as the (accumulation of merit) of the Disciples and Pratyekabuddhas; and also the wholesome roots which as a result of hearing the demonstration of Dharma have been planted by the common people, by the devas, Nagas, Yakshas, Gandharvas, Asuras, Garudas, Kinnaras and Mahoragas, by members of good warrior families, etc. *to*: by the gods up to the gods of the Pure Abode;—all that he piles up, rolls into one lump, and weighs up, and, then, having rejoiced over it with the most excellent and sublime jubilation, which has none above it, is unequalled, and equals the unequalled, he turns all this over into the supreme enlightenment. And if he again turns over while being aware that those dharmas are extinct, stopped, departed, reversed, and that that dharma also into which it (i.e. the wholesome root) is turned over is empty in its own-being, then it (i.e. the wholesome root) becomes something which has been turned over into full enlightenment. And so it does if he turns over while aware that dharmas cannot turn over dharmas, because all dharmas are empty in their own-being. It is thus that a Bodhisattva who courses in the perfection of wisdom and the other perfections is without perverted perception, thought, or view. And why? Because he does not settle down in those turnings over, and, since he does not review those wholesome roots and that thought of enlightenment, he cannot settle down in it. This is the supreme turning over of a Bodhisattva, a great being.

II 8,4. THE ISOLATEDNESS OF THE FACTORS INVOLVED IN TURNING OVER.

The accumulation of the foundations of meritorious work furthermore becomes something which the Bodhisattva has turned over into full enlightenment if he remains aware that this accumulation of the foundations of meritorious work is isolated from the skandhas, elements, and sense fields, from the 37 dharmas which act as wings to enlightenment, etc. *to*: from the 18 special dharmas of a Buddha; and if furthermore he remains aware that the foundation of meritorious work associated with rejoicing is isolated in its own-being, that the Buddhas and Lords are isolated from the own-being of a Buddha, that also the wholesome roots are isolated from the own-being of wholesome roots, the accumulations from the own-being of the accumulations, the thought of enlightenment from the own-being of the thought of enlightenment, the thought of turning over from the own-being of turning over, enlightenment from the own-being of enlightenment, the perfection of wisdom from the own-being of the perfection of wisdom, etc. *to*: the Buddhadharmas are isolated from the own-being of the Buddhadharmas. It is thus that a Bodhisattva should course in the isolated perfection of wisdom. This is the perfection of wisdom of a Bodhisattva, a great being.

II 8,5. MINDFUL RECOLLECTION OF THE OWN-BEING OF THE WHOLESOME ROOTS OF THE BUDDHAS.

Moreover, a Bodhisattva should mindfully recollect all the wholesome roots of those Buddhas and Lords and turn them over in such a way that he is aware that such as that turning over so is that thought by which one turns over; both are of the same kind, have the same own-being. When he remains aware of that, it (i.e. the wholesome root) becomes something that has been turned over into full enlightenment. When he turns over in this way he is without perverted perception, thought, or view. If, however, the Bodhisattva who courses in perfect wisdom becomes aware of that wholesome root of those Buddhas and Lords by way of a sign, then he does not succeed in turning it over into full enlightenment. And even if he brings to mind that the Buddhas and Lords of the past who have entered Parinirvana are without a sign and without an objective sphere, and if he treats that as a sign, then he does not succeed in turning over those wholesome roots into full enlightenment, and he has perverted perception, perverted thought, and perverted views. But if he does not perceive the Buddhas and Lords, nor those wholesome roots, nor those accumulations, nor those productions of thought, and if he does not make them into a sign, then the wholesome roots become something that has been turned over into full enlightenment, and the Bodhisattva is then without perverted perception, thought, or view.

II 8,6. THE TURNING OVER IN ITS ASSOCIATION WITH SKILL IN MEANS.

Maitreya: How, Rev. Subhuti, does the Bodhisattva turn over without making a sign?

Subhuti: The Bodhisattva should train himself in the skill in means contained in this perfection of wisdom. For the Bodhisattva should know about skill in means from this perfection of wisdom, and without resorting to the perfection of wisdom he cannot possible turn over the foundation of meritorious work.

Maitreya: One should surely not say, Ven. Subhuti, that those Buddhas and Lords do not exist in the perfection of wisdom, nor those wholesome roots, nor those accumulations, nor those productions of thought, etc. *to*: one should not say that one does not turn over into full enlightenment?

Subhuti: A Bodhisattva who courses in perfect wisdom should consider as follows: Stopped are those personal lives, those wholesome roots, those accumulations and those productions of thought. But it is only when one has made a sign that the Buddhas and Lords are discriminated, as well as those wholesome roots, those accumulations, and those productions of thought. And the Tathagatas withhold their sanction from the rejoicing of someone who in this way turns over by way of a sign. And why? For this becomes to him a great basis that he makes into a sign the Buddhas and Lords who have entered Parinirvana, that he discriminates and apprehends them.

Therefore a Bodhisattva who wants to turn over the wholesome roots should not turn them over after having apprehend them and made them into a sign, for the Tathagatas have not ascribed great wonderworking power to the turning over carried out by one who perceives a basis or a sign. And why? Because that turning over is poisonous and thorny.

II 8,7. The turning over as signless.

It is just as with food that seems excellent, but has been mixed with a poison which is concealed under its (apparently desirable) colour and taste. Some foolish person might think that it should be eaten. When he eats it, it appears good in its colour and taste, but its transformation (in someone who eats it) leads to a painful conclusion. Just so someone who has badly seized (the teaching), badly distinguished it, and who badly repeats it, and who neither knows its meaning nor understands it, will instruct others as follows: Come here, you son of good family, and consider the wholesome roots which the Buddhas and Lords of the past, future, and present have effected in the interval between their first production of the thought of enlightenment, up to their achievement of the supreme enlightenment, up to their entry into final Nirvana in the Nirvana-element which leaves nothing behind, and up to the vanishing of the good Dharma, by coursing in the perfection of wisdom and in the other perfections; and also the wholesome roots associated with the four trances, etc. *to*: the 18 Buddhadharmas, through the accumulation of which the Buddha-fields are purified and beings matured; and of those Buddhas and Lords the mass of morality, concentration, wisdom, emancipation, and the mass of the vision and cognition of emancipation, as well as their cognition of the knowledge of all modes, the cognition of the state of being always mindful, the dwelling always in evenmindedness; and also the wholesome roots effected by the Disciples and by those predestined to Pratyekabuddhahood; and also the wholesome roots effected by gods, Nagas, Yakshas, Gandharvas, Asuras, Garudas, Kinnaras, and Mahoragas; and, then, having piled all these up, rolled them into one lump, and weighed them up, turn them over into the supreme enlightenment! Thus this turning over, since it is carried out by means of a sign and a basis, causes people to partake of poisonousness. It is just like the poisonous food mentioned before. There can be no turning over for one who perceives a basis. And why? For a basis is poisonous (has a range), and is connected with signs, causes, and conditions. One who turns over in this way has not been well taught by the Tathagata, he does not preach what the Tathagata has said, he does not preach the Dharma. Followers of the Bodhisattva-vehicle should not train in this way.

II 8,8. The turning over as enjoined by the Buddhas.

Maitreya: How, then, should one turn over the wholesome roots of the past, future, and present Buddhas and Lords, after having rejoiced over them, from the production of their first thought of enlightenment, to their awakening to the supreme enlightenment, to the period when their good Dharma remains established, including their congregations of Disciples, all the wholesome roots which they have effected during this interval, until they have attained all-knowledge, etc. *to* : how should one, after having rejoiced over them, turn over the wholesome roots planted by gods, Nagas, Yakshas, Gandharvas, Asuras, Garudas, Mahoragas, humans and nonhumans? And how should one turn over so that those wholesome roots are actually turned over into the supreme enlightenment?

Subhuti: Here a follower of the great vehicle, who courses in the perfection of wisdom and who does not want to calumniate the Tathagata, should turn over as follows: As the Tathagatas cognize with their unsurpassed Buddha-cognition those wholesome roots, their kind such as it is, their own-being such as it is, their marks such as they are, and as they exist in their own dharmic nature, just so I rejoice, and as the Buddhas and Lords cognize it, so also I turn over into the supreme enlightenment. It is thus that a follower of the great vehicle should turn those wholesome roots over into the supreme enlightenment. When he turns over in such a way, he does not calumniate the Tathagatas, he preaches what the Tathagata has said and he preaches Dharma. It is thus that the Bodhisattva's turning over becomes nonpoisonous.

II 8,9. THE TURNING OVER IS UNINCLUDED IN WHAT BELONGS TO THE TRIPLE WORLD.

Furthermore, someone who has set out in the great vehicle and who courses in the perfection of wisdom, should turn over those wholesome roots while he realizes that form is unincluded in the world of sense desire, the world of form and the formless world, and so are feelings, etc. *to* : conditioned coproduction, and so also the perfection of wisdom and the other perfections, and so Suchness, Dharmahood, the element of Dharma, the Reality limit and the unthinkable element, and so are a Tathagata's morality, concentration, wisdom, emancipation, vision and cognition of emancipation, his knowledge of all modes, his state of being always mindful, and his always dwelling in evenmindedness. But what is unincluded that is not past, future, or present. And why? Because just as that is unincluded (in the triple world), so is also the turning over, and the dharmas which and into which one turns over, and he who turns over, and also the Buddhas and Lords and their wholesome roots, and also the Disciples and Pratyekabuddhas and their wholesome roots. But what is unincluded that is not past, future, or present. If, however, the Bodhisattva who courses in perfect wisdom perceives that form, etc. *to*: the (Tathagata's) state of always dwelling in mindfulness are unincluded in the triple world, and that which is unincluded is not past, future, or present, he must remain aware that it is not possible to turn over these (dharmas) by way of a sign or a basis. And why? Because a dharma's own-being does not exist; and that of which an own-being does not exist is nonexistence; but it is impossible to turn over nonexistence by way of nonexistence. It is thus that a Bodhisattva's turning over becomes nonpoisonous. If, however, a follower of the great vehicle turns over these wholesome roots by way of a sign and a basis, then he turns them over wrongly; but the Buddhas and Lords do not praise the wrong turning over as the right turning over. Such a one does not turn over with the turning over which the Buddhas and Lords praise; he does not turn over in the perfection of giving, etc. *to*: in the perfection of wisdom; he thus will not fulfill the six perfections, etc. *to*: the Buddhadharmas, he will not fulfill the concentrations or the Dharani-doors; he will not purify the Buddha-field or mature beings. But if he does not purify the Buddha-field or mature beings, then he will not fully know the supreme enlightenment. And why? Because his turning over is spoiled by poison. Moreover, the Bodhisattva who courses in the perfection of wisdom should thus consider: 'As the Buddhas and Lords cognize it, through that Dharmahood should that wholesome root be turned over. Then it will actually and successfully be turned over. In this way I turn it over through this Dharmahood to the supreme enlightenment'.

II 8,10. THE TURNING OVER AS GIVING RISE TO GREAT MERIT—WHICH IS WEAK.

The Lord: Well said, Subhuti, well said, you who explain the mass of turning over to the Bodhisattvas, the great beings, by way of the signless and baseless, by way of nonproduction and nonmanifestation, by way of nondefilement and nonpurification, by way of nonexistence and of the emptiness of own-marks, by way of the Dharma-element, of Suchness, of nonfalseness, of unaltered Suchness. If all the beings in the great trichiliocosm were to become recipients of the ten ways of wholesome action, of the four trances, etc. *to*: of the five superknowledges, would they on the strength of that beget much merit?

Subhuti: They would, O Lord.

The Lord: A merit greater than this would that son or daughter of good family beget who would turn over the wholesome roots by a turning over which is without any stain. For such a turning over on the part of that son or daughter of good family is proclaimed the most excellent of all.

II 8,11. THE TURNING OVER AS GIVING RISE TO GREAT MERIT—WHICH IS MEDIUM.

Moreover, Subhuti, if all the beings in the great trichiliocosm were to become Streamwinners, etc. *to*: Arhats, and if someone would during his entire life honour, revere, and worship them, with robes, etc. would he on the strength of that beget much merit?

Subhuti: He would, O Lord.

The Lord: Greater than his would be the merit of someone who would turn over the wholesome roots by a turning over which is without stain. Moreover, Subhuti, if all beings in the great trichiliocosm were to become Pratyekabuddhas, and if someone would during his entire life, honour, revere, and worship them, with robes, etc. would he on the strength of that beget much merit?

Subhuti: He would, O Lord.

The Lord: Greater than his would be the merit of someone who would turn over wholesome roots by a turning over which is without stain.

II 8,12. THE TURNING OVER AS GIVING RISE TO GREAT MERIT—WHICH IS STRONG.

Moreover, Subhuti, if all beings in this great trichiliocosm would set out for the supreme enlightenment; and if in all the ten directions all the beings in the countless world systems would for countless aeons honour, revere, and worship one single Bodhisattva with robes, etc. and furnish him with all he might need—would those sons and daughters of good family on the strength of that beget a great deal of merit?

Subhuti: A great deal indeed, O Lord. That merit would in fact be infinite. It would not be easy to find a comparison for this foundation of meritorious work. If that foundation of meritorious work were a material thing, it would not find room even in all the world systems countless like the sands of the Ganges.

The Lord: Well said, Subhuti, well spoken was that which you have just said. Greater than that would be the merit of someone who would thus turn over wholesome roots into the supreme enlightenment by a turning over which is without stain. Such a turning over of wholesome roots is proclaimed as the most excellent of all. The mass of merit previously mentioned will be infinitesimal compared with the mass of merit due to the turning over which is without stain. And why? Because those who were endowed with the ten ways of wholesome action, the four trances, etc. *to*: the five superknowledges, were also perceivers of a basis. And so were those who honoured, revered, and worshipped, with robes, etc. all those beings who had become Streamwinners, etc. *to*: Arhats and Pratyekabuddhas, and furnished them with all they might need. For this was only a matter of honouring, revering, and worshipping Bodhisattvas who are based on something. Thereupon the *Four Great Kings* and twenty thousand gods belonging to their host paid homage to the Lord with folded hands and said: A great transformation surely, O Lord, is this (turning over) by which the Bodhisattva, the great being, with his skill in means—in a manner which takes nothing as a basis, which is without stain, which is without a sign—turns over those wholesome roots into the utmost, right, and perfect enlightenment, and turns them over in such a way that he approaches neither duality nor non-duality. Thereupon *Śakra*, Chief of Gods, together with (one hundred thousand) gods of the Thirty-three, worshipped the Lord with heavenly flowers, incense, lamps, perfumes, wreaths, ointments, aromatic powders, garments, parasols, banners, and with music from heavenly musical instruments and cymbals. And they spoke as follows: A great transformation . . . nonduality.

Further again a Suyāma god, a Samtushita, a Nirmanarati, a Paranirmitavaśavartin god, together with many hundreds of thousands of *deities* said to the Lord: A great transformation . . . non-duality. Thereupon many hundreds of thousands of kotis of niyutas of the *Brahmaparshadi gods* came to where the Lord was, saluted the Lord's feet with their heads, raised their voices, and uttered the following words: It is wonderful, O Lord, how much a Bodhisattva, a great being who has been taken hold of by the perfection of wisdom and by skill in means, surpasses the wholesome roots of those previously mentioned Bodhisattvas and sons and daughters of good family who are based on something. And so spoke seventeen other classes of gods, up to the Highest Gods. Thereupon *the Lord* said to those gods, from the gods belonging to the Four Great Kings up to the Highest Gods: If, O gods, all the beings in the great trichiliocosm had all set out for full enlightenment, and if they all, by way of taking something as a basis, would, after they had piled them up, and rejoiced at them, turn over into full enlightenment the following wholesome roots—i.e. those of the past, future, and present Tathagatas, Arhats, fully Enlightened Ones, with their congregations of Disciples, and with (their) Pratyekabuddhas—beginning with the first thought of enlightenment, going on until the time when they have fully known the utmost, right, and perfect enlightenment, going on until they have entered Parinirvana in the Nirvana-element which leaves nothing behind, and up to the establishment of their good Dharma, i.e. the wholesome root (acquired by) those Buddhas and Lords in that interval, and by those Disciples and by those Pratyekabuddhas, and by all those beings different from them, the wholesome root which has issued from the perfection of giving, etc. *to*: the perfection of wisdom—the mass of morality, the mass of concentration, the mass of wisdom, the mass of emancipation, the mass of the cognition and vision of emancipation, and in addition the other measureless Buddhadharmas. And if on the other hand a son or daughter of good family has set out for full enlightenment, and turns the above wholesome roots over into full enlightenment, after he has piled them all up, heaped them up, weighed them all up, and has rejoiced over them with the most excellent rejoicing, and (he turns over) in the manner of not taking anything as a basis, by way of nonduality, without a sign, without a stain, treating all dharmas as inactive. Then, that second son or daughter of good family begets much more merit than the previously mentioned sons or daughters of good family, and their wholesome root is incomparably superior to theirs. This turning over of the Bodhisattva which takes nothing as a basis is the one which is described as the most excellent, etc. *to* : as something quite unsurpassed.

II 9. Rejoicing.

Subhuti: How is it that a jubilation becomes the most excellent, etc. *to*: something quite unsurpassed?

The Lord: The jubilation of a Bodhisattva becomes the most excellent, etc. *to*: something quite unsurpassed when he does not seize upon or release the wholesome dharmas of the Tathagatas of the past, future, and present, together with their Pratyekabuddhas, and also the wholesome dharmas of all other beings, and if he does not mind them, not despise them, not apprehend them; but if he thinks to himself that therein no dharma is produced or stopped, defiled or purified, and that of those dharmas there is no diminution or growth, no coming or going, no heap and no nonexistence; and if he resolves to rejoice in accordance with the Suchness, nonfalseness, and unaltered Suchness of those dharmas, with their dharmic nature, the established order of Dharma, and the fixed sequence of Dharma; and if after having rejoiced, he turns it over into the supreme enlightenment. All other kinds of rejoicing are infinitely inferior to this one, and by comparison with them this rejoicing is called the most excellent. Moreover, a son or daughter of good family who has newly set out in the vehicle and who wants to rejoice over the wholesome roots of the past, future, and present Tathagatas, together with their Disciples and the Pratyekabuddhas, acquired between the production of the first thought of enlightenment and the period when their Dharma remains established, associated with the perfection of giving, etc. *to*: associated with the immeasurable Buddhadharmas; as well as over the wholesome roots of all other beings, due to giving, morality, and meditational development; he should rejoice as follows: As the resolve so the gift, the morality, etc. *to*: the wisdom; as the resolve, so form, etc. *to*: consciousness; as the resolve, so the elements, etc. *to*: the Buddhadharmas; as the resolve so the vision and cognition of emancipation; as the resolve so the rejoicing; as the resolve, so the past, future, and present Buddhadharmas; as the resolve, so the Buddhas and Lords; as the resolve, so the full enlightenment of those Buddhas and Lords; as the resolve, so the Parinirvana of those Buddhas and Lords; as the resolve, so the Disciples and Pratyekabuddhas of those Buddhas and Lords; as the resolve, so the Parinirvana of the Disciples and Pratyekabuddhas;

as the resolve, so the Dharmahood of those Buddhas and Lords; as the resolve, so the Dharmahood of those Disciples and Pratyekabuddhas; as the resolve so is the Dharmahood of all dharmas and of all beings who are unliberated (?), devoid of calm, undefiled, and unpurified, the Dharmahood of those dharmas which are unborn, unarisen, unproduced, and unstopped; in this way he turns over to the supreme enlightenment, although nothing passes on and nothing is destroyed. This is the most excellent rejoicing of the Bodhisattvas. When he is endowed with this rejoicing, the Bodhisattva quickly knows full enlightenment. Moreover, Subhuti, if some follower of the great vehicle should during the whole of his life honour, revere, and worship, with robes, etc. those Buddhas and Lords, together with their congregations of Disciples, who abide in all the ten directions, in each single direction, in the world systems countless like the sands of the Ganges, and would give them everything that they might need; and if day and night he would put forth zeal to honour, revere, and worship those Buddhas and Lords, with flowers, etc.; and if, by way of taking something as a basis he would stand in morality, develop patience, exert vigour, enter into trance and develop wisdom; and if on the other hand someone who has set out for the supreme enlightenment, coursing in the six perfections without taking anything as a basis, turns these wholesome roots over into the supreme enlightenment, then compared with his accumulation of merit and his accumulation of wholesome roots the previously mentioned accumulation of merit is infinitesimally small. This is the turning over which is proclaimed as the most excellent, etc. *to*: as something quite unsurpassed. It is thus that the Bodhisattva, who courses in the six perfections, and who has rejoiced over those wholesome roots by way of skill in means and by way of taking nothing as a basis, should turn these wholesome roots over into the supreme enlightenment.

CHAPTER 34

GLORIFICATION OF THE VIRTUES OF CONSUMMATION

II 10. Glorification of the Marks of Consummation.

II 10,1. ITS OWN BEING.

Śariputra: The perfection of wisdom gives light, O Lord. She is worthy of homage; I pay homage to the perfection of wisdom! She is unstained. She removes the darkness from everyone in the triple world. She does her utmost to bring about the forsaking of the blinding darkness caused by the defilements and by false views. She makes us seek the safety of all the dharmas which act as wings to enlightenment. She brings light, so that all fear, terror, and distress may be forsaken. She shows the path to beings, so that they may acquire the five organs of vision. To beings who have strayed on to the wrong road she brings about the knowledge of all modes through the avoidance of the two extremes, on account of the forsaking of all the defilements together with their residues. The perfection of wisdom is the mother of the Bodhisattvas, the great beings, on account of her generation of the Buddhadharmas. She is neither produced nor stopped, on account of the emptiness of own-marks. She liberates from birth-and-death because she is not unmoved nor destroyed. She protects the unprotected, on account of her being the donor of all dharmas. She brings about the ten powers (of a Buddha), because she cannot be crushed. She sets in motion the wheel of Dharma with its three revolutions and its twelve aspects on account of its being neither turned forward nor backward. The perfection of wisdom shows forth the own-being of all dharmas, on account of the emptiness of the nonexistence of own-being.

II 10,2. ITS EXCELLENCE.

How, O Lord, should one stand in the perfection of wisdom?

The Lord: As in the Teacher, so should one stand in the perfection of wisdom. As one should pay homage to the Teacher, so also to the perfection of wisdom. And why? For just this perfection of wisdom is the Teacher; the Teacher is not one thing and the perfection of wisdom another; just the Teacher is the perfection of wisdom, just the perfection of wisdom is the Teacher. For from this perfection of wisdom all Tathagatas come forth, and also all Bodhisattvas, great beings, all Pratyekabuddhas, Arhats, Never-returners, Once-returners, and Streamwinners. From it have come forth the ten wholesome ways of acting, etc. *to*: the Buddhadharmas and the knowledge of all modes.

Thereupon it occurred to *Śakra*, Chief of Gods: Wherefrom, and for what reason, has this question of the Ven. Śariputra arisen?

The Ven. *Śariputra* read Śakra's thoughts and replied: This question has arisen for the reason that it has been said that 'taken hold of by the perfection of wisdom the Bodhisattvas, the great beings, through skill in means dedicate to the knowledge of all modes all the wholesome roots of the Buddhas and Lords of the past, future, and present, in the interval beginning with the first thought of enlightenment, up to their full knowledge of the supreme enlightenment, up to the abiding of the good Dharma.' This perfection of wisdom of the Bodhisattvas surpasses the(ir) perfection of giving, etc. *to*: the(ir) perfection of meditation. Just as, Kauśika, people born blind, one hundred, one thousand, or one hundred thousand of them, cannot, without a leader go along a road and much less enter into a city; just so, Kauśika, without an eye the five perfections are as if born blind, without the perfection of wisdom they are unable to ascend the path to enlightenment, and still less can they enter into the city of the knowledge of all modes. When, however, the five perfections have been taken hold of by the perfection of wisdom, then they acquire an organ of vision, and, taken hold of by the perfection of wisdom, these five perfections deserve to be called 'perfections'.

Śakra: As the Rev. Śariputra has said, 'taken hold of by the perfection of wisdom, the five perfections deserve to be called 'perfections'. But they do not deserve to be called 'perfections' because they are taken hold of by the perfection of giving, etc. *to*: by the perfection of meditation?

Śariputra: So it is, Kauśika, so it is. Therefore, then, this perfection of wisdom has been proclaimed as superior to the other five perfections.

II 10,3. THE NONEFFECTING OF ALL DHARMAS.

Śariputra: How should, O Lord, the perfection of wisdom be consummated?

The Lord: Through the nonconsummation of form, etc. *to*: the Buddhadharmas. Through the nonconsummation of all dharmas, etc. *to*: through the nonconsummation of the knowledge of all modes.

Śariputra: How should from the nonconsummation of form, etc. *to*: of the knowledge of all modes, the perfection of wisdom be consummated?

The Lord: The perfection of wisdom should be consummated from the nonbringing-about of form, etc. *to*: the knowledge of all modes, from their nonproduction, nonstopping, nonexistence, no birth, nondestruction, and from their baselessness.

II 10,4. THE PROCURING OF REUNION BY NOT TAKING ALL DHARMAS AS A BASIS.

Śariputra: What dharma does the perfection of wisdom procure when consummated in such a way?

The Lord: None whatsoever. That is why it is styled 'perfection of wisdom'.

Śariputra: What dharma does it not procure?

The Lord: No dharma which is wholesome or unwholesome, faulty or faultless, with or without outflows, conditioned or unconditioned, defiled or purified, belonging to Samsara or to Nirvana. And why? Because the perfection of wisdom has not been set up for the sake of providing a basis. For that reason it procures no dharma.

Śakra: Then, O Lord, does this perfection of wisdom not even procure the knowledge of all modes?

The Lord: The perfection of wisdom does not procure or apprehend any dharma, and therefore also not the knowledge of all modes.

Śakra: How then, O Lord, does the perfection of wisdom not procure or apprehend the knowledge of all modes?

The Lord: The perfection of wisdom does not procure or apprehend any dharma and therefore also not the knowledge of all modes.

Śakra: How then, O Lord, does the perfection of wisdom not procure or apprehend the knowledge of all modes?

The Lord: The perfection of wisdom does not procure it as if it were a mental process, a sign, or a volitional act.

Śakra: How then, again, does it procure?

The Lord: To the extent that one does not approach anything, does not grasp at anything, does not take one's stand on anything, does not forsake anything, does not settle down in anything, to that extent one procures, i.e. to the extent that one does not procure any dharma, does not set it free or acquire it. It is thus that one does not procure all dharmas, does not set them free, does not acquire them.

Śakra: It is wonderful, O Lord, to see the extent to which this perfection of wisdom has been set up for the nonproduction of all dharmas, for their nonstopping, their noneffecting, their nonapprehension and their nondestruction.

Subhuti: If, O Lord, the Bodhisattva who courses in perfect wisdom should perceive that 'the perfection of wisdom does not procure all dharmas', then he will treat the perfection of wisdom as worthless and keep far away from it?

The Lord: There is some way in which the Bodhisattva may treat the perfection of wisdom as worthless and keep away from it. If the Bodhisattva, coursing in the perfection of wisdom, perceives that 'this perfection of wisdom is worthless, insignificant, unsubstantial and void', then he will treat it as worthless and move far away from it.

Subhuti: Which dharma become restored when the perfection of wisdom has been restored?

The Lord: Not form, etc. *to*: not the supreme enlightenment.

Subhuti: How is it that when the perfection of wisdom has been restored no form, etc. *to*: no knowledge of all modes has been restored?

The Lord: When form, etc. *to*: the knowledge of all modes are not apprehended, then the perfection of wisdom is restored.

II 10,5. IT IS THAT WHICH BRINGS ABOUT THE GREAT AIM.

Subhuti: A great perfection is this perfection of wisdom, O Lord!

The Lord: What do you think, Subhuti, in what manner is this perfection of wisdom a great perfection?

Subhuti: There is nothing that it makes great or small, that it extends or contracts, that it strengthens or weakens. If, again, a Bodhisattva who has newly set out in this vehicle, perceives because of the perfection of wisdom, etc. *to*: because of the perfection of giving that 'the perfection of wisdom makes nothing great or small, nor does it strengthen or weaken anything', then, when he thus perceives, the Bodhisattva does not course in the perfection of wisdom. And why? Because that cannot be an outcome of the perfection of wisdom. It is not an outcome of the perfection of wisdom that form, etc. *to*: the Buddhadharmas are made large or small. And why? Because Bodhisattvas do not perceive a basis. Thus the perfection of wisdom should be seen from the no-birth of beings. From the no-birth of form, etc. *to*: the Buddha should the no-birth of the perfection of wisdom be seen. One should see that the perfection of wisdom has no own-being, because beings, as well as form, etc. *to*: the Buddhas have no own-being. One should know the nonexistence of the perfection of wisdom, its emptiness, signlessness, and wishlessness from the fact that beings as well as form, etc. *to*: the Buddhas are nonexistent, empty, signless, and wishless. One should know the nonbeingness of the perfection of wisdom, its unthinkability, and indestructibility from the fact that beings are nonbeings, unthinkable, and indestructible. One should know that the perfection of wisdom does not actually undergo the process which leads to enlightenment because beings do not, nor does form, etc. do so. One should know that 'the perfection of wisdom is not endowed with the powers because beings are not endowed with the powers, and because form, etc. *to*: the Buddhas are not endowed with the powers'. In this manner also is the perfection of wisdom a great perfection for the Bodhisattvas, the great beings.

CHAPTER 35

THE HELLS

II 11. Absolute Purity.

II 11,1. THE CAUSES OF THE PRODUCTION (OF FIRM BELIEF IN THE DHARMA).

II 11,1,1. TENDING THE BUDDHAS.

Śariputra: The Bodhisattva, the great being, who resolutely believes in this deep perfection of wisdom—wherefrom has he deceased before he came here? For how long has that son or daughter of good family set out for the supreme enlightenment? How many Tathagatas has he honoured? For how long has he coursed in the six perfections, he who resolutely believes in this perfection of wisdom according to the meaning and the method?

The Lord: This Bodhisattva will be one who is reborn here after he has deceased (in other world systems) where he has honoured the Tathagatas in the ten directions.

II 11,1,2. THE FULFILMENT OF THE SIX PERFECTIONS.

That Bodhisattva has for incalculable and immeasurable hundreds of thousands of niyutas of kotis of aeons perfected himself for the supreme enlightenment, and beginning with the first thought of enlightenment he has coursed in the six perfections, and then he has come here. And when he sees and hears the perfection of wisdom he will produce the thought, 'I have seen the Teacher', 'I have heard the Teacher'. And he will obtain this perfection of wisdom according to the meaning and the method, by way of the signless, the nondual, and the baseless.

Subhuti: Can one then see or hear the perfection of wisdom?

The Lord: No, Subhuti. Those who hear and see the perfection of wisdom, they do not actually see or hear the perfection of wisdom, on account of the fact that Dharma is their real field. They do not see or hear the emptinesses, the applications of mindfulness, etc. *to*: the enlightenment of a Buddha, on account of the fact that Dharma is their real field.

II 11,1,3. SKILL IN MEANS.

Subhuti: For how long has the Bodhisattva coursed who makes endeavours about this deep perfection of wisdom?

The Lord: One must make a distinction in this. It is possible that a Bodhisattva, beginning with the first thought of enlightenment, makes endeavours about this deep perfection of wisdom and about the other perfections, and that with skill in means. He does not reject any dharma and sees no accumulation or taking away. He never becomes lacking in the six perfections, and those Buddhas and Lords whom he desires to honour, and worship with various kinds of worship, with regard to them his various kinds of worship succeed as soon as he has produced a thought of them. He passes on from Buddha-field to Buddha-field, he is no more reborn in the belly of a mother, he is never again deprived of the super-knowledges, and he does not become partial to any defilement, or to a Disciple-thought or Pratyekabuddha-thought.

II 11,2. THE CAUSES OF THE NONPRODUCTION (OF FIRM BELIEF IN THE DHARMA).

II 11,2,1. DEEDS CONDUCIVE TO THE RUIN OF DHARMA.

On the other hand there are sons and daughters of good family who use the great vehicle, and who have seen countless Buddhas, and who, training themselves in their presence, have given gifts, guarded morality, etc. *to*: developed wisdom, but all that by was of basing themselves on something. When the deep perfection of wisdom is being taught to them, they lack in faith, and walk out (of the assembly). In their lack of respect these sons and daughters of good family even walk away when the Buddhas and Lords teach this deep perfection of wisdom. Even here there are assembled sons and daughters of good family, belonging to the great vehicle, who, when the deep perfection of wisdom is being taught, will walk away. And why? Because in the past also when the deep perfection of wisdom was being taught, they have walked away, therefore, also just now they walk away when the deep perfection of wisdom is being taught. There is no concord either in their bodies or their thoughts, and they will heap up a karma conducive to weakness in wisdom. Having done and heaped up this karma conducive to weakness in wisdom, they will refuse this deep perfection of wisdom when it is being taught, and by this refusal they will refuse the all-knowledge of the past, future, and present Buddhas and Lords. By this rejection of all-knowledge, and by having done and heaped up karma conducive to the ruin of Dharma, they will be hurled for many thousands of niyutas of kotis of years into the great hells. While they pass on from one great hell to another, their world system will be destroyed by fire, water, or wind. When such a destruction of their world system takes place, they will be hurled into the great hells in other world systems. When they have been reborn there, they will pass on from one great hell to another, and after the destruction of that world system they will again in other world systems be hurled into the great hells. When also those world systems will be destroyed, they will, having deceased in these great hells, be again reborn just here, while their karma conducive to the ruin of Dharma is still unexhausted. Again they will pass on from one great hell to another. When they are reborn in these great hells, they will experience many sharp pains, and that until the time that this world system is once more destroyed. When that destruction has taken place, they will again, having deceased here, be reborn in other world systems in the great hells. Thereafter they will in all the ten directions be reborn as animals. Then they will, reborn in the ten directions in the world of Yama, experience very painful feelings there, and thereby they will exhaust that karma. Having exhausted the karma which led to so many painful feelings, they will somewhere and at some time acquire a human body, and wherever they may be reborn they will be born blind, or be reborn among born-blind families, or in the families of outcasts, or refuse workers, or among keepers of oxen, hogs, or . . ., or in families which are mean, contemptible and low-class. And when they are thus reborn they will be blind, or ugly, or . . ., or without hands, feet, ears, or nose; and where they are they will not hear the words, 'Buddha', 'Dharma' or 'Samgha', or the words 'Bodhisattva', 'Pratyekabuddha' or 'Arhat'. All this from their having done and heaped up this karma conducive to ruin of Dharma.

Śariputra: Are not even the five deadly sins similar (in their after-effects) to the doing and heaping up of this karma conducive to the ruin of Dharma?

The Lord: One should not say that there is anything similar (in magnitude) to this karma conducive to the ruin of Dharma which has been done and heaped up by those who think that they should oppose the perfection of wisdom when it is being taught and who say that 'one should not train therein; this is not Dharma, this is not Vinaya, this is not the Teacher's religion, this has not been taught by the Tathagatas, the Arhats, the fully enlightened Buddhas'. They themselves will decide to oppose it, and other beings also they will dissuade from it. Not content with having injured their own continuities, they will try to injure those of others also. Having poisoned their own continuities, they will poison those of others also. Themselves lost they will also destroy others. They themselves do not cognize or understand the deep perfection of wisdom, and they decide to oppose it, and others also they will persuade to do the same. To these persons I do not even grant permission to hear (the perfection of wisdom), how much less do I grant a vision of it, and still less the ability to stand in it. And why? Persons of this kind should be known as defamers of Dharma. Sons of good family of this kind should be known as mere rubbish and vipers. Those who think that they should listen to them and believe them will be ruined through their lack of method. For someone who defames My perfection of wisdom should be known as a person who defames Dharma.

Śāriputra: The Lord has not told us about the length of time during which such a person who has defamed Dharma will be reborn under the influence of this deed.

The Lord: Leave that alone, Śāriputra. And why? If this were announced, those who hear it would have to beware lest hot blood spurt out of their mouths, lest they should incur death or deadly pain, or be afflicted by the dart of sorrow, lest they shrivel up or wither away, turn blue-black or a sicklish green or .... So great is the length of time during which a person who has defamed Dharma will be reborn under the influence of that deed. So great are its faults!

But the Lord gave no opportunity to the Ven. Śāriputra to learn for exactly how long that person would have to suffer for his deed.

Śāriputra: Proclaim, O Lord, as a guidance for future generations, for how long the Dharma-defaming persons will continue to suffer from their deeds conducive to the ruin of Dharma!

The Lord: May this be a guidance to future generations that through having done and heaped up this karma conducive to the ruin of Dharma he will experience many sufferings in the great hells. That is the measure and magnitude of his sufferings that he will experience sufferings for just so long. In this way virtuous sons and daughters of good family will turn away from these deeds conducive to the ruin of Dharma. Even to save their lives they will not reject the Dharma, because they fear they might meet with such sufferings.

Subhuti: A son or daughter of good family should become well restrained in the deeds of their body, speech, or mind. For they do not want to experience such sufferings, and do not wish to be prevented from seeing the Tathagata, from hearing the Dharma and from seeing the Samgha, do not want to be reborn outside the Buddha-fields and without encountering a Buddha, do not want to live among poverty-stricken humans and .... For when this action, expressed by speech, which rejects Dharma has been done and heaped up, then an action conducive to the ruin of Dharma has been done and heaped up.

The Lord: When this action, expressed by speech, which rejects all dharmas has been done and heaped up, then an action conducive to the ruin of Dharma has been done and heaped up. Just here there will be deluded persons who have left the world for the well-taught Dharma-Vinaya, and who will decide to defame and oppose this perfection of wisdom. But to defame and oppose the perfection of wisdom means to defame and oppose the enlightenment of the Buddhas and Lords;

and to defame and oppose that means to defame and oppose the all-knowledge of the Buddhas of the past, future, and present; and to defame and oppose that means to oppose the Dharma; to oppose the Dharma means to oppose the Samgha. And when the Samgha is opposed then the worldly right views and the supramundane are opposed, as well as the six perfections, the 37 dharmas which act as wings to enlightenment, the holy truths, etc. *to*: all-knowledge is opposed. When all-knowledge has been opposed, then an infinite mass of demerit has been acquired. And when such a mass of demerit has been acquired, then also an infinite mass of ill and sadness has been acquired.

II 11,2,2. The four causes of the karma obstacles.

Subhuti: Those who oppose this deep perfection of wisdom, O Lord, by what modes do they oppose it?

The Lord: By four modes do these deluded men oppose this deep perfection of wisdom. Which four? These deluded men are (1) under the influence of Mara, (2) they are unpractised in deep dharmas, and have no serene confidence (in them), (3) they have settled down in the five skandhas, and (4) they have fallen into the hands of bad spiritual directors, practise in faulty ways, exalt themselves, and depreciate others. Endowed with these four modes those deluded men will reject the deep perfection of wisdom.

Subhuti: It is hard to gain confidence in the deep perfection of wisdom for one who is unpractised, lacks in wholesome roots, and is in the hands of a bad spiritual advisor.

The Lord: So it is, Subhuti.

Subhuti: How deep then, O Lord, is the perfection of wisdom, since it is so hard to gain confidence in it?

The Lord: Form, etc. is neither bound nor freed, because form, etc. is without the own-being of form, etc. The past starting point of form, etc. is neither bound nor freed, because it has nonexistence for its own-being. The future end of form, etc. is neither bound nor freed, because it has nonexistence for its own-being. A present form, etc. is neither bound nor freed, because it has nonexistence for its own-being.

Subhuti: It is hard to gain confidence in the perfection of wisdom, if one is unpractised, has planted no wholesome roots, is in the hands of a bad teacher, has come under the sway of Mara, is lazy, of small vigour, robbed of mindfulness and without self-possession.

The Lord: So it is, Subhuti.

II 11,3. The general character of absolute purity.

The purity of form, etc. is identical with the purity of the fruit. Moreover, the purity of form, etc. *to*: the purity of the knowledge of all modes is the purity of the fruit, the purity of the fruit is the purity of the perfection of wisdom, the purity of the perfection of wisdom is the purity of form, etc. *to*: the knowledge of all modes. It is thus that the purity of form, etc. *to*: the knowledge of all modes, and the purity of the fruit, and the purity of the perfection of wisdom are not two nor divided, are not broken apart, not cut apart.

II 11,4. The different forms of absolute purity.

II 11,4,1. The disciples are purified of the obstacle of the defilements.

Moreover, Subhuti, what is the purity of self that is the purity of form, and what is the purity of form that is the purity of self. It is thus that the purity of self and the purity of form are not two nor divided, are not broken apart, not cut apart. So with the purity of a being, a living soul, a person, etc. *to*: of one who sees. Etc. *to*: The purity of one who sees is the purity of the knowledge of all modes; the purity of the knowledge of all modes is the purity of one who sees; for they are not two nor divided, are not broken apart, not cut apart. Moreover, Subhuti, from the perfect purity of self results the perfect purity of form etc., from the perfect purity of form, etc. results the perfect purity of self, etc. It is thus that the perfect purity of self, etc. and the perfect purity of form etc. are not two nor divided, are not broken apart, not cut apart. Moreover, Subhuti, from the perfect purity of greed, hate, and delusion results the perfect purity of form, etc. *to*: the perfect purity of the knowledge of all modes. It is thus that the perfect purity of greed, hate, and delusion and the perfect purity of form, etc. *to*: of the knowledge of all modes are not two nor divided, are not broken apart, not cut apart. Moreover, Subhuti, from the perfect purity of greed-hate-delusion results the perfect purity of form, etc. etc.

II 11,4,2. The pratyekabuddhas as purified of a part of the obstacle of the cognizable.

Moreover, Subhuti, the purity of form, etc. *to*: consciousness is the purity of the fruit. And so on, until we come to the purity of ignorance. From the purity of the karma formations results the purity of consciousness, from the purity of consciousness results the purity of name-and-form, etc. *to*: from the purity of old age, death, sorrow, lamentations, pain, sadness, and despair results the purity of all-knowledge. It is thus that the purity of old age, death, sorrow, lamentation, pain, sadness, and despair and the purity of all-knowledge are not two nor divided, not broken apart, not cut apart.

II 11,4,3. THE BODHISATTVAS AS PURIFIED OF (THE COVERING ON) THE PATH OF THE TRIPLE VEHICLE.

Moreover, the purity of the perfection of giving results from the purity of the perfection of giving; and so for the other perfections, for the various kinds of emptiness, etc. *to*: from the purity of the special Buddhadharmas results the purity of all knowledge. It is thus that the purity of all knowledge and the purity of the special Buddhadharmas is not two nor divided, not broken apart, not cut apart.

(II 11,5. THE VARIETIES OF ABSOLUTE PURITY).

II 11,5,1. THE WEAKEST PATH.

Moreover, the purity of the perfection of wisdom is the purity of form, the purity of form is the purity of everything up to the knowledge of all modes. It is thus that the purity of the perfection of wisdom and the purity of form and the purity of the knowledge of all modes are not two nor divided, not broken apart, not cut apart. And so for the other skandhas, and for the perfections.

II 11,5.2. THE MEDIUM WEAK PATH.

Moreover, from the purity of inward emptiness, etc. *to*: from the purity of the emptiness of the nonexistence of own-being results the purity of the knowledge of all modes. It is thus that the purity of inward emptiness, etc. *to*: the purity of the emptiness of the nonexistence of own-being and the purity of the knowledge of all modes are not two nor divided, not broken apart, not cut apart. From the purity of the skandhas, elements, sense fields and conditioned coproduction, etc. *to*: from the purity of the ten powers, the grounds of self-confidence, and the special Buddhadharmas results the purity of the knowledge of all modes. It is thus that the purity of the skandhas, elements, sense fields and conditioned coproduction, and the purity of the perfections, the dharmas which act as wings to enlightenment, the holy truths, the Unlimited, the trances, the formless attainments, the eight emancipations, the nine successive attainments, the emptiness, signless and wishless, the superknowledges, of all concentrations and all dharani-doors, and the purity of the ten powers, the grounds of self-confidence, the analytical knowledges and the special Buddhadharmas, and the purity of the knowledge of all modes are not two nor divided, not broken apart and not cut apart. Moreover, the purity of the knowledge of all modes and the purity of the perfection of wisdom are not two nor divided, not broken apart nor cut apart.

II 11,5,3. THE STRONGEST WEAK PATH.

Moreover, from the purity of the conditioned results the purity of the unconditioned, and from the purity of the unconditioned the purity of the conditioned. It is thus that the purity of the conditioned and the purity of the unconditioned are not two nor divided, not broken apart, not cut apart. Moreover, Subhuti, from the purity of the past results the purity of the future, from the purity of the future the purity of the past, from the purity of the past and future the purity of the present, from the purity of the present the purity of the past and future. It is thus that the purity of the past and future and the purity of the present are not two nor divided, are not broken apart, are not cut apart.

CHAPTER 36

THE EXPOSITION OF THE PURITY OF ALL DHARMAS

II 11,5,4. THE WEAK-MEDIUM PATH.

Śāriputra: This purity is deep, O Lord.

The Lord: Because of absolute purity.

Śāriputra: Because of the purity of what?

The Lord: Because of the purity of form etc. *to*: the knowledge of all modes.

II 11,5,5. THE MEDIUM-MEDIUM PATH.

Śāriputra: A true light, O Lord, is the perfection of wisdom.

The Lord: Because of absolute purity.

Śāriputra: Because of the purity of what?

The Lord: The purity of the infinite light results from the purity of the six perfections, the various kinds of emptiness, etc. *to*: of the knowledge of all modes.

II 11,5,6. THE STRONG-MEDIUM PATH.

Śāriputra: Not subject to rebirth is the perfection of wisdom.

The Lord: Because of absolute purity.

Śāriputra: The purity results from the nonpassing-on of what?

The Lord: The fact that form, etc. *to*: the knowledge of all modes are not subject to passing on or to rebirth, that is the purity.

II 11,5,7. THE STRONG-WEAK PATH.

Śāriputra: Undefiled, O Lord, is purity.

The Lord: Because of the absolute absence of all defilement.

Śāriputra: Through the nondefilement of what is the purity?

The Lord: The purity results from the fact that form, etc. *to*: the knowledge of all modes are in their essential original nature free from the defilements.

II 11,5,8. THE STRONG-MEDIUM PATH.

Śāriputra: The purity is without attainment or reunion.

The Lord: Because there is absolutely no attainment or reunion.

Śāriputra: Through the nonattainment of what and through the nonreunion with what is there purity?

The Lord: Through the nonattainment of form, etc. *to*: the knowledge of all modes, and through the nonreunion with them.

II 11,5,9. THE STRONG-STRONG PATH.

Śāriputra: Purity, O Lord, does not reproduce itself.

The Lord: Because absolutely there is no reproduction.

Śāriputra: The purity results from the nonreproduction of what?

The Lord: It results from the nonreproduction of the five skandhas.

II 11x. THE PATH AS OPPOSED TO THE WORLD.

Śāriputra: Purity means no rebirth, whether in the world of sense desire or the world of form, or the formless world.

The Lord: Because of absolute purity.

Śāriputra: How is it that purity means no rebirth in the triple world?

The Lord: Because, when the own-being is considered, there is no rebirth in any of the three worlds.

II 11xx. THE PATH AS OPPOSED TO THE DUALITY BETWEEN THE COGNITION AND THE COGNIZABLE.

Śāriputra: Purity, O Lord, does not cognize.

The Lord: Because of absolute purity.

Śāriputra: How is it that purity does not cognize?

The Lord: Because one is benumbed by Dharma.

Śāriputra: Purity does not cognize the skandhas.

The Lord: Because of absolute purity.

Śāriputra: How is it that purity does not cognize the skandhas?

The Lord: On account of the emptiness of own-marks.

Śāriputra: Purity does not cognize all dharmas.

The Lord: Because of absolute purity.

Śāriputra: How is it that purity does not cognize all dharmas?

The Lord: Because it does not apprehend them.

II 11xxx. REFUTATION OF AN OBJECTION WITH REGARD TO THE PATH. CONCLUSION OF THE DUAL PURITY OF THE PATH OF DEVELOPMENT.

Śāriputra: The perfection of wisdom neither helps nor hinders all-knowledge.

The Lord: Because of absolute purity.

Śāriputra: How is it that the perfection of wisdom neither helps nor hinders all-knowledge?

The Lord: Because of the established order of Dharma.

Śāriputra: The purity of the perfection of wisdom does not take hold of any dharma.

The Lord: Because of absolute purity.

Śāriputra: How is it that the purity of the perfection of wisdom does not take hold of any dharma?

The Lord: Because the Dharma-element has been taken hold of.

Subhuti: The purity of the skandhas, O Lord, is due to the purity of the self.

The Lord: Because of absolute purity.

Subhuti: For what reason is the purity of the skandhas due to the purity of (the) self?

The Lord: The absolute purity results from the unreality of both self and the skandhas.

Subhuti: The purity of the perfections, etc. *to*: the 18 special Buddhadharmas is due to the purity of self.

The Lord: Because of absolute purity.

Subhuti: The purity of all dharmas is due to the purity of self.

The Lord: Because of absolute purity.

Subhuti: For what reason is the purity of self the purity of all dharmas?

The Lord: It is purity because of the unreality of the self.

Subhuti: To the purity of the self is due the purity of the fruit of a Streamwinner; and so is that of the fruit of a Once-returner, a Never-returner, of Arhatship, and of the enlightenment of a Pratyekabuddha.

The Lord: On account of the emptiness of own-marks.

Subhuti: To the purity of the self is due the purity of enlightenment.

The Lord: Because of absolute purity.

Subhuti: For what reason is the purity of enlightenment due to the purity of the self?

The Lord: On account of the emptiness of own-marks.

Subhuti: To the purity of self is due the purity of all-knowledge.

The Lord: Because of absolute purity.

Subhuti: For what reason is the purity of all-knowledge due to the purity of the self?

The Lord: On account of the emptiness of own-marks.

Subhuti: The dual purity is not attainment or reunion.

The Lord: Because of absolute purity.

Subhuti: For what reason is the dual purity not attainment or reunion?

The Lord: Because in Dharma nondefilement and nonpurification are the same.

Subhuti: The boundlessness of the skandhas is due to the boundlessness of the self.

The Lord: Because of absolute purity.

Subhuti: For what reason is the boundlessness of the skandhas due to the boundlessness of the self?

The Lord: On account of absolute emptiness and of the emptiness without beginning or end.

Subhuti: This then, O Lord, is the perfection of wisdom of the Bodhisattva, the great being.

The Lord: Because of absolute purity.

[*Subhuti*: For what reason is this the perfection of wisdom of the Bodhisattva, the great being?

The Lord: On account of the knowledge of the modes of the path.]

III. ALL-KNOWLEDGE.

III 1-2. Unestablished in either Samsara or Nirvana.

Subhuti: The perfection of wisdom of the Bodhisattvas, the great beings, O Lord, is not got at on the shore this side, or on the shore beyond, or in between the two.

The Lord: Because of its absolute purity, Subhuti.

Subhuti: For what reason is the perfection of wisdom of the Bodhisattvas, the great beings, not got at on the shore this side, or on the shore beyond, or in between the two?

The Lord: Because of its absolute purity, Subhuti, on account of the fact that all dharmas are the same in the three periods of time.

III 3. Farness (from Perfect Wisdom) owing to Lack of Skill in Means.

Subhuti: If again, O Lord, a son or daughter of good family who belongs to the great vehicle would, unskilled in means, cognize the perfection of wisdom by making it into a basis, he will (thereby) part from this perfection of wisdom and get far away from it.

The Lord: Well said, Subhuti, well said; so it is, Subhuti. For also names and signs are sources of attachment. And why? Because all dharmas are signless and nameless.

Subhuti: How, O Lord, are also names and signs sources of attachment?

The Lord: Here, Subhuti, a son or daughter of good family who belongs to the great vehicle seizes on the perfection of wisdom through a name, seizes on it through a sign. And, having seized on it through a sign and a name they will part from the perfection of wisdom, will get far away from it; by minding it they will part from the perfection of wisdom, will get far away from it.

III 4. Nearness (to Perfect Wisdom) owing to Skill in Means.

Subhuti: It is wonderful, O Lord, to see the extent to which this perfection of wisdom of the Bodhisattvas, the great beings, has been well taught, and well rounded off.

III 5. (The Cognition of) Entities (as a Point to be Shunned).

Śāriputra: What, Ven. Subhuti, is attachment on the part of the

Bodhisattvas who course in perfect wisdom, and what is nonattachment?

Subhuti: Here, Ven. Śariputra, a Bodhisattva, or a son or daughter of good family, unskilled in means will perceive the skandhas as empty—and that is an attachment; unskilled in means he will perceive past dharmas as past dharmas, future dharmas as future dharmas, present dharmas as present dharmas—and that is an attachment. Moreover, it is an attachment if a Bodhisattva, while perceiving a basis, courses, beginning with the first thought of enlightenment, in the six perfections.

III 6. Points to be Shunned and Antidotes.

III 6,ab. Antidotes (and points to be shunned).

As again, Ven. Śariputra, you have said, 'What is the nonattachment of the Bodhisattvas, the great beings, who course in perfect wisdom?' The Bodhisattva, the great being, who courses in perfect wisdom and who is skilled in means does certainly not perceive form as form, feeling as feeling, etc.; not past dharmas as past dharmas, etc. Nor does it occur to him: I give a gift, to him I give a gift, this gift I give; I guard morality, this morality I guard, through that do I guard morality; etc. *to*: I beget merit, thus I beget (merit). I enter on the Bodhisattva's certainty of salvation; I will purify the Buddha-field; I will mature beings; I shall reach all-knowledge. The Bodhisattvas who course in perfect wisdom and are skilled in means do not make any of these discriminations. And why? On account of the twenty kinds of emptiness. These are the nonattachments of a Bodhisattva, a great being, who courses in perfect wisdom and who is skilled in means.

III 6c. Once more the points to be shunned.

Śakra: In which manner, Subhuti, is there attachment on the part of a Bodhisattva?

Subhuti: Here, Kauśika, the Bodhisattva perceives thought, perceives giving, etc. *to*: wisdom, the 20 kinds of emptiness, perceives the Buddhas, the Lords. He perceives the wholesome roots which have been planted under the Buddhas, and after he has heaped up all these, rolled them into one lump, and weighed them up, he converts them into the utmost, right, and perfect enlightenment. This is an attachment on the part of a Bodhisattva, and through it he does not course in nonattachment. And why? For it is impossible to turn over the essential original nature of form, feeling, etc.

III 6d. Once more the antidote.

Moreover, Kauśika, a Bodhisattva who wants to instruct others in the supreme enlightenment, who wants to instigate them, fill them with enthusiasm for it, encourage them towards it, he should do so with a mind which keeps in agreement with true reality, and also in such a way that, when he courses in perfect wisdom, he does not produce such discursive ideas as 'I give a gift', etc. It is thus that a Bodhisattva rouses and incites others. In that way he does not cast his self away, and the manner in which he rouses others has the sanction of the Buddhas. It is thus that a Bodhisattva should rouse and incite to the supreme enlightenment. And it is in this way that that son or daughter of good family succeeds in abandoning all the points of attachment.

III 6e. SUBTLE ATTACHMENTS.

The Lord: Well said, Subhuti, you who point out to the Bodhisattvas, the great beings, these points of attachment. I will now announce to you other, more subtle, attachments. Listen to them well, and pay good attention! I will teach them to you. "So be it, O Lord!" and the Ven. *Subhuti* listened in silence.

The Lord: Here, Subhuti, a son or daughter of good family who has set out for the supreme enlightenment attends to the Tathagatas through a sign. But, so many signs, so many attachments. Whatever wholesome root there may be on the part of those Tathagatas in the interval (of time) which begins with the first thought of enlightenment, until full enlightenment has been fully known, until they have reached final Nirvana in the Nirvana-element which leaves nothing behind, and until the establishment of the Good Law,—to all that he attends through a sign, and, having attended to it, dedicates it to the supreme enlightenment. But as long as he attends through a sign, so long there is attachment. And as to the wholesome roots, which are quite free from attachment, of those Tathagatas, who are themselves free from all attachment, and as to the wholesome roots of other beings as well—to those also he attends through a sign, and, having attended to them, he dedicates them to the supreme enlightenment. But as long as he attends through a sign, so long there is attachment. And why? For the Tathagatas should not be attended to through a sign, nor should the wholesome roots of those others be attended to through a sign.

III 6f. THE DEPTH OF DHARMA.

Subhuti: Deep, O Lord, is the perfection of wisdom.

The Lord: Because all dharmas are isolated in their essential original nature.

Subhuti: I pay homage, O Lord, to the perfection of wisdom!

The Lord: For the perfection of wisdom is unmade, it has not been brought about, and so it has not been fully known by anyone.

III 6g. THE ABANDONMENT OF ALL ATTACHMENTS.

Subhuti: Hard to know fully are all dharmas.

The Lord: Because they have the essential nature of Buddhadharmas. Their nature is a no-nature. May a Bodhisattva thus cognize and see the essential nature as a no-nature which has not been brought about. All points of attachment will then be abandoned.

III 6h. THE FACT THAT IT IS HARD TO UNDERSTAND.

Subhuti: Hard to know fully, O Lord, is the perfection of wisdom!

The Lord: Because the perfection of wisdom has not been seen by anyone, nor heard, nor felt, nor discerned, nor fully known.

III 6i. UNTHINKABILITY.

Subhuti: Unthinkable, O Lord, is the perfection of wisdom.

The Lord: Because the perfection of wisdom has not been discerned by anyone, and it has not been cognized by form, etc. *to*: by the Buddhadharmas.

Chapter 37

UNSUPPORTED ANYWHERE

Subhuti: Inactive is the perfection of wisdom.
The Lord: Because all dharmas cannot be apprehended.

III 7. The Endeavours of the Cognition of Entities.

III 7,1. The endeavours with regard to the skandhas.

Subhuti: How, O Lord, should a Bodhisattva course in perfect wisdom?

The Lord: Here, Subhuti, if a Bodhisattva, who courses in perfect wisdom, does not course in form, etc., then he courses in perfect wisdom.

III 7,2. The endeavours with regard to the impermanence, etc. of the skandhas.

If he does not course in the idea that 'form is not permanent or impermanent', 'not ease or ill', etc. then he courses in perfect wisdom. And why? That form does not exist in such a way that impermanent or permanent, ease or ill, self or not-self, attractive or repulsive (can be predicated) of it; and so for feeling, etc.

III 7,3. The endeavours with regard to the completeness or incompleteness of the skandhas.

Moreover, if a Bodhisattva who courses in perfect wisdom does not course in the idea that 'form, etc. is incomplete or complete', then he courses in perfect wisdom. And why? For what is the incompleteness or completeness of form, etc. *to*: all-knowledge, that is not form, etc. *to*: all-knowledge. If also thus he does not course, then he courses in perfect wisdom.

III 7,4. The endeavours with regard to nonattachment to the skandhas.

Subhuti: It is wonderful, O Lord, to what an extent both the attachment and the nonattachment of the Bodhisattvas, the great beings, have been explained!

The Lord: So it is, Subhuti. They have been well explained by the Tathagata, the Arhat, the fully enlightened Buddha. Moreover, Subhuti, if a Bodhisattva who courses in perfect wisdom does not course in the idea that 'form is with attachment or without attachment', then he courses in perfect wisdom. Coursing thus, the Bodhisattva, the great being, does not perceive form, etc., as 'with or without attachment'.

III 7,5. THE ENDEAVOURS WITH REGARD TO THE IMMUTABILITY (OF PERFECT WISDOM).

Subhuti: It is wonderful, O Lord, how demonstration does not diminish this deep perfection of wisdom, nor does nondemonstration diminish it; demonstration does not increase it, and also nondemonstration does not increase it.

The Lord: So it is, Subhuti, nondemonstration of the perfection of wisdom does not diminish, demonstration does not increase it. It is as if a Tathagata should, during his entire life, speak in praise or dispraise of space—and yet the volume of space would not increase when he praises it and would not diminish when he does not praise it. For space does not increase through praise, nor does it diminish through nonpraise.

III 7,6. THE ENDEAVOURS WITH REGARD TO THE ABSENCE OF AN AGENT.

Or it is as with an illusory man. Praise does not make him grow, nor does he waste away when there is no praise. Praise does not win him over, and when there is no praise he is not frustrated. Just so the true nature of dharmas is just as much as it is, whether it be demonstrated or not.

III 7,7. THE ENDEAVOUR TO DO THAT WHICH IS HARD TO DO.

III 7,7a. THE ULTIMATE AIM IS HARD TO REALIZE.

Subhuti: A doer of what is hard is the Bodhisattva who, while coursing in perfect wisdom, does not lose heart when the perfection of wisdom is being preached, and does not mentally turn away from it, who persists in making endeavours about the perfection of wisdom and who does not turn back on the supreme enlightenment. And why? This development of perfect wisdom is like the development of space. But in space there can be no development of perfect wisdom and the perfection of wisdom cannot be conceived in space, nor the other perfections, nor the skandhas, etc. *to*: nor the supreme enlightenment.

Subhuti: I pay homage to the Bodhisattvas, the great beings, who are armed with this armour. Those who for the sake of beings put on the armour want to exert themselves and to struggle for the sake of space, and they want to liberate space. Armed with the great armour are the Bodhisattvas who put on the armour for the sake of dharmas which are like space.

III 7,7b. THE TRAINING IS DIFFICULT.

They want to get rid of space or the firmanent, those who for the sake of beings put on the armour.

III 7,7c. THE ACTIVITY IS DIFFICULT.

A great perfection of vigour has the Bodhisattva who wants to know the supreme enlightenment for the sake of beings. And why? If this great trichiliocosm were quite full of Tathagatas, like a thicket of reeds, a bamboo wood, a sugar cane forest, a forest of Saccharum Sara reed or like a rice field, and if these Tathagatas would demonstrate Dharma for an aeon or for the remainder of an aeon; and if each single Tathagata would lead countless beings to Nirvana; still one could not conceive of the depletion or repletion of the world of beings. And why? On account of the unreality of beings, on account of their isolatedness. And the same would be true if all the world systems in all the ten directions were considered. It is by way of this method that I say: Space would those want to liberate who for the sake of beings want to know full enlightenment.

III 7,8. THE ENDEAVOUR IS NOT BARREN.

Thereupon, it occurred to a *certain monk*: I pay homage, O Lord, to the perfection of wisdom of the Lord, in which no dharma is either produced or stopped. The mass of morality is not conceived in it, the mass of concentration, etc. *to*: the fruit of a Streamwinner, etc. is not conceived in it.

Śakra: If, Ven. Subhuti, a Bodhisattva were to make endeavours about this deep perfection of wisdom, what would his endeavours be about?

Subhuti: About space he would make endeavours, if he would endeavour to train in this deep perfection of wisdom.

III 7,9. THE ENDEAVOUR IS NOT CONDITIONED BY ANYONE ELSE.

Śakra: I will arrange for the shelter, defense, and protection of that son or daughter of good family who will take up, etc. this perfection of wisdom.

Subhuti: Can you, Śakra, see that dharma which you wish to shelter, defend, and protect?

Śakra: No, I cannot.

Subhuti: When a son or daughter of good family stand in perfect wisdom as it has been expounded, then just that will be their shelter, defense, and protection. On the other hand, when they are lacking in the perfection of wisdom as it has been expounded, then (hostile) men and ghosts will get a chance to harm them. One would think of arranging shelter, defense, and protection for space if one would think of arranging shelter, defense, and protection for the Bodhisattvas who course in perfect wisdom. What do you think, Kauśika, are you able to arrange shelter, defense, and protection for a magical illusion, a mirage, a dream, an echo, a reflection, an image, a city of the Gandharvas?

Śakra: Not so, Ven. Subhuti.

Subhuti: So it is, Kauśika, One who would think of arranging shelter, defense, and protection for Bodhisattvas who course in perfect wisdom would wear himself out to no purpose. What do you think, Kauśika, are you able to arrange shelter, defense, and protection for a Tathagata, or for a Tathagata's magical creation?

Śakra: Not so, Ven. Subhuti.

Subhuti: So it is, Kauśika. One who would think of arranging shelter, defense, and protection for Bodhisattvas who course in perfect wisdom would wear himself out to no purpose. What do you think, Kauśika, are you able to arrange shelter, defense and protection for the Dharma-element, for the Reality limit, for Suchness, for the unthinkable element?

Śakra: Not so, Ven. Subhuti.

Subhuti: Just so with the Bodhisattvas.

III 7,10. THE COGNITION OF THE SEVEN ASPECTS (OR POINTS OF) COMPARISON.

Śakra: To what an extent has a Bodhisattva who courses in perfect wisdom comprehended all dharmas as like a dream, a mock show, a mirage, an echo, a reflected image, a city of the Gandharvas, an illusory magical creation?

Subhuti: To the extent that Bodhisattvas do not put their minds even to the dream, or do not mind through the dream, or do not think that 'this is my dream', or do not mind in the dream—and so for the other six—to that extent have they comprehended that all dharmas are like a dream, etc.

III 8. The Sameness of the Endeavours.

Moreover, Kauśika, a Bodhisattva who courses in perfect wisdom does not put his mind even to form, does not mind through form, does not mind in a dream, does not think 'mine is the dream', does not think 'this is a dream'; and so on with the usual variations.

III 9. The Path of Vision.

III 9a. THE INTIMATION OF THE PRESENCE OF THE 16 MOMENTS OF THE PATH OF VISION.

Thereupon through the Buddha's might the Four Great Kings in this great trichiliocosm, and the other gods up to the gods of the Pure Abode, scattered heavenly sandalwood powder and came to where the Lord was. They reverently saluted the Lord's feet with their heads and stood on one side. Thereupon through the Buddha's might the minds of all these deities were impressed by (the sight of) a thousand Buddhas in the act of teaching the Dharma, in these very syllables, in these very words, with monks called Subhuti asking questions about just this deep perfection of wisdom as well as demonstrating it, and with Śakras, Chiefs of Gods, asking counterquestions about it. And so for the world systems in all the ten directions.

The Lord: Subhuti, just at this spot of earth the Bodhisattva Maitreya will, after he has won supreme enlightenment, teach this very same perfection of wisdom. At just this spot of earth will the Tathagatas of this Auspicious Aeon teach this very same perfection of wisdom, after they have won the supreme enlightenment.

III 9,1. ACCEPTANCE OF COGNITION OF DHARMA IN SUFFERING: NEITHER PERMANENT NOR IMPERMANENT. (Aspect: Impermanent).

Subhuti: By which modes, O Lord, by which characteristics, by which signs will the Bodhisattva Maitreya teach this perfection of wisdom, after he has won the supreme enlightenment?

The Lord: Here, Subhuti, the Bodhisattva Maitreya will, after he has won the supreme enlightenment, teach Dharma to the effect that form is not permanent or impermanent, not ease or ill, not self or not-self, not attractive or repulsive; that it is neither bound nor freed; that it is not past, future, or present. And so for everything up to the Buddhadharmas.

III 9,2. COGNITION OF DHARMA IN SUFFERING: BOTH ETERNITY AND ANNIHILATION ARE LEFT BEHIND. (Aspect: Ill).

Subhuti: How again will the Bodhisattva Maitreya demonstrate Dharma after he has known the supreme enlightenment?

The Lord: He will demonstrate Dharma to the effect that 'form, etc. is absolutely pure, absolutely pure'.

III 9,3. ACCEPTANCE OF SUBSEQUENT COGNITION OF SUFFERING: PURE. (Aspect: Empty).

Subhuti: Perfectly pure, O Lord, is the perfection of wisdom.

The Lord: Because of the perfect purity of form, etc.

III 9,4. SUBSEQUENT COGNITION OF SUFFERING: NOT PRODUCED OR STOPPED, NOT DEFILED OR PURIFIED. (Aspect: Impersonal).

Subhuti: How is it that the perfection of wisdom is perfectly pure because of the perfect purity of form, etc.?

The Lord: The perfect purity of form, etc. lies in its nonproduction and nonstopping, its nondefilement and nonpurification.

III 9,5. Acceptance of cognition of dharma in origination: like space. (Aspect: Cause).

Moreover, Subhuti, because of the perfect purity of space is the perfection of wisdom perfectly pure.

Subhuti: How is that, O Lord?

The Lord: The perfection of wisdom is like space and is perfectly pure because of the nonproduction, nonstopping, nondefilement and nonpurification of form, etc. *to*: all-knowledge.

III 9,6. The cognition of dharma in origination: unstained by primary and secondary defilements. (Aspect: Origination)

The perfection of wisdom is perfectly pure because of the stainlessness of space.

Subhuti: How is that, O Lord?

The Lord: The perfection of wisdom is like space and perfectly pure because of the stainlessness of form, etc. *to*: all-knowledge.

III 9,7. Acceptance of subsequent cognition of origination: set free. (Aspect: Product).

Moreover the perfection of wisdom is perfectly pure because of the fact that space cannot be seized upon.

Subhuti: How is that, O Lord?

The Lord: The perfection of wisdom is like space and perfectly pure because form, etc. *to*: all-knowledge cannot be seized upon.

III 9,8. Subsequent cognition of origination: inexpressible. (Aspect: Condition).

The perfection of wisdom is perfectly pure because of the inexpressibility of space.

Subhuti: How is that, O Lord?

The Lord: Just as in space an echo is the sound of a non-duality, just so the perfection of wisdom is like space and it is perfectly pure because form, etc. *to*: all-knowledge are inexpressible.

III 9,9. Acceptance of cognition of dharma in stopping: unobtainable. (Aspect: Stopping).

The perfection of wisdom is perfectly pure because of the incommunicability of space.

Subhuti: How is that, O Lord?

The Lord: There can be no conventional utterance about space. Just so the perfection of wisdom is perfectly pure because form, etc. *to*: all-knowledge are incommunicable.

III 9,10. COGNITION OF DHARMA IN STOPPING: WITHOUT A GROUND FOR APPREHENSION. (Aspect: Calm Quietude).

The perfection of wisdom is perfectly pure because, like space, it offers no basis for apprehension.

Subhuti: How is that, O Lord?

The Lord: Because there can be no basis for the apprehension of space. Just so the perfection of wisdom is perfectly pure because form, etc. *to*: all-knowledge offer no basis for apprehension.

III 9,11. ACCEPTANCE OF SUBSEQUENT COGNITION IN STOPPING: PURITY. (Aspect: Sublime).

The perfection of wisdom is perfectly pure because all dharmas are not produced or stopped, not defiled or purified.

Subhuti: How is that, O Lord?

The Lord: The perfection of wisdom is perfectly pure because of the absolute purity of form, etc. *to*: all-knowledge.

III 9,12. SUBSEQUENT COGNITION OF STOPPING: NONPRODUCTION OF ALL KINDS OF DISEASE. (Aspect: Definite Escape).

Subhuti: If some son or daughter of good family will take up this perfection of wisdom, bear it in mind, preach it, study it, and wisely attend to it, then he will have no disease in his eyes, ears, nose, tongue, body or mind, he will not have tiny limbs or a senile body. Nor will that son or daughter of good family die a violent death. And many thousands of deities will follow closely behind them so as to hear the Dharma. The gods of the Four Great Kings, etc. *to*: the gods of the Pure Abode will follow closely behind them. On the eighth, fourteenth, and fifteenth day a large number of deities will congregate where that son or daughter of good family preach the Dharma and teach this perfection of wisdom. And when he teaches this perfection of wisdom that son or daughter of good family will beget a great deal of merit—immeasurable, incalculable, measureless, inconceivable and incomparable.

The Lord: So it is, Subhuti, so it is. That son or daughter of good family will beget a great deal of merit, immeasurable, incalculable, measureless, inconceivable and incomparable, when they teach this perfection of wisdom on the eighth, fourteenth, and fifteenth day and a congregation of deities will follow closely behind them. And why? Because this perfection of wisdom is a great treasure.

III 9,13. ACCEPTANCE OF COGNITION OF DHARMA IN THE PATH: CESSATION OF THE STATES OF WOE. (Aspect: Path).

When this most precious perfection of wisdom is properly tended, it will liberate from the hells, the animal world, the world of Yama and from poverty among men. One will be reborn in good families—among warriors, Brahmins and wealthy house holders—or among the various kinds of gods. This perfection of wisdom is a donor of the fruit of a Streamwinner, etc. *to*: of the supreme enlightenment. And why? For in this perfection of wisdom have the ten wholesome paths of action been explained in detail, and in it all the spiritual practices are conceived, as well as their fruits, up to the Tathagatas themselves. That is why it is called a most precious perfection.

III 9,14. COGNITION OF DHARMA IN THE PATH: ABSENCE OF THOUGHT-CONSTRUCTION. (Aspect: Correct Method).

But in this most precious perfection no dharma whatsoever is produced or stopped, defiled or purified, acquired or rejected. And why? Because there are no dharmas which could be produced or stopped, defiled or purified, acquired or rejected. Nor can in this most precious perfection any dharma be apprehended which is wholesome or unwholesome, worldly or supramundane, with or without outflows, conditioned or unconditioned. By this method this most precious perfection is without basis.

III 9,15. ACCEPTANCE OF SUBSEQUENT COGNITION OF THE PATH: ABSENCE OF CONTACT WITH SIGNS. (Aspect: Progress).

Nor is this most precious perfection of wisdom stained by any dharma whatsoever. And why? Because those dharmas cannot be apprehended by which it could be stained, and therefore this perfection of wisdom is free from all stains.

III 9,16. SUBSEQUENT COGNITION OF THE PATH: NONGENESIS OF THE DIFFERENCE BETWEEN THE COGNITION AND ITS VERBAL EXPRESSION. (Aspect: Factor of Release).

If, Subhuti, the Bodhisattva, the great being who courses in perfect wisdom, does even thus not cognize, does even thus not apprehend, does even thus not get delayed (by thinking multiple thoughts), then he courses in perfect wisdom, develops wisdom, pleases the Buddhas and Lords, and passes on from Buddha-field to Buddha-field so as to honour, revere, and worship the Buddhas and Lords. Passing on from Buddha-field to Buddha-field, maturing beings and purifying the Buddha-field, he will reach all-knowledge.

(III 10. The Résumé of I to III).

III 10,1. THE INDICATION THAT THE FIRST TOPIC, I.E. ALL-KNOWLEDGE, IS CONCLUDED.

And again, Subhuti, this perfection of wisdom does not bring near any dharma nor remove one, it does not show one up or define one, does not bestow one or take one away, does not produce or stop one, does not annihilate one or make it eternal, it has not one single meaning or a manifold meaning, does not make (a dharma) come or go away, does not defile or purify one, does not diminish one or make it grow. Nor is it past, future, or present.

III 10,2. Indication that the second topic, the knowledge of the paths, is concluded.

And again, Subhuti, this perfection of wisdom does not transcend the world of sense-desire, nor does it establish it; and so with the world of form and the formless world. She does not bestow the perfection of giving, nor does she take it away; and so with the emptinesses, etc. *to*: all-knowledge.

III 10,3. Indication that the third topic, that of the knowledge of all modes, is concluded.

And again, Subhuti, this perfection of wisdom does not bestow the Buddhadharmas nor take them away; and so for the dharmas of the foolish common people, the dharmas of the Disciples and Pratyekabuddhas, and the Buddhadharmas; and so for the conditioned element and the unconditioned element. And why? Whether Tathagatas are produced (in the world) or are nor produced, fixed is this Dharmahood of dharmas, the Dharma-element, the fixedness of Dharma, the fixed sequence of dharma(s). Those the Tathagata fully knows, and realizes intuitively. Having fully known them and having realized them intuitively, he describes them, demonstrates them, uncovers them, analyzes them, enlarges on them, and reveals them.

Thereupon a great many hundreds of thousands of *gods* who stood up high in the intermediate space called out aloud with cries of joy, waved their garments, and hurled heavenly blue, red, and white lotuses and mandarava flowers (into the air). And they said, "Now, indeed, we see the second turning of the wheel of Dharma taking place in Jambudvipa!" And when the perfection of wisdom was being expounded, many thousands of gods acquired the patient acceptance of dharmas which fail to be produced.

The Lord: This is not, Subhuti, the second turning of the wheel of Dharma, nor the first. Nor has this perfection of wisdom been set up for the sake of turning forward any dharma, or of turning it backward—on account of the emptiness of the nonexistence of own-being.

Subhuti: What, O Lord, is the emptiness of the nonexistence of own-being, in consequence of which this perfection of wisdom has not been set up for the sake of turning any dharma forward or backward?

The Lord: The perfection of wisdom is empty of the perfection of wisdom; and so is the perfection of meditation empty of the perfection of meditation; etc.

Subhuti: A great perfection for the Bodhisattvas, the great beings, O Lord, is this perfection of wisdom. For the own-being of all dharmas is empty of the own-being of all dharmas. It is thanks to the perfection of wisdom that the Bodhisattvas, the great beings know full enlightenment, although they do not fully know any dharma. They turn the wheel of Dharma, but they do not turn any dharma forward or backward. They do not behold any dharma, nor do they demonstrate any dharma. And why? Because that dharma cannot be apprehended which could turn forward or backward. For one absolutely does not settle down in all dharmas. And why? Because emptiness does not proceed or recede, nor does the Signless or Wishless. To demonstrate that is the proclamation of the perfection of wisdom, its narration, its disclosure, its dispatching, its explanation, its analysis, its indication, its amplification, its revelation. This is the perfectly pure demonstration of the perfection of wisdom. No one has demonstrated it, no one has received it, no one has realised it. And since no one has realised it, no one has therein gone to final Nirvana. Nor has this demonstration of Dharma ever made anyone worthy of gifts.

CHAPTER 38

WITHOUT BASIS

IV. THE FULL UNDERSTANDING OF ALL MODES.

IV 1. Modes.

IV 1,1.(27) MODES OF ALL-KNOWLEDGE.

Subhuti: A perfection of what is not is this, O Lord, i.e. the perfection of wisdom.

The Lord: Because space is not something that is.

Subhuti: A perfection of sameness is this, i.e. the perfection of wisdom.

The Lord: Because all dharmas are equally uncomprehended.

Subhuti: This is an isolated perfection.

The Lord: On account of absolute emptiness.

Subhuti: This is a perfection which cannot be crushed.

The Lord: Because all dharmas cannot be apprehended.

Subhuti: This is a trackless perfection.

The Lord: Because both body and mind are absent.

Subhuti: This is a perfection like space.

The Lord: Because breathing in and breathing out cannot be apprehended.

Subhuti: This is an incommunicable perfection.

The Lord: Because thought applied and thought discursive cannot be apprehended.

Subhuti: This is a nameless perfection.

The Lord: Because feelings, perceptions, impulses, and consciousness cannot be apprehended.

Subhuti: This is a perfection which does not go away.

The Lord: Because all dharmas do not go away.

Subhuti: One cannot partake of this perfection.

The Lord: Because no dharma can be seized.

Subhuti: This perfection is inexhaustible.

The Lord: Because all dharmas are extinguished in absolute extinction.

Subhuti: This perfection has no genesis.

The Lord: Because all dharmas are not produced or stopped.

Subhuti: This is a perfection without an agent.

The Lord: Because no agent can be apprehended.

Subhuti: This is a perfection without a cognizer.

The Lord: Because no cognizer can be apprehended.

Subhuti: This is a perfection which does not pass on.

The Lord: Because decease and rebirth cannot be apprehended.

Subhuti: This is a perfection which does not discipline.

The Lord: Because all dharmas in their essential original nature do not need any discipline.

Subhuti: This perfection is like a dream.

The Lord: Because one cannot apprehend the one who sees the dream.

Subhuti: This perfection is like an echo.

The Lord: Because one cannot apprehend the one who makes the noise (ghoshādāra?)

Subhuti: This perfection is like a reflected image.

The Lord: Because both mirror and image cannot be apprehended.

Subhuti: This perfection is like a mirage.

The Lord: Because no mass of water can be apprehended.

Subhuti: This perfection is like an illusion.

The Lord: Because its sign cannot be apprehended.

Subhuti: This perfection is free from defilement.

The Lord: Because the own-being of the defilements cannot be apprehended.

Subhuti: This perfection knows no purification.

The Lord: Because no defiled being can be apprehended.

Subhuti: This perfection is spotless.

The Lord: Because space cannot be apprehended.

Subhuti: This perfection is without impediments.

The Lord: Because it uproots all impediments.

Subhuti: This perfection has no mental attitudes.

The Lord: Because it uproots all mental attitudes.

Subhuti: This perfection is unshakeable.

The Lord: Because of the stability of the Realm of Dharma.

IV 1,2(36) MODES OF THE KNOWLEDGE OF THE PATHS.

Subhuti: This perfection has turned away from greed.

The Lord: Because its dispassion cannot be apprehended.

Subhuti: This is a perfection which takes its stand nowhere.

The Lord: Because all dharmas are not discriminated.

Subhuti: This perfection is calm.

The Lord: Because the nonfalseness of all dharmas is not fully understood (?).

Subhuti: This perfection is free from greed.

The Lord: Because of the nonapprehension of greed.

Subhuti: This perfection is free from hate.

The Lord: Because of the unreality of hate.

Subhuti: This perfection is free from delusion.

The Lord: Because the blinding darkness of delusion has been dispelled.

Subhuti: This perfection is undefiled.

The Lord: Because imagination is something that is not.

Subhuti: No living being is found in this perfection.

The Lord: Because no being can be apprehended.

Subhuti: This perfection is unlimited.

The Lord: Because all dharmas do not rise up.

Subhuti: This perfection does not follow after the duality of opposites.

The Lord: Because of absolute nonapprehension.

Subhuti: This perfection is undifferentiated.

The Lord: Because all dharmas are.

Subhuti: This perfection is untarnished.

The Lord: Because it has transcended the level of both Disciples and Pratyekabuddhas.

Subhuti: This perfection is undiscriminated.

The Lord: Because of the nonapprehension of nondiscrimination.

Subhuti: This perfection is immeasurable.

The Lord: Because all dharmas are without measure and cannot be apprehended.

Subhuti: This perfection is unattached.

The Lord: Because all dharmas in their own-being are the same as space.

Subhuti: Impermanent is this perfection.

The Lord: Because no dharma is ever destroyed.

Subhuti: Ill is this perfection.

The Lord: Because it is not bent on all dharmas but joined to Dharma itself (?).

Subhuti: Empty is this perfection.

The Lord: Because it brings forth no fruits (?).

Subhuti: Not-self is this perfection.

The Lord: Because there is no settling down in all dharmas.

Subhuti: Markless is this perfection.

The Lord: Because all dharmas are signless.

Subhuti: This is a perfection of the emptiness of the subject.

The Lord: Because inward dharmas cannot be apprehended.

Subhuti: This is a perfection of the emptiness of the object.

The Lord: Because outward dharmas cannot be apprehended.

Subhuti: This is a perfection of the emptiness of both subject and object.

The Lord: Because both inward and outward dharmas cannot be apprehended.

Subhuti: This is a perfection of the emptiness of emptiness.

The Lord: Because the emptiness of emptiness cannot be apprehended. And so for the great emptiness, the emptiness of ultimate reality, the conditioned emptiness, the unconditioned emptiness, the infinite emptiness, the emptiness without beginning or end, the emptiness of non-repudiation, the emptiness of essential nature.

Subhuti: This is a perfection of the emptiness of all dharmas.

The Lord: Because of the nonapprehension of all dharmas.

Subhuti: This is a perfection of the emptiness of own-marks.

The Lord: Because by its own marks it is perfectly isolated.

Subhuti: This is a perfection of the unascertainable emptiness.

The Lord: Because in the three periods of time the three ...? ... cannot be apprehended.

Subhuti: This is a perfection of the emptiness of the nonexistence of own-being.

The Lord: Because the emptiness of the nonexistence of own-being cannot be apprehended.

IV 1,3.(110) Modes of the knowledge of all modes.

IV 1,3a. 37 modes corresponding to the path of all-knowledge.

1-4. *Subhuti*: A perfection of the applications of mindfulness is this, O Lord, i.e. the perfection of wisdom.

The Lord: On account of the nonapprehension of body, feelings, thought, and dharmas.

5-8. *Subhuti*: It is a perfection of the right efforts.

The Lord: On account of the nonapprehension of wholesome and unwholesome dharmas.

9-12. *Subhuti*: It is a perfection of the bases of psychic power.

The Lord: On account of the nonapprehension of desire-to-do, vigour, thought, and exploration.

13-17. *Subhuti*: It is a perfection of the faculties.

The Lord: On account of the nonapprehension of faith, etc. (i.e. vigour, mindfulness, concentration, and wisdom).

18-22. *Subhuti*: It is a perfection of the powers.

The Lord: On account of the nonapprehension of the five powers.

23-29. *Subhuti*: It is a perfection of the limbs of enlightenment.

The Lord: On account of the nonapprehension of the seven limbs of enlightenment.

30-37. *Subhuti*: It is a perfection of the path.

The Lord: On account of the nonapprehension of the holy eight-fold path.

IV 1,3b. 34 MODES CORRESPONDING TO THE PATH OF THE KNOWLEDGE OF THE PATHS.

1. *Subhuti*: This is a perfection of Emptiness.

The Lord: Because no false views are apprehended.

2. *Subhuti*: This is a perfection of the Signless.

The Lord: Because no discoursings are apprehended.

3. *Subhuti*: This is a perfection of the Wishless.

The Lord: Because no plans for the future are apprehended.

4-11. *Subhuti*: This is a perfection of the eight deliverances.

The Lord: Because they cannot be apprehended.

12-20. *Subhuti*: This is a perfection of the nine successive stations.

The Lord: Because they cannot be apprehended.

21-24. *Subhuti*: This is a perfection of the four Truths.

The Lord: Because ill, origination, stopping, and path cannot be apprehended.

25. *Subhuti*: This perfection of wisdom is a perfection of giving.

The Lord: Because no meanness is apprehended.

26. *Subhuti*: It is a perfection of morality.

The Lord: Because no immorality is apprehended.

27. *Subhuti*: It is a perfection of patience.

The Lord: Because no ill will is apprehended.

28. *Subhuti*: It is a perfection of vigour.

The Lord: Because no indolence is apprehended.

29. *Subhuti*: It is a perfection of meditation.

The Lord: Because no distraction is apprehended.

30. *Subhuti*: It is a perfection of wisdom.

The Lord: Because no stupidity is apprehended.

31. *Subhuti*: It is a perfection of skill in means.

The Lord: Because no lack of skill in means is apprehended.

32. *Subhuti*: It is a perfection of the Vow.

The Lord: Because no lack of vows is apprehended.

33. *Subhuti*: It is a perfection of strength.

The Lord: Because no weakness is apprehended.

34. *Subhuti*: It is a perfection of cognition.

The Lord: Because no noncognition is apprehended.

IV 1,3c. 39 MODES CORRESPONDING TO THE PATH OF THE KNOWLEDGE OF ALL MODES.

1-10. *Subhuti*: This perfection of wisdom is a perfection of the ten powers.

The Lord: On account of the nonapprehension of all dharmas.

11-14. *Subhuti*: It is a perfection of the four grounds of self-confidence.

The Lord: On account of uncowedness in the knowledge of all the modes of the path.

15-18. *Subhuti*: It is a perfection of the analytical knowledges.

The Lord: Because the cognition which reaches everywhere is unattached and unobstructed.

19-36. *Subhuti*: It is a perfection of the eighteen special Buddha-dharmas.

The Lord: On account of the complete transcending of the dharmas of all Disciples and Pratyekabuddhas.

37. *Subhuti*: It is a perfection of the Tathagata.

The Lord: On account of the Suchness that is taught by all the Buddhas.

38. *Subhuti*: It is a perfection of the Self-Existent.

The Lord: On account of its sovereignty over all dharmas.

39. *Subhuti*: It is a perfection of the Buddhadharmas.

The Lord: On account of the full understanding of all dharmas in all their modes.

CHAPTER 39

THE TRADITION IN THE NORTH

IV 2. Endeavours.

IV2,A. FOUR ASPECTS OF THE PERSON WHO IS SUITABLE TO MAKE THE ENDEAVOURS.

Thereupon it occurred to *Śakra*, Chief of Gods: Those sons and daughters of good family who come to hear this perfection of wisdom must have fulfilled their duties under the Jinas of the past, must have planted wholesome roots under (those) Tathagatas and must have been taken hold of by good spiritual friends. How much more so those who take it up, bear it in mind, preach and study it, wisely attend to it, and who, in addition, progress to Thusness. They must have honoured many Buddhas if, on hearing this perfection of wisdom, they take it up, etc. *to*: progress to Thusness. They must have questioned the Tathagatas of the past again and again, must have tended, loved and honoured them, if, on hearing this perfection of wisdom, they do not tremble, are not frightened or terrified. Under many kotis of Buddhas they must have coursed in the six perfections if, on hearing this perfection of wisdom, they do not tremble, are not frightened or terrified.

Śāriputra: Those sons and daughters of good family, O Lord, who, having heard this deep perfection of wisdom, will not tremble, be frightened or terrified, but will take it up, bear it in mind, recite and study it, and wisely attend to it, as irreversible Bodhisattvas, great beings, should these sons and daughters of good family be borne in mind. And why? Because the perfection of wisdom is deep, and therefore someone who has not in the past practised the six perfections cannot believe in it. But again those who now decide to reject this deep perfection of wisdom, they have also rejected it in the past. And that is the reason why with regard to this deep perfection of wisdom they have no faith, no serene confidence, no affection, and no resolve. And those sons and daughters of good family have not repeatedly questioned the Buddhas, the Bodhisattvas, the Pratyekabuddhas, or Disciples as to how the six perfections should be practised, or as to how the emptinesses etc. *to*: the Buddhadharmas should be developed.

Śakra: Deep, Ven. Śariputra, is the perfection of wisdom! It is not at all astonishing that Bodhisattvas who in the past did not believe in this deep perfection of wisdom, or in the perfection of giving, etc. *to*: the Buddhadharmas, should now reject it. There is nothing astonishing about that. I pay homage to the Blessed Perfection of Wisdom! One pays homage to the cognition of the all-knowing when one pays homage to the perfection of wisdom.

The Lord: So it is. For from it has come forth the knowledge of all modes of the Buddhas, the Lords, and, conversely, the perfection of wisdom is brought about as something which has come forth from the knowledge of all modes. A son or daughter of good family should stand in the perfection of wisdom, if they want to transcend all-knowledge, to stand in the knowledge of the paths, to produce the knowledge of all modes, to uproot all the defilements and their residues, to fully know the supreme enlightenment and to turn the wheel of Dharma. Likewise, if a Bodhisattva wants to establish beings in the fruit of a Streamwinner, or in the enlightenment of a Pratyekabuddha, or in the supreme enlightenment, or if he wants to foster the order of monks, he should make endeavours about this perfection of wisdom.

Śakra: How does a Bodhisattva become established in the six perfections, and how does he make endeavours about them? And how, coursing in the perfection of wisdom, does he make endeavours about the emptinesses, etc. *to*: the Buddhadharmas?

The Lord: Well said, Kauśika, well said. It is good that you have decided to question the Tathagata about this matter. In that also you have been inspired by the Buddha's might. Therefore then, Kauśika, listen and attend well, I will explain this to you.

IV2B. THE METHODS OF TRAINING.

IV2B,1. THE METHOD OF TRAINING WHICH DOES NOT INSIST ON THE REALITY OF THE SKANDHAS.

Here, Kauśika, a Bodhisattva who courses in perfect wisdom does not stand in form, etc. and in consequence makes no endeavour about form, etc. It is thus that he makes endeavours about the perfection of wisdom. And why? Because he does not apprehend that form, etc. wherein he could abide, or whereabout he could make endeavours.

IV2B,2. THE METHOD OF TRAINING WHICH IS WITHOUT EFFORT.

Moreover the Bodhisattva does not apply himself to form, etc.; it is thus that he makes endeavours about them. And why? Because he does not apprehend form, etc. where it begins, or where it ends, or in its middle either.

IV2B,3. THE METHOD OF TRAINING WHICH IS DEEP.

Śāriputra: Deep, O Lord, is the perfection of wisdom.

The Lord: Through the depth of the Suchness of form; so with feeling, etc.

IV2B,4. THE METHOD OF TRAINING WHICH IS HARD TO FATHOM.

Śāriputra: Hard to fathom is the perfection of wisdom.

The Lord: Because form is hard to fathom; so with feeling, etc.

IV2B,5. ITS IMMEASURABLENESS. (+3 subdivisions).

Śāriputra: Unlimited is the perfection of wisdom.

The Lord: Because form is unlimited; so with feeling, etc. *to*: the Buddhadharmas.

Śāriputra: How does the Bodhisattva course in the perfection of wisdom?

The Lord: If the Bodhisattva, when he courses in perfect wisdom does not course in the notion that 'form, etc. is deep'. And why? The depth of form is not form; and so with feeling, etc. And again, Śariputra, if the Bodhisattva, who courses in perfect wisdom, does not course in the notion that 'form, etc. is hard to fathom', then he courses in the perfection of wisdom. And why? Because the unfathomability of form is not form; and so with feeling, etc. Moreover, if the Bodhisattva, when he courses in perfect wisdom, does not course in the notion that 'form, etc., is unlimited', then he courses in the perfection of wisdom. And why? The unlimitedness of form, that is not form; and so with feeling, etc.

IV2B,6. UNDERSTANDING IS ATTAINED PAINFULLY AND SLOWLY.

Śāriputra: So deep is this perfection of wisdom, so hard to fathom, so hard to understand, so unlimited that it should not be taught in front of Bodhisattvas who have newly set out in the vehicle. May they not, when they hear this deep perfection of wisdom, tremble, be frightened, be terrified! In front of an irreversible Bodhisattva should it be taught! When he has heard this perfection of wisdom, he will not tremble, be frightened or terrified, he will not hesitate or doubt, and he will resolutely believe in it when he hears it.

Śakra: If, Rev. Śariputra, this deep perfection of wisdom were taught in front of a Bodhisattva who has newly set out in the vehicle, what fault would there be?

Śāriputra: If, Kauśika, this perfection of wisdom were taught in front of a Bodhisattva who has newly set out in the vehicle, he would tremble, be frightened and terrified, and it is quite possible that he may be put off, may reject it, may not believe in it. And if that Bodhisattva who has newly set out in the vehicle should, on hearing it, reject this deep perfection of wisdom, then he would heap up a karma which leads him into an evil destiny and he would awake to full enlightenment only with much trouble and slowly.

IV2B,7. The method of training connected with the gaining of the prediction.

Śakra: Are there, then, Ven. Śariputra, Bodhisattvas who are still unpredicted, and who, on hearing this perfection of wisdom, will not tremble, be frightened or terrified?

Śāriputra: Those who, on hearing this perfection of wisdom, will not tremble, be frightened or terrified, before long will gain the prediction to full enlightenment. Before they have passed by one, or two, or three Tathagatas, they will gain the prediction to full enlightenment.

The Lord: So it is, Śariputra, so it is. Set out for long in the vehicle will be those Bodhisattvas, for long will they have coursed in the six perfections, many Buddhas will they have honoured if, on hearing this deep perfection of wisdom, they will not tremble, be frightened or terrified, and if, after having heard it, they will take it up, bear it in mind, recite and study it, and will stand in the perfection of wisdom as it has been explained.

Śāriputra: It has become clear to me, O Lord, it has become clear to me, O Well-Gone!

The Lord: Make it clear then, Śariputra.

Śāriputra: If in a dream a son or daughter of good family who has set out in the great vehicle were to develop the perfection of wisdom and the other perfections, etc. *to*: were to sit on the terrace of enlightenment, then one should know that he is actually near to the supreme enlightenment. How much more will one who, while awake, develops the six perfections be quite near to the supreme enlightenment!

IV2B,8. Irreversibility.

Those sons and daughters of good family who come to hear of this deep perfection of wisdom, and who, on hearing it, progress in it, have matured their wholesome roots for a long time. They will have set out for a long time in the vehicle, will have planted wholesome roots, have honoured many Buddhas, will have been taken hold of by the good spiritual friends if, after having heard this deep perfection of wisdom, they will take it up, bear it in mind, recite and study it, and wisely attend to it. They will be quite near to the supreme enlightenment and will receive the prediction to it (?). Or those will be irreversible from the supreme enlightenment to whom this perfection of wisdom appears on its own accord, and who then take it up, bear it in mind, recite and study it, and wisely attend to it.

IV2B,9. Definite going forth.

A man coming out of a huge wild forest, one hundred up to five hundred miles big, might see certain signs which indicate a town or other inhabited place—such as cowherds, cattle keepers, boundary lines, gardens, woods, groves, or the signs of groves, or a village, city, market town, capital or royal city. From these signs he will infer the nearness of an inhabited place. He feels relieved and is no longer afraid of robbers, outcasts, fierce beasts of prey, hunger or thirst. Just so a Bodhisattva to whom the perfection of wisdom appears of its own accord, and who then takes it up, bears it in mind, recites and studies it, and wisely attends to it, should know that he is quite near the prediction to the supreme enlightenment and before long he will be fully enlightened. Nor should he be afraid of the level of the Disciples and Pratyekabuddhas. Because he has had these indications, i.e. that he has received this deep perfection of wisdom for vision, praise, worship, and hearing.

The Lord: So it is, Śariputra, so it is.

IV2B,10. He reaches a state free from impediments.

Go on, Śariputra, and, through the might of the Buddha, make the problem still clearer!

Śāriputra: A man desirous of seeing the great ocean, might travel towards it. As long as on his travels he would see a tree or the signs of a tree, a mountain or the sign of a mountain, he would know that the great ocean is still far away, and not at all near. Because in the neighbourhood of the great ocean no tree or sign of a tree can be seen, no mountain or sign of a mountain. But if he no longer sees any tree or mountain, then it occurs to him that he is no longer far from the great ocean, but near it. Because in the neighbourhood of the great ocean no tree or sign of a tree can be seen, no mountain or sign of a mountain. Although that man may not yet see the great ocean directly before his eyes, he nevertheless can be quite certain that: 'I am near the great ocean, quite near here is the great ocean, not much farther from here is the great ocean'. Just so, O Lord, this Bodhisattva who hears the perfection of wisdom, takes it up, bears it in mind, recites and studies it, and wisely attends to it, should know and reflect that 'although face to face with the Lord I have not been predicted to full enlightenment—i.e. 'after so many aeons, so many hundreds of aeons, etc. *to*: so many hundreds of thousands of niyutas of kotis of aeons you will fully know the utmost enlightenment!',—in spite of that he should know: 'I am now quite near to the prediction to the utmost, right, and perfect enlightenment. And why? Because I have received this deep perfection of wisdom for the sake of vision, praising, worship, and hearing, and, having heard it, I take it up, bear it in mind, recite and study it, and attend wisely to it'.

IV2B,11. Nearness to supreme enlightenment.

When spring approaches, the withered leaves on the trees act as tokens to the men of Jambudvipa who then know that quite soon new leaves, flowers and fruits will manifest themselves. For when these symptoms have appeared on the trees, before long leaves, flowers, and fruits will manifest themselves. When they have seen these symptoms on the trees, the men of Jambudvipa will be overjoyed. Just so, when a Bodhisattva receives his deep perfection of wisdom for vision, praise, worship, and hearing, and if, on having heard it, he takes it up, bears it in mind, recites and studies it, and wisely attends to it, he should be known as one who has matured his wholesome roots for a long time, as one who has honoured many Buddhas. That Bodhisattva should know that through his previous wholesome roots he moves in the direction of (?) the supreme enlightenment. He also should know that, since he has received this deep perfection of wisdom for vision, praise, and worship, and since he makes progress in the perfection of wisdom as it has been expounded, those divinities who have seen the Buddhas of the past will be overjoyed, exultant, and jubilant. For they feel that before long this Bodhisattva will receive his prediction to the supreme enlightenment, since also with the Bodhisattvas of the past these were the symptoms of their coming prediction to full enlightenment.

IV2B,12. SPEEDY PROGRESS TO FULL ENLIGHTENMENT.

When a pregnant women comes nearer and nearer to her confinement, her body becomes more and more twisted (Note: unsteady, agitated, hemmed in), excessive sufferings and weariness arise in her body, she does not walk about a great deal, does not have her wits very much about her, takes little food, finds little rest, and, because these unpleasant feelings proceed in her, she speaks little. She also abstains from habitual cohabitation because she realizes that she experiences these unpleasant feelings as a result of indulging in unwise attention in the past, developing and practising it. One knows, by comparison with what befalls other women, that when these symptoms appear in this woman she will before long give birth to a child. Just so when in Bodhisattvas—who have planted wholesome roots, honoured many Buddhas, observed and practised good conduct, who have been taken hold of by the good spiritual friends and who have matured their wholesome roots for a long time—this deep perfection of wisdom appears, and then they take it up, bear it in mind, recite and study it, and attend to it wisely—then one should know that before long they will have their prediction to the supreme enlightenment.

The Lord: Well said, Śariputra. In this also you have been inspired by the Buddha's might.

IV2B,13. ENDEAVOURS FOR THE WELFARE OF OTHERS.

Subhuti: It is wonderful to see the extent to which these Bodhisattvas have been helped and well encompassed by the Tathagata.

The Lord: It is because these Bodhisattvas have practiced for the weal and happiness of the many, out of pity for the world. For the benefit, weal, and happiness of a great mass of people, both gods and men, they have set out for the supreme enlightenment and on the course of a Bodhisattva. They assist innumerable beings with the help of the four means of conversion. They are established in giving. They themselves course in the perfection of giving, etc. *to*: the perfection of wisdom, and also others they establish in them. Thanks to the perfection of wisdom and through skill in means they establish beings in the fruit of a Streamwinner, etc. *to*: in the enlightenment of a Pratyekabuddha, but they themselves do not realize them. They themselves enter on the irreversible stage and others also they establish in it. They themselves purify the Buddha-field, and also others they instigate to purify the Buddha-field. Themselves they mature beings and others also they instigate to do the same. Themselves they produce the superknowledges and others also they instigate to win them. Themselves they purify the Dharani-door and others also they instigate to purify it. Themselves they acquire the accomplishment of ready speech and others also they instigate to acquire it. Themselves they acquire a perfect physical body and others also they instigate to do likewise. Themselves they acquire the accomplishment of the marks and others also they instigate to do likewise. Themselves they achieve the position of a Crown Prince and others also they instigate to do likewise. Themselves they accomplish the dharmas, which act as wings to enlightenment, and others also they instigate to accomplish them. Themselves they produce the eight deliverances, nine attainments of successive stations, the Emptiness-Signless-Wishless (deliverance) and the dharani-doors, and others also they instigate thereto. Themselves they produce the four grounds of self-confidence and the four analytical knowledges, and others also they instigate to win them. Themselves they develop to the end the great friendliness, the great compassion, the great sympathetic joy and the great impartiality, and others also they instigate to develop the four Unlimited to the end. Themselves they accomplish the eighteen special dharmas of a Buddha and others also they instigate to do likewise. Themselves they forsake all the defilements with their residues and others also they instigate to do likewise. Themselves they fully know the supreme enlightenment and others also they instigate to fully know the supreme enlightenment. Themselves they turn the wheel of Dharma and others also they instigate to do likewise.

IV2B,14. Neither growth nor diminution.

Subhuti: It is wonderful, O Lord, it is wonderful, O Sugata, with how many virtues those Bodhisattvas are endowed who for the sake of all beings course in the perfection of wisdom and fully know the supreme enlightenment. How does the development of perfect wisdom on the part of the Bodhisattvas reach its fulfillment?

The Lord: When a Bodhisattva, while coursing in perfect wisdom, does not review the growth of form, etc. nor its diminution.

IV2B,15. NEITHER DHARMA NOR NON-DHARMA ARE TAKEN AS A BASIS.

The Bodhisattva's development of perfect wisdom reaches its fulfillment, if, when he courses in perfect wisdom, he does not review 'dharma' or 'nondharma', 'past', 'future', or 'present', 'wholesome, unwholesome, or indeterminate', 'conditioned' or 'unconditioned', the world of sense desire, the world of form, the formless world, the perfection of giving, etc. *to*: the knowledge of all modes. And why? Because this is on account of the essential marks of Dharma, on account of irreversibility, of nullity, vanity, unsubstantiality, and voidness.

IV2B,16. THE ENDEAVOUR WHICH PERCEIVES THE ASPECT OF UNTHINKABILITY.

Subhuti: The unthinkable, O Lord, is here demonstrated.

The Lord: Because of the unthinkability of form, etc. If, when coursing in perfect wisdom, the Bodhisattva does not perceive that 'form etc. it unthinkable', then he fulfills the perfection of wisdom.

IV2B,17. ABSENCE OF ALL DISCRIMINATION.

Subhuti: Who will zealously believe in this deep perfection of wisdom?

The Lord: A Bodhisattva will zealously believe in this perfection of wisdom if already in the past he has practiced the six perfections, if he has planted wholesome roots under the Tathagatas, if he has honoured many Buddhas, if he has been taken hold of by good spiritual friends.

Subhuti: To what extent, O Lord, has such a Bodhisattva in the past already practiced the six perfections, etc. *to*: has been taken hold of by good spiritual friends?

The Lord: Here, Subhuti, a Bodhisattva who courses in perfect wisdom does not construct form, or discriminate it; and so with: the sign of form, the own-being of form; and so with; feelings etc. *to*: all-knowledge. And why? Because form is unthinkable, and so is feeling etc. *to*: all-knowledge. It is certainly thus that the Bodhisattva is one who already in the past has been taken hold of by good spiritual friends.

Subhuti: Deep, O Lord, is the perfection of wisdom!

The Lord: Because of the depth of form, etc. *to*: because of the depth of all-knowledge.

IV2B,18. THE BESTOWAL OF THE PRECIOUS JFWEL OF THE FRUITS (OF THE HOLY LIFE).

Subhuti: A heap of treasure is the perfection of wisdom, a bestower of precious jewels. This perfection of wisdom, which turns the Wheel of Dharma, bestows the fruit of a Streamwinner, etc. *to*: the supreme enlightenment.

IV2B,19. PURITY.

A pure heap of all dharmas is the perfection of wisdom.

The Lord: On account of the purity of form, etc. *to*: all-knowledge.

IV2B,20. THE DELIMITATION OF TIME.

Subhuti: It would not be surprising if many obstacles should arise to this deep perfection of wisdom being taught.

The Lord: So it is, Subhuti, so it is. There will be many obstacles to this deep perfection of wisdom. Therefore one should hurry with one's task of copying it out, of explaining it, etc. *to*: of developing it. One should prevent all obstacles from becoming effective. If a son or daughter of good family have one month, or up to a year, in which to copy out the perfection of wisdom, etc. *to*: to develop it, they should try to finish their task within that period. Because it is a fact that in respect of very precious things many obstacles are wont to arise.

Subhuti: It is not surprising that Mara, the Evil One, should exert himself to cause obstacles to this deep perfection of wisdom, i.e. to its being copied out, etc. *to*: its being developed.

The Lord: In spite of that he cannot produce any really effective obstacle to a Bodhisattva who wishes to copy it out, etc. *to*: develops this perfection of wisdom.

IV 3. Qualities.

IV3,1. THE ANNIHILATION OF MARA'S POWER.

Śāriputra: Through whose might, O Lord, is Mara, the Evil One, prevented from causing obstacles to the Bodhisattvas who copy out, etc. *to*: develop this perfection of wisdom?

The Lord: It is through the might of the Buddha, and also through the might of those Buddhas and Lords who abide in all the ten directions. For those Buddhas and Lords bring to mind and assist those Bodhisattvas, and Mara, the Evil One, cannot cause an obstacle to Bodhisattvas who are assisted by the Buddhas and Lords, when they copy out this perfection of wisdom, etc. *to*: develop it. For Mara, the Evil One, is just incapable of causing an obstacle to Bodhisattvas assisted by the Buddhas and Lords. For it is in the nature of things that countless Tathagatas who abide in all the ten directions in inumerable world systems should bring to mind the Bodhisattvas who copy out, etc. *to*: develop this perfection of wisdom.

IV3,2. ONE IS BROUGHT TO MIND BY THE BUDDHAS AND IS AWARE OF THE FACT.

It is through the Buddha's might that a son or daughter of good family copies out, etc. *to*: develops this deep perfection of wisdom.

Śāriputra: Any such son or daughter of good family who do so do so through the Buddha's might, and they are all upheld by the Buddha?

The Lord: So it is, Śariputra.

IV3,3. ONE IS PLACED INTO THE SIGHT OF THE BUDDHAS.

Śāriputra: The Buddhas and Lords who abide in all directions in innumerable world systems know those sons and daughters of good family with their cognition and see them with their fleshly eye, when they copy out this deep perfection of wisdom, etc. *to*: progress to Thusness?

The Lord: So it is, Śariputra.

IV3,4. ONE IS QUITE NEAR TO ENLIGHTENMENT.

And of these sons and daughters of good family who belong to the great vehicle one should know that they are quite near to the supreme enlightenment.

IV3,5. ONE REALISES THE GREAT AIM, ETC.

If, after having copied out this deep perfection of wisdom and made it into a book, they will bear it in mind, then they will gain an abundance of resolute faith in it. If they honour, revere, and worship it, they are known and seen by the Buddhas and Lords, and the Tathagatas see them with their Buddha-eye. And it will be greatly profitable to those sons and daughters of good family, a great advantage, fruit and reward that, having copied out this deep perfection of wisdom, they bear it in mind. Through that wholesome root they will never again be deprived of the Buddhas, the Lords; they will never again be reborn in the states of woe; when reborn among gods and men they will never be deprived of the Buddhas and Bodhisattvas, and they will transcend the irreversible stage. Nor will they, as a result of this wholesome root, ever be deprived of the six perfections, the emptinesses, the applications of mindfulness, etc. *to*: the Buddhadharmas, or of all-knowledge.

IV3,6. ONE CAN JUDGE THE CHARACTER OF DIFFERENT COUNTRIES.

And this Perfection of Wisdom will, after the passing away of the Tathagata, appear in the South; from there it will move to the East, and from there to the North. In each of these directions monks and nuns, laymen and laywomen will copy out this deep perfection of wisdom, take it up, bear it in mind, recite and study it, and attend to it wisely. As a result of this wholesome root they will not go to the great distress of some wretched destiny. Having succeeded in experiencing life among gods or men, they are elevated by the six perfections. They honour, revere, and worship the Buddhas and Lords, and gradually they will go forth by one of the three vehicles, i.e. the Disciple-vehicle, the Pratyekabuddha-vehicle, or the great vehicle.

Therein this deep perfection of wisdom does the work of a Buddha. And why? For when the Dharma-Vinaya is like freshly made cream the good Dharma does not disappear. I bring to mind those sons and daughters or good family who will copy out this deep perfection of wisdom, etc. *to*: progress to its Thusness. And also those sons and daughters of good family who copy out this deep perfection of wisdom, honour, revere, and worship it, they also as a result of this wholesome root will not go to the great distress of some wretched destiny. Having succeeded in experiencing life among gods and men, they are elevated by the six perfections. They honour, revere, and worship the Buddhas and Lords, and gradually go forth by one of the three vehicles, i.e. the Disciple-vehicle, the Pratyekabuddha-vehicle, or the great vehicle. For they are seen by the Tathagata with his Buddha-eye, they are praised by the Tathagata. And the Buddhas and Lords who abide in all the world systems which extend in all the ten directions all around, also those Tathagatas see those sons and daughters of good family with their Buddha-eye, praise, and extol them.

Śāriputra: Will then this deep perfection of wisdom in the last time, in the last period, be widespread in the Northern direction?

The Lord: Yes, it will. In the last time, in the last period, there will be sons and daughters of good family who will hear this deep perfection of wisdom, will copy it out, take it up, bear it in mind, recite and study it, wisely attend to it, and progress to its Thusness; and they will have set out for a long time in the vehicle, will have honoured many Buddhas, will have planted wholesome roots under the Tathagatas.

Śāriputra: How many of these sons and daughters of good family will there be?

The Lord: In the last time, in the last period, at the extinction of the Dharma, there will be in the North many sons and daughters of good family, who belong to the Bodhisattva-vehicle, but there will be few who, having heard this deep perfection of wisdom, will believe; who, having believed, will read, write, take it up, bear it in mind, study, recite, expound, and preach it, attend wisely to it, develop it (by meditation) and progress to its Thusness.

IV3,7. All dharmas without outflows are perfected.

And they, having heard this deep perfection of wisdom being taught, will not be cowed or despondent, will not tremble, be frightened or terrified. And why? Because these sons and daughters of good family have pursued the Tathagatas, have questioned and counterquestioned them, by resorting to just this deep perfection of wisdom. And why? Because these sons and daughters of good family will become quite full of the perfection of wisdom, of the perfection of meditation, etc. *to*: of the eighteen kinds of emptiness, etc. *to*: of the eighteen special Buddha-dharmas. And why? Supported by their wholesome roots they will work the weal and ease of many people, with reference to just this utmost, right, and perfect enlightenment.

IV3,8. One becomes a person who can communicate the doctrine.

And why? Because I, Śariputra, have preached to them sermons connected with the knowledge of all modes. Those also who in a past period have been Tathagatas, they also have for those sons and daughters of good family preached sermons connected with the knowledge of all modes. Even when they have passed beyond (this) birth, just these ideas, i.e. referring to the utmost, right, and perfect enlightenment, will persist by force of habit. They again will preach to others just these sermons, i.e. with reference to the utmost, right, and perfect enlightenment.

IV3,9. One cannot be deflected from enlightenment.

And again these sons and daughters of good family will be united in harmony in the utmost, right, and perfect enlightenment. But Mara, or the deities of Mara's host, will not be able to deflect such a one from the utmost, right, and perfect enlightenment; how much less can he be deflected by other evil wishes or habitual ideas; that is not possible.

IV3,10. Genesis of an uncommon store of merit.

And again, those sons and daughters of good family who belong to the Bodhisattva-vehicle, will, having heard this deep perfection of wisdom, acquire an uncommon degree of zest, serene faith, and elation, and they will establish many people in wholesome dharmas, i.e. with reference to the utmost, right, and perfect enlightenment.

IV3,11. The pledge is genuinely redeemed.

And these sons and daughters of good family in my presence when they were face to face with Me, have said: 'We, O Lord, will establish many hundreds of living beings, yea, many hundreds of thousands of kotis of living beings in wholesome roots, with a view of their winning the supreme enlightenment; we shall hold up perfect enlightenment to them, instigate, encourage, and incite them to win it, and help them to be predicted to irreversibility! And why? For I have rejoiced at the words of these sons and daughters of good family who belong to the Bodhisattva-vehicle, and also when I had surveyed their thought with my thought I certainly rejoiced at those sons and daughters of good family. Those Bodhisattvas, coursing towards enlightenment, will establish innumerable beings in the supreme enlightenment, instigate, encourage, and incite them to win it, and help them to be predicted to irreversibility.

IV3,12. One receives a sublime reward.

And these sons and daughters of good family will have sublime aspirations with regard to forms, sounds, smells, tastes, touchables, and dharmas. They will give sublime gifts and thereby effect sublime wholesome roots. In consequence they will receive a sublime reward, and for the sake of other beings they will continue to acquire one reward after another.

IV3,13. One is active for the weal of beings.

To those beings they renounce all their belongings, be they inward or outward. Through their wholesome root they will seek rebirth in other Buddha-fields where they will come face to face with the Tathagatas demonstrating Dharma. And when they have heard from them just this perfection of wisdom, they will also in their Buddha-field instigate, encourage, and incite innumerable living beings to win the supreme enlightenment.

Śāriputra: It is wonderful to see the extent to which there is not any dharma which the Tathagata has not fully understood, or the Suchness of any dharma, or the conduct of any being. For he has cognized the Bodhisattvas, Buddha-fields and Disciples of the Tathagatas of the past, of the future Tathagatas, and of the present Tathagatas, i.e. of those Tathagatas who just now abide in the world systems in all the ten directions and there demonstrate Dharma.

IV3,14. One is certain to win perfect wisdom.

And there are Bodhisattvas who make efforts about these six perfections, and who seek and search for them. Among them some will get them and others will not.

The Lord: As a rule these six perfections will appear to these sons and daughters of good family. And why? Because they have made efforts about them.

Śāriputra: And will also the very deep Sutras connected with the six perfections come to them?

The Lord: Yes, they will.

Śāriputra: To which sons and daughters of good family will they come?

The Lord: To those who, with intense faith, make efforts about these six perfections with utter disregard for their body and life. And why? For it so happens that to those who instigate, encourage, and incite beings to win the supreme enlightenment the six perfections will appear after they have passed through this present birth. And proceeding with the six perfections as they have been expounded they will not relax their vigour until they purify the Buddha-field, mature beings, and know full enlightenment.

Chapter 40

MARA

IV 4. Faults.

IV4,1. Attainment with great difficulty.

Subhuti: The Lord has proclaimed these virtues of those sons and daughters of good family who have set out for the supreme enlightenment, and who will course in the six perfections, mature beings, and purify the Buddha-fields. Which obstacles will, on the other hand, arise to them?

The Lord: Only after a long time will they understand (this perfection of wisdom). This should be known as Mara's deed to the Bodhisattvas.

Subhuti: For what reason will they understand only after a long time?

The Lord: Here the Bodhisattva, who courses in perfect wisdom, will very laboriously fulfill the perfection of wisdom, and the other perfections. In this way he will understand only after a long time.

IV4,2. Sudden flashes of ideas arise too quickly.

Moreover, sudden flashes of ideas will arise too quickly. This also should be known as Mara's deed to the Bodhisattvas.

Subhuti: In what way does to the Bodhisattvas a deed of Mara arise from the sudden spread of their flashes of insight?

The Lord: Here to a Bodhisattva who courses in the six perfections, but who is without the wholesome root of skill in means, sudden flashes of ideas arise too quickly.

IV4,3. Threefold unsuitable bodily behaviour.

Moreover, they will copy out this perfection of wisdom while yawning, while laughing, and while sneering at one another.

IV4,4. Threefold unsuitable mental behaviour.

Moreover they will copy it out with their thoughts disturbed; they will copy it out with their minds on other things. Or it will occur to these Bodhisattvas that 'we do not derive any enjoyment from this', and with these words they will get up from their seats and take their leave.

IV4,5. Recitation for the wrong reasons.

Furthermore they will yawn, get up from their seats, and take their leave. Or yawning they will study, bear in mind, recite, demonstrate, and attend. Or, laughing at one another they will learn, bear in mind, recite, study, and wisely attend. Or, sneering at one another they will write, learn, etc. *to*: wisely attend. Or, with thoughts disturbed they will learn, etc. Or they will learn, etc. with their minds on other kinds of talk.

IV4,6. CONSIDERATION OF REASONS FOR REJECTING THE SUTRA.

Subhuti: As the Lord has said: 'We do not derive any enjoyment from this', with these words they will get up from their seats and take their leave. This also should be known as Mara's deed to the Bodhisattvas. For what reason do they not derive any enjoyment from this?

The Lord: Because in the past also they have not coursed in the six perfections. Furthermore, it is another deed of Mara that it occurs to the Bodhisattvas that they are not predestined for this perfection of wisdom, and so, their thoughts devoid of serene faith, they will get up from their seats and leave.

Subhuti: For what reason do they feel that they are not predestined for the perfection of wisdom?

The Lord: Bodhisattvas who have not definitely set out (on the career of a Bodhisattva) are certainly not predicted to the supreme enlightenment, and they have no serene faith in this perfection of wisdom because their name is not mentioned in it.

Subhuti: For what reason are the names of Bodhisattvas not proclaimed in this deep perfection of wisdom?

The Lord: Certainly the names of unpredicted Bodhisattvas are not proclaimed. They think to themselves that 'my name is here not proclaimed, nor that of the village, city, market place, royal city, or nation (?) where I was born', and then decide that the perfection of wisdom is not worthwhile their listening to and that they had better leave that assembly. And each time they decide to leave they get away from the Buddhadharmas. As often as they have the thought of leaving, for so many aeons they will have to take to (Birth-and-death) and make new efforts again and again.

IV4,7. DESERTION OF THE CAUSE OF BUDDHAHOOD (*i.e. the Prajñāpāramitā*)

Having spurned the perfection of wisdom which nourishes the cognition of the all-knowing, they will seek and search for those Sutras which do not nourish it. In this way those sons and daughters of good family will decide to spurn the root of the obtainment of the cognition of all-knowledge, and to look instead for support in what are mere branches, leaves, and foliage.

Subhuti: Which are the Sutras that do not nourish the cognition of the all-knowing and which they decide to study?

The Lord: They are the Sutras associated with the vehicle of the Disciples and Pratyakabuddhas. They enjoin the applications of mindfulness, the right efforts, etc. *to*: the doors to deliverance which consist in emptiness, the signless, the wishless. When they have stood in these, the sons and daughters of good family attain the fruit of a Streamwinner, etc. *to*: the enlightenment of a Pratyekabuddha. These are the Sutras associated with the level of the Disciples and Pratyekabuddhas which are conducive to nourishing the vehicle of all-knowledge, and which (those people) decide to study after they have spurned the perfection of wisdom. And why? For the Bodhisattvas have issued from the perfection of wisdom, and when they train in perfect wisdom they will go forth to the worldly and supramundane spiritual dharmas and train in them.

IV4,8. Loss of taste for this most sublime (teaching).

Just as a dog would spurn a morsel (of food or a sip of water) from a servant; just so, in the future, some persons belonging to the great vehicle will spurn this deep perfection of wisdom which is the root of all the Buddhadharmas, and decide instead to study the Sutras associated with the vehicles of the Disciples and Pratyekabuddhas, Sutras which are like branches, leaves, and foliage. This also will be Mara's deed to them. Furthermore, there will be in the future some adherents of the Bodhisattva-vehicle who, having spurned this deep perfection of wisdom, will decide to study the Sutras associated with the vehicle of the Disciples and Pratyekabuddhas for the sake of gain and honour.

IV4,9. Desertion of the supreme vehicle.

If a man who wants an elephant were to get hold of one and then be content to examine his foot, would that man be an intelligent person?

Subhuti: No, Lord!

The Lord: The same is true of those persons who belong to the Bodhisattva-vehicle and who, having spurned this deep perfection of wisdom, decide to study the Sutras associated with the vehicles of the Disciples and Pratyekabuddhas. What do you think, Subhuti, would these followers of the great vehicle be very intelligent?

Subhuti: No, Lord.

The Lord: This also should be known as Mara's deed to the Bodhisattvas.

IV4,10. Desertion of the highest goal.

Just as a person would want to see the great ocean; on having seen it he would look for a puddle in a cow's footprint. On having seen that he would say to himself that it is of the same size as the great ocean. What do you think, Subhuti, would that be a very intelligent person?

Subhuti: No, Lord!

The Lord: The same is true of the followers of the great vehicle who, after they have heard and obtained this perfection of wisdom, abandon it to learn the Sutras associated with the Disciples and Pratyekabuddhas. What do you think, Subhuti, would they be very intelligent people?

Subhuti: No, Lord.

The Lord: This also should be known as Mara's deed to the Bodhisattvas.

IV4,11. Desertion of both the cause (of Buddhahood) and the fruit connected with it.

Just as a mason, or mason's apprentice, would want to build a palace of the size of the Vaijayanta palace and would take his measure from the size of the sun and moon, would that be an intelligent thing to do?

Subhuti: No, Lord!

The Lord: Just so there will be in the future some followers of the Bodhisattva-vehicle who, after they have heard and obtained this deep perfection of wisdom, will spurn and reject it and will decide to search for the knowledge of all modes in the Sutras associated with the Disciples and Pratyekabuddhas. Would these people be very intelligent?

Subhuti: No, Lord!

The Lord: This also should be known as Mara's deed to Bodhisattvas.

IV4,12. Desertion of the highest possible (form of existence).

Suppose some person sees the commander of a fort and thinks to himself that he is like the universal monarch in his complexion and shape. Having observed the aspects, signs, and tokens of the complexion and shape of the commander of a fort he would say that these are the distinctive aspects of the complexion and shape of the universal monarch. What do you think, Subhuti, would that be an intelligent person?

Subhuti: No, Lord!

The Lord: Just so there will be in the future some followers of the great vehicle who, after they have heard and obtained this deep perfection of wisdom, will spurn and reject it and will decide to search for the knowledge of all modes in the Sutras associated with the Disciples and Pratyekabuddhas. Would these people be very intelligent?

Subhuti: No, Lord.

The Lord: This also should be known as Mara's deed to the Bodhisattvas.

IV4,13. The production of many flashes of ideas, and of distracting thoughts directed towards a great variety of objects.

Moreover to those sons and daughters of good family who copy out this perfection of wisdom, many flashes of ideas will arise, which will disturb their writing of this deep perfection of wisdom. These flashes of ideas will concern sight objects, sounds, etc. *to* : Buddhadharmas and the supreme enlightenment. And why? For the perfection of wisdom is without flashes or ideas, it is unthinkable and inconceivable. It is not produced or stopped, not defiled or purified. It cannot be disturbed, it is inexpressible, it is without basis. And why? Because in this deep perfection of wisdom those dharmas do not exist. If some follower of the Bodhisattva-vehicle is disturbed by these dharmas when they hear or copy out this deep perfection of wisdom, then that also is Mara's deed to him.

IV4,14. ONE SETTLES DOWN IN THE IDEA THAT THIS TEXT IS COPIED OUT.

Subhuti: Is it then possible to write down the perfection of wisdom?

The Lord: No, Subhuti. And why? Because the own-being of the perfection of wisdom does not exist, nor that of the other perfections, the emptinesses, the Buddhadharmas or all-knowledge. That of which the own-being does not exist, that is nonexistence; what is nonexistence cannot be written down by the nonexistent.

IV4,15. ONE SETTLES DOWN IN THE IDEA THAT IT IS NONEXISTENCE. (Note: Differs from printed AA.)

If again some followers of the great vehicle have the notion that this perfection of wisdom is a nonexistent, this also will be an act of the Evil One.

IV4,16. ONE ADHERES TO IT AS IN THE LETTERS.

Subhuti: If some followers of the great vehicle, after they have copied out this deep perfection of wisdom in written letters, should think that 'the deep perfection of wisdom has been written down by me', then they form an attachment to the written letters as representing this deep perfection of wisdom. This also should be known as Mara's deed to them.

IV4,17. ONE ADHERES TO IT AS NOT IN THE LETTERS.

And why? Because this perfection of wisdom is not in the letters, nor are the other perfections, etc. *to*: all-knowledge. But if followers of the great vehicle settle down in the perfection of wisdom, etc. as not in the letters, then that also should be known as Mara's deed to them.

IV4,18. ATTENTION TO WORLDLY OBJECTS, SUCH AS A PLEASANT COUNTRY-SIDE.

Moreover, when these sons and daughters of good family copy out this perfection of wisdom, their minds will be on the landscape. This also should be known as Mara's deed to them. Furthermore, they will pay attention to villages, cities, market towns, royal cities, nations, gods, and teachers; their attentions will be associated with mother, father, brother, sister, son, daughters, and relatives, with robbers and outcasts, with discoursings about sense pleasures, with the company of others, and many other things. In this way also Mara, the Evil One, will arrange obstacles and disturbances to those who copy out this deep perfection of wisdom, expound and repeat it, wisely attend to it.

IV4,19. A taste for gain, honour, and fame.

Furthermore, they will relish the thought of gain, honour, and fame, be concerned about their robes, almsbowl, lodging, and medicinal appliances for use in sickness. This also is Mara's deed to them.

IV4,20. One seeks for skill in means where it cannot be found.

Furthermore, Mara, the Evil One, will bring along very deep Sutras to the Bodhisattvas who copy out this deep perfection of wisdom, expound and repeat it, and wisely attend to it. But Bodhisattvas who are skilled in means should not long for those very deep Sutras which Mara has brought along. And why? Because they do not nourish all-knowledge. But Bodhisattvas, who have no skill in means, will, after they have heard it, reject this deep perfection of wisdom in which I have extensively explained skill in means and in which it can be extensively found. That these followers of the great vehicle should, having rejected this deep perfection of wisdom, seek for skill in means in those Sutras associated with the vehicle of the Disciples and Pratyekabuddhas, that also should be known as Mara's deed.

Chapter 41

THE ABSENCE OF MARA'S HOSTS

IV4,21. Maladjustment between the zealous and the indolent.

Furthermore, it may be that the pupil is zealous to copy out this perfection of wisdom, to recite, explain and repeat it, whereas the teacher is indolent.

IV4,22. Maladjustment through geographical separation, although both be zealous.

Furthermore it may be that the teacher is untiring in his desire to copy out, etc. this deep perfection of wisdom, whereas the pupils move off into a different district. Or vice versa, the pupils want to copy, etc. the perfection of wisdom, but the teacher moves into a different district.

IV4,23. The one values gain and honour, the other is easily satisfied.

Furthermore it may be that the teacher attaches weight to gain, honour, and fame, and is passionately fond of robes, food, lodgings, and of a supply of medicinal appliances for sickness, whereas the pupils have few wishes, are easily contented, energetic, mindful, inwardly collected, one-pointed in their thought, and wise. This discord affecting the copying, etc., of the perfection of wisdom should also be known as Mara's deed to the Bodhisattvas. Or, on the contrary, the teacher may have few wishes, be easily contented, quite detached, energetic, etc. *to* : wise, whereas the pupils have many wishes, are attached to gain, honour, and fame, and to robes, food, lodgings, and medicinal appliances for use in sickness. This also is a deed of the Evil One.

IV4,24. The one has undergone austerities, the other has not.

Furthermore it may be that the teacher is a forest dweller, or begs his food from door to door without accepting invitations, or wears clothes made of rags taken from dung heaps, or never eats any food after midday, or eats his meal in one sitting, or lives on alms-food, or inhabits and frequents cemeteries, or lives in an open unsheltered place, or dwells at the foot of a tree, or even in his sleep remains in a sitting posture, or sleeps at night wherever he may happen to be, or possesses no more than three robes, whereas the pupils undergo none of these ascetic practices. Or, on the contrary, a pupil undergoes the (12) ascetic practices whereas the teacher does not. This discord is another deed of Mara which affects the study of the perfection of wisdom.

IV4,25. The one is lovely in his character, the other is not.

Furthermore, it may be that the pupil is full of faith, lovely in his character, and desirous of copying, expounding, and repeating this deep perfection of wisdom, whereas the teacher has no faith, is not lovely in his character, and does not desire to copy, expound, and repeat this deep perfection of wisdom. Or, on the contrary, it may be that the teacher is full of faith, lovely in his character, and desirous of giving this deep perfection of wisdom so that it may be copied out and its meaning understood, whereas none of this is found in the pupil. This discord is another deed of Mara which affects the study of the perfection of wisdom.

IV4,26. The one is generous, the other stingy.

Furthermore it may be that the teacher is one who gives away everything, without niggardliness in his heart, whereas the pupil is stingy, with many wishes, with evil wishes, and attaches weight to gain, honour, fame, robes, etc. On the other hand it may be that the pupil is the one who gives away everything and has no niggardliness in his heart, whereas the teacher is stingy and niggardly. This discord is another deed of Mara which affects the study of the perfection of wisdom.

IV4,27. The one is willing to give advice, the other not willing to accept.

Furthermore it may be that the pupil is willing to give robes, etc. to the teacher, but that the teacher is not willing to accept them. This discord, a deed of Mara, also affects the study of the perfection of wisdom. On the other hand, it may be that the teacher is willing to accept from the pupil, but that the pupil is not willing to give. This discord again is Mara's work.

IV4,28. The one requires a brief explanation, and the other gives a detailed one.

Furthermore it may be that the teacher understands as soon as the main points are mentioned, whereas the pupil needs elaborate instructions, cannot understand unless all the details are explained, and insists on verbal expressions being laboriously explained. Or conversely, the pupil understands at a mere hint, whereas the teacher needs lengthy explanations. This discord is again Mara's work.

IV4,29. The one has the higher knowledge of the Dharma (as expounded in) the Sutras, while the other has not.

Furthermore it may be that the teacher knows the exposition of

Dharma (dharmāntara? Note!), i.e. the Discourses, Discourses in Prose and Verse Mingled, Predictions, Verses, Summaries, Origins, Thus-was-said, Birth-Stories, Expounded Texts, Marvels, Tales and Expositions, whereas the pupils do not. This discord also is Mara's work.

IV4,30. THE ONE IS ENDOWED WITH THE SIX PERFECTIONS, THE OTHER IS NOT.

Furthermore it may be that the teacher is endowed with the six perfections, whereas the pupil is not. Or, alternatively, the pupils may be endowed with the six perfections, whereas the teacher is not. This discord also is Mara's work.

IV4,31. THE ONE HAS SKILL IN MEANS, THE OTHER HAS NOT.

Furthermore the teacher may have skill in means with regard to the six perfections, whereas the pupils have none. Alternatively, the pupils have skill in means with regard to the six perfections, whereas the teacher has none. This discord also is Mara's work.

IV4,32. THE ONE HAS A POWERFUL MEMORY, THE OTHER HAS NOT.

Furthermore the teacher may have acquired the Dharanis, whereas the pupils have not. This discord also is Mara's work.

IV4,33. THE ONE LOVES TO WRITE, ETC. THIS TEXT, THE OTHER DOES NOT.

Furthermore it may be that the teacher is willing to copy out, bear in mind, recite, and repeat, etc. *to* : attend, whereas the pupils have no such desires. Or it may be that the pupils who are willing to copy out, etc. whereas the teacher has no such desire. This discord also is Mara's work.

IV4,34. THE ONE HAS SENSE DESIRES, ETC., THE OTHER IS FREE FROM THEM.

Furthermore it may be that the teacher is free from sense desire, ill will, sloth and torpor, excitedness and sense of guilt, or doubt, whereas the pupils are not free from them. Or alternatively, the pupils are free from the hindrances, whereas the teacher is not. This discord also is Mara's work.

IV4,35. THE AVERSION TO BEING REBORN IN THE STATES OF WOE.

Moreover someone will come along to those who copy, etc. *to*: who develop this deep perfection of wisdom, and disparage life in the hells, among the animals or the Pretas, saying 'so ill are the hells, so ill is the animal world, so ill is life among the Pretas. Do make an end of ill just here and now; what point is there in your fully knowing the supreme enlightenment?' This is another one of Mara's deeds.

IV4,36. DELIGHT AT THE THOUGHT OF GOING TO A BLISSFUL EXISTENCE.

Moreover someone will come along to those who copy, etc. *to*: who wisely attend to this deep perfection of wisdom, and praise life among the (27) kinds of gods. 'So happy is life among the gods, in the world of sense desire because of the enjoyment of sense pleasures, in the world of form because of the trances and transic attainments, and in the formless world because of its calm. All this, however, is impermanent, ill, empty, not the self or belonging to a self, doomed to reversal, fall, cessation, and stopping. Do attain the fruit of a Streamwinner just here and now, etc. *to*: do attain the enlightenment of a Pratyekabuddha just here and now! Do not err about in Samsara for a long time!' This is another one of Mara's deeds.

IV4,37. THE ONE IS FOND OF SOLITUDE, THE OTHER OF COMPANY.

Furthermore it may be that the teacher lives alone, without a second, and does everything by and for himself, whereas the pupil prefers the company of others. Or, conversely, the pupil may live alone, whereas the teacher prefers the company of others. This discord also is Mara's deed.

IV4,38. THE PUPIL WISHES TO ASSOCIATE WITH THE TEACHER WHO GIVES HIM NO OPPORTUNITY.

Furthermore the teacher may say 'to those who come to where I am I will give this perfection of wisdom, so that they can copy it, etc. *to*: develop it', whereas the pupil refuses to come. Conversely, the pupil may wish to go where the teacher is, but the teacher gives him no opportunity to do so. This is another one of Mara's deeds.

IV4,39. THE ONE NEEDS SOME MATERIAL HELP, THE OTHER IS UNWILLING TO GIVE IT.

Furthermore the teacher is willing to give this perfection of wisdom in return for some material help, but the pupil does not wish to approach him for fear of having to offer it. This is another one of Mara's deeds.

IV4,40. THE ONE GOES TO A PLACE OF DANGER, THE OTHER TO A SAFE PLACE.

Furthermore the teacher may want to go to a district where he is in danger of his life, but the pupil does not want to go there. Or conversely the pupil may want to go to a district where he is in danger of his life, but the teacher does not want to go there. This is another one of Mara's deeds.

IV4,41. THE TEACHER GOES TO A PLACE WHICH IS SHORT OF FOOD, AND THE PUPIL REFUSES TO COME WITH HIM.

Furthermore the teacher may want to go to a place which is short of food and water, but the pupil will not want to go there. Or the teacher may have gone to a place where there is plenty of food and water, and the pupils will follow him there. He, however, will say to them : 'You may think that it is a good thing for you to come here, because you think that your material needs will be supplied. But I am afraid that you will regret having come, when you see how little alms-food can be had here'. In this way the teacher refuses Dharma by means of a subtle device. And they will in disgust interpret his remarks as signs of refusal, and not as signs of willingness to give. This is another one of Mara's deeds.

IV4,42. The teacher goes to a place haunted by robbers, etc.

Furthermore the monk who is a teacher may move to a place where there is danger from robbers, outcasts, desperadoes, fierce beasts of prey, vipers, wild jungles, and treacherous roads. And the pupils who wish to hear this deep perfection of wisdom will follow him there. To them this monk will say, 'why do you want to go where there are all these dangers?' Though the pupils, desirous of hearing this deep perfection of wisdom, are willing to follow the teacher, the monk who is the teacher does not wish to teach them, and does not wish to see to it that this deep perfection of wisdom is copied out, proclaimed or heard. Having heard the teacher's remark, they do in their disgust not go to where he goes. This is another one of Mara's deeds.

IV4,43. The teacher likes to see the families who feed him.

Furthermore the teacher may be one of those who attach weight to their relations with the families who give them alms, constantly go to see them, and refuse their prospective pupils on the ground that they have to see those families and pay visits to them. Refused, those pupils will turn back. This is another one of Mara's deeds.

IV4,44. Mara, the Evil One, makes an effort to dissuade from wisdom.

Moreover, Mara, the Evil One in the guise of a monk bestirs himself to prevent, by many devices, anyone from copying this perfection of wisdom, etc. *to* : from attending to it.

Subhuti : For what reason does he do so?

The Lord : Because as a result of the perfection of wisdom all beings can forsake their defilements. Moreover, Mara, the Evil One, will come along in the guise of a monk, in order to cause dissension and he will say that 'this Sutra as it has come to you is not the perfection of wisdom' in order to dissuade people from copying etc. the perfection of wisdom. Moreover, approaching in the guise of a monk, Mara, the Evil One, will say, 'a Bodhisattva who courses in this deep perfection of wisdom realizes the reality limit, and attains the fruit of a Streamwinner, etc. *to*: the enlightenment of a Pratyekabuddha'. Some of those who have heard those words will then not course in the perfection of wisdom. This is another one of Mara's deeds.

IV4,45. MARA ARRANGES A COUNTERFEIT (PERFECTION OF WISDOM).

Moreover to those who copy, etc. *to*: develop this deep perfection of wisdom many deeds of Mara will arise which will cause obstacles. A Bodhisattva should avoid them.

Subhuti: Which are the deeds of Mara that a Bodhisattva should recognise and avoid?

The Lord: Mara will produce counterfeits of the perfection of wisdom and the other perfections, and of the 18 kinds of emptiness. Others of his deeds will be connected with the Disciples and Pratyekabuddhas, and he will say: 'study these (?) and then attain the fruit of a Streamwinner, etc. *to*: Arhatship! Develop these four applications of mindfulness, etc. *to*: the wishless door to deliverance! What is the point of your fully knowing the supreme enlightenment?' In this way Mara will arrange many deeds of this kind.

IV4,46. MARA PRODUCES A LONGING FOR UNDESIRABLE THINGS.

Moreover, Mara, the Evil One, will approach in the guise of the Buddha, with a body all shining like gold and the halo extending for a fathom around him. When the Bodhisattva has seen Him, longing will rise up in him, and he will fail to win all-knowledge. Moreover, Mara, the Evil One, will exhibit in front of those sons and daughters of good family a community of monks headed by the Buddha. Longing will thereupon arise in the Bodhisattva, and he will think that 'I also will at a future period be such a Tathagata, and I will likewise foster a host of monks. As this Tathagata, so will I also demonstrate Dharma!' As a result of this longing he will fail to win all-knowledge. Moreover, Mara, the Evil One, will exhibit many hundreds and thousands of Bodhisattvas who course in the six perfections, Some Bodhisattvas will feel longing for those illusory magical creations conjured up by Mara, and as a result they will fail to win all-knowledge. And why? Because in this deep perfection of wisdom no form exists, no feeling, etc. *to*: no enlightenment. And when no form exists, etc. *to*: no enlightenment, there also Buddhas, Bodhisattvas, and Disciples do not exist. And why? Because all dharmas are in their own-being empty.

IV4,47. THE BUDDHA'S GREAT MIGHT AS ILLUSTRATED BY THE SIMILE OF THE PRECIOUS THINGS IN JAMBUDVIPA, AND SO ON.

Moreover this perfection of wisdom will be bound up with many obstacles for those who bear it in mind, recite, explain and study it, and wisely attend to it. Just as the precious things that there are in Jambudvipa, such as gold, gems, pearls, lapis lazuli, conch shells, crystal, coral, silver, etc. are subject to many obstacles and provoke much hostility; just so those who copy, etc. *to*: develop this deep perfection of wisdom will endure many obstacles and much hostility.

Subhuti: So it is, O Lord, so it is, O Sugata. The Sutras associated with the perfection of wisdom will provoke much hostility. Beset by Mara, of small and sluggish intelligence will be those deluded persons who will cause obstacles to this deep perfection of wisdom being copied, etc. *to*: being developed. Nor will their intelligence be able to function in these very sublime dharmas if they do not copy, etc. *to*: develop this deep perfection of wisdom, or if they cause obstacles to those who copy, etc. *to*: develop it.

The Lord: So it is, Subhuti, so it is. Those people who will not copy out, etc. *to*: wisely attend to this deep perfection of wisdom and who will cause obstacles to it being copied out, etc. *to*: developed, they will be beset by Mara, they will have newly set out in the vehicle, they have planted no wholesome roots, have but tiny wholesome roots, have not done their duties under the Jinas of the past and have not been taken hold of by the good spiritual friends. Small, sluggish, and limited will be their intelligence, and their thought will be unable to stride up into very sublime dharmas. But although these deeds of Mara are bound to arise when this deep perfection of wisdom is being copied out, etc. *to*: is being developed, nevertheless it is due to the Buddha's might that often no deeds of Mara and no obstacles arise to the study of this deep perfection of wisdom and that in addition sons and daughters of good family can perfect the other five perfections, as well as the emptinesses, etc. *to*: the Buddhadharmas and the knowledge of all modes. Those Buddhas and Lords who abide in the ten directions and demonstrate Dharma will make efforts on behalf of those sons and daughters of good family who copy out, etc. *to*: attend to this deep perfection of wisdom. And so will the irreversible Bodhisattvas in the ten directions, and they will bring help.

It is as with a woman who has many children—five, ten, twenty, forty, fifty, or one hundred, one thousand, one hundred thousand. If she feels ill, they will all exert themselves so that their mother may not meet with any obstacle to her life, so that she may live long, so that no unpleasant touch may hit her body. For they feel that she is their genetrix and has given them their body and their life. They will therefore look well after their mother, protect her well, and hope that she will meet with no obstacle to her life, that her body will not become excessively weak, and that she be free from pain caused by stinging insects, mosquitos, crawling animals, by a fall, or by cold, hunger or thirst. In this way the sons give their mother everything that can make her happy, make much of her and cherish her, because they are aware that she has instructed them in the ways of the world. In this way the Tathagatas bring this deep perfection of wisdom constantly and always to mind with their Buddha-eye. And why? Because they are aware that this deep perfection of wisdom is the genetrix of the Tathagatas and their instructress in the cognition of all the Buddhadharmas, and the maker (?) of the world. And the Buddhas and Lords who abide in all the ten directions in countless world systems, they also constantly and always bring to mind just this deep perfection of wisdom with their Buddha-eye. And why? Because this deep perfection of wisdom is the genetrix of the Tathagatas and their instructress in the cognition of the all-knowing. It is because of this that the Tathagatas, motivated by gratitude, constantly and always bring this deep perfection of wisdom to mind with their Buddha-eye, And why? From it have come forth for the Tathagatas the six perfections, the (18) kinds of emptiness, etc. *to*: the eighteen Buddhadharmas, the six super-knowledges, the knowledge of all modes of all the Buddhas, the countless and numberless Buddhadharmas. From it have come forth the Stream-winners, etc. *to*: the Tathagatas, Arhats, fully enlightened Buddhas. All the Tathagatas who have known, do know, and will know the supreme enlightenment, they all do so thanks to this deep perfection of wisdom. And those followers of the great vehicle who will copy out this deep perfection of wisdom, etc. *to*: attend to it, they also will all be brought to mind constantly and always by the Tathagatas with their Buddha-eye, and the Tathagatas will constantly and always arrange for them shelter, defense, and protection, so that they may not fail to win the supreme enlightenment.

CHAPTER 42

SHOWING THE WORLD

IV 5. Marks

IV5,1. THE MARKS OF COGNITION.

IV5,1a. THE MARKS OF THE COGNITION AS REGARDS ALL-KNOWLEDGE

IV5,1a,1. COGNITION OF THE APPEARANCE OF THE TATHAGATA.

Subhuti: The Lord has said that 'the perfection of wisdom is the genetrix of the Tathagatas and their instructress in this world.' How then is she the genetrix of the Buddhas and Lords? How is she their instructress in the world? How has the Tathagata been generated by the deep perfection of wisdom? And what is it that the Tathagata has proclaimed as 'the world'?

The Lord: The ten powers of a Tathagata have been generated by this deep perfection of wisdom, and likewise the four grounds of self-confidence, the great friendliness, the great compassion, the 18 special dharmas of a Buddha and his knowledge of all modes. It is through these dharmas that a 'Tathagata' becomes manifest. That is why it is this deep perfection of wisdom which has generated the Tathagata.

IV5,1a,2. COGNITION OF THE WORLD.

Subhuti: What is it that the Tathagata has proclaimed as 'the world'?

The Lord: The five skandhas.

Subhuti: And how have the five skandhas been shown up by the perfection of wisdom?

The Lord: The perfection of wisdom does not show up these five skandhas as crumbling or crumbling away, as being produced or stopped, as being defiled or purified, as undergoing growth or diminution, toiling or withdrawal from it, nor does it show up past, future or present dharmas. And why? Because emptiness does not crumble, nor crumble away, and so also the Signless, the Wishless, the Uneffected, Nonproduction, Stopping, Nonexistence and the absence of own-being. It is thus that the Tathagata has proclaimed the deep perfection of wisdom as the instructress in the world.

IV5,1a,3. COGNITION OF THE THOUGHTS AND DOINGS OF ALL BEINGS.

It is also thanks to the perfection of wisdom that those who know the thoughts of others can wisely know the thoughts and doings of countless beings. Though in this deep perfection of wisdom no being or concept of a being can be apprehended; no form or concept of form; etc. *to*: no knowledge of all modes, or concept of the knowledge of all modes. It is thus that this deep perfection of wisdom instructs the Tathagatas in the world, but she does not show up form, etc. *to*: all-knowledge. And why? Because even the perfection of wisdom itself does not exist in the perfection of wisdom, nor can it be apprehended in it; how much more so with form, etc. *to*: the knowledge of all modes.

IV5,1a,4-5. COGNITION OF COLLECTED AND DISTRACTED THOUGHTS.

Moreover the Tathagata wisely knows collected and distracted thoughts as they really are as 'collected and distracted thoughts', and that applies to the thoughts of all beings, as many as there are, conceived under the concept of beings—with or without form, with or without perception, and with neither perception nor nonperception, in this world system or in other world systems in the ten directions. And how does he do so? Through Dharmahood.

Subhuti: Through which kind of Dharmahood?

The Lord: Through that Dharmahood in which even the Dharmahood cannot be apprehended, how much less collected thoughts and distracted thoughts.

IV5,1a,6. THE COGNITION OF THE MODE OF NONEXTINCTION OF THOUGHTS.

Moreover the Tathagata wisely knows as they really are the collected and distracted thoughts of those beings under the aspect of nonextinction. And how does he do so? He wisely knows those thoughts in the aspect of their stopping, their forsaking, their peaceful calm, their vanity, and their isolatedness.

IV5,1a,7-8. THE COGNITION OF THOUGHTS WITH AND WITHOUT GREED, ETC.

Moreover the Tathagata wisely knows as they really are thoughts with greed, hate, or delusion, and thoughts without greed, hate, or delusion.

Subhuti: And how does the Tathagata wisely know thought with greed, hate, or delusion, as it really is?

The Lord: The thought which is with greed, hate, or delusion is not the thought as it really is. And why? Because thought as it really is cannot be apprehended, nor can the dharmas which constitute thought, how much less so thought that is with greed, hate, or delusion! And how does the Tathagata wisely know thought without greed, hate, or delusion as it really is? A thought marked by absence of greed is not a thought marked by its presence. And why? Because there can be no meeting of two thoughts. The same applies to hate and delusion.

IV5,1a,9. THE COGNITION OF EXTENSIVE THOUGHTS.

Moreover, the Tathagata, thanks to this deep perfection of wisdom, wisely knows as it really is the extensive thought of other beings and persons as 'extensive thought'. And how does he do so? Here the Tathagata wisely knows as it really is that the thought of other beings and persons is neither expanded nor contracted, for it does not grow or diminish, does not come or go. And why? Because of a thought no own-being can be apprehended which could effect an expansion, etc. *to*: which could come.

IV5,1a,10. THE COGNITION OF THOUGHT WHICH HAS GONE GREAT.

Moreover the Tathagata, thanks to this perfection of wisdom, wisely knows as it really is of other beings and persons the thought which has gone great as 'thought which has gone great'. And how does he do so? Because he does not review of those thoughts the coming or going, the production or stopping, the stability or alteration. And why? Because those thoughts have no own-being which could come or go, be produced or stopped, be stable or altered.

IV5,1a,11. THE COGNITION OF UNLIMITED THOUGHTS.

Moreover thanks to this perfection of wisdom, the Tathagata wisely knows as it really is of other beings and persons the unlimited thought as 'unlimited thought'. And how does he do so? Because with regard to this thought He does not review that it is, nor that it is not, nor does He review it as discontinuous, or as not discontinuous. And why? Because unlimited trends of thought have no support, since for them there exists no foundation on which they could be firmly grounded.

IV5,1a,12. THE COGNITION OF THOUGHTS AS UNDEFINABLE.

Moreover thanks to this perfection of wisdom the Tathagata wisely knows as it really is of other beings and persons the undefinable thought as 'undefinable thought'. And how does he do so? Because he wisely knows as they really are those thoughts as without marks, as devoid of ownbeing, on account of the emptiness of own-marks.

IV5,1a,13. THE COGNITION OF THOUGHTS AS IMPERCEPTIBLE.

And the same with imperceptible thoughts. Because those thoughts of others are not perceived by the five eyes of the Tathagata.

IV5,1a,14. THE COGNITION OF THOUGHTS WITH AFFIRMATION, ETC.

Moreover thanks to the perfection of wisdom the Tathagata wisely knows as they really are of other beings and persons the thoughts which affirm or negate, which are drawn in or stretched out. And how does he do so? He wisely knows that wherever they may arise they are all dependent on the five skandhas. If we take such statements as—'The Tathagata continues to exist after death'. 'The Tathagata does not continue to exist after death', 'The Tathagata neither does nor does not continue to exist after death'—then these statements refer to the skandhas only. The same applies to statements such as, 'Eternal are self and the world—just that is the truth, everything else is delusion'. And so if one considers that self and the world are noneternal, both eternal and noneternal, neither eternal nor noneternal. Likewise if one maintains that self and the world are finite, or not finite, or both finite and not finite, or neither finite nor not finite. Or, finally, if one says 'that which is the soul, that is the body', or 'one thing is the soul, another the body'.

IV5,1a,15. THE COGNITION OF THE MODE OF SUCHNESS.

Moreover the Tathagata, thanks to this perfection of wisdom, perceives form, etc. as identical with Suchness and nonfalseness, as immutable, indiscriminate, signless, impassive, unimpeded, and inapprehensible. It is thus that the Tathagata, thanks to the perfection of wisdom, cognizes of other beings and persons the thoughts which affirm or negate, which are drawn in or stretched out, just as he cognizes Suchness, etc. *to*: the inapprehensible.

IV5,1a,16. THE COGNITION WHICH UNDERSTANDS THE SUCHNESS OF THE FULLY ENLIGHTENED BUDDHAS AND CAN COMMUNICATE IT TO OTHERS.

In this way the Suchness of the affirmations and negations, of the contractions and expansions is the Suchness of the skandhas, elements, sense fields and conditioned coproduction; and that is the Suchness of all dharmas and the Suchness of the six perfections; and that is the Suchness of the 37 dharmas which act as wings to enlightenment; etc. *to*: the Suchness of the 18 special dharmas of a Buddha is the Suchness of all-knowledge; and that is the Suchness of wholesome and unwholesome dharmas; and that again is the Suchness of the dharmas which are worldly and supramundane, with or without outflows, with and without faults, with and without defilements, defiled or purified, conditioned or unconditioned. And the Suchness of the conditioned and unconditioned is the Suchness of past, future, and present dharmas; and that again is the Suchness of the Streamwinner, and that the Suchness of the fruit of a Streamwinner, etc. *to*: the Suchness of the enlightenment of a Pratyekabuddha is the Suchness of the utmost, right, and perfect enlightenment;

that again is the Suchness of a Tathagata, and that the Suchness of all beings. It is thus that the Suchness of the Tathagata and the Suchness of all beings are just one single Suchness, an indistinct Suchness. As indistinct this Suchness is indistinguishable and because it is indistinguishable it is not divided. This is the Suchness of all dharmas which, thanks to the perfection of wisdom, the Tathagata has fully known. In this way this Suchness of the perfection of wisdom is the genetrix of the Tathagatas, and in this way this perfection of wisdom is the instructress in the world. It is thus that the Tathagata cognizes the Suchness of all dharmas, their nonfalseness, their unaltered Suchness. And it is because of this Suchness that the Tathagata is called a 'Tathagata'.

Subhuti: Deep, O Lord, is this Suchness of all dharmas, their non-falseness, their unaltered Suchness. It is through this Suchness that the enlightenment of the Buddhas, the Lords has been revealed. Who else, O Lord, could firmly believe in it, except for irreversible Bodhisattvas, great beings, or persons who have achieved right reviews, or Arhats whose outflows have dried up; etc. *to*: these deep dharmas have first been fully known by the Tathagata and then they have been declared.

The Lord: For Suchness, Subhuti, is inexhaustible. And why is it inexhaustible? Because of the inexhaustibility of all dharmas. This is the Suchness of all dharmas which the Tathagata proclaimed after he had fully known the supreme enlightenment.

CHAPTER 43

UNTHINKABLE

IV5,1b. THE MARKS OF COGNITION AS REGARDS THE KNOWLEDGE OF THE PATH.

Thereupon all the *gods* of the realm of sense desire and of the realm of form in this great trichiliocosm scattered sandal wood powder, came to where the Lord was, saluted the Lord's feet with their heads, stood on one side, and said : Deep, O Lord, is the perfection of wisdom which is being revealed. Which, O Lord, are the marks of the deep perfection of wisdom?

IV5,1b,1. THE COGNITION OF EMPTINESS.

The Lord: Emptiness, Gods, is the mark of this deep perfection of wisdom,

IV5,1b,2. THE COGNITION OF THE SIGNLESS.

Signlessness,

IV5,1b,3. COGNITION OF THE WISHLESS.

Wishlessness and Uneffectedness;

IV5,1b,4. COGNITION OF NONPRODUCTION.

nonproduction,

IV5,1b,5. COGNITION OF NONSTOPPING.

nonstopping,

IV5,1b,6. COGNITION OF NONDEFILEMENT.

nondefilement,

IV5,1b,7. COGNITION OF NONPURIFICATION.

nonpurification,

IV5,1b,8. COGNITION OF NONEXISTENCE.

nonexistence,

IV5,1b,9. COGNITION OF OWN-BEING.

absence of own-being, having nonexistence for own-being,

IV5,1b,10. Cognition of lack of support.
lack of support.

IV5,1b,11. Cognition of having the mark of space.

This deep perfection of wisdom is marked like unto space. In this way, Gods, this deep perfection of wisdom is nonmarked, and it has been verbally expressed by the Tathagata by way of worldly convention, but not by way of ultimate reality.

IV5,1b,12. Cognition of the nature of dharma as undisturbed. (As something that cannot be upset?)

Gods, those marks cannot possibly be altered by the world with its gods, men, and Asuras. And why? Because that world with its gods, men, and Asuras has also that very same mark. For a mark cannot alter a mark. A mark cannot wisely know a mark, nor can a mark wisely know a no-mark, nor can a no-mark wisely know a mark, nor can a no-mark wisely know a no-mark. Therefore then as to mark, no-mark, and mark plus no-mark, there is no possibility for them to be wisely known, nor can anyone wisely know them.

IV5,1b,13. Cognition of the unconditioned.

Gods, these marks have not been brought about by form, etc. *to*: they have not been brought about by the knowledge of all modes. For these marks are neither human nor nonhuman, with or without outflows, worldly or supramundane, conditioned or unconditioned.

IV5,1b,14. Cognition of nondiscrimination.

And the Lord furthermore said to those gods of the realms of sense desire and of form: If someone were to say that space has some kind of mark, would he be speaking correctly?

The Gods: No, Lord, because space is unconditioned.

The Lord: Whether Tathagatas are produced or not produced, just this markless element is established. As it is established, so the Tathagata has fully known it. Therefore is he called the Tathagata.

IV5,1b,15. Cognition of the distinctions (between dharmas).

The Gods: These deep marks have been fully known by the Tathagata. Because of his full knowledge of them there proceeds the Tathagata's unattached vision and cognition, and, having stood in these marks, the Tathagata has revealed all the marks. It is because of the nonattachment of the perfection of wisdom that the Lord has revealed the marks. It is wonderful to see how the deep perfection of wisdom is the range of the Tathagatas, coursing in which the Tathagata has fully known the supreme enlightenment and thereafter has made a distinction between all marks, between the marks of all dharmas like form, etc.

IV5,1b,16. COGNITION OF THE ABSENCE OF MARKS.

The Lord: The Tathagata has fully known the marklessness of form marked by molesting (being liable to destruction); and so with feeling marked by experiencing, perception marked by taking up, the impulses marked by together-making, consciousness marked by recognition; the perfection of giving marked by renunciation, the perfection of morality marked by celibacy, the perfection of patience marked by immovability, the perfection of vigour marked by uncrushability, the perfection of concentration marked by comprehension, the perfection of wisdom marked by nonattachment; the four trances, the four Unlimited, the four formless attainments marked by immovability; the 37 dharmas which act as wings to enlightenment marked by leading forth; emptiness as a door to deliverance marked by detachment, the signless as a door to deliverance marked by quiet calm, the wishless as a door to deliverance marked by the removal of suffering; the deliverances marked by delivering, the powers marked by being well determined, the grounds of self-confidence marked by being well established, the analytical knowledges marked by being indestructable, the great friendliness marked by providing what is beneficial, the great compassion marked by protection, the great sympathetic joy marked by rejoicing, the great impartiality marked by noncommingling; the 18 special Buddhadharmas marked by being something to which no one else has a claim; and the cognition of the knowledge of all modes marked by being 'before the eye'. It is thus that the Tathagata has fully known all dharmas as unmarked, and that is why the Tathagata is called the one who has the cognition of nonattachment.

IV5,1c. THE MARKS OF COGNITION AS REGARDS THE KNOWLEDGE OF ALL MODES.

IV5,1c,1. THE COGNITION OF THE FACT THAT (THE BUDDHA) DWELLS AS ONE WHO HAS TAKEN RECOURSE TO HIS OWN DHARMA.

The Lord: The perfection of wisdom, Subhuti, is the genetrix of the Tathagata. The perfection of wisdom instructs him in this world. For this reason the Tathagata dwells taking recourse to this Dharma;

IV5,1c,2. THE COGNITION OF HONOURING.

he honours that Dharma,

IV5,1c,3. THE COGNITION OF VALUING GREATLY.

values it greatly,

IV5,1c,4. THE COGNITION OF REVERING.
reveres,

IV5,1c,5. THE COGNITION OF WORSHIP.
and worships it, i.e. the perfection of wisdom. This is the Dharma, i.e. the perfection of wisdom, which the Tathagata honours, values greatly, reveres, and worships. And why? Because it is from this perfection of wisdom that the Buddhas, the Lords manifest themselves. Grateful is the Tathagata, the Arhat, the fully enlightened Buddha, thankful is the Tathagata, the Arhat, the fully enlightened Buddha. Rightly would he speak who would say of the Tathagata that he is 'grateful and thankful'. And how is the Tathagata grateful and thankful? The Tathagata honours, values greatly, reveres and worships, favours and cherishes that vehicle on which he has come and that progressive path by which he has won full enlightenment.

IV4,1c,6. THE COGNITION OF THE ABSENCE OF AN AGENT.
Moreover the Tathagata has, relying on the signlessness of all dharmas, fully known all dharmas as not made on account of the nonbeingness of an agent. He has fully known them as not unmade, on account of the nonbeingness of their suppression. This, also, Subhuti, should be seen as the gratitude and thankfulness of the Tathagata. Thanks to the perfection of wisdom He has thus fully known the inactivity of all dharmas.

IV5,1c,7. THE COGNITION WHICH REACHES EVERYWHERE.
Moreover it is thanks to the perfection of wisdom that the Tathagata's cognition has proceeded in all dharmas as unmade as though really it has not proceeded, and the proceeding is only a matter of convention. In this way the perfection of wisdom is the genetrix of the Tathagata, and instructs him in this world.

IV5,1c,8. THE COGNITION THAT (THE BUDDHA) CAN SHOW THAT WHICH IS IMPERCEPTIBLE.
Subhuti: If all dharmas, O Lord, are unknowable and imperceptible, how can the perfection of wisdom be the genetrix of the Tathagata and his instructress in this world?

The Lord: So it is, so it is. All dharmas are unknowable and imperceptible. And why are they so? Because all dharmas are empty, worthless, insignificant, void, and insubstantial. In this way all dharmas are unknowable and imperceptible. Moreover, Subhuti, all dharmas are unknowable and imperceptible because they are unsupported and unincluded. It is thus that the perfection of wisdom is the genetrix of the Tathagata and his instructress in this world. And she is an instructress because form, etc.

to : the knowledge of all modes cannot be viewed. It is thus that the perfection of wisdom is the Tathagata's genetrix and his instructress in this world.

Subhuti : How does she become the instructress through the nonviewing of form, etc.?

The Lord: Where, Subhuti, there arises an act of consciousness which has none of the skandhas for an objective support, there she becomes an instructress through a nonviewing of the world. It is thus, Subhuti, that this deep perfection of wisdom is the genetrix of the Tathagata and his instructress in the world.

IV5,1c,9. THE COGNITION OF THE WORLD FROM THE POINT OF VIEW OF EMPTINESS.

Furthermore how is the perfection of wisdom the genetrix of the Tathagata and his instructress in the world? Here the perfection of wisdom indicates that the world is empty. And why does she do so? Here in the world the five skandhas are empty, the 12 sense fields are empty, etc. *to* : the knowledge of all modes is empty. It is thus that the perfection of wisdom is the genetrix of the Tathagata and his instructress in this world.

IV5,1c,10. COGNITION OF THE FACT THAT THE BUDDHA CAN INDICATE THE WORLD'S EMPTINESS.

How does the perfection of wisdom show up the world as empty?

IV5,1c,11. COGNITION OF THE FACT THAT THE BUDDHA CAN MAKE KNOWN THE WORLD'S EMPTINESS.

IV5,1c,12. COGNITION OF THE FACT THAT HE CAN SHOW UP THE WORLD'S EMPTINESS.

She shows up the fact that the world and the five skandhas are 'empty'. It is thus that the perfection of wisdom is the Tathagata's genetrix and his instructress in the world.

IV5,1c,13. COGNITION OF UNTHINKABILITY.

Moreover the perfection of wisdom shows up to the Tathagata the world as unthinkable. How? It shows up that the five skandhas are the world which is unthinkable. Moreover the perfection of wisdom shows up to the Tathagata the world, in other words the five skandhas, as isolated, as absolutely empty, as empty of own-being, as empty through the nonexistence of own-being.

IV5,1c,14. THE COGNITION OF QUIESCENCE.

Moreover the perfection of wisdom shows up to the Tathagata the world, or the five skandhas, as calmly quiet.

IV5,1c,15. THE COGNITION OF THE CESSATION (OF THE WORLD).

Moreover the perfection of wisdom shows up to the Tathagata the world, or the five skandhas, as just emptiness.

IV5,1c,16. THE COGNITION OF THE CESSATION OF THE PERCEPTION OF THE WORLD.

And again how does this deep perfection of wisdom show up the world? So that no perception of this world or the other world takes place. And why? Because those dharmas do not exist through which a perception of this world or a perception of the other world could take place.

IV5,2. THE DISTINCTIVE MARKS.

IV5,2,1. ACCEPTANCE OF COGNITION OF DHARMA IN SUFFERING: UNTHINKABILITY.

Subhuti: For the sake of a great performance, O Lord, has this perfection of wisdom been set up, for the sake of an unthinkable, incomparable, immeasurable, and equal to the unequalled (P: incalculable) performance.

The Lord: So it is, Subhuti, so it is. And how has the perfection of wisdom been set up as a great performance? It is a great performance on the part of the Tathagatas that they protect all beings and do not abandon them. And how has the perfection of wisdom been set up as an unthinkable performance? Unthinkable is Buddhahood, Tathagatahood, Self-Existence, and the state of all-knowledge. In this way has the perfection of wisdom been set up for an unthinkable performance on the part of the Tathagatas, the Arhats, the fully enlightened Buddhas.

IV5,2,2. COGNITION OF DHARMA IN SUFFERING: INCOMPARABILITY.

And how has the perfection of wisdom been set up for an incomparable performance? There is no being whatsoever, among those who are comprehended under the term 'beings,' who would be able to think Buddhahood, Tathagatahood, Self-Existence, and the state of all-knowledge, or to compare it.

IV5,2,3. ACCEPTANCE OF THE SUBSEQUENT COGNITION OF SUFFERING: IMMEASURABILITY.

And how has the perfection of wisdom been set up for an immeasurable performance? The Buddhahood, Tathagatahood, Self-Existence, and state of all-knowledge of the Tathagatas is immeasurable, and it cannot be measured by anyone.

IV5,2,4. Subsequent cognition of suffering : incalculability.

And how has the perfection of wisdom been set up for a performance which equals the unequalled? Because nothing can be quite equal to the Tathagatas, the Arhats, the fully Enlightened Ones, how much less can anything be superior to them!

Subhuti: Are then Buddhahood, Tathagatahood, Self-Existence, and the state of all-knowledge unthinkable, incomparable, immeasurable, and equal to the unequalled?

The Lord: Yes, they are. And so are also form, etc. *to* : all-knowledge. All dharmas in fact are unthinkable, immeasurable, and equal to the unequalled. With regard to the Dharmahood of all dharmas no thought, and no dharmas belonging to thought, can be apprehended. Form also, as unthinkable, etc. cannot be conceived, and so up to the knowledge of all modes.

Subhuti: For what reason can form, etc. as unthinkable, etc. not be conceived?

The Lord: Because with regard to form, etc. one cannot conceive of the thinking, the comparing, the measuring, the equality or inequality.

Subhuti: And for what reason is that so?

The Lord: Because also of form, etc. the own-being is unthinkable, etc. What do you think, Subhuti, can form, etc. be apprehended in what is unthinkable, etc.?

Subhuti: No, O Lord!

The Lord: In that manner all dharmas are unthinkable, etc. And these Tathagata-dharmas of the Tathagata are unthinkable, etc. They are unthinkable because thinking has ceased and been transcended, comparing and measuring have ceased and been transcended, equality and inequality have ceased and been transcended. 'Unthinkable', that is a synonym of incomparable, etc. These Tathagata-dharmas of the Tathagata are unthinkable because space is unthinkable, incomparable because space is incomparable, etc. etc. This also is of the Tathagata the Tathagata-unthinkability, -incomparability, -immeasurability, and -equality to the unequalled, which cannot be thought or compared by the world with its gods, men, and Asuras. Thus are the Buddhas immeasurable, thus are the Buddhadharmas immeasurable.

When this chapter on the Tathagata's unthinkability, etc. was being taught, the minds of 500 monks were freed, without further clinging, from the outflows, and so were the minds of 2,000 nuns; 6,000 lay brethren obtained with regard to dharmas the pure, dispassionate, unstained Dharma-eye, 20,000 Bodhisattvas won the patient acceptance of dharmas which fail to be produced, and the Lord has predicted that they will become Buddhas in this very Bhadra-kalpa.

CHAPTER 44

THE CONGREGATION

IV5,2,5. ACCEPTANCE OF COGNITION OF DHARMA IN ORIGINATION: COMPRISING ALL THE HOLY PERSONS.

Subhuti: Deep, O Lord, is the perfection of wisdom. For a great performance (enterprise) has this perfection of wisdom been set up, for an enterprise which is unthinkable, incomparable, immeasurable, equal to the unequalled.

The Lord: So it is, Subhuti, so it is. For entrusted to this perfection of wisdom are the five perfections, entrusted to it are the various kinds of emptiness, the four applications of mindfulness, etc. *to*: the knowledge of all modes. Just as an anointed king, a Kshatriya, who feels strong and secure in his kingdom, entrusts all his business concerning the kingly office and the kingdom to his minister; he himself has few cares and his burden is light as regards the business concerning his kingly duties and his activities concerning the kingdom; just so, Subhuti, whatever dharmas of the Disciples, the Pratyekabuddhas, the Bodhisattvas, or the Buddhas there may be, they are all entrusted to the perfection of wisdom, and the perfection of wisdom in them does the work. Therefore, then, has the perfection of wisdom been set up for a great performance, for a performance which is unthinkable, incomparable, immeasurable, equal to the unequalled. And why? Because this deep perfection of wisdom has been set up so that one should not take hold of form, etc. *to*: the supreme enlightenment, nor settle down in them.

Subhuti: How, O Lord, has this perfection of wisdom been set up so that one should not take hold of form, etc. *to*: supreme enlightenment, nor settle down in them?

The Lord: What do you think, Subhuti, can you review that form, etc. *to*: that knowledge of all modes, or that fruit of a Streamwinner, etc. *to*: that supreme enlightenment, which could be taken hold of or settled down in, or do you review that dharma which one could take hold of or settle down in, or that dharma whereby one could take hold of or settle down in?

Subhuti: No, O Lord.

The Lord: Well said, Subhuti, well said! I also do not review form, etc. *to*: the supreme enlightenment; because I do not review it I do not take hold of it; because I do not take hold of it I do not grasp at it.

I also do not review the level of a Buddha, all-knowledge, the knowledge of all modes, and Tathagatahood; not reviewing it I do not take hold of it; not taking hold of it I do not settle down in it. And why? The Bodhisattva, Subhuti, should not take hold of form, etc. *to* : Tathagatahood, and he should not settle down in them.

IV5,2,6. COGNITION OF DHARMA IN ORIGINATION : THE KNOWLEDGE OF THE ABSOLUTE IS ACCESSIBLE TO THE EXPERIENCE OF THE WISE.

The Gods of the realm of sense desire and of form : Deep, O Lord, is this perfection of wisdom, hard to see, hard to understand, inaccessible to reasoning and discursive thought, calm, subtle, delicate, to be felt only by the learned and discerning. Those beings who firmly believe in this perfection of wisdom will be such as have fulfilled their duties under the Jinas of the past, they will have been taken hold of by the good spiritual friends, and they will have planted wholesome roots.

IV5,2,7. ACCEPTANCE OF THE SUBSEQUENT COGNITION OF ORIGINATION : UNCOMMONNESS.

If, O Lord, all beings in this great trichiliocosm would become Faith-followers, Dharma-followers, people on the eighth-lowest stage, Stream-winners, Once-returners, Never-returners, Arhats, or Pratyekabuddhas, compared with their cognition and forsaking the cognition of this deep perfection of wisdom for one single day, the willingness to find pleasure in it, the reflection on it, the weighing up of it, the exploration and investigation of it, will be superior. And why? Because the patient acceptance of the Bodhisattva, the great being who has gained the patient acceptance of dharmas which fail to be produced, is superior to the cognition and forsaking of the Faith-followers, etc. *to*: Pratyekabuddhas.

IV5,2,8. SUBSEQUENT COGNITION OF ORIGINATION : QUICK UNDERSTANDING.

The Lord: So it is, O Gods, so it is. One may expect that those sons and daughters of good family who will listen to this deep perfection of wisdom, copy it out, explain and repeat it, and wisely attend to it, will go forth more quickly than those others, who belong to the vehicle of the Disciples and Pratyekabuddhas, who are lacking in perfect wisdom, and who course on the stage of a Faith-follower, etc. for an aeon or for the remainder of an aeon. And why? Because in this deep perfection of wisdom that patient acceptance of dharmas which fail to be produced has been explained in detail, and in that the Faith-followers, etc. *to* : the Pratyekabuddhas should train, in that the Bodhisattvas, the great beings should train, and because they have trained in that perfection of wisdom the Tathagatas have fully known the supreme enlightenment, do fully know it, will fully know it.

Thereupon the gods of the realm of sense desire and the realm of form gave forth this shout of triumph: A great perfection is this perfection of wisdom, O Lord, etc. *to*: a perfection which equals the unequalled is this perfection of wisdom! It is because they have trained in this deep perfection of wisdom that the Faith-followers, etc. *to*: the Pratyekabuddhas have gone forth, do go forth, and will go forth, and that the Bodhisattvas, the great beings, have gone forth to the supreme enlightenment, do go forth to it, will go forth to it.

IV5,2,9. ACCEPTANCE OF COGNITION OF DHARMA IN STOPPING: NEITHER DECREASE NOR INCREASE.

And of this deep perfection of wisdom neither deficiency nor completeness can be conceived.

Thereupon the gods of the realm of sense desire and of form saluted the Lord's feet with their heads, thrice walked round the Lord, and then moved away from the presence of the Lord. Before they had gone far, they disappeared from sight, and the gods of the realm of sense desire departed for the world of sense desire, and the gods of the realm of form for the realm of form.

IV5,2,10. COGNITION OF DHARMA IN STOPPING: INTENSE PROGRESS.

Subhuti: If a Bodhisattva, on merely hearing it, immediately believes in this deep perfection of wisdom—where has he deceased, where is he reborn?

The Lord: Here, Subhuti, a Bodhisattva, a great being, immediately on hearing this deep perfection of wisdom firmly believes in it, does not become cowed or stolid, is not stupefied, does not hesitate or doubt, but delights in hearing this deep perfection of wisdom, and on hearing this deep perfection of wisdom does not become lacking in those attentions and does never let go those attentions, wherever he goes, comes, stands, or sits, and he constantly and always follows that reciter of Dharma. Just as a cow does not abandon her young calf, just so, Subhuti, the Bodhisattva who knows this deep perfection of wisdom by heart, who has become thoroughly familiar with it through his mindfulness, who has well investigated it with his mind, who has well penetrated it with his vision,—that person belonging to the vehicle of the Bodhisattvas has deceased among men, has been reborn among men. And why? Because this son or daughter of good family, belonging to the vehicle of the Bodhisattvas, has in the past also copied this deep perfection of wisdom, made it into a book, honoured, revered, adored, and worshipped it with flowers, etc. Through that wholesome root he has, deceased among men, been reborn among men, and has firmly believed in this deep perfection of wisdom immediately on hearing it.

IV5,2,11. Acceptance of subsequent cognition of stopping: full attainment.

Subhuti: Could a Bodhisattva, a great being, who is endowed with these qualities, and who firmly believes in this deep perfection of wisdom immediately on hearing it, who copies it out, explains and studies it, and wisely attends to it—could that Bodhisattva have deceased near other Buddhas and Lords whom he has honoured, before he was reborn here?

The Lord: So it is, Subhuti, so it is. That is quite possible. And why? Because that Bodhisattva, that great being, has in the presence of these Buddhas and Lords heard this deep perfection of wisdom, borne it in mind, preached and studied it, and has wisely attended to it. Through just that wholesome root and through just these attentions he has been reborn here. Moreover, the Bodhisattva, the great being, has been reborn among the Tushita gods and he should be known as endowed with just these same qualities. And why? Because that Bodhisattva, that great being, has questioned and counterquestioned Maitreya, the Bodhisattva, the great being, about this deep perfection of wisdom and through that wholesome root he has been reborn here. But if that Bodhisattva, that great being in the past, when he heard this deep perfection of wisdom, has not asked questions and counterquestions about it, then, when now this deep perfection of wisdom is being preached, he feels hesitation, stupefaction, and despondency of thought. And so when the other five perfections, or the various kinds of emptiness, or the supreme enlightenment are being preached. Moreover, Subhuti, some Bodhisattva, a great being has in the past heard this deep perfection of wisdom for one, two, three, four, or five days, has asked questions and counterquestions about it, and has pursued it for that time, but afterwards he has again withdrawn from it and feels no longer like asking questions about it. And why? For it is a fact that if a Bodhisattva has in the past not all the time asked questions and counterquestions about this deep perfection of wisdom, and pursued it, and if only for a time he has been intent and keen on it, then he will later at some time feel the urge to pursue it, but not so at other times; he will again withdraw from it, and through his unsteady intelligence he will become like cotton wool. That Bodhisattva, that great being should merely be known as one who has but lately set out in the vehicle, as one who has not been taken hold of by the good spiritual friends, as one who has not honoured the fully enlightened Buddhas. He will no further explain this deep perfection of wisdom, study it or wisely attend to it. He has not been trained in the perfection of wisdom, or the other five perfections, etc. *to*: in the knowledge of all modes. That Bodhisattva, that great being should be known as one who has newly set out in the vehicle. Endowed with but a little faith and little love, he will no longer be able to copy out this deep perfection of wisdom, or to preach, explain or study it, or to wisely attend to it. But if a son or daughter of good family does not copy out this deep perfection of wisdom, or explains or studies it, or wisely attends to it, and does not get hold of the beyond of this deep perfection of wisdom, etc. *to*: of the knowledge of all modes, does not comply with this deep perfection of wisdom, etc. *to*: with the knowledge of all modes, then one of two stations or levels should be expected of them, i.e. the level of a Disciple or Pratyekabuddha. And why? It is because in the past they have not copied, etc. this deep perfection of wisdom, because they have not got hold of the beyond of this deep perfection of wisdom, and have not complied with it, that of these sons or daughters of good family these two levels should be expected.

Chapter 45

THE SHIP

IV5,2,12. Subsequent cognition of stopping: the distinctive objective support.

Just as, Subhuti, if a ship breaks up on the ocean, one should know that those people who cannot find the support of a log, gravel bank, plank, tree-trunk, or a corpse, or get hold of one of these, will surely meet with their end in the ocean before they have reached the shore. But those people who, when a ship breaks up in the ocean, think of seeking the support and of getting hold of a log, gravel-bank, plank, tree-trunk, or corpse—one should know, Subhuti, that those people do not meet with their end in the great ocean, but they will safely cross over the great ocean, and unhurt, uninjured, and safe they will again stand on dry land. Just so, Subhuti, those sons and daughters of good family who belong to the vehicle of the Bodhisattvas, and who are endowed with just a little faith, a little serene belief, a little affection, but who do not read this perfection of wisdom, do not explain or study it, do not wisely attend to it, do not seek their support in it—and likewise with the perfection of giving etc. *to*: the knowledge of all modes—one should know, Subhuti, that those sons and daughters of good family who belong to the vehicle of the Bodhisattvas, will in the middle of the way experience a loss of enlightenment and, without having obtained the knowledge of all modes, they will realize the level of a Disciple or Pratyekabuddha. But those persons who belong to the Bodhisattva-vehicle, and who have faith, patience, serene belief, resolution, willingness to find pleasure in this, renunciation, and persistence in trying to win the supreme enlightenment, they will copy this deep perfection of wisdom, explain and study it, wisely attend to it, and seek their support in it. Thus whatever of the perfection of wisdom etc. *to*: the knowledge of all modes, those sons and daughters of good family, who have faith, patience, serene belief, resolute intentions, joyous will, resolve, renunciation, and persistence in trying to win the supreme enlightenment, have got hold of, with regard to that they will not midway come to ruin. Having transcended the level of the Disciples and Pratyekabuddhas, having matured beings and purified the Buddha-field, they fully know the supreme enlightenment.

IV5,2,13. ACCEPTANCE OF COGNITION OF DHARMA IN THE PATH: ITS DISTINCTIVE FOUNDATION.

Just as if a woman or man would want to carry water in a jar which is badly baked or quite unbaked, one should know that that jar will not last long, but will quickly fall to pieces and melt away. And why? Because in its unbaked condition it would actually soon come to an end on the ground. Just so, although sons and daughters of good family who belong to the Bodhisattva-vehicle may have faith, etc. *to*: persistence in trying to win supreme enlightenment, but if they have not been taken hold of by the perfection of wisdom, or by skill in means, or by the five perfections, or the various kinds of emptiness, or the knowledge of all modes, then they will midway come to ruin and fall on the level of a Disciple or Pratyekabuddha. But if some woman or man would carry water in a well-baked jar, from a ... or any other water-bearing place, then that jar will safely go to where it is meant to go. Just so the Bodhisattva, the great being who has faith, etc. *to*: persistence in trying to win the supreme enlightenment, and who has also been taken hold of by the perfection of wisdom, by skill in means and by the knowledge of all modes, will not midway come to ruin, on the level of the Disciples or Pratyekabuddhas, and he will, unhurt and uninjured, fully know the supreme enlightenment.

IV5,2,14. COGNITION OF DHARMA IN THE PATH: THE FULL COMPLEMENT.

Just as if some man were to launch into the great ocean a ship which has not been properly repaired or caulked, and has been overloaded with goods; one should know, Subhuti, that that ship will soon flounder, and that the ship will soon be in one place and the goods in another. That merchant, who is without skill in means, will thus suffer a great disadvantage and lose a huge fortune. Just so, although a Bodhisattva may have faith, etc., if he has not been taken hold of by the perfection of wisdom, by skill in means, etc. *to*: by the knowledge of all modes, one should know, Subhuti, that this Bodhisattva will suffer ruin midway, will be separated from a great advantage and will lose great wealth, i.e. the wealth of the knowledge of all modes, and he will fall unto the level of the Disciples and Pratyekabuddhas. But if an intelligent man were to launch into the great ocean a ship which is well repaired and well got ready, and were to place the load properly on it, then one should know that this ship will not flounder in the water, and that it will go to the place which it is meant to go to. Just so, if a Bodhiśattva has faith, etc. and has also been taken hold of by the perfection of wisdom, by skill in means, etc. *to*: by the knowledge of all modes, then one should know that he will not founder midway before he reaches the supreme enlightenment. And why? Because under such circumstances he cannot fall on the level of a Disciple or Pratyekabuddha.

IV5,2,15. Acceptance of subsequent cognition of the path: the assistance.

Just as if a man were one hundred years old, very aged, advanced in years, and decrepit, and if some illness were to arise in his body—from the wind, bile, phlegm or combination of the humours—what do you think, Subhuti, could he rise from his bed on his own?

Subhuti: No, Lord! If even he could get up, he would not have the strength to walk for half a mile. Wasted away by both old age and illness he could, even if he managed to get up, not walk about.

The Lord: So it is, Subhuti. Even though a Bodhisattva may have faith, etc. if he has not been taken hold of by the perfection of wisdom, by skill in means, etc. *to*: by the knowledge of all modes, then one should know, Subhuti, that midway he will fall down unto the level of the Disciples or Pratyekabuddhas. And why? Just because he has not been taken hold of by the perfection of wisdom, by skill in means, etc. *to*: by the knowledge of all modes. Just as if that man who is so sick and old would wish to get up; and two strong men, one to his right and one to his left, would carefully lift him up and promise him that he may go wherever he wishes—then he will have no fear of falling down on his way to where he wants to go. Just so, if a Bodhisattva has faith, etc. and if he has been taken hold of by the perfection of wisdom, skill in means, etc. *to*: by the knowledge of all modes, then one should know that that Bodhisattva will not collapse midway, and he will be able to reach the place he wants to go to, i.e. the supreme enlightenment. And why? Because he is not lacking in perfect wisdom and skill in means.

Subhuti: How does the person belonging to the Bodhisattva-vehicle, who has not been taken hold of by perfect wisdom and skill in means, fall on the level of Disciple or Pratyekabuddha?

The Lord: Well said, Subhuti, well said, you who think that for the sake of the persons belonging to the Bodhisattva-vehicle you should ask the Tathagata about this matter. Here, Subhuti, a Bodhisattva from the beginning gives gifts, but with a mind that has fallen into I-making and Mine-making; he guards morality, etc. etc. When he gives a gift, etc. it occurs to him, I give a gift, to him I give that gift, I am a giver; I guard morality, etc. He puts his mind to that gift, he thinks by means of that gift, he thinks I am a giver, etc. And why? Because in the perfection of wisdom these discriminations do not exist, for the perfection (*pāramitā*) of giving has abstained (*āramitā*) from them, etc. And so for the other perfections. And that person belonging to the Bodhisattva-vehicle neither knows the not-beyond nor the Beyond. Not taken hold of by the perfection of giving, etc. *to*: the knowledge of all modes, he falls on the level of a Disciple or Pratyekabuddha, and does not go forth to the knowledge of all modes.

And how, Subhuti, does a person who belongs to the Bodhisattva-vehicle become unskilled in means? Here, Subhuti, from the beginning without skill in means he gives a gift, guards morality, develops patience, etc. And it occurs to him, I give a gift, this gift I give, to him I give, etc. He puts his mind to the gift, he thinks 'I am a giver', etc. And why? Because in the perfection of giving these discriminations do not exist, as he discriminates them. And why? Because that perfection of giving is really a nonperfection. And he knows neither the not-beyond nor the Beyond. Not taken hold of by the perfection of giving, etc. *to* : by skill in means, etc. *to* : by the knowledge of all modes, he falls on the level of a Disciple or a Pratyekabuddha, and he does not go forth to the knowledge of all modes.

And how, Subhuti, does a person who belongs to the Bodhisattva-vehicle, and has been taken hold of by perfect wisdom and by skill in means, not fall on the level of a Disciple or Pratyekabuddha, and attain full enlightenment? Here, Subhuti, a person who belongs to the Bodhisattva-vehicle gives gifts from the beginning, but not with a mind that has fallen into I-making and Mine-making; and so he guards morality, develops patience, exerts vigour, develops the trances, develops wisdom. It does not occur to him, I give a gift, to him I give a gift, etc *to* : I develop wisdom. He does not put his mind to the gift, he does not think through the gift, he does not think : I am a giver, I am moral, I am patient, I am energetic, I am capable of the trances, I am wise. And why? Because there in the perfection of giving these discriminations do not exist to which he could put his mind. For a non-perfection is this, i.e. the perfection of giving, etc. But that Bodhisattva does not put his mind to a non-perfection, or to a perfection. Taken hold of by the perfection of giving, etc. *to* : by the knowledge of all modes, he does not fall on the level of a Disciple, and attains to the knowledge of all modes.

And how does a Bodhisattva become one who has been taken hold of by skill in means? Here, from the beginning, just with skill in means he gives a gift, etc. It does not occur to him, I give a gift, etc. *to* : I develop wisdom. He does not think of a gift, nor through it, etc. *to* : I am wise. And why? Because in the perfection of wisdom these discriminations do not exist by which he could discriminate. And why? Because there that is a nonperfection, i.e. the perfection of giving, etc. Taken hold of by the perfection of giving, etc. *to* : by that skill in means, he does not fall on the level of a Disciple and attains to the knowledge of all modes.

Chapter 46

EXPOSITION OF THE OWN-BEING OF ALL DHARMAS

IV5,2,16. Subsequent cognition of the path: the absence of relishing.

Subhuti: How, O Lord, should a Bodhisattva, a great being who is a beginner, train in the perfection of wisdom and the other five perfections.

The Lord: Here, Subhuti, a Bodhisattva, who is a beginner and who wants to train in the perfection of wisdom and the other five perfections, should tend, love, and honour the good spiritual friends, who explain to him this deep perfection of wisdom, as follows: 'Come here, son of good family, whatever gift you may have given, whatever morality you may have guarded, etc. *to*: whatever wisdom you may have developed—all that, having made it common to all beings, do dedicate to the supreme enlightenment! But do not misconstrue the supreme enlightenment as form or as any other skandha! Do not misconstrue it as one of the perfections, one of the emptinesses, etc. *to*: the knowledge of all modes! And why? For the skandhas when not misconstrued, reach an all-knowledge which is also not misconstrued. Nor should you produce any longing for the skandhas, etc. *to*: a Bodhisattva's special way of salvation, etc. *to*: the supreme enlightenment. And why? Because all these are not worth longing for. And why? Because all dharmas are empty of own-being.'

IV5,3. The marks of activity.

Subhuti: Doers of what is hard are the Bodhisattvas, the great beings who, when all dharmas are empty of own-marks, strive for the supreme enlightenment and want to fully know it.

The Lord: So it is, Subhuti, so it is. And yet, Subhuti, although they have known all dharmas as like a mock show or a dream, the Bodhisattvas, the great beings have set out towards the supreme enlightenment for the benefit and welfare of the world, so that they can become a shelter for the world, a refuge, a place of rest, the final relief, islands, torchbearers, caravan leaders and light bringers, and leaders of the world.

IV5,3,1. He brings benefits.

How then has a Bodhisattva, who wants to fully know the supreme enlightenment, set out for the benefit of the world? Here the Bodhisattva liberates beings from the five places of rebirth, and places them on the shore where there is nothing to fear, into the safety of Nirvana.

IV5,3,2. He brings ease.

And how has the Bodhisattva set out for the world's Ease? Here the Bodhisattva, the great being who wants to fully know the supreme enlightenment, liberates beings from physical ills, mental sadness, and despair, and places them on the shore where there is nothing to fear, into the safety of Nirvana.

IV5,3,3. He gives shelter.

And how does the Bodhisattva who wants to fully know the supreme enlightenment become the world's shelter? He protects beings from all the sufferings which belong to Samsara; he demonstrates Dharma so that these sufferings might be forsaken, and he leads the beings who have heard that Dharma gradually to Nirvana through the three vehicles.

IV5,3,4. He gives refuge.

And how does the Bodhisattva who wants to fully know the supreme enlightenment become a refuge for beings? He sets free from birth, decay, death, sorrow, lamentation, pain, sadness, and despair those beings who are doomed to undergo these conditions, and he leads them to the realm of Nirvana which leaves nothing behind.

IV5,3,5. He provides a place of rest.

And how does the Bodhisattva, who wants to fully know the supreme enlightenment, become a resting place for beings? He demonstrates Dharma to beings so that they may learn not to embrace anything.

Subhuti: How does the nonembracing of all dharmas come about?

The Lord: The nonembracing of form, etc. *to*: of the knowledge of all modes, is the same as their nonconnection; and that is the same as their nonproduction, and that is the same as their nonstopping.

IV5,3,6. He provides final relief.

And how does the Bodhisattva who wants to fully know the supreme enlightenment become the final relief of beings? He demonstrates to beings the Dharma as follows: The Beyond of form, etc. that is not form. And as form, so all dharmas.

Subhuti: If as form so all dharmas, then a Bodhisattva must surely have fully known all dharmas. And why? Because in the Beyond of form, etc. there is no discrimination, to the effect: this is form, this is feeling, etc. *to*: this is the knowledge of all modes.

The Lord: So it is, Subhuti, so it is. In the Beyond of form, etc. there is no discrimination at all. This also is most hard for the Bodhisattvas that they meditate on all these calm dharmas, and yet do not become cowed, (but are resolved that) 'in this way should all these dharmas be fully known, and, when the supreme enlightenment has been won, I will reveal these dharmas to others.'

IV5,3,7. He acts as an island.

And how does a Bodhisattva, when he has fully known the supreme enlightenment, become the world's island? Islands are pieces of land limited all round by water, in rivers, or great oceans. Just so form, etc. is limited at its beginning and end, and so everything up to the knowledge of all modes. By this limitation of their beginning and end are all dharmas circumscribed. And this limitation of all dharmas at their beginning and end is the Calm Quiet, the Sublime, That which really is, i.e. emptiness, nonbasis, the nonannihilation of Dharma, the extinction of craving, the nonembracing, dispassion, stopping, Nirvana. It is thus that the Bodhisattva, when he has fully known the supreme enlightenment, reveals these dharmas, so calm, so sublime. And how does the Bodhisattva, when he has fully known the supreme enlightenment, become a torch-bearer of beings, a light bringer to them? He reveals to beings the true meaning associated with the four means of conversion, and establishes them in it.

And how does the Bodhisattva, when he has fully known the supreme enlightenment, become a caravan leader to beings? He points out to beings who have set out on a bad road or who find themselves at some crossroads the one single suitable path, which is conducive to purity, the transcending of sorrows and misfortunes, the going to rest of physical ills and mental sadness, the attainment of the methodically correct Dharma, and the realisation of Nirvana.

IV5,3,8. He acts as a leader.

And how does the Bodhisattva, when he has fully known the supreme enlightenment, become a leader of beings? He demonstrates and reveals dharma for the sake of the nonproduction, nonstopping, nondefilement and nonpurification of form, etc. *to* : of the supreme enlightenment.

IV5,3,9. He does not turn towards anything.

And how does the Bodhisattva, when he has fully known the supreme enlightenment, become the resort of beings? He demonstrates dharma to beings to the effect that form, etc. is situated in space; that the emptiness of form, etc. is situated so that it has not come, i.e. it neither comes nor goes. And why? For all dharmas are situated in emptiness and from that situation they do not depart. And why? For of emptiness no coming or going can be apprehended. And so for the Signless and Wishless. Situated in the Uneffected are all dharmas and they do not depart from that situation. And why? Because of the Uneffected no coming or going can be apprehended.

IV5,3,10. THE (NON?) REALIZATION OF THE FRUIT.

For all dharmas are situated in nonproduction and nonstopping, and from that situation they do not depart. And why? Because of nonproduction and nonstopping no coming or going can be apprehended. And the same formula is applied to : nondefilement and nonpurification; dream, magical illusion, echo, reflection, mirage, firewheel, magical creation; endless and boundless; unrecoverable and unremovable; nonaddition and nonsubtraction. For all dharmas have not come, and from that situation they do not depart. And why? Because noncoming, coming, and going cannot be apprehended. Likewise all dharmas are situated in non-toiling and absence of toiling; they are situated in nonbinding and unbinding, they are situated in nonjoining and disjoining. They are situated in the self and from that situation they do not depart. And why? Because absolutely a self does not exist; how could its coming and going take place? And as for the self, so for being, living soul, etc. *to*: one who sees. And in the same sense all dharmas are situated in permanence, ease, the self, the lovely; and likewise in impermanence, ill, not-self, and the unlovely; in greed, hate, delusion, wrong views; for an entity made by false views does not exist, how can the false views themselves take place? For situated in Suchness are all dharmas, and from that situation they do not depart. And why? Because the coming or going of Suchness cannot be apprehended. And so for the Dharma-element, the Reality limit, Sameness, the unthinkable element, and immobility.

IV5,3,11. HE BECOMES A MEANS OF SALVATION.

For all dharmas are situated in form, and from that situation they do not depart. And why? Because absolutely form does not exist; how could its coming or going take place? And so for the other four skandhas, the six perfections, the various kinds of emptiness, the fruits, etc. *to*: the supreme enlightenment.

Subhuti: Who will there firmly believe in this so deep perfection of wisdom?

The Lord: Those Bodhisattvas, great beings, Subhuti, who have formerly coursed in the direction of full enlightenment, who have done their duties under the Jinas of the past, have matured wholesome roots under the Jinas of the past, have honoured many hundreds of thousands of niyutas of kotis of Buddhas, and have been taken hold of by the good spiritual friends—they will firmly believe in this deep perfection of wisdom.

IV5,4. THE MARKS OF OWN-BEING.

Subhuti: What again, O Lord, will be of those Bodhisattvas, great beings, who firmly believe (who cognize P) this deep perfection of wisdom, the tokens, signs, and modes (attributes)?

CHAPTER 47

THE DISCIPLINING OF GREED

IV5,4,1. ISOLATED FROM THE DEFILEMENTS.

The Lord: They will in their own-being be isolated from (the need for the) disciplining of greed, hate, and delusion.

IV5,4,2. ISOLATED FROM THE TOKENS OF THE DEFILEMENTS.

They will in their own-being be isolated from the tokens of greed, hate, and delusion.

IV5,4,3. ISOLATED FROM THE SIGNS OF THE DEFILEMENTS.

They will in their own-being be isolated from the signs of greed, hate, and delusion.

IV5,4,4. ISOLATED FROM BOTH THE POINTS TO BE SHUNNED AND FROM THEIR ANTIDOTES.

In their own-being isolated from the attributes of greed, hate, and delusion will be those Bodhisattvas, great beings, who resolutely believe in this deep perfection of wisdom.

Subhuti: Destined (*gatika*) for what will be those Bodhisattvas, great beings, who will understand this deep perfection of wisdom?

The Lord: They will be destined for the knowledge of all modes.

Subhuti: Will the Bodhisattva, the great being, who is destined for the knowledge of all modes, be the resort (*gati*) of all beings?

The Lord: Yes, Subhuti.

IV5,4,5. IT IS HARD TO DO.

Subhuti: Doers of what is hard are those Bodhisattvas, great beings who have put on this armour, 'all beings we will lead to Nirvana'. And yet therein no being and no concept of a being is apprehended.

The Lord: So it is, Subhuti, so it is. Moreover, Subhuti, the armour of that Bodhisattva, that great being, is not tied up with form, etc. And why? Because absolutely form, etc. does not exist, and also not the Bodhisattva's armour. Therefore it is said that not tied up with form surely is this armour. And so with feeling, etc. *to*: the knowledge of all modes.

IV5,4,6. IT IS DEVOTED TO ONE AIM ONLY.

Subhuti: Of that Bodhisattva, that great being who has thus put on the great armour, 'all beings we will lead to Nirvana', two stations should not be expected, i.e. the level of a Disciple or the level of a Pratyekabuddha. It is impossible, O Lord, it cannot be that a Bodhisattva, a great being who has thus put on the armour, 'I will lead all beings to Nirvana', should fall on the level of a Disciple or Pratyekabuddha. That cannot possibly be. And why? Because the Bodhisattva, the great being has not, hemmed in by boundaries, put on the armour for the sake of beings.

The Lord: For what reason do you, Subhuti, say that of that Bodhisattva, that great being, who thus puts on the armour and courses in this deep perfection of wisdom, neither of these two levels can be expected, i.e. the level of a Disciple or of a Pratyekabuddha?

IV5,4,7. THE PROGRAMME.

Subhuti: Because there, O Lord, that Bodhisattva, that great being has not put on the armour for the sake of a limited number of beings or for the sake of a limited kind of cognition. And why? For the sake of leading all beings to Nirvana and for the sake of the cognition of the knowledge of all modes has the Bodhisattva, the great being, put on the armour.

The Lord: So it is, Subhuti, so it is. It is not for the sake of a limited number of beings that the Bodhisattva, the great being, has put on the armour. But on the contrary, for the sake of leading all beings to Nirvana and for the cognition of the knowledge of all modes has the Bodhisattva, the great being put on the armour.

IV5,4,8. IT OFFERS NO BASIS.

Subhuti: Deep, O Lord, is this perfection of wisdom. She is not to be developed by anyone, nor should anything be developed, nor should one develop anywhere. And why? Because in this deep perfection of wisdom one does not get at the full reality of any dharma, which would develop, or which he would develop, or through which he would develop. A development of space, O Lord, is this development of the perfection of wisdom. A development of all dharmas, a development of what is not, a development of not taking hold of, a development which is really an undevelopment, that is this development of the perfection of wisdom.

The Lord: Of what, Subhuti, is the development of the perfection of wisdom an undevelopment of development?

Subhuti: Of form this is an undevelopment of development; of feeling, etc. *to*: the knowledge of all modes.

The Lord: So it is, Subhuti, so it is. This development of perfect wisdom is an undevelopment of the development of form, etc. *to*: the knowledge of all modes.

IV5,4,9. NO SETTLING DOWN.

And the Lord further said (āmantrayate) to the Ven. Subhuti: The irreversible Bodhisattva, great being, should thoroughly ponder on this deep perfection of wisdom, for then he does not settle down in this deep perfection of wisdom (as if it were a real thing). And so he should thoroughly ponder on the other five perfection, etc. *to* : on the knowledge of all modes, for then he does not settle down in the knowledge of all modes. For then that irreversible Bodhisattva, great being, who courses in this deep perfection of wisdom, does not look upon the critical arguments and hints of others as having validity; he does not go by someone else whom he puts his trust in; he does not pertake of thoughts connected with greed, hate, and delusion; he is not deprived of the six perfections; and when this deep perfection of wisdom is being taught, he will not tremble, be frightened or terrified, nor will his mind turn back; but he delights in hearing this deep perfection of wisdom, and, having heard it, he takes it up, studies it, bears it in mind, teaches it, attends wisely to it, and progresses to Thusness. One should know, Subhuti, that in a former life already that irreversible Bodhisattva, great being, has asked questions and counterquestions about this deep perfection of wisdom, and has learned it and wisely attended to it. And why? Because the irreversible Bodhisattva, when this deep perfection of wisdom is being taught, does not tremble, is not frightened or terrified, is not cowed or despondent, and his mind does not turn back on it. In addition, when he has heard it, he learns and studies it, bears it in mind, and preaches it, and wisely attends to it.

Subhuti : How should a Bodhisattva who, when this deep perfection of wisdom is being taught, does not tremble, etc. *to* : does not allow his mind to turn back on it, apprehend this deep perfection of wisdom?

IV5,4,10. The objective support.

The Lord: The Bodhisattva, the great being, should apprehend this deep perfection of wisdom through a series (of thoughts) inclined to the knowledge of all modes.

Subhuti : How does the Bodhisattva, the great being, through a series (of thoughts) inclined to the knowledge of all modes have an apperception of this deep perfection of wisdom?

The Lord : The Bodhisattva has an apperception of this deep perfection of wisdom through a series (of thoughts) inclined to emptiness, the signless, the wishless, to space, etc. *to* : nonproduction and nonstopping, to nondefilement and nonpurification, to Suchness, the Dharma-element, the Reality limit, Sameness, the unthinkable element, to the Uneffected, to a dream, etc. *to* : a magical creation.

Subhuti : When the Bodhisattva, the great being, has an apperception of this deep perfection of wisdom through a series (of thoughts) inclined to emptiness, etc. *to* : a dream and a magical creation, does he then apperceive form, or feeling, etc. *to* : the knowledge of all modes?

The Lord: When a Bodhisattva courses in perfect wisdom, he does not apperceive form, etc. *to* : consciousness, etc. *to* : the knowledge of all modes. And why? Because the knowledge of all modes has not been made or unmade, it has not come from anywhere nor gone to anywhere, it does not stand in any spot or place, and its definition cannot be apprehended, nor its coming or going. But that of which no definition and no coming or going can be apprehended, that cannot possibly be fully known by anyone, not through form, or any of the other skandhas. And why? Because form is not the knowledge of all modes, nor is any of the other skandhas. And why? For the Suchness of form and the Suchness of the knowledge of all modes are just one single Suchness. And so for feeling, and everything up to the eighteen special Buddha-dharmas.

Chapter 48

SETTLEMENT IN THE TRAINING OF A BODHISATTVA

Thereupon *the gods* of the realm of sense desire and of the realm of form took heavenly sandalwood powder, took heavenly blue lotuses, pink lotuses, night lotuses, and white lotuses, and scattered them over the Lord. They approached to where the Lord was, respectfully saluted his feet with their heads, stood on one side, and said to the Lord : Deep, O Lord, is the perfection of wisdom, hard to see, hard to understand, incomprehensible, engaged in incomprehensibilities, subtle, delicate, to be felt only by the learned and discerning. In antagonism to the entire world is the enlightenment of the Tathagatas, by which the Tathagatas (are able to) expound this so deep perfection of wisdom. Form, etc. is just the knowledge of all modes, the knowledge of all modes is just form, etc. The Suchness of form, etc. *to* : the Buddha, and the Suchness of the knowledge of all modes, are just one single Suchness, they are not two or divided.

IV5,4,11. Antagonism to the entire world.

The Lord: So it is, O Gods. When he considers this sequence of reasoning, the thought of the Tathagata is inclined to carefree nonaction and not to the demonstration of Dharma. And why? Because surely this Dharma, i.e. the enlightenment of the Tathagata is deep, hard to see, hard to understand, incomprehensible, engaged in incomprehensibilities, subtle, delicate, to be felt only by the learned and discerning, and antagonistic to the entire world. It has not been fully known by anyone, not at any time, nor anywhere. This is the depth of dharmas wherein the habitual idea of duality does not exist. This Dharma is deep through the idea of space, of Suchness, of the Dharma-element, of the Reality limit, of the unthinkable element, of the Endless and Boundless, of that which neither comes nor goes, of the full knowledge of nonproduction and nonstopping, of nondefilement and nonpurification, of the full knowledge of the Uneffected, of the self, etc. *to* : one who sees, of form and the other skandhas, of the perfections, the various kinds of emptiness, etc. *to* : the knowledge of all modes.

The *gods* : Surely, as in antagonism to the entire world has this Dharma been expounded. And why? Because this Dharma, O Lord, is not demonstrated for the sake of taking up form, nor for the sake of not taking it up;

and so with feeling, etc. *to* : the 18 special Buddhadharmas; the fruit of a Streamwinner, etc. *to* : the knowledge of all modes. But it is in taking up that the world courses : Mine is form, I am form, etc. *to* : mine is the knowledge of all modes, I have the knowledge of all modes.

The Lord: So it is, Gods, so it is. This Dharma is not demonstrated for the sake of taking up form, etc. *to* : the knowledge of all modes, nor for the sake of not taking them up. But those, Gods, who course for the taking up of form, etc. or for not taking it up, they are not capable of developing the perfection of giving, etc. *to* : the perfection of wisdom, etc. *to* : the knowledge of all modes.

IV5,4,12. NOWHERE OBSTRUCTED.

Subhuti: In agreement with all dharmas is this Dharma. In agreement with which all-dharmas? It is in agreement with the perfection of wisdom, etc. *to*: the perfection of giving; the emptiness of the subject, etc. *to*: the knowledge of all modes. And this Dharma is not anywhere obstructed. By what is it not obstructed? By form, etc. *to* : by the knowledge of all modes. Marked with nonobstruction is this Dharma, on account of its sameness with space, Suchness, the establishment of the Dharma-element, the Reality limit, the unthinkable element, Emptiness, the Signless, the Wishless, Nonproduction, Nonstopping, Nondefilement and Nonpurification. Nonproduced is this Dharma, on account of the nonapprehension of the production of form, etc. *to* : of the knowledge of all modes.

IV5,4,13. GROUNDLESS.

Trackless (*apado*) is this Dharma, on account of the nonapprehension of form, etc. *to* : the knowledge of all modes.

IV5,4,14. WITHOUT A RESORT.

The *gods* of the realm of sense desire and of the realm of form : Born after the image of the Lord, O Lord, is the Elder Subhuti. And why? Because whatever the Elder Subhuti demonstrates, all that he just demonstrates starting from Emptiness, from the Signless, from the Wishless.

Subhuti: As you say, O Gods, born after the image of the Tathagata is Subhuti the Elder. It is because he is born after the image of the Tathagata! As the Tathagata's Suchness has neither come nor gone, so also that of Subhuti the Elder. For from the very beginning has Subhuti the Elder come to be born after the image of the Tathagata. As the Tathagata's Suchness, so is that of all dharmas. And the Suchness of all-dharmas is the same as that of the Tathagata. But the Tathagata's Suchness is a no-Suchness. It is thus also that Subhuti the Elder has been born after the image of the Tathagata. As the Tathagata-Suchness, so has Subhuti the Elder been established and he has been born after the image of the Tathagata. As the Tathagata's Suchness is immutable and indiscriminate, so also that of Subhuti the Elder. As the Tathagata's Suchness is nowhere obstructed, so also that of all dharmas. The Suchness of the Tathagata, and the Suchness of all dharmas, they are both one single Suchness, not two or divided. Unmade is that Suchness, and there is nothing of which it is not the Suchness; that is why it is not two or divided. It is in this sense that the Elder Subhuti is born after the image of the Tathagata. Everywhere this Suchness is immutable, indiscriminate, and undifferentiated, and so is also the Suchness of Subhuti. Just as the Tathagata's Suchness is not broken apart, unbroken, unbreakable, and unapprehensible, so is that of Subhuti. It is thus that Subhuti the Elder is born after the image of the Tathagata. As the Suchness of the Tathagata cannot fail to be the Suchness of each and every dharma, just such is that Suchness; just so is Subhuti the Elder born after the image of the Tathagata because he is not other than Him. But he is not born after the image of anything. It is thus that Subhuti the Elder is born after the image of the Tathagata. As the Suchness of the Tathagata is not past, future, or present, so also the Suchness of all dharmas. It is thus that Subhuti the Elder is called born after the image of the Tathagata, born after the image of Suchness. Through the Suchness of the sameness of the past is the Suchness of the sameness of the Tathagata; through the sameness of the Suchness of the Tathagata is the Suchness of the sameness of the past. And so for the future and present. In consequence the Suchness of the past, future, and present, and the Suchness of the Tathagata, are not two or divided. Through the Suchness of the Tathagata is the Suchness of form, etc. In consequence the Suchness of form, etc., and the Suchness of the Tathagata, are not two or divided. And so for the Suchness of the self, etc. *to* : one who sees, of the six perfections, the various kinds of emptiness, etc. *to* : of the knowledge of all modes. It is because he has fully known this Suchness in Suchness that a Bodhisattva, a great being comes to be called a 'Tathagata'.

IV5,4,15. UNBORN.

When this disquisition on Suchness had been taught, this great trichiliocosm shook in six ways, stirred, quaked, was agitated, resounded, and rumbled etc. Thereupon the *gods* of the realm of sense desire and of form scattered and showered heavenly sandalwood powder over the Lord and over Subhuti the Elder, and pronounced these words : It is wonderful, O Lord, how much this Subhuti the Elder is born after the image of the Tathagata through the Suchness of the Tathagata!

Subhuti : But Subhuti the Elder, O Gods, is not born after the image of form, or anything other than form, or born after the image of the Suchness of form, or anything other than the Suchness of form; etc. *to* : he is not born after the knowledge of all modes, nor anything other than the knowledge of all modes; not born after the Suchness of the knowledge of all modes, nor anything other than the Suchness of the knowledge of all modes; not born after the conditioned or anything other than the conditioned; not born after the Suchness of the conditioned, or anything other than the Suchness of the conditioned; and so with the unconditioned. And why? Because all these dharmas do not exist and are not apprehended, neither he that has been born after, nor that through which he has been born after, nor he who would be born after, nor that through which he would be born after, nor he who would make him be born after, nor that through which he would be made to be born after.

IV5,4,16. The nonapprehension (even) of suchness.

Śāriputra: Deep, O Lord, is the Suchness, nonfalseness, unaltered Suchness, the Dharmahood, Dharma-element, the established nature of Dharma, the fixed nature of Dharma, the Reality limit—in which no form, etc. is apprehended, nor form-Suchness, etc. Form is just not apprehended, how could the Suchness of form be apprehended? Etc. *to* : the knowledge of all modes.

The Lord: So it is, Śāriputra, so it is. Deep is this Suchness in which no form is apprehended, nor the Suchness of form. Form is just not apprehended, how could its Suchness be apprehended. Etc. *to* : the knowledge of all modes.

Again, Śāriputra, when this chapter on Suchness, Nonfalseness, Unaltered Suchness, was being taught, the thought of 200 monks were freed from the outflows without any further clinging. To 500 nuns there arose the dispassionate, unstained Dharma-eye in dharmas; and 5,000 Bodhisattvas—gods and men—acquired the patient acceptance of dharmas which fail to be produced, and 6,000 Bodhisattvas were freed from the outflows without any further clinging. And these Bodhisattvas, great beings, have honoured 500 Buddhas, and have everywhere given gifts, guarded their morality, developed their patience, exerted their vigour, produced the trances, and developed wisdom. But they were not upheld by perfect wisdom and skill in means. They gave gifts while coursing in manifoldness, 'this gift we will give to him, but not to him; we will guard this morality, develop this patience and vigour, enter into these trances, develop this wisdom'. Lacking in perfect wisdom and not upheld by skill in means they give gifts, etc. *to* develop wisdom. Coursing in the notion of not-self and the nonapprehension of not-self, they have not entered on a Bodhisattva's special method of salvation. They have attained the fruit of a Streamwinner, etc. *to*: Arhatship, but although the Bodhisattva, the great being, has the path (of) Emptiness, the Signless, and the Wishless—because he is lacking in perfect wisdom and not upheld by skill in means, he has realized the Reality limit and become a Disciple or Pratyekabuddha.

Śāriputra: For what reason do they, when developing the dharmas of Emptiness, the Signless, and the Wishless, because they lack in skill in means, realise the Reality limit and become Disciples and Pratyekabuddhas, whereas the Bodhisattvas, developing just these same dharmas of Emptiness, the Signless, and the Wishless, because they have been taken hold of by the perfection of wisdom, thanks to their skill in means fully know the supreme enlightenment?

The Lord: Here, *Śāriputra*, some, lacking in the thought of the knowledge of all modes, developing the dharmas of Emptiness, the Signless, and the Wishless, become, thanks to their (lack of?) skill in means, Disciples and Pratyekabuddhas. Here, again, the Bodhisattvas, the great beings, (not?) lacking in the thought of the knowledge of all modes, developing the dharmas of Emptiness, the Signless and Wishless, thanks to their skill in means enter on a Bodhisattva's special way of salvation. Suppose there is a very huge bird, with a body about 100 or up to 500 miles large. That bird would intend to fly from the Gods of the Thirty-Three down to here, but it would be deficient in wings. It would take off from the Gods of the Thirty-Three, and decide to land here in Jambudvipa. What do you think, Śāriputra, if that bird would in the middle of its journey wish to have stayed with the Gods of the Thirty-Three, would it be able to do so?

Śāriputra: No, O Lord.

The Lord: And could it hope to come down in Jambudvipa without damage or injury?

Śāriputra: No, O Lord. It is bound to get damaged and injured, and when it drops down on Jambudvipa it will incur death or deadly pain. And why? Because of the fact that, whereas its body is huge, its wings are insufficient.

The Lord: So it is, Śāriputra. Although a Bodhisattva may for aeons countless as the sands of the Ganges give gifts, etc. *to*: enter on the trances, and although his setting forth may be great, and his thought of enlightenment, and his effort to win the supreme enlightenment; but if he is lacking in perfect wisdom and skill in means, he falls on the level of a Disciple or Pratyekabuddha. And why? Because as one who is lacking in the thought of the knowledge of all modes has that Bodhisattva given gifts, etc. *to*: has he produced the trances. And that Bodhisattva, lacking in perfect wisdom and not upheld by skill in means falls on the level of the Disciples and Pratyekabuddhas. And although that Bodhisattva brings to mind the morality, concentration, wisdom, emancipation, and the vision and cognition of the emancipation of the past, future, and present Buddhas and Lords, retains it in mind and makes it into a sign, he does nevertheless not cognize the morality of the Tathagatas, etc. *to*: their vision and cognition of emancipation; uncognizing, without understanding, he hears talk about Emptiness, the Signless, the Wishless. He makes that talk into a sign and dedicates it to the supreme enlightenment. Thus dedicating, the Bodhisattva will stand on the level of a Disciple or Pretyekabuddha. And why? For it is a fact, Śāriputra, that, lacking in perfect wisdom and skill in means, he dedicates these wholesome roots to the supreme enlightenment.

IV 6. The Aids to Emancipation.

IV6a. The aids to emancipation in general.

And again, Śāriputra, the Bodhisattva, the great being, beginning with the first thought of enlightenment, not lacking in the thought of the knowledge of all modes, gives gifts, but does not make that into a sign; he develops the applications of mindfulness, etc. but does not make that into a sign.

IV6b. Fivefold division of the aids to emancipation.

IV6b,1. The aid to emancipation which consists in faith.

And, not lacking in perfect wisdom and skill in means, he brings to mind of the past, future, and present Buddhas the mass of morality, concentration, wisdom, emancipation, and the mass of the vision and cognition of emancipation—but all that he does not make into a sign. He does not make the emptiness-concentration into a sign, etc. One should know, Śāriputra, that this Bodhisattva, this great being, will not stand on the level of a Disciple or Pratyekabuddha, but unhurt and uninjured he will know full enlightenment.

IV6b,2. The aid to emancipation which consists in vigour.

And why? For by that Bodhisattva, that great being, beginning with the first thought of enlightenment, gifts have been given, but that has not been made into a sign; morality has been guarded, etc.; of the past, future, and present Buddhas and Lords the morality, etc. *to*: the vision and cognition of emancipation have not been made into a sign. This, Śāriputra, is of the Bodhisattvas, the great beings, the skill in means, that with a mind devoid of signs they have given gifts, etc. *to*: that they course in all-knowledge and yet do not make that into a sign.

IV6b,3. The aid to emancipation which consists in mindfulness.

Śāriputra: As I understand the meaning of the Lord's teaching, the

Bodhisattva, the great being, who, beginning with the first thought of enlightenment, is not lacking in perfect wisdom and skill in means will indubitably win full enlightenment.

IV6b,4. THE AID TO EMANCIPATION WHICH CONSISTS IN CONCENTRATION.

And why? For the Bodhisattva, the great being has, beginning with the first thought of enlightenment, apprehended no dharma which fully knows, or by which he fully knows, i.e. form, etc. *to* : the knowledge of all modes. But of sons and daughters of good family, who belong to the great vehicle, and who are lacking in perfect wisdom and skill in means, of them full enlightenment is not to be expected. And why? Because they, lacking in perfect wisdom and skill in means, have made into a sign all the gift they have given, all the morality they have guarded, etc. *to* : all the wisdom they have apperceived. In consequence it is more than doubtful whether full enlightenment can be expected of them. Therefore then the Bodhisattva, the great being who wants to know full enlightenment, should become one not lacking in perfect wisdom and in skill in means. Having stood in perfect wisdom and in skill in means, without taking anything as a basis, and with a mind connected with the Signless, he should give gifts, etc. *to* : course in the knowledge of all modes.

IV6b,5. THE AID TO EMANCIPATION WHICH CONSISTS IN WISDOM.

The *gods* who belong to the realm of sense desire and the realm of form : Hard to come up to, O Lord, hard to believe in is the utmost enlightenment! For here the Bodhisattva, the great being, should fully know all dharmas in all their modes and yet these dharmas do not exist and cannot be apprehended.

The Lord: So it is, O Gods, so it is. Hard to come up to, hard to believe in is the utmost enlightenment. By me, however, have all dharmas been fully known in all their modes, and yet no dharma has by me been got at which would fully know, by which one would fully know, and which one would fully know. And why? Because of the absolute purity of all dharmas.

IV6c. THREE DEGREES OF STRENGTH OF THE AIDS TO EMANCIPATION.

IV6c,1. THE HIGHEST AIDS TO EMANCIPATION.

Subhuti: The Lord has said, 'hard to come up to is the supreme enlightenment'. As I, however, understand the meaning of the Lord's teaching, and as I think it out for myself—easy to win is the supreme enlightenment. And why? For no one fully knows, by no one is anything fully known, there is nothing that should be fully known. For, O Lord, all dharmas are empty. And when all dharmas are empty, that dharma does not exist which would fully know, or by which one would fully know, or which one would fully know. And why? For all dharmas, O Lord, are empty. And that dharma, for the sake of the growth or diminution of which he would give gifts, guard morality, etc. *to*: train in the knowledge of all modes—these dharmas do not exist. And what he fully knows, and that whereby he fully knows, and that which he fully knows, all these dharmas are empty. In this manner, O Lord, easy to win is the supreme enlightenment of the Bodhisattvas, the great beings. And why? Because form, etc., is empty of the own-being of form, etc.

IV6c,2. The weak aids to emancipation.

Śāriputra: In this manner, Ven. Subhuti, the supreme enlightenment is hard to come up to. And why? For it does not occur to space, 'I shall know full enlightenment'. Just so it does not occur to the Bodhisattva, the great being, 'I shall know full enlightenment'. And why? Because the same as space are all dharmas. And it is after he has firmly believed in all dharmas as the same as space that the Bodhisattva, the great being, knows full enlightenment. If again on the part of the Bodhisattva, the great being who has firmly believed that all dharmas are the same as space, the supreme enlightenment were easy to win, not hard to come up to, then Bodhisattvas countless like the sands of the Ganges would not turn away from full enlightenment. In this manner, Ven. Subhuti, one can discern that the supreme enlightenment is hard to come up to, and not easy to win.

IV6c,3. Medium aids to emancipation.

Subhuti: What do you think, Śāriputra, does form turn away from the supreme enlightenment?

Śāriputra: No, Ven. Subhuti.

And so in detail for feeling, etc. *to*: the knowledge of all modes.

Subhuti: Is then the dharma which turns away from full enlightenment other than form, etc.?

Śāriputra: No, Subhuti.

Subhuti: Does the Suchness of form, etc. turn away from full enlightenment?

Śāriputra: No, Subhuti.

Subhuti: Is the dharma which turns away from full enlightenment other than the Suchness of form, etc.?

Śāriputra: Does Suchness turn away from full enlightenment, or does Dharmahood, the Dharma-element, the established order of Dharma, the fixed sequence of Dharma, the reality limit or the inconceivable Element?

Śāriputra: No, Subhuti.

Subhuti: Is the dharma which turns away from full enlightenment other than Suchness, Dharmahood, etc. *to*: the inconceivable Element?

Śāriputra: No, Subhuti.

Subhuti: Since thus, in ultimate truth and as things stand, those dharmas cannot be apprehended as real, what is that dharma which is turned away from full enlightenment?

Śāriputra: When one adopts the method of considering dharmas in their ultimate reality, which Subhuti the Elder uses in his exposition, then indeed there is no Bodhisattva who will turn away from the supreme enlightenment. But then there will no longer be any ground for the distinction of those who have set their hearts on enlightenment into three kinds of persons, who, as described by the Tathagata, differ with respect to the vehicle which they have chosen. According to the exposition of the Ven. Subhuti, there should be only one single kind of Bodhisattva, i.e. the one who belongs to the Bodhisattva-vehicle.

Pūrna, the son of Maitrayani: First of all, Ven. Śāriputra, Subhuti the Elder should be asked whether he looks for even one single kind of Bodhisattva!

Śāriputra: Do you, Ven. Subhuti, look for even one single kind of Bodhisattva—one who belongs to the vehicle of the Bodhisattvas?

Subhuti: Do you, Ven. Śāriputra, look in Suchness for three kinds of Bodhisattvas—Bodhisattvas who use the Disciple-vehicle, Bodhisattvas who use the Pratyekabuddha-vehicle, and Bodhisattvas who use the Bodhisattva-vehicle?

Śāriputra: No, Subhuti.

Subhuti: Can then three kinds of Bodhisattvas be apprehended in Suchness?

Śāriputra: No, Subhuti.

Subhuti: Can then Suchness be apprehended as being of one, two, or three kinds?

Śāriputra: No, Subhuti.

Subhuti: Can one in Suchness then apprehend one single (kind of) Bodhisattva?

Śāriputra: No, Subhuti.

Subhuti: Since, in ultimate truth and as things stand, such dharmas cannot be apprehended, wherefrom does the Ven. Śāriputra get the idea that 'this Bodhisattva belongs to the Disciple-vehicle, that Bodhisattva to the Pratyekabuddha-vehicle, and that Bodhisattva again to the Buddha-vehicle'? If a Bodhisattva who thus identifies all dharmas in Suchness does not become cowed or stolid in mind, has no regrets, and is not frightened, then he is bound to go forth to the supreme enlightenment.

The Lord: Well said, Subhuti, well said! Through the Buddha's might you have been inspired to say this.

Śāriputra: To which enlightenment, O Lord, will that Bodhisattva go forth?

The Lord: To the supreme enlightenment.

IV 7. The Aids to Penetration.

IV7a. HEAT.

IV7a,1. WEAK HEAT.

Subhuti: How should a Bodhisattva, a great being behave, if he wants to go forth to the supreme enlightenment?

The Lord: Here the Bodhisattva, who wants to know full enlightenment, should behave towards beings with an even mind. Towards all beings he should produce an even mind, and he should not produce an uneven mind. All beings he should make into an object with an even, and not an uneven mind. Towards all beings he should produce the great friendliness and the great compassion. He should handle all beings with a friendly thought, with the thought of great compassion. He should towards all beings produce a thought which has slain pride and he should be honest towards all of them.

IV7a,2. MEDIUM HEAT.

He should produce towards all beings a thought of benefit and not of no-benefit; he should make them into an object with a thought of benefit and not of no-benefit. Towards all beings he should produce a thought free from aversion, and he should make them into an object with a thought free from aversion. Towards all beings he should produce a thought of no-harming, and he should make them into an object with a thought of no-harming.

IV7a,3. STRONG HEAT.

He should handle all beings as if they were his mother, father, brother, sister, son, or daughter, his friends, relatives, or kinsmen. It is thus that a Bodhisattva should behave if he wants to go forth to the supreme enlightenment.

IV7b. SUMMITS.

IV7b,1. LOW SUMMITS.

He himself should become one who abstains from taking life, and also others he should induce to abstain from taking life; he should speak in praise of the abstention from taking life, and he should praise also those other people who abstain from taking life—one acquiescent. It is thus that a Bodhisattva should stand if he wants to go forth to the supreme enlightenment. And what is said of the abstention from taking life applies also *to*: the taking of what is not given, to sexual misconduct, to lying speech, harsh speech, malicious speech, senseless prattling, covetousness, ill will and wrong views; to the four trances, the four Unlimited, and the four formless trances.

IV7b,2. MEDIUM SUMMITS.

He himself should fulfill the perfection of giving, etc. and also others he should induce to fulfill the perfection of giving, etc. etc. *to*:—one acquiescent.

IV7b,3. HIGH SUMMITS.

He himself should develop the emptiness of the subject, etc. the four applications of mindfulness, etc. *to*: the ten powers of a Tathagata, the four grounds of self-confidence, the four analytical knowledges, the eighteen special Buddhadharmas, the great friendliness and the great compassion, and others also he should induce, etc. He himself should accomplish the conditioned coproduction in direct and reverse order, and others also he should induce, etc. And that without taking anything as a basis.

IV7c. PATIENCE.

IV7c,1. WEAK PATIENCE.

He himself should comprehend ill, forsake origination, realize stopping, and develop the path; and others also he should induce, etc.

IV7c,2. MEDIUM PATIENCE.

He himself should produce cognition for the realization of the fruit of a Streamwinner, etc. *to*: for the enlightenment of a Pratyekabuddha, but he should not realize the Reality limit; and others also he should induce, etc.

IV7c,3. STRONG PATIENCE.

He himself should enter on a Bodhisattva's special way of salvation and others also he should induce, etc. And that without taking anything as a basis.

IV7d. HIGHEST MUNDANE DHARMAS.

IV7d,1. WEAK HIGHEST MUNDANE DHARMAS.

He himself should mature beings and others also he establishes in the maturing of beings; and he praises the maturing of beings and also those others who mature beings—one acquiescent. He himself should purify the Buddhafield, etc. *to*:

IV7d,2. MEDIUM HIGHEST MUNDANE DHARMAS.
produce a Bodhisattva's superknowledges, etc. *to*:

IV7d,3. STRONG HIGHEST MUNDANE DHARMAS.
produce the cognition of the knowledge of all modes, and others also he should induce, etc. He himself should forsake all defilements together with their residues, and others also he should induce, etc. *to* : one acquiescent. It is thus that a Bodhisattva, who wants to go forth to the supreme enlightenment, should behave and that without taking anything as a basis. He himself should acquire the accomplishment of a long lifespan, etc. *to* :—one acquiescent. He himself should acquire the stability of his good Dharma, etc. *to* :—one acquiescent. It is thus that a Bodhisattva should train in perfect wisdom and skill in means. When he thus trains and abides, then form, etc. *to* : the stability of the Good Dharma, will be uncovered to him. And why? Because the seizing of form, etc. is not form, etc. And when this station of a Bodhisattva was being taught, two thousand Bodhisattvas acquired the patient acquiescence in the fact that no dharma has ever been produced.

CHAPTER 49

IRREVERSIBILITY

IV 8. The Community of Irreversible Bodhisattvas.

IV8,1. THE MARK OF IRREVERSIBILITY ON THE LEVEL OF THE AIDS TO PENETRATION.

Subhuti: What, O Lord, are the attributes, tokens and signs of an irreversible Bodhisattva, great being, and how can we know that this particular Bodhisattva, great being, is irreversible?

The Lord: Here, Subhuti, what has been called the level of the common people, the level of the Disciples, the level of the Pratyekabuddhas, and the level of the Tathagatas—they are all in Suchness without modification, indiscriminate, not two nor divided. Just as Suchness is indiscriminate, so he does not discriminate. Thus he enters into Suchness without discrimination. When he has thus entered on it, and has heard of Suchness just as it is, then he does not doubt. And he does not take that Suchness as single or double. He does not prattle away about everything that comes into his head. He only speaks when it is profitable (to others), and not when it is not profitable. He does not look down on what others have or have not done. He becomes one who seeks to speak well. Endowed with these attributes, tokens, and signs a Bodhisattva should be known as irreversible.

Subhuti: Through which attributes, tokens, and signs should a Bodhisattva be known as irreversible?

The Lord: But all dharmas are without attributes, tokens, and signs!

Subhuti: If all dharmas are without attributes, tokens, and signs, from which dharmas must a Bodhisattva have turned away in order to be pointed out as irreversible?

(*A. Heat*).

IV8,1,1. THE TURNING AWAY FROM FORM, ETC.

The Lord: That Bodhisattva has turned away from form and the other skandhas. A Bodhisattva should be known as irreversible if he has turned away from the six perfections, the various kinds of emptiness, the applications of mindfulness, etc. *to*: the 18 special Buddhadharmas, from the level of the Disciples and Pratyekabuddhas, etc. *to*: from enlightenment.

Such a Bodhisattva should be known as irreversible.

And why? Because form, etc. *to* : enlightenment has no own-being in which the Bodhisattva could find support.

IV8,1,2. THE EXTINCTION OF DOUBT.

Furthermore a Bodhisattva does not pander to Sramanas and Brahmins of other schools, telling them that they know what is worth knowing, that they see what is worth seeing. It is quite impossible that they should be able to form a conception of what is the right view. He does not undergo doubt, does not fall into the contagion of mere rule and ritual or into false views, nor does he need to wipe away any occasion for remorse due to sin. He pays no homage to strange gods, offers them no flowers, garlands, perfumes, etc. He does not think that he should give to them, or pay homage to them. Endowed with these attributes, etc.

IV8,1,3. THE EXTINCTION OF THE EIGHT KINDS OF INAUSPICIOUS REBIRTH.

Moreover, the irreversible Bodhisattva is no more reborn in the hells, etc. *to* : in the eight kinds of inauspicious places of rebirth. Nor does he ever again become a woman.

IV8,1,4. ONESELF ESTABLISHED IN WHOLESOME DHARMAS, ONE ENJOINS THEM ON OTHERS ALSO.

Moreover the irreversible Bodhisattva undertakes to observe the ten wholesome ways of action. He himself abstains from taking life, and also others he establishes in the abstention from taking life; he praises the abstention from taking life, and also those others who abstain from taking life; one acquiescent. And so for (the abstention from : taking what is not given, sexual misconduct, intoxicants as tending to cloud the mind, lying speech, malicious speech, indistinct prattling, covetousness, ill will and) wrong views. Endowed with these attributes, etc. Moreover the irreversible Bodhisattva even in his dreams commits no offence against the ten wholesome ways of acting, how much less when he is awake. Endowed with these attributes, etc.

IV8,1,5. THE REWARDS FOR GIVING, ETC. ARE TURNED OVER TO ALL BEINGS.

Moreover the irreversible Bodhisattva, when he proceeds in the perfection of giving, etc. *to* : in the perfection of wisdom, gives gifts for the sake of all beings, etc. *to* : develops wisdom for the sake of all beings. Endowed with these attributes, etc. Moreover the irreversible Bodhisattva studies Dharma, i.e. the Discourses, Discourses with Prose and Verse Mingled, Predictions, etc. *to* : Tales and Expositions, out of concern for the welfare of all beings. And when he gives the gift of Dharma he thinks to himself, 'may the intentions of all beings be fulfilled by this gift of Dharma!' Having made that gift of Dharma common to all beings, he dedicates it to the supreme enlightenment. Endowed with these attributes, etc.

IV8,1,6. NO HESITATION WITH REGARD TO DEEP DHARMAS.

Moreover the irreversible Bodhisattva has no hesitation or doubt with regard to deep dharmas.

Subhuti: For what reason has the irreversible Bodhisattva no hesitation, perplexity, or doubt with regard to deep dharmas?

The Lord: The irreversible Bodhisattva does not review any dharma, from form to enlightenment, with regard to which he could have hesitation, perplexity, or doubt.

IV8,1,7. FRIENDLY DEEDS OF BODY, VOICE, AND MIND.

Moreover the irreversible Bodhisattva is endowed with gentle deeds of body and his thoughts are free from hostility for all beings. Endowed with these attributes, etc. Moreover the irreversible Bodhisattva is constantly and always endowed with friendly deeds of body, speech, and mind. Endowed with these attributes, etc.

IV8,1,8. ONE DOES NOT MEET WITH THE FIVE HINDRANCES.

Moreover the irreversible Bodhisattva does not meet with the five hindrances, i.e. with sensuous desire, ill will, sloth and torpor, excitedness and sense of guilt, or doubt. Endowed with these attributes, etc.

IV8,1,9. LOSS OF ALL LATENT TENDENCIES TO IGNORANCE, ETC.

Moreover the irreversible Bodhisattva does not have in any way whatsoever the latent biases towards evil. Endowed with these attributes, etc.

IV8,1,10. MINDFULNESS AND SELF POSSESSION.

Moreover whether the irreversible Bodhisattva goes out or comes back, his mind does not wander, but his mindfulness is fixed before him. Mindfully he comes, goes, walks about, stands, sits and lies down. When he lifts up or puts down his foot on the ground, he knows what he does. Endowed with these attributes, etc.

IV8,1,11. CLEANLINESS OF THE ROBE HE WEARS, ETC.

Moreover the robe of the irreversible Bodhisattva is free from lice, his habits are clean, he is salubrious, smells clean and his afflictions are few. Endowed with these attributes, etc.

(*B. Summits*).

IV8,1,12. The 80,000 families of worms cannot arise in his body.

Moreover the 80,000 families of worms which men have in their bodies and which eat their bodies, they do not exist at all in the body of the irreversible Bodhisattva. And why? Because his wholesome roots have lifted him above all the world and are the most excellent in all the world, for that reason that Bodhisattva does not have these 80,000 families of worms in his body. And as those wholesome roots of his go on increasing, to that extent he acquires in due course the perfect purity of body, speech, and thought. Endowed with these attributes, etc.

IV8,1,13. No crookedness in his heart.

Subhuti: How does the Bodhisattva's perfect purity of body, speech, and thought take place?

The Lord: As those wholesome roots of his go on increasing, to that extent the craftiness of his body, thought, and speech, the crookedness of his body, thought, and speech are being purified by these wholesome roots. By way of his body he courses well in three ways, by way of his speech in four ways, by way of his mind in three ways. This is the Bodhisattva's perfect purity of body, speech, and thought. And through that perfect purity of body, speech, and thought he transcends the level of the Disciples or Pratyekabuddhas, and he does not realize the Reality limit. Endowed with these attributes, etc.

IV8,1,14. He takes upon himself the twelve ascetic practices.

Moreover the irreversible Bodhisattva is not one to attach weight to gain, honour, and fame, etc. *to*: he does not attach weight to the triple robe. And he takes upon himself the twelve ascetic practices. Endowed with these attributes, etc.

IV8,1,15. Nonproduction in his mind of states which are hostile to the perfections, such as meanness, etc.

Moreover in the irreversible Bodhisattva no thought of meanness arises, nor of immorality, anger, sloth, unconcentratedness, or stupidity; nor does a thought of envy arise in him. Endowed with these attributes, etc.

IV8,1,16. Moving towards a junction with the perfection of wisdom which is not in conflict with the true nature of dharmas.

Moreover the intelligence of the irreversible Bodhisattva becomes steady and goes deep. With respect he hears the Dharma from others and unites all of it with the perfection of wisdom. And also all worldly activities he unites, thanks to the perfection of wisdom, with the nature of dharmas. There is not any dharma which he does not see as yoked to the

Dharma-element, and all that he sees as making an effort towards the perfection of wisdom. These should be known as the irreversible marks of the irreversible Bodhisattvas.

IV8,1,17. THE DESIRE TO GO INTO THE HELLS FOR THE GOOD OF OTHERS.

If again, Mara, the Evil One, conjures up the eight great hells in front of the irreversible Bodhisattvas, and in each one of them many thousands, etc. *to* : many hundreds of thousands of niyutas of kotis of Bodhisattvas, burning, boiling ... and experiencing sharp pains, having conjured them up, he shows them to that Bodhisattva, and says to him : 'These Bodhisattvas have been predicted as irreversible by the Tathagata; they have been reborn here in the hells. You also have been predicted by the Tathagata to irreversibility, but in fact you have been predicted to rebirth as a being in hell. Reject that thought of enlightenment! Then you will not be reborn in hell, but you will be one who goes to heaven'. If the thought of the Bodhisattva is not disturbed, if he does not hesitate or doubt, then one should know that this Bodhisattva has been predicted by the Tathagatas of the past, that he is predestined (to Buddhahood), and firmly established in the irreversible element. It is impossible, it cannot be that the irreversible Bodhisattva should be reborn in hell, among the animals, or in the world of Yama. That cannot possibly be. Endowed with these attributes, etc.

(*C. Patience.*)

IV8,1,18. ONE CANNOT BE LED ASTRAY BY OTHERS.

Moreover approaching in the guise of a Sramana, Mara, the Evil One will say : 'What you have learnt, i.e. that you should purify the perfection of giving, etc. *to* : that you should know full enlightenment, that has been wrongly learnt. You must confess that it was erroneous. What you have been told, i.e. that you should rejoice at all the wholesome roots of the Tathagatas of the past, future, and present, and of their disciples, beginning from the production of the first thought of enlightenment up to the abiding of their true Dharma—of that you must confess it was erroneous; that you must reject! What you have heard, that is not the Buddha-word, that has not been taught by the fully enlightened Buddha. It is mere poetry. What I teach is the Buddha-word, that is as taught by the Tathagata'. If the Bodhisattva, the great being, is agitated, hesitates, and doubts, one should know that this Bodhisattva, this great being has surely not been predicted by the Tathagata, etc.; not fixed surely is that Bodhisattva, nor is he established in the irreversible element. But if the Bodhisattva, the great being, does not get agitated, does not hesitate and doubt, but does flee back to the true nature of Dharma, to the Unconditioned, to Nonproduction, then he does not put his faith in someone else, then he does not go by someone else whom he puts his trust in, as concerns the six perfections, etc. *to*: enlightenment. Just as an Arhat, with his outflows dried up, does not go by someone else whom he puts his trust in, but places the true nature of Dharma directly before his eyes, and cannot be assailed by Mara, the Evil One, just so, Subhuti, does the irreversible Bodhisattva become uncrushable by persons belonging to the Disciple-vehicle or the Pratyekabuddha-vehicle; he cannot by his nature go back on the supreme enlightenment, he is predicted (to Buddhahood) and firmly established in the irreversible element; and he becomes someone who does not go by someone else whom he puts his trust in. He does not go by his faith in the Tathagata, how much less in those who belong to the Disciple-vehicle or the Pratyekabuddha-vehicle, how much less in Mara, the Evil One, how much less in the heretical wanderers! It is impossible that he should trust them. And why? Because he does not review any dharma in which he could put his faith, be it form, etc. *to* : the Suchness of enlightenment. Endowed with these attributes, tokens, and signs a Bodhisattva should be known as irreversible.

IV8,1,19. ONE RECOGNIZES THE MARAHOOD OF MARA WHEN HE POINTS OUT A COUNTERFEIT PATH.

Moreover, Subhuti, Mara the Evil One, approaching in the guise of a monk, will say to the Bodhisattva, the great being: 'A wandering in birth-and-death is this, and not the wandering of a Bodhisattva; just here do you, monk, make an end of ill!' And again, that Mara the Evil One will expound to the Bodhisattva a counterfeit of the Path. He expounds this counterfeit path by worldly modes belonging to the plane of birth-and-death. Of the perception of bones, the first trance, etc. *to* : the fourth formless attainment he says that 'this, your worship, is the path, these are its progressive steps. Through this path, through these progressive steps you will reach the fruit of a Streamwinner, etc. to Arhatship. Through this path, through these progressive steps, do you make, just here, an end of ill! No longer will you experience those sufferings which belong to the plane of birth-and-death. Ah, surely, you will first of all not produce this personality of yours. How would you think of taking hold of another personality?' If again, Subhuti, the thought of the Bodhisattva, the great being, is not agitated, and does not waver, and if in addition he thinks to himself, 'very helpful to me is this monk who expounds a counterfeit to the holy path. That counterfeit path is not conducive to the realization of the fruit of a Streamwinner, etc. *to*: of Arhatship or Pratyekabuddha-enlightenment, etc. *to*: of full enlightenment.' He then laughs, 'very helpful to me is that monk who expounds attachment to me! When I have understood that attachment, I should train in all the three vehicles.' When Mara, the Evil One, has noticed the laughter of the Bodhisattva, the great being, he says to him: 'You wish, son of good family, to see the Bodhisattvas, the great beings who have presented to Buddhas and Lords, countless as the sands of the Ganges, robes, almsbowl, lodging, medicinal appliances for use in sickness; who have, in the presence of Tathagatas countless as the sands of the Ganges, fulfilled the six perfections; who have honoured, questioned, and counterquestioned Buddhas and Lords countless as the sands of the Ganges, for the sake of this very Bodhisattva-vehicle, (asking:) how should the Bodhisattva, the great being, stand in the Bodhisattva-vehicle, while coursing in the six perfections, the applications of mindfulness, etc. *to*: the great compassion. They have stood, coursed, made efforts in that which those Buddhas and Lords have taught, and yet to this very day not known full enlightenment!' And he adds: 'Though they have been thus instructed, have thus stood, thus trained, they have not reached the knowledge of all modes! How then will you reach full enlightenment ever?' If, when he is thus being dissuaded, the Bodhisattva undergoes no change of heart, if he remains unafraid, and if, in addition, he laughs and says to himself, 'very helpful to me is this monk who expounds attachment to me, and who suggests that through these attachments the fruit of a Streamwinner, etc. *to*: the knowledge of all modes can be reached!', then Mara, the Evil One, having noticed the uncowedness of his mind, conjures up a great many monks in that very spot of earth and says, 'All these are Arhats with their outflows dried up who have set out for the supreme enlightenment. But they have all stopped short at Arhatship. How will you ever know full enlightenment?' But if it occurs to the Bodhisattva, the great being, 'surely, Mara, the Evil One, expounds a counterfeit path, 'then, coursing in the perfection of wisdom, he does not go back on the supreme enlightenment, and does not fall back on the level of a Disciple or Pratyekabuddha; and in addition it occurs to him, 'it is impossible, it cannot be that the Bodhisattva, the great being, who courses in the perfection of giving, etc. *to*: who develops the knowledge of all modes, does not fully know the supreme enlightenment. That cannot possibly be!'

(*D. Supreme Dharmas*).

IV8,1,20. He takes up the progressive practice in which everywhere the Buddhas have rejoiced.

Moreover the Bodhisattva who courses in perfect wisdom thinks to himself, 'if, having trained as the Tathagata has taught, if, not lacking in this practice, one dwells in attentions associated with these perfections, then one will not fail in the six perfections, etc. *to*: in the knowledge of all modes.' Moreover, the Bodhisattva thinks to himself, 'one who recognizes the deeds of Mara, he does not fail in the supreme enlightenment.' Endowed with these attributes, etc.

IV8,2. The marks of irreversibility of one who stands on the path of vision.

IV8,2,1. Patient acceptance of the cognition of dharma in ill: rejection of understanding dharmas as form, etc.

Subhuti: Wherefrom does the irreversible Bodhisattva turn away?

The Lord: He turns away from the perception of form, and the other skandhas: of the elements, sense fields, etc. *to*: of the Buddha. And why? Because the irreversible Bodhisattva through dharmas which are empty of own-marks enters on the certainty that he will win salvation as a Bodhisattva. He does not apprehend even that dharma and so he cannot put it together or produce it. One therefore says that 'a Bodhisattva who patiently accepts nonproduction is irreversible'. Endowed with these attributes, tokens, and signs should a Bodhisattva be known as irreversible.

Chapter 50

EXPOSITION OF THE TOKENS OF IRREVERSIBILITY

IV8,2,2. Cognition of dharma in ill : firmness of the thought of supreme enlightenment.

Moreover Mara, the Evil One, approaches the Bodhisattva, and tries to dissuade him with the words, 'the same as space is this knowledge of all modes; with nonexistence for their own-being are all dharmas, empty of own-marks; these dharmas also are the same as space, with nonexistence for own-being, empty of own-marks. When all dharmas have the own-being of space, have no own-being for own-being, and are empty of own-marks, no dharma can be apprehended, which could know full enlightenment or by which it could be known. All these dharmas are the same as space, have no own-being for own-being, and are empty of own-marks. It is useless for you to resist. A deed of Mara is this doctrine that 'one should know full enlightenment'. It is not the Buddha's teaching. May you, son of good family, not fall into these attentions in the hope that they will allay (all ill). On the contrary, this is not conducive to advantage, benefit, or happiness, but leads to a state of punishment.' When that son or daughter of good family has heard this kind of abuse, they should consider that 'this is a deed of Mara that I am being dissuaded from the supreme enlightenment. Those beings do not cognize, see, or understand that all dharmas are the same as space, have nonexistence for own-being, are empty of own-marks. Therefore we, having put on the armour which is the same as space, has nonexistence for own-being and is empty of own-marks, will, having fully known the knowledge of all modes, demonstrate Dharma to all beings, and establish (even) the beings in hell in the fruit of a Streamwinner, etc. *to*: in the supreme enlightenment.' The Bodhisattva should, beginning with the first thought of enlightenment, having heard this Dharma, make this thought firm, unshakeable, and unconquerable. Endowed with a thought which is firm, unshakeable, and unconquerable he enters, coursing in the six perfections, into a Bodhisattva's special way of salvation.

IV8,2,3. Patient acceptance of subsequent cognition of ill : turning away from the thought of disciples and pratyekabuddhas.

Subhuti: Can then an irreversible Bodhisattva be called reversible or a reversible Bodhisattva irreversible?

The Lord: An irreversible Bodhisattva may be called reversible and a reversible Bodhisattva may be called irreversible.

Subhuti: How may the irreversible, and the reversible, Bodhisattva be so called?

The Lord: The Bodhisattva who has turned away from the level of the Disciples and Pratyekabuddhas, this reversible Bodhisattva should be called irreversible. But the Bodhisattva who does not turn away from the level of the Disciples or Pratyekabuddhas, this irreversible Bodhisattva would be called reversible. This should be known as the irreversible mark of the Bodhisattva who is endowed with these attributes, tokens, and signs. Endowed with these attributes, tokens, and signs the irreversible Bodhisattva cannot be dissuaded by Mara, the Evil One, from the supreme enlightenment.

IV8,2,4. Subsequent cognition of ill : the mastery over the limbs of the trances, etc.

Moreover according to plan the irreversible Bodhisattva enters on the first trance, etc. *to* : on the attainment of cessation. Moreover, according to plan the irreversible Bodhisattva enters on the four applications of mindfulness, etc. *to*: he consummates the five superknowledges. He becomes a complete master over the four trances, the four Unlimited, the four formless attainments, and the attainment of cessation; he develops the four applications of mindfulness, etc. *to* : he enters on the path and the concentrations on emptiness, the signless and wishless, etc. *to* : he consummates the five superknowledges. But he does not take hold of the trances, etc. *to* : the fruit of the attainment of cessation, he does not take hold of the fruit of a Streamwinner, etc. *to* : the enlightenment of a Pratyekabuddha. According to plan and at will he takes hold of a new personality, through which he can work the weal of beings. Endowed with these attributes, etc.

IV8,2,5. Patient acceptance of the cognition of dharma in origination : lightness of body and mind.

Moreover the irreversible Bodhisattva becomes endowed with attention to enlightenment; not lacking in the thought of enlightenment, he does not become one who attaches weight to form, or the marks, or the physical basis, or giving, morality, etc. *to*: the Unlimited, etc. *to* : the enlightenment. He does not become one who attaches weight to the purification of the Buddhafield, the maturing of beings, the vision of the Buddhas, or the planting of wholesome roots. And why? Because when all dharmas are empty of own-marks, the Bodhisattva does not see any dharma whereto he should attach weight, or whereby he could do so. And why? Because all dharmas are the same as space, have nonexistence for own-being, are empty of own-marks. And that Bodhisattva, endowed with attention to enlightenment, remains unbewildered in the four postures; he is unbewildered whether he goes out or comes back, stands or walks about, sits or lies down. Mindful he comes, mindful he goes, walks about, stands, sits, and lies down. Endowed with these attributes, etc.

IV8,2,6. COGNITION OF DHARMA IN ORIGINATION: ENJOYMENT OF SENSE PLEASURES WITHOUT SETTLING DOWN IN THEM.

Moreover if the Bodhisattva lives the life of a householder, he possesses all pleasant things through skill in means and for the sake of maturing beings. He gives gifts to all beings, food to those in need of food, etc. He himself courses in the perfection of giving, he establishes others also in the perfection of giving; he praises the perfection of giving and also those who course in it, one acquiescent. And so for the other perfections.

IV8,2,7. PATIENT ACCEPTANCE OF SUBSEQUENT COGNITION OF ORIGINATION: ONE ALWAYS LEADS A CHASTE LIFE.

And again that irreversible Bodhisattva who lives the life of a householder gives gifts, having filled Jambudvipa, etc. *to*: the great trichiliocosm, with the seven precious things. But he does not really derive enjoyment from the sense pleasures. Constantly and always he remains chaste. And he does not generate anything which could overpower him or blight his spirit. Endowed with these attributes, etc. Moreover the yaksha Vajrapani constantly and always follows close behind the irreversible Bodhisattva, so as to protect and defend him. This Bodhisattva will fully know the supreme enlightenment, and until that time Vajrapani and his clan will constantly and always follow behind him. He cannot be assailed by men or ghosts, and he cannot be crushed by gods, Maras, or Brahmas, or by anyone else in the world, with justice.

IV8,2,8. SUBSEQUENT COGNITION OF ORIGINATION: PURITY OF LIVELIHOOD BY PROVIDING RIGHTLY FOR IT.

His mind is not distracted from attentions to enlightenment until the time that he fully knows the supreme enlightenment. The faculties of that Bodhisattva are not deficient, i.e. his eye-faculty, etc. *to*: his body-faculty, or his faculties of faith, vigour, mindfulness, concentration, and wisdom. He is a true man, not a contemptible person.

Subhuti: Through what is a Bodhisattva a true man, and not a contemptible person?

The Lord: If a Bodhisattva's thought is not disturbed, that is why he is a true man and not a contemptible person. Endowed with these attributes, etc. Moreover the irreversible Bodhisattva, endowed with attentions to enlightenment, does not in any way embark on those spells, herbs, magical formulas, and medical incantations which are the work of women. Nor does he indulge in making marvellous predictions, saying to women or men, 'you will have a son, or daughter; you will have a family; you will live long'. And why? Because the Bodhisattva does not see a sign in dharmas which are empty of own-marks. Not seeing a sign, he becomes one who is perfectly pure in his livelihood. Endowed with these attributes, etc.

IV8,2,9. PATIENT ACCEPTANCE OF THE COGNITION OF DHARMA IN STOPPING: NEGATION OF THE DWELLING IN OCCUPATION OR PREOCCUPATION WITH SKANDHAS OR SENSE FIELDS.

Furthermore, Subhuti, I will demonstrate the attributes, tokens, and signs, endowed with which a Bodhisattva should be known as irreversible. Listen to them, and attend to them well. I will teach them to you.—

'So be it, O Lord,' and the Ven. *Subhuti* listened in silence to the Lord.

The Lord: Here the Bodhisattva who courses in perfect wisdom and who is not lacking in attentions to enlightenment, is not preoccupied with the skandhas, elements, or sense fields. And why? Because the Bodhisattva has well attended to the emptiness of the skandhas, elements, and sense fields. He is not preoccupied with society. And why? Because he has well attended to the emptiness of the essential original nature. He is not preoccupied with talk about kings. And why? Because, standing in the emptiness of the essential original nature, he does not review of any dharma the inferiority or difficulty.

IV8,2,10. COGNITION OF DHARMA IN STOPPING: NEGATION OF THE DWELLING IN OCCUPATIONS OR PREOCCUPATIONS WITH TALK CONCERNING THINGS WHICH COULD ACT AS POSSIBLE OBSTACLES TO FULL ATTAINMENT.

He is not preoccupied with talk about robbers. And why? Because in dharmas which are empty of own-marks he does not review of any dharma a bringing along or taking away.

IV8,2,11. PATIENT ACCEPTANCE OF SUBSEQUENT COGNITION OF STOPPING: NEGATION OF THE DWELLING IN OCCUPATION OR PREOCCUPATION WITH TALK ABOUT ARMIES (WHICH IS HELD TO REFER TO THE MANY VARIOUS THINGS SUCH AS) GIVING, ETC. WHICH ARE THE TRUE EQUIPMENT FOR ENLIGHTENMENT.

He does not dwell preoccupied with talk about armies. And why? Because one who is established in the emptiness of the essential original nature does not review of any dharma the fewness or abundance.

IV8,2,12. SUBSEQUENT COGNITION OF STOPPING: NEGATION OF THE DWELLING IN OCCUPATION OR PREOCCUPATION WITH THE TALK ABOUT BATTLES, KILLERS AND THEIR VICTIMS, HOSTILE STATES AND ANTIDOTES.

He does not dwell preoccupied with talk about battles. And why?

Because, established in the dharmahood of all dharmas, he does not see any affection or aversion on the part of any dharma whatever. He does not dwell preoccupied with talk about villages. And why? Because, established in the emptiness of all dharmas, he does not see the assemblage or nonassemblage of any dharma. He does not dwell preoccupied with talk about cities. And why? Because established in the emptiness of space he does not review the attraction or nonattraction of any dharma. He does not dwell preoccupied with talk about market towns. And why? Because established in the Reality limit, he does not review the accumulation or taking away of any dharma whatever. He does not dwell preoccupied with talk about self, etc. *to* : about one who knows, one who sees. He dwells preoccupied with nothing at all outside the perfection of wisdom, and he is not lacking in mental activities associated with the cognition of all modes.

IV8,2,13. PATIENT ACCEPTANCE OF THE COGNITION OF DHARMA IN THE PATH : NEGATION OF OCCUPATION AND PREOCCUPATION WITH MEANNESS, IMMORALITY, ETC.

Coursing in the perfection of giving, he does not dwell preoccupied with meanness; and so for the perfection of morality and immorality, etc. *to* : the perfection of wisdom and stupidity. Coursing in the dharmahood of all dharmas he is one who wants dharma and not its opposite. Coursing in the Dharma-element he does not speak in praise of a broken Dharma. He wants friendship. Sons and daughters of good family, who belong to the vehicle of the Disciples and Pratyekabuddhas, and whom he encounters in the presence of the Buddhas, the Lords, and of the Bodhisattvas, great beings—them also he establishes in supreme enlightenment, incites them to it, disciplines them in it. He pleases the Tathagatas, so that he may have a vision of them. He is reborn in those world systems in which the Tathagatas stand, hold, and maintain themselves. According to plan he is reborn near them, and he dwells in those attentions. i.e. the attentions on the Buddha. And why? Because as a rule the irreversible Bodhisattvas, when they have produced attentions associated with the world of sense desire, and have observed the ten wholesome ways of action, are reborn in those Buddha-fields; having produced the first trance, etc. *to* : the fourth formless attainment, they are reborn there. And there they are face to face with the Tathagatas who stand, hold, and maintain themselves. Endowed with these attributes, etc.

IV8,2,14. COGNITION OF DHARMA IN THE PATH : ONE DOES NOT TAKE EVEN THE LEAST DHARMA AS A BASIS.

Moreover the irreversible Bodhisattva who courses in the perfection of wisdom, and who is established in subjective emptiness, etc. *to* : in the knowledge of all modes, in the doors to deliverance of Emptiness, the

Signless and Wishless, does not think to himself: I am irreversible and not reversible. No such doubt arises in him. He has no uncertainty about the stage he has made his own. And why? Because he does not review these dharmas, i.e. him who turns away or him who does not turn away. Just as a man who stands on the stage of a Streamwinner has no hesitation or doubts about it if that is the stage which is his by right, and so up *to*: the Buddha-stage. Just so the Bodhisattva, when he stands on the stage which is his own by right, has no hesitations or doubts about it. Established on that irreversible stage he purifies the Buddha-fields and matures beings. And he quickly sees through any deed of Mara that may have arisen and does not come under its influence. He understands all these deeds of Mara and turns away from them. Just as, Subhuti, a man who has committed one of the deadly sins will never again, until his death, lose the thought of that sin; but it will follow after him; he cannot shake off the (irresistible drive towards) the states of woe; its overwhelming effect follows him until the time of his death. Just so the irreversible thought of the irreversible Bodhisattva has been truly established, he cannot be deflected from the irreversible stage, and the whole world with its gods, men, and Asuras cannot divert him from it. And why? That irreversible thought, having transcended the world with its gods, men, and Asuras, has entered on the certainty of salvation. Having stood on the stage which is his by right, he has achieved the complete perfection in the superknowledges, purifies the Buddha-field, and matures beings; he passes on from Buddha-field to Buddha-field, and he plants in these Buddha-fields wholesome roots which allow him to have a vision of the Buddhas, the Lords, to salute them respectfully, to honour them, and to hear the Dharma from them. And in all these Buddha-fields he questions the Buddhas and Lords, counterquestions and honours them. And that Bodhisattva who has thus stood recognises for what they are any deeds of Mara that may have arisen, and he does not come under their influence. And he cleanses those deeds of Mara through skill in means at the Reality limit. He has no hesitations or doubts about the stage which is his by right. And why? He has no uncertainties about the Reality limit, and he does review the Reality limit as either one or two. When he has cognized this, even after he has passed through this present life, he will produce no thought on the level of the Disciples and Pratyekabuddhas. And why? Because the Bodhisattva does not, when all dharmas are empty of own-marks, review the production of any dharma, or its stopping, its defilement, or purification.

IV8,2,15. PATIENT ACCEPTANCE OF THE SUBSEQUENT COGNITION OF THE PATH: HE IS ESTABLISHED IN THE CERTAINTY ABOUT THE TRIAD OF HIS OWN LEVELS, WHICH IS ESSENTIALLY THE SAME AS THE TRIPLE OMNISCIENCE.

But when that Bodhisattva has passed through this present life, he will think, 'it is not the case that I shall not win full enlightenment; I will in fact win it! And why? Because the supreme enlightenment is empty of own-marks'. When the Bodhisattva has thus stood firm on the stage which is his by right, he cannot be led astray or crushed by others. And why? Because, as he has stood firm on it, he becomes endowed with an insuperable cognition. If again Mara, the Evil One, in the guise of the Buddha (himself) were to come to him and say, 'Realise Arhatship here and now! You are not predestined to full enlightenment. You have not acquired the patient acceptance of dharmas which fail to be produced and without that you cannot be predicted by the Tathagatas to full enlightenment. You have not the attributes, tokens, and signs which a Bodhisattva must be endowed with to be predicted to full enlightenment'. If a Bodhisattva when he has heard these words, does not become terrified in his mind, then this Bodhisattva should know that he has been predicted to full enlightenment by the Tathagatas. And why? Because he knows that he has the dharmas endowed with which a Bodhisattva is predicted to the supreme enlightenment.

IV8,2,16. Subsequent cognition of the path: renunciation of one's life for the sake of Dharma, which consists in the knowledge of all modes.

If Mara, the Evil One, having approached in the guise of a Buddha, or of some person under the influence of Mara, should predict the Bodhisattva to the level of the Disciples or Pratyekabuddhas, then the Bodhisattva thinks to himself, 'this one, who wants to establish me on the level of a Disciple or Pratyekabuddha, is surely Mara, the Evil One, who has come along in the guise of the Buddha, or this is a person under Mara's influence.' When the Bodhisattva reads and studies the Extensive Sutras, then Mara, the Evil One, comes to him in the guise of the Buddha and says to him, 'these have not been taught by the Lords or their Disciples. Taught by Mara are these Sutras in which you course.' But that Bodhisattva should know that it is surely Mara, the Evil One, or someone under Mara's influence, who tries to dissuade him from the supreme enlightenment. If he does know that, then he has been predicted to full enlightenment by the Tathagatas of the past and he is firmly established on the irreversible stage.

And why? Because he has the attributes, tokens, and signs of the irreversible Bodhisattvas. Endowed with these attributes, etc. Moreover, Subhuti, an irreversible Bodhisattva who courses in perfect wisdom gives up even his self and life so that he may gain the True Dharma. But that Dharma he does not give up. The irreversible Bodhisattva makes great efforts to gain the True Dharma. He gains the True Dharma of the past, future, and present Buddhas and Lords, and he does not give up the Buddhas. And why? He thinks that because they have gained the True Dharma the past, present, and future Buddhas have been worshipped. And what is the True Dharma for the sake of which the Bodhisattva gives up his self? Here the Tathagatas demonstrate Dharma to the effect that 'all dharmas are empty'. A few deluded persons then contradict and say that this is not the Dharma, not the Vinaya, not the Teacher, not the Teaching. But the Bodhisattva for the sake of that Dharma gives up even his self. He becomes convinced that he also will be reckoned as one of the future Buddhas, that he also has been predicted (to full enlightenment) and that his also is the True Dharma for the sake of which he is willing to give up even self and life. The Bodhisattva has also these considerations in mind when he renounces even his self for the sake of gaining the True Dharma. Endowed with these attributes, etc. Moreover, Subhuti, when the Tathagata demonstrates Dharma, the irreversible Bodhisattva does not hesitate or doubt. But whatever Dharma the Buddhas may teach, all that he does not forget. And why? Because he has acquired the Dharanis.

Subhuti: What dharanis has he acquired so that he no longer forgets the Sutras taught by the Tathagata?

The Lord: The dharani which causes inexhaustibility, the Seal of the Ocean, and the Lotus Array.

Subhuti: (Does the Bodhisattva's absence of hesitation and doubt refer only to) the Tathagata's teachings, and not also to those of Disciples, gods, Nagas, Gandharvas, Asuras, Garudas, Kinnaras and Mahoragas?

The Lord: Whatever may be said or spoken by anyone, with regard to that the Bodhisattva has no hesitation and doubts. And why? Because he has acquired that dharani. Endowed with these attributes, tokens, and signs a Bodhisattva should be known as irreversible from the supreme enlightenment.

Chapter 51

THE EXPOSITION OF SKILL IN MEANS

IV8,3. The mark of irreversibility of one who stands on the path of development.

IV8,3,A. The depth of the path of development.

IV8,3,A,1. Deep is the path of development.

Subhuti: Endowed with great qualities, O Lord, is the irreversible Bodhisattva, great being. Endowed with immeasurable, incalculable, unmeasured qualities is the Bodhisattva, the great being. Endowed with measureless qualities is the irreversible Bodhisattva, great being.

The Lord: So it is, Subhuti, so it is. Endowed with, etc. *to*: great being. And why? Because he has acquired an endless and boundless cognition, which is not shared by all the Disciples and Pratyekabuddhas. And, having stood in this cognition, the irreversible Bodhisattva, great being, consummates the analytical knowledges, and in consequence he cannot, when questioned by the world with its gods, men, and Asuras, be overcome by counterarguments.

Subhuti: The Tathagata, O Lord, could for aeons countless like the sands of the Ganges go on explaining the attributes, tokens, and signs through which an irreversible Bodhisattva, great being is exalted. It would be well, O Lord, if now those very deep stations were explained, established in which the Bodhisattva, the great being, coursing in the six perfections, fulfills the four applications of mindfulness, etc. *to*: the knowledge of all modes.

IV8,3,A,2. The depth of the path of development.

The Lord: Well said, Subhuti, well said. It is good that you, for the sake of the irreversible Bodhisattvas, great beings, should question the Tathagata about the very deep stations. 'Deep', Subhuti, of emptiness that is a synonym, (of the Signless, the Wishless, the Uneffected, the Unproduced, of No-birth, Nonexistence, Dispassion, Cessation, Nirvana and Departing. So A).

Subhuti: Is it a synonym only of Nirvana or of all dharmas?

The Lord: It is a synonym of all dharmas. And why? For form, etc. *to*: enlightenment is deep. How is form, etc. *to*: enlightenment, deep?

As deep as the Suchness of form, etc. to enlightenment, so deep is form, etc. to enlightenment.

IV8,3,A,3. THE PATH OF DEVELOPMENT IS FREE FROM THE EXTREMES OF ATTRIBUTION AND NEGATION.

Subhuti: What is the Suchness of form, etc.?

The Lord: The Suchness in which there is no form, etc. and which yet is no other than form, etc.

Subhuti: It is wonderful, O Lord, how by a subtle device the irreversible Bodhisattva has impeded form, etc., and indicated Nirvana at the same time. All dharmas which one might seize upon have been impeded—whether they be worldly or supramundane, common or uncommon, with or without outflows—and Nirvana has been indicated.

IV8,3,B. THE DISTINCTIVE FEATURES OF THE PATH OF DEVELOPMENT.

IV8,3,B,1. THE ROAD TO DEVELOPMENT.

The Lord: If again, Subhuti, the Bodhisattva, the great being, will reflect on these very deep stations associated with the perfection of wisdom, will weigh them up, will meditate on them,

IV8,3,B,2. THE ROAD TO DEVELOPMENT WITH THE AIDS TO PENETRATION, ETC.

'thus must I stand as it is commanded in the perfection of wisdom, thus must I train myself as it has been explained in the perfection of wisdom, thus must I progress as it is pointed out in the perfection of wisdom';—this Bodhisattva, this great being who thus perfects himself, thus meditates, thus investigates, thus makes an effort, thus strives, thus struggles,

IV8,3,B,3. THE THREEFOLD ADVANTAGE.

through that production of thought he will gain incalculable, immeasurable, and innumerable wholesome roots. For an immeasurable aeon he will spurn Samsara; how much more so if, coursing in the perfection of wisdom exclusively, he dwells in attentions associated with enlightenment. Suppose a man, moved by considerations of greed, had made a date with a handsome, attractive and good-looking woman; but, held back by someone else, she could not leave her house; what do you think, Subhuti, with what would that man's thought be connected?

Subhuti: With the woman, of course. He thinks of her going out, coming to him, and how he will fall down on her and have sexual intercourse with her.

The Lord: How many such ideas will he have in the course of a day and night?

Subhuti: Many indeed, O Lord.

The Lord: As many ideas as that man has in the course of a day and night, for so many aeons a Bodhisattva spurns Samsara, turns his back on it, if he trains in this deep perfection of wisdom as it has been expounded, investigates it and meditates on it, and if he endeavours to get rid of those faults which turn him from the supreme enlightenment. If, engaged in these endeavours, the Bodhisattva for only one day dwells, as it has been explained in the perfection of wisdom, in that dwelling, then the wholesome root which he thereby acquires is infinitely greater than the wholesome root which results from filling countless world systems (with gifts).

IV8,3,C. THE DISTINCTION OF (9 OR 18) KINDS ON THE PATH OF DEVELOPMENT.

IV8,3,C,1. THE DISCRIMINATION (HOSTILE STATE) IS VERY STRONG.

If, Subhuti, a Bodhisattva, great being, lacking in perfect wisdom, gives gifts for aeons countless like the sands of the Ganges to the triple Jewel, would he, on account of that, beget a great deal of merit?

Subhuti: He would, O Lord.

IV8,3,C,2. THE PATH (ANTIDOTE) IS VERY WEAK.

The Lord: Greater is the merit which a son or daughter of good family beget by making endeavours about this deep perfection of wisdom as it has been explained. And why? For this is the method by which the supreme enlightenment is fully known.

IV8,3,C,3. THE DISCRIMINATION IS MEDIUM STRONG.

What do you think, Subhuti, if, lacking in perfect wisdom, a Bodhisattva would for aeons countless like the sands of the Ganges bestow donations upon Streamwinners, etc. *to*: upon the Tathagatas, would that Bodhisattva on account of that beget much merit?

Subhuti: He would, O Lord.

IV8,3,C,4. THE PATH IS MODERATELY WEAK.

The Lord: Greater is the merit which a son or daughter of good family would beget by making endeavours about this deep perfection of wisdom as it has been explained. And why? Because when he courses in this perfection of wisdom a Bodhisattva, having transcended the level of the Disciples and Pratyekabuddhas, enters on a Bodhisattva's way of salvation, until he fully knows the supreme enlightenment.

IV8,3,C,5. THE DISCRIMINATION IS WEAKLY STRONG.

What do you think, Subhuti, if, lacking in perfect wisdom, a Bodhisattva would for aeons countless like the sands of the Ganges give gifts, guard his morality, perfect his patience, exert vigour, enter into the trances and develop wisdom, would he on account of that beget much merit?

Subhuti: He would, O Lord.

IV8,3,C,6. THE PATH IS FAIRLY WEAK.

The Lord: A son or daughter of good family would beget greater merit if, having stood in this deep perfection of wisdom as it has been explained, they would for only one day give gifts, guard morality, perfect patience, exert vigour, enter the trances, and develop wisdom. And why? Because the perfection of wisdom is the mother and genetrix of the Bodhisattvas, the great beings. Having stood in this perfection of wisdom, the Bodhisattvas fulfill all dharmas until they know fully the supreme enlightenment.

IV8,3,C,7. THE DISCRIMINATION IS STRONGLY MEDIUM.

What do you think, Subhuti, if, lacking in perfect wisdom, a Bodhisattva for aeons countless like the sands of the Ganges were to give the gift of Dharma, would he on account of that beget much merit?

Subhuti: He would, O Lord.

IV8,3,C,8. THE PATH IS WEAKLY MEDIUM.

The Lord: Greater would be the merit which a son or daughter of good family would beget if, having stood in this deep perfection of wisdom as it has been explained, they would give the gift of Dharma for one single day only. And why? Because the Bodhisattva who lacks perfect wisdom also lacks the knowledge of all modes; the Bodhisattva who does not lack perfect wisdom also does not lack the knowledge of all modes. Therefore, then, should a Bodhisattva who wants to fully know the supreme enlightenment become one who is not lacking in perfect wisdom.

IV8,3,C,9. THE DISCRIMINATION IS MODERATELY MEDIUM.

What do you think, Subhuti, if, lacking in perfect wisdom, a Bodhisattva would for aeons countless like the sands of the Ganges make endeavours about the four applications of mindfulness, etc. *to*: about all the concentrations, what do you think, Subhuti, would he on account of that beget much merit?

Subhuti: He would, O Lord.

IV8,3,C,10. THE PATH IS MODERATELY MEDIUM.

The Lord: Greater is the merit which a son or daughter of good family beget if they make endeavours for one single day only in this deep perfection of wisdom as it has been explained, in the four applications of mindfulness, etc. *to* : in the eighteen special Buddha-dharmas. And why? It is impossible, it cannot be that a Bodhisattva who is not lacking in perfect wisdom should turn away from the knowledge of all modes. That is quite impossible. But it could be that a Bodhisattva who is lacking in perfect wisdom might turn away from the knowledge of all modes. Therefore, then, should the Bodhisattva become one who is not lacking in perfect wisdom.

IV8,3,C,11. THE DISCRIMINATION IS WEAKLY MEDIUM.

What do you think, Subhuti, if, lacking in perfect wisdom, a Bodhisattva would for aeons countless like the sands of the Ganges dedicate those material gifts, that gift of Dharma and those attentions associated with meditative seclusion to the supreme enlightenment, would he on account of that beget much merit?

Subhuti: He would, O Lord.

IV8,3,C,12. THE PATH IS STRONGLY MEDIUM.

The Lord: Greater would be the merit which a son or daughter of good family beget if, having stood in this deep perfection of wisdom, they dedicate for one single day only to the supreme enlightenment those material gifts, the gifts of Dharma and those attentions associated with meditative seclusion. And why? For this dedication (in the spirit) of the perfection of wisdom is the best of all rejoicings and dedications. Therefore, then, a Bodhisattva who wants to fully know the supreme enlightenment should become one who is skilled in the dedication (in the spirit) of the perfection of wisdom.

IV8,3,C,13. THE DISCRIMINATION IS FAIRLY WEAK.

What do you think, Subhuti, if. lacking in perfect wisdom, a Bodhisattva would for aeons countless like the sands of the Ganges dedicate to the supreme enlightenment all the wholesome roots of the past, future, and present Buddhas and Lords, as well as those of their congregations of Disciples, would he on account of that beget much merit?

Subhuti: He would, O Lord.

IV8,3,C,14. THE PATH IS WEAKLY STRONG.

The Lord: Greater would be the merit which a son or daughter of good family beget, if, having stood in this deep perfection of wisdom as it has been explained, they would dedicate to the supreme enlightenment the root of merit (produced) during one single day. And why? Because all his dedicating will be guided by the perfection of wisdom. Therefore, then, should a Bodhisattva who wants to fully know the supreme enlightenment become skillful in the dedication (in the spirit) of the perfection of wisdom.

IV8,3,C,15. THE DISCRIMINATION IS MODERATELY WEAK.

Subhuti: How can that son or daughter of good family beget a greater merit, since the Lord has described all (karmic) accumulation as mere imagination. For without (karmic) accumulation one cannot produce right views, or enter on the right way of salvation, or gain the fruit of a Streamwinner, etc. *to*: fully know the supreme enlightenment.

IV8,3,C,16. THE PATH IS MEDIUM STRONG.

The Lord: So it is, Subhuti, so it is. Without (karmic) accumulation it is not possible to produce right views, or to enter on the right way to salvation, or to gain the fruit of a Streamwinner, etc. *to*: to fully know the supreme enlightenment. But also that gift of a Bodhisattva who courses in perfect wisdom is without (karmic) accumulation, because it has been declared to be just empty, null, vain, and insubstantial. And why? Because the Bodhisattva is well trained in all the (18) kinds of emptiness.

IV8,3,C,17. THE DISCRIMINATION IS VERY WEAK.

To the extent that a Bodhisattva, having stood in these emptinesses, goes on contemplating all karma-formations in this manner, to that extent he becomes one who does not lack perfect wisdom.

IV8,3,C,18. THE PATH IS VERY STRONG.

And to the extent that the Bodhisattva does not lack in perfect wisdom, to that extent he begets an incalculable, immeasurable, and measureless merit.

IV8,3,D. (THE MARK OF ENLIGHTENMENT).

IV8,3,D,1. THE IMPLICATIONS OF 'INCALCULABLE', ETC.

Subhuti: What is the distinction and difference between the incalculable, the immeasurable, and the measureless?

The Lord: 'Incalculable' is that which has no number, or that to which calculation does not apply. 'Immeasurable' is that of which no measure can be apprehended in past, future, or present dharmas. 'Measureless' is that which one cannot measure.

Subhuti: Would there be a reason to assume that the skandhas are incalculable, immeasurable, and measureless?

The Lord: Yes, there would be.

IV8,3,D,2. THE MARK OF THE OWN-BEING OF 'INCALCULABLE', ETC.

Subhuti: In what manner are the skandhas incalculable, etc.?

The Lord: They are empty, and (therefore) incalculable, etc.

Subhuti: Are only the skandhas empty or also all dharmas?

The Lord: What do you think, Subhuti, have I not declared all dharmas to be empty?

Subhuti: As 'empty', O Lord, have all dharmas been described by the Tathagatas. And they that are empty and inextinguishable, they are also incalculable, immeasurable, and measureless. Of emptiness no number is got at, nor measure, nor limitation.

IV8,3,D,3. ONE RAISES THE PROBLEM AND EXPLAINS (THESE TERMS) AS OUTPOURINGS OF THE TATHAGATA'S COMPASSION.

Therefore, then, no distinction can be apprehended between these dharmas by way of their meaning or method.

The Lord: So it is, Subhuti. As inexpressible has this been talked about by the Tathagata. An exposition of the outpourings of demonstration are the words used by the Tathagata, i.e. 'inextinguishable', 'incalculable', 'immeasurable', 'measureless', 'empty', 'signless', 'wishless', 'uneffected', 'nonproduction', 'dispassion', 'stopping', and 'Nirvana'.

IV8,3,D,4. THE PROBLEM RAISED BY THE ABSENCE OF GROWTH AND DIMINUTION IN AN INEXPRESSIBLE ENTITY.

Subhuti: It is wonderful to see the extent to which the Tathagata has demonstrated the true nature of all these dharmas although that Dharmahood is inexpressible. As I understand the meaning of the Lord's teaching, all dharmas cannot be talked about in any proper sense?

The Lord: So it is, Subhuti. All dharmas are inexpressible. The inexpressibility of all dharmas is their emptiness. And emptiness cannot be expressed in words.

Subhuti: Can an inexpressible object have growth or diminution?

The Lord: No, Subhuti.

Subhuti: But if there is no growth or diminution of an inexpressible object, then there can be no growth or diminution of the six perfections, etc. *to*: of the Buddhadharmas. The nonexistence of the six perfections, etc. *to*: the Buddhadharmas, will be a fact. Because of the nonexistence of these dharmas also the nonexistence of the knowledge of all modes will be a fact, and because of the nonexistence of the knowledge of all modes, who could fully know the supreme enlightenment?

IV8,3,D,5. ITS SOLUTION.

The Lord: So it is, Subhuti, so it is. There is no growth or diminution of an inexpressible object. But it does not occur to the Bodhisattva, the great being, who courses in the perfection of wisdom, develops it, makes efforts about it, and is skilled in means that 'I grow in perfect wisdom; I grow in perfect vigour,' etc. On the contrary it occurs to him, 'a mere designation is that, i.e. this perfection of giving, etc.' When he courses in the perfection of giving, etc. *to* : in the perfection of wisdom, he dedicates those attributes, those productions of thought, and those wholesome roots to the utmost, right, and perfect enlightenment. And he dedicates so as to conform to that which the utmost, right, and perfect enlightenment actually is.

IV8,3,D,6. THE MARK OF ENLIGHTENMENT.

Subhuti: And what again is this utmost, right, and perfect enlightenment?

The Lord: It is the Suchness of all dharmas.

Subhuti: And what is this Suchness of all dharmas which is the utmost, right, and perfect enlightenment?

The Lord : The Suchness of form, etc. *to*: of Nirvana—that neither grows nor diminishes. Therefore the Bodhisattva who regularly and abundantly dwells as one who is not lacking in perfect wisdom, does not review the growth or diminution of any dharma whatever. It is thus that there is no growth or diminution of an inexpressible object. It is thus that there is no growth or diminution of the six perfections, etc. *to* : of the analytical knowledges. It is thus that the Bodhisattva should course in the perfection of wisdom, by way of no-growth and no-diminution.

IV8,3,E.

IV8,3,E,I.

IV8,3,E,I,1.

Subhuti: Does the Bodhisattva, the great being, awake to the utmost, right, and perfect enlightenment by means of the first production of the thought (of enlightenment), or rather by means of the last production of the thought (of enlightenment)? If, O Lord, the Bodhisattva, the great being, would, by means of the first production of the thought (of enlightenment) fully awake to the utmost, right, and perfect enlightenment—that first production of the thought (of enlightenment) is not in touch with the last production of the thought (of enlightenment); the last production of the thought (of enlightenment) is not in touch with the first. When thus, O Lord, the dharmas which constitute thought and its concomitants are not in touch with each other, how do the wholesome roots go on accumulating? But without the wholesome roots being accumulated, it is impossible to fully know the utmost, right, and perfect enlightenment.

IV8,3,E,I,2. THE SIMILE OF THE LAMP.

The Lord: Therefore, then, Subhuti, will I give you a simile, so that you can understand this matter. Through a simile discerning people will understand the meaning of the teaching. What do you think, Subhuti, in a burning oil lamp, is the wick burnt by the first incidence of the flame, or by the last incidence of the flame?

Subhuti: Not, O Lord, is the wick burnt by means of the first incidence of the flame, nor independent of it.

The Lord: What do you think, Subhuti, has now that wick burnt up?

Subhuti: It is burnt up, O Lord, it is burnt up, O Sugata!

The Lord: Just so, Subhuti, does the Bodhisattva, the great being not fully awake to the utmost, right, and perfect enlightenment by means of the first production of the thought (of enlightenment), nor independent of it; not by means of the last production of the thought (of enlightenment), nor independent of it. And yet the Bodhisattva, the great being, does fully awake to the utmost, right, and perfect enlightenment. Because, Subhuti, the Bodhisattva, the great being, coursing in this perfection of wisdom, on account of the first thought (of enlightenment), having fulfilled the ten stages, does awake to the utmost, right, and perfect enlightenment.

Subhuti: How, O Lord, does the Bodhisattva, the great being, having fulfilled the ten stages, awake to the utmost, right, and perfect enlightenment?

The Lord: Having fulfilled the stage of bright insight does the Bodhisattva, the great being, awake to full enlightenment; having fulfilled the stage of becoming one of the clan, etc. to the Bodhisattva-stage does the Bodhisattva, the great being, awake to full enlightenment. Training himself in the ten stages, the Bodhisattva, the great being, does not by means of the first production of the thought (of enlightenment) fully know the utmost, right, and perfect enlightenment, nor independent of it; nor by means of the last thought (of enlightenment), nor independent of it; and yet he fully knows the utmost, right, and perfect enlightenment.

IV8,3,E,II. THE EIGHTFOLD DEPTH.

IV8,3,E,II,1. THE DEPTH OF ITS (MODE OF) PRODUCTION.

Subhuti: Deep, O Lord, is conditioned coproduction. For the Bodhisattva, the great being, does not by means of the first production of the thought (of enlightenment) fully know the utmost, right, and perfect enlightenment, nor independent of it; nor by means of the last production of the thought (of enlightenment), nor independent of it; and yet he fully knows the utmost, right, and perfect enlightenment.

The Lord: What do you think, Subhuti, the thought which has been stopped, will that again arise?

Subhuti: No, O Lord.

IV8,3,E,II2. THE DEPTH OF ITS STOPPING.

The Lord: The thought which has (not?) been produced, is that doomed to stop.

Subhuti: It is doomed to stop, O Lord, it is doomed to stop, O Sugata.

The Lord: What is doomed to stop, will that be stopped?

Subhuti: No, O Lord.

IV8,3,E,II3. THE DEPTH OF ITS SUCHNESS.

The Lord: Will it abide just as Suchness does?

Subhuti: Yes, it will.

The Lord: When it will abide just as Suchness does, it would certainly no be unmoved?

Subhuti: No, O Lord.

The Lord: Is Suchness deep?

Subhuti: It is deep.

IV8,3,E,II4. THE DEPTH OF THE COGNIZABLE.

The Lord: Is that thought like Suchness?

Subhuti: No, O Lord.

The Lord: Is the thought other than Suchness?

Subhuti: No, O Lord.

The Lord: Is Suchness other than the thought?

Subhuti: No, O Lord.

The Lord: Is thought in Suchness?

Subhuti: No, O Lord.

IV8,3,E,II5. THE DEPTH OF THE COGNITION.

The Lord: Does then Suchness review Suchness?

Subhuti: No, O Lord.

IV8,3,E,II6. THE DEPTH OF THE PRACTICE.

The Lord: One who courses thus, does he course in the deep perfection of wisdom?

Subhuti: Yes, he does.

The Lord: One who courses thus, where (whither) does he course?

Subhuti: One who courses thus, he does not course anywhere. And why? Because in the Bodhisattva, the great being, who courses in the perfection of wisdom, these habitual ideas do not proceed, they do not happen in him. To one who stands in Suchness, nothing happens, nor can anything happen to him.

The Lord: The Bodhisattva, the great being, who courses in the perfection of wisdom, where does he course?

IV8,3,E,II7. THE DEPTH OF ITS NONDUALITY.

Subhuti: He courses in (by means of) ultimate reality, wherein the idea of duality does not exist.

The Lord: One who courses in ultimate reality courses in ideas, courses in signs?

Subhuti: No, O Lord.

The Lord: Has, then, by him the perception of a sign been annihilated?

Subhuti: No, O Lord.

IV8,3,E,II8. THE DEPTH OF THE SKILL IN MEANS.

The Lord: Has, then, by the Bodhisattva, the great being, the perception of a sign (been developed, or the perception of the signless) been annihilated?

Subhuti: That Bodhisattva, the great being who courses in the perfection of wisdom, does not apply himself thus, 'I will develop the sign or I will annihilate the signless'. Here again the Bodhisattva, the great being who courses in the perfection of wisdom, awakens to full enlightenment not without having fulfilled the ten powers of a Tathagata, etc. *to* : the Buddhadharmas. This again is of the Bodhisattva, the great being, the skill in means, by which he does not make any dharma into something existent or something nonexistent. And why? Because there the Bodhisattva, the great being, established in the own-mark-emptiness of all dharmas, enters into the three concentrations, for the sake of beings whom he matures through them. It is thus that the Bodhisattva, the great being, enters the three concentrations. How, O Lord, does the Bodhisattva, the great being, enter into the three concentrations for the sake of beings whom he matures through them?

The Lord: Here a Bodhisattva, a great being, having stood in the three concentrations establishes in emptiness those beings who course in the perception of discrimination, in the signless those who course in the sign, and enjoins the wishless on those who course in making plans. It is thus that the Bodhisattva, the great being, coursing in the perfection of wisdom, having stood in the three concentrations, matures beings.

CHAPTER 52

THE FULFILLMENT OF SKILL IN THE SIX PERFECTIONS

IV 9. The Identity of Nirvana and Samsara.

Sāriputra: Ven. Subhuti, the Bodhisattva, the great being, who in his dreams enters into the three concentrations—emptiness, the signless, the wishless—does he, then, grow in perfect wisdom?

Subhuti: If, Ven. Śāriputra, he grows through the development by day, then he also grows in a dream. And why? Because dream and waking are indiscriminate. If the Bodhisattva who courses by day in the perfection of wisdom has a development of the perfection of wisdom, then also the Bodhisattva, the great being, who dreams will have a development of the perfection of wisdom.

Śāriputra: If again, Ven. Subhuti, the Bodhisattva, the great being, does a deed in his dream, will there by of that deed a heaping up or accumulation? If all dharmas are said to be like a dream, there will be no heaping up or accumulation of it. And why? Because in a dream no heaping up or accumulation of a dharma can be apprehended. But when one wakes up and thinks it over, then there is a heaping up or accumulation of it.

Subhuti: One who had committed a murder in his dream, and, on waking, would think it over like this, 'he has been well killed by me, (A : it is right that he was killed, it is just that he was killed, it was I who killed him!' Such thoughts are equivalent to the conscious notion that he wants to kill someone).

Śāriputra: Not without an objective support does a deed arise or an act of will.

Subhuti: So it is, Śāriputra, not without an objective support does a deed arise or an act of will. Only with an objective support is a deed produced, or an act of will, and not without. In seen, heard, and known dharmas does intelligence proceed, and not in unseen, unheard, unknown dharmas. Therein some intellectual acts take hold of defilement, and some of purification. Therefore, then, Śāriputra, it is with an objective support that a deed or act of will arises and not without objective support.

Śāriputra: If, Ven. Subhuti, the Bodhisattva, the great being, in his dream would give gifts, guard morality, perfect himself in patience, exert vigour, enter the trances and develop wisdom, and would turn that wholesome root over to full enlightenment, would it (actually) become turned over by him into full enlightenment?

Subhuti: Maitreya, this Bodhisattva, this great being, has experienced (this) face to face, he is bound to only one more birth, his irreversibility has been declared by the Lord, he should be asked, he will dispose of this.

Maitreya: As the Ven. Subhuti, the Elder has said: 'Maitreya, this Bodhisattva, this great being, has experienced (this) face to face, he is bound to one more birth only, his irreversibility has been declared by the Lord, he should be asked, he will dispose of this'. Will now that designation 'Maitreya, the Bodhisattva, the great being' dispose of this matter, or will form dispose of it, or feeling, etc.? Or the emptiness of form, etc.? Or the Suchness of form, etc.? The emptiness of form, etc. that is not capable of disposing (replying). The Suchness of form, etc. that is not capable of disposing. I do not review (see) that dharma which would dispose, or by which one would dispose, or wherein one would dispose. Nor that dharma which has been predicted to full enlightenment, or whereby it has been predicted, or wherein it has been predicted. All these dharmas are nondual and undivided.

Śāriputra: Have by you these dharmas then perhaps been realised in the way in which you teach this dharma?

Maitreya: No, they have not.

Thereupon it occurred to the Ven. *Śāriputra*: Profoundly wise surely is Maitreya, this Bodhisattva, this great being, how he makes this explanation after he has coursed for a long time in the six perfections and in baselessness.

The Lord: What do you think, Śāriputra, do you see (review) that dharma by which you are dignified as an 'Arhat'?

Śāriputra: No indeed, O Lord.

The Lord: In the same way, Subhuti, it does not occur to the Bodhisattva, the great being, who courses in the perfection of wisdom: 'that good dharma is being predicted; that good dharma has been predicted; that good dharma fully knows the utmost, right, and perfect enlightenment!' Coursing thus, the Bodhisattva, the great being, courses in the perfection of wisdom. Nor does there arise a doubt in him: 'I will not fully know the utmost, right, and perfect enlightenment.' 'I will just know fully the utmost, right, and perfect enlightenment,' (that he knows). One who courses thus, he courses in the perfection of wisdom. Thus coursing the Bodhisattva, the great being, will not tremble, will not be frightened or terrified: 'Not shall I not fully know the utmost, right, and perfect enlightenment; but just I will fully know the utmost, right, and perfect enlightenment'.

IV 10. The Purity of the Buddha-field.

Subhuti: How, O Lord, does the Bodhisattva, the great being, fulfill the six perfections and come near to the knowledge of all modes?

The Lord: Here, Subhuti, the Bodhisattva, the great being, who courses in the perfection of giving should, having seen beings who are hungry, thirsty, ill housed, ill clad, and devoid of beds and seats, consider as follows: 'Just so will I course in the perfection of giving that, when I have won full enlightenment, all these faults of those beings will in each and every way not take place and not be conceived. Just like the possessions enjoyed by the various classes of gods, from the Gods belonging to the Four Great Kings, to the Highest Gods, so will be the possessions enjoyed by the beings in that Buddha-field'. When he courses thus, the Bodhisattva, the great being, fulfills the perfection of giving and comes near to full enlightenment. Moreover, Subhuti, the Bodhisattva, the great being, who courses in the perfection of morality, having seen beings who take life, take what is not given, commit sexual misconduct, speak falsely, speak harshly, speak maliciously, prattle away, are covetous, with minds full of ill will, with false views, short-lived, with many afflictions, with many troubles, ugly to look at, insignificant, with few possessions, of low-class families, badly dressed, and mutilated—he should thus consider: 'In such a way will I course in the perfection of morality that, when I have won full enlightenment, in that Buddha-field those beings will not have those faults and that they will not even be conceived'. Thus coursing, the Bodhisattva, the great being, fulfills the perfection of morality and comes near to full enlightenment.

Moreover, Subhuti, the Bodhisattva, the great being, who courses in the perfection of patience, having seen beings who are full of ill will for each other, and having seen beings who belabour each other with clods, beatings, and swords, rob each other of their lives, and use staffs, clubs, and so on, on each other, he should consider thus: 'In such a way will I course in the perfection of patience that, when I have won full enlightenment, in that Buddha-field those beings shall not have these faults, that they shall become inconceivable. And the minds of all beings will become like that of a mother, father, brother, sister, son, or daughter'. When he courses thus, the Bodhisattva, the great being, fulfills the perfection of patience and comes near to full enlightenment. Moreover, Subhuti, the Bodhisattva, the great being, who courses in the perfection of vigour, having seen beings who are of little vigour, lazy, indolent, averse from making efforts, trivial beings who have set out in the three vehicles, the Disciple-vehicle, the Pratyekabuddha-vehicle, or the Bodhisattva-vehicle—he will thus consider: 'So will I practise the perfection of vigour that, when I have won full enlightenment, in that Buddha-field those beings shall not have those faults, and that they shall become inconceivable'. When he courses thus, the Bodhisattva, the great being, fulfills the perfection of vigour and comes near to full enlightenment. Moreover, Subhuti, the Bodhisattva, the great being, who courses in the perfection of meditation, having seen beings who proceed with the five hindrances, i.e. with the obstacles of sense desire, ill will, sloth and torpor, excitedness and sense of guilt, and doubt; beings who are bewildered, confused in their mindfulness, who are lacking in the four trances, in friendliness, compassion, sympathetic joy and impartiality, and in the four formless attainments, he should thus consider: 'In such a way will I practise the perfection of meditation that, when I have won full enlightenment, in that Buddha-field those beings shall not have these faults and that they shall become inconceivable'. When he courses thus, the Bodhisattva, the great being, fulfills the perfection of meditation and comes near to full enlightenment.

Moreover, Subhuti, the Bodhisattva, the great being, who courses in the perfection of wisdom, having seen beings who are stupid and devoid of wisdom, who are devoid of either mundane or supramundane right views, who teach that actions have no karmic result, who teach nihilism, annihilation, eternity, and oneness, otherness or bothness, he should thus consider: 'Thus will I practise the perfection of wisdom that, when I have won full enlightenment, in that Buddha-field those beings shall not have those faults, and that they shall become inconceivable'. When he courses thus, the Bodhisattva, the great being, fulfills the perfection of wisdom and comes near to full enlightenment.

Moreover, a Bodhisattva, a great being, who courses in the six perfections and who has seen beings proceeding in the three heaps—those destined (for salvation), those destined for perdition, and those whose destiny is not fixed either way—should consider as follows: 'For so long will I course in the six perfections, purify the Buddha-field and mature beings until, when I have known full enlightenment, in that Buddha-field even the word for beings who are destined (for salvation), destined for perdition, not destined either way, will no longer be or be conceived'. When he courses thus, a Bodhisattva fulfills the six perfections and comes near to the knowledge of all modes. Moreover, a Bodhisattva, a great being, who courses in the six perfections, and who has seen the beings in the hells, the beings in the animal world, and the beings in the world of Yama, should consider as follows: 'For so long will I course, etc. *to*: even the word for the three states of woe will no longer be or be conceived'. When he courses thus, etc.

Moreover the Bodhisattva, the great being, who courses in the six perfections, and who has seen that this great earth is full of jungles, rocky crags, precipices, sewers, and cesspools, should consider as follows: 'For so long will I course, etc. *to*: these faults of beings will no longer be conceived, and this my Buddha-field will be (flat and) even like the palm of a hand'. When he courses thus, etc.

Moreover the Bodhisattva, etc. *to*: who has seen this great earth made chiefly of clay, with very little gold and silver, should, etc. *to*: this great earth will be covered with rivers of gold'. When he courses thus, etc. Moreover the Bodhisattva, etc. *to*: who has seen beings indulging in the seizing on Mine-making, should, etc. *to*: these beings will no longer seize on Mine-making'. When he courses thus, etc.

Moreover the Bodhisattva, etc. *to*: who has seen beings divided into the four castes, should, etc. *to*: even the words for the four castes will no longer exist'. When he courses thus, etc.

Moreover the Bodhisattva, etc. *to*: who has seen the inferiority, superiority, and middlingness of beings, and (their distribution) into inferior families, middling families, and superior families, should, etc. *to*: those beings will no longer have these faults. When he courses thus, etc.

Moreover the Bodhisattva, etc. *to*: who has seen the difference in the beauty of beings, should, etc. *to*: no difference in the beauty of beings will any longer be or be conceived. But all beings shall be handsome, attractive, good-looking, endowed with the supreme excellence of loveliness and beauty'. When he courses thus, etc.

Moreover the Bodhisattva, etc. *to*: who has seen sovereignty, should, etc. *to*: not even the concept of sovereignty will be known, except with reference to the King of Dharma, the Tathagata, the Arhat, the fully Enlightened One'. When he courses thus, etc.

Moreover the Bodhisattva, etc. *to*: who has seen the differentiation among beings of the places of rebirth, should, etc. *to*: the differentiation of the places of rebirth among beings will not be or be conceived, i.e. the hells, the animal world, the world of Yama, the gods and men. But all beings will be of one karma and not lacking in the four applications of mindfulness, etc. *to*: the four analytical knowledges'.When he courses thus, etc.

Moreover the Bodhisattva, etc. *to*: who has seen the four modes of rebirth of beings, i.e. egg-born, born from a womb, moisture-born or miraculously born, should, etc. *to*: three of these modes of rebirth will not be or be conceived, i.e. the egg-born, those born from a womb and the moisture-born. But all beings will be miraculously born'. When he courses thus, etc.

Moreover the Bodhisattva, etc. *to*: who has seen beings deficient in the five superknowledges, should, etc. *to*: all beings will have the five superknowledges'. When he courses thus, etc.

Moreover the Bodhisattva, etc. *to*: who has seen all beings brought forth among faeces, etc, should, etc. *to*: all beings will be nourished on trance and on joyous zest for the Dharma'. When he courses thus, etc.

Moreover the Bodhisattva, etc. *to*: who has seen beings lacking in halos, should, etc. *to* : each being will have his own halo'. When he courses thus, etc.

Moreover the Bodhisattva, etc. *to*: who has seen among beings (the difference between) night, day, month, half-month and year, should, etc. *to* : even the words for night, day, month, half-month, and year will among those beings not be or be conceived'. When he courses thus, etc.

Moreover the Bodhisattva, etc. *to*: who has seen that beings are shortlived, should, etc. *to* : all beings will have an immeasurable lifespan'. When he courses thus, etc.

Moreover the Bodhisattva, etc. *to* : who has seen that beings are without the marks, should, etc. *to*: beings will be endowed with the thirty-two marks of the Superman'. When he courses thus, etc.

Moreover the Bodhisattva, etc. *to* : who has seen that beings are lacking in wholesome roots, should, etc. *to*: all beings will be endowed with wholesome roots and, as endowed with these wholesome roots, they will attend on the Buddhas, the Lords'. When he courses thus, etc.

Moreover the Bodhisattva, etc. *to*: who has seen beings subject to diseases, should, etc. *to* : beings will not have the four kinds of diseases, i.e. those caused by wind, bile, phlegm, or the disorder of the humours'. When he courses thus, etc.

Moreover the Bodhisattva, etc. *to* : who has seen beings defiled by the three defilements, should, etc. *to*: the three defilements will not be or be conceived. Which three? Greed, hate, and delusion. But all beings will be free from greed, hate, and delusion'. When he courses thus, etc.
Moreover the Bodhisattva, etc. *to* : who has seen beings of inferior resolve, should, etc. *to* : even the words for the two vehicles will not be, i.e. for the Disciple-vehicle or the Pratyekabuddha-vehicle. But all beings will have set out for all-knowledge'. When he courses thus, etc.

Moreover the Bodhisattva, etc. *to*: who has seen conceited beings, should, etc. *to* : even the word 'conceit' will not be, and all beings shall be free from conceit'. When he courses thus, etc.

Moreover Subhuti, the Bodhisattva, the great being, who courses in the six perfections should thus produce a thought : 'For so long shall I not fully know the supreme enlightenment until, when I have known the supreme enlightenment, I will have in that Buddha-field an immeasurable lifespan, an infinite halo, and an infinite congregation of monks'. When he courses thus, etc.

Moreover the Bodhisattva, the great being, who courses in the six perfections should thus consider, 'I will not win full enlightenment before among all the countless Buddha-fields I have at least one single Buddha-field for my own'. When he courses thus, etc.

Moreover, Subhuti, the Bodhisattva, the great being, who courses in the six perfections should consider that 'long standing, surely, is this Samsara, infinite surely is this world of beings!' And he should thus wisely attend to it: 'Bounded by space surely is Samsara, bounded by space surely is this world of beings! Here no one wanders in Samsara, no one wins Parinirvana'. When he courses thus, Subhuti, the Bodhisattva, the great being, fulfills the six perfections and comes near to the knowledge of all modes.

CHAPTER 53

THE PREDICTION OF THE GANGES GODDESS

Thereupon *a goddess from among the gods of the Ganges* came to that assembly and sat down in it. She rose from her seat, put her upper robe over one shoulder, saluted the Lord with folded hands, and said : "I also, O Sugata, when I have coursed in the six perfections, will take hold of such a Buddha-field, as it has been explained by the Tathagata in the *Prajñāpāramitā*."

Thereupon that woman took golden flowers and silvery flowers, flowers from water plants and flowers from land plants, and all the requisite ornaments, as well as golden-coloured and yellow flowers yoked together, and hurled them to where the Lord was. And immediately after she had done so, through the Buddha's might there stood out high up in the firmament above the Lord's head a pointed tower, with four pillars, quadrangular, well-proportioned, enjoyable, pleasing to the mind. And that woman, having made this pointed tower common to all beings, dedicated it to their supreme enlightenment.

Thereupon the Lord, having perceived that woman's resolute intention, on that occasion manifested a smile. But such is the dharmic nature of the Buddhas and Lords that, when they manifest a smile, then various-coloured rays issue from the Lord's mouth—rays blue, yellow, red, white, crimson, crystal, silverish, and golden. Their lustre spread into endless and boundless world systems, and then again returned from there, thrice circulated round the Lord and then vanished in the head of the Lord.

Thereupon the Ven. *Ānanda* rose from his seat, put his upper robe over one shoulder, placed his right hand on the earth, stretched his folded hands towards the Lord, and said to the Lord : What is the cause, what is the reason for this manifestation of a smile? For it is not without cause or reason that the Tathagatas manifest a smile.

The Lord replied : This goddess of the Ganges, Ananda, will in a future period, in the starlike aeon, appear in the world as a fully enlightened Tathagata, 'Golden Flower' by name. This is the last time that this Ganges goddess has been reborn as a woman. She will (in her next birth) cease to be a woman and become a man. He will be reborn in Abhirati, the Buddha-field of the Tathagata Akshobhya and will therein lead the holy life. And that Bodhisattva, that great being, will have the name of 'Golden Flower'. After his decease there he will pass from Buddha-field to Buddha-field, and he will never be without the Buddhas, the

Lords. Just as the universal monarch can pass from palace to palace, without ever, during his entire life up to the time of his death, treading upon the earth with the soles of his feet; just so will that Bodhisattva Golden Flower, that great being, pass from Buddha-field to Buddha-field until he has known the supreme enlightenment.

Thereupon the *Ven. Ānanda* thought to himself: All those Bodhisattvas, great beings, who will be assembled in that Buddha-field should be known as the congregation of the Tathagata?

The Lord read the Ven. Ānanda's thought and said to him: So it is, Ānanda, as you say. That assembly of Bodhisattvas, great beings, should be known as the congregation of the Tathagata. In addition, the community of the disciples in the Buddha-field of the Tathagata Golden Flower will not be bound by any measure, and it will be impossible to measure the extent of his community of disciples by saying that there are so many disciples, or so many hundreds of disciples, or so many thousands of disciples, etc. *to*: or so many hundreds of thousands of niyutes of kotis of disciples. All one can say is that these disciples will be countless, innumerable, and immeasurable. And furthermore, Ananda, in the Buddha-field of the Tathagata Golden Flower, after he has known the supreme enlightenment, these faults which have been enumerated in this *Prajnāpāramitā* will in no way whatsoever either be or be conceived.

Ānanda: Where, O Lord, has that Ganges goddess (first) planted her wholesome root?

The Lord: It was in the presence of the Tathagata Dipankara that she planted her wholesome root, raised her thought to the supreme enlightenment, and dedicated that wholesome root to the supreme enlightenment. It was when, aspiring for the supreme enlightenment, she had scattered golden flowers over the Tathagata Dipankara. That was at the same time when I, aspiring for the supreme enlightenment, strewed five lotus flowers over the Tathagata Dipankara, and when that Tathagata, having known that I was endowed with the requisite roots, predicted my future enlightenment with the words: 'You will in a future period become a Tathagata, Śakyamuni by name—endowed with knowledge and virtue, Well-Gone, a worldknower, unsurpassed, tamer of men to be tamed, teacher of gods and men, a Buddha, a Blessed Lord!' Thereupon when she had heard my prediction, that goddess produced a thought to the effect that: 'Certainly, like that young man I also would like to be predicted to the supreme enlightenment!' It is thus, Ānanda, that that goddess has in the presence of that Tathagata Dipankara raised the first thought to the supreme enlightenment.

Ānanda: This Ganges goddess is one who has made the necessary preparations for the supreme enlightenment.

The Lord: So it is, Ānanda, so it is. As you say, this Ganges goddess has made the necessary preparations for the supreme enlightenment.

Chapter 54

DEMONSTRATION OF THE DEVELOPMENT OF SKILL IN MEANS

IV 11. Training in Skill in Means.

Subhuti: How, O Lord, should the Bodhisattva, the great being who courses in the perfection of wisdom, make a complete conquest of emptiness, how should he achieve the emptiness-concentration? How should the four applications of mindfulness be developed? How should he gain mastery over the right efforts, how should the right efforts be developed? So with: the bases of psychic power, etc. etc.

The Lord: Here, Subhuti, the Bodhisattva, the great being who courses in the perfection of wisdom, should contemplate form, etc. as empty. And he should contemplate in such a way that, when he contemplates, his thought does not get disturbed. With his own thought undisturbed he does not review his own dharmas. Not reviewing his own dharmas, he does not realise. And why? Because that Bodhisattva, that great being, should train in all dharmas as empty of own-marks, and so he does not bring about the separation of any dharma—either of one who would realise, or of one which would realise, or of one through which he would realise. All these dharmas he does not review.

Subhuti: As the Lord has just said: 'empty dharmas should not be realised by the Bodhisattva, the great being.' How then does the Bodhisattva, the great being, who has stood in emptiness, realise emptiness?

The Lord: When, Subhuti, the Bodhisattva, the great being, contemplates the emptiness furnished with the best of all modes, he does not contemplate 'I do realise', 'I will realise' or 'I should realise'; he contemplates: 'I will gain mastery', and not 'I should realise'; he contemplates that 'this is the time for effecting complete conquest and not the time for realization'. Just unconcentrated Bodhisattva, the great being, ties his thought to an objective support. Meanwhile, the Bodhisattva, the great being, does not become destitute of the dharmas which act as wings to enlightenment, but he does not realize the extinction of the outflows. And why? The Bodhisattva, the great being, becomes endowed with an exalted cognition, if, having stood in the dharmas which constitute the wings of enlightenment, he discerns thus: 'This is the time for complete conquest, this is not the time for realisation.' That Bodhisattva, that great being who courses in the perfection of wisdom, should surely contemplate: 'For the six perfections is this the time; for the development of the applications of mindfulness is this the time, etc. *to*: for the development of the Path, of the concentrations on emptiness, the signless and the wishless, for the acquisition of the superknowledges, of the concentrations, etc. *to*: of the four analytical knowledges. But this is not the time for the realisation of the fruit of a Streamwinner, etc. *to*: of the cognition of a Pratyekabuddha. It is the time for the nonrenunciation of the acquisition of the knowledge of all modes'. It is thus, Subhuti, that the Bodhisattva who courses in the perfection of wisdom makes complete conquest of emptiness; and he dwells in emptiness; and so with the signless; of the wishless he makes complete conquest and he dwells in the wishless. He develops the holy eightfold path, but he does not realize (it); etc. *to*: he develops the applications of mindfulness and dwells in them. It is thus, Subhuti, that the Bodhisattva makes complete conquest of the dharmas which constitute the wings of enlightenment, develops them, and dwells through them. But he does not realise the fruit of a Streamwinner, etc. *to*: Arhatship.

IV 11,1–10. THE OBJECTIVE RANGE OF SKILL IN MEANS.

IV 11,1. THE OVERCOMING OF HOSTILE STATES.

Suppose, Subhuti, that there were a man who is a hero, vigorous, of high social position, handsome, attractive, and fair to behold, endowed with the supreme excellence of loveliness and beauty; in archery he has gone as far as one could go, he is successful in warding off all manner of attacks, accomplished in all the sixty-four arts, and foremost in all crafts. He is dear and pleasant to many. Whatever work he may undertake will win him much gain and honour, and for that reason he would be honoured, revered, and worshipped by the manyfolk. More and more he would feel ever increasing joy and zest. Taking his parents and children with him on some business or other, he enters on a wild forest. The foolish among them would feel terror and hair-raising fear. He, however, would fearlessly say to his family: 'Do not be afraid! I will soon get you out of this fearful wild forest. I will protect you and soon set you free!' If then many unfriendly, destructive, hostile, and inimical forces should rise up against him in that wild forest, this heroic man would be endowed with the power of supreme wisdom. Having taken his parents and children out of that fearful forest, having set them free, he will securely and safely reach a village, city or market town, a country district or a place in a country district, and will dwell there full of joy and happiness, unhurt and uninjured. Nor does he become angry in his mind with those hostile and inimical beings. And why? Because he is well skilled in all the arts. In consequence he can in that wild forest conjure up forces which are more powerful than those which oppose him, and all the forces hostile and inimical to him will flee in fright. And thereupon that man will dwell at ease, after he has safely rescued his parents and children. Just so, at the time when a Bodhisattva dwells radiating towards all beings a thought of friendliness, compassion, sympathetic joy, and impartiality, he does not on that occasion through the realisation of the signless concentration get established on the level of the Disciples or the level of the Pratyekabuddhas.

IV11,2. To dwell without support.

A bird on its wings courses in the air and does not fall to the ground. It dwells just in space, just in the air, but it does not stand therein nor does it get established therein. Just so the Bodhisattva achieves mastery over emptiness and dwells in the emptiness; he achieves mastery over the signless and dwells in the signless; he achieves mastery over the wishless and dwells in the wishless. But he does not realise emptiness, the signless, and the wishless in such a way that, as a result of this realisation, he would fall on the level of the Disciples or Pratyekabuddhas, without having completed the ten powers of a Tathagata, etc. *to*: the eighteen Buddhadharmas, the great friendliness and the great compassion. But, having coursed in innumerable Buddhadharmas, he reaches the knowledge of all modes.

IV 11,3. The carrying out of the vows made in the past.

It is as with a powerful master of archery, well-trained in archery. He would first shoot an arrow upwards and would then by a regular succession of other arrows prevent it from falling down on the ground. In fact, the first arrow would not fall down on the ground until that man would decide that it should do so. In order that the first arrow should fall unto the ground, he does not send up the last arrow, with the result that the whole succession of arrows falls unto the ground. In the same way a Bodhisattva, who courses in perfect wisdom and who is upheld by skill in means, does not realise that farthest Reality limit until his wholesome roots are matured in the supreme enlightenment. Only when those wholesome roots are matured in the supreme enlightenment, only then does he realise that farthest Reality limit. Therefore, then, Subhuti, a Bodhisattva, who courses in perfect wisdom, should thus contemplate and meditate the dharmic nature of these dharmas.

IV 11,4. The skill which is uncommon.

Subhuti: A doer of what is hard is the Bodhisattva, if he trains in this Dharmahood, in the Reality limit, in the Dharma-element, etc. *to*: in the three doors to freedom, and yet does not collapse midway before he has known full enlightenment. Wonderful is this, O Lord, most wonderful, O Sugata!

The Lord: For, Subhuti, all beings have not been abandoned by the Bodhisattva, the great being. As he has not abandoned all beings, he can have this extraordinary vow. The Bodhisattva whose thought aspires thus, 'all beings should not be abandoned, by me they should be set free', when he proceeds in dharmas which are not, if he aspires to the concentration of emptiness, the signless, and the wishless, which are the doors to freedom, the Bodhisattva should at that time be known as endowed with skill in means. But he does not midway realise the Reality limit, until he reaches the knowledge of all modes.

IV 11,5. THE SKILL WHICH IS UNATTACHED.

Moreover, Subhuti, when the Bodhisattva, the great being, becomes one who wants to contemplate these very deep stations—i.e. the emptiness of the subject, etc. *to*: the emptiness of the nonexistence of own-being, the four applications of mindfulness, etc. *to*: the holy eightfold path, the three doors to deliverance, his thought should aspire thus: 'For a long time those beings, through the perception of a self, of a being, etc. *to*: of one who feels, course in a basis. So that they may forsake the view of a basis, I will, after I have fully known the utmost, right, and perfect enlightenment, demonstrate dharmas.' At that time the Bodhisattva, the great being, enters into the emptiness-concentration, a door to freedom, but he does not realise the Reality limit, by the realisation of which he would attain the fruit of a Streamwinner, etc. *to*: Pratyekabuddha-enlightenment. At the time when the Bodhisattva, the great being, develops the signless concentration, a door to freedom, at that time he enters the signless concentration, a door to freedom, but does not realise the Reality limit, by the realisation of which he would win the fruit of a Streamwinner, etc. *to*: Arhatship, or Pratyekabuddha-enlightenment. Thus, Subhuti, the Bodhisattva, the great being, endowed with this production of thought, and with these wholesome roots, does not midway realise the Reality limit, nor does he become destitute of the four trances, etc. *to*: the Buddhadharmas. Thus, Subhuti, does the Bodhisattva, the great being, at that time become endowed with all the dharmas which constitute the wings to enlightenment. But he does not fail until he fully knows the utmost, right, and perfect enlightenment. The Bodhisattva, the great being, who has been taken hold of by skill in means, grows in pure dharmas and his faculties become keener, unlike those of Disciples and Pratyekabuddhas.

IV 11,6. THE SKILL WHICH IS WITHOUT BASIS.

Moreover it occurs to the Bodhisattva, the great being: 'For a long time those beings have coursed in the four perverted views, in the notions of permanence, of ease, of loveliness, of self; for their sake I will, when I have known full enlightenment, demonstrate dharma to the effect that they may form the habitual idea that this is impermanent, ill, unlovely, and not-self.' Endowed with this production of thought and with skill in means, he courses in the perfection of wisdom. He does not enter on the concentration of a Buddha before having completed the ten powers of a Tathagata, etc. *to* : the eighteen Buddhadharmas, the great friendliness, and the great compassion. At that time the Bodhisattva develops the doors to deliverance which consist in the concentration on emptiness, the signless and the wishless, and enters upon them, but he does not realise the Reality limit until he fully knows the supreme enlightenment. Moreover the Bodhisattva thinks to himself: 'For a long time these beings have coursed in a basis, i.e. in 'a self, a being, a living soul, etc. *to* : one who does, one who feels, one who knows, one who sees'; in 'form', 'feeling', etc. For them I will act in such a way that, when I have fully known the supreme enlightenment, the beings will not have the faults connected with assuming a basis.' Endowed with these productions of thought and with this skill in means, he courses in perfect wisdom and does not realise the Reality limit, without first having completed the ten powers of a Tathagata, etc. *to* : the great compassion. At that time the door to deliverance which consists in concentration on emptiness reaches for that Bodhisattva the fulness of its development.

IV 11,7. THE SKILL WHICH IS SIGNLESS.

Moreover the Bodhisattva who courses in perfect wisdom, thinks to himself: 'For a long time these beings have coursed in signs, in the signs of women and man, in the signs of form and the formless. For those beings I will act in such a way that, when I have fully known the supreme enlightenment, they will no more have these faults.' Endowed with this production of thought and with this skill in means, he courses in perfect wisdom and does not realise the Reality limit before he has completed the ten powers of a Tathagata, etc. *to* : the great compassion. When he is endowed with that production of thought, then, at that time the door to deliverance which consists in concentration on the signless reaches for the Bodhisattva the fulness of its development.

IV 11,8. THE SKILL WHICH IS WITHOUT WISHES FOR THE FUTURE.

Moreover the Bodhisattva, the great being who courses in perfect wisdom, thinks to himself: 'For a long time these beings, under the influence of hopes for the future, have been eager to become Śakras, Brahmas, world guardians or world rulers. They have been eager for forms, etc. For their sake I will, when I have fully known the full enlightenment, demonstrate Dharma to beings to the effect that they see the faults of having hopes for the future'. When the Bodhisattva, the great being, through these wholesome roots and through this skill in means courses in the perfection of wisdom, then the door to freedom which consists in the concentration on the wishless arrives at the fulness of its development. But he does not realise the Reality limit, without having fulfilled the ten powers, etc. *to* : the great compassion and until he has fully known the supreme enlightenment. It is impossible, it cannot be that a Bodhisattva, a great being who courses in the six perfections, in the various kinds of emptiness, in the four applications of mindfulness, etc. *to* : in the Buddha-dharmas, and who has made a complete conquest and is thus endowed with vision and cognition, should fall into the Uneffected, or become intimate with what belongs to the triple world. That cannot possibly be.

IV 11,9. THE SKILL WHICH IS THE TOKEN OF IRREVERSIBILITY.

Moreover the Bodhisattva, the great being, who courses in the dharmas which act as wings to enlightenment, and makes a complete conquest, may be asked : 'How can a Bodhisattva, who wants to fully know the supreme enlightenment, after he has coursed in the dharmas which act as wings to enlightenment and made a complete conquest, manage not to realise emptiness, or to penetrate the Reality limit, with the result that he might reach the fruit of a Streamwinner, etc. *to*: Pratyekabuddha-enlightenment? How can he realise emptiness, the signless, the wishless, the Uneffected, nonproduction and nonexistence, and how can he develop the perfection of wisdom?' If the Bodhisattva, when thus questioned by Bodhisattvas, would explain that 'just emptiness should be attended to, just the signless, the wishless, the Uneffected, nonproduction and nonexistence should be attended to, and yet all beings should not be abandoned,' then one should know that that Bodhisattva has been predicted by the Buddhas, the Lords to the supreme enlightenment. And why? Because he indicates the complete conquest of an irreversible Bodhisattva, great being, declares and exalts it. If a Bodhisattva, when questioned, explains that 'not should a complete conquest be made of emptiness, of the signless, the wishless, the Uneffected, of nonproduction, of nonexistence; but one should make a complete conquest of the dharmas which act as wings to enlightenment and one should not hang on to all beings', then one should know that this Bodhisattva has not been predicted to the supreme enlightenment. And why? Because he does not indicate the complete conquest of an irreversible Bodhisattva, does not declare or exalt it; and in consequence the Bodhisattvas, the great beings, should know that that Bodhisattva, having made a complete conquest, has transcended the stage of an irreversible Bodhisattva.

IV 11,10. The skill which is unlimited in its objective range.

Subhuti: Is therein some manner in which a Bodhisattva is irreversible?

The Lord: He is irreversible if, having heard the six perfections, he answers as an irreversible Bodhisattva would. He then should by the Bodhisattvas be known as irreversible.

Subhuti: There are, O Lord, many Bodhisattvas who course towards enlightenment, but few only who answer as an irreversible Bodhisattva would, either on the preparatory or the nonpreparatory stage.

The Lord: So it is, Subhuti, so it is. And why? Because few only are the Bodhisattvas who have been predicted to the irreversible stage in which this cognition becomes possible. But those who have been predicted to it, they will give the correct answer. One should know that they have planted splendid wholesome roots, and that the whole world, with its gods, men, and Asuras, cannot overwhelm them.

Chapter 55

THE EXPOSITION OF THE FORSAKING OF DISCRIMINATION.

V. THE FULL UNDERSTANDING AT ITS SUMMIT

V 1. The Characteristics. (Heat).

V 1,1. The characteristic of contemplating all dharmas as similar to a dream.

V 1,2. The characteristic of not producing a thought of longing for the level of the disciples, etc.

Thereupon the *Lord* said to the Ven. Subhuti: Moreover, Subhuti, for the Bodhisattva, the great being, even in his dreams the level of a Disciple or Pratyekabuddha, or anything that belongs to the triple world, does not become an object of his longing, or appears advantageous to him. He beholds all dharmas as like a dream, like an echo, etc. *to*: like a magical creation. But he does not realize (his escape from this illusory world).[1] This, Subhuti, should be known as the irreversible mark of the irreversible Bodhisattva.

V 1,3. The characteristic of having a vision of the Tathagata.

It is another mark if even in his dreams he sees the Tathagata, the Arhat, the fully enlightened Buddha demonstrating Dharma, in the midst of an immensely large assembly, surrounded and revered by monks and nuns, laymen and laywomen, gods, Nagas, Yakshas, Gandharvas, Asuras, Garudas, Kinnaras, and Mahoragas. Having heard this Dharma, he dwells, so as to win the assurance that he will come to understand[2] its meaning, as one who makes progress towards the Dharma and its logical sequence,[3] who makes progress in conformity (with that

[1] *H* 764: He does not realise the Dharma which is really real, so as not to definitely turn his back on the world of beings.

[2] *ājñāsyāmīti*. This is a technical term for the first of a series of 'supramundane' faculties which mark the growth in wisdom. It pertains to the Streamwinners. See *P* 209.

[3] *anudharma*; or 'the method behind' the Dharma. *Ad* f. 232b, *anudharmatā*, *rjes-su mthun-pa'i chos*. For the sense of this phrase see Edgerton s. v. *anudharma, H* 862, PTS Dict. 173b, DN ii 224, iii 119, SN iii 40 sq., AN iii 176, Lamotte, *La Somme du Grand Vèhicule,* II 27, *Bodhisattvabhūmi* 107, *Madhyāntavibhāga* 213-233, W. & M. Geiger, *Pali Dhamma,* 115-118, J. May, *Prasannapadā,* 219.

Dharma) and who courses in its logical sequence. This also should be known as the irreversible mark of an irreversible Bodhisattva.

V 1,4. THE CHARACTERISTIC OF HAVING A PERCEPTION OF THE WONDER-WORKING POWERS OF A BUDDHA.

Moreover even in his dreams the Bodhisattva, the great being, sees the Tathagata rising up high into the air and demonstrating Dharma to the community of monks, endowed with the 32 marks of the superman, as he exhibits the halo extending a fathom (round his body) and manifold miracles, and conjures up magical creations through which he does a Buddha's work in other world systems; this also, Subhuti, should be known as the irreversible mark of an irreversible Bodhisattva.

V 1,5. THE CHARACTERISTIC OF THE PRODUCTION OF A THOUGHT BY WHICH HE DEMONSTRATES DHARMAS AS SIMILAR TO A DREAM.

Moreover if a Bodhisattva even in his dreams feels no fear when confronted with the sacking of a village or city, or some huge conflagration; if he feels no sorrow, fear, terror, or fright, when he sees ferocious wild animals or fierce beasts of prey,[4] or when he perceives that his head is about to be cut off, or sees other fearful and terrible things which bring suffering, mental agony, and despair, sees those who are hungry and thirsty, sees the death of his mother or father, his brother or sister, of those dear to him, of his relatives and kinsmen; but if immediately on waking up from his dream he reflects that 'like a dream indeed is all this that belongs to the triple world! And when I have woken up to full enlightenment, I shall demonstrate that all dharmas in the triple world are like a dream!', then, this also, Subhuti, should be known as the irreversible mark of an irreversible Bodhisattva.

V 1,6. THE CHARACTERISTIC OF THE RECOLLECTION[5] BY WHICH HE ABOLISHES THE STATES OF WOE IN HIS OWN BUDDHA-FIELD.

Moreover, Subhuti, how can one discern that in the Buddha-field of the irreversible Bodhisattva, when he has become a fully enlightened Buddha, the three states of woe will in no way whatsoever be? If that Bodhisattva, when he has in ((f. 216a)) his dream seen hellish beings, or animal beings, or beings in the world of Yama,[6] turns his mindful attention upon them[7] and thinks to himself, 'thus will I act, thus will I progress that, when I have known full enlightenment, in my Buddha-field these three states of

[4]*cāṇḍālamṛgajātāni, gcan-gzan khro-bo'i rigs dag*; more likely = *caṇḍa*, as in *Mhvy. A* xx 381, *ksudramṛgajātīn*.

[5]*smṛti = anusmaraṇa H.*

[6]*yamalaukikān*; A xx 382: *preta-gatān.*

[7]*evaṃ* (*'di lta-bu' i*) *smṛtiṃ pratilabhate.*

woe will in no way whatsoever be!' And why? Because the state of dreaming and the state of being awake, all that is (dharmically) not two nor divided. This also, Subhuti, should be known as the irreversible mark of an irreversible Bodhisattva.

V 1,7. THE CHARACTERISTIC OF THE SUCCESS IN THE SUSTAINING POWER OF THE TRUTH,[8] WHEN ONE APPEASES A CONFLAGRATION IN A CITY, ETC.

Moreover, Subhuti, a Bodhisattva, a great being, may, either in his sleep or on waking up from it, see a town on fire[9] and think to himself, 'if I have the attributes, tokens, and signs which I have seen in my dream or on waking up from it as those with which an irreversible Bodhisattva, great being, is endowed, then, because of this Truth, because of the enunciation of this Truth, let that town fire be appeased, cooled down, and extinguished!' If that fire is then appeased, cooled down, and extinquished, then one should know that that Bodhisattva has been predicted as irreversible from the supreme enlightenment. If, however, that mass of fire, overpowering this anunciation of the Truth, spreads from house to house, from road to road, if it burns some houses and not others, some roads and not others, then, Subhuti, one should know that the Bodhisattva must at some time have heaped up a karma conducive to the rejection of Dharma by these beings,[10] and through that the houses of some of these beings now burn while others do not. It is their karma which now matures in this very life; it is the karma left over from the rejection of Dharma which now comes to fruition. This is the cause of a Bodhisattva's irreversibility, this is its condition. Through these causes and conditions should the irreversible Bodhisattva, great being, be known.

V 1,8. THE CHARACTERISTIC OF ACCOMPLISHING A TRUTHFUL UTTERANCE WHICH INDUCES GHOSTS, SUCH AS YAKSHAS, ETC. TO GO AWAY.

And once more, Subhuti, I will demonstrate the attributes, tokens, and signs by which an irreversible Bodhisattva, great being, should be

[8]*satyādhiṣṭhāna*. This refers to the Indian belief that an "Act of Truth" is all-powerful and irresistible. It is a formal declaration of fact, accompanied by a command or resolution or prayer, that the purpose of the agent shall be accomplished. cf. 2 Kings I 10-12, Elijah: "If I be a man of God, then let fire come down from heaven to consume thee and thy men with thee!", and with that, came fire from heaven, and he and his fifty were consumed. For further information see JRAS 1917, 429-467. JAOS 1944. *Milindapañha* 119-123.

[9]so *AdT*: *groṅ-khyer tshig-pa mthoṅ na*.

[10]*ebhiḥ sattvaiḥ, AdT*: *sems-can 'di-dag-gis*; not in *A* where it is the Bodhisattva who has rejected the Dharma. *H* 767: His previous rejection of the Good Law matures in this life when he experiences sadness from seeing the ineffectiveness of his Act of Truth. The Large *Prajñāpāramitā* seems, however, to feel that justice demands that these persons who lose their houses through fire should also in some way be karmically responsible for their misfortune.

known. If some woman or man were possessed by[11] a ghost, then the Bodhisattva should think to himself: 'If it is true that the Tathagatas of the past have predicted me to full enlightenment, then to the extent that my earnest intention to win full enlightenment, and my attention to it, are perfectly pure, to that extent I have left behind the thoughts of the Disciples and Pratyekabuddhas, and I surely will win full enlightenment! Nor shall I not win full enlightenment! Surely, I shall win full enlightenment![12]. There is nothing that the Buddhas and Lords who reside in countless world systems and demonstrate Dharma have not cognized, seen, known, realized, or fully known. I am sure to win full enlightenment, for these Buddhas and Lords know my earnest intention to do so. ((f. 216b)) By this Truth, by this enunciation of the Truth may that ghost depart who possesses and torments this woman or man!' If as a result of this utterance of the Bodhisattva the ghost does not depart, then one should know that that Bodhisattva has not been predicted by the former Tathagatas to full enlightenment. But if he departs one should know that the Bodhisattva has had his prediction to full enlightenment. As endowed with these attributes, tokens, and signs should the irreversible Bodhisattva, great being, be known.

(*Mara's Deeds*).[13] Moreover, in connection with the sustaining power of the Truth, Mara, the Evil One, may approach a Bodhisattva unpractised in the six perfections, deficient in skill in means, unpractised in the four applications of mindfulness, etc. *to*: in the doors to freedom which consist in Emptiness, the Signless, and the Wishless, and who has not entered on a Bodhisattva's specific course of salvation. When the Bodhisattva effects his Act of Truth, i.e. 'by this Truth, by the enunciation of the Truth that the Tathagatas of the past have predicted my full enlightenment, may that ghost depart!', then Mara, the Evil One, will eagerly try himself to remove the ghost. And why? As Mara's efforts become ever more forceful and vehement, in the end the ghost will actually be removed by Mara's power; but the Bodhisattva will think to himself, 'it is through my might that that ghost has departed!', and will fail to cognize that his departure was in fact due to Mara's might. In consequence he will despise other Bodhisattvas, deride, mock, condemn, and depreciate them, in the belief that he himself has been predicted to full enlightenment by the Tathagatas of the past, but those others have not. As he grows in conceit and produces (thoughts of) conceit, so he moves far away from the knowledge of all modes, from the utmost Buddha-cognition. When such a being, so greatly lacking in skill in means, produces this kind of excessive conceit,

[11]*AdT*: *byin-gyis rlabs* (*adhiṣṭhāna*) *śin babs-par gyur* (*āviṣṭa*).

[12]The construction of this sentence is obscure, and I have understood it as in my translation of *A* xx 384.

[13]This corresponds to the beginning of *A* ch. XXI.

then two levels may be expected of him. Which two? The level of the Disciples or that of the Pratyekabuddhas. It is thus that a deed of Mara will arise to that Bodhisattva through the sustaining power of the Truth. He will omit to tend, love, and honour the good spiritual friends, and thus he will further tighten the hold which Mara has over him. And why? Because he has not practised the six perfections, because he has not been taken hold of by skill in means. This also should be known by the Bodhisattva, the great being, as Mara's deed.

And how is it that Mara, the Evil One, approaches the Bodhisattva in connection with the prediction of his name,[14] if the Bodhisattva is unpractised in the six perfections, etc. *to* : has not entered on a Bodhisattva's special way of salvation? Here Subhuti, Mara, the Evil One approaching the Bodhisattva in some guise or other, will say to him : 'You, son of good family, have by the Tathagata ((f. 217a)) been predicted to the supreme enlightenment. This is your name, these the names of your mother, father, brother, sister, friends, relatives, kinsmen, and relations.' Backwards through seven generations he will recite the names of your parents, and he will tell you the country and region from which you have come, as well as the country, town, or village in which you were born. If the Bodhisattva has a dull nature, he will tell him that also in the past he has been dull; if he is keen, he will claim that likewise in the past he was keen. If the Bodhisattva is a forest dweller, or begs his food from door to door without accepting invitations, or wears clothes made of rags taken from dust heaps, or never eats any food after midday, or eats his meal in one sitting, or lives on alms food,[15] or lives in and frequents cemeteries, or lives in an open unsheltered place, or dwells at the foot of a tree, or even in his sleep remains in a sitting posture, or sleeps at night wherever he may happen to be, or possesses no more than three robes,[16] if he has few wishes, is easily contented, quite detached, etc. *to*: wise, frugal, soft in his speech[17] or soft in his talk[18]—in each case Mara will tell him that also in the past he has had the same quality. And why? Because since you have these ascetic practices now, you must in all certainly have

[14]*nāma-adhiṣṭhāna*. *A* xxi 386 distinguishes the *nāma-apadeśa* and the *nāma-adhiṣṭhāna*. The first is the annunciation of the name which the Bodhisattva will have as a Buddha. This takes place at the 'prediction', in the case of Śākyamuni at the time of Dipaṅkara. This second is the announcement of other details and circumstances connected with the annunciation of the name, such as the name of his mother, etc. (*H*). Since the connection with the normal meaning of *adhiṣṭhāna* is not immediately obvious, the Tibetan sometimes translates *miṅ-la brten-pa* (at *A* xxi 387), or *miṅ-gi gshi-las,* at *R* xxi 2. The whole subject requires further investigation.

[15]*prāptapiṇḍiko, pattapiṇḍika* in Pali, but not in other Buddhist Sanskrit documents.

[16]This gives 12 ascetic practices, as against the 13 of the Pali tradition. Most of the above terms are explained in *H* 774-5.

[17]*mandabhāṣyo, smra-ba ñuṅ-ba.*

[18]*mandamantro, brjod-pa ñuṅ-ba.*

undergone the austerities also in the past. Through that previous annunciation of his name and clan, and through this persent assurance that he has undergone the austerities of the ascetic practices, he will produce conceitedness. And Mara, the Evil One, aware of his foolishness, will approach him and say: 'Predicted you are, son of good family, by the Tathagata to a state of irreversibility from the supreme enlightenment, because you have[19] the qualities necessary for it.'[19] Sometimes he will approach in the guise of a monk, sometimes in that of a nun, or a householder, or his mother or father, and he will say: 'Predicted you are, son of good family, by the Tathagata to the supreme enlightenment. And why? Because you have the qualities of an irreversible Bodhisattva'. But those modes, tokens, and signs of an irreversible Bodhisattva which I have declared, they do not exist in that Bodhisattva. One should know, Subhuti, that this Bodhisattva, compared with those other Bodhisattvas,[20] is truly under Mara's influence. And why? Because the modes, tokens, and signs of an irreversible Bodhisattva do not exist in him. As a result of this annunciation of his name he will despise other Bodhisattvas, deride, mock, condemn, and depreciate them. This also should be known as a deed of Mara which happens to a Bodhisattva through the prediction of his name. Here is another deed of Mara which may happen to a Bodhisattva through the prediction of his name. And how? For here the Bodhisattva, who does not course in the six perfections, does not cognize the Skandha-Mara,[21] because he does not cognize form, feelings, perceptions, impulses, and consciousness. And to him ((217b)) Mara, the Evil One, will predict that 'when you have known full enlightenment you shall have this name!' When thereupon that Bodhisattva ponders and reflects on this name, then to him, who is stupid and without skill in means it occurs that 'just this very name which I thought of in my own mind, just that will be my name when I have known full enlightenment'. He follows the suggestions of Mara, the Evil One, or the deities of Mara's host, or a monk who is under Mara's influence, and thinks to himself: 'The name of which I have thought in my own mind, and that which has been indicated to me by that monk, they are the same; that is the name under which I have been predicted by that Tathagata to the supreme enlightenment'. But those modes, tokens, and signs of an irreversible Bodhisattva which I have declared, they do not exist in that Bodhisattva. Devoid of them he will, as a result of this annunciation of his name and prediction, look down on the other Bodhisattvas, great beings. Through

[19]'performed the ascetic practices', *S. AdT.*

[20]? *tad anyair bodhisattvair*; 'he should be known by the other Bodhisattvas': *A* xxi 388, *de-la ... gshan-gyis*, but *AdT*: *de-las gshan-pa' i.*

[21]Māra appears in four different forms, as 1. the defilements, 2. the skandhas, 3. death, and 4. as a divinity of the heavenly host.

his contemptuousness he remains far from full enlightenment. Of him who is lacking in skill in means, in perfect wisdom, and in the good spiritual friends, two levels should be expected, i.e. that of a Disciple or Pratyekabuddha. Or, alternatively, he will only after erring and wandering about in Samsara for a long time, for a good long time, know full enlightenment thanks to this very perfection of wisdom. But if the Bodhisattva does not repeatedly win good spiritual friends—to observe, obey, and honour—and if in his new incarnation[22] he does not censure his former ideas and see their error,[23] then only two levels can be expected of him, i.e. that of a Disciple or Pratyekabuddha. Among the monks who follow the vehicle of the Disciples anyone guilty of any of the four capital offences[24] ceases to be a monk, a Śramana, a son of the Sakya, and cannot, while in this body, gain any of the four fruits of a Śramana. More serious still are the ideas[25] associated with conceitedness which a Bodhisattva has because of the annunciation of his name, and which make him despise other Bodhisattvas and look down on them. In this way subtle deeds of Mara take place as a result of this annunciation of the name. Not only more serious than the four capital offences, but even than the five deadly sins[26] are these conceited ideas which stem from the annunciation of the name.

Moreover by way of declaring the virtues of detachment Mara, the Evil One, approaches the Bodhisattva and says: 'The Tathagata has spoken in praise of detachment'. But I, Subhuti, do not speak of the detachment of a Bodhisattva in the way of his residing in the remote forest, in forest jungle, or in far-away places. ((f. 218a))

Subhuti: What then is a Bodhisattva's detachment, if it is different from his residing in the remote forest, in forest jungle, or in far-away places?

The Lord: If a Bodhisattva becomes detached from attentions associated with the Disciples and Pratyekabuddhas, then he dwells detached, though not in the remote forest, forest jungle, or far-away places. If he dwells day and night in the detachment which I have enjoined, then the Bodhisattva dwells truly detached. And the detachment which I have enjoined for the Bodhisattvas differs from that which Mara, the Evil One, recommends, and which consists in residing in the remote forest,

[22]*ātmabhāvapratilābhena, lus rñed-pa*; *A* xxi 390, *-pratilambhena, lus yoṅs-su grub-pa,* 'in his new-found outlook on life'?

[23]'confesses his fault', which lay in having held them.

[24]*mūla=pradhāna H* 779. They are: murder, theft. unchastity, and false claims to 'superhuman states or the fulness of the insight of the Saints'. In the *Prātimokṣasūtra* they are the four offences which are punished by expulsion from the order of monks.

[25]*cittotpādo*.

[26]Murder of mother, father, or an Arahant; causing dissension in the order of monks; deliberately causing a Tathagata's blood to flow.

in forest jungle, in far-away places. He who is contaminated by that detachment, who is not lacking in the attentions associated with the level of the Disciples and Pratyekabuddhas, who does not apply himself to the perfection of wisdom, he will not fulfill the knowledge of all modes. His attentions are by no means perfectly pure, and yet he looks down on those other Bodhisattvas who dwell near a village, although their attentions are perfectly pure and uncontaminated by Disciple-thoughts, Pratyekabuddha-thoughts, or any other ideas, and they have reached the full comprehension of the trances, emancipations, concentrations, attainments and superknowledges.[27] But that Bodhisattva who has no skill in means—though he may spend up to hundreds of thousands of niyutas of kotis of years or more, in wild forests, hundreds of miles wide, with no other company than[28] beasts of prey, deer and birds, thieves and outcasts, snakes, Rakshasas and a few stray hunters—he will still not cognize this detachment[29] by which Bodhisattvas dwell as having set out with earnest intention. But contaminated is that Bodhisattva and polluted when he leans on this kind of detachment, clings to it and is bent on it. He will not gladden my heart with such thoughts as these. But that which I have declared to be the detachment of Bodhisattvas, that does not appear in him who is endowed with this kind of detachment. And why? Because he is without it. And to him Mara, the Evil One, standing high up in the air, will say: 'Well done, well done, son of good family! This is the true detachment which the Tathagata has declared. Do dwell in it! Then you shall quickly know full enlightenment!' He now proudly imagines that his kind of detachment is the most valuable of all, returns to the neighbourhood of a village, and despises the monks belonging to the vehicle of the Bodhisattvas who live there, although their thoughts and mental activities are perfectly pure, and although they are well behaved and lovely in character; and he believes that they dwell in a contaminated dwelling. He exhorts those Bodhisattvas who dwell in (true) detachment ((f. 218b)) to live in what is in fact a contaminated,[30] a crowded[31] dwelling. But those who live in a contaminated dwelling, he credits with dwelling in detachment and feels respect for them. But where he ought to feel respect, there he feels pride. And why? Because he imagines, 'ghosts exhort me, ghosts inform me! How can this happen to one living near a village?' It is thus that the Bodhisattva despises other sons of good family who belong to the Bodhisattva-vehicle. This person should be known as an outcast among Bodhisattvas,[32] a defamer of

[27]So *AdT*.

[28]*anapagata*; *A, P*: *apagata*, 'without even the company of'; *AdT*: *med-pa*.

[29]which is the result of the perfection of wisdom and of skill in means. *H*.

[30]by the ideas of the Disciples, etc. *H*.

[31]as lying outside the Mahayana. *H*.

[32]because other Bodhisattvas do not wish to have any contact with him. *H*.

Bodhisattvas,[33] a counterfeit Bodhisattva,[34] a thief [35] of the world with its gods, men and Asuras in the guise of a Śramana. Sons and daughters of good family who belong to the vehicle of the Bodhisattvas should not tend, love, or honour such a person. And why? Because, Subhuti, he must be regarded as greatly conceited.

V 1,9. The characteristic of courageously advancing on one's own initiative to the higher knowledge, and of tending the good spiritual friend.

A Bodhisattva, a great being, who has not abandoned the knowledge of all modes or the supreme enlightenment, that Bodhisattva, that great being, who earnestly intends to know full enlightenment and to work the weal of all beings, should not tend such persons, love, or honour them. But he should devote himself to his own welfare,[36] always alarmed at Samsara and afraid of it, unsubmerged by the triple world. And even towards outcast Bodhisattvas he should also produce a thought of friendliness, of compassion, of sympathetic joy, of impartiality. He should produce a thought, 'thus will I act that in future all these faults of mine shall in no way whatsoever either happen or be produced. And if they should be produced, I will train myself to quickly forsake them!' This should be known as the courageous advance of these Bodhisattvas towards their own higher knowledge.[37] Furthermore the Bodhisattva, the great being, who earnestly intends to know the utmost, right, and perfect enlightenment, should tend, love, and honour the good spiritual friends.

Subhuti: Who, then, O Lord, should be known as the good spiritual friends of the Bodhisattvas, the great beings?

The Lord: The Buddhas, the Lords should be known as the good spiritual friends of the Bodhisattvas, the great beings; and so should the Bodhisattvas, the great beings, and also the Disciples; and so should those who tell them about[38] the six perfections. ((219a)) Moreover, the six perfections should be known as the good spiritual friends of the Bodhisattvas, the great beings; and so should the four applications of mindfulness, etc. *to*: the 18 special Buddhadharmas; and also Suchness, the Reality limit and the Dharma-element. Moreover the six perfections

[33]because he defames, or disgraces, his own thought of enlightenment, and that of others. *H.*

[34]because he is devoid of the attributes (*dharma*) of a Bodhisattva. *H.*

[35]because he enjoys his alms without any proper justification. *H.*

[36]*AdT*: *raṅ-gi don sbyar-ba-la rjes-su brtson-par bya'o.*

[37]*svayam-abhijñā-parākramo.* Wogihara's edition of *A*, p. 784, reads *abhijñāya*. But the Tibetan, both at *A* and *AdT* has *raṅ-gi mṅon-par śes-pas*, 'by, or through, their own higher knowledge'.

[38]The text here gives eight synonyms.

should be known as the teachers of the Bodhisattvas, the great beings; they are the Path, the Light, the torch, the illumination, the intelligence, the sagacity, the wisdom; the six perfections are the protection of the Bodhisattvas, the great beings, their refuge and final relief; they are the parents of the Bodhisattvas, the great beings.[39] The four applications of mindfulness (should be known as the teachers of the Bodhisattvas, the great beings) etc. *to* :[40] the knowledge of all modes is conducive to the forsaking of all the defilements together with their residues. And why? These dharmas which constitute the wings to enlightenment[41] were the parents also of those Buddhas and Lords who were Tathagatas in the past period; they will be the parents of those Buddhas and Lords who will be Tathagatas in a future period; and they are also the parents of those Buddhas and Lords who just now in the world systems in the ten directions stand, hold, and maintain themselves. And why? Because from these dharmas have issued the past, future, and present Buddhas and Lords. Therefore, then, Subhuti, the Bodhisattva, the great being who wants to win full enlightenment, to purify the Buddha-field, to mature beings, should win over beings through the four means of conversion. Which four? Through gifts, kind words, helpfulness, and consistency between words and deeds. Surveying also this reasoning, Subhuti, I say: These dharmas which are the wings to enlightenment are of the Bodhisattvas, the great beings, the teachers, the parents, the place of rest, the refuge, and the final relief.

V 1,10. THE CHARACTERISTIC OF TRAINING IN PERFECT WISDOM IN ALL MANNERS AND WAYS.

Therefore, then, Subhuti, the Bodhisattva, the great being, who wants to go to a state where he cannot be led astray by others, and to maintain himself in it, who wants to terminate the uncertainties of all beings, to purify the Buddha-field and to mature beings, should train himself in just this perfection of wisdom. And why? Because here in this perfection of wisdom those dharmas are pointed out in detail in which the Bodhisattva, the great being, should train.

V 1,11. THE CHARACTERISTIC OF NOT SETTLING DOWN IN ANYTHING.

Subhuti: How is the perfection of wisdom marked?

The Lord: Like space, the perfection of wisdom is marked by non-

[39]Most of these terms are explained by *H* on p. 787.

[40]The *yāvat* represents a long list in *S*. This seems to suggest that *Ad* is later than *S* and represents a contraction of it.

[41]The later Mss give their number as 37, i.e. the 4 applications of mindfulness, 4 right efforts, 4 roads to psychic power, 5 dominants (or 'cardinal virtues'), 5 powers, 7 limbs of enlightenment, 8 limbs of the Path.

attachment.[42] But the perfection of wisdom is not a mark ((f. 219b)) nor does it have one.

Subhuti : Might perhaps all dharmas exist[42a] through that mark through which the perfection of wisdom exists[42a]?"

The Lord: So it is, Subhuti, so it is. All dharmas exist by just that mark by which the perfection of wisdom exists. And why? Because all dharmas are isolated in their own-being, empty of their own-being. In that way all dharmas exist through the mark by which the perfection of wisdom exists, i.e. through the mark of emptiness, the mark of isolatedness.

Subhuti: If all dharmas are isolated from all dharmas, if all dharmas are empty of all dharmas, how then can the defilement and purification of beings be conceived? Because what is isolated is not defiled or purified. Emptiness is not defiled or purified. Neither the isolated nor emptiness fully knows the utmost, right, and perfect enlightenment. The isolated cannot apprehend any dharma in emptiness. The isolated cannot apprehend in emptiness any being who knows full enlightenment. How then shall we understand the meaning of this teaching?

The Lord: What do you think, Subhuti, do beings for a long time course in I-making and Mine-making?

Subhuti: So they do, O Lord.

The Lord: Are then I-making and Mine-making isolated and empty?

Subhuti: Yes, they are.

The Lord: Is it because of I-making and Mine-making that beings run and wander about in birth-and-death?

Subhuti: So it is, O Lord.

The Lord: It is surely thus that the defiling of beings is conceived. No I-making and Mine-making and in consequence no taking up. No taking up, and then no beings run and wander about in birth-and-death. And so there is no defilement. In the same way should the purification of beings be conceived.

V 1,12. THE CHARACTERISTIC OF BEING NEAR THE ENLIGHTENMENT OF A BUDDHA.

Subhuti: Thus coursing, the Bodhisattva does not course in form, etc.; not in the applications of mindfulness, etc. *to* : not in the 18 special Buddhadharmas. And why? Because there all those dharmas are not apprehended—he who courses, that whereby he courses, that wherein he would course. When he courses thus, the Bodhisattva, the great being, cannot be crushed by the whole world with its gods, men and Asuras or surpassed by any of the Disciples or Pratyekabuddhas. And why? Because

[42] *A* xii 400 omits "like space" and has only *asaṅga-lakṣaṇā* = *anabhiniveśa-svabhāvā, H.*
[42a] *saṃvidyate*; or 'is found', 'be found'.

this Bodhisattva's special way of salvation is an insuperable position. For unsurpassable is the Bodhisattva who is not devoid of attentions to the knowledge of all modes. ((f. 220a))

V 2. The Growth. (Summits).

V2,1. THE GROWTH OF THIS MERIT IS SUPERIOR TO THAT WHICH THE BEINGS OF JAMBUDVIPA, ETC. GAIN FROM HONOURING THE TATHAGATAS, ETC.

The Lord: If, Subhuti, all beings in Jambudvipa should acquire a human personality, and thereafter know full enlightenment; and suppose that some son or daughter of good family should all their lives honour, revere, adore, and worship them, and should dedicate the merit thus gained[43] to the supreme enlightenment—would they on the strength of that beget much merit?

Subhuti: They would, O Lord.

The Lord: A greater merit does that son or daughter of good family beget who demonstrates[44] the perfection of wisdom to others, and dwells in attentions associated with it. Likewise, if a son or daughter of good family should establish all beings in the great trichiliocosm, after they have acquired a human personality, in the ten paths of wholesome action, in the four trances, the four Unlimited, the four formless attainments, etc. *to*: in the fruit of a Streamwinner, etc. *to*: in Pratyekabuddhahood, and in full enlightenment, and would dedicate the merit thus gained to the supreme enlightenment—would they on the strength of that beget much merit?

Subhuti: They would, O Lord.

The Lord: A greater merit does that son or daughter of good family beget who demonstrates the perfection of wisdom to others, and dwells in attentions associated with the knowledge of all modes. He then reaches a cognition where he becomes worthy of the donations of all beings.[45] And why? No other being has such a dwelling as the Bodhisattva, the great being, except of course the Tathagata. And why? Because these sons of good family, when they course in the perfection of wisdom, aspire for the great friendliness, and see all beings as on the way to their slaughter; they aspire for the great compassion. Dwelling in that dwelling, they rejoice with the great sympathetic joy, and aspire for the great sympathetic joy. But they do not become intimate with that sign,[46] but acquire the great impartiality. This, Subhuti, is of those Bodhisattvas, the great

[43]literally: 'that wholesome root'.

[44]The text here gives 8 synonyms.

[45]i.e. *puṇyakṣetratāṃ pratipadyate*. *H*.

[46]*A* xxii 403: "But he does not make either this, or anything else, into a sign to which he becomes partial". *Sārdhaṃ saṃvasati* also at *A* xx 379. *P* f. 275.

light of wisdom—the light of the six perfections. Even before they are fully enlightened they become worthy of the donations of all beings, for they do not turn away from full enlightenment. Dwelling in attentions associated with the perfection of wisdom, they purify[47] the donations of those who give them the requisites of life, ((220b)) and they are near the knowledge of all modes. Therefore, then, Subhuti, the Bodhisattva should constantly and always dwell in this mental work associated with perfect wisdom, if he does not want to consume his alms fruitlessly, if he wants to point out the path to all beings, to shed light over a wide range, to liberate the beings imprisoned in the triple world, to produce the supreme Eye of Wisdom in all beings. If the Bodhisattva dwells in these attentions associated with perfect wisdom, he should also preach sermons associated with the perfection of wisdom.

V2,2. In its distinctive own-being the growth consists in attentions to the perfection of wisdom.

When he has preached sermons associated with the perfection of wisdom, he should dwell in just these attentions associated with the perfection of wisdom, and give no opportunity to other mental activities. Day and night he should persistently dwell in just these attentions associated with the perfection of wisdom. If a man had newly acquired a very precious gem, he would be overjoyed. If he lost it again, he would be most sad and distressed. Constantly and always mental activities associated with that precious gem would proceed in him, and he would regret being parted from it. Just so should the Bodhisattva, the great being, recognizing this (perfect wisdom) as a precious jewel, not lack in attentions associated with the knowledge of all modes.

Subhuti: Since, however, all mental activities are lacking in own-being, are empty of own-being, how then can the Bodhisattva become one who is not lacking in acts of attention associated with the knowledge of all modes? For how can one apprehend the Bodhisattva, his acts of attention and the knowledge of all modes, in that which is deprived of them?[48]

The Lord: If the Bodhisattva cognizes thus: 'devoid of own-being are all dharmas; they have not been made by the Disciples, nor by the Pratyekabuddhas, nor even by the Buddhas, the Lords; but just a fact is the Dharmahood of these dharmas, the established order of Dharma, the fixed sequence of dharmas, the Suchness, nonfalseness, unaltered Suchness, the Dharma-element, the Reality limit', then the Bodhisattva

[47]*samyak-phalavatīṃ kurvanti. H.*

[48]*virahite, AdT*: *'bral-ba-la.*—The authors of the *Prajñāpāramitā* were rather fond of disquisitions in which they juggle with the words *virahita, avirahita, viharati* and *manasikāra.* It is almost impossible to do them justice in English.

is not lacking in perfect wisdom. ((221a)) And why? Because this perfection of wisdom is in its own-being isolated and empty, and it neither increases nor decreases.[49]

V2,3. THE GROWTH WHICH IN ITS OWN FORM IS THE GAINING OF THE PREEMINENT PATIENT ACCEPTANCE OF THAT WHICH FAILS TO BE PRODUCED.

Subhuti: If, O Lord, the perfection of wisdom in its own-being is isolated and empty, how is it that the Bodhisattva, the great being, thanks to the full possession of the perfection of wisdom[50] wins full enlightenment?

The Lord: When in full possession of the perfection of wisdom, the Bodhisattva, the great being, neither increases nor decreases; nor does the Reality limit or the Dharma-element. And why? Because the perfection of wisdom is neither one nor two. If the Bodhisattva, when this is being taught, is not cowed, does not lose heart, and remains unafraid, then one can be quite certain that he stands in the irreversible element,[51] and is in fact one who courses in perfect wisdom.

Subhuti: Is it, then, this emptiness of the perfection of wisdom, its nullity, insignificance, voidness and insubstantiality,[52] which courses in perfect wisdom?

The Lord: No, Subhuti.

Subhuti: Can one, then, outside the perfection of wisdom apprehend a dharma which courses in perfect wisdom?

The Lord: No, Subhuti.

Subhuti: Does, then, perhaps the perfection of wisdom course in perfect wisdom?

The Lord: No, Subhuti.

Subhuti: Does, then, perhaps the emptiness course in emptiness?

The Lord: No, Subhuti.

Subhuti: Does, then, perhaps something outside emptiness course in perfect wisdom?

The Lord: No, Subhuti.

Subhuti: Do, then, the skandhas course in perfect wisdom?

The Lord: No, Subhuti.

[49]*H* 796: The perfection of wisdom is empty and in actual fact devoid of growth and diminution. When the attention makes the emptiness of all dharmas into its object, the fact that it is turned on emptiness guarantees its unpervertedness (see *P* 198), and in that sense the perfection of wisdom is not lacking in attention.

[50]*prajñāpāramitāyāṃ samudāgamya*; *AdT*: *śes-rab-kyi pha- rol-tu phyin-pa-la yaṅ-dag-par bsgrub-par bgyis*; *A* xxii 405, *bodhaye* (*byaṅ-c̱hub-kyi-phyir*) *samudāgacchati*, "how can a Bodhisattva arrive, without an increase in perfect wisdom, at the full attainment of enlightenment?"

[51]*AdT*: stage, or, level.

[52]For a definition of these terms see *H* 706.

Subhuti: Do, then, the six perfections course in perfect wisdom, etc. *to*: do the 18 special dharmas of a Buddha course in perfect wisdom?

The Lord: No, Subhuti.

Subhuti: Does, then, the emptiness of form, its nullity, vanity, insubstantiality, Suchness, nonfalseness, unaltered Suchness, its Dharmahood, Dharma-element, fixed sequence of Dharma, Reality limit, course in the perfection of wisdom?

The Lord: No, Subhuti.

Subhuti: Does, then, the emptiness, etc. *to*: Reality limit of all dharmas up to the 18 special Buddhadharmas course in the perfection of wisdom?

The Lord: No, Subhuti.

Subhuti: If, O Lord, these dharmas do not course in perfect wisdom, how then again does the Bodhisattva, the great being, course in perfect wisdom?

The Lord: What do you think, Subhuti, do you review that dharma which ((f. 221b)) courses in the perfection of wisdom?

Subhuti: No, O Lord.

The Lord: What do you think, Subhuti, do you review[53] that perfection of wisdom in which the Bodhisattva should course?

Subhuti: No, O Lord.

The Lord: What do you think, Subhuti, can one perhaps apprehend that dharma which you do not review?

Subhuti: No, O Lord.

The Lord: What do you think, Subhuti, that dharma which one cannot apprehend, will that be produced or stopped?

Subhuti: No, O Lord.

The Lord: This, Subhuti, is of the Bodhisattvas, the great beings, the patient acceptance of dharmas which fail to be produced.[54] Endowed with this kind of patience, a Bodhisattva is predicted by the Buddhas, the Lords to the supreme enlightenment. He is bound to progress to the Tathagata's grounds of self-confidence and his analytical knowledges.[55] When he thus courses, thus strives, and struggles, then it is quite impossible that the Bodhisattva should not reach the cognition of the supremely enlightened Buddhas, the great cognition, the cognition of the knowledge of all modes. And why? Because that Bodhisattva has attained the patient acceptance of dharmas which fail to be produced. And he cannot lose any of these dharmas[56] until he has known full enlightenment.

[53]*tattvato, H.*

[54]*sarvadharmānupalambhād eva paramārtha-dvāreṇa-anupapattau māyopama-bhāvanayā saṃvṛtyā caraṇād anutpattikeṣu dharmeṣu viśiṣṭādhimuktir bhavati. H.*

[55]The sense is none too clear, and the text is here corrupt. I follow *AdT* and *A*.

[56]*AdT*: because he will remain intent on it (*gshol-bar*=*nimna*).

V2,4. THE GROWTH WHICH HAS FOR ITS MARK THE FACT THAT IT OFFERS NO BASIS FOR THE APPREHENSION OF THE REAL EXISTENCE OF THE PERSONS WHO WIN ENLIGHTENMENT, OR OF THE DHARMA WHICH IS KNOWN TO ENLIGHTENMENT.

Subhuti: Is it, then, for the production[57] of all dharmas that a Bodhisattva is predicted to full enlightenment?

The Lord: No, Subhuti.

Subhuti: Is it, then, for the nongenesis[58] of all dharmas that a Bodhisattva is so predicted?

The Lord: No, Subhuti.

Subhuti: Is it, then, for neither genesis nor nongenesis that he is so predicted?

The Lord: No, Subhuti.

Subhuti: If he is predicted neither for genesis[59] nor for nongenesis,[60] how then does just now here the prediction of this Bodhisattva to full enlightenment take place?

The Lord: Do you see[61] as real that dharma which is predicted to full enlightenment?

Subhuti: No, O Lord. I do not see as real that dharma which is predicted to full enlightenment, or also that dharma which is fully known, or whereby it is fully known, or him who fully knows it.

The Lord: So it is, Subhuti, so it is. When he does not apprehend all dharmas, it does not occur to the Bodhisattva: 'I will fully know, through this (dharma) I will fully know, this one will fully know'. And why? Because all these discriminations do not exist in the Bodhisattva who courses in perfect wisdom. ((f. 222a)) And why? Because the perfection of wisdom does not discriminate.

[57]So *AdT*. Ms has: *anutpādāya*, but in view of Subhuti's next questions this seems preferable.

[58]*anutpattikatāya S*; *AdT*: *skye-ba ma mchis-pa'i slad-du.*

[59]*Ad*: *utpatti, skye-ba.*

[60]*Ad*: *anutpatti, skye-ba ma mchis-pa.*

[61]*samanupaśyasi*, review.

Chapter 56

EVEN TRAINING

V2,5. THE GROWTH WHICH IS ESSENTIALLY AN (INCREASING) ENDOWMENT WITH DISTINGUISHED (AND SUPERIOR) WHOLESOME ROOTS.

Śakra, Chief of Gods: Deep, O Lord, is this perfection of wisdom, hard to see, hard to understand, inaccessible to reasoning and discursive thought, etc. *to* : it is subtle, delicate, to be felt only by the learned and discerning—on account of its absolute isolatedness. Not will those beings be endowed with a puny wholesome root who will hear this perfection of wisdom, learn it, bear it in mind, preach and study it, and will progress to its Thusness[1] and give no occasion[2] to any other mental dharmas[3] until they know full enlightenment!

The Lord: So it is, Kauśika, so it is. What do you think, Kauśika, if all the beings of Jambudvipa were endowed with the ten ways of wholesome action, the four trances, etc. *to* : the five superknowledges, and if a son or daughter of good family were to learn this deep perfection of wisdom, bear it in mind, preach and study it, and after that he would progress to its Thusness, then his wholesome root would be immeasurably superior to that of the former wholesome root?

Thereupon *a monk* said to Śakra, Chief of Gods : This son or daughter of good family who will learn this deep perfection of wisdom with undistracted thought, bear it in mind, preach and study it, who will progress to its Thusness and who will not give any occasion to other mental dharmas until he will know full enlightenment, has surpassed all those beings of Jambudvipa who were endowed with the ten ways of wholesome action, the four trances, etc. *to*: the five superknowledges.

Śakra : The Bodhisattva, O monk, who has raised even a single thought to enlightenment has surpassed all those beings of Jambudvipa who are endowed with the ten ways of wholesome action, with the four trances, the four Unlimited, the four formless attainments, and the five superknowledges; how much more so if he will learn this deep perfection of wisdom, bear it in mind ((f. 222b)) and study it, and thereafter will progress to its Thusness. He will surpass the world with its gods, men and Asuras, he will come to surpass it. And he will in addition come to surpass

[1]*tathatva* or *tathātva*; *de-bshin ñid-du*; i.e. its true meaning.

[2]room, opportunity.

[3]*cittacaitasikā dharmā*, 'the dharmas which constitute thought and its concomitants'.

all the Streamwinners, etc. *to*: Pratyekabuddhas; and also those Bodhisattvas who, without skill in means and perfect wisdom, course in the perfection of giving, etc. *to*: the perfection of meditation. But those Bodhisattvas who course in the perfection of wisdom as it has been explained, them the world with its gods, men and Asuras cannot surpass. The Bodhisattva who courses in the perfection of wisdom as it has been explained and complies with it, he works for the noninterruption of the lineage of the knowledge of all modes,[4] he does not keep aloof from[5] the Tathagatas. He will, when he progresses thus, not turn back on the terrace of enlightenment, for he wants to extricate beings from (the mud of the defilements) into which they have sunk.[6] When he thus trains, he trains in the training of a Bodhisattva, and not that of a Disciple or Pratyekabuddha.

V2,6. The growth which by its own-being (induces) the whole multitude of the gods to approach (the Bodhisattva).

When he thus trains, the Four Great Kings will think of approaching him, and, having approached him, they will say to him: "Quickly train yourself, great man, nimbly train yourself! Here are the four begging bowls which the former Tathagatas have received,[7] and which you also shall receive when you will be seated on the terrace of enlightenment, after you have known full enlightenment." And also the divinities belonging to the Four Great Kings will think of approaching the Bodhisattva who thus trains in perfect wisdom. And not only they, but also the Gods of the Thirty-three, the deva kings headed by Suyāma, the deva kings headed by Samtuṣita, the deva kings headed by Nirmito (who magically create their own enjoyments), those who control the enjoyments magically created by others, Brahmā Sahampati and the gods connected with him, the shining gods, the altogether lovely gods, those who have a great fruition, the lowest of the five Gods of the Pure Abode, the Atapa gods, ((f. 223a)) the gods who are good to see, the gods who are good to behold, the Gods of the Pure Abode.[8] The Tathagatas will constantly bring to mind the Bodhisattva who courses in this deep perfection of wisdom as it has been explained. When he thus courses in this deep perfection as it has been explained, then all the worldly ills which may befall his body as the result of hostile influences from the outside will never befall his body or assail it. These, O monk, will be the qualities which a

[4]*A* XXIII 413 speaks of the "lineage of all all-knowing", and *S* i 77 of *buddhavaṃśa* (*rigs*) *-anupacchedāya sthātukāmena* etc. *AdT* here: *gduṅ*.

[5]or 'disdain', 'belittle', 'reject'. See *A* VII 174, VIII 190, XI 239.

[6]*A* xxiii 414, *kleśapaṅke saṃsīdamānān uddhariṣyati.*

[7]*Buddhacarita* XIV 104.

[8]For this list see Edgerton s.v. *deva.*

Bodhisattva who courses in this deep perfection of wisdom gains in this very life. All the illnesses that there are, which may befall him,[9] such as eye-disease, ear-, nose-, and tongue-diseases, bodily illness, mental illness—they all cannot arise in his body or assail it. These qualities belonging to this very life should be expected of the Bodhisattva who courses in this deep perfection of wisdom.

V2,7. THE GROWTH WHICH IN ITS OWN FORM IS THE ABILITY TO OVERCOME ALL MARAS.

Thereupon it occurred to the *Ven. Ānanda*: Does this Śakra, Chief of Gods, expound by his own insight[10] the perfection of wisdom and its virtues and advantages or by the Buddha's might?

Śakra read his thoughts, and said to the Ven. Ānanda : As the Buddha's might should this be known when I expound the perfection of wisdom and its virtues and advantages.

The Lord: So it is, Ānanda, so it is. It is through the Tathagata's might, it is through His sustaining power, that Śakra, Chief of Gods, expounds the perfection of wisdom, and its virtues and advantages. At the time when, Ānanda, a Bodhisattva trains in perfect wisdom, makes endeavours about it and develops it, all the evil Maras in the great trichiliocosm are in a state of uncertainty, 'Will this Bodhisattva realise the Reality limit and then reach the fruit of a Streamwinner, etc. *to*: Pratyekabuddhahood, or will he know full enlightenment?' Moreover, at the time when the Bodhisattva becomes one who is not without perfect wisdom, Mara, the Evil One, is pierced by the dart of sorrow.[11] Moreover the Evil Maras will let loose a shower of meteors, so as to generate fear in him, to cow him, to make his hairs stand on end, to discompose his mind, to cause one thought at least to be distracted away from attentions to the knowledge of all modes.

Ānanda: Does then, O Lord, Mara, the Evil One, attempt to hurt all Bodhisattvas?

The Lord: No, he does not.

Ānanda: What kind of persons does he then try to hurt? (223b))

The Lord: Mara attempts to hurt those Bodhisattvas who, when this deep perfection of wisdom was being taught in the past have had no

[9]lit. 'from the union of the humours'.

[10]*pratibhāna*, also 'inspiration'. The English language has no exact equivalent. It is the fourth of the 'analytical knowledges' (see *A.K.* vii 91-2), and one of the faculties of a Bodhisattva which he requires less for his own salvation than for the conversion of others (see *SaPu* x v. 34, *DaBhu* 76, 24 sq.). It means both 'flashes of ideas', 'due to mental flexibility', and readiness to express them in speech, to make them clear. cf. *H* to *A* i 4, iii 83, xi 232, xx 371.

[11]because the Bodhisattva has transcended their realm and has moved outside the range of their influence, they are filled with deep sorrow (*vaimanasya*), *H* 814.

firm belief in it. And also those who have been seized by uncertainties about this deep perfection of wisdom, and who thought that 'perhaps this perfection of wisdom is so, perhaps not.' And also Bodhisattvas who lack the good spiritual friend, and who, not seeing him, do not hear this deep perfection of wisdom, do not cognize it, and in consequence do not progress to its Thusness, and do not know how to develop it. And Mara also has a chance with a Bodhisattva who, being without perfect wisdom, takes hold of what is not the true Dharma. Moreover when a Bodhisattva, being without perfect wisdom, speaks in praise of what is not the true Dharma, then it occurs to Mara, the Evil One: 'One who speaks in praise of what is not the true Dharma, he is my adherent[12] and in him I have found an advocate[12] among many who belong to the Bodhisattva-vehicle. He will fulfill my intention, which is that those who belong to the Bodhisattva-vehicle should stand on either of two levels—that of a Disciple or Pratyekabuddha.' What other kind of a Bodhisattva will Mara, the Evil One, gain entry to? If a Bodhisattva, when this deep perfection of wisdom is being taught, says, 'Deep is this perfection of wisdom! What point is there in your listening to it, etc. *to* : in your studying it! Even I do not get to the bottom of it. How then can you?', then Mara will gain entry to him. Moreover when a Bodhisattva despises other Bodhisattvas, and thinks, 'I course in the perfection of giving, etc. *to* : in the perfection of wisdom, but you do not!', then Mara gains entry to him. Moreover when a Bodhisattva fancies and exalts himself, then Mara, the Evil One, becomes contented, elated, enraptured, he becomes overjoyed, exultant and jubilant, and can gain entry to him. Moreover when of a Bodhisattva the assumption of a name or clan[13] is proclaimed, then he may regard that as a sufficient reason to look down on other Bodhisattvas, however well behaved and lovely in character[14] they may be. He exalts himself and depreciates others. He has not got the qualities which are the attributes, tokens, and signs of irreversible Bodhisattvas. Because he has not got them, he gives rise to defilement, exalts himself and depreciates others and says: 'In this Bodhisattva-vehicle, in this Bodhisattva-clan you do not make such a good figure[15] as I do.' So he will condemn and depreciate those persons belonging to the Bodhisattva-vehicle. Mara, the Evil One, then thinks to himself: 'My realm will not remain empty, but crowded will be the hells, the animal kingdom, ((f. 224a)) the world of Yama, and the range of the Pretas'. More and more will Mara, the Evil One, sustain that Bodhisattva, so that he will in due course become a plausible talker. 'Because of his plausible talk many

[12]*sahāyako, grogs.*
[13]*miṅ smos sam, rus smos te.*
[14]As f. 218a.
[15]*yaṅ-dag-par snaṅ-ba.*

people will listen to him and believe him, they will imitate what they have seen and heard, and will in consequence not[16] train in Thusness; not[16] training in Thusness, not[16] progressing in it, they will increase their defilements. Whatever deed they may do with their perverted personality[17]—by body, voice and mind—that will lead them to what is unserviceable, disagreeable, and unpleasant. In consequence the great hells will become crowded, the animal kingdom, the world of Yama, and the range of the Pretas. The realm of Mara will be crowded!' When he considers this sequence of events, Mara becomes enraptured, overjoyed, and jubilant. Moreover, if a person belonging to the Bodhisattva-vehicle disputes with a son of good family, who belongs to the vehicle of the Disciples, and claims to be superior to him, then Mara, the Evil One, thinks to himself: 'Surely, this son of good family will keep far away from the knowledge of all modes and will not come near it!' And why? Because these quarrels, fights, battles, and disputes do not lead to the knowledge of all modes, but to the hells, to animal births, to the world of Yama. Because they are not the way to the knowledge of all modes.

Moreover if a person belonging to the vehicle of the Bodhisattvas quarrels, fights, battles, and disputes with someone else who likewise belongs to that vehicle, then Mara, the Evil One, thinks to himself, 'both these remain far away from the knowledge of all modes! Both these will not know full enlightenment!' And why? Because this path, this progress on which the sons of good family have set out leads not to the knowledge of all modes, but to the hells, the animal world, the world of Yama! Moreover if a Bodhisattva, who has not had his prediction, cherishes malice for one who has had it, and quarrels, fights, battles, and disputes with him, then he must put on the armour for as many aeons as he has produced in himself those evil thoughts, which cause quarrelling, fighting, battles, and disputes, unless, of course, he has altogether abandoned the knowledge of all modes.

Ānanda: Is there an escape from (the aftereffects of) these thoughts, or is he definitely condemned to go on putting on the armour for all those aeons?

The Lord: I have, Ananda, demonstrated a Dharma which includes the possibility of escape—for persons of the vehicles of the Disciples, Pratyekabuddhas, and Bodhisattvas. As to the person who belongs to the vehicle of the Bodhisattvas, and who quarrels with someone else who also belongs to it, or disputes with him, insults, or reviles him; if he does not confess his fault, but harbours a latent tendency (to hostility)—of

[16]So *A* xxiv 419. But Ms and *AdT* both omit *na*. 'Thusness' then must refer to the meaning of the falsehoods contained in his 'plausible talk'.

[17]*AdT*: "whatever mental deed they may do with perverted mind, body, or voice"; see *A* xxiv 419.

that person I do not teach the escape (from the consequences of his action.) Quite definitely that person must go on putting on the armour for all these aeons unless, of course, he has altogether abandoned the knowledge of all modes. But if the Bodhisattva confesses his fault, harbours no latent tendency (to hostility), effects restraint in future (and reflects): 'It is indeed a loss to me and not a gain, that I, who ought to remove suffering from all beings, should, when I am spoken to, answer back; that I, who should be to all beings a bridge across the sea of birth-and-death, should speak unkindly to others and contradict them. This is not how I should act! I should behave like a senseless idiot or a dumb sheep, and nothing should deflect me from this earnest intention. ((224b)) When after having won full enlightenment I should lead those beings to final Nirvana, yet nevertheless I bear ill will towards them and get angry with them! I should not bear ill will towards them, should not be angry with them!' Of such a Bodhisattva I teach the escape, and Mara, the Evil One, cannot gain entry to him. Moreover the Bodhisattva should have no commerce with persons belonging to the Disciple-vehicle. But if he does, then he should never bear ill will towards anyone, never get angry with anyone. And why? 'For that is not seemly to me that I should bear ill will towards them or get angry with them. And why? Because when I have known full enlightenment I should liberate them from all ills.'

V2,8. THE GROWTH WHICH HAS FOR ITS OWN-MARK THE FACT THAT (A BODHISATTVA) TREATS (ALL OTHER BODHISATTVAS) ALIKE, (REVERING THEM) AS IF THEY WERE THE TEACHER HIMSELF.

Ānanda: How then should a Bodhisattva behave towards persons who belong to the vehicle of the Bodhisattvas?

The Lord: As to the Teacher himself. And why? 'For he is my companion,[18] we have both mounted on the same ship, we should both be trained in the same ways and the same things, i.e. in the perfection of giving, etc. *to*: in the knowledge of all modes'. And he should think that 'he is to me one who shows me the way to the perfect enlightenment'. But if that Bodhisattva should dwell in a contaminated dwelling, without attentions associated with the knowledge of all modes, then I should not train therein. But if he should dwell not without attentions associated with the knowledge of all modes, then I also should train therein'. When he thus trains, the Bodhisattva, the great being, becomes one who trains evenly.[19]

[18]*sahāyaka, grogs.*

[19]*samaśikṣo bhavati, bslab-pa mñam-pa yin no.*

CHAPTER 57

PRACTICES

Subhuti: What then, O Lord, is the sameness of the Bodhisattvas, the great beings, in which the Bodhisattva should train?

The Lord: The various kinds of emptiness[1] are the sameness of the Bodhisattvas, the great beings. That 'form is empty of form', etc. *to*: 'enlightenment is empty of enlightenment', that is the sameness of the Bodhisattvas, the great beings, having stood in which the Bodhisattva knows full enlightenment.

V2,9. THE GROWTH WHICH IN ITS OWN-FORM IS THE PERFECTLY PURE TRAINING IN SKILL IN MEANS.

Subhuti: Does then the Bodhisattva train in the knowledge of all modes when he trains for the extinction of form, etc. *to*: enlightenment, for their dispassion,[2] stopping, and nonproduction? ((f. 225a))

The Lord: With regard to what Subhuti the Elder has said, what do you think, Subhuti, does the Suchness of form, etc. *to*: enlightenment, etc. *to*: the Suchness of the Tathagata by which he is conceived as a Tathagata,[3] does that Suchness get extinct, or is it stopped, or can it be forsaken?

Subhuti: No indeed, O Lord, no indeed, O Well-Gone!

The Lord: When he trains thus, Subhuti, the Bodhisattva trains in Suchness, trains in the knowledge of all modes. But Suchness does not get extinct, is not stopped, cannot be forsaken. When he trains thus, the Bodhisattva trains in Suchness, trains in the knowledge of all modes. When he trains thus, the Bodhisattva trains in the six perfections, in the four applications of mindfulness, etc. *to*: in the 18 special Buddhadharmas, and he trains in the knowledge of all modes. When he trains thus, the Bodhisattva reaches the perfection of all training. He cannot be overcome by Mara or the divinities of his host. Quite soon he shall reach the irreversible level. He courses in the range of the Tathagata, which is his own ancestral[4] range. He trains in the dharmas which make him into a saviour; he trains in the great friendliness and the great com-

[1]see e.g.f. 263b.

[2]*virāga,* dispassion from them.

[3]*tathateti sarvajñatā buddhatvam iti yāvat. H.* 821.

[4]Or 'paternal'. *A* xxv 425 has simply *svake gocare carati, raṅ-gi spyod-yul-la slob-bo.*

passion; he trains for the purification of the Buddha-field and the maturing of beings. He trains for the turning of the wheel of the Dharma, with its three revolutions and twelve aspects.[5] He trains so as to lead all beings to Nirvana to ensure the noninterruption of the lineage of the Tathagatas,[6] to open the door to the Undying, to make the unconditioned element visible.[7] But inferior beings cannot train in this sublime training. That Bodhisattva trains so as to extricate all beings from Samsara. When he trains thus, he is not reborn in the hells among animals, or in the world of Yama; nor in outlying districts, or among refuse workers, or outcasts; nor is he one-eyed, hunchbacked, or lame; nor crippled, deaf, or utterly destitute[8] or deficient in his faculties; he becomes one who has all his faculties and does not lack any of them; he does not become one who takes life ((f. 225b)), takes what is not given, commits sexual misconduct, who speaks falsely, maliciously or harshly, or who prattles indistinctly, or who is covetous, harbours ill will in his heart or has wrong views, and he does not earn his livelihood in the wrong fashion. He does not seize on what is unreal or immoral. When he trains thus, the Bodhisattva is not reborn among the long-lived gods.[9] And why? Because he is endowed with skill in means. And what is that? In this very perfection of wisdom that skill in means has been explained which consists in that he enters on the trances, Unlimited, and formless attainments, but does not get reborn through their influence.[10] When he trains thus, the Bodhisattva incurs the perfect purity of all the dharmas and powers of a Buddha, because he is perfectly pure of the level of the Disciples and Pratyekabuddhas.

Subhuti: If all dharmas are by nature perfectly pure, of which dharma does then the Bodhisattva incur the perfect purity?

The Lord: As you say, Subhuti, all dharmas are by nature perfectly pure. When in spite of this fact a Bodhisattva, who courses in perfect wisdom, does not lose heart and remains uncowed, then that is his perfection of wisdom. Because all the foolish common people do not know or see that nature of dharmas, for their sake the Bodhisattvas course in the six perfections, etc. *to*:[11] in the knowledge of all modes. When he

[5]The three *parivartas* refer to the paths of vision, of development, and of the adepts; when they are multiplied by the four truths, they give the 12 *ākāras*.

[6]see note 4 to ch. 56.

[7]*(saṃ)darśayiṣyāmīti, yaṅ-dag-par bstan-par bya'o shes.*

[8]See the Sanskrit text, which is none too satisfactory.

[9]Because there he would be so wrapped up in his own happiness that he would be of no use to other beings.

[10]Each level of trance corresponds to one or other of the 28 heavens in which the gods dwell, and the achievement of a trance entitles to rebirth among the corresponding gods. The Bodhisattva voluntarily foregoes this reward of his trances, so as to be useful to others and share their misfortunes.

[11]So *AdT*.

thus courses in all dharmas, the Bodhisattva acquires the powers and the state of self-confidence, and does not fall on the level of the Disciples or Pratyekabuddhas. He then goes beyond the throbbing thoughts and doing of all beings.

V2,10. THE GROWTH WHICH HAS FOR ITS MARK THE FACT THAT ONE BECOMES ONE WHO BELONGS TO THE CLAN OF THE BUDDHAS.

Just as, Subhuti, few are on this great earth the spots where, as in the Jambu River, gold and silver are found; just so, Subhuti, few are the beings who train in this perfect-wisdom-training, much more numerous those who have set out for the level of the Disciples or Pratyekabuddhas.

V2,11. THE GROWTH WHICH CONSISTS ESSENTIALLY IN THE SIGN OF (THE ASPIRATION FOR) THE ATTAINMENT OF THE FRUIT OF BUDDHAHOOD.

Just as, Subhuti, few are the beings who have done deeds conducive to universal kingship, and much more numerous those who have done deeds conducive to their becoming commanders of a fort, just so, few are the beings who have mounted on this path leading to all-knowledge, and much more numerous those who have mounted on the path of the Disciples and Pratyekabuddhas. Fewer than the Bodhisattvas who have set out for full enlightenment are those who progress to Thusness, but more numerous are those who stand in Discipleship and Pratyekabuddhahood. Much more numerous than the sons of good family who belong to the Bodhisattva-vehicle and who, dwelling in this deep perfection of wisdom, are without any doubt bound to enter on the irreversible stage, are those who do not manage to enter on it. ((f. 226a)) Therefore, then, Subhuti, a Bodhisattva who wants to reach the irreversible stage, who wants to be numbered among those who belong to that stage, should train in this deep perfection of wisdom.

V2,12. THE GROWTH WHICH IN ITS OWN-BEING IS THE NONPRODUCTION IN THOUGHT OF STATES HOSTILE TO THE PERFECTIONS.

Moreover, Subhuti, when the Bodhisattva courses in perfect wisdom, no thoughts associated with meanness arise in his mind, no thoughts associated with immorality, anger, sloth, distraction, or stupidity; with greed, hate, or delusion; or with rigidity.

V2,13. THE GROWTH WHICH . . .[12]

Or with form, etc. *to* : enlightenment. And why? For when the Bodhisattva courses in this deep perfection of wisdom, he does not apprehend any dharma, and in consequence he does not raise his thought to

[12]Haribhadra (p. 824 n. 5) has failed to indicate the name of the 13th *vivṛddhy-artha*. The Ms of *P* has only *iti trayodaśī.*

any dharma. It is thus that the Bodhisattva, the great being who trains in this deep perfection of wisdom, has taken hold of all the six perfections, has procured them, has conformed to them. And why? Because in this deep perfection of wisdom all the perfections are contained.

V2,14. THE GROWTH WHICH HAS FOR ITS MARK THE COGNITION WHICH COMPRISES ALL PERFECTIONS.

Just as the view of individuality includes the 62 false views, just so all the perfections are included in this deep perfection of wisdom. When a man has died, the stopping of his life faculty implies the stopping of all his faculties; just so, when the Bodhisattva courses in this deep perfection of wisdom, all the other perfections are included. Therefore, then, Subhuti, the Bodhisattva who wants to go to the beyond of all the perfections,[13] should train in this deep perfection of wisdom.

V2,15. THE GROWTH WHICH IMPLIES THE ACQUISITION OF ALL THE ACCOMPLISHMENTS.

Again, when he trains in this deep perfection of wisdom, the Bodhisattva trains in that which is the highest possible degree of perfection for any being. What do you think, Subhuti, if you consider all the beings in the great trichiliocosm, would they be many?

Subhuti: Many, O Lord, many, O Well-Gone! There are many beings even in Jambudvipa alone, and how many more in the great trichiliocosm!

The Lord: If all beings in the great trichiliocosm would sooner or later, after acquiring a human body, know full enlightenment; and if one single Bodhisattva, during his entire life were to furnish them all with robes, almsbowls, lodgings, medicinal appliances for use in sickness, what do you think, Subhuti, does this Bodhisattva on the strength of that beget much merit?

Subhuti: He does, O Lord. ((f. 226b))

The Lord: Much greater merit will that son or daughter of good family beget who will take up this deep perfection of wisdom, bear it in mind, preach and study it, will wisely attend to it, and who will progress to its Thusness. And why? So greatly profitable is the perfection of wisdom of the Bodhisattvas, the great beings, as productive of the supreme enlightenment! A Bodhisattva should therefore train in just this perfection of wisdom if he wants to arrive at the supreme position among all beings, to become a saviour of all those who are helpless, a refuge and final relief to those who so far have found no refuge or final relief; an eye to the blind, a lamp to those plunged into the darkness of ignorance; if he wants to reach Buddhahood, to arrive at the domain of the Buddhas, to

[13]*sarva-pāramitānāṃ pāraṃ gantu-kāmena*; *pha-rol-tu phyin-pa thams-cad-kyi pha-rol-tu 'gro-bar' dod-pas*. Cf. *P* 29, 94: *serva-dhamāṇāṃ pāraṃ gantu-kāmena*. Cf. *A* xxv 428.

sport with a Buddha's sport, to roar a Buddha's lion's roar, to beat the drum and to blow the conch-shell of a Buddha, and to explain the Dharma as only a Buddha can do.[14] And why? When the Bodhisattva trains in perfect wisdom, he acquires all the accomplishments which he should acquire.

Subhuti: Should he also acquire the accomplishments of a Disciple or Pratyekabuddha?

The Lord: Yes, he should, but he should not abide therein, or rely thereon. After having viewed them with his cognition and vision, he should pass above them, and enter on a Bodhisattva's special way of salvation. When he trains thus, the Bodhisattva comes near to the knowledge of all modes, and will know the supreme enlightenment. He reaches a condition where he becomes worthy of the donations of the world with its gods, men and Asuras. He surpasses others who are worthy of donations, if they are Disciples and Pratyekabuddhas, and he comes near to the knowledge of all modes. He does not part from the perfection of wisdom, but he courses in it, is not without it. When he courses thus in this deep perfection of wisdom, he will never again lose interest in the knowledge of all modes, he keeps away from the level of a Disciple or Pratyekabuddha, and comes near to the supreme enlightenment.

V2,16. The growth in its own-being is the nearness to full enlightenment.

But when he thinks to himself, 'this is the perfection of wisdom, here is the perfection of wisdom, by this perfection of wisdom shall I bring about the knowledge of all modes', when he cognizes thus, then he does not course in perfect wisdom. On the contrary, he does not cognize this perfection of wisdom; that 'this is the perfection of wisdom, here is the perfection of wisdom', that also he does not cognize or see, or likewise that 'this one has the perfection of wisdom, by that is the perfection of wisdom', or 'him who, going forth by this perfection of wisdom, ((f. 227a)) comes to know full enlightenment'. But if it occurs to him, 'Not is this the perfection of wisdom, nor is the perfection of wisdom here, nor does through this perfection of wisdom any dharma go forth, because fixed and established is the Dharma-element, is Suchness, is the Reality limit'—when he courses thus, then the Bodhisattva courses in perfect wisdom.

[14]*buddhasāṃkathyam*; *A* xxv 432, *dharmasāṃkathyam*; *AdT*: *saṅs-rgyas-kyi chos daṅ 'brel-ba' i gtam zer-bar 'dod-pa*.

CHAPTER 58

EXPOSITION OF NONDISCRIMINATION THROUGH SIMILES

V 3. Firm Position. (Patience).

V3,1. THE FIRM POSITION IN THE UTMOST FULFILLMENT OF THE DHARMAS OF THE THREE KINDS OF OMNISCIENCE.

Thereupon it occurred to *Śakra, Chief of Gods*: Even when he only courses in these six perfections, etc. *to*: in the 18 special Buddhadharmas, a Bodhisattva surpasses all beings, how much more so when he will have known full enlightenment! How fortunate are those beings, how good is the life which they live when their thought strides forth to the knowledge of all modes, how much more so when they raise their thought to full enlightenment! To be envied[1] are those beings who have raised their thought to the supreme enlightenment, or who will raise it, and who can listen to this perfection of wisdom!

Thereupon Śakra, Chief of Gods, seized Mandarava flowers, approached to where the Lord was, scattered them over the Tathagata and spoke thus: May those persons belonging to the Bodhisattva-vehicle who thus hang on to[2] the supreme enlightenment, fulfill through this wholesome root[3] the Buddhadharmas, the dharmas of the knowledge of all modes, just these dharmas of the Self-Existent, just these dharmas without outflows!

V3,2. THE FIRM POSITION WITH REGARD TO THE NONABANDONMENT OF THE WELFARE OF BEINGS.

For I have not even the slightest suspicion that a person belonging to the Bodhisattva-vehicle, who has set out for full enlightenment, could turn back on it; or that, having turned back on it, he could fall into Discipleship or Pratyekabuddhahood. But on the contrary, he will generate zest for the supreme enlightenment, and his resolve to win it will increase more and more; desirous of the welfare of the world with its gods, men and Asuras, desirous to benefit it, to make it happy, to make it secure, the Bodhisattva, when he has seen these ills which afflict

[1]*spṛhaṇīya*; also: 'to be emulated'; *AdT*: *'dod-par bya-ba.*

[2]*adhyālambante, dmigs-pa.* Also at f. 239a, where *lhag-par dmigs-la.*

[3]i.e. as a result of the merit they have gained by aspiring for the supreme enlightenment. Cf. *A* xxvi 434.

beings on the plane of Samsara, produces an attitude of mind in which he reflects: 'Having crossed over, we shall help across those beings who have not yet crossed! Freed we shall free those beings who are not yet free! Recovered we shall help to recovery those beings who have not yet recovered! ((f. 227b)) Gone to Nirvana we shall lead to Nirvana those beings who have not yet gone there!' How much merit will that son or daughter of good family beget who rejoices in the productions of thought of the Bodhisattvas, the great beings, who have first set out in the vehicle, of those who have for long coursed in it, of those who are irreversible, and of those who are bound to one more birth only?

V 4. Complete Stabilization of Thought. (Highest Mundane Dharmas).

The Lord: One might be able, Kauśika, to take the measure of a four-continent world system, or a great trichiliocosm, with a tip of straw, but there can be no measure of the merit derived from these productions of thought connected with jubilation. One might be able to lift all the water of the great oceans in the great trichiliocosm drop by drop with the fine point of the tip of hair split a hundredfold, but there can be no measure of the merit derived from these productions of thought connected with jubilation.

Śakra: Under Mara's influence will be those beings who do not rejoice at these productions of thought, partisans of Mara, deceased in Mara's realm. And why? Because shatterers of Mara's realm are those beings who have aspired to these productions of thought and dedicate (the resulting merit) to the supreme enlightenment. One should rejoice at those productions of thought which have been raised to the supreme enlightenment. Those who have not abandoned the Buddha, Dharma, or Sangha should rejoice at these productions of thought, and then dedicate (the resulting merit) to the supreme enlightenment, but in such a way that there is no notion of either duality or nonduality.

The Lord: So it is, Kauśika, so it is, just as you say. Those who rejoice at these productions of thought will soon please the Tathagatas, and not again displease them. Thus those who become endowed with these wholesome roots of the productions of thought which are connected with jubilation—wherever they may be reborn, there they shall be honoured, respected, revered, and worshipped. Never again shall they see unpleasant sights, hear unpleasant sounds, smell unpleasant smells, taste unpleasant tastes, come into contact with anything unpleasant to touch, or become aware of unpleasant mind-objects. Nor will they ever again be deprived of the Buddhas and Lords. ((f. 228a)) They will pass on from Buddha-field to Buddha-field, honour therein the Buddhas and Lords and plant wholesome roots (with them). And why? For these sons and daughters of good family have rejoiced at the wholesome roots of innumerable Bodhisattvas, great beings, who have first set out in the vehicle, of those who stand on the second stage, on the third stage, etc. *to* : on the tenth stage, etc. *to* : of those who are bound to one more birth only. As these wholesome roots grow, they come near to full enlightenment, and when they have won full enlightenment, they will lead countless beings to Nirvana. In this way also, Kauśika, should that son or daughter of good family, having rejoiced at the wholesome roots of the Bodhisattvas, the great beings who have first set out in the vehicle[4] dedicate (the resulting merit) to the supreme enlightenment, but in such a way that they do not treat (these productions of thought) as either thought or as other than thought.[5]

V 5. The Path of Vision. (At its Summit).

V5a. THE TWO DISCRIMINATIONS OF THE OBJECT.

V5a,1. THE FIRST DISCRIMINATION OF THE OBJECT, REFERRING TO THE WHOLE OF WORLDLY ACTIVITY.

And likewise, having rejoiced at the wholesome roots of the Bodhisattvas who course on the pilgrimage, who are irreversible, and who are bound to one more birth only, one should dedicate (the resulting merit) to the supreme enlightenment, but in such a way that one does not treat (these productions of thought) as either thought or as other than thought.[6]

V5a,2.[7] THE SECOND DISCRIMINATION OF THE OBJECT, REFERRING TO THE ALTERNATIVE OF WITHDRAWAL FROM ACTIVITY. ((f. 229b))

Śāriputra : Is now, Subhuti, just the perfection of wisdom indiscriminate, or are also the other five perfections indiscriminate?

Subhuti : Also the other five perfections are indiscriminate.

Śāriputra : Is, Ven. Subhuti, also form indiscriminate, etc. *to* : consciousness; eye, etc. *to* : mind; form etc. *to* : dharmas; eye-consciousness, etc. *to* : mind-consciousness; eye-contact, etc. *to* : mind-contact; feeling born of eye-contact, etc. *to* : feeling born of mind-contact? Are also the trances, Unlimited, and formless attainments indiscriminate? Are also the applications of mindfulness indiscriminate, etc. *to* : the Path, and Emptiness, the Signless and the Wishless? Are also the ten powers of a Tathagata, the four grounds of self-confidence, the four analytical knowledges, the great friendliness, the great compassion, etc. *to* : are

[4]So Ms. *AdT* and *P* : "who have had the first thought of enlightenment".

[5]*AdT* : *ci nas kyaṅ sems de-la-'aṅ ma yin shiṅ, sems gshan-la-'aṅ ma yin-pa.*

[6]*P* : "that there is no perception of either duality or nonduality". This alteration is due to a desire to adapt the argument to the theme of '*AA* V 5a?

[7]V 5d continues with folio 243 A.

also the eighteen special dharmas of a Buddha indiscriminate? Is the conditioned element, is the unconditioned element indiscriminate?

Subhuti: All dharmas, Ven. Śāriputra, are indiscriminate.

Śāriputra: Since all dharmas are indiscriminate, whence then has come this division of Samsara into the five places of rebirth, i.e. hells, animals, world of Yama, gods, and men, and whence has come this distinctive manifestation of Streamwinners, Once-Returners, Never-Returners, Arhats, Pratyekabuddhas, Buddha and Lords?

Subhuti: Those beings, Śāriputra, who effect deeds arisen from perverted views—by body, voice, or mind—they reproduce themselves in suchlike sense fields; having taken hold of the retribution for a karma which is rooted in their desire-to-do, and which has arisen from discrimination, they reproduce themselves in the realms[8] of the hells, animals, the world of Yama, of gods and men. When again the Ven. Śāriputra has said: 'How are the Streamwinners distinguished, etc. *to*: and how the fully enlightened Buddhas?' From nondiscrimination are the Streamwinners, etc., distinguished, from nondiscrimination is the Pratyekabuddha, from nondiscrimination is the Pratyekabuddha-enlightenment, from nondiscrimination are the Buddhas, from nondiscrimination is their enlightenment. Also those who in a past period have been Tathagatas, those Buddhas and Lords also were without discrimination, had forsaken all discriminations; just so those in a future period will be without discrimination; and those Buddhas and Lords also who just now in the ten directions in the present period win full enlightenment, they also are without discrimination, have forsaken all discrimination. It is by this method, Śāriputra, that one should know: all dharmas are indiscriminate when measured by the standard of indiscriminate Suchness, the Reality-limit-Suchness, the Dharma-element-Suchness. It is surely thus, Śāriputra, that the Bodhisattva, the great being, should course in the undiscriminating perfection of wisdom, and thereby he fully knows all dharmas as without discrimination.

[8]*gati*, above = destiny.

Chapter 59

NONATTACHMENT

V5b. The two discriminations of the subject.

V5b,1. The first discrimination of the subject: referring to common people as being substantial entities.

Śāriputra: In the core verily ((f. 230a)), Ven. Subhuti, courses the Bodhisattva, the great being, who courses in perfect wisdom! In the core[1] verily courses the Bodhisattva, the great being!

Subhuti: Not in the core[2] verily, Ven. Śāriputra, courses the Bodhisattva, the great being who courses in the perfection of wisdom. And why? For without a solid core[3] is the perfection of wisdom, and everything up to the knowledge of all modes. And why? A Bodhisattva, a great being who courses in the perfection of wisdom, can obviously not apprehend or review that which is without a solid core; how then again could he get at the core? Etc. *to*: he cannot apprehend the knowledge of all modes which has no solid core; how then could he apprehend its core?

Thereupon it occurred to a great many of the *Gods of the sphere of sense desire and form*: Worthy of homage are those sons and daughters of good family who have raised their thought to the utmost, right, and perfect enlightenment, and who course here in this deep perfection of wisdom as it has been explained, and who, although they course in this meaning,[4] do not realize the Reality limit, by the realisation of which they would be situated on the level of the Disciples or Pratyekabuddhas. In this way also are the Bodhisattvas, the great beings worthy of homage, for they do not realise this Dharmahood.[5]

Subhuti: Not that, O Gods, is hard for the Bodhisattvas, the great beings, that they do not realise this Dharmahood, when its realisation would situate them on the level of the Disciples or Pratyekabuddhas. But this, O Gods, is extremely hard for them that they put on the armour of the resolution to lead countless beings to Nirvana, when absolutely those beings whom they would lead to Nirvana cannot be apprehended.

[1]*sāre, sñiṅ-po-la.*

[2]*asāre.* So read also at *A* xxvii 444. H: *sāratva-avagraha-abhāvād.*

[3]*asārikā*, or 'unsubstantial'.

[4]*artha*, see note 15.

[5]who, out of respect for the sameness of everything, do not realize these dharmas, *AdT.*

When he courses thus, the Bodhisattva, the great being, becomes one who has set out for the supreme enlightenment, for he has decided to discipline all beings. One would think of disciplining space if one were to think of disciplining beings. And why? From the isolatedness of space should the isolatedness of beings be seen; from the emptiness of space should the emptiness of beings be seen, from the unsubstantiality of space the unsubstantiality of beings, from the vanity of space the vanity of beings. In this way also, O Gods, are doers of what is hard the Bodhisattvas, the great beings who put on the armour for the sake of beings who do not exist. Those who for the sake of beings put on the armour are like people who would want to dispute with space. And that armour which has been put on by the Bodhisattva, the great being, and those beings for the weal of whom he has put on that armour—they likewise are not apprehended. And why? From the isolatedness of beings should the isolatedness of the armour be seen. If a Bodhisattva, a great being, when this is being taught, does not lose heart, then he courses in perfect wisdom. And why? For from the isolatedness of form, etc. should be inferred the isolatedness of beings, as well as that of the knowledge of all modes. If, when the isolatedness of all dharmas is being taught, a Bodhisattva does not lose heart, feels no despondency and does not tremble in his mind, then he courses in perfect wisdom.

V5b,2. THE SECOND DISCRIMINATION OF THE SUBJECT: REFERRING TO THE HOLY PERSONS AS BEING CONCEPTUAL ENTITIES.

The Lord: For what reason, Subhuti, does the Bodhisattva, the great being ((f. 230b)) not lose heart in the perfection of wisdom?

Subhuti: Because of the nonbeingness of all dharmas does the Bodhisattva, the great being, not lose heart in the perfection of wisdom, because of their isolatedness, their calm, their unproducedness. It is for that reason that he does not lose heart in the perfection of wisdom. And why? For he is not apprehended who would lose heart, or that whereby he would lose heart, or that whereabout he would lose heart. All these dharmas do not exist. If a Bodhisattva, a great being, when this is being taught, does not lose heart, is not cast down, does not get cowed, depressed, or stolid, and remains unafraid, then he courses in perfect wisdom. And why? For all those dharmas do not exist—he who would lose heart, that whereby he would lose heart, or that whereabout he would lose heart. When he courses thus, the gods round Indra, round Brahma, round Prajāpati pay homage to the Bodhisattva, the great being.

The Lord: These are not the only gods to pay homage to the Bodhisattva, the great being, who thus courses in perfect wisdom; but also those gods who have quite passed beyond materiality[6] of any kind, the

[6]lit. 'colour'; *AdT*: *kha-dog las śin-tu 'das-pa.*

Śubhakritsna gods, the Vṛhatphala gods, etc. *to*: the Gods of the Pure Abode[7] pay homage to him. And the Tathagatas who reside in countless world systems, they also bring him to mind. This Bodhisattva, who courses in perfect wisdom, fulfills the perfection of giving, etc. *to*: the knowledge of all modes. But the Bodhisattva who courses in perfect wisdom, and whom the Buddhas and Lords bring to mind, he should be borne in mind as a candidate to Buddhahood. If all beings in world systems countless like the sands of the Ganges should become evil Maras, and if each evil Mara would conjure up just as many evil Maras, they all would be powerless to obstruct that Bodhisattva, that great being. Endowed with two dharmas does the Bodhisattva become one hard to assail by the evil Maras: he surveys all dharmas from emptiness, and does not abandon any being. Endowed with two other dharmas does the Bodhisattva, the great being who courses in perfect wisdom, become one hard to assail by the evil Maras: as he speaks so he acts, and he is brought to mind by the Buddhas, the Lords. When a Bodhisattva courses thus, deities will think of approaching him, they will honour him, will ask questions and counterquestions, and will strengthen his determination by saying to him: 'Soon, son of good family, shall you reach the enlightenment of a Buddha! Therefore, then, son of good family, do dwell just in this dwelling, i.e. the dwelling of Emptiness, of the Signless, of the Wishless! ((f. 231 a)) And why? For dwelling in this dwelling, you shall become a saviour of the helpless, a refuge to those without refuge, a shelter of the defenseless, the final relief of those who are without one, a place of rest for those without resting place, an island to those without one, and a true light to the blind.' And why? Because the Buddhas and Lords who reside in countless world systems, and who demonstrate Dharma surrounded by the congregation of monks, they will, proclaiming the name and clan of this Bodhisattva, this great being, who dwells in this dwelling of perfect wisdom, who courses in perfect wisdom, and who is endowed with these virtues, i.e. the virtues of perfect wisdom, demonstrate Dharma, and exult.[8] Just as, Subhuti, I just here and now, proclaiming the name of the Bodhisattva Ratnaketu, the great being, demonstrate Dharma, and exult; and likewise that of the Bodhisattva Śikhin, the great being. And of the Bodhisattvas, the great beings, who lead the holy life with Akshobhya, the Tathagata, and who are not lacking in this perfection of wisdom, of them also proclaiming the name I demonstrate Dharma, and exult. And the Buddhas, the Lords who reside in each of the ten directions and demonstrate Dharma, they demonstrate the Dharma with a thrill and with much exultation to the Bodhisattvas, the great beings, who with them thus lead the holy life, and who are not

[7]cf. f. 222b-223a.

[8]*ched-du brjod-pa' aṅ ched-du brjod-pa mdzad-pa.*

without this perfection of wisdom; and likewise to the Bodhisattvas who, beginning with the first thought of enlightenment, purify the path to enlightenment, until they reach the knowledge of all modes. And why? Because doers of what is hard are the Bodhisattvas, the great beings, who make progress so that She who is the Guide of the Buddhas should suffer no interruption.

Subhuti: Of which Bodhisattvas, great beings do the Buddhas, the Lords, proclaim the name when they demonstrate Dharma—of the irreversible or the reversible?

The Lord: There are, Subhuti, ((f. 231b)) irreversible Bodhisattvas, great beings who course in perfect wisdom, and there are also unpredicted Bodhisattvas who do so. To them the Buddhas and Lords demonstrate Dharma with a thrill and with much exultation.

Subhuti: And who are they, O Lord?

The Lord: Those who under Akshobhya, the Tathagata, course on the pilgrimage of a Bodhisattva and dwell engaged on regular training,[9] these are the irreversible Bodhisattvas, great beings to whom the Buddhas and Lords demonstrate Dharma with a thrill and with much exultation. And likewise those who course on the pilgrimage of a Bodhisattva while learning from Ratnaketu, the Bodhisattva, the great being. Moreover, Subhuti, those Bodhisattvas, great beings who course in perfect wisdom, and who resolutely believe in the fact of the nongenesis of all dharmas, although they have not acquired the patient acceptance of dharmas which fail to be produced; and likewise those who, although they have not acquired the patient acceptance of dharmas which fail to be produced, resolutely believe that all dharmas are empty, that they are calmly quiet, that they are nullities, insignificant, void and unsubstantial—to them also the Buddhas and Lords demonstrate the Dharma with a thrill and with much exultation. But the Bodhisattvas, the great beings, to whom the Buddhas and Lords, while proclaiming their name, demonstrate Dharma and exult, they have forsaken the level of the Disciples and Pratyekabuddhas, and they are predicted to the supreme enlightenment. For a Bodhisattva, who courses in perfect wisdom, and of whom the Buddhas and Lords proclaim the name, will stand in irreversibility, and, having stood therein, he will reach the knowledge of all modes. Moreover, Subhuti, the Bodhisattva, the great being who, when the deep perfection of wisdom is being taught, on hearing it will not hesitate, or doubt, or be stupefied, (but will know) 'so it is as the Tathagata has taught', and will listen to it in greater detail, in the presence of the Tathagata Akshobhya and of those sons of good family who belong to the Bodhisattva-vehicle; this son of good family belonging to the Bodhisattva-vehicle will, as one who resolutely believes in this perfection of wisdom

[9] *rjes-su slob-pa'i tshul-gyis.*

as taught by the Tathagata, stand in irreversibility. For even merely to hear of the perfection of wisdom achieves much for the Bodhisattvas, the great beings, how much more (will be achieved) by those who resolutely believe in it, who, having believed, will stand in Thusness, and progress to Thusness, and who thereafter will stand firmly in the knowledge of all modes!

Subhuti: If again, O Lord, ((f. 232a)) when he has stood in Thusness and progressed to it, no dharma has been apprehended, how will he stand firmly in the knowledge of all modes? Since as distinct from Suchness no separate dharma can be apprehended,[10] who then will stand in Suchness, or who will, having stood in Suchness, fully know the supreme enlightenment and demonstrate Dharma? The Suchness, to begin with, cannot be apprehended, how much more so he who, having stood in Suchness, knows full enlightenment and demonstrates Dharma. That cannot possibly be!

The Lord: So it is, Subhuti, so it is, just as you say. And why? Whether Tathagatas are produced, or whether Tathagatas are not produced, there stands firmly established this Suchness of dharmas, their nonfalseness, unaltered Suchness, Dharmahood, there stands just this Dharma-element of dharmas, the established order of Dharma, the fixed sequence of Dharma, the Reality limit. In this Suchness no one will stand, nor will anyone, having stood in Suchness, know full enlightenment or demonstrate Dharma. And why? For therein in this Suchness no production is apprehended, no passing away, no alteration of what is established, and in such a dharma no one can stand, nor can he, having stood in it, know full enlightenment and much less can he demonstrate Dharma. That cannot possibly be!

Śakra: Deep, O Lord, is this perfection of wisdom, doers of what is hard are the Bodhisattvas, who want to know full enlightenment. And why? For no dharma, O Lord, can be apprehended, nor can anyone stand in Suchness, or know full enlightenment, or demonstrate Dharma. And yet that does not cow them, nor do they hesitate, nor are they stupefied.

V5c.[11] The first discrimination of the object (referring to the alternative of the whole of worldly activity). ((f. 228a))

V5c,1. The discrimination in its own-being.

Subhuti: How can an illusory thought know full enlightenment?

[10] *AdT*, Ms.: 'Since the magical creation of a Tathagata cannot be apprehended' as a dharma. This seems to be a corruption of *A* xxvii 453: 'Since as distinct from Suchness (*tathatā-vinirmukto*) no other dharma can be apprehended'. *AdT* takes the same view at f. 232a 5.

[11] V 5a2-V 5b2 are found at fol. 229b-232a; V5c belongs to *Ad* ch. 581 !

The Lord: What do you think, Subhuti, can you review (as a separate reality) that illusory thought?

Subhuti: No indeed, O Lord! I can review neither illusion nor a thought which is like illusion.

The Lord: What do you think, Subhuti, can that thought, wherein you can review neither illusion nor an illusory thought, know full enlightenment?

Subhuti: No indeed, O Lord!

The Lord: What do you think, Subhuti, can you, then, review that dharma which will know full enlightenment as something other than an illusion or an illusory thought?

Subhuti: No, I cannot, O Lord. Since I cannot see any dharma outside (this world of illusoriness), to which dharma can I point, and say 'it is' or 'it is not'? To a dharma which is absolutely isolated,[12] no is-ness or not-is-ness can be attributed. A dharma cannot know full enlightenment if it is absolutely isolated, or if it does not exist. And why? Because all the dharmas which could defile or purify do not exist. And why? Because the perfection of wisdom, as well as the other five perfections, as well as enlightenment—they are all absolutely isolated ((f. 228b)). And a dharma which is absolutely isolated, that should not be developed nor undeveloped.[13] Nor does this perfection of wisdom, because it is absolutely isolated, bring about any dharma. The perfection of wisdom is absolutely isolated,—how then can a Bodhisattva, by resorting to it, know full enlightenment? Even full enlightenment is absolutely isolated—how then can the isolated understand the isolated?

The Lord: Well said, Subhuti, well said! So it is, Subhuti, so it is! For the perfection of wisdom is absolutely isolated, and so are the other five perfections, enlightenment, and the knowledge of all modes. And insofar as the perfection of wisdom, etc. *to*: the knowledge of all modes, are absolutely isolated, insofar is an absolutely isolated supreme enlightenment fully known. If the perfection of wisdom, etc. *to*: the knowledge of all modes, were not absolutely isolated, then they would not be the perfection of wisdom and the knowledge of all modes. Therefore, then, Subhuti, insofar as the perfection of wisdom, etc. *to*: the knowledge of all modes are absolutely isolated, the full enlightenment cannot be known by resorting to[14] the perfection of wisdom. For the isolated cannot fully know the isolated. And yet the supreme enlightenment is fully known, but not without resorting to the perfection of wisdom.

[12]*atyantatayā vivikto. H*: No isness can be attributed to a dharma which is empty in its own-being, because it has never been produced. And since its existence has no real significance, the same is true of the correlative notion of nonexistence.

[13]*na sa bhāvayitavyo na vibhāvayitavyah, rnam-par gshig-par bgyi-ba*. The latter term is somewhat obscure and needs further clarification.

[14]*AdT*: *brten-nas*... *ma yin-la*; *Ms*: *na*... *anāgamya*; *A* xxvi 440 *āgamya*+*anāgamya*.

Subhuti: In a deep object courses the Bodhisattva, the great being, O Lord!

The Lord: So it is, Subhuti, so it is. In a deep object courses the Bodhisattva, the great being. A doer of what is hard is the Bodhisattva, the great being, when he courses in a deep object, but does not realize that object,[15] i.e. on the level[16] of Disciple or Pratyekabuddha.

Subhuti: As I understand the meaning of the Lord's teaching, the Bodhisattva, the great being, does not do anything that is hard to do—how can he be a doer of what is hard? And why? Because that object[15] cannot be apprehended which could be realized, nor that perfection of wisdom through which he would realize, nor that dharma which would realize. When all dharmas cannot be apprehended, what is the object he will realize, what is the dharma he will realize, so that he can know full enlightenment? This is the Bodhisattva's coursing in the Baseless through which he loses his blindness[17] for all dharmas. If, when this is being taught, a Bodhisattva does not despond, or become cowed, or afraid, then, thus coursing, a Bodhisattva courses in perfect wisdom. He does not, however, review the fact that he courses, nor the perfection of wisdom, nor that he will know full enlightenment. And to that Bodhisattva who courses in perfect wisdom it does not occur: 'I keep away from the level of the Disciples and Pratyekabuddhas, I am near to ((229a)) the knowledge of all modes'.

V5c,2. THE DISCRIMINATION OF THE LINEAGE.

Just, O Lord, as it does not occur to space,[18] 'I am near this or I am far from that'. And why? Because of the unbrokenness of space, its immobility, its nondiscriminativeness. Just so it does not occur to the Bodhisattva, the great being who courses in perfect wisdom, 'the Disciple-level or the Pratyekabuddha-level is far from me, the utmost, right, and perfect enlightenment is near to me'. And why? Because of the lack of discrimination on the part of the perfection of wisdom.

V5c,3. THE DISCRIMINATION OF (THE PROCESS WHICH LEADS TO) FULL ATTAINMENT.

Just as it does not occur to an illusory man, 'the illusion is far from me, the conjuror is near to me, again this assembled crowd of people, that is far from me or near to me'. And why? Because of the lack of discrimination on the part of the illusory man. Just so it does not occur to the Bodhisattva, the great being who courses in perfect wisdom, 'the

[15]*artha*, also 'gain'.

[16]So *A* xxvi 440 : *-bhūmau*; Ms. : "i.e. the stage of a Disciple etc.".

[17]*anandhakāratām anuprāpnoti.*

[18]*Ad* and *S* 165a have *abhyavakāśa*, *P* 435b *ākāśa*, *AdT nam-mkha*'.

Disciple-level or the Pratyekabuddha-level is far from me, the utmost, right, and perfect enlightenment is near to me'.

V5c,4. THE DISCRIMINATION OF THE OBJECT (OF UNMISTAKEN COGNITION).

Just as it does not occur to a reflected image,[19] 'the object by which the reflected image has arisen, that is near to me; but again those who have approached in that mirror or bowl of water, they are far from me'. And why? Because of lack of discrimination on the part of the reflected image. Just so it does not occur to the Bodhisattva, the great being who courses in the perfection of wisdom, 'the Disciple-level or the Pratyekabuddha-level is far from me, the utmost, right, and perfect enlightenment is near to me'. And why? Because of the lack of discrimination on the part of the perfection of wisdom. For, O Lord, to the perfection of wisdom nothing is dear or undear. And why? Because the own-being of that which would be dear or undear cannot be apprehended.

V5c,5. THE DISCRIMINATION OF POINTS TO BE SHUNNED AND ANTIDOTES.

Just as for the Tathagata, the Arhat, the Fully Enlightened One nothing dear or undear exists, just so also for the perfection of wisdom.

V5c,6. THE DISCRIMINATION OF ONE'S OWN SPIRITUAL ACHIEVEMENTS.

Just as the Tathagata is one who has forsaken all constructions and discriminations, just so has the perfection of wisdom forsaken all constructions and discriminations, on account of (its) nondiscrimination.

V5c,7. THE DISCRIMINATION OF THE DOER.

Just as it does not occur to a magical creation of the Tathagata, 'the Disciple-level or the Pratyekabuddha-level is far from me, full enlightenment is near to me'. And why? Because of the lack of discrimination on the part of the Tathagata and of his magical creation. Just so also it does not occur to a Bodhisattva, a great being, who courses in the perfection of wisdom, 'the Disciple-level or the Pratyekabuddha-level is far from me, full enlightenment is near to me.'

V5c,8. THE DISCRIMINATION OF THE ACTIVITY.

Just as, when the Tathagata conjures up a (fictitious) magical creation, he, for whose sake the magical creation performs its work,[20] and that magical creation (itself), are undiscriminated, undifferentiated; just so that for the sake of which the perfection of wisdom is developed and does its work, and that perfection of wisdom (itself) are undiscriminated, undifferentiated.

[19]*pratibimba, gzugs brñan*; *P*: *pratibhāsa*.

[20]*AdT*: *de ni de ni gaṅ-gi slad-du sprul-pa de'i bgyi-ba bgyid*; cf. *A* xxvi 443.

V5c,9. THE DISCRIMINATION OF THE ACTIONS WITH THEIR FRUITS.

Just as an expert mason or mason's apprentice may have made a machine, in the shape of a woman, a man, an elephant, or a bull; for whatever work it has been made, that work it performs. And that machine has no discrimination. Just so the perfection of wisdom performs the work for the sake of which it is developed and yet it is indiscriminate. ((f. 229a))

V5d.[20a] THE SECOND DISCRIMINATION OF THE OBJECT, (REFERING TO THE ALTERNATIVE OF WITHDRAWAL FROM ACTIVITY, WHICH IS NINEFOLD.) ((f. 243A))

V5d,1. THE DEFICIENCY IN SPIRITUAL ACHIEVEMENT (WHICH RESULTS WHEN SAMSARA AND NIRVANA, OR BECOMING AND QUIETUDE, ARE ALLOWED TO FALL APART).

Subhuti: For how long, then, has this Bodhisattva, this great being, set out who is endowed with this skill in means?

The Lord: For countless hundreds of thousands of niyutas of kotis of aeons.

Subhuti: How many Buddhas and Lords have these Bodhisattvas honoured?

The Lord: They have honoured Buddhas and Lords countless as the sands of the Ganges.

Subhuti: How large[21] is the wholesome root which they have planted?

The Lord: From the first thought of enlightenment onwards there is no perfection of giving, etc. *to*: no perfection of wisdom which they have not fulfilled.

Subhuti: It is wonderful, O Lord, how these Bodhisattvas are endowed with this skill in means!

The Lord: So it is, Subhuti, so it is. Just as the disk of the sun and moon light up[22] the four continents, follow them and revolve round them; just so the perfection of wisdom does the work of the five perfections, and the five perfections follow it and revolve round it. When they do not lack in the perfection of wisdom the five perfections get the designation of 'perfections', but not so when they do lack in it. Just as the World Ruler, when he lacks in the seven precious things,[23] does not get the name of World Ruler', just so, when they lack in perfect wisdom, the five perfections do not get the designation of 'perfections'.

[20a] V 5d-V 5f belongs to *Ad* ch. 63!

[21] *S*: *kin*; *P*: *kiyadbhir*; *AdT*: *ji-tsam shig*.

[22] so *AdT*; *S, P*: "do the work in".

[23] For the list see V 5d, 9.

V5d,2. THE DISCRIMINATION OF THE ABSENCE OF ASSISTANCE (FROM THE GOOD FRIEND AND FROM SKILL IN MEANS).

Just as, Subhuti, a woman without a husband is easily assailed by rogues, just so, Subhuti, the five perfections, when lacking in the perfection of wisdom, are easily assailed by Mara, the Evil One, and by the divinities of his host.

V5d,3. THE DISCRIMINATION OF THE INCOMPLETENESS OF THE PROGRESS.

Just as, Subhuti, in battle a man who is armed with a complete armour is hard to assail by hostile kings, enemies, or foes, just so, when they are not lacking in the perfection of wisdom, the five perfections are hard to assail by Mara, the Evil One, by the divinities of his host, by conceited persons, etc. *to*: by those who are outcasts among Bodhisattvas.

V5d,4. THE DISCRIMINATION OF THE FACT THAT ONE GOES TO OUTSIDERS FOR HELP.

Just as, Subhuti, the commanders of forts act in obedience to the World Ruler, and are at all times ready to serve him, just so the five perfections, when taken hold of by the perfection of wisdom, arrive at where the knowledge of all modes is.

V5d,5. THE DISCRIMINATION OF GOING BACK ON THE PROGRAMME.

Just as, Subhuti, whatever small rivers there are, they all flow into the river Ganges and come to the great ocean together with it, just so the five perfections, when taken hold of by the perfection of wisdom, arrive at where the knowledge of all modes is.

V5d,6. THE DISCRIMINATION OF (BEING CONTENT) WITH A LIMITED ACTIVITY.

The perfection of wisdom may be likened to a man's right hand, which does all his work; the five perfections may be likened to his left hand.

V5d,7. THE DISCRIMINATION OF THE DIFFERENTIATION BETWEEN (VARIOUS KINDS OF) SPIRITUAL ACHIEVEMENTS.

Just as all the water in the small and large rivers becomes of one taste once it has flows into the great ocean, just so the five perfections, taken hold of by the perfection of wisdom, enter together with it into the knowledge of all modes, and get the name of 'perfections'.[24]

V5d,8. THE DISCRIMINATION OF NONCOGNITION AS TO STANDING AND SETTING OUT.

Just as, Subhuti, the jewel of the Wheel precedes the four-fold army

[24] *S* adds: "and they become of one taste, i.e. the taste of the knowledge of all modes".

of the World Ruler, and stays there; and wherever the World Ruler places it for the sake of food, there he refreshes his army, and that jewel of the Wheel does not move away from that position; just so, Subhuti, the perfection of wisdom is the leader of these five perfections, and they follow it to the knowledge of all modes. Therein they will stand, and, having stood therein, they will not move away from that position.

V5d,9. THE DISCRIMINATION OF GOING FORTH (ONLY) AFTERWARDS.

Just as the jewel of the Wheel, that of the General, the Householder, the Wife, the Gem, the Elephant, and the Horse precede the fourfold army of a World Ruler, just so the perfection of wisdom precedes these five perfections, and stands (still) where the knowledge of all modes is. And yet it does not occur to the perfection of wisdom, 'May the perfection of giving ((243b)) follow me', etc. *to*: 'may the perfection of meditation follow me'. Nor does it occur to the perfection of giving, 'I will follow the perfection of wisdom', and so for the other perfections. And why? Because this is their own-being that they are incapable of doing anything,[25] empty in their own-being, vanities, a mere mirage.

Subhuti: If, O Lord, all dharmas are empty of own-being, how then does the Bodhisattva, coursing in the perfection of giving, etc. *to*: in the perfection of wisdom, awake to full enlightenment?

The Lord: Here it occurs to the Bodhisattva, who courses in the six perfections: 'a perverted thought surely is this fabrication of the world. Without skill in means it cannot possibly be set free from birth-and-death; for the sake of these beings I should course in the perfection of giving, etc. *to*: in the perfection of wisdom'. For the sake of these beings he renounces his inward and outward possessions, but thinks: 'not anything have I renounced'. And why? Because he knows that possession to be empty of own-being. When he considers thus, the Bodhisattva fulfills the perfection of giving. He also, for the sake of these beings, gives no occasion to immorality. And why? For he thinks to himself: 'that would not be seemly for me that I who have set out for full enlightenment should take life, etc. *to*: have false views, or should strive after sense objects, or the condition of a god or Brahma, or the level of a Disciple or Pratyekabuddha'. When he considers thus, the Bodhisattva courses in the perfection of morality. For the sake of those beings he also does not become angry in his mind, when abused and reviled with sharp and harsh words; nor does he feel hatred when struck with blows from clods, sticks, swords, or stones, or when his body is broken, or cut limb from limb. And why? Because all that he regards as no more than an echo.

[25]*akiṃcitsamartha, nus-pa cuṅ-zad kyaṅ med-la*; also at f. 258b, 259a where *AdT* has: *byed-pa'i mthu med ciṅ*. At *f.* 235b 'incapable of doing anything' renders *akriyāsamartha, bya-ba-la mthu med-pa*.

He regards form as a mass of foam, etc. *to* : consciousness as like an illusion.[26] ((f. 244a)) When he considers thus, the Bodhisattva courses in the perfection of patience. For the sake of just those beings he never, while on his way to full enlightenment, produces a lazy thought, but diligently he searches for all that is wholesome. And why? Because he thinks to himself, 'the lazy can neither work the weal of beings nor know full enlightenment'. When he considers thus, the Bodhisattva, the great being, courses in the perfection of vigour. For the sake of those beings he never, while on his way to full enlightenment, has distracted thoughts. When he considers thus, the Bodhisattva, the great being, courses in the perfection of meditation. For the sake of those beings he also, while on his way to full enlightenment, never again becomes lacking in wisdom. And why? For he knows that he could not mature beings except by entering into the perfection of wisdom, and that therefore he should not produce even one single stupid thought. It is thus that the Bodhisattva, the great being, just for the sake of beings courses in the perfection of wisdom.

Subhuti : If there is no difference between the perfections, how is it that this perfection of wisdom has been called the foremost of the five perfections, the principal, the best, the choicest, the most excellent, the most sublime, the highest, the utmost, the unequalled?

The Lord : So it is, Subhuti, so it is. There is no difference at all between the perfections. But if there were no perfect wisdom, then these five perfections would not get the designation of 'perfections'. For it is thanks to the perfection of wisdom that they get this designation. Just as, Subhuti, various kinds of bodies, when they have approached Sumeru, the king of mountains, become of one colour, just so, Subhuti, thanks to the perfection of wisdom, these five perfections get the designation of 'perfections' and when they have entered into the knowledge of all modes, they become of one colour, i.e. of the colour of perfect wisdom, and no more distinction between them is conceived, (so that one could say :) 'this is the perfection of giving,' etc. *to* : 'this is the perfection of wisdom'. And why? Because they have no own-being—for that reason no distinction (between them) is conceived.

Subhuti : If, O Lord, of any dharma which is modelled on an objective entity[27] no distinction or difference is conceived, how is it that the perfection of wisdom has been declared to be among the perfections the foremost, the principal, etc. *to* : the unequalled?

The Lord : So it is, Subhuti, so it is. No distinction or difference is conceived of any dharma which is modelled on an objective entity. But

[26]For the full list see f. 241a.

[27]*artha-anupratipannasya P*; *arthaprāptau* Ms *Ad*; *don-gyi rjes-su shugs-pa*. I have not really understood this term.

it is in order to free beings from the round of birth-and-death that through agreed symbols and worldly convention the perfection of giving, etc. *to* : the perfection of wisdom have been conceived. But all those beings are not born, do not die, have not deceased, are not reborn, are not beings. From the nonbeingness of beings should the nonbeingness of all dharmas be known. By this method the perfection of wisdom has been declared to be among the perfections the foremost, etc. *to* : ((f. 244b)) the unequalled. As, Subhuti, among the women of Jambudvipa, however many there may be, one may be called the most precious, just so the perfection of wisdom has been declared among the perfections to be the foremost, etc. *to* : the unequalled.

Subhuti : What is here the intent in declaring the perfection of wisdom to be the foremost, etc.?

The Lord: Because this perfection of wisdom, having taken hold of all wholesome dharmas, will stand in the knowledge of all modes by way of not taking a stand there.

V5e. The first discrimination of the subject : referring to the common people as being substantial entities : which is ninefold.

V5e,1. With regard to taking hold of, and liberation.

Subhuti : Does then the perfection of wisdom take hold of any dharma or does it release one?

The Lord: No, it does not. And why? Because all these dharmas are neither seized nor released.

Subhuti: Which all dharmas does the perfection of wisdom neither seize nor release?

The Lord: Form, etc. *to* : enlightenment.

V5e,2. The discrimination of attention.

Subhuti : How does form, etc. *to* : the knowledge of all modes, become something that has not been taken hold of?

The Lord: Through the nonattention to form, etc. Through the nonattention to the knowledge of all modes enlightenment becomes something that has not been taken hold of. It is thus that form, etc. *to* : enlightenment become something that has not been taken hold of.

Subhuti: If, O Lord, one should not attend to form, etc. how then, with form, etc. being unattended, do the wholesome roots grow? And how, when they do not grow, are the six perfections fulfilled? And how, without the six perfections being fulfilled, can the knowledge of all modes be reached?

The Lord: When the Bodhisattva does not attend to form, etc. *to* : enlightenment, then his wholesome roots will grow, the six perfections be fulfilled, the knowledge of all modes be reached. And why? After he has not attended to form, etc. *to*: enlightenment, he will know full enlightenment.

V5e,3. THE DISCRIMINATION OF THE (NON) ADHERENCE TO THAT WHICH BELONGS TO THE TRIPLE WORLD.

Subhuti: What is the reason why, not having attended to form, etc. *to*: enlightenment, he will reach the knowledge of all modes?

The Lord: Because through his nonattention he does not cling to the world of sense desire, the world of form, or the formless world. By this nonattention he does not cling to anything. It is thus indeed that the Bodhisattva, the great being, who courses in perfect wisdom, should not cling to any dharma whatever.

V5e,4. THE DISCRIMINATION OF THE STANDING PLACE.

Subhuti: When the Bodhisattva, ((f. 245a)) the great being, thus courses in perfect wisdom, where then will he stand?

The Lord: When he courses thus the Bodhisattva, the great being, will not stand in forms, or in anything else up *to*: the knowledge of all modes.

V5e,5. THE DISCRIMINATION OF SETTLING DOWN IN THE DISCRIMINATION BETWEEN EXISTENTS AND NONEXISTENTS.

Subhuti: For what reason does he not stand even in this knowledge of all modes?

The Lord: Because of his not settling down (anywhere) does he not stand anywhere. And why? Because he does not review all the dharmas in which he might settle down or abide. It is thus that the Bodhisattva, the great being courses in perfect wisdom by way of not settling down, by way of not taking his stand (anywhere).

V5e,6. THE DISCRIMINATION BETWEEN OBJECTIVE AND NOMINAL ENTITIES.

But if it occurs to the Bodhisattva, the great being, that 'he who courses thus, who develops thus, he courses in perfect wisdom, he develops perfect wisdom; I course in perfect wisdom, I develop perfect wisdom',—if he perceives thus, then he moves away from perfect wisdom, he gets far away from the perfection of wisdom, and from the other perfections, etc. *to*: from the knowledge of all modes. And why? Because the perfection of wisdom does not settle down in any dharma, nor is it capable of doing so. And why? Because that wherein one could settle down has no own-being. If again the Bodhisattva, the great being, perceives even the perfection of wisdom, then he has fallen away from it. When he falls away from the perfection of wisdom, then he falls away from all dharmas. If it occurs to him, 'the perfection of wisdom takes hold of the five perfections, etc. *to*: of the knowledge of all modes', then the Bodhisattva, the great being has fallen away from the perfection of wisdom. But someone who has failed in the perfection of wisdom is not able to know full enlightenment. If again it occurs to him: 'one who has stood in this perfection of wisdom will be predicted to full enlightenment', then the Bodhisattva, the great being, has fallen away from the perfection of wisdom. And someone who has fallen away from the perfection of wisdom is not predicted to full enlightenment. If again it occurs to him, 'a Bodhisattva, a great being who has stood in this perfection of wisdom consummates[28] the perfection of giving, etc. *to*: the great compassion', then the Bodhisattva, the great being, has fallen away from the perfection of wisdom. And why? Because someone who has fallen away from the perfection of wisdom is not capable of consummating the perfection of giving, etc. *to*: the great compassion. If again it occurs to him, 'the Tathagata has taken hold of all dharmas; on his own he has fully known them, and then he has proclaimed, demonstrated and revealed them', then the Bodhisattva, the great being, has fallen away from the perfection of wisdom. And why? Because the Tathagata does not conceive any dharma,[29] how much less will he fully know one! That is quite impossible.

V5e,7. THE DISCRIMINATION OF ATTACHMENT.

Subhuti: How can a Bodhisattva, a great being who courses in perfect wisdom, be without these faults?

The Lord: If the Bodhisattva, the great being who courses in perfect wisdom, perceives that all dharmas, as unattached[30] and not taken hold of, cannot be fully known—if he courses thus, then he courses in perfect wisdom. But if he settles down in a dharma which he cannot possibly take hold of, then he lacks ((f. 245b)) in perfect wisdom. And why? Because the perfection of wisdom cannot be expressed by way of settling down.

V5e,8. THE DISCRIMINATION OF ANTIDOTES.

Subhuti: Is, then, the perfection of wisdom not lacking in the perfection of wisdom, etc. *to*: is the knowledge of all modes not lacking in the knowledge of all modes? If that were so,

V5e,9. THE DISCRIMINATION OF THE IMPAIRMENT OF THE ABILITY TO GO WHEREVER ONE WISHES TO GO.

how then can the perfection of wisdom be consummated, etc. *to*: how

[28]*abhinirharati, mṅon-par bsgrub-par bya'o,* cf. ch. 61 n. 2.

[29]The Tibetan has: 'because he does not even apprehend visible dharmas, how much less one which he could fully know!'

[30]So *AdT*, *P*. Ms: nonexistent.

can the knowledge of all modes be consummated?

The Lord: Here the Bodhisattva, the great being who courses in perfect wisdom, does not settle down in 'form', in 'this is form', or 'his is this form', and so for everything up to the knowledge of all modes. He does not settle down in form, etc. *to* : the knowledge of all modes by way of permanence or impermanence, ease or ill, self or not self, calm or not calm, empty or not empty, sign or signless, wish or wishless, isolated or not isolated. And why? Because a dharma which has no own-being cannot aspire[31] for permanence or impermanence, etc. *to* : for isolatedness or nonisolatedness.[32] An own-being which is empty of own-being is incapable of consummation. This Bodhisattva, this great being again will, when he courses thus in this perfection of wisdom, etc. *to* : in the perfection of giving ((f. 246a)), stand in the knowledge of all modes. Just as, Subhuti, the four-fold army of the World Ruler goes just where the World Ruler goes, just so, Subhuti, wherever the perfection of wisdom may go, there these five perfections go likewise, and where the knowledge of all modes is, there they come to a stand.

V5f. THE SECOND DISCRIMINATION OF THE SUBJECT: REFERRING TO (THE HOLY PERSONS) AS BEING CONCEPTUAL ENTITIES; WHICH IS NINEFOLD.

V5f,1. THE DISCRIMINATION OF NOT GOING FORTH ACCORDING TO THE PROGRAMME.

Just as a charioteer, having mounted on a chariot drawn by four horses, goes along on the right[33] road, just so the perfection of wisdom acts as a charioteer for these five perfections, and by the right road it arrives where the knowledge of all modes is.

V5f,2. THE DISCRIMINATION OF THE COGNITION OF WHAT IS THE PATH AND WHAT IS NOT THE PATH.

Subhuti: What is of the Bodhisattvas, the great beings, the path, and what is not the path?

The Lord: The paths of the Disciples and Pratyekabuddhas are not the paths of the Bodhisattvas, the great beings, but the path to the knowledge of all modes is the path of the Bodhisattvas, the great beings. These are both the path and the no-path of the Bodhisattvas, the great beings.

V5f,3. THE DISCRIMINATION BETWEEN PRODUCTION AND STOPPING.

Subhuti: For a great performance has this perfection of wisdom of the

[31] *abhinirhartum.*
[32] *abhinirhartum.*
[33] *sama, mñam-pa*; *P*: *samyak.*

Bodhisattvas, the great beings, been set up, for it guides to 'this is the path, this is not the path'.

The Lord: So it is, Subhuti, so it is. For a great performance on the part of the Bodhisattvas, the great beings, has the perfection of wisdom been set up, since she shows up the path and the no-path. For an immeasurable and incalculable performance has the perfection of wisdom of the Bodhisattvas, the great beings, been set up. But, although the perfection of wisdom lends lustre[34] to the performance, it does not take hold of form, etc. *to* : consciousness. Nor has it been set up for the sake of taking hold of Discipleship or Pratyekabuddhahood, but on the contrary, this perfection of wisdom is the leader of the Bodhisattva, the great being, to full enlightenment. She does not lead to the level of the Disciples or Pratyekabuddhas, but to the acquisition[35] of the knowledge of all modes. It is thus that this perfection of wisdom neither produces nor stops any dharma, if the fixed nature of Dharma is made into the standard.

Subhuti: If the perfection of wisdom neither produces nor stops any dharma, how then should the Bodhisattva, the great being who courses in perfect wisdom, give gifts, how guard morality, etc. *to* : how develop wisdom?

The Lord: After he has made the knowledge of all modes into his objective support, he should give gifts. Having made these wholesome roots common to all beings, he should dedicate them to supreme enlightenment. Then the six perfections go in him to their full development, and so does the ((f. 246b)) knowledge of all modes. A Bodhisattva, a great being who is not lacking in the six perfections, is also not lacking in the knowledge of all modes. A Bodhisattva, a great being who wants to know full enlightenment, should therefore train in the six perfections. When he courses in the six perfections, then the Bodhisattva, the great being, having fulfilled all the wholesome roots, will reach the knowledge of all modes. Therefore, then, should the Bodhisattva, the great being, make efforts about the six perfections.

V5f,4. The discriminations between conjunction (samyoga) and disjunction (visamyoga).

Subhuti: How should the Bodhisattva, the great being make efforts (*yoga*) about the six perfections?

The Lord: Here the Bodhisattva, the great being should contemplate thus: Form, etc. is neither conjoined nor disjoined. It is thus that the Bodhisattva, the great being, should make efforts about the six perfections.

[34]*varṇayati* seems to be taken in a special sense here, but I am not sure that I have guessed it correctly.

[35]So *AdT*.

V5f,5. THE DISCRIMINATION OF THE STANDING ON FORM, ETC.

Moreover the Bodhisattva, the great being, should make efforts in the sense, 'I will not stand in form, etc.' And why? Because form, etc. is not established anywhere. It is thus, by not taking his stand anywhere, that the Bodhisattva, the great being, should know full enlightenment.

V5f,6. THE DISCRIMINATION OF THE LOSS OF THE LINEAGE.

It is just as if a man would want to eat mangoes or bread fruits. First of all he must plant mangoes or bread fruits; having planted them, he must in due season and at regular times water them, and carefully look after them; as they gradually grow branches and boughs, his fruits will get ready and obtain the full complement of conditions; and he will be able to eat those mangoes and bread fruits. Just so the Bodhisattva, the great being who wants to know full enlightenment, should, after he has trained in the six perfections, help beings with gifts, with morality, patience, vigour, trance, and wisdom, and should liberate them from the round of birth-and-death.

V5f,7. THE DISCRIMINATION OF THE ABSENCE OF STRIVING.

Therefore, then, a Bodhisattva, a great being, who wants to gain a state where he cannot be led astray by others, to purify the Buddha-field, to sit on the terrace of enlightenment, and to turn the wheel of Dharma, should train in the six perfections.

Subhuti: You say that he should through perfect wisdom train in perfect wisdom?

The Lord: So I do. I say also that he should train in perfect wisdom if he wants to gain the development of sovereignty over all dharmas.

V5f,8. THE DISCRIMINATION WITH REGARD TO THE ABSENCE OF A CAUSE.

And why? Because this perfection of wisdom through which one gains the stage of the sovereignty over all dharmas, is the door to all dharmas. Just as, Subhuti, the great ocean is the door of all rivers, so is the perfection of wisdom the door to all dharmas.[36] Whether persons belong to the vehicle of the Disciples, or to that of the Pratyekabuddhas, or to that of the Bodhisattvas, they all should train in just this perfection of wisdom. Therefore, then, the Bodhisattva, the great being, should train in the six perfections ((f. 247a)), etc. *to*: in the knowledge of all modes.

V5f,9. THE DISCRIMINATION OF THE APPREHENSION OF HOSTILE DHARMAS.

Just as a teacher of archery, Subhuti, when he has found a suitable

[36]*AdT* and *P* add that, as the waters of the rivers, once they have flown into the ocean, become all of one taste, so also all dharmas, once they have reached the perfection of wisdom, all become perfect wisdom.

bow, cannot be overpowered by his enemies or foes, just so the Bodhisattva, the great being, when he courses in perfect wisdom, cannot be overpowered by Mara or the divinities of his host. Therefore, then, the Bodhisattva, the great being, who wants to know full enlightenment, should train in perfect wisdom. And when he courses in perfect wisdom, then the past, future, and present Buddhas and Lords bring him to mind.

Subhuti: How do the Buddhas and Lords bring to mind the Bodhisattva, the great being who courses in the perfections, in the emptinesses, etc. *to*: in the knowledge of all modes?

The Lord: Here, Subhuti, the past, future, and present Buddhas and Lords bring to mind the Bodhisattva, the great being, who courses in the six perfections, but in such a way that thereby no giving, morality, etc. *to*: wisdom is apprehended. Through nonapprehension they thus bring to mind the Bodhisattva, the great being. Moreover, the Buddhas and Lords do not bring the Bodhisattva, the great being, to mind through form, etc. *to*: through the knowledge of all modes.

V5g.[37] THREE REASONS FOR THE ATTAINMENT OF FULL ENLIGHTENMENT.

V5g,1. THE INDICATION OF THE GREAT ACHIEVEMENT TO OTHERS.

Subhuti: When you say, Kauśika, 'Doers of what is hard are the Bodhisattvas, the great beings, who have neither hesitation nor stupefaction about these deep dharmas'—where all dharmas are empty, who can have any hesitation or stupefaction about them?

Śakra: Whatever Subhuti the Elder may expound, all that he expounds with reference to emptiness, and he does not get stuck anywhere. Just as an arrow shot into the air does not get stuck anywhere, just so Subhuti the Elder's demonstration ((f. 232b)) of Dharma.

[37]V 5c has been placed to f. 228a. We here return to *Ad* ch. 59.

CHAPTER 60

ENTRUSTING

Śakra: Then, perhaps, O Lord, when I teach and explain thus,[1] I will become one who repeats what the Lord has said, a preacher of Dharma, one who correctly states the Dharma and also its logical sequence?[2]

The Lord: When, Kauśika, you teach and explain thus, you become one who repeats what the Tathagata has said, you preach Dharma, and you state both the Dharma and its logical sequence!

Śakra: It is wonderful, O Lord, how the Elder Subhuti makes everything clear with reference to Emptiness, the Signless, and the Wishless; to the applications of mindfulness, etc. *to*: to enlightenment.

The Lord: The Elder Subhuti, Kauśika, dwells in emptiness,[3] and so he does not apprehend the six perfections, how much less him who courses in them. And so for the other practices and achievements.[4] And why? For the Elder Subhuti is one who dwells in the isolatedness of all dharmas, who dwells in the Baseless, in Emptiness, the Signless, and the Wishless. And yet this dwelling of Subhuti the Elder is of infinitesimal value compared with the dwelling of a Bodhisattva, a great being, who courses in perfect wisdom. ((f. 233a)) And why? Except for the dwelling of a Tathagata this dwelling of a Bodhisattva, a great being who courses in perfect wisdom, is the supreme dwelling, superior to that of the Disciples and Pratyekabuddhas. Therefore then, Kauśika, the Bodhisattva, the great being, who wants to go to what is the highest possible degree of perfection for all beings should dwell in this dwelling of the perfection of wisdom. And why? When he courses in this perfection of wisdom the Bodhisattva, the great being, passes above the level of the Disciples and Pratyekabuddhas, he enters on a Bodhisattva's specific salvation, and after that he perfects the Buddhadharmas, and then reaches the cognition of the knowledge of all modes. On reaching the cognition of the knowledge of all modes, he becomes one who has a Tathagata's forsaking of all the defilements and their residues.

[1] *A* adds: 'in conformity with (*ārabhya*) the Ven. Subhuti'.

[2] *H* 862 explains *dharmasya cānudharmam* of *A* xxvii 454 as *yathā praṇihitasya śūnyatā-dharmasya pratipattim*.

[3] *śūnyatayā, stoṅ-pa ñid-kyis*.

[4] Here a list of 7 lines is omitted.

Thereupon the Gods of the Thirty-three in that assembly seized Mandarava flowers and strewed, scattered, and spread them over the Lord. And *six thousand monks* rose from their seats, put their upper robes over one shoulder, placed their right knees on the ground, and saluted the Lord with folded hands and with their wide-open eyes firmly fixed upon Him.[5]

Thereupon through the Buddha's might the cupped hands of these monks were filled with Mandarava flowers, and they strewed, scattered, and spread them over the Tathagata, and exclaimed : 'We, O Lord, shall dwell by means of this wholesome root in the utmost dwelling, to which all Disciples and Pratyekabuddhas have no access!' And when the Lord knew of the resolve of these monks, he manifested on that occasion a smile. But such is the nature of the Buddhas and Lords that, when they manifest a smile, many-coloured, various-coloured rays issue from their mouths—rays blue, yellow, red, white, crimson, crystal, silverish, and golden. These rays, after they have irradiated the great trichiliocosm with their lustre, return again to the Lord, circulate thrice round Him, and then vanish again in the Lord's head.

Thereupon the *Ven. Ānanda* rose from his seat, put his upper robe over one shoulder, placed his right knee on the ground, bent his folded hands towards the Lord, and said : What is the cause, O Lord, what the reason for the manifestation of a smile? It is not without cause or reason that Tathagatas manifest a smile.

The Lord: These six thousand monks, Ānanda, will in the starlike aeon know full enlightenment, they all will in the world be Tathagatas by the name of Avakīrṇakusuma—with an equal congregation of monks, an equal Buddha-field, an equal[6] lifespan of one thousand years. ((f. 233b)) Wherever they may leave home, wherever they will take up the homeless life, wherever they will know full enlightenment, there showers of Kusuma flowers, of all the five colours, shall rain down on all of them. Therefore, then, Ānanda, the Bodhisattva, the great being, who wants to dwell in the highest dwelling, in the dwelling of the Tathagata, should course in the perfection of wisdom.

V5g,2. With enlightenment for cause the entrusting of the perfection of wisdom.

V5g,2a. Introduction.[7]

And, Ānanda, any son or daughter of good family who courses in

[5] *animiṣābhyāṃ cakṣurbhyāṃ prekṣamāṇā*; *mig mi 'dzum-pas*.

[6] *sama*, 'equal' rather than 'identical'?

[7] *Upodghāta*, or 'preface'.—The three subdivisions of V5g,2 are not found in *P*, and are here added from *AAA* pp. 869-874.

this deep perfection of wisdom should be quite certain that he has been reborn here after just having deceased among men or the heavenly hosts of the Tushitas.[8] For only men and the heavenly hosts of the Tushitas hear this perfection of wisdom in detail. As beheld by the Tathagatas should those Bodhisattvas, great beings, be seen who will course in this deep perfection of wisdom. And if any son or daughter of good family will hear this deep perfection of wisdom, learn it, bear it in mind, preach and study it, and wisely attend to it, and if he will also instruct and admonish in it persons belonging to the Bodhisattva-vehicle, then this follower of the Bodhisattva-vehicle may be quite certain that 'face to face I will be with the Tathagatas, this deep perfection of wisdom I will hear from them, learn it, bear it in mind, preach and study it, and wholesome roots will be planted with those Tathagatas'. That son or daughter of good family should know that they have not planted wholesome roots with Disciples, and that this deep perfection of wisdom cannot be learned from them. The son or daughter of good family who will hear this deep perfection of wisdom, bear it in mind, preach and study it, and pursue it according to its meaning, contents, and method,[9] should be quite certain that he will be face to face with the Tathagata. If a son or daughter of good family, when they hear this perfection of wisdom being taught, do not reject or oppose it, but acquire a serene faith in it, as one who has fulfilled his duties under the Jinas of the past such a son of good family should be known, as one who has planted wholesome roots, as one who has been taken hold of by the spiritual friend. The wholesome root which that son of good family has planted in the presence of the Tathagatas, he does not go back on that—into Discipleship or Pratyekabuddhahood.[10] The Bodhisattva, the great being, should become one who has well penetrated when he courses in the perfection of giving, and the other perfections, etc. *to* : in the knowledge of all modes ((f. 234a)), for then he will not stand in Discipleship or Pratyekabuddhahood.

V5g,2b. THE ENTRUSTING IN CONNECTION WITH THE TATHAGATA.

Therefore, then, Ānanda, I entrust to you this deep perfection of wisdom. If, Ānanda, as concerns the Dharma I have demonstrated, you would, after learning and studying it, again forget all that demonstration of Dharma except for the perfection of wisdom, and discard it, that, Ānanda, would not be a great offence against me. But if, Ānanda,

[8]The same argument also in *Ad* ch. 44=*P* 340-341.

[9]This is a tentative and inadequate rendering of *arthataś ca dharmataś ca vyañjanataś ca* (*tshul-las*). *A* xxviii 460 has *nayatas* for *vyañjanatas*. At *A* v 112 *vyañjana* 'the letter' is contrasted with *artha*, 'the meaning', and also at *A* xxviii 461 and xxx 491 it clearly refers to the verbal expression of the teaching.

[10]Ms adds: Or Buddhahood, ND omits this. *H.* at *A* 460: he does not give over the reward or karmaresult to Discipleship or Pratyekabuddhahood.

when you have learned this perfection of wisdom, you would forget even a single verse of it, that would be a serious offence against me. If, however, when you have learned this deep perfection of wisdom, you would not again forget and discard it, then you would not offend me. Therefore, then, Ānanda, I entrust to you this deep perfection of wisdom so that, when it has been learned, it should be borne in mind, preached, and studied; one should well attend to it, well take hold of it, well study it, well bear it in mind, and one should well analyse and learn it, letter by letter, syllable by syllable, word by word. The son or daughter of good family who learns this deep perfection of wisdom will be one who bears in mind the enlightenment of the past, future, and present Buddhas and Lords, and he assists[11] that enlightenment. If someone wishes, face to face with Me, to honour, adore, revere, and worship Me with flowers, garlands, perfumes, unguents, aromatic powders, robes, parasols, flags, and banners, then he should learn, bear in mind, preach and study this perfection of wisdom, and thereafter honour, adore, revere, and worship it with flowers, etc. *to*: with banners. Those who honour this perfection of wisdom, they thereby worship Me, as well as the Buddhas and Lords of the past, future, and present. If anyone, when this deep perfection of wisdom is being preached, feels respect, affection, and serene faith for it, then he feels respect, affection and serene faith also for the Buddhas and Lords of the past, future, and present. If, Ānanda, I am dear and pleasing to you, and you do not abandon Me,[12] let this perfection of wisdom become dear and pleasing to you, and may you not abandon it, so that you may not forget even a single word of it. For long could I speak to you, Ānanda, about this bestowal of the perfection of wisdom. To cut it short, Ānanda, just as I am your Teacher, so is ((ff. 234b)) this perfection of wisdom. Therefore, then, Ānanda, with a measureless bestowal I again entrust[13] to you this perfection of wisdom. In front of the world with its gods, men, and Asuras I solemnly declare: One who does not want to abandon the Buddha, Dharma, or Samgha, nor the past, future, and present Buddhas and Lords, or their enlightenment, let him not abandon this perfection of wisdom! And this is My admonition to you: those sons or daughters of good family who will learn this deep perfection of wisdom, bear it in mind, preach and study it, place their trust in it, wisely attend to it, and who will declare it also to others by various methods and in detail, will demonstrate it, make it known, set them going in it, explain it, analyse it, enlarge on it, and reveal it, they shall quite soon know full enlightenment, they are quite near to the knowledge of all modes. And why? Because from this perfection of

[11]*anuparigṛhīta, rjes-su yoṅs-su bzuṅ-bar 'gyur ro.*

[12]This refers to the many years of Ānanda's personal service on the Buddha.

[13]*anuparindāmi,* at 234a trsl: 'entrust'.

wisdom has issued the supreme enlightenment of the Buddhas and Lords,

V5g,2c. THE ENTRUSTING IN CONNECTION WITH THE BODHISATTVA.

—whether they were Tathagatas in the past, or will be Tathagatas in a future period, or are Tathagatas who just now reside in world systems in all the directions and demonstrate Dharma. Therefore, then, Ānanda, a Bodhisattva who wants to know full enlightenment should course in these six perfections. And why? Because this perfection of wisdom, Ānanda, is the genetrix of the Bodhisattvas, the great beings. All those Bodhisattvas, great beings who train in the six perfections, shall go forth to full enlightenment. Therefore, then, Ānanda, these six perfections I again and again entrust to you. And why? For this storehouse of the six perfections is the Tathagata's inexhaustible storehouse of Dharma. And those Tathagatas who just now reside in world systems in all the directions and demonstrate Dharma, they derive their demonstration from this storehouse of the six perfections. And those who in a past period were Tathagatas, they have, after they had trained in just these six perfections, known full enlightenment and demonstrated Dharma. And that holds good also of the Tathagatas of the future. ((f. 235a)) And also all the Disciples of the past, future and present Buddhas and Lords will win Nirvana after they have trained in just this perfection of wisdom.

V5g,3. THE MARK OF THE ABUNDANCE OF MERIT CAUSED BY THE (UNINTERRUPTED) ATTAINMENT OF THE GREAT ENLIGHTENMENT.

If, Ānanda, you should demonstrate Dharma on the level of the Disciples to persons belonging to the vehicle of the Disciples, and if, as a result of your demonstration of Dharma, all the beings in the great trichiliocosm would realise Arhatship, nevertheless you would thereby not yet have done your duty as my disciple. But if you, Ānanda, would demonstrate and reveal to a Bodhisattva, a great being, even one single verse connected with the perfection of wisdom, then I would be pleased with you as my disciple, and you would have done your duty as my disciple. And if by your former demonstration of Dharma the beings in the great trichiliocosm would all realise sooner or later Arhatship—would then the foundation of their meritorious work, consisting in giving, morality, and development, be a great one?

Ānanda: It would be, O Lord.

The Lord: A merit greater than that, Ānanda, would a person belonging to the Disciple-vehicle beget who would demonstrate to a Bodhisattva, a great being, the Dharma associated with the perfection of wisdom, for one single day even, or just for half a day, or for one forenoon, for half an hour, for the time of a fingersnap, or just only for a moment, an inkling, a mere second. He begets the greater merit and surpasses the wholesome roots of all sons or daughters of good family who belong to the Disciple-vehicle or the Pratyekabuddha-vehicle. And so does a Bodhisattva, a great being, who demonstrates to persons belonging to the Bodhisattva-vehicle the Dharma associated with the perfection of wisdom—for even one single day, or half a day, or a forenoon, or half an hour, or a moment, or an inkling, or a mere second. And why? Because he himself wants to know full enlightenment, and others also he encourages to full enlightenment, incites them, instigates them, settles, and establishes them. It is thus impossible, Ānanda, that the Bodhisattva, the great being, coursing in the four applications of mindfulness, etc. *to* : the knowledge of the modes of the path, growing in wholesome roots, could fail to win full enlightenment; that cannot possibly be.

When this Perfection of Wisdom was being taught, the Lord in front of the four assemblies, and of the gods, men, Yakshas, Gandharvas, Asuras, Garudas, Kinnaras, and Mahoragas who had gathered around Him, exerted his psychic power in such a way that they all saw Akshobhya, the Tathagata, surrounded and revered by his congregation of monks, demonstrating Dharma to an assembly vast like the ocean[14] and imperturable[15]—all of them Arhats, with their outflows dried up, undefiled, fully controlled, quite freed in their hearts, well freed and wise, thoroughbreds, great Serpents, ((f. 235b)) their work done, their task accomplished, their burden laid down, their own weal accomplished, with the fetters that bound them to becoming extinguished, their hearts well freed by right understanding, in perfect control of their whole minds[16]—and also to the Bodhisattvas, the great beings who had an intelligence vast like the ocean. Thereupon the Lord again withdrew that psychic power, and in consequence the four assemblies no longer saw the Tathagata Akshobhya, or the persons belonging to the Disciple-vehicle or the Bodhisattva-vehicle, nor that Buddha-field of the Tathagata Akshobhya. That congregation of monks headed by the Buddha no longer came within the range of their vision. And why? Because the Lord, the Tathagata, had withdrawn that exercise of psychic power. That is why they could no longer see it.

The Lord: Ānanda, do you see that Buddha-field of the Tathagata Akshobhya, and that congregation of monks and Bodhisattvas?

Ānanda : That Buddha-field, O Lord, does not come within the range of the eye, nor that Tathagata, nor that congregation of monks, nor that congregation of Bodhisattvas.

[14]*sarvaguṇaratnākaratvāt sāgaropamā. H.*

[15]*sarva-Māra-viṣaya-atikrāntatvād akṣobhyā. H.*

[16]All these attributes are explained at *H* p. 9.

The Lord: Just so, Ānanda, all dharmas come not within the range of the eye. No dharma comes within the range of a dharma, no dharma sees a dharma, no dharma cognizes a dharma. Just as this Tathagata Akshobhya, these Disciples, those persons belonging to the Bodhisattva-vehicle, and that Buddha-field, do not come within the range of the eye, just so, Ānanda, all dharmas; a dharma does not come within the range of a dharma, does not see a dharma, does not cognize a dharma. For all dharmas are unknowable, unseeable, incapable of doing anything. And why? All dharmas are unoccupied, unseizable, on account of the fact that they are unoccupied, like space; all dharmas are unthinkable like an illusory man; all dharmas cannot be known,[17] because they elude all thought, have the mark of being set up as mere fabrications, and on account of their insubstantiality.[18] When he courses thus, the Bodhisattva, the great being, courses in the perfection of wisdom, but settles down in no dharma whatever. When he trains thus he courses in the perfection of wisdom. A Bodhisattva, a great being, who wants to fulfill all the perfections, should train in the perfection of wisdom. For this training has been declared to be the highest, the best, the principal, the choicest, the most excellent, the sublime, the foremost, the utmost, the unsurpassed; bent on the benefit and happiness of the entire world, a protector of the unprotected, ordained and extolled by the Buddhas. Having stood in it, the Tathagatas could lift up this great trichiliocosm with their right hands and then just drop it again; and yet it would not occur to these beings[19] that 'this great trichiliocosm has been lifted up or dropped down'. And why? As a result of training in this perfection of wisdom there has arisen in the Buddhas and Lords an unattached vision and cognition of past, future, and present dharmas. Of all trainings that there are, this training in perfect wisdom has been declared to be the highest, etc. *to*: the unsurpassed. ((f. 236a)) To think of seizing the measure[20] or boundary of[21] the perfection of wisdom would be like thinking of seizing the measure or boundary of space.[22] And why? Because without measure is the perfection of wisdom, and I have set no measure to it. The body of names, the body of words, the body of letters are bound by measure, but the perfection of wisdom is not.[23]

[17]*avedaka, rig-pa(r) med-pa.*

[18]The text is here not very clearly transmitted, and *AdT* differs substantially from the Ms of *Ad.*

[19]*A*: 'to those Buddhas and Lords'. *H* comments: *vineya-jana-pratibhāsa-apekṣayā-ucyate, na tu Bhagavatāṃ vikalpaḥ samudācarati.*

[20]*H*: *pratyakṣeṇa svarūpa-paricchedaḥ pramāṇam.*

[21]*H*: *Āgamenobhābhyaṃ veyattā 'vadhāraṇaṃ paryantaḥ.*

[22]*H* explains: *yathā-ākāśasya dravya-abhāva-mātra-svabhāvatvāt pramāṇa-ādi grahītuṃ na śakyate tathā Mātur api.*

[23]cf. *H* p. 878.

V5h. THE GREAT ENLIGHTENMENT.

V5h,1. THE GREAT ENLIGHTENMENT CONSISTING IN THE COGNITIONS OF EXTINCTION AND OF NONPRODUCTION.

Ānanda: For what reason, O Lord, is the perfection of wisdom not bound by measure?

The Lord: Because of nonextinction, because of isolatedness.[24] Those Buddhas and Lords who in a past period have been Tathagatas, they have come forth[25] from just this perfection of wisdom,[26] and yet the perfection of wisdom has not got extinguished. Those Buddhas and Lords who in a future period will be Tathagatas, they also will come forth from just this perfection of wisdom, and yet this perfection of wisdom will not get extinguished. Those Tathagatas who just now reside in the world in the ten directions and demonstrate Dharma, they also come forth from just this perfection of wisdom, and yet the perfection of wisdom does not get extinguished. And why? One would think, Ānanda, of extinguishing space if one were to think of extinguishing the perfection of wisdom. But the perfection of wisdom has not got extinguished, does not get extinguished, will not get extinguished. And the same holds good of the other five perfections. For of these dharmas there is no production. That of which there is no production, how can of that the extinction be conceived?

V5h,2. THE REASON FOR BEING CONFIRMED IN THE CONVICTION OF THE GREAT ENLIGHTENMENT.

Thereupon *the Lord* stretched out his tongue, covered his whole face with it, and said to the Ven. Ānanda: What do you think, Ānanda, could such a tongue speak what is false, what is otherwise?

Ānanda: No, O Lord, no, O Sugata!

The Lord: Therefore, then, Ānanda, do reveal this perfection of wisdom to the four assemblies, explain it, encourage it, analyse it, explain it, enlarge on it, and reveal it in detail! For in this deep perfection of wisdom have all dharmas been pointed out in detail wherein the persons belonging to the Disciple-vehicle, the Pratyekabuddha-vehicle, the Bodhisattva-vehicle should be trained. When trained therein, as instructed, they will each stand on their own level. And this deep perfection of wisdom is the entrance to all the syllables[27] and the door to the dhāraṇīs in which the Bodhisattva, the great being, should be trained. The Bodhisattvas, the great beings, who bear in mind these dhāraṇīs will come face to face with

[24]*H*: *utpāda-abhāvena-anutpāda-jñāna-svabhāvatvāt.*

[25]*prabhāvitā*; cf. also ff. 229b, 248a, 253a.

[26]i.e. from the *kṣaya-anutpāda-jñāna H.*

[27]*sarva-akṣarāṇāṃ praveśaḥ* (*'jug go*). *P*: *pradeśaḥ*, cf. *S* IX 1450.

all the flashes of insight and all analytical knowledges.[28] I have taught this deep perfection of wisdom as the inexhaustible storehouse of the true Dharma of the past, future, and present Buddhas and Lords. Therefore, then, Ānanda, I solemnly declare to you, I make known to you, that one who will take up this deep perfection of wisdom, bear it in mind, recite and study it, he will bear in mind the enlightenment of the past, future, and present Buddhas and Lords. ((f. 236b)) I have taught this perfection of wisdom as a dhāraṇī. When you bear in mind those dhāraṇīs of the perfection of wisdom,[29] you bear all dharmas in mind.

[28]*pratibhāna-pratisaṃvida.*

[29]These dhāraṇīs are enumerated in *P* 212-214.

CHAPTER 61

NONEXTINCTION

V5i. THE COGNITIONS OF EXTINCTION AND OF NONPRODUCTION.

Thereupon the Ven. *Subhuti* thought to himself: Deep, to be sure, is this enlightenment of the Tathagatas. Let me question the Tathagata about it. The Ven. Subhuti then said to the Lord: Inexhaustible,[1] O Lord, is the perfection of wisdom.

The Lord: Because, like space, it cannot be extinguished.

Subhuti: How should one aspire for[2] the perfection of wisdom?

The Lord: Through the nonextinction of form, etc. *to*: of the knowledge of all modes, and furthermore through the space-like nonextinction of form, etc. *to*: of the knowledge of all modes. Moreover, through the space-like nonextinction of the karma formations, etc. *to*: through the space-like nonextinction of old age and death, of sorrow, lamentation, pain, sadness, and despair. ((f. 237a)) It is thus that the Bodhisattva, the great being, should aspire for the perfection of wisdom. This is the surveying of conditioned coproduction which avoids the extremes.[3] To survey conditioned coproduction in such a manner, that is the special dharma of a Bodhisattva who is seated on the terrace of enlightenment.[4] When he thus surveys conditioned coproduction, he will gain the cognition of the all-knowing. A Bodhisattva who, coursing in perfect wisdom through this aspiration for space-like nonextinction, surveys conditioned coproduction, cannot stand on the level of Disciples or Pratyekabuddhas, but will stand in full enlightenment. If persons belonging to the Bodhisattva-vehicle turn away (from full enlightenment),[5] they do so because they have not resorted to the attentions on this perfection of wisdom. They fail to cognize how a Bodhisattva who courses in perfect wisdom

[1]*akṣayā*. See *H* p. 880.

[2]*abhinirhartavyā* = *H ādhigamyeta*, with the qualification *ādikarmika-avasthāyām upalambha-abhiniveśena bhāvanāyām*. This rather speaks for the translation 'aspire to' than 'consummate'.

[3]i.e. of eternity and annihilation, acc. to *H*. Cf. the whole passage at *A* xxviii 469-471, of which this is an abbreviation.

[4]This refers to the Buddha, in the third watch of the night, just before his enlightenment, surveying the 12 links of *pratītyasamutpāda*; e.g. *Buddhacarita* xiv 52-83. v. 83: as a result of his insight into conditioned coproduction "the great seer had achieved a correct knowledge of all there is to be known, and he stood out in the world as a Buddha".

[5]*A* and *P* add this.

should survey conditioned coproduction through the aspiration for space-like nonextinction. Persons who belong to the Bodhisattva vehicle, and who yet turn away from full enlightenment do so because they have failed to resort to this skill in means. Those Bodhisattvas, great beings, however, who do not turn away from full enlightenment, do so because they all have resorted to this perfection of wisdom. The Bodhisattva, the great being, who courses in skill in means and in the perfection of wisdom should through the aspiration for space-like nonextinction survey the perfection of wisdom and aspire to it. When he thus surveys conditioned coproduction, a Bodhisattva certainly does not see any dharma that is being produced without a cause,[6] nor does he review a dharma that is permanent and never stopped.[7] He reviews no dharma as a self, a being, a soul, a creature, a man, a youth, a person, a personality, a doer, one who feels,[8] one who knows, one who sees; nor does he review a dharma as permanent or impermanent, as ease or ill, as self or not-self, as appeased or not appeased. It is certainly thus that a Bodhisattva, a great being who courses in perfect wisdom, should survey conditioned coproduction. At the time when the Bodhisattva courses in perfect wisdom, he does not review form, etc. *to* : the knowledge of all modes, as permanent or impermanent, as ease or ill, as self or not-self, as appeased or not appeased. ((f. 237b)) He does not review the perfection of wisdom, etc. *to* : he does not review enlightenment, nor that dharma by which he would review enlightenment; nor does he review that dharma by which he would effect the forsaking of all residues of the defilements. It is thus that a Bodhisattva should course in the perfection of wisdom, without taking any dharma as a basis. At the time when the Bodhisattva, without taking any dharma as a basis, courses in the perfection of wisdom, at that time Mara, the Evil One, is afflicted with the dart of sorrow. Just as a man whose parents have died is afflicted with the dart of sorrow, the dart of the deepest sorrow, just so Mara, the Evil One, in respect to the Bodhisattva, the great being, who courses in perfect wisdom and takes no dharma as a basis.

Subhuti : Is this affliction confined to just one Mara, or does it extend to all the Maras in the great trichiliocosm, to each one on his own seat?[9]

The Lord : All Evil Maras in the great trichiliocosm are afflicted with the dart of the deepest sorrow, and they do not enjoy themselves where they are.[10] If a Bodhisattva, a great being, becomes not lacking in the dwelling of the perfection of wisdom, then the entire world with its

[6]Because in the conventional world causes do exist. *H*.

[7]*H* 883-4 explains *nitya* and its synonyms.

[8]The translation of the synonyms of 'self' has been slightly abbreviated.

[9]so *AdT*.

[10]lit. 'and they cannot sit still on their respective seats'.

gods, men, and Asuras cannot gain entry to him, nor can it find any ground for taking hold of him and turning him away (from full enlightenment).[11] Therefore, then, Subhuti, the Bodhisattva who wants quickly to know full enlightenment should dwell in the dwelling of perfect wisdom.

V5k. THE ACCOMPLISHMENT OF THE DEVELOPMENT OF THE SIX PERFECTIONS.[12]

In a Bodhisattva who dwells in the dwelling of perfect wisdom, the perfection of giving, etc. *to*: the perfection of wisdom, arrive at their most perfect development. In a Bodhisattva who dwells in the perfection of wisdom all the perfections arrive at their most perfect development.

Subhuti: How does in a Bodhisattva, who courses in perfect wisdom, the perfection of giving, etc. *to*: the perfection of wisdom arrive at their most perfect enlightenment?

The Lord: Here a Bodhisattva dedicates to the knowledge of all modes the gift which he gives. In the same way, dedicating them to the knowledge of all modes, ((f. 238a)) he guards morality, perfects patience, exerts vigour, enters concentration, and develops wisdom.

Subhuti: How, O Lord, does a Bodhisattva who has stood in the perfection of Giving acquire the perfection of Morality?

The Lord: Here, when the Bodhisattva gives gifts, and dedicates them to the knowledge of all modes, a friendly deed of body, friendly deed of voice, friendly deed of mind is set up towards all beings. On that occasion he acquires the perfection of morality.

Subhuti: How than does the Bodhisattva, having stood in the perfection of Giving, acquire the perfection of Patience?

The Lord: When the Bodhisattva gives gifts, and their recipients abuse and revile him, use unsupportable and harsh words against him, he does not feel any anger for them.

Subhuti: How does the Bodhisattva, having stood in the perfection of Giving, acquire the perfection of Vigour?

The Lord: When the Bodhisattva gives gifts, and their recipients abuse and revile him, use insupportable and harsh words against him, he nevertheless remains determined to give and to renounce: 'I should give gifts! Not should I not give gifts!' So he generates physical and mental vigour in himself. ((f. 238b))

Subhuti: How does the Bodhisattva, having stood in the perfection of Giving acquire the perfection of Meditation?

The Lord: A Bodhisattva who gives gifts does not dedicate them to the level of a Disciple and Pratyekabuddha, but outside the knowledge of all modes his thought does not proceed.

[11]See *A* xxviii 472.

[12]So *H* 886, 23. *P* has no separate heading here.

Subhuti: How does the Bodhisattva, when he gives gifts with skill in means, acquire the perfection of wisdom?

The Lord: When the Bodhisattva gives gifts and renounces them, the intelligent appreciation that he has to do with an illusion is always set up with regard to those gifts, and he does not see that these gifts have bestowed anything on any being or taken away anything from anyone.

CHAPTER 62

THE SUPREME ATTAINMENT[1]

Subhuti: How, O Lord, does the Bodhisattva, having stood in the perfection of Morality, acquire the perfection of Giving?

The Lord: Here the Bodhisattva, the great being, having stood in the perfection of morality, does not adhere[2] by any of his bodily, vocal, or mental engagements[3] to the level of the Disciples and Pratyekabuddhas. When he stands in this perfection of morality, he does not rob beings of life, does not take what is not given, etc. *to* :[4] does not have false views. When he has stood in that perfection of morality, then any gift which he gives—whether it be food to those who want food, drink to those who want drink, and likewise cars, clothes, flowers, garlands, perfumes, ointments, lodgings, asylum, livelihood, and services to those who want them, in short all kinds of things useful to humans—that gift he makes common to all beings and dedicates it to full enlightenment, but not to the level of the Disciples or Pratyekabuddhas.

Subhuti: How does the Bodhisattva, having stood in the perfection of Morality, acquire the perfection of Patience?

The Lord: Here, the Bodhisattva, the great being, who has stood in the perfection of morality, when all beings cut off all his limbs, never gets angry or feels ill will, but just thinks to himself: 'How good it is that this should have happened to me! For through my renunciation of this stinking body I shall win the heavenly, the adamantine body of a Tathagata!' ((f. 239a))

Subhuti: How does the Bodhisattva, having stood in the perfection of Morality, acquire the perfection of Vigour?

The Lord: Here the Bodhisattva, the great being, does not relax his physical and mental vigour, (and he is determined that he) 'will rescue all beings from Samsāra, and establish them in the Deathless element.'

Subhuti: How does the Bodhisattva, having stood in the perfection of Morality, acquire the perfection of Concentration?

The Lord: When the Bodhisattva, the great being, enters on the trances,

[1]*vyutkrāntakasamāpatti?*, *thod-rgyal-du sñoms-par 'jug-pa*. J. May (p. 353) would prefer *thod (b)rg(y)al-gyi sñoms-par jug-pa*, which he translates as 'Concentration du Saut.'

[2]*na parāmṛśati, mchog-tu 'dzin-par mi byed ciṅ.*

[3]*saṃcara*; *sdom-pa gaṅ yin pa'i.*

[4]For the full list see f. 225b.

he does not hang on to[5] the level of the Disciples or Pratyekabuddhas, but thinks to himself that 'having stood here in the perfection of concentration, I should liberate all beings from Samsāra'.

Subhuti: How does the Bodhisattva, the great being, having stood in the perfection of Morality, acquire the perfection of Wisdom?

The Lord: Here the Bodhisattva, the great being, having stood in the perfection of morality, does not see any dharma as conditioned or unconditioned; he does not see existence as conditioned or nonexistence as unconditioned; he does not see the sign as conditioned or the signless as unconditioned; he does not review the beingness or nonbeingness of any dharma, except in such a way that he does not transgress against the Suchness of all dharmas. And through that perfection of wisdom and skill in means he does not fall on the level of a Disciple or Pratyekabuddha.

Subhuti: How does the Bodhisattva, having stood in the perfection of Patience, acquire the perfection of Giving?

The Lord: As the Bodhisattva—from the first thought of enlightenment onwards and up to his being seated on the terrace of enlightenment—gives gifts—if all beings should abuse and revile him, and cut him limb from limb, still, firmly established in the perfection of patience, he thinks to himself, 'I should give to these beings, not should I not give gifts!' To those who want food he gives food, etc. Having made these wholesome roots common to all beings, he dedicates them to the knowledge of all modes, but in such a way that the triple intellectual act does not take place, i.e. (concerning) him who dedicates, that which dedicates, that whereto it is dedicated.

Subhuti: How does the Bodhisattva, having stood in the perfection of Patience, acquire the perfection of Morality?

The Lord: Here the Bodhisattva, the great being, beginning with the first thought of enlightenment, until he is seated on the terrace of enlightenment, does not rob any being of life, does not take what is not given, etc. *to*: ((f. 239b)) he has no false views, and his thought does not stride forth to the level of the Disciples or Pratyekabuddhas. And he makes these wholesome roots common to all beings and dedicates them to full enlightenment, etc. as before.

Subhuti: How does the Bodhisattva, the great being, having stood in the perfection of Patience, acquire the perfection of Vigour?

The Lord: Here the Bodhisattva, the great being, having stood in the perfection of Patience, generates vigour in this manner: 'I will travel for one mile, for a hundred miles, or up to a distance of thousands of kotis of world systems for the sake of one single being whom I could establish in the (art of) taking refuge (with the Triple Jewel), in the moral rules, or in patience, or in the fruit of a Streamwinner, etc. *to*: in full

[5] *adhyālambate*; cf. ch. 58 n. 2.

enlightenment. So he should exert vigour, and, having made these wholesome roots common to all beings, he dedicates them to the supreme enlightenment.

Subhuti: How does the Bodhisattva, the great being, having stood in the perfection of Patience, acquire the perfection of Concentration?

The Lord: Here, Subhuti, the Bodhisattva, the great being, having stood in the perfection of patience, detached from sense desires, detached from evil and unwholesome dharmas, dwells in the attainment of the first trance, which is with thoughts adjusted and discursive, born of detachment, full of rapture and ease. And so he dwells in all trances up to the fourth and up to the attainment of cessation. All those dharmas which constitute thought and its concomitants,[6] and which are connected with wholesomeness, he dedicates to the knowledge of all modes, but in such a way that on that occasion he does not apprehend the trances or their limbs.

Subhuti: How does the Bodhisattva, having stood in the perfection of Patience, acquire the perfection of Wisdom?

The Lord: Having stood in the perfection of patience the Bodhisattva dwells as one who surveys dharmas in their modes as isolated, calm and nonextinct, but he does not realise that Dharmahood until he is seated on the terrace of enlightenment, and there wins the knowledge of all modes, immediately thereafter to turn the wheel of Dharma. It is thus that the Bodhisattva, the great being, having stood in the perfection of patience, acquires the perfection of wisdom, but in such a way that he neither rejects it nor seizes upon it.

Subhuti: How does the Bodhisattva, having stood in the perfection of Vigour, ((f. 240a)) acquire the perfection of Giving?

The Lord: Here the Bodhisattva, having stood in the perfection of vigour, does not, either in body or thought, lay aside his duties. 'Without any doubt should I know full enlightenment! Not should I not know it!' Firmly established in the perfection of vigour he travels for the sake of beings for one mile, etc. *to*: over the distance of hundreds of thousands of kotis of world systems, if only to bring just one single being to enlightenment. If he can find no persons belonging to the Bodhisattva-vehicle, he will establish a person belonging to the Disciple-vehicle in Discipleship, or one belonging to the Pratyekabuddha-vehicle in Pratyekabuddhahood. One single being even he establishes in the ten wholesome paths of action. Having given that gift of Dharma, he gratifies beings also with material gifts. He does not, however, dedicate that wholesome root to the level of the Disciples or Pratyekabuddhas, but, having made it common to all beings, dedicates it to full enlightenment.

Subhuti: How does the Bodhisattva, having stood in the perfection of Vigour, acquire the perfection of Morality?

[6]*utpanno 'nutpannāṃś ca cittacaitasikān dharmān.*

The Lord: Here the Bodhisattva, beginning with the first thought of enlightenment, until he is seated on the terrace of enlightenment, himself abstains from taking life, and also others he induces to abstain from taking life; he speaks in praise of the abstention from taking life, and he praises also those other people who abstain from taking life, one acquiescent;[7] etc. *to*: he himself abstains from wrong views, and also others he induces to abstain from them; he speaks in praise of the abstention from wrong views, and he praises also those others who abstain from wrong views, one acquiescent. But through that perfection of morality, he does not base himself on[8] the world of sense desire, the world of form, or the formless world; nor on the level of the Disciples or Pratyekabuddhas. But he makes these wholesome roots common to all beings and dedicates them to full enlightenment, as before.

Subhuti: How does the Bodhisattva, having stood in the perfection of Vigour, acquire the perfection of Patience?

The Lord: As the Bodhisattva, the great being, advances from the first thought of enlightenment to his seat on the terrace of enlightenment, if a man or ghost distracts his mind,[9] or if his limbs are cut off from his body and carried away, the Bodhisattva, firmly established in the perfection of vigour, does not think 'someone cuts or breaks or kills me.' But on the contrary he thinks to himself: 'How fortunate ((f. 240b)) that just those should destroy my body for whose sake I look after it!' Or he learns to attend well to the true nature of dharmas. And he does not dedicate these wholesome roots to the level of the Disciples or Pratyekabuddhas, but, having made them common to all beings, dedicates them to the supreme enlightenment.

Subhuti: How does the Bodhisattva, having stood in the perfection of Vigour, acquire the perfection of Concentration?

The Lord: Here the Bodhisattva, the great being, enters on the trances, the Unlimited, the formless attainments, but he does not take hold of their karma result. He is reborn only where he can work the weal of beings, whom he matures through the six perfections. He passes on from Buddha-field to Buddha-field, for the sake of honouring the Buddhas and Lords and of planting wholesome roots.

Subhuti: How does the Bodhisattva, having stood in the perfection of Vigour, acquire the perfection of Wisdom?

The Lord: Here the Bodhisattva, the great being, having stood in the perfection of vigour, does not review the perfection of giving, etc. as an actual reality,[10] or as an existent, or as a sign. And so for the appli-

[7]*samanujña, rjes-su dga'-bar byed do.*
[8]*pratitiṣṭhati, don-du (mi) gñer.*
[9]So *AdT.*
[10]*dravyatas, rdzas*; also f. 251a.

cations of mindfulness, etc. *to* : the knowledge of all modes. Reviewing all dharmas as without actual reality, existence, or sign, he does not make his home in any dharma. And as he speaks, so he acts.

Subhuti: How does the Bodhisattva, having stood in the perfection of Concentration, acquire the perfection of Giving?

The Lord: Here the Bodhisattva, the great being, having entered on the trances, etc. having stood in the perfection of concentration, with undistracted mind ((f. 241a)) gives to beings gifts both material and spiritual.[11] He himself gives material and spiritual gifts, and others also he instigates to give material and spiritual gifts, he speaks in praise of giving material and spiritual gifts, and he praises also those other beings who give them, one acquiescent. And those wholesome roots he does not dedicate to the level of the Disciples or Pratyekabuddhas, but, having made them common to all beings, he dedicates them to the supreme enlightenment.

Subhuti: How does the Bodhisattva, having stood in the perfection of Concentration, acquire the perfection of Morality?

The Lord: Here the Bodhisattva, the great being, who has stood in the perfection of concentration, does not produce a thought connected with greed, hate, delusion, or harming; he dwells only in attentions associated with the knowledge of all modes. And these wholesome roots, etc. as before.

Subhuti: How does the Bodhisattva, having stood in the perfection of Concentration, acquire the perfection of Patience?

The Lord: Here the Bodhisattva, the great being, having stood in the perfection of concentration, contemplates form as a mass of foam, feeling as a bubble, perception as a mirage, the drives as a plantain tree, consciousness as like a mock show. When he contemplates thus, the conviction is set up in him that the five grasping skandhas are insubstantial. And when he thus contemplates, he thinks to himself: 'when all my limbs are cut off, who is it that cuts, or what is it that is being cut? Whose is the body, whose the feeling, whose this perception, whose the drives, whose the consciousness?' When he thus contemplates he thinks to himself: 'who is it that reviles or abuses, or feels ill will when reviled or abused?'

Subhuti: How does the Bodhisattva, having stood in the perfection of Concentration, acquire the perfection of Vigour?

The Lord: Here the Bodhisattva, the great being, who has stood in the perfection of concentration, enters into the first, second, third and fourth trances. He does not take up[12] the sign of those trances and trance limbs, and with a thus concentrated thought (1) he experiences the

[11]lit. Gift of Dharma.

[12]So *AdT, P, S*; Ms: 'he takes up the sign'.

various kinds of psychic power. (2) With the heavenly ear-element he hears sounds both heavenly and human. (3) Likewise he wisely knows the thought of other beings and persons, etc. *to* :[13] he wisely knows, as it really is, a thought without anything above it as a 'thought without anything above it'. (4) He remembers his various previous lives. (5) With the heavenly eye, pure and surpassing that of men, (he sees beings as they die, and are reborn), etc. *to* : he sees that beings fare according to their deeds. This should be worked out in detail.[14] ((f. 241b)) Based on these five superknowledges, he passes on from Buddha-field to Buddha-field, honouring the Buddhas and Lords, planting wholesome roots, maturing beings and purifying the Buddha-field. And he does not dedicate these wholesome roots to the level of the Disciples and Pratyekabuddhas, etc. as before.

Subhuti : How does the Bodhisattva, having stood in the perfection of Concentration, acquire the perfection of Wisdom?

The Lord: Here the Bodhisattva, the great being, having stood in the perfection of concentration, does not apprehend form, or any of the other skandhas; or the perfections, the applications of mindfulness, etc. *to* : the knowledge of all modes, the conditioned element, the uncontitioned element. Not apprehending them, he does not put them together.[15] Not putting them together, he does not produce or stop them. And why? Because, whether Tathagatas are produced or not, firmly established is the established order of these dharmas, firmly established is the Dharma-element, and that is neither produced nor stopped. Undistracted in his thought he becomes one who is not lacking in attentions associated with the knowledge of all modes.

Subhuti : How does the Bodhisattva, having stood in the perfection of Wisdom, acquire the perfection of Giving?

The Lord: Here the Bodhisattva, the great being, coursing in the perfection of wisdom reviews all dharmas as empty.

Subhuti : How does he do so?

The Lord: Here, Subhuti, the Bodhisattva, the great being, coursing in the perfection of wisdom, does not apprehend the inward emptiness as 'inward emptiness', etc. for 14 kinds of emptiness, up to the emptiness of own-marks. Having stood in these 14 kinds of emptiness the Bodhisattva, the great being, does not apprehend form ((f. 242a)) as empty or not empty, nor anything else, up to the unconditioned element. Coursing in this perfection of wisdom, the Bodhisattva, the great being, does not review the gift which he gives, whether it be food, etc. or anything else

[13] The whole list in *P* 85.

[14] The text consists of various scraps from the formula to be found in extenso in *P* 83-89, *S* 301-306.

[15] *na-abhisaṃskaroti.*

as empty; nor does he review him who gives, or him to whom he gives as empty. There is then no occasion for thoughts of meanness or acquisitiveness.[16] And why? There are no such discriminations for the Bodhisattva who courses in perfect wisdom, beginning with the first thought of enlightenment, up to his being seated on the terrace of enlightenment. Just as no thought of meanness or acquisitiveness arises to the Tathagata who has known full enlightenment, just so with the Bodhisattva who courses in perfect wisdom. Just this perfection of wisdom is the Teacher of the Bodhisattva, the great being.

Subhuti: How does the Bodhisattva, having stood in the perfection of Wisdom, acquire the perfection of Morality?

The Lord: Here the Bodhisattva, the great being, having stood in the perfection of wisdom, gives no opportunity to the thoughts of the Disciples or Pratyekabuddhas. And why? Because he does not apprehend the level of the Disciples and Pratyekabuddhas, nor that thought which he would dedicate to the level of the Disciples or Pratyekabuddhas. From the first thought of enlightenment until the terrace of enlightenment he demonstrates Dharma so that the taking of life might be forsaken. He himself abstains from taking life, etc. as at f. 240a. And through that morality he does not adhere to any dharma, to Discipleship, Pratyekabuddhahood, or Buddhahood—how much less to any other.

Subhuti: How does the Bodhisattva, having stood in the perfection of Wisdom, acquire the perfection of Patience?

The Lord: Here, Subhuti, there arises to the Bodhisattva, the great being, who has stood in the perfection of wisdom, the adaptable patience. And he thinks to himself: 'no dharma is here produced or stopped, is born, grows old[17] or dies, is abused or reviled, cut, broken, or ((f. 242b)) struck'. From his first thought of enlightenment up to the terrace of enlightenment, whenever any being may abuse or revile him, cut or break him by belabouring him with clods, sticks, fists, or swords, he thinks to himself: 'Ah, this dharmahood of dharmas! For there is no dharma here that is abused, or reviled, cut, broken, struck, or bound.'[17]

Subhuti: How does the Bodhisattva, having stood in the perfection of Wisdom, acquire the perfection of Vigour?

The Lord: Here the Bodhisattva, the great being, having stood in the perfection of wisdom and in the four bases of psychic power, endowed with skill in means, generates physical and mental vigour, travels over the distance of one world system, etc. *to*: hundreds of thousands of niyutas of kotis of world systems, and demonstrates the dharmas which act as the wings to enlightenment, the fruits of the holy life, but in such a way that he establishes them neither in the conditioned nor in the unconditioned element.

[16]*āgrahacitta, kun-tu 'dzin-pa' i sems.*
[17]om. *AdT.*

Subhuti: How does the Bodhisattva, having stood in the perfection of Wisdom, acquire the perfection of Concentration?

The Lord: Here the Bodhisattva, the great being, having stood in the perfection of wisdom, enters on all the concentrations, as many as there are—be they those of the Disciples, the Pratyekabuddhas or the Bodhisattvas—with the exception of those of the Tathagatas. Having stood in these concentrations, in direct and reverse order he enters on and emerges from the eight deliverances. Which eight? (1) Here the Bodhisattva, the great being, having form, sees forms; (2) not perceiving inward form, he sees outward forms; (3) he becomes resolved on the lovely;[18] (4) completely overcoming all perceptions of form, by the going to rest of the perception of impact, by not attending to the perceptions of manifoldness, thinking 'endless space', he dwells in the attainment of endless space; (5) by completely overcoming the station of endless space, and thinking 'infinite consciousness', he dwells in the attainment of the station of infinite consciousness; (6) by completely overcoming the station of infinite consciousness, and thinking that 'there is not anything', he dwells in the attainment of the station of the field of nothing whatever; (7) by completely overcoming the station of Nothing Whatever, he dwells in the attainment of the station of neither perception non nonperception; (8) through having in every way overcome the station of neither perception nor nonperception, he dwells in the attainment of the trance of the cessation of perception and feeling. ((f. 243a)) And in direct and reverse order he enters on the nine attainments of successive stations, and emerges from them. Which nine? The four trances, the four formless attainments, the trance of the cessation of perception and feeling. Having made a classification[19] of these eight deliverances and of the nine attainments of successive stations, he enters on this concentration which is like the lion's yawn.[20]

V 6. The Path of Development.

V6a. The crowning assault.[21]

And what, Subhuti, is of the Bodhisattva, the great being, the concentration which is like the lion's yawn? Here, Subhuti, the Bodhisattva, detached from sense pleasures, detached from evil and unwholesome dharmas, dwells in the attainment of the first trance, which is with thought adjusted and discursive, born of detachment, full of rapture and ease. So he dwells in all the trances up to the attainment of the cessation of

[18]the empty?—See the same list at *P* 210. See S. Konow, *Daśasāhasrikā*, pp. 19-20.

[19]*vibhaṅga, rnam-par dbye-ba.*

[20]*seṅ-ge rnam-par bsgyiṅs-pa.*

[21]*avaskandha-samāpatti H.* So *AA* v 25 *(thod rgyal-du)*. See n. 23.

feeling and perception. Having emerged from the attainment of cessation, he enters into the attainment of the station of neither perception nor nonperception, and so (descending one by one) he enters the first trance. Having made a classification[22] of this concentration which is like the lion's yawn, he enters into the concentration which represents the crowning assault.[23]

And what is a Bodhisattva's concentration which represents the crowning assault? Here a Bodhisattva, detached from sense pleasures, detached from evil and unwholesome dharmas, dwells in the attainment

[22]So *AdT, P.*—Ms. and *S*: "having reaped the merit from", or "having activated the karma result of this concentration".—cf. f. 264b where the Lord, before cultivating the various superknowledges, activates the merit due to him from his *dhyānas* (*vipākī-kṛtvā,* no Tib.).

[23]*viṣkandaka* (root *SKAND,* Tib. (*b*)*rgal*). The terminology concerning this *samādhi* suffers from an *embarras de richesse. P*'s *avaskandaka* and *Ad's viṣkandaka* both emphasize the aspect of 'leaping, jumping, skipping'. At *P* 71, where under the heading of *kāyasākṣin* part of this *samādhi* is described, the word *avaskandakena* is used; *S* i 273 has instead *viṣ-kadya, rnam-par mnan ciṇ.* The equivalent of *AdT, thod-rgyal-gyi,* also stands for *vyut-krāntaka-samāpatti,* and at *VM* xii 2, 5 Buddhaghosa uses the word *ukkantika* in the sense of 'skipping', '*ueberspringen*'. Das has *rgal,* the translation of *AK brgal,* which Edgerton rather rashly assumes to be the correct form. Both *AA* and *AdT* have *rgyal,* and the notion of 'victory' seems implied (*H* 888 calls it *vaśitva-lakṣaṇam*). *S's viṣṭambhaka* appears to express a quite different idea, and I would provisionally assume that we have to deal with the unwarranted correction of a Nepalese scribe. J. May (*Hobogirin* 356-357) sums up the less detailed account of Kumārajīva's *P* (*T* 223 xx 368a12-cl). For some more Chinese equivalents see *T* 220 cccl, 800-1; *T* 1509 lxxxi, 630b.

The 'concentration which is like the lion's yawn' is the one which the Buddha underwent immediately before his Parinirvāṇa (*Das Mahāparinirvāṇasūtra,* ed. E. Waldschmidt, 1951, pp. 394-397. *Buddhacarita* xxvi 89-91, trsl. in my *Buddhist Scriptures,* 1959, p. 63). The 'overleaping *samādhi*' is a method of 'thought-control' (*cittaṃ paridametabbam, VM* xii 2) and of winning 'mastery over the trances' (*AK* viii 174). It is described in *AK* viii 18-19 (quot. *H* 888), and according to Vasubandhu's commentary, it is the privilege of the Arhats of the *asamayavimukta* type, i.e. of those who cannot fall back, and whose deliverance does not depend on circumstances. But even they cannot leave out more than one stage at a time. The Bodhisattva, on the other hand, from the 8th stage onwards (acc. to Asanga) can (1) jump from any one stage to any other, and (2) can even from any transic stage directly return into a condition of unconcentrated distraction.

The term *siṃha-vijṛmbhita-samādhi,* above interpreted as the concentration of the lion who 'yawns', while he frowns and scowls at the same time, can also be understood as the concentration of the lion who darts, or springs, forward. As we read in a Chinese commentary (quot. by J. May, p. 357): 'One says of a lion that he springs forth so as to 1. remove the dust from his coat, and 2. so as to run much faster than the other animals, whether he flees or attacks. Just so this trance springs forth so as to 1. remove the dirt of ignorance, and 2. so that one can enter rapidly and immediately into the higher concentrations, as well as emerge from them again.'

For further information see J. May's article CHŌJŌ in *Hobogirin* IV, 1970, pp. 353-360; *H* 888-889; BEFEO xliv 2, p. 429; Chih-i, 'The successive stages of the *dhyānapāramitā*", fasc. 10, who comments on this very *Prajñāpāramitā* passage.

of the first trance, which is with thoughts adjusted and discursive, born of detachment, full of rapture and ease; emerged from it he dwells in all the trances, up to the attainment of the station of neither perception nor nonperception; emerged from the attainment of the station of neither perception nor nonperception he enters on the attainment of the cessation of feeling and perception; emerged from that he dwells in the attainment of the second trance; emerged from the second trance he enters on the attainment of cessation; emerged from that he enters on the third trance; emerged from that he enters on the attainment of cessation; emerged from that he enters on the fourth trance; emerged from that he enters on the attainment of cessation; emerged from that he enters on the attainment of the station of endless space; emerged from that he enters on the attainment of cessation; emerged from that he enters on the station of infinite consciousness; emerged from that he enters on the attainment of cessation; emerged from that he enters on the attainment of the station of nothing whatever; emerged from that he enters on the attainment of cessation; emerged from that he enters on the attainment of the station of neither perception nor nonperception; emerged from that he enters on the attainment of cessation; emerged from that he enters on the attainment of the station of neither perception nor nonperception. Emerged from the attainment of the station of neither perception nor nonperception, he falls into unconcentrated thought; from unconcentrated thought he enters into the attainment of cessation; emerged from the attainment of cessation he abides in unconcentrated thought; ((f. 243b)) from unconcentrated thought he enters into the attainment of cessation; emerged from that he abides in unconcentrated thought; from unconcentrated thought he enters on the attainment of the station of neither perception nor nonperception; emerged from that he abides in unconcentrated thought; from unconcentrated thought he enters on the attainment of the station of nothing whatever; emerged from that he abides in unconcentrated thought; from unconcentrated thought he enters on the attainment of the station of infinite consciousness; emerged from that he abides in unconcentrated thought; from unconcentrated thought he enters on the attainment of the station of endless space; emerged from that he abides in ((f. 243A)) unconcentrated thought; from unconcentrated thought he enters on the fourth trance; emerged from that he abides in unconcentrated thought; from unconcentrated thought he enters on the third trance, emerged from that he abides in unconcentrated thought; from unconcentrated thought he enters on the second trance; emerged from that he abides in unconcentrated thought; from unconcentrated thought he enters on the first trance; emerged from that he abides in unconcentrated thought. After he has stood in this concentration which represents the crowning assault, he reaches the sameness of all dharmas.[24] It is thus that the Bodhisattva, the great being, having stood in the perfection of Wisdom, acquires the perfection of Meditation.[25]

[24] *P* adds : "The wholesome roots (which he derives from this practice) he makes common to all beings, and dedicates them to full enlightenment. But he turns them over without the threefold discernment, i.e. of him who turns over, of that which turns over, of that whereto he turns over. It is thus that the Bodhisattva enters into the concentration which represents the crowning assault, and emerges from it".

[25] If we number the pretrance state 0 and the trances as 1-9, then this is the sequence envisaged here : [0] - 1 - 2 - 3 - 4 - 5 - 6 - 7 - 8 - 9 - (1 - 9 -) - 2 - 9 - 3 - 9-4 - 9 - 5 - 9 - 6-9-7-9 - 8 - 9 - 8 - 0 - 9 - 0 - 9 - 0 - 8 - 0 - 7 - 0 - 6 - 0 - 5 - 0 - 4 - 0 - 3 - 0 - 2 - 0 - 1 - 0. See *AA V vv*. 24-5. J. May, Hobogirin p. 357a differs.

Chapter 63

MANY QUESTIONS CONCERNING THE DUALITY OF DHARMAS

V6b. Ninefold discrimination of the object.

V6b,1-2. Discrimination of condensed and detailed cognition.

Subhuti: A Bodhisattva should be trained in many stations and yet he should not be trained in anything?

The Lord: So it is, Subhuti, so it is. A Bodhisattva should be trained in many stations and yet he should not be trained in anything. For the dharmas in which the Bodhisattva should train cannot be apprehended.

Subhuti: A Bodhisattva who wants to know full enlightenment should, in what the Tathagata has taught about dharmas briefly and in detail, study those six perfections in brief and in detail. After he has studied them he should become thoroughly familiar with them in his speech, and then repeatedly consider them with his mind, but in such a way that the dharmas which constitute thought and its concomitants do not proceed.

The Lord: So it is, Subhuti, so it is. A Bodhisattva who trains briefly and in detail in these six perfections ((f. 247b)) will also cognize all dharmas briefly and in detail.

Subhuti: And how will he do that?

The Lord: When he cognizes the Suchness of form, etc. briefly and in detail, he will in that way cognize all dharmas briefly and in detail.

Subhuti: What then is the Suchness of form, etc.?

The Lord: That Suchness of which no production, abiding, or alteration is conceived, that is the Suchness of form, etc. in which the Bodhisattva should train. When he knows the Reality limit, a Bodhisattva will cognize all dharmas briefly and in detail.

Subhuti: What is that Reality limit?

The Lord: A no-limit is the Reality limit. When he trains in this limit a Bodhisattva will cognize all dharmas briefly and in detail. When he cognizes the Dharma-element, a Bodhisattva will cognize all dharmas briefly and in detail.

Subhuti: What is that Dharma-element?

The Lord: A no-element is the Dharma-element. Of that Dharma-element no cutting-off is conceived, and no limitation. When he courses thus and cognizes the Dharma-element, a Bodhisattva will cognize all dharmas briefly and in detail.

Subhuti: How should he cognize all dharmas briefly and in detail?

The Lord: He should see all dharmas as neither conjoined nor disjoined.

Subhuti: Which are these all-dharmas that are neither conjoined or disjoined?

The Lord: Form, etc. *to*: the conditioned element and the unconditioned element, are neither conjoined nor disjoined. And why? Because they have no own-being which could be conjoined or disjoined. And what has no own-being that is a nonexistent, and what is a nonexistent that is not conjoined with a nonexistent or disjoined from it. Thus should all dharmas be cognized. This again is the abridgement for a Bodhisattva, a great being. For in this abridged perfection should a Bodhisattva train as a beginner and until he has stood on the tenth stage. When he trains in this abridgement, a Bodhisattva will cognize all dharmas briefly and in detail.

Subhuti: Is this an introduction for a Bodhisattva whose faculties are keen?

The Lord: This is an introduction also for a Bodhisattva whose faculties are dull, or of a medium kind, or unconcentrated. This is an introduction for any Bodhisattva who wants to train, but not for one who is lazy, inferior in vigour, confused in his mindfulness, disturbed in his thought; it is an introduction for one who exerts vigour, who is not lazy, whose mindfulness is well established, and who wants to train on the irreversible stage and to reach the knowledge of all modes.

V6b,3. THE FACT THAT HE IS NOT UPHELD BY THE BUDDHA'S AID.

If a Bodhisattva will train in the perfection of wisdom as it has been explained, he will, having trained in the perfection of giving, etc. *to*: the perfection of wisdom ((f. 248a)) reach the knowledge of all modes. Whatever deeds of Mara may arise to a Bodhisattva who courses in perfect wisdom, he will at once get rid of them again. Therefore a Bodhisattva who wants to gain skill in means should train in the perfection of wisdom. At the time when a Bodhisattva courses in the perfection of wisdom, develops it, and makes endeavours about it, at that time the Buddhas and Lords who reside in countless world systems and demonstrate the Good Dharma, bring that Bodhisattva to mind, as he courses in perfect wisdom. And why? The past, future, and present Buddhas and Lords have issued from the six perfections. A Bodhisattva who courses in perfect wisdom should therefore expect that also he will reach those dharmas which the past, future, and present Buddhas and Lords have reached, will reach, and do reach. It is thus that a Bodhisattva who courses in perfect wisdom should exert effort. When he exerts himself in such a way, then he will quickly know full enlightenment. A Bodhisattva should therefore become one who is not lacking in attentions to the knowledge of all modes. If a Bodhisattva, thus coursing in the knowledge of all modes, develops perfect wisdom even for the time of a mere finger-snap, then he will beget a greater amount of merit than if he were to gratify all beings in the great trichiliocosm with gifts, or were to establish them in morality, in concentration, in wisdom, in emancipation, in the vision and cognition of emancipation, in the fruit of a Streamwinner, etc. *to* : Pratyekabuddha-enlightenment. And why? Because all these, from giving to Pratyekabuddha-enlightenment, have issued from this (perfect wisdom). Those Buddhas and Lords also, who reside in the world systems in the ten directions and demonstrate Dharma, they also have issued from this perfection of wisdom. All the past, future, and present Buddhas have come forth from this perfection of wisdom. Furthermore if, for a second, or a day, or a hundred days, or a year, or one hundred years, or an aeon, or for one hundred aeons, or for countless thousands of aeons, a Bodhisattva were to develop this perfection of wisdom with attentions which have the knowledge of all modes for their objective basis, he will beget a greater merit than one who were to gratify all beings in world systems equal to the sands of the Ganges with gifts, or would establish them in morality, etc. *to*: in Pratyekabuddha-enlightenment. And why? ((f. 248b)) Because from this have issued those Buddhas and Lords who have arranged[1] this foundation of meritorious deeds consisting in giving, etc. *to* : the Pratyekabuddha-enlightenment.

V6b,4. The nonexistence of (the virtuous qualities) on the path of training.

Furthermore one should expect a Bodhisattva to be irreversible if he stands in the perfection of wisdom as expounded here. One should expect him to be endowed with the Tathagatas, if he is endowed with this skill in means. One should expect him to have honoured many hundreds of thousands of niyutas of kotis of Buddhas, to have planted wholesome roots, to have been taken hold of by the good spiritual friend, to have coursed for long in the six perfections, to have developed the fourteen[2] kinds of emptiness, and so on, until we come to : one should expect him to have developed the four analytical knowledges, to possess the six superknowledges, to be a true Crown Prince,[3] full of good intentions, not lacking in the vision of the Buddhas, or in wholesome roots, or in the

[1]*prajñapta*; *btags-pa,* which can also mean *upanīta.*

[2]*P* says : 20.

[3]*kumārabhūta, gshon-nur gyur-pa.*

Buddha-field, with his inspired speech never interrupted, one who has acquired the dhāraṇīs, who has achieved an accomplished body, who has achieved the prediction, who can be reborn at will, who is skilled in entering on the letters and on what cannot be expressed by letters,[4] skilled in what can and what cannot be expressed by worldly convention, skilled in finding one synonym, two synonyms, many synonyms, skilled in the words of women, men, and neuters, skilled in the past, future, and present, skilled in form and the other skandhas, in Nirvana, in the mark of the Dharma-element, of the Conditioned and the Unconditioned, skilled in existence and in nonexistence, own-being and other-being, in what is associated, dissociated, both associated and dissociated, neither associated nor disassociated, skilled in Suchness, nonfalseness, unaltered ((f. 249a)) Suchness, in the Dharma-element, the fixed sequence of Dharma, skilled in causes and conditions, skilled in what has no conditions, skilled in the skandhas, elements, and sense fields, in the truths, in conditioned coproduction, skilled in the trances, Unlimited and formless attainments, in the six perfections, the four applications of mindfulness, etc. *to* : in the knowledge of all modes, skilled in the conditioned element, the unconditioned element, in the element and the non-element, skilled in attention to form, etc. *to* : the knowledge of all modes, skilled in the understanding that 'form is empty of form', etc. *to* : that 'consciousness is empty of consciousness', etc. *to* : that 'enlightenment is empty of enlightenment', skilled in the path of quiescence and the path of nonquiescence, skilled in production, in stopping, in the alteration of what has been established, skilled in greed, hate, and delusion, as well as in no-greed, no-hate, and no-delusion, skilled in views and in no-views, in false views and not-false views, etc. *to* : skilled in all views; skilled in name, in name and form, in objective supports, in the decisive condition, in modes, in marks, in ill, origination, stopping and the path, in the hells, animal births, world of Yama, men and ghosts, skilled in the path which leads to (beings being reborn as) men, in the gods, in the path which leads to (rebirth among) the gods, in the fruit of a Streamwinner, in the path which leads to the fruit of a Streamwinner, etc. *to* : in Arhatship, in the path which leads to Arhatship, in Pratyekabuddha-enlightenment, in the path which leads to Pratyekabuddha-enlightenment, in the knowledge of the modes of the path, in the path which leads to the knowledge of the modes of the path, in the knowledge of all modes, in the path which leads to the knowledge of all modes, in the faculties, in the perfection of the faculties, skilled in quick wisdom, keen wisdom, swift wisdom, penetrating wisdom, vast wisdom, unequalled wisdom, skilled in the past, future, and present period, skilled in means, skilled

[4]Ms adds: "skilled in the dwelling of a Bodhisattva"; but not in *AdT*, and seems to be out of place here.

in the intentions of beings and their earnest intentions, skilled in the meaning, skilled in the method, skilled in the establishment in the triple vehicle. These advantages, Subhuti, should be expected of that Bodhisattva, that great being, when he courses in perfect wisdom,

V6b,5. THE NONEXISTENCE OF (THE VIRTUOUS QUALITIES) ON THE PATH OF VISION.

aspires for it,[5]

V6b,6. THE NONEXISTENCE OF (THE VIRTUOUS QUALITIES) ON THE PATH OF DEVELOPMENT,

develops it.

V6b,7. THE COGNITION OF THE PATH OF TRAINING.

Subhuti: How, O Lord, should one course in perfect wisdom, how aspire for it, how develop it?

The Lord: One should course in perfect wisdom through the calmness of form, etc. through its voidness, its vanity, its insubstantiality.

V6b,8. THE COGNITION OF THE PATH OF VISION.

You ask, Subhuti, how one should aspire for the perfection of wisdom. Through the aspiration for the emptiness of space.

V6b,9. THE COGNITION OF THE PATH OF DEVELOPMENT.

You ask, Subhuti, how the perfection of wisdom should be developed. ((f. 249b)) Through the undevelopment of development.

V6c. THE SECOND DISCRIMINATION OF THE OBJECT.

V6c,1. THE NONPRODUCTION OF THE THOUGHT OF ENLIGHTENMENT.

Subhuti: For how long must that Bodhisattva course in perfect wisdom?

The Lord: From the first thought of enlightenment onwards,

V6c,2. THE NONATTENTION TO THE TERRACE OF ENLIGHTENMENT.

until he is seated on the terrace of enlightenment, he[6] should course in perfect wisdom, aspire for it, develop it!

V6c,3-4. THE NONATTENTION TO THE VEHICLE OF THE DISCIPLES AND PRATYEKABUDDHAS.

[5]*abhiṇirharataḥ, mṅon-par sgrub-pa.*

[6]*P*: "does not attend to the terrace of enlightenment. It is thus that he should course, etc."

Subhuti: Should one then course in perfect wisdom while giving opportunity to thoughts of another kind?

The Lord: One should course in perfect wisdom as one who does not give an opportunity to other acts of attention, and so one should aspire for it, and develop it.

V6c,5. The nonattention to full enlightenment.

Without ever abandoning the attentions to the knowledge of all modes should one course in perfect wisdom, aspire for it, and develop it, but in such a way that the dharmas which constitute thought and its concomitants do not proceed.

Subhuti: Will then one who courses in perfect wisdom, aspires for it, and develops it, reach the knowledge of all modes?

The Lord: No, Subhuti.

V6c,6. The development.

(*Subhuti*: Will then one who develops it reach it?

The Lord: No, Subhuti.)[7]

V6c,7. The nondevelopment.

Subhuti: Will then someone reach it who does not develop it?

The Lord: No, Subhuti.

(*Subhuti*: Will then someone who both develops and does not develop reach it?

The Lord: No, Subhuti.)[8]

V6c,8. Neither development nor nondevelopment.

Subhuti: Or one who neither develops nor not develops it?

The Lord: No, Subhuti.

V6c,9. It is not considered as it really is.

Subhuti: How then can he ever reach the knowledge of all modes?

The Lord: As Suchness.

Subhuti: How Suchness?

The Lord: As the Reality limit.

Subhuti: How the Reality limit?

The Lord: As the Dharma-element.

V6d. The first discrimination of the subject.

V6d,1. The conceptual existence of beings.

Subhuti: How the Dharma-element?

[7]Only in *P*.
[8]Not in *P*.

The Lord: As the element of a self, of a being, of a soul, of a person.

Subhuti: What then is the element of a self, of a being, of a soul, of a person?

The Lord: What do you think, Subhuti, can one apprehend a self, a being, a soul or a person?

Subhuti: No, O Lord.

The Lord: When one cannot apprehend a self, a being, a soul or a person, how can I make (people) conceive of the element of a self, a being, a soul or a person? In this way, without conceiving the perfection of wisdom, or all dharmas, one will reach the knowledge of all modes.

Subhuti: Are then the six perfections inconceivable?

The Lord: Not only is the perfection of wisdom inconceivable, but so are all dharmas, be they conditioned or unconditioned, be they Disciple-dharmas, or Pratyekabuddhadharmas, (or even Buddhadharmas).[9]

Subhuti: If all dharmas are inconceivable, how can one conceive the hells, the animal kingdom, the world of Yama, men or gods, how the Streamwinners, etc. *to*: the fully enlightened Buddhas?

The Lord: What do you think, Subhuti, can one apprehend the concept of a being?

Subhuti: No, O Lord.

The Lord: How then, if beings cannot be apprehended, can one conceive of the hells, etc. *to*: the fully enlightened Buddhas? It is thus that a Bodhisattva who courses in perfect wisdom should train in dharmas which are inconceivable.

V6d,2. THE CONCEPTUAL EXISTENCE OF DHARMAS.

Subhuti: Should then a Bodhisattva, who courses in perfect wisdom, not be trained in form, etc. *to*: ((f. 250a)) in the knowledge of all modes?

V6d,3. THE DISCRIMINATION OF EMPTINESS.

The Lord: He should be trained in form, etc. without adding or subtracting anything.

Subhuti: How should he be trained in form, etc. without adding or subtracting anything?

The Lord: He should train in nonproduction and nonstopping.

Subhuti: How should he train in that?

The Lord: He should train in what has not been brought about, and there should be no development, nor undevelopment, of the karma formations.

Subhuti: How should he train in what has not been brought about?

The Lord: By seeing all dharmas as empty of own-marks.

Subhuti: How should all dharmas be seen as empty of own-marks?

[9]Not in Ms, but in *P*.

The Lord: Form should be seen as empty of form, etc. *to* : enlightenment as empty of enlightenment. It is thus, Subhuti, that the Bodhisattva, the great being, who courses in perfect wisdom, should train in all dharmas as empty of own-marks.

Subhuti: If, O Lord, form should be seen as empty of form, etc. *to* : enlightenment as empty of enlightenment, how can of a Bodhisattva who courses in perfect wisdom the coursing take place?

The Lord: A noncoursing is the Bodhisattva's coursing in perfect wisdom.

Subhuti: For what reason?

The Lord: Because no perfect wisdom can be apprehended, no Bodhisattva, no coursing, no one who courses, nor that whereby or wherein he courses. It is thus that a Bodhisattva's coursing in perfect wisdom is a noncoursing in which all these discoursings are not apprehended.

Subhuti: If the coursing in perfect wisdom is a noncoursing, how should a Bodhisattva, who is a beginner, course in perfect wisdom?

The Lord: From the first thought of enlightenment onwards he should train in all dharmas as baseless. When he gives a gift, he should do so without taking anything as a basis. And so when he guards morality, etc. *to* : when he develops wisdom, etc. *to* : ((f. 250b)) when he develops the knowledge of all modes.

Subhuti: By what is there a basis, and by what is there not?[10]

The Lord: In so far as there is duality, there is Basis. Nonduality, that is Nonbasis.

Subhuti: What then is duality?

The Lord: In so far as there is eye and form, etc. *to* : mind and mind objects, etc. *to* : in so far as there is enlightenment and the enlightened, that is duality.

Subhuti :[11] And what is nonduality?

The Lord: In so far as there is no eye and form, etc. *to* : no mind and mind objects, etc. *to* : no enlightenment and no enlightened, that is nonduality.

V6d,4. THE DISCRIMINATION OF ATTACHMENT.

Subhuti: Is then the apprehended nonbasis, or the nonapprehended?[12]

The Lord: Neither.[13] But on the contrary it is the sameness of basis

[10]*AdT*: *ji-tsam-gyis na mi dmigs-par 'gyur, ji-tsam-gyis na dmigs-par 'gyur lags*?

[11]So *AdT*, *P*, *S*. Ms omits.

[12]*kiṃ punar upalabhyo 'nupalambhaḥ athānupalabhyo' nupalambha*. This is not clear to me.—*AdT*: *ci dmigs-su ma mchis-pa mi dmigs lags sam, on te gñis-su mchis-pa mi dmigs lags?*—*P*: *kiṃ punar Bhagavann upalambhaḥ, athānupalambha upalambha?*

[13]*na Subhūte anupalaṃbhyo 'nupalambha, na-anupalabhyo' nupalambhaḥ*—*P*: *na S-e upalambho 'nupalambhaḥ.*—*AdT*: *dmigs-su yod-pas mi dmigs-pa' aṅ ma yin, dmigs-su med-pas mi dmigs-pa' aṅ ma yin mod-kyi.*

and nonbasis which is the Nonbasis. It is thus that a Bodhisattva should train in the sameness of basis and nonbasis.[14] Thus coursing, he becomes one who observes no basis[15] in perfect wisdom.

Subhuti: When a Bodhisattva who courses in perfect wisdom does not get attached to either basis or nonbasis, how can he, coursing in perfect wisdom, fulfil one stage after another and reach the knowledge of all modes?

The Lord: A Bodhisattva, coursing in perfect wisdom, who stands on a basis does not fulfil the stages one after another, because he cannot possibly do so. And why? The perfection of wisdom has no basis, enlightenment has no basis, and he also cannot be apprehended who courses in perfect wisdom. It is thus that a Bodhisattva should course[16] in perfect wisdom.

V6d,5. THE DISCERNMENT OF DHARMAS.

Subhuti: If no perfect wisdom can be apprehended, no enlightenment, and also no one who courses towards it, how can a Bodhisattva, who courses in perfect wisdom, effect a discernment of all dharmas.[17] (determining) this as form, that as feeling, etc. *to*: that as enlightenment?

The Lord: A Bodhisattva, a great being who courses in perfect wisdom, does not effect his discernment of dharmas in such a way that he apprehends form, etc. *to*: enlightenment.

V6d,6. THE DISCRIMINATION OF ENTITIES.

Subhuti: If the Bodhisattva, the great being who courses in perfect wisdom, does not apprehend form, etc. *to*: enlightenment, how, then, can he, after fulfilling the six perfections, enter on a Bodhisattva's special way of salvation, and how thereafter purify the Buddha-field, mature beings, reach the knowledge of all modes, turn the wheel of Dharma, do the work of a Buddha and liberate beings from Samsāra?

The Lord: The Bodhisattva, the great being, does not course in perfect wisdom for the sake of form, etc. *to*: enlightenment. ((f. 251a))

Subhuti: For the sake of what, then, does he course in perfect wisdom?

The Lord: For the sake of nothing whatever. And why? Because all dharmas are not made, not brought about, and that applies also to the perfection of wisdom, to enlightenment, and to the Bodhisattva. It is thus that the Bodhisattva should course in perfect wisdom, by way of its being unmade and not brought about.

[14]So *AdT*, *P*; *Ms*: "in the sameness of the basis".

[15]*anaupalambhika, dmigs-pa med-pa. Aupalambhika* occurs at *A* vi 158, vii 172, xxviii 473 (*dmigs-pa daṅ bcas-pa*, and *dmigs-pa can*), *Suv.* ii 23b, *Sapt.* 208.

[16]*AdT*: "train".

[17]*AdT* adds: "which are devoid of own-being".

V6d,7. THE DISCRIMINATION OF THE TRIAD OF VEHICLES.

Subhuti: If all dharmas are not made and not brought about, how can there be a distinctive definition of these three vehicles, i.e. of the Disciple-vehicle, the Pratyekabuddha-vehicle, the great vehicle?[18]

The Lord: No distinctive definition can be apprehended of dharmas which are not made and not brought about, but only of dharmas which are brought about and arranged (into concrete things and events).[19] And why? Because foolish, untutored common persons, having settled down in the five skandhas, in form to consciousness, etc. *to*: in the knowledge of all modes, put their minds to form, etc. up to enlightenment, apprehend form, etc. up to enlightenment. And it occurs to them, 'I shall know full enlightenment, I shall liberate beings from Samsāra'. In this way they imagine what does not exist. And why? Because, although the Buddhas with their five[20] eyes have not apprehended this form, etc. *to*: enlightenment, these deluded persons, blind, without eyes, who give the lie to the Buddhas,[21] want to liberate beings from Samsāra!

Subhuti: If the Tathagata with his five eyes has not apprehended the beings whom he liberates from Samsāra, how then could the Lord, having knows full enlightenment, predict beings to the three heaps[22]—those destined for salvation, those destined for perdition, those whose destiny is not fixed either way?

The Lord: Not have I after knowing full enlightenment apprehended any being as destined for salvation, destined for perdition, or as one whose destiny is not fixed either way. All I do is to restrain from seizing on what is unreal those beings who perceive actual reality as that which is not actually real—but by way of worldly convention and not in ultimate reality.

Subhuti: Has, then, the Lord known full enlightenment after having stood in ultimate reality?

The Lord: Not so.

Subhuti: Or having stood in perverted views?

The Lord: Not so.

Subhuti: If he has not known full enlightenment having stood in either ultimate reality or in perverted views[23] then surely the Tathagata has not at all known the supreme enlightenment!

[18]*AdT*: "the Buddha-vehicle".

[19]*AdT*: mṅon-par bsags-pa.

[20]Described in *P* 77-83=*S I* 290-303.

[21]So only *AdT*.

[22]For the three *rāśīs* see de la Vallée Poussin, *Abhidharmakośa*, III 137-138, Introd. p. LIII. "Salvation" is literally "righteousness"; "perdition" "wrongness". *Mithyātva* means rebirth in the hells, as an animal, or as a *preta*.

[23]The "perverted views" may refer back to the "perceiving of actual reality in that which is not actually real". *AdT* seems to have read *ṛddhiparyāye(ṇa)*, "by way of his magical power". It is difficult to decide between these two readings.

The Lord: The Tathagata has known the supreme enlightenment, but he has not stood anywhere, in the conditioned or unconditioned element. Just as a Tathagata's magical creation does not stand[24] anywhere, in the conditioned or unconditioned element, and yet it goes and comes, stands up and sits down, and courses in the six perfections and the other practices ((f. 251b)) up to the eighteen special dharmas of a Buddha. If in the course of his turning of the wheel of Dharma[25] that magical creation were to conjure up countless beings, and predict them to the three heaps, what do you think, Subhuti, would that magical creation have in fact predicted any being at all?

Subhuti: No indeed, O Lord.

The Lord: Just so a Tathagata has cognized all dharmas as like a magical creation, and in consequence He has apprehended or disciplined no being at all. It is thus that the Bodhisattva should course in perfect wisdom, i.e. like a Tathagata's magical creation.

Subhuti: If all dharmas are like a magical creation, what is the difference, what the distinction, between the Tathagata and his magical creation? What is the purpose (of this teaching)?

The Lord: No difference or distinction can be apprehended between the Tathagata and his magical creation. For without difference are the Tathagata and his magical creation. And why? Because that deed which the Tathagata does, that his magical creation does.

Subhuti: Is it, then, when there is the Tathagata that the magical creation does its work?

The Lord: It does so, Subhuti.

Subhuti: Or is it when there is no Tathagata that the magical creation does its work?

The Lord: Let us assume that with calm determination the Tathagata, without apprehending the Bodhisattva,[26] had conjured up a Tathagata-frame,[27] and then gone to final Nirvana; that magical creation had, then, for up to an aeon done a Buddha's work; therefore, after having been predicted, that Bodhisattva, that great being[28] would be called 'one who has won final Nirvana'; nevertheless that magical creation undergoes neither production nor Parinirvana. It is thus that the Bodhisattva should course in the perfection of wisdom, i.e. with the firm belief that all dharmas are like magical creations.

[24]*AdT*: "is not apprehended", *mi dmigs.*

[25]The punctuation is not quite clear here.—*pravartanāyai* is *bskor-bar 'gyur-la* in *AdT.*

[26]*blo-gros shi-bas byaṅ-chub sems-dpa 'ma dmigs-nas.*

[27]*AdT*: "magical creation".

[28]Or is it the *nirmita* which gets the prediction, and is treated as a Bodhisattva? The construction is obscure to me. *des phyi byaṅ-chub sems-dpa 'luṅ bstan-nas yoṅs-su mya-ṅan lus-' da 'shes skye-bo rnams-kyis kun-tu śes kyaṅ.*

V6d,8. THE NONPURITY OF HIS ACCEPTANCE OF OFFERINGS.

Subhuti: If there is no difference between a magical creation and a Tathagata, how can there be a perfect purity of donations? For there are beings, desirous of merit, desirous of Nirvana, who establish for a Tathagata a donation, which never again becomes extinct until they have all entered Nirvana in the realm of Nirvana which leaves nothing behind. Can just so also for the magical creation a donation be established which never again becomes extinct until all the donors have entered Nirvana in the realm of Nirvana which leaves nothing behind?

The Lord: The dharmic fitness[29] by which the Tathagata becomes worthy of the donations of the world with its gods, men, and Asuras, by that very same dharmic fitness also the magical creation becomes worthy of them. But let us leave aside the gifts established for the Tathagata and his magical creations. If, Subhuti, any son or daughter of good family will lovingly attend to the Tathagata, they all will, when they have reached the limit of this wholesome root, make an end of ill. Leaving aside the loving attention, if a son or daughter of good family has attended to the Tathagata and honoured him by hurling a flower into the air, they all will, before having reached the limit of that wholesome root, make an end of ill. Leaving aside the loving attention and the flower in space, if any son or daughter of good family pay homage to the Buddha, they all will ((f. 252a)) gradually make an end of ill. So greatly profitable indeed is the donation established for the Tathagata, so greatly advantageous. By this method also should one know that there is no difference between the Tathagata and his magical creation, if the dharmic nature[30] of dharmas is taken as the standard.

V6d,9. THE DISTURBANCE OF HIS PRACTICES.

It is thus that a Bodhisattva should course in perfect wisdom, having entered into the dharmic nature of dharmas. And that dharmic nature of dharmas should not be disturbed by saying, 'this is perfect wisdom, this is the dharmic nature of perfect wisdom', and so for the other five perfections, and for all dharmas.

Subhuti: If the dharmic nature of all dharmas should not be disturbed, has it, then, not been disturbed by the Tathagata when he has pointed out dharmas as form, etc. *to*: consciousness, or when he has pointed out dharmas as inner and outer, as wholesome and unwholesome, with and without outflows, worldly and supramundane, common and uncommon, conditioned and unconditioned? Has not thereby the dharmic nature of dharmas been disturbed?

The Lord: No indeed, Subhuti. Through names and signs have I pointed out these dharmas, have I indicated them, so as to introduce

[29] *dharmatā*.

others to them. But the dharmic nature of dharmas has not thereby been disturbed.

Subhuti: If names and signs are used[30] for the sake of introducing others (to the dharmas named), how then can dharmas which are obviously nameless and signless, be verbally expressed through names and signs?

V6e. THE SECOND DISCRIMINATION OF THE SUBJECT; IN GENERAL.

The Lord: Verbal expression does not necessarily imply a settling down in names and signs. Only with reference to suffering do I use verbal expressions, not for the settling down in name and sign. For a Tathagata, or his disciple, does not settle down in name and sign. If name could settle down in name, sign in sign, emptiness in emptiness, the signless in the signless, the wishless in the wishless, Suchness in Suchness, the Reality limit in the Reality limit, the Dharma-element in the Dharma-element, the Unconditioned in the Unconditioned, then the Tathagata, or his disciples, would settle down in name or sign. But since all dharmas are mere words, they do not abide in them. It is thus that a Bodhisattva, having taken his stand on mere words and signs, should course in perfect wisdom, but not settle down in it.

Subhuti: If all dharmas[31] are mere words and signs, what is the point of a Bodhisattva's raising his thought to enlightenment, and why should he experience the manifold misfortunes of the karma formations, why go on the pilgrimage of a Bodhisattva, and give various gifts, guard morality, etc. *to*: develop wisdom, course in emptiness, etc. *to*: fulfil the great friendliness and the great compassion?

The Lord: As Subhuti has asked, 'if thus all dharmas[31] are but names and signs, what is the point of a Bodhisattva's going on his pilgrimage?' It is just because everything conditioned is mere name and sign, and those names are empty of names ((f. 252b)), those signs are empty of signs, that a Bodhisattva, coursing on his pilgrimage, reaches the knowledge of all modes, and then turns the wheel of Dharma, thereby leading beings to Nirvana through the three vehicles. But of that name or sign no production, passing away or alteration can be conceived.[32]

V6e,1. THE BEWILDERMENT ABOUT THE KNOWLEDGE OF ALL MODES.

Subhuti: 'Knowledge of all modes, knowledge of all modes', you say, O Lord?

The Lord: So I do, Subhuti.

Subhuti: The Tathagata has spoken of the knowledge of all modes,

[30]So *AdT*.

[31]So *AdT*. Ms: "everything conditioned". This may well be the better, though less obvious, reading.

[32]*AdT* "apprehended".

the knowledge of the modes of the path, and all-knowledge. What is the difference, what the distinction, between these three kinds of omniscience?

The Lord: The knowledge of all modes belongs to the Tathagata, the knowledge of the paths to the Bodhisattvas, the great beings, and all-knowledge of the Disciples and Pratyekabuddhas.

Subhuti: What is the reason for this?[33]

V6e,2. THE BEWILDERMENT CONCERNING ALL-KNOWLEDGE.

The Lord: Everything that there is, both inner and outer dharmas, that has been cognized by the Disciples and Pratyekabuddhas—but not all the paths, and not in all respects. As Subhuti has asked:

V6e,3. THE BEWILDERMENT CONCERNING THE KNOWLEDGE OF THE PATHS.

'For what reason does the knowledge of the modes of the path belong to the Bodhisattvas, the great beings?' The Bodhisattva, the great being, should produce and cognize all paths. The paths of the Disciples and Pratyekabuddhas, and those of the Bodhisattvas—those paths should be fulfilled, and through them should be done what ought to be done on them. But the Reality limit should not be penetrated.

Subhuti: Why should a Bodhisattva, who ought to fulfil the Buddha-path, not realise the Reality limit?[34]

The Lord: The Bodhisattva should not realise the Reality-limit without having completely purified his Buddha-field and matured beings.[35]

V6e,4. THE BEWILDERMENT CONCERNING THE PATH.

Subhuti: Should then a Bodhisattva, having stood in the path, realise the Reality limit?

The Lord: No, Subhuti.

Subhuti: Having stood in the no-path?

The Lord: No, Subhuti.

Subhuti: Having stood in both path and nonpath?

The Lord: No, Subhuti.

Subhuti: Having stood in neither path nor no-path?

The Lord: No, Subhuti.

[33]*P* then adds: "*Subhuti*: For what reason does the knowledge of all modes belong to the Tathagata? *The Lord*: As many as there are the modes, tokens, and signs by which dharmas are indicated, all those modes, tokens, and signs have been understood by the Tathagata. Therefore one speaks of a Tathagata's knowledge of all modes. *Subhuti*: For what reason does all-knowledge belong to the Disciples and Pratyekabuddhas?"—*P* also reverses the order.

[34]or, as *AdT* seems to take it: If the Bodhisattva should not fulfil the Buddhapath (which is not mentioned in the above answer), why then should he not just as well realize the Reality limit?

[35]*P* adds: "For that reason one speaks of the Bodhisattva's knowledge of the paths".

Subhuti: How then can a Bodhisattva actually realise the Reality limit?

The Lord: What do you think, Subhuti, have you, by having stood in the path, freed your thought from the outflows without further clinging?

Subhuti: No, O Lord.

The Lord: Or by having stood in the no-path, or in both path and no-path, or in neither path nor no-path?

Subhuti: No, O Lord, My thought has not been freed from the outflows without further clinging in so far as I am one who has stood anywhere; but it has been freed in so far as I have stood nowhere.

The Lord: Just so a Bodhisattva who has stood nowhere should realise the Reality limit. And as to the term 'knowledge of all modes', it is through one single mode that one speaks of that, i.e. through the mode of calm. Moreover, Subhuti, all the modes, tokens and signs ((f. 253a)) by which dharmas are indicated have been thoroughly understood by the Tathagata; therefore one speaks of 'the knowledge of all modes'.

Subhuti: Again, concerning the three kinds of omniscience—the knowledge of all modes, the knowledge of the paths, and all-knowledge—is there some differentiation as to the forsaking of the defilements in respect of them, in the sense that this one has a forsaking with, and that one a forsaking without remainder?

The Lord: There is no such differentiation in the forsaking of the defilements; but the Tathagatas forsake not only the defilements, but also the residues connected with them, whereas the Disciples and Pratyekabuddhas do not.

Subhuti: Have they not (all) reached the Unconditioned, and can one apprehend a differentiation within the Unconditioned?

The Lord: One cannot, Subhuti.

Subhuti: If no such differentiation can be apprehended, how is it that the Lord has distinguished between those who have forsaken all the defilements and the residues connected with them, and those who have not (also forsaken the residues)?

The Lord: There are really no defilements, and no residues connected with them. But there is on the part of the Disciples and Pratyekabuddhas a forsaking of greed, hate, and delusion, though their physical afflictions continue to proceed; these are harmful to foolish common people, but not to the Disciples; and the Tathagatas do not have them at all.

Subhuti: If, O Lord, nonexistence is the Path, nonexistence is Nirvana, how can one distinguish between Streamwinners, etc. *to*: Pratyekabuddhas, Bodhisattvas, great beings, and fully enlightened Tathagatas?

The Lord: All these have been brought forth from the Unconditioned[36] —Streamwinners, etc. *to*: fully enlightened Tathagatas.

Subhuti: Is it, then, perhaps the Unconditioned which causes the

[36]See my *Vajracchedikā*, 1957, pp. 98-9.

distinction between them?

The Lord: It certainly does not. Taking language as a standard, one can talk (of Streamwinners, etc.), but in ultimate reality no such distinction can be caused. And why? Because the paths of speech do not lead to any valid concept.

Subhuti: How can the final limit[39] be conceived?

The Lord: Having made worldly convention into a standard, one can conceive of the final limit of those who have cut off[38] the limit,[39] but not by way of ultimate reality. Moreover, those whose former limit has been cut off, of them the final limit is conceived.

Subhuti: When all dharmas are empty of own-marks, how can one conceive of a former or a final limit?

The Lord: So it is, Subhuti. Since all dharmas are empty of own-marks, one cannot conceive of a former limit; how again of a final limit? That cannot possibly be. But on the other hand, to those beings who do not cognize dharmas as empty of own-marks, just to them it has been explained that this is the former, this the final limit. But in dharmas which are empty of own-marks no former or final limit can in fact be apprehended. It is thus that a Bodhisattva should course in perfect wisdom in dharmas which are empty of own-marks. He, then, does not settle down anywhere, not in inner or outer dharmas, not in conditioned or unconditioned ones, not in those of the Disciples or Pratyekabuddhas.

Subhuti: In what sense does one speak of the 'perfection of wisdom'?

The Lord: It has reached the highest[41] perfection of all dharmas—in that sense one speaks of the 'perfection of wisdom'. ((f. 253b)) Furthermore it is through this perfection of wisdom that all Disciples, Pratyekabuddhas, Bodhisattvas, and Tathagatas have gone beyond[42] all dharmas, do go beyond, will go beyond—in that sense one speaks of 'perfection of wisdom'. Moreover in the ultimate sense[43] the objectivity[44] of dharmas is unbroken. Through this perfection of wisdom the Tathagatas have not apprehended a Beyond[45] in all dharmas—in that sense one speaks of the 'perfection of wisdom'.

V6e,5. THE BEWILDERMENT CONCERNING THE CONJUNCTION WITH AND THE DISJUNCTION FROM SUCHNESS.

Furthermore in this perfection of wisdom, Suchness is contained, the

[37]*paścimā koṭi, phyi-ma'i mtha'.*
[38]*S*: "not cut off"?
[39]*anta, mtha'.*
[41]*parama, pha-rol dam-pa ste.*
[42]*pāram, pha-rol-tu son-pas.*
[43]*parama-arthena.*
[44]*artha,* don.
[45]*pāro.*

Reality limit, the Dharma-element—in that sense one speaks of 'the perfection of wisdom'. Furthermore perfect wisdom is not conjoined with any dharma, nor disjoined from it; it is not definable nor undefinable, not resisting nor nonresisting. And why? Because this perfection of wisdom is immaterial, undefinable, nonresisting, with one mark only, i.e. no-mark.

V6e,6. THE BEWILDERMENT CONCERNING THE ABSENCE OF A STATE OF SAMENESS.

Moreover, this perfection of wisdom is the practice of all dharmas, it bestows an uninterrupted (flow of) flashes of insight and illuminations, it cannot be overpowered by Mara or the deities of his host, or by the persons who belong to the vehicle of the Disciples and Pratyekabuddhas, nor can this perfection of wisdom of the Bodhisattva, the great being, be taken away by any heretics or bad spiritual friends. And why? Because all these[46] cannot be apprehended in this perfection of wisdom, on account of the emptiness of own-marks. It is thus, Subhuti, that the Bodhisattva, the great being, should course in this perfection of wisdom.

V6e,7. THE BEWILDERMENT CONCERNING THE TRUTHS OF ILL, ETC.

Moreover, Subhuti, the Bodhisattva, the great being, who courses in the meaning of this deep perfection of wisdom, should course in the meaning of impermanence, ill and not self; in the meaning of the cognition of ill, of origination, of stopping, of the path; in the cognition of extinction, nonproduction, the dharma, the subsequent dharma, ultimate truth, etc. *to* : in the meaning of the cognition of what is just so.[47] It is thus that the Bodhisattva should course in the meaning of perfect wisdom.

V6e,8. THE BEWILDERMENT CONCERNING THE ESSENTIAL NATURE OF THE DEFILEMENTS.

Subhuti: If in this deep perfection of wisdom no meaning[48] and no nonmeaning[49] is apprehended, how should the Bodhisattva, the great being, course in the meaning of the perfection of wisdom?

The Lord: Here the Bodhisattva, the great being, who courses in the deep meaning of perfect wisdom, should course as follows : He should not course in 'greed is useful or harmful to me'[50] and so with : hate, delusion, wrong views, etc. *to* : all that pertains to false views. And why? Because the Suchness of greed, hate, and delusion, etc. *to* : the various false

[46]*AdT* in greater detail : "this taking away, he who takes away and that which is taken away".

[47]The enumeration in *AdT* differs; cf. also *P* 208-9 = *S* 1440-1, and the numerous parallels.

[48]*artha, don-la don.*

[49]*anartha, don ma lags-pa.*

[50]*me 'rtho' anartha iti, bdag-gi don ci 'am, bdag-la gnod-pa shes.*

views, does not bring about the welfare[51] or misfortune[52] of anything. He should not course in 'form is useful[53] or harmful[54] to me', and so with everything up to enlightenment. And why? Because the Tathagata, when he has known full enlightenment, has not apprehended any dharma which would do him good[55] or harm.[56] Whether Tathagatas are produced or not produced, firmly established is just this Dharmahood of dharmas, the established nature of dharmas, the element of Dharma, and these do not do any good or harm. It is thus that the Bodhisattva, the great being, should, having relinquished all thought of good[57] and evil,[58] course in the perfection of wisdom.

Subhuti: For what reason does the perfection of wisdom no good and no harm?

The Lord: Because the perfection of wisdom has no effect on the conditioned and unconditioned dharmas,[59] for that reason ((f. 254a)) it does no good or harm to anything.

Subhuti: Does, then, the Unconditioned not benefit[60] all holy men—the Buddhas and their disciples?

The Lord: The Unconditioned benefits all holy men—the Buddhas and their disciples. But it has not been set up so as to benefit[61] or not benefit[62] anything. Just as the Suchness of space has not been set up to benefit or not benefit anything, just so likewise the perfection of wisdom of the Bodhisattva, the great being.

Subhuti: Does, then, the Bodhisattva, the great being, having trained in the unconditioned perfection of wisdom, not reach the knowledge of all modes?

The Lord: Yes, he does, but not by way of duality.

V6e,9. THE BEWILDERMENT CONCERNING THE NONEXISTENCE OF DUALITY.

Subhuti: Does then again a nondual dharma reach a nondual dharma?

The Lord: No, Subhuti.

Subhuti: Does, then, a dual dharma reach a dual dharma?

The Lord: No, Subhuti.

Subhuti: Does then a dual dharma reach a nondual dharma?

[51]*artha, don.*
[52]*anartha, gnod-pa.*
[53]*artha, don.*
[54]*anartha, gnod-pa.*
[55]*artha, don.*
[56]*anartha, gnod-pa.*
[57]*artha, don.*
[58]*anartha, gnod-pa.*
[59]The text is here corrupt.
[60]*artha, don.*
[61]*upakāra, phan-pa*; at f. 238a as 'bestowal'.
[62]*anupakāra, gnod-pa.*

The Lord: No, Subhuti.

Subhuti: Does then a nondual dharma reach a dual dharma?

The Lord: No, Subhuti.

Subhuti: How then is it just now attained?

The Lord: When neither a dual dharma nor a nondual dharma is apprehended. In this way the knowledge of all modes is attained by way of taking nothing at all as a basis.[63,64]

[63]So *AdT. S*: "And why? For attainment is without basis and cannot be attained either by the baseless or by that which has a basis".

[64]V 6f. The achievement of a virtuous condition.—This item, described in *AA* V vv. 35-36, is absent from all the *Prajñāpāramitā* texts I have seen.

Chapter 64

RIGHT EXPOSITION

V 7. The Unimpeded Concentration.

The cognition of the nonexistence of the object of the knowledge of all modes.

Subhuti: Deep, O Lord, is the perfection of wisdom. Doers of what is hard are the Bodhisattvas who set out towards full enlightenment, and who, although no being is got at, nor the concept of a being, nevertheless for the sake of beings set out towards full enlightenment. The Bodhisattva, who would wish to reach the knowledge of all modes for the sake of beings, would be just like a man who would wish to plant a tree in space when space can give no ground for its support.

The Lord: So it is, Subhuti, so it is. Doers of what is hard are the Bodhisattvas who, for the sake of beings, set out towards the knowledge of all modes and who, having fully known that knowledge of all modes, will then set beings free from their attachment.[1]

The Unimpeded Concentration.

Just as if, Subhuti, a man would want to plant a tree. At first (before it is planted) he would not know[2] the root of that tree, nor its branches, nor its trunk, leaves, flowers, or fruits. Having planted the sapling, he would from time to time look after it and water it; gradually that tree would become fully grown, with branches, leaves, flowers, and fruits; and the man would enjoy its leaves, flowers, and fruits. Just so, Subhuti, those Bodhisattvas, who for the sake of all beings set out for full enlightenment, they will, coursing gradually in the six perfections, reach the knowledge of all modes. And they will serve all beings as if they were leaves, flowers, and fruits. Here, Subhuti, a Bodhisattva acts like a leaf in that thanks to him beings are liberated from the three states of woe.[3] (f. 254b)) He is a flower in that thanks to the Bodhisattva, the great being, beings are reborn in good warrior families, good Brahmin families, good house-holder families, that they are reborn in the realm of the Four Great Kings, etc. *to*: among the gods of the realm of neither

[1]So *AdT*. *Ad* Ms. *S*: *sattvagrāhāt*; *P*: "from Samsāra".

[2]*na jānīyāt*; *mi śes*.

[3]the hells, animal world, world of Yama.

perception nor nonperception. The Bodhisattva, the great being, is a fruit in that, after he has reached the knowledge of all modes, he establishes those beings in the fruit of a Streamwinner, etc. *to* : in the enlightenment of a Pratyekabuddha. It is thanks to just this Bodhisattva, this great being, that they reach the knowledge of all modes and when they have reached it, they will also serve all beings as if they were leaves, flowers, and fruits. And those who give them donations, they all will gradually reach the final Nirvana through the three vehicles, i.e. by the vehicle of the Disciples, the vehicle of the Pratyekabuddhas, or the great vehicle they will win full enlightenment. And although they do not conceive of any being or the concept of a being, they will set free those beings from their attachment to themselves.[4] It is thus that the Bodhisattva, the great being, should course in perfect wisdom, i.e. in the conviction that 'those beings for whose sake I will reach the knowledge of all modes cannot be apprehended or conceived'.

Subhuti: That Bodhisattva, that great being, should verily be known as a Tathagata. And why? For it is thanks to the Bodhisattva that all the hells are cut off, all animal births, all worlds of Yama, all untoward moments and states of woe, all poverty-stricken states, all inferior destinies, and the whole world of sense desire, the whole world of form, the whole formless world.

The Lord: So it is, Subhuti, so it is. Just as a Tathagata should the Bodhisattva be known. If, however, Subhuti, there were no Bodhisattvas,[5] then the full enlightenment of the past, future, and present Buddhas and Lords would not be conceivable, there could be no manifestation of Pratyekabuddhas in the world, nor of Arhats, etc.; and the hells etc. *to* : the formless world could not be cut off. Moreover, Subhuti, when you say that 'just as a Tathagata should the Bodhisattva be known' so it is, Subhuti, so it is, just as a Tathagata should the Bodhisattva, the great being, be known! And why? ((f. 255a)) Because that Suchness through which the Tathagata is conceived, that Suchness through which the Pratyekabuddha and all holy men, through which form, etc. *to* : consciousness, as well as the conditioned and the unconditioned element are conceived—they are all just that Suchness.[6] Therefore is it called 'Suchness'. When he has stood in that Suchness a Bodhisattva, a great being, will reach the knowledge of all modes. That is why he may be called a 'Tathagata'. By this method should the Bodhisattva, the great being, be known as just a Tathagata, when Suchness is taken as the standard. It is thus, Subhuti, that the Bodhisattva, the great being, should train in the perfection of wisdom which is Suchness; he then

AdT; *Ad* Ms, *S*, *sattvagrāhāt*, as note 1.

[5] *AdT*, *S* add: "who have set out for full enlightenment".

[6] *P sarvasattvānāṃ tathatā tathāgatatathatā ca prajñapyate.*

trains in the Suchness of all dharmas, and perfects it; then he will win the development of sovereignty over the Suchness of all dharmas, become skilled in the faculties of all beings,[7] gain the skill in perfecting the faculties,[8] cognize that all that concerns beings is their own work, perfect the cognition which results from resolve,[9] and purify the cognition of the three periods of time; coursing in the pilgrimage of a Bodhisattva, he will work the weal of beings, purify the Buddhafield, reach the knowledge of all modes, turn the wheel of Dharma, establish beings in the three vehicles, and lead them to the realm of Nirvana which leaves nothing behind. It is thus, Subhuti, that the Bodhisattva, the great being, on seeing all the(se) virtues and advantages, should raise his own thought to full enlightenment, and likewise that of others.

Subhuti: Worthy of homage, O Lord, by the world with its gods, men, and Asuras are those Bodhisattvas, great beings, who course in this perfection of wisdom as it has been expounded!

The Lord: So it is, Subhuti, so it is.

Subhuti: How much merit, O Lord, does the Bodhisattva, the great being, who has had his first thought of enlightenment, beget when for the sake of all beings he wants to know fully the supreme enlightenment?

The Lord: If, Subhuti, all beings in the great trichiliocosm, as many as there are, would be established on the level of Disciple or Pratyekabuddha, would, then, these beings beget much merit?

Subhuti: Much, O Lord, much, O Well-Gone! An infinite merit, O Lord, a boundless merit, O well-Gone!

The Lord: Yet the merit which would result from all beings in the great trichiliocosm becoming followers of the Disciple- or the Pratyekabuddha-vehicle is infinitesimal when compared with the equipment of merit of the Bodhisattva who has had his first thought of enlightenment. ((f. 255b)) And why? Because the Disciples and Pratyekabuddhas have been begotten by the Bodhisattvas, whereas the Bodhisattvas, the great beings, have not been begotten by the Disciples and Pratyekabuddhas. And the same holds good if all those beings were endowed with the virtues of the Disciples and Pratyekabuddhas, because the virtues of the Disciples and Pratyekabuddhas have been begotten by the Bodhisattvas, and not the other way round. And the same holds good if all those beings were established on the stage of right insight, or on the stage where they become one of the clan, or on any other stage up to the stage of a Pratyekabuddha; and likewise if they had all entered on a Bodhisattva's special way of salvation, then their merit would be infinitesimal compared with that of a Bodhisattva, a great being.[9a] And if again all beings in the

[7] *sattvendriyakuśala, sems-can thams-cad-kyi dbaṅ-po-la mkhas-pa.*

[8] *indriyaparipūrīkuśalatā, dbaṅ-po yoṅs-su rdzogs-par bya-ba-la mkhas-pa.*

[9] *praṇidhijñāna, smon-nas śes-pa.*

[9a] I do not understand this sentence.

great trichiliocosm were to become candidates for enlightenment, then their merit would still be infinitesimal compared with that of the Tathagata.

The mark of the knowledge of all modes, or of Buddhahood.

Subhuti: Should the Bodhisattva, the great being, O Lord, who has had his first thought of enlightenment, attend to the knowledge of all modes?

The Lord: Yes, he should.

The objective support, dominant function, and mode of the knowledge of all modes.

Subhuti: What, O Lord, is of the knowledge of all modes the existence,[10] what the objective support, what the dominant function,[11] what the mode, what the mark?

The Lord: 'Knowledge of all modes'—that is nonexistent, markless, signless, impassive,[12] nonproduction, nonmanifestation. And again, as to what Subhuti has said, 'what is the objective support of the knowledge of all modes, what the dominant function, what the mode, what the mark?' Its objective support is nonexistence, its dominant function is mindful recalling, its mode is calm, its mark is a no-mark. This is the objective support of the knowledge of all modes, its dominant function, mark, and mode. ((f. 256a))

V 8. The Sixteen Errors.

V8,1. ERROR WITH REGARD TO THE GENESIS OF THE OBJECTIVE SUPPORT.

Subhuti: Is, then, just the knowledge of all modes nonexistence, or also form, and everything up to the unconditioned element?

The Lord: The knowledge of all modes is nonexistence, and so is form, etc. *to*: the unconditioned element. And why? Because, Subhuti, the knowledge of all modes has no own-being. And what has no own-being, that is nonexistence.

Subhuti: For what reason has the knowledge of all modes no own-being?

The Lord: It has no own-being acting in causal connection. And that which has no own-being acting in causal connection, that is nonexistence. It is by this method that all dharmas have nonexistence for own-being.

V8,2. THE ERROR WITH REGARD TO THE ACCURATE DETERMINATION OF THE OWN-BEING OF THE OBJECTIVE SUPPORT.

Moreover, Subhuti, all dharmas have emptiness for own-being, the

[10]*bhāva, dṅos-po.*
[11]*ādhipateya, dbaṅ bgyid-pa.*
[12]*anābhoga, lhun-gyis grub-pa.*

signless, the wishless. Moreover, Subhuti, all dharmas have Suchness for own-being, the Reality limit, the Dharma-element. By this method also, Subhuti, should one know that all dharmas have nonexistence for own-being.

Subhuti: If, O Lord, all dharmas have nonexistence for their own-being, then endowed with which skill in means does the Bodhisattva, the great being, who has had his first thought of enlightenment, coursing in the perfection of giving, etc. *to* : in the knowledge of all modes, purify the Buddha-field and mature beings?

The Lord: Just that is the skill in means of the Bodhisattva, the great being, that he gets fully acquainted[13] with all dharmas as having non-existence for own-being, and yet purifies the Buddha-field and matures ((f. 256b)) beings, and that he cognizes that Buddha-field and those beings as having nonexistence for own-being. Furthermore that Bodhisattva, that great being, coursing in the six perfections, etc. *to* : in the knowledge of all modes, gets fully acquainted with the path to enlightenment, and he cognizes that path to enlightenment as having nonexistence for own-being. And that Bodhisattva, that great being, who courses in the six perfections continues to get more fully acquainted with that path to enlightenment until he has been endowed with the ten powers of a Tathagata, etc. *to* : the 18 special dharmas of a Buddha, the great friendliness, and the great compassion. Having stood in that path to enlightenment he will fulfill the perfections and, then, through a wisdom associated with one single moment[14] reach the knowledge of all modes. Thereupon he will forsake all his defilements together with their residues, through a forsaking which fails to be produced.

V8,3. THE ERROR WITH REGARD TO THE COGNITION OF THE KNOWLEDGE OF ALL MODES.

Surveying the great trichiliocosm with the Buddha-eye, he does not apprehend nonexistence, how much less an existent. It is thus that the Bodhisattva, the great being, should course in the perfection of wisdom, i.e. in all dharmas as having nonexistence for own-being. And that is just of the Bodhisattva, the great being, the skill in means that he does not apprehend 'nonexistence', how much less an existent. Furthermore that Bodhisattva, that great being, who, coursing in perfect wisdom, gives a gift, does not have any imaginations about that gift, does not make it into a sign, and does not attend to it by way of existence or nonexistence. And likewise for the recipient and the giver. And also that thought of enlightenment he does not apprehend, or make it into a sign or objective

[13]*paricayaṃ karoti, yoṅs-su 'dris-par byed ciṅ.* Also at f. 259, *'dres-par byed-la,* 'gains mastery over'. The term *paricaya,* in Nepalese Mss often *parijaya,* deserves further study.

[14]*AdT*; *P* : 'mark'.

support, and he does not review it. And so everything, including the perfection of wisdom, him who develops the perfection of wisdom, and the beings for whose sake he develops it, he does not imagine, does not make into a sign, does not attend to by way of existence or nonexistence. And why? Because, if all dharmas are nonexistent,[15] then they have not been made by the Buddhas, Disciples, or Pratyekabuddhas. For all dharmas are without an agent, devoid of an agent.

Subhuti: Are then, O Lord, dharmas devoid of dharmas?

The Lord: Yes, they are.

Subhuti: If, O Lord, dharmas are devoid of dharmas, how, then, can a dharma which is devoid of itself cognize as existence or nonexistence a dharma which is devoid of itself? For a nonexistent dharma cannot cognize an existent dharma, nor an existent dharma a nonexistent one, nor a nonexistent dharma a nonexistent one, nor an existent dharma an existent one. When all dharmas are thus uncognizable, how can it occur to the Bodhisattva, the great being, that there is 'existence' or non-existence'?

The Lord: It is on account of worldly convention that the Bodhisattva, the great being who courses in perfect wisdom, points to 'existence' or 'nonexistence', and not in ultimate truth.

V8,4. THE ERROR WITH REGARD TO THE ULTIMATE AND CONVENTIONAL TRUTH.

Subhuti: Is again, O Lord, worldly convention one thing, and ultimate truth another?

The Lord: Worldly convention is not one thing and ultimate truth another. What is the Suchness of worldly convention, that is the ((f. 257 a)) Suchness of ultimate reality. It is because perverted beings do not know or see that Suchness, that for their sake the Bodhisattva, the great being, points to 'existence' or 'nonexistence' by way of worldly convention. These beings moreover perceive the five skandhas as existence, and do not cognize them as 'nonexistence'. For their sake, in an effort to make them understand that the skandhas are nonexistence has the Bodhisattva spoken of 'existence' and 'nonexistence', but leaving intact[16] the undifferentiatedness of dharmas. It is thus that the Bodhisattva, the great being, should course in the perfection of wisdom.

[15]So Ms. *Ad. AdT*: *dṅos-po med-pa'i ṅo-bo-ñid de, dṅos-po med-pa de'aṅ. S*: *abhāva-svabhāvās.*

[16]*upādāyā, phyir.*

CHAPTER 65

THE SKILL IN HONOURING, TENDING AND REVERING THE GOOD FRIENDS

V8,5. THE ERROR WITH REGARD TO THE ENDEAVOURS.

Subhuti: One speaks of a 'Bodhisattva's pilgrimage'. Of what is that a synonym?

The Lord: As a pilgrimage towards enlightenment[1] is it called a 'Bodhisattva's pilgrimage'.

Subhuti: Where[2] is that Bodhisattva-pilgrimage of the Bodhisattva, the great being?

The Lord: He courses in that 'form, etc. is empty'. In the same way he courses in the inner and outer sense fields, in the six perfections, the 18 kinds of emptiness, the trances, etc. *to*: the 18 special dharmas of a Buddha; in the purification of the Buddha-field, the maturing of beings, in ready speech,[3] in the aspirations for the letters,[4] in the entrances to the letters,[5] in the entrance to what cannot be expressed in letters,[6] in the dhāraṇis, in the conditioned element, in the unconditioned element. But he courses in such a way that no dual intellectual act takes place. It is thus that, coursing in perfect wisdom, the Bodhisattva courses towards enlightenment.[7]

V8,6. THE ERROR WITH REGARD TO THE JEWEL OF THE BUDDHA.

Subhuti: One speaks of a 'Buddha', O Lord. Of what is that a synonym?

The Lord: He is called 'Buddha' as the truly real fact.[8] Moreover he has fully known the truly real Dharma, ((f. 257b)) he has penetrated to the real meaning, he has fully known all dharmas as they really are—therefore is he called a 'Buddha'.

V8,7. THE ERROR WITH REGARD TO THE JEWEL OF THE DHARMA.

Subhuti: One speaks of 'enlightenment'. Of what is that a synonym?

[1]*bodhaye*; *byaṅ-chub-kyi phyir.*
[2]*kva*; *gaṅ-la.*
[3]*pratibhāna.*
[4]*akṣara-abhinirhāra.*
[5]*aksara-praveśa.*
[6]*anakṣara-praveśa.*
[7]Ms: *bodhau.* P: *bodhaye.*
[8]*bhūto 'rtho*; *yaṅ-dag-pa' i don.*

The Lord: 'Enlightenment', that is a synonym of emptiness, of Suchness, of the Reality limit, of the Dharma-element. Moreover enlightenment is Suchness, nonfalsehood, unaltered Suchness, unaltered existence,[9] therefore is it called 'enlightenment'. Moreover 'enlightenment' is a mere word and sign, therefore is it called 'enlightenment'. Moreover 'enlightenment' means an undifferentiated object.[10] Moreover because the Buddhas, the Lords have it, therefore is it called 'enlightenment'. Moreover the Buddhas and Lords have fully known it, therefore it is called 'enlightenment'.

V8,8. THE ERROR WITH REGARD TO THE JEWEL OF THE SAMGHA.

Subhuti: A Bodhisattva who courses towards this enlightenment,[11] does he course in the six perfections until he dwells in the knowledge of all modes? And of which wholesome roots is there an accumulation or removal, a diminution or growth, a production or stopping, a defilement or purification?

The Lord: A Bodhisattva who courses towards this enlightenment courses in the six perfections, etc. *to*: the knowledge of all modes, but to him no accumulation of any dharma takes place or its removal, no diminution or growth, no production or stopping, no defilement or purification. And why? Because the enlightenment of a Bodhisattva, who courses in perfect wisdom, is not set up through making any dharma into an objective support, or for an accumulation or removal, a diminution or growth, a production or stopping, a defilement or purification.

Subhuti: If a Bodhisattva's enlightenment has not been set up through making any dharma into an objective support, how then can the Bodhisattva acquire the six perfections, course in the emptinesses, trances, etc. *to*: in the great compassion, course on the ten stages of a Bodhisattva, transcend the level of Disciples and Pratyekabuddhas, and enter on the Bodhisattva's special way of salvation?

The Lord: It is because a Bodhisattva's intellect does not course in duality. For it is not through duality that he courses in the six perfections. It is thus that the Bodhisattva acquires the six perfections and in the end reaches the knowledge of all modes. ((f. 258a))

Subhuti: If a Bodhisattva does not course in the six perfections by way of duality, how is it possible for the Bodhisattva's wholesome roots to grow steadily from the first thought of enlightenment to the last?

The Lord: The wholesome roots of those who course in duality do not grow. And why? Because all the foolish common people lean on duality, and their wholesome roots do not grow. A Bodhisattva, on the contrary,

[9] *ananyathābhāva*; or: 'unaltered nonexistence'.

[10] *abhedārtho*, om. *AdT*.

[11] *iha bodhaye*; *byaṅ-chub 'di-la*; *P*: *imāyai bodhaye*.

courses in nonduality, and his wholesome roots[12] grow from the first to the last thought of enlightenment. The world with its gods, men and Asuras can then not overpower him and he will not fall on the level of the Disciples or Pratyekabuddhas, or partake of any other unwholesome dharmas which would prevent the increase of his wholesome roots while he courses in the six perfections, etc. *to* : in the knowledge of all modes. It is thus that a Bodhisattva should course in perfect wisdom.

Subhuti : Should, then, a Bodhisattva course in perfect wisdom for the sake of wholesome roots?

The Lord: No, indeed, Subhuti. A Bodhisattva courses in perfect wisdom not for the sake of wholesome, and still less for the sake of unwholesome roots. Though a Bodhisattva cannot reach the knowledge of all modes without having honoured the Buddhas, the Lords, having fulfilled the wholesome roots, or having gained good spiritual friends.

Subhuti : How does a Bodhisattva reach the knowledge of all modes after he has honoured the Buddhas, the Lords, won the wholesome roots, and gained good spiritual friends?

The Lord: Here a Bodhisattva, from the first thought of enlightenment onwards, honours the Buddhas, the Lords. He learns[13] all the dharmas which they teach, i.e. the Sutra, Geya, Prediction, Verses, Shouts of Triumph, Origins, Thus-was-said, Birth Stories, Expanded Texts, Marvels, Tales and Exposition,[14] becomes thoroughly familar with them in his speech, repeatedly considers them with his mind, penetrates them well with his vision, gains the dhāraṇis, and produces the analytical knowledges. From then onwards he never again, even after he has died,[15] forgets these dharmas until he reaches the knowledge of all modes. He also plants wholesome roots in the presence of the Tathagatas (whom he honours). Upheld by these wholesome roots he is never again reborn in the states of woe, or in unpropitious circumstances. And through these wholesome roots he acquires the perfect purity of the physical basis.[16] With this foundation he purifies the Buddha-field and matures beings. Upheld by these wholesome roots he is never again lacking in good spiritual friends—Buddhas and Lords, Bodhisattvas, great beings, and Disciples who speak to him in praise of the Buddha-vehicle. It is thus that a Bodhisattva who courses in perfect wisdom should honour the Buddhas and Lords, plant wholesome roots and tend the good spiritual friends. ((f. 258b))

[12]So Ms; *AdT*: "wholesome dharmas", *P*: *kuśalamūlair dharmair*.

[13]*udgṛhnāti*.

[14]This rather archaic list of the 12 branches of the Scriptures occurs often in the Large *Prajñāpāramitā*, e.g. *P* 31 = *S* 100, *P* 158, *P* 218 = *S* ×1460.

[15]Lit. "after he has passed through this present birth".

[16]*āśraya Ad, āśaya P*; *AdT* : *bsam-pa*. At *P* 532a *the āśraya (lus)—pariśuddhi* is mentioned as one of the four *pariśuddhayah*; cf. also *P* 526a. 'Resolute intentions' is, however, equally possible.

Chapter 66

EXPOSITION OF SKILL IN MEANS

Subhuti: But a Bodhisattva who would not honour the Buddhas, not fulfil the wholesome roots, not be upheld by the good friends, he would surely not reach the knowledge of all modes?

The Lord: Certainly not. And why? Even though he has honoured the Buddhas, planted wholesome roots, tended the good spiritual friends, he is quite incapable of reaching the knowledge of all modes. How much more so if he has not honoured the Buddhas, the Lords, not planted wholesome roots, not tended the good spiritual friends—that under those circumstances he should reach the knowledge of all modes, that cannot possibly be. Therefore then, Subhuti, a Bodhisattva who is in truth eager for full enlightenment and wants quickly to know it, should honour the Buddhas, the Lords, plant wholesome roots, and tend the good spiritual friends.

Subhuti: For what reason does a Bodhisattva who has honoured the Buddhas, the Lords, planted wholesome roots, and tended the good spiritual friends, not reach the knowledge of all modes?

The Lord: Because from lack of skill in means he has not listened to the Buddhas, the Lords, has not planted wholesome roots in their presence, and has not tended those good spiritual friends who could have explained skill in means to him.

V8,9. The error with regard to skill in means.

Subhuti: What is the skill in means, endowed with which the Bodhisattva reaches the knowledge of all modes?

The Lord: Here a Bodhisattva, a great being, beginning with the first thought of enlightenment, coursing in the perfection of Giving, gives gifts, with attentions associated with the knowledge of all modes—to Buddhas and Lords, to Pratyekabuddhas or Disciples, to men or ghosts. Endowed with attentions associated with the knowledge of all modes, he has with regard to the gift no notion of a gift, with regard to the recipient no notion of a recipient, with regard to the donor no notion of a donor. And why? Because he cognizes all dharmas as empty of own-marks, and sees them as not really existing, not totally real, uncreated. He enters into the dharma-mark of dharmas. (Seeing that) 'all dharmas are incapable of doing anything', he enters on the mark of their ineffectiveness.[1] Endowed with this skill in means he grows in wholesome dharmas, courses in the perfection of giving, matures beings and purifies the Buddha-field. But he does not aspire for any fruit of his giving which he could enjoy in Samsāra, and it is only for the purpose of protecting beings, of liberating them, that he courses in the perfection of giving.

[1]*asaṃskāra, mṅon-par 'du byed-pa med-pa.*

Chapter 67

MORALITY

Again, Subhuti, the Bodhisattva, the great being, coursing in the perfection of Morality, beginning with the first thought of enlightenment, guards morality with attentions associated with the knowledge of all modes. No greed obscures his thought, no hatred, no delusion; no evil tendencies or obsessions; nor any other evil, unwholesome dharmas which might obstruct enlightenment, such as niggardliness, immorality, wrathfulness, indolence, inferior ((f. 259a)) vigour, mental confusion or stupidity; or pride, contempt for others, conceit or self-conceit; or the thought of a Disciple or Pratyekabuddha. And why? For he cognizes all dharmas as empty of own-marks, and sees them as not really existing, not totally real, uncreated. And he enters into the dharma-mark of dharmas. (Seeing that) 'all dharmas are incapable of doing anything' he enters on their mark as being unconditioned.[1] Endowed with this skill in means, he grows in wholesome roots, courses in the perfection of morality, matures beings, and purifies the Buddha-field. But he does not aspire for any fruit from his morality, which he could enjoy in Samsāra, and it is only for the purpose of protecting and maturing beings that he courses in the perfection of morality.

[1]*asaṃskṛta, mṅoṅ-par 'du byed-pa med-pa.*

CHAPTER 68

GROWTH

Likewise with the perfections of Patience, Vigour, and Concentration. Moreover, Subhuti, the Bodhisattva, the great being, coursing in the perfection of Wisdom, beginning with the first thought of enlightenment, develops wisdom with attentions associated with the knowledge of all modes. And his thought is not obscured by greed, etc. *to* : the thought of the Disciples and Pratyekabuddhas. And why? Because he cognizes all dharmas as empty of own-marks, and sees them as not really existing, not totally real, uncreated. He enters into the dharma-mark of dharmas. (Seeing that) 'all dharmas are incapable of doing anything', he enters on their mark as being unconditioned. Endowed with this skill in means he grows in wholesome roots, courses in the perfection of wisdom, matures beings, and purifies the Buddha-field. But he does not aspire for any fruit of his wisdom which he could enjoy in Samsāra, and it is only for the purpose of protecting and liberating beings that he courses in the perfection of wisdom.

CHAPTER 69

EXPOSITION OF THE PATH-DEVELOPMENT

And again, the Bodhisattva, the great being, enters into the trances, Unlimited and formless attainments. But he does not take hold of his reward.[1] And why? Because he is endowed with the skill in means through which he cognizes the trances, Unlimited and formless attainments as empty of own-marks, etc. *to*: as uncreated. Moreover, Subhuti, the Bodhisattva, the great being who courses in perfect wisdom, beginning with the first thought of enlightenment, endowed with skill in means courses in the paths of vision, development and forsaking,[2] but does not attain the fruit of a Streamwinner, of a Once-Returner, or Never-Returner, or Arhatship. And why? Because he cognizes all dharmas as empty of own-marks, etc. *to*: as uncreated, and so, though he courses in these dharmas which act as wings to enlightenment, he transcends the level of the Disciples and Pratyekabuddhas. This, Subhuti, is the Bodhisattva's, the great being's, patient acceptance of dharmas which fail to be produced. Moreover, Subhuti, the Bodhisattva, the great being who courses in perfect wisdom, enters on the eight deliverances and the nine attainments of successive stations, but does not attain the fruit of a Streamwinner, etc. *to*: Arhatship. And why? Because he cognizes all dharmas as empty of own-marks ((f. 259b)), etc. *to*: as uncreated. Moreover, the Bodhisattva, the great being, gains mastery[3] over the ten powers of a Tathagata, the four grounds of self-confidence, the four analytical knowledges, the 18 special dharmas of a Buddha, the great friendliness, and the great compassion. But he does not reach the knowledge of all modes before his Buddha-field has been quite purified, and beings have been matured. It is thus that the Bodhisattva, the great being, should course in perfect wisdom.

Subhuti: Of the highest intelligence, O Lord, is the Bodhisattva, the great being, who courses in dharmas as deep as these, and who yet does not take hold of a reward.

The Lord: So it is, Subhuti, so it is. And why? Because the Bodhisattva, the great being, does not swerve from the own-being.

[1]cf. ch. 62 n. 22.

[2]*darśana-bhāvanā-prahātavya ca mārge*, *S*; *AdT*: *mthoṅ-ba daṅ bsgom-pas spoṅ-ba'i lam-la*.

[3]*paricayaṃ karoti*; see note 13 to ch. 64.

Subhuti: From the own-being of what does he not swerve?

The Lord: He does not swerve from nonexistence. And as to what the Ven. Subhuti has asked, 'from the own-being of what does he not swerve'? He does not swerve from the own-being of form, etc. And why? Because the own-being of these dharmas is nonexistence. Nonexistence cannot possibly be fully known through nonexistence.

V8,10. THE ERROR WITH REGARD TO THE REUNION WITH (OF) THE TATHAGATA.

Subhuti: Is it possible to fully know existence through existence?

The Lord: No, Subhuti.

Subhuti: Or nonexistence through nonexistence?

The Lord: No, Subhuti.

Subhuti: Or existence through nonexistence?

The Lord: No, Subhuti.

Subhuti: Or nonexistence through existence?

The Lord: No, Subhuti.

Subhuti: Then there will be neither attainment nor reunion, if there is no reunion of nonexistence with nonexistence, nor of existence with existence, nor of existence with nonexistence, nor of nonexistence with existence!

The Lord: There is reunion, but not through this aspiration after the four alternatives.[4]

Subhuti: How then, O Lord, does a reunion actually take place?

The Lord: Where there is neither nonexistence nor existence, that is the reunion in which these multiplicities[5] do not exist. For reunion takes place where these obstacles to spiritual progress are absent and do not impede.[6]

V8,11. THE ERROR WITH REGARD TO THE PERVERTED VIEWS.

Subhuti: What, then, is it that delays[7] the Bodhisattva, the great being?

The Lord: (The conviction that) 'form is permanent or impermanent' that delays the Bodhisattva, the great being; so for feeling, etc. ((f. 260a)) (The conviction that) 'form etc. is at ease or ill', that it is 'the self or not the self', 'calm or not calm', that 'it should or should not be comprehended'—all that delays the Bodhisattva, the great being. It delays him to think that 'the holy Truth of ill should be comprehended', 'origination forsaken', 'stopping realised' and the 'Path developed'; that 'the four trances, Unlimited and formless attainments should be developed';

[4]So *L, S, AdT*: *P*: *prakāra*: *cātuṣkoṭika* is the more usual term.

[5]*prapañca*; obstacles to spiritual progress.

[6]*aprapañcyo niṣprapañcyo*.

[7]*prapañca*.

etc. for the four applications of mindfulness, etc.; that 'I shall transcend the fruit of a Streamwinner, etc. *to* : Arhatship', or 'I shall transcend the enlightenment of a Pratyekabuddha', 'I shall fulfill the ten stages of a Bodhisattva', 'I shall enter on a Bodhisattva's certain way of salvation', 'I shall purify the Buddha-field', 'I shall mature beings', 'I shall produce the ten powers of a Tathagata, etc. *to* : the 18 special Buddhadharmas', 'I shall reach the knowledge of all modes', 'I shall forsake all the defilements and the residues relating to them'. Therefore, then, the Bodhisattva, the great being, who courses in the perfection of wisdom, does not cause any delay[8] by thinking that 'form is permanent or impermanent', etc. *to* : 'I shall forsake all the defilements and the residues relating to them'. And why? For own-being causes no delay to own-being, nor nonexistence to nonexistence. And apart from own-being and nonexistence one cannot apprehend any other dharma which could cause delay, or whereby or wherein one could be delayed. Therefore, then, Subhuti, free from all multiplicity[9] is form, etc. *to* : the knowledge of all modes. It is thus that the Bodhisattva, the great being, should course in a perfection of wisdom which is free from all multiplicity. Moreover, Subhuti, form, etc. has no ownbeing. What has no own-being ((f. 260b)) is free from all multiplicity. For that reason form, etc. is free from all multiplicity. It is thus that the Bodhisattva who courses in perfect wisdom enters on the Bodhisattva's way of certain salvation.

Subhuti : If of no dharma an own-being is apprehended, by which path does the Bodhisattva enter on the Bodhisattva's way of certain salvation, by the path of the Disciples, of the Pratyekabuddhas or the Buddhas?

The Lord: Not by either the path of the Disciples, or that of the Pratyekabuddhas, or that of the Buddhas. But the Bodhisattva enters on the Bodhisattva's way of certain salvation after he has trained in all the paths. Just as the Arhat,[10] after he has trained in all paths,[11] enters on the certainty that he will win salvation by the methods appropriate to the Disciples,[12] but does not attain the fruit (of Arhatship) until the fruit of the path arises,[13] just so the Bodhisattva, after he has produced all the paths, enters on a Bodhisattva's way of certain salvation, but does not reach the knowledge of all modes until the adamantine concentration[14] has been acquired. Through the acquisition of this con-

[8]*aprapañcyan na prapañcayati, spros-par bya-ba ma yin-pa spros-par mi byed do.* Also : 'he forms no discursive ideas about all that'.

[9]*niṣprapañcya, spros-pa med.*

[10]So *AdT, P*; Ms, L : 'the Eighth-lowest', i.e. the candidate to Streamwinnership.

[11]so *AdT, L, P*; Ms, 'dharmas'.—The preceding paths are meant?

[12]*samyaktvanyāma,* in contrast to *bodhisattvanyāma.*

[13]*ji-srid-du lam-gyi 'bras-bu ma bskyed-pa.*

[14]See my *Prajñāpāramitā Literature,* 1960, p. 109.

centration he then reaches the knowledge of all modes by means of the wisdom which is conjoined with one single moment.[15]

V8,12. THE ERROR WITH REGARD TO THE PATH.

Subhuti: If the Bodhisattva after having fulfilled all the paths should enter on the Bodhisattva's way of (certain) salvation—is it not so that the path of the Eighth-lowest[16] is one path, that of the Streamwinner another, that of the candidate to Once-returnership another, that of the Once-returner another, that of the candidate to Never-returnship another, that of the Never-returner another, that of the candidate to Arhatship another, that of the Arhat another, that of the Pratyekabuddha another, and that of the fully enlightened Tathagata another? If these paths are different from one another, how is it that the Bodhisattva, after he has fulfilled all of them, should enter on a Bodhisattva's way of (certain) salvation? If a Bodhisattva should fulfill all the paths, how could the Bodhisattva, the great being, on producing the Eighth-lowest path be the Eighth-lowest, on producing the path of vision be a Streamwinner, on producing the path of development a candidate to Once-returnership, a Once-returner, a candidate to Never-returnership, a Never-returner, a candidate to Arhatship, and an Arhat, and on producing the path of a Pratyekabuddha a Pratyekabuddha? For it is quite impossible and it cannot be that a Bodhisattva, after having been the Eighth-lowest, should enter on a Bodhisattva's way of special salvation—that is out of the question; and likewise that after entering on a Bodhisattva's way of salvation he should reach the knowledge of all modes; or likewise that, after he has attained the fruit of a Streamwinner, etc. *to*: Pratyekabuddha-enlightenment, he should enter on a Bodhisattva's way of salvation and then reach the knowledge of all modes. How then, O Lord, shall we understand this, i.e. that the Bodhisattva, the great being, after he has fulfilled all the paths, enters on a Bodhisattva's way of salvation, and then reaches the knowledge of all modes, and forsakes the defilements together with their residues?[17]

The Lord: So it is, Subhuti, so it is. It is first of all impossible that a Bodhisattva, once he has become the Eighth-lowest, or after attaining the fruit of a Streamwinner, etc. *to*: Pratyekabuddha-enlightenment, should enter on a Bodhisattva's way of salvation. And without that he cannot reach the knowledge of all modes. ((f. 261a)) But the Bodhisattva, the

[15]So L. P: mark. cf. ch. 64 n. 14.

[16]For the meaning of this term see n. 10.

[17]It is not quite clear to me what particular difficulty Subhuti has in mind when he asks this long question. There is something in this whole disquisition on the *bodhisattvanyāma* which continues to elude me, and I can only hope that one of my successors will do better than I did.

great being, beginning with the first thought of enlightenment, coursing in the six perfections, transcends the eight stages (of the Disciples and Pratyekabuddhas) with his cognition and vision. Which eight? The stage of bright insight, the stage of becoming one of the clan, the eight-lowest stage, the stage of vision, the stage of refinement, the stage of turning away from passion, the stage of him who has done, the stage of a Pratyekabuddha. Having gone beyond these eight stages with his cognition and vision, he enters, by the knowledge of the modes of the path,[18] on the Bodhisattva's special way of salvation, and through the cognition of the knowledge of all modes he forsakes the last residues of the defilements. There, Subhuti, the Bodhisattva, the great being, patiently accepts the cognition of the Eighth-lowest and likewise the cognition and forsaking of the Streamwinner, etc. *to*: Pratyekabuddha. Having fulfilled the paths of the Disciples and Pratyekabuddhas, the Bodhisattva, with the help of the cognition of the knowledge of the modes of the path, enters on a Bodhisattva's special way of salvation, and through the cognition of the knowledge of all modes forsakes the last residues of the defilements. It is thus that the Bodhisattva, after he has fulfilled all the paths, knows full enlightenment, and thereafter becomes a life-giving fruit[19] for (all) beings.

Subhuti: As regards these paths, i.e. the path of the Disciples, the path of the Pratyekabuddhas, the path of the Buddhas, what then is among them the path envisaged by the knowledge of the modes of the path?

The Lord: Here the Bodhisattva should produce the purity of the knowledge of the modes of the path. And this is it: the Bodhisattva should fully know those modes, tokens, and signs by which the path is indicated, and then proclaim them to others, demonstrate and reveal them, make them known to them and establish them in them, so that they may be disciplined in them, and thoroughly know them. He should be able to utter and retain in his mind all the languages, agreed symbols and meaningful sounds[20] which are used for communication in the great trichiliocosm, though always looking upon them as just so many echoes. In this way also should the Bodhisattva, the great being, fulfill the knowledge of the modes of the path, and thereafter he should know the mentality[21] of all beings. Of the beings in hell the path should be known, the root cause[22] and the fruit, and thereupon their path, root cause, and fruit should be impeded. Likewise for the animals and those in the world of Yama. Of the Kinnaras, Mahoragas, Nagas, Yakshas, and men should

[18] *AdT* here omits this clause of *S*.

[19] *phalopājīvyo, 'bras-bu ltar' tsho-bar ('gyur ro).*

[20] *skad daṅ, brda daṅ, sgra.*

[21] *(āśayā?), sems-pa*; *āśayatā, bsam-pa.*

[22] *hetu, rgyu.*

the path, root cause, and fruit be known; and so for ((f. 261b)) 14 classes of gods. The four applications of mindfulness, etc. *to*: the 18 special Buddhadharmas should be known. And the beings who should be established in the fruit of a Streamwinner etc. *to*: enlightenment, these he establishes therein. This is the knowledge of the modes of the path. When the Bodhisattva, the great being, has trained in it, he can enter into the mentality[21] of beings and demonstrate Dharma accordingly.[23] In that way his demonstration of Dharma becomes unforgetful and fruitful. And why? Because, having known the higher and lower faculties of beings, he can well discern and understand them.[23] He wisely knows the going and coming of beings, their decease and rebirth. It is thus that the Bodhisattva should course in the perfection of wisdom in which all the paths are contained, as well as the dharmas which act as wings to enlightenment, in which the Bodhisattva, the great being should course, just as do the Disciples and Pratyekabuddhas.

Subhuti: If, O Lord, the dharmas which act as wings to enlightenment, as well as enlightenment itself, are all dharmas which are neither conjoined nor disjoined, immaterial, undefinable, nonreacting, with one mark only, i.e. no mark, how can these dharmas which act as wings to enlightenment bring enlightenment about? For a dharma which is not conjoined, nor disjoined, etc., that cannot bring about any dharma, or remove one. Just as space cannot bring about or remove any dharma, just so a dharma which is empty of own-marks.

The Lord: So it is, Subhuti, so it is. A dharma which is empty of own-marks cannot bring about or remove any dharma. But for the sake of those beings who do not cognize dharmas as empty of own-marks, it has been explained that 'these dharmas which act as wings to enlightenment lead to enlightenment'.

V8,13-14. THE ERROR WITH REGARD TO HOSTILE STATES AND ANTIDOTES.

But, Subhuti, form, etc. *to*: ((f. 262a)) the knowledge of all modes, all these dharmas (mentioned) in this holy Dharma-Vinaya[24] are not conjoined or disjoined, immaterial, undefinable, nonresisting, with one mark only, i.e. no mark. And they have, Subhuti, only been expressed in words by the Tathagata for the sake of introducing[25] beings to them, by way of worldly convention, and not as if they were ultimate realities. Therein, Subhuti, the Bodhisattva, the great being, should train in every way through cognition and vision. When he has done so, some dharmas should, some dharmas should not, be penetrated. And which

[23]The translation follows *AdT*.

[24]This is a classification of the Scriptures even older than the one mentioned at ch. 65 n. 14.

[25]*avataraṇā, gzud-pa* ('convert'); also f. 252a, *khoṅ-du chud-par bgyi-ba*.

dharmas should the Bodhisattva, the great being, who has trained in them through cognition and vision, not penetrate? Which dharmas should be penetrate? He should not penetrate the dharmas of a Disciple and Pratyekabuddha after he has trained in them through cognition and vision; but through the cognition of the knowledge of all modes he should penetrate all dharmas in every respect.[26] It is thus that the Bodhisattva, the great being, should train in the holy Dharma-Vinaya, (i.e.) in this perfection of wisdom.

Subhuti: 'The holy Dharma-Vinaya, the holy Dharma-Vinaya', says the Lord. By how much[27] is the holy Dharma-Vinaya so called?

The Lord: Here, Subhuti, the Disciples, the Pratyekabuddhas, the Bodhisattvas, the great beings, and the fully enlightened Tathagatas are not conjoined with greed, nor disjoined from it; and so for : hate, delusion, the view of individuality; doubt, the contagion of mere rule and ritual, sensuous greed and ill will, greed for form and the formless, ignorance, conceit and excitedness, the first, etc. *to* : the fourth trance; friendliness, etc. *to*: impartiality; the four applications of mindfulness, etc. *to*: the unconditioned element. Therefore they are called 'holy'. And because theirs is this Dharma-Vinaya, therefore it is called 'the *holy* Dharma-Vinaya'. And why? Because all those dharmas are immaterial, undefinable, nonresisting, with one mark only, i.e. no mark. The immaterial is not conjoined with the immaterial, nor disjoined from it; and the same holds good of the undefinable, the nonresisting and the markless. This, Subhuti, is the immaterial, undefinable, nonresisting, one-marked, no-marked perfection of the Bodhisattvas, the great beings, ((f. 262b)) in which the Bodhisattva, the great being, should train. And when he has trained in it, he does not apprehend the mark of any dharma whatever.

V8,15. THE ERROR WITH REGARD TO THE MARKS.

Subhuti: One should, you say, O Lord, not train in the mark of form, or anything else. If one should not train in the marks of these dharmas, how, then, will the Bodhisattva, the great being, not having trained in the mark(s) of all dharmas, and in the marks of the conditioned factors,[28] transcend the level of the Disciples and Pratyekabuddhas? How, without having transcended the level of the Disciples and Pratyekabuddhas, will he enter on a Bodhisattva's special way of salvation? How without having entered on a Bodhisattva's special way of salvation will he reach the knowledge of all modes? How without having reached the knowledge of all modes will he turn the wheel of Dharma? How without having turned the wheel of Dharma will he set beings free from Samsāra, by the

[26]*rnam-pa thams-cad-du*, 'in each one of their modes'.
[27]*kiyatā, ji-tsam-gyis*.
[28]*P* : *saṃskāra*, *AdT* : *'du-byed*.

vehicle of the Disciples, the vehicle of the Pratyekabuddhas, or the great vehicle?

The Lord: If any dharma had a mark, then the Bodhisattva, the great being, should train in these marks. But because all dharmas are without marks, immaterial, undefinable, nonresisting, with one mark only, i.e. no mark, therefore the Bodhisattva, the great being, should train neither in their mark(s)[29] nor in their no-mark(s). And why? For it is not so that they were formerly without marks and that they got marks later on. But because formerly just as now these dharmas were without marks, therefore the Bodhisattva, the great being, should not train in their mark(s) or their no-mark(s). And why? Whether the Tathagatas are produced or not, just so is this unmarked Element established. ((f. 263a))

V8,16. The error with regard to the development.

Subhuti: If all dharmas are without marks, without differentiating marks,[30] how does, on the part of the Bodhisattva, the great being, the development of perfect wisdom take place? Because, without having developed the perfection of wisdom, the Bodhisattva, the great being, cannot transcend the level of the Disciples and Pratyekabuddhas; and without having done so he cannot enter on the Bodhisattva's special way of salvation; and without that he cannot produce the patient acceptance of dharmas which fail to be produced; and without that he cannot produce the superknowledges; and without them he cannot purify the Buddha-field and mature beings; and without that he cannot reach the knowledge of all modes; and without that he cannot turn the wheel of Dharma; and without that he cannot establish beings in the fruits of a holy life, or in the foundations of meritorious action due to giving, morality, and (meditational) development.

The Lord: So it is, Subhuti, so it is. Without marks, without differentiating marks are all dharmas.

Subhuti: How can with regard to markless dharmas development in perfect wisdom take place?

The Lord: A markless development is the Bodhisattva's, the great being's, development of the perfection of wisdom.

Subhuti: How then does a markless development of perfect wisdom take place?

The Lord: An undevelopment[31] of all dharmas is the development of perfect wisdom.

Subhuti: What is the undevelopment of all dharmas?

The Lord: A development of the undevelopment of form is the deve-

[29]The Sanskrit has here the singular, the Tibetan the plural.

[30]*na vilakṣaṇā* in *S* and *P*. *AdT*: *mtshan-ñid tha-dad-pa' aṅ ma lags-la.*

[31]*bsgom-pa rnam-par 'jig-pa.*

lopment of perfect wisdom. And so for the following categories : feeling, perception, impulses, consciousness; eye, ear, nose, tongue, body, mind; forms, sounds, smells, tastes, touchables, dharmas; toiling and withdrawal;[32] the four trances; friendliness, compassion, sympathetic joy, and impartiality; the station of endless space, etc. *to*: the station of neither perception nor nonperception; the recollection of the Buddha, of the Dharma, of the Samgha, of morality, of renunciation, of the deities, of agitation, of breathing in and out, of death, of what pertains to the body; the perception of impermanent, ill, not-self, unlovely; conditioned coproduction; the perception of a self, a being, a living soul, a creature, a man, a young man, ((f. 263b)) a personality, a person, a doer, an agent; the perception of permanence, ease, loveliness and self; the applications of mindfulness, the right efforts, bases of psychic power, faculties, powers, limbs of enlightenment, the holy eightfold path; the concentration on emptiness, the signless, the wishless; the eight emancipations, the nine successive attainments; the concentration which is with both thought applied and discursive, the concentration which is without thought applied and merely with thought discursive, the concentration without either thought applied or discursive; the holy truths of ill, origination, stopping, the path; the cognition of ill, origination, stopping, the path; the cognition of extinction, the cognition of nonproduction, the cognition of dharma, the subsequent cognition, the cognition conforming to worldly convention, the cognition of mastery, the cognition of what really is;[33] the six perfections; inward emptiness, outward emptiness, inward and outward emptiness, the emptiness of emptiness, the great emptiness, the emptiness of ultimate reality, the conditioned emptiness, the unconditioned emptiness, the absolute emptiness, the emptiness without beginning an end, the emptiness of nonrepudiation, the emptiness of essential nature, the emptiness of all dharmas, the emptiness of own-marks, the emptiness of nonexistence, the emptiness of own-being, the emptiness of nonexistence of own-being;[34] the 10 powers of a Tathagata, etc. *to*: the great compassion; the fruit of a Streamwinner, etc. *to*: a development of the undevelopment of the knowledge of all modes is the development of perfect wisdom. A development of the undevelopment of the forsaking of all the defilements and of the residues relating to them is the development of perfect wisdom.

Subhuti: How is it that the development of the undevelopment of form, etc. *to*: of the forsaking of all the defilements together with their residues, is the development of perfect wisdom?

The Lord: Here, Subhuti, a Bodhisattva, coursing in the perfection of

[32]*āyūha, niryūha*; *blaṅ-ba, dor-ba.*

[33]see ch. 63 n. 47.

[34]cf. *P* 195.198 = *S* vii 1407-1411.

wisdom, does not develop the notion that 'form, etc., is existence'. ((f. 264a)) And why? Because in anyone who has the notion of existence no development of the six perfections can take place, etc. *to* : no development of the knowledge of all modes. And why? Because when he is attached to existence[35] he forms an attachment to giving, morality, patience, vigour, meditation, and wisdom. And one who is thus attached[35] can have no emancipation. One who has the notion of existence cannot have a development of the applications of mindfulness, etc. *to* : of the knowledge of all modes. And why? Because he is attached to existence.

Subhuti: What is 'existence', what 'nonexistence'?

The Lord: Duality is existence, nonduality nonexistence.

Subhuti: What is duality?

The Lord: The perception of form, etc., is duality, etc. *to* : the perception of a Buddha and of enlightenment, the perception of the conditioned element and the unconditioned element, etc. *to* : all perception and nonperception, that is duality. As far as there is duality, there is existence; as far as there is existence there are the karma formations; as far as there are the karma formations, beings are not liberated from birth, decay, sickness, and death, from sorrow, lamentation, pain, sadness, and despair. Also by this method, Subhuti, should one know: One who perceives duality has no giving, morality, patience, vigour, meditation or wisdom; no path, attainment or reunion. He cannot even have adaptable patience, how much less a comprehension of form, etc. *to* : of the knowledge of all modes. And one who has no development of the path, how can he have the fruit of a Streamwinner, etc. *to* : how Arhatship, how Pratyekabuddha-enlightenment, how the forsaking of all the residues of the defilements?

[35]through his attachment to the two extremes (of eternalism and annihilationism), which is the result of his self-assertion. *S. P. AdT.*

CHAPTER 70

THE EXPOSITION OF THE CONSUMMATION OF THE TRAINING IN GRADUAL ACTIVITY

Subhuti: If, O Lord, one who perceives existence has not even adaptable patience, how much less still attainment and reunion, can then someone who perceives nonexistence have adaptable patience, or the stage of bright insight, etc. *to*:[1] the stage of a Pratyekabuddha, of a Bodhisattva, or of a Buddha? Or the development of the path, thanks to which he could forsake the defilements associated with the Disciples and Pratyekabuddhas? As one covered with these defilements he cannot enter on a Bodhisattva's special way of salvation, without that he cannot reach the knowledge of all modes and without that he cannot forsake all the defilements together with their residues. For (to one who perceives nonexistence) there is no production of a dharma that is being produced;[2] how can he, then, without having produced these dharmas, reach the knowledge of all modes?

The Lord: So it is, Subhuti, so it is. Someone who perceives nonexistence does not have the adaptable patience, etc. *to*: he does not have the forsaking of all the defilements together with their residues.

Subhuti: Does, then, the Bodhisattva, the great being who courses in perfect wisdom, have a perception of existence or of nonexistence; or a perception of form, etc. *to*: a perception of the knowledge of all modes; of greed or the forsaking of greed; and so for hate ((f. 264b)), delusion, ignorance, karma formations, consciousness, name-and-form, etc. *to*: sorrow and lamentation; ill, origination, stopping, the path; etc. *to*: a perception of the knowledge of all modes, or of the forsaking of all the defilements with their residues?

The Lord: No, Subhuti, not so. The Bodhisattva, the great being who courses in the perfection of wisdom, has with regard to no dharma whatever the perception of existence or nonexistence. And just this is of the Bodhisattva, the great being, the adaptable patience that he has no perception of existence and nonexistence. This is just the development of his path, this is just his fruit, when there is no perception of either existence or nonexistence. Nonexistence in fact is the path of the Bodhi-

[1]For this list see f. 261a.

[2]So Ms. *AdT*: 'there is no production or abiding of any dharma'. The addition in brackets is from *P*

sattva, the great being, just nonexistence is his reunion. By this method also, Subhuti, you should know that with nonexistence for own-being are all dharmas.

Subhuti: If all dharmas have nonexistence for own-being, how has the Tathagata fully known all dharmas which have nonexistence for ownbeing? And how has he, by fully knowing them, reached the dominion over the range of all dharmas?[3]

The Lord: Here, I, formerly coursing on the Bodhisattva-course, coursing in the six perfection, detached from sense desires, etc. dwell in the attainment of the first, up to the fourth, trance; but I do not take up the sign[4] of these trances and trance-limbs,[5] do not put my mind to these trances, do not relish or apprehend them. I enter on these trances as they are pure in all their modes, and, having activated their karma result,[6] I incline my thought[7] to the realisation of the various wonder-working powers, of the cognition of the heavenly ear, of the cognition of others' mental make-up, of the cognition of the recollection of former lives, of the cognition of the heavenly eye. Not taking up the sign of these realizations, I do not mind those superknowledges, do not relish, do not apprehend them. Seeing those (five) superknowledges as identical with space, I enter (into trance). Again, having fully known the utmost, right, and perfect enlightenment through a wisdom which is conjoined with one single moment,[8] having fully understood as it really is that 'this is ill, this the origination of ill, this the stopping of ill, this the progressive path which leads to the stopping of ill', and, endowed with the ten powers of a Tathagata, the four grounds of self-confidence, etc. *to*: the 18 special dharmas of a Buddha, I predict beings to the three groups.[9]

Subhuti: How is it ((f. 265a)) that the Tathagata has produced the four trances and the six superknowledges which yet have nonexistence for their ownbeing, and how has he predicted to the three groups beings who have the character of not being beings?

The Lord: If the sense desires, or the evil unwholesome dharmas, had an own-being, or some inward existence, or an other-being,[10] then I, Subhuti, formerly coursing in the Bodhisattva-course, having known the sense desires or the evil, unwholesome dharmas as nonexistent in

[3]*chos thams-cad-kyi yul-la mṅa' brñes-ipar gyur.*

[4]*mtshan ma bzuṅ.*

[5]The five 'factors' of *dhyāna* are thought applied, thought discursive, joyful zest, ease, and one-pointedness of mind.

[6]not in *AdT*.

[7]*(mṅon sum-du bya-ba'i phyir) sems mṅon-par gshol-bar byas te.*

[8]So *AdT*; P: 'mark'.

[9]distinguished at f. 251a.

[10]*ṅo-bo-ñid cig yod-par gyur tsam, raṅ-gi dṅos-po 'am, gshan-gyi dṅos-po shig yod-par gyur na ni.*

their own-being, would not have dwelt in the attainment of the four trances. But because sense desires and the evil, unwholesome dharmas have no own-being, no inward existence, and no other-being, except for the fact that they have just nonexistence for their own-being, therefore have I, formerly coursing in the Bodhisattva-course, dwelt in the attainment of the first trance, which is detached from sense desires, detached from evil, unwholesome dharmas, with applied and discursive thought, born of detachment, full of joy and ease. And so for the other trances, up to the fourth. If the superknowledges had existence, or own-being, or an other-being, then I would not, after I had known all the superknowledges as having non existence for own-being, have fully known the supreme enlightenment. But because all these superknowledges have no existence, no own-being, no other-being, except for the fact that they have just nonexistence for their own-being, therefore I have as a Tathagata, after I had known all the superknowledges as nonexistent in their own-being, fully known the supreme enlightenment.

VI. GRADUAL REUNION.

VIa. Gradual reunion in general.

Subhuti: If the Bodhisattva knows full enlightenment although all dharmas have nonexistence for own-being, how can one, when all dharmas have nonexistence for own-being, conceive of a Bodhisattva's gradual activity, training, and progress, through which he (gradually) knows full enlightenment?

The Lord: Here the Bodhisattva has heard previously, in the presence of the Buddhas and Lords, of the Bodhisattvas who have honoured the dharmas of the Buddhas, of the Arhats, etc. *to*: of the Streamwinners, that, since the Buddhas and Lords have nonexistence for own-being, and so have the Bodhisattvas, the Pratyekabuddhas, etc. *to*: all holy men—all conditioned things have no own-being even as little as the tip of a hair. And that Bodhisattva thinks to himself: Just nonexistence are the Buddhas, the Lords, etc. *to*: the Streamwinners. Whether I will, or will not, know full enlightenment, just nonexistent are all dharmas. When I have known full enlightenment, I should establish all beings who course in the notion of the existence (of dharmas) (in the belief) in their nonexistence. And that Bodhisattva, who has set out for full enlightenment for the sake of leading all beings to Parinirvana, exerts himself in the gradual activity, training, and progress in which the Bodhisattvas of the past have trained with the result that they have known full enlightenment.

VI 1-6. The Six Perfections.

Just from the first they train in the six perfections, (f. 265b), i.e. the perfection of giving, etc. *to*: the perfection of wisdom.

VI 1. The Perfection of Giving.

When he courses in the perfection of giving, he himself gives gifts and also others he establishes in the perfection of giving. And he praises giving as well as those others who course in the perfection of giving, one acquiescent. Through those gifts he acquires great wealth, and he renounces and gives his gifts with a heart free from stinginess—food to those who are in need of food, etc. Through those gifts he guards that morality which constitutes an essential portion of his spiritual practices, and he acquires an exalted position as a god or human, . . . and he acquires a mass of morality, etc. *to*: the mass of the vision and cognition of emancipation. Endowed with this giving he transcends the levels of a Disciple or Pratyekabuddha and enters on a Bodhisattva's certainty of salvation, purifies the Buddha-field, matures beings, and reaches the knowledge of all modes. It is thus that, through giving, the Bodhisattva's gradual activity is conceived, his gradual training, his gradual progress. And all that cannot be apprehended. And why? Because it has no own-being.

VI 2. The Perfection of Morality.

Moreover the Bodhisattva, from the first thought of enlightenment onwards, himself courses in the perfection of morality, and establishes others also in the perfection of morality. He praises morality and also those others who course in the perfection of morality, one acquiescent. Through that morality he acquires an exalted position as a god or a human, and through it he establishes beings in giving, etc. *to*: in the vision and cognition of emancipation. Endowed with that morality he transcends the levels of the Disciples and Pratyekabuddhas, and thereafter through that mass of morality, etc. *to*: that mass of the vision and cognition of emancipation . . . establishes beings in the triple vehicle and frees them from Saṃsāra. It is thus that one conceives a Bodhisattva's gradual activity, training, and progress. But all that cannot be apprehended. And why? Because it has no ownbeing.

VI 3. The Perfection of Patience.

As at VI 2. ((f. 266a))

VI 4. The Perfection of Vigour.

As at VI 2–3.

VI 5. The Perfection of Concentration.

As at VI 2–4.

VI 6. The Perfection of Wisdom.

Moreover the Bodhisattva, from the first thought of enlightenment onwards, courses in perfect wisdom and establishes beings in giving, in morality, etc. *to* : in the vision and cognition of emancipation. ((f. 266b)) When he courses in perfect wisdom, he himself gives gifts, guards morality, achieves patience, exerts vigour, enters on the trances, and develops wisdom. He establishes also others in giving, etc. *to*: wisdom and he speaks in praise of them. And those also who give gifts, etc. *to* : develop wisdom, them also he praises, one acquiescent. With the help of these six perfections, he transcends the levels of the Disciples and Pratyekabuddhas, enters on the Bodhisattva's certainty of salvation, purifies the Buddha-field, matures beings, and reaches the knowledge of all modes. Having established beings in the triple vehicle, he frees them from Samsara. But all that cannot be apprehended. And why? Because it has no own-being.

VI 7-12. The Six Recollections.

Moreover the Bodhisattva trains in the gradual activity, the gradual training, the gradual progress. From the first thought of enlightenment onwards he has, with his attentions associated with the knowledge of all modes, resolutely believed in all dharmas as having nonexistence for own-being. And he develops the recollection of the Buddha, of the Dharma, of the Samgha, of morality, of renunciation, and of the deities.

VI 7. The Recollection of the Buddha.

And how does the Bodhisattva develop the recollection of the Buddha? Here he does not attend to the Tathagata through the skandhas. And why? Because they have no own-being, and what has no own-being that is a nonexistent. And why? A nonrecollection and a nonattention is the recollection of the Buddha.—A Tathagata further should not be attended to through the 32 marks of the superman, nor through his golden-coloured body, (nor through the effulgence of his halo or his eighty minor characteristics). And why? Because the effulgence of his body and the minor characteristics have no ownbeing, and what has no own-being that is nonexistent. And why? A nonrecollection and a nonattention is the recollection of the Buddha.—The Tathagata should further not be attended to from his mass of morality, etc. *to* : the mass of his vision and cognition of emancipation. And why? Because all these have no own-being, and what has no own-being that is nonexistent. And why? Because the recollection of a Buddha is a nonrecollection and a nonattention.—Furthermore the Tathagata should not be attended to through the ten powers of a Tathagata, the four grounds of self-confidence, the four analytical knowledges, the great friendliness, the great compassion, or the eighteen special dharmas of a Buddha. And why? Because they have no own-being, ((f. 267a)) and that which has no own-being that is nonexistent. And why? Because the recollection of the Buddha is a nonrecollection and a nonattention.—Furthermore a Tathagata should not be attended to from conditioned coproduction. And why? Because it has no own-being and that which has no own-being that is nonexistent. And why? Because the recollection of the Buddha is a nonrecollection and a nonattention.—It is thus that the Bodhisattva who courses in perfect wisdom should attend to the recollection of the Buddha. It is thus that his gradual activity, training, and progress is conceived, and it is by training himself in these that he fulfils by gradual methods the four applications of mindfulness, etc. *to* : the knowledge of all modes, and that through the nonexistence of own-being. He will fully know all dharmas as just nonexistent, and he will with regard to them no longer even have the notion of an own-being.

VI 8. The Recollection of the Dharma.

And how should the Bodhisattva develop the recollection of the Dharma. Here the Bodhisattva, who courses in perfect wisdom, should not attend to wholesome or unwholesome dharmas, to determinate or indeterminate dharmas, to worldly or supramundane ones, to fleshly or spiritual ones, to holy or unholy ones, to (dharmas) with or without outflows, not to dharmas included in the world of sense desire, in the world of form, or in the formless world, (nor to conditioned or unconditioned dharmas.) And why? Because these dharmas have no own-being, and what has no own-being that is nonexistent. Because the recollection of the Dharma is a nonrecollection and a nonattention. Here . . . fully knows, and therein there is not even the notion of the existence of the notion of an own-being. It is thus that the Bodhisattva who courses in perfect wisdom should develop the recollection of the Dharma.

VI 9. The Recollection of the Samgha.

And how should the Bodhisattva develop the recollection of the Samgha? Here the Bodhisattva, endowed with morality, concentration and wisdom, emancipation and the vision and cognition of emancipation, should attend to the community of the Lord's disciples, the four pairs of men and the eight great personages through the absence of own-being. And why? Because they have no own-being and are nonexistent. For the recollection of the Samgha is a nonrecollection and a nonattention. It is thus that the Bodhisattva should develop the recollection of the Samgha.

VI 10. The Recollection of Morality.

And how should the Bodhisattva develop the recollection of morality? Here the Bodhisattva who courses in perfect wisdom should from the first thought of enlightenment onwards attend to the unbroken, flawless, unspotted, pure, untarnished morality, which has been lauded by the wise ((f. 267b)) which one has well taken upon oneself, which is conducive to concentration—all these acts of morality should be attended to by way of the nonexistence of own-being, so that with regard to them there is not even an act of recollection, how much less the departure of a recollection. And why? It is thus that the Bodhisattva should attend to the recollection of morality, i.e. that there is in it not even the notion of an own-being.

VI 11. The Recollection of Renunciation.

And how should the Bodhisattva who courses in perfect wisdom develop the recollection of renunciation? Here, Subhuti, the Bodhisattva should, through the nonexistence of own-being, attend to renunciation, be it a renunciation of fleshly things or a renunciation of Dharma. And when he renounces (things) in such a way he should not produce a thought thus: 'I give or I do not give. I renounce or I do not renounce.' (Even when he gives up all his limbs he should not produce such a thought). And why? Because all this has no own-being. When he thus courses in the recollection of renunciation and trains in it, he will gradually advance up to the knowledge of all modes.

VI 12. The Recollection of Deities.

And how should the Bodhisattva, who courses in perfect wisdom, develop the recollection of the deities? Here the Bodhisattva should attend, through the nonexistence of own-being, to those gods who have been reborn in the various heavens. And why? Because they have no own-being. And so should those deities be attended to, that there is with regard to them not even the action of recollection. When he attends thus the Bodhisattva gradually attends to everything up to the knowledge of all modes. And also the Non-Returners should be attended to as nonexistent. And why? Because they have no own-being, and what has no own-being that is nonexistent. And so they should be attended to in such a way that there is with regard to them not even the action of recollection. When he attends thus he gradually attends to everything up to the knowledge of all modes.

It is thus that one conceives of the Bodhisattva who attends thus to the six recollections the gradual activity, training, and method.

VI 13. The Cognition of the Nonexistence of Own-being in Dharmas.

Moreover it is the gradual activity, training, and method of a Bodhisattva, who courses in perfect wisdom, that he should, through the nonexistence of own-being train in the emptinesses, etc. *to*: in the great compassion. When he thus trains in the path to enlightenment, he shall fully know dharmas as nonexistent in their own being. With regard to them there is not even the action of recollection, how much less can there possibly be form, etc. *to*: the knowledge of all modes! It is thus that one conceives of the gradual activity, training, and method of the Bodhisattva who courses in perfect wisdom.

Subhuti: If all dharmas are nonexistent in their own-being then there is no form, etc. *to*: no attainment and reunion, etc. *to*: no all-dharmas.

The Lord: Is then is-ness or not-is-ness apprehended in dharmas which have a nonexistent own-being?

Subhuti: No certainly not, O Lord!

The Lord: How then can it be ((f. 268a)) that, if all dharmas have a nonexistent own-being, then there is no form, etc. *to*: no all-dharmas.

Subhuti: Not do I, O Lord, hesitate and doubt with regard to these dharmas. But on the other hand there will be in a future period monks who belong to the vehicle of the Disciples, or to that of the Pratyekabuddhas, or to that of the Bodhisattvas, and who will speak thus: If all dharmas are nonexistent in their own-being, who then can be defiled or purified by them? Since these people fail to cognize the defilement or purification (which these dharmas may cause), they will fail in their morality, views, and conduct, and in consequence one must expect them to be reborn in one or other of three places of rebirth—in the hells, in the animal world, or in the world of Yama. It is because I consider this future peril that I question the Tathagata about this subject, but it is not because I hesitate or doubt with regard to these dharmas.

The Lord: Well said, well said, Subhuti, so it is as you say.

CHAPTER 71

THE NATURE OF DHARMAS IS SIGNLESS AND CANNOT BE APPREHENDED

Subhuti: If all dharmas have a nonexistent own-being, as a result of which reasoning does the Bodhisattva for the sake of beings set out to fully know the utmost, right, and perfect enlightenment?

The Lord: To the extent that all dharmas are nonexistent in their own-being, to that extent the Bodhisattva sets out for the supreme enlightenment. And why? Something base[1] is a basis, and there can be no attainment, reunion, or full enlightenment for someone who has the notion of a basis.

Subhuti: Is there, then, an attainment of the baseless, a reunion with it or a full enlightenment with regard to it?

The Lord: Just the baseless is attainment, just the baseless is reunion, just the baseless is full enlightenment, on account of the fact that the Realm of Dharma should not be upset.[2] One would wish to upset the Realm of Dharma if one were to wish for the attainment of the baseless, for reunion with it, or for full enlightenment with regard to it.

Subhuti: If there is no attainment of the baseless, no reunion with it, and no full enlightenment with regard to it, but if just the baseless is attainment, just the baseless is reunion, just the baseless is the supreme enlightenment—how then again can there be of a Bodhisattva the first, etc. *to*: the tenth stage, how the patient acceptance of dharmas which fail to be produced; how can there be those karma-resultant superknowledges and that karma-resultant giving, etc. *to*: wisdom, which enable him to mature beings, to purify his Buddha-field and to serve upon the Buddha and Lords with food, etc. *to*: other benefits useful to humans, and which will not be snatched away from him before his karma result becomes exhausted at the time when, on having entered final Nirvana, he leaves his relics and disciples.[3]

The Lord: Just in so far as there is the baseless, just so far there are the ten stages, the karma-resultant five superknowledges, the karma-resultant perfections, as well as the karma-resultant wholesome roots

[1]vile, sordid.

[2]Lit. the nonbeing-upsetness of the Realm of Dharma. Perhaps, 'has not been upset'.

[3]The last clause of this sentence puzzles me, and the translation is only approximately right.

by which he works the weal of beings until, on having entered final Nirvana, he becomes an object of worship.

Subhuti: What is the distinction, what the difference, between the baseless on the one side, and the perfections and superknowledges on the other?

The Lord: There is no difference between them. ((f. 268b)) But with regard to the unstained perfections and superknowledges a difference has been laid down.

Subhuti: What is that difference?

The Lord: Here the Bodhisattva, who courses in perfect wisdom, gives gifts without having apprehended the gift, or the renunciation, or the donor or the recipient; he guards morality without having apprehended morality, etc. *to*: he purifies the Buddha-field without having apprehended the Buddha-field, and he fully knows enlightenment without having apprehended the Buddhadharmas. It is thus that the Bodhisattva courses in a perfection of wisdom which does not act as a basis. It is thus that the Bodhisattva courses in perfect wisdom, and that, coursing in it, he becomes unassailable by Mara, the Evil One, or by the divinities of Mara's host.

VII. THE SINGLE INSTANTANEOUS REUNION.

VIIa. THE REUNION BY ONE SINGLE THOUGHT IN GENERAL.

Subhuti: How does the Bodhisattva, the great being, coursing in the perfection of wisdom, acquire with one single thought the six perfections, etc. *to*: the eighty accessory marks of a superman?

VII 1. The Single Instantaneous Reunion with Regard to All Dharmas without Outflows and without Karma Result (This Not Having Yet Matured (?)).

The Lord: Here whatever gift a Bodhisattva may give that is not taken hold of apart from perfect wisdom. And so for all other spiritual practices. ((f. 269a))

Subhuti: How does a Bodhisattva who has been taken hold of by perfect wisdom acquire with one single production of thought the six perfections, etc. *to*: the eighty accessory marks of a superman?

The Lord: Here when the Bodhisattva, who courses in perfect wisdom, gives gifts, then, taken hold of by perfect wisdom, he is not one who perceives duality in that. And so for the other spiritual practices.

Subhuti: How can a Bodhisattva, who courses in perfect wisdom, accomplish these spiritual practices without becoming one who perceives duality therein?

The Lord: Here a Bodhisattva, coursing in perfect wisdom, fulfils the *perfection of giving*. He gives gifts after having included in that perfection of giving all the six perfections. And likewise he fulfils all the dharmas which constitute the wings to enlightenment, etc. *to* : he develops the path after having included in it all the six perfections. And why should that be so? At the time when the Bodhisattva, coursing in perfect wisdom, gives a gift, he does so having stood in a thought without outflows, and he does not review a sign, i.e. him who gives, him to whom he gives, what he gives, who am I that gives. He gives his gifts with a thought free from signs, without outflows, free from craving and ignorance. He does not review that thought, nor that gift, and so on up to all the Buddhadharmas. Moreover with a thought free from signs he practises the other five perfections, as well as the remaining spiritual practices, and in each case he fails to review them and their constituents.

Subhuti: How does the Bodhisattva fulfil these spiritual practices when all dharmas are without signs and uneffected? ((f. 269b))

The Lord: Here the Bodhisattva gives to all who ask for them gifts with a thought free from all signs—food to those who desire food, drink to those who desire drink, etc. And if someone who has come along should say to him, 'what is the use of your giving a gift which is no help at all!' then that Bodhisattva, who courses in perfect wisdom. thinks to himself, "although those beings do abuse me and say 'what is the use of your giving such a trifling [4] gift!'—nevertheless I should give gifts, and I should not not give them!" Having made that gift common to all beings, he dedicates it to the supreme enlightenment. But he dedicates it in such a way that, when dedicating, he does not review a sign, i.e. this is the gift, to him I give, (by) that I give, or who is it that gives. Or, I do dedicate, to what do I dedicate, wherewith do I dedicate, who is it that dedicates. He does not review the entity which he would give away or which, having given it away, he would dedicate to the supreme enlightenment. And why? Because all such entities are empty through thirteen kinds of emptiness. And when he thus considers whereto he will dedicate, what he will dedicate and whereby he will dedicate, then his dedication will be actually effective.[5] Furthermore he matures beings and acquires a Buddha-field. He fulfils the perfection of giving, etc. *to* : the eighteen special Buddhadharmas. And from the very beginning he fulfils the perfection of giving without seizing on its reward. Just as the Paranirmitavasavartin gods satisfy all their needs by mind alone, so does the Bodhisattva. Through that gift he serves upon the Buddhas and Lords, he gladdens the world with its gods, men and Asuras, and establishes those beings in the triple vehicle through his having taken up that

[4]*asthira*, = transient = doubtful in value.

[5]*P* : when he dedicates in such a way, his dedication becomes a nonpoisonous dedication, a dedication to the realm of Dharma.

perfection of giving, as well as through his skill in means. It is thus that the Bodhisattva, coursing in perfect wisdom, fulfils the perfection of giving with a thought free from signs.

And how does the Bodhisattva fulfil the *perfection of morality*? Here the Bodhisattva fulfils the perfection of morality while coursing in perfect wisdom. He acquires that morality which is holy, without outflows, which is included within the path, and which is acquired in the nature of things.[6] And his morality becomes unimpaired, flawless, pure, untarnished, something which sets free (from the slavery of craving), which it is good to concentrate upon, and which has been lauded by the wise.[7] And in respect of that morality he does not misconstrue any dharma, from form ((f. 270a)) to the achievement of world rulership. But, having made this morality common to all beings, he dedicates it to the knowledge of all modes, by way of a dedication which is signless, baseless and nondual, and which is also by way of worldly convention and not by way of ultimate reality. And through having fulfilled that perfection of morality, he produces through his skill in means the four trances, without wishing to enjoy their fruits. He further achieves the heavenly eye. With that heavenly eye, relating to moral discipline,[8] he sees the Buddhas and Lords who in all the ten directions stand, hold, and maintain themselves, and who demonstrate Dharma. And he does not lose that vision before he has known full enlightenment. With the heavenly ear, pure and surpassing that of men, he hears the words of those Buddhas and Lords when they preach (the doctrine). And he does not forget what he has heard before he has worked, as a result of what he has heard, the weal of himself and of others. With the cognition of others' mental make-up he wisely knows with his own mind the mental processes of those Buddhas and Lords, and with the help of that cognition of others' mental make-up he works the weal of all beings. With the help of the recollection of former lives he appraises the past merits of those beings, and through those meritorious deeds he (still further) encourages those beings, with the result that they become people of specific attainment(s).[9] With the cognition of the extinction of the outflows he establishes beings in the fruits of the holy life, from that of a Streamwinner to the supreme enlightenment. In fact he establishes beings in wholesome dharmas in accordance with their capabilities. It is thus that the Bodhisattva fulfils the perfection of morality with a mind free from signs.

And how does he fulfil the *perfection of patience*, when dharmas are signless, impassive, baseless, and uneffected? Here the Bodhisattva,

[6]*dharmatā-prātilambhikam*.

[7]cf. f. 273.

[8]*vainayika*. *E*: *vaināyika*, Buddhist (?). So the Ms, but *AdT* has "due to karma result".

[9]So *E* who explains: grasping one thought so intently that *dhyāna* is attained.

beginning with the first thought of enlightenment until he is seated on the terrace of enlightenment, even if all beings should give him blows with clods, sticks, and swords, should not give an occasion to even one single thought associated with rage. In fact, the Bodhisattva should develop two kinds of patience. Which two? He should endure of all beings the abuse and revilings,[10] as well as the blows with clods, sticks, and swords; and he should also produce the patient acceptance of dharmas which fail to be produced. As to the first, the Bodhisattva should, when abused or reviled, or when he receives blows with clods, sticks, or swords, reflect as follows: who is it that abuses or reviles me, or gives me blows with clods, sticks, or swords? And to whom does he give these? He should contemplate the own-being of (all) dharmas and, when he does so, he apprehends not even dharmas, how much less the own-being of Dharma itself. ((f. 270b)) And when he contemplates the own-being of Dharma, he thinks to himself: who cuts or breaks me? When he contemplates the own-being of Dharma in this manner, then he acquires the patient acceptance of dharmas which fail to be produced. And what is the patient acceptance of dharmas which fail to be produced? It is of two kinds: The one results from the nongenesis of the defilements, and the other from the noncutting off of cognition. Having stood in these two kinds of patience, he will fulfil the four trances, etc. *to*: the eighteen special Buddhadharmas. Having stood in these dharmas which are holy, without outflows, supramundane, not shared by all the Disciples and Pratyekabuddhas, he fulfils at the same time the holy superknowledges. When he has fulfilled them he reaches the fulness of the six perfections. And when he has stood in the five superknowledges which are without outflows, then he sees with his heavenly eye, in all the ten directions, the Buddhas and Lords, and as a result he acquires the recollection of the Buddhas. And that Buddha-recollection of his will not be cut off again before he knows full enlightenment. With the heavenly ear he learns all that these Buddhas and Lords have taught, and he thereupon teaches beings the Dharma just as it is. And he will understand with his own mind the mental processes of these Buddhas and Lords. And after he has, through his cognition of others' mental make-up, understood with his own mind the mental processes of all beings, he will teach Dharma just as it is. After he has appraised, through his cognition of the recollection of former lives, the wholesome roots of those beings, he will as a result of[11] that former wholesome root, encourage them still further. And through his cognition of the extinction of the outflows he will exhort those beings to the triple vehicle, and establish them therein. And that Bodhisattva, coursing in perfect wisdom, will, through skill in means,

[10]rebukes.

[11]by reminding them of?

mature beings, purify the Buddha-field, and, coursing in the knowledge of all modes, he will, having fulfilled the knowledge of all modes and having won full enlightenment, turn the wheel of Dharma. It is thus that the Bodhisattva who courses in perfect wisdom fulfils the perfection of patience.

How then does the Bodhisattva who courses in perfect wisdom fulfil the *perfection of vigour,* although dharmas are signless, impassive, baseless, nonmanifest, and uneffected? Here the Bodhisattva, who courses in perfect wisdom, becomes endowed with physical vigour. He dwells having entered upon the four trances, one after the other. When he has achieved the fourth trance he experiences manifold wonderworking powers, etc. *to*: with his hands he handles even the sun and moon, and up to the world of Brahma he holds sway with his body. Endowed with this physical vigour he travels, by means of his wonderworking powers, to the many hundreds of thousands of world systems in the ten directions where the Buddhas and Lords dwell, and he serves upon those Buddhas and Lords with robes, almsbowls, etc. And his robes, almsbowls, etc. will not get exhausted before he knows full enlightenment. And when he has won full enlightenment, then the world with its gods, men and Asuras will become happy through these robes, almsbowls, etc. And when he has entered final Nirvana his relics will be worshipped. Having travelled (to other world systems) by means of his wonderworking powers, he hears the Dharma from those Buddhas and Lords, and before he wins full enlightenment he will never again forget what he has heard. And he matures beings and acquires a Buddha-field, while coursing in the knowledge of all modes. It is thus ((f. 271a)) that the Bodhisattva, endowed with physical vigour, fulfils the perfection of vigour.

And how, then, does the Bodhisattva fulfil the perfection of vigour when he is endowed with a mental vigour which takes place on the holy Path without outflows and is included in the Path? Here the Bodhisattva, who courses in perfect wisdom and is endowed with mental vigour, gives no opportunity to unwholesome deeds of body or speech.[12] He does not misconstrue anything whatsoever as 'permanent' or 'impermanent', 'ease' or 'ill', 'self' or 'not-self', 'conditioned' or 'unconditioned', —be it the world of sense desire, the world of form or the formless world; the element with outflows or the element without outflows; or the transic concentrations; or friendliness, compassion, sympathetic joy or impartiality; or the formless concentrations; or the applications of mindfulness, etc. *to*: the Buddhadharmas. Nor does he misconstrue the fruits of the holy life, from the fruit of a Streamwinner to Bodhisattvahood, as 'permanent' or 'impermanent', etc. and he does not (mistakenly say) that these beings have been exalted by Vision, those by the stage of refine-

[12] *P*, but not *Ad*, either Sanskrit or Tibetan, adds: deeds of mind.

ment, those by the removal of the lower fetters, those by the removal of the higher fetters, those by Pratyekabuddhahood, or by the knowledge of the modes of the path or by the knowledge of all modes. And why? Because there does not exist the own-being of all these (states) by which they (the beings) could be exalted. Endowed with this mental vigour even at the time of his dying he works the weal of beings, but without apprehending them. He fulfils the perfection of vigour, but does not apprehend it. He fulfils the Buddhadharmas, but does not apprehend them. He purifies the Buddha-field, but does not apprehend it. Endowed with this physical and mental vigour he fulfils all the wholesome dharmas, but does not cling to them. Not clinging to them he passes on from Buddha-field to Buddha-field, and works the weal of beings. He works miracles with the help of whichever wonderworking powers he desires to use—whether it be a rain of flowers, or an emission of scents, or by songs and music, or an earthquake, or the splendour of his appearance, or a display of a world system made up of the seven precious things, or whether he sacrifices himself for the sake of those who want to regain their youth, or of those who are blind to the light, or whether he discharges scents, or bestows great oblations—but without taking any life in the process—or introduces countless beings to the Path, etc. *to*: whether he induces them to desist from the taking of life, etc. *to*: whether he frees them from wrong views. Some he helps by giving, others by morality, for the sake of others again he renounces all his limbs. To some he gives sons and daughters, and to others a kingdom. For the sake of others he sacrifices himself. In this way he works the weal of beings by whatever device it can be worked. It is thus that the Bodhisattva, who courses in perfect wisdom and is endowed with mental vigour, fulfils the perfection of vigour even though dharmas be signless.

And how does the Bodhisattva, who courses in perfect wisdom, fulfil the *perfection of meditation,* in spite of the fact that he has stood in dharmas as nameless and signless? Here the Bodhisattva, who courses in perfect wisdom, fulfils all the concentrations, with the exception of that of the Tathagata. ((f. 271b)) Detached from sense desires and other evil and unwholesome dharmas he dwells as one who has entered on the first trance, which is with applied and discursive thought, born of detachment, full of rapture and ease. And so for the other trances.[13] He dwells as one who has irradiated the entire world with a mind associated with friendliness, etc. *to*: with impartiality, etc. *to*: he dwells as one who has entered on the station of neither perception nor nonperception. Having stood in that perfection of meditation he enters on the eight emancipations in direct and in reverse order, and emerges from them. He dwells as one who has entered the nine successive meditational achievements, as well

[13]So *P*.

as the concentration on emptiness, the signless concentration and the wishless concentration. He dwells as one who has entered on the unimpeded concentration, the concentration which is like lightning, the right concentration, and the adamantine concentration. Having stood in this perfection of meditation he dwells as one who has entered the thirty-seven dharmas which act as wings to enlightenment. Having stood in this perception of meditation with the help of the cognition of the knowledge of the modes of the path he sees that all concentrations are included in the knowledge of the modes of the path, he transcends the stage of bright insight, the stage of becoming one of the clan, the eighth-lowest stage, the stage of vision, the stage of the attenuation of the defilements, the stage where one is without greed, the stage of a Pratyekabuddha, and then moves into a Bodhisattva's certainty of salvation and fulfils the stage of a Buddha. And although he courses in these stages, he does not midway attain their fruit[14] before he reaches the cognition of the knowledge of all modes. Having stood in this perfection of meditation, he passes on from Buddha-field to Buddha-field, honouring the Buddhas and Lords. He honours those Buddhas and Lords, plants wholesome roots in their presence, matures beings and purifies the Buddha-field. He passes on from world system to world system and works the weal of beings. Some he wins over with gifts, etc. *to*: some with the vision and cognition of emancipation. Some he establishes in the fruit of a Streamwinner, etc. *to*: some he establishes in (full) enlightenment. By whatever wholesome dharmas the beings may be lifted up, just those he enjoins on them. Having stood in this perfection of meditation, he consummates all dharani-doors, and acquires the four analytical knowledges. And he becomes a recipient of the superknowledges which are born of karma result. Never again is he born in the belly of a mother and never again does he pursue sense pleasures. There is no kind of rebirth that he does not take up,[15] though he is not polluted by the faults (which are apt to attend a) rebirth. And why? Because he has well seen that all dharmas are like a magical illusion. Having known that all conditioned things are like a magical illusion, he works the weal of all beings without, however, apprehending therein any beings or the concept of a being. Himself nonapprehending he establishes beings in the baselessness of all dharmas—though on account of worldly convention and not in ultimate reality. Having stood in this perfection of meditation, he courses in all the trances, emancipations, concentrations, and meditational attainments, and he will never again be lacking in the perfection of meditation until the time that he wins the supreme enlightenment. Having stood in this knowledge of the modes of the path he consummates the knowledge of

[14]*P*: the fruit of the trances.

[15]*PT* adds: so as to be able to mature beings.

all modes. Having stood therein he forsakes the residues of all the defilements. He then works his own weal and that of others. Thereupon he becomes worthy of gifts from the world with its gods, men and Asuras. It is thus that the Bodhisattva who courses in perfect wisdom fulfils the perfection of meditation.

VII 2. The Single Instantaneous Reunion with Regard to All Dharmas without Outflows Which Have Reached the State Where Their Karma Result Has Matured.

And how does the Bodhisattva, who courses in perfect wisdom, among signless dharmas go to the fulfilment of the development of the *perfection of wisdom*? Here ((f. 272a)) the Bodhisattva who courses in perfect wisdom does not review any dharma as truly real, or as totally real. But he does not review that true or total reality with regard to the skandhas; nor does he review their production, the door of their arrival, or their heaping together. *And so on, until we come to* : he does not review the door of arrival of all dharmas with and without outflows, but he reviews them as just vanities or nullities. And when he considers thus he does not apprehend the own-being of any dharma. Coursing in perfect wisdom he firmly believes that all dharmas have nonexistence for own-being. Having firmly believed that, he courses in the emptinesses, and does not settle down in any dharma whatsoever. Coursing in a perfection of wisdom which is nonexistent in its own-being he fulfils the path of a Bodhisattva, i.e. the six perfections, etc. *to* : the eighty minor characteristics. Having stood in the path to enlightenment which has the nature of being a karma result, when he has fulfilled the six perfections, the thirty-seven wings to enlightenment, and the superknowledges which are born from karma result, he helps with gifts those beings who should be helped with gifts. And so he helps them with morality, patience, vigour, concentration, wisdom, emancipation, and the vision and cognition of emancipation. He establishes in the fruit of a Streamwinner those who should be established in the fruit of a Streamwinner, etc. *to* : he establishes in (full) enlightenment those who should be established in full enlightenment. And so all this should be done in full detail. Working miracles with his manifold wonderworking powers he travels to world systems numerous as the sands of the Ganges, and he conjures up all those precious things which he planned to produce. Fulfilling the intentions of beings ((f. 272b)) he passes on from Buddha-field to Buddha-field. When he has seen those world systems, he acquires the Buddha-field which he wishes to acquire, —and therein there will be all the enjoyments and their objects which are found among the gods who hold sway over (the enjoyments) magically created by others, or which can be had in other Buddha-fields without having to strive for them. Through those karma-resultant six perfections and superknowledges, as well as the path to enlightenment which is born of karma result, he attains, coursing in the knowledge of the modes of the path, the fulfilment of all dharmas and will reach the knowledge of all modes. And so on, if all dharmas have not been taken hold of, then for someone who has known the supreme enlightenment all the enjoyments and objects of enjoyment in this Buddha-field will be something that he has not taken hold of. And why? Because all dharmas have not been taken hold of, on account of their baselessness. And he teaches the Dharma to beings so that they may not take hold of any dharma. It is thus that the Bodhisattva, who courses in perfect wisdom, fulfils the perfection of wisdom by way of signlessness.

Chapter 72

EXPOSITION OF MARKLESSNESS

VII 3. The Single Instantaneous Reunion, Which Sees All Dharmas as Devoid of Marks.

Subhuti: How can there be a fulfilment of the development of the six perfections if all dharmas are undifferentiated, signless, and empty of own-marks? How can one conceive of a difference between those dharmas which are with and those which are without outflows? How can one form a concept of (the difference between) these dharmas with their distinguishing marks when in fact they have one mark only, i.e. no mark?

The Lord: Here the Bodhisattva, who courses in perfect wisdom, having stood in the conviction that the five skandhas are like a dream, an echo, an image, a mirage, a magical illusion or an apparition, practises the five cardinal virtues. (For) the five skandhas are like a dream, an image, a mirage, a magical illusion, an apparition, and devoid of marks. And why? Because a dream has no own-being, nor has an echo, etc. And that which has no own-being, that has no mark. That which has no mark, that has one mark only, i.e. no mark. By this method also one should know that the gift is without mark, and so is the giver and recipient. One who gives gifts after having cognized this, fulfils the *perfection of giving*, but does not turn away ((f. 273a)) from the other five perfections. Having stood in these six perfections, he fulfils the four trances, etc. *to*: the eighteen special Buddhadharmas. Having stood in these dharmas without outflows which are born of karma result he travels to the world systems in the ten directions with the help of his wonderworking powers, and there honours and serves the Buddhas and Lords. *And so on, until we come to*: he works the weal of beings by helping them in every way. He wins over by gifts those who should be won over by gifts, etc. *to*: he wins over by all wholesome dharmas those who should be won over by all wholesome dharmas. Endowed with these wholesome roots he accepts rebirth in Samsāra, as one who is a sovereign over all dharmas, but he is not contaminated by the sufferings which pertain to Samsāra. For the sake of beings he accepts rebirth in the (relatively) prosperous condition of gods and men, and that enables him to win over beings. He cognizes all dharmas as without marks, and also cognizes the fruit of a Streamwinner, but does not take his stand on it. And so on up to the enlightenment of a Pratyekabuddha. And why? Because, when he has cognized all dharmas, he should reach the knowledge of all modes which is not shared by any of the Disciples and Pratyekabuddhas. It is thus that the Bodhisattva, having cognized all dharmas as without marks, cognizes the six perfections, etc. *to*: all Buddhadharmas as without marks.

Moreover, the Bodhisattva, coursing in perfect wisdom, having stood in the conviction that the five grasping skandhas are like a dream, etc. *to*: like an apparition, fulfils the *perfection of morality*. Having cognized the five grasping skandhas as like a dream, etc. *to*: like an apparition, he fulfils the markless perfection of morality, which is unimpaired, flawless, unspotted, pure, untarnished, which sets free (from the slavery of craving), which has been lauded by the wise, which one has well taken upon oneself, and which is holy, without outflows, included within the Path and supramundane.[1] Having stood therein he guards the morality (1) which consists in the (verbal) intimation that one has undertaken to observe the moral precepts,[2] (2) which is acquired in the nature of things,[3] (3) which is due to restraint,[4] (4) which is announced[5] ((f. 273b)), (5) which is habitual,[6] and (6) which is nonhabitual.[7] Endowed with these kinds of morality he does not misconstrue (the situation by thinking)[8]: through this (practice of morality) I shall be reborn in good warrior families, or in good Brahmin families, or in the families of wealthy householders, or as a universal monarch, or as the commander of a fort, or among the gods; or, alternatively, I shall win the fruit of a Streamwinner, etc. *to*: enlightenment. And why? Because all dharmas are without marks, with one mark only, i.e. with the mark of having nonexistence for their own-being. And a markless dharma cannot win a markless dharma. Nor

[1]cf. f. 269.

[2]i.e. one verbally makes a promise, or takes a resolution, to the effect that 'I will not do either this or that'.

[3]Here there is no deliberate resolution, but morality arises spontaneously or automatically because (1) by dissociating oneself from the defilements of the world of sense desire, one takes hold of a state of concentrated trance in which taking of life, etc. becomes quite out of the question, or (2) because by abstaining from certain actions one enters upon the Path.—One may compare *Aṭṭhasālinī* p. 103, where there is mention of an abstention due to a definite undertaking *(samādānavirati)* as distinct from an abstention due to cutting off those factors which make for evil deeds *(samucchedavirati)*.

[4]"Restraint is that which destroys or arrests the flow of immorality" *(Abhidharmakoṣa-bhāṣya*, ed. P. Pradhan, Patna, 1967, p. 208,1).

[5]i.e. to others. One declares to others that one renounces the taking of life, etc. esp. in the course of the Prātimokṣa ceremony.

[6]This is how I normally translate *samudācāra*. Prof. Lamotte tells me that he has not found this or the following term in his sources, and he believes that they refer to two stages of sanctity *(āryatva)*—in the first morality still requires an effort, while in the second it does not. The Tibetan *(yaṅ-dag-par spyod-pa)* for *samudācāra* can in fact also mean *samyak-prayoga* (right effort).

[7]om. Tib.

[8]*Ku*: does not make a vow.

can a dharma with distinguishing marks win a dharma with distinguishing marks. Nor can dharmas which are markless and without distinguishing marks attain dharmas which are markless and without distinguishing marks. It is thus that the Bodhisattva, coursing in perfect wisdom, fulfils the markless perfection of morality and then enters on the Bodhisattva's way of certain salvation. Thereafter he acquires the patient acceptance of dharmas which fail to be produced. He courses in the knowledge of the modes of the path, acquires the five superknowledges which are born of karma result, establishes himself in the five hundred dharani doors and the five hundred concentration doors, and acquires the four analytical knowledges. Thereafter he passes on from Buddha-field to Buddha-field, honours the Buddhas and Lords, matures beings and acquires a Buddha-field (for himself). He wanders about in the world of birth-and-death with its five places of rebirth, but he is not contaminated by the karma which is bound up with the world of birth-and-death or by its results. Just as a magical creation walks about, stands, sits, and lies down, though its coming is not observed (as a real fact) nor its going, nor its standing, sitting, or lying down, just so he works the weal of beings, but does not apprehend a being or the concept of a being. Just as the Tathagata who has won full enlightenment, after he has known full enlightenment, (has) turned the wheel of Dharma and led countless beings to Nirvana through the two vehicles, does not apprehend any Bodhisattva whom he might have predicted to the supreme enlightenment. Having let go the factors which make for a long life, he has entered Nirvana which leaves nothing behind after he has conjured up a magical creation. And that magical creation, after he has predicted (the enlightenment of) that Bodhisattva after an aeon has elapsed, wins final Nirvana through the supreme enlightenment. But one cannot apprehend any entity in him who has won final Nirvana, i.e. none of the skandhas. It is thus that the Bodhisattva works the weal of beings, although he does not apprehend a being or the concept of a being. In this way the Bodhisattva, who courses in perfect wisdom, fulfils the perfection of morality, and in its fulfilment all dharmas are contained.

Moreover the Bodhisattva, who courses in perfect wisdom, having stood in the conviction that the five grasping skandhas are like a dream, etc. *to*: are apparitions, fulfils the markless *perfection of patience*. And how does the Bodhisattva, having stood in markless dharmas, fulfil the perfection of patience? Here he fulfils the perfection of patience by way of two kinds of patience. Which two? The patience which means toleration and the patience which can look through to dharmas.[9] What, then, is the patience which means toleration? ((f. 274a)) During the entire time which elapses between his first thought of enlightenment and his being seated

[9] *dharma-avabodha-kṣānti.*

on the terrace of enlightenment, even though all beings should again and again revile and abuse him, and should use (towards him) mendacious and harsh words, or would give him blows with clods, sticks, or swords, the Bodhisattva, who desires to fulfil the perfection of patience, should not produce even one single thought associated with rage or ill will. And with regard to these beings he should intensely reflect that they are surely afflicted with the defilements and that he should produce towards them a thought which contains no evil. And he should think that 'when I have taken hold of these skandhas I have taken hold of what are deadly enemies'. When, as he thus reflects, he becomes full of friendliness and compassion, then one speaks of the patience which means toleration. And what is the patience which can look through to dharmas? It consists in that he does not apprehend even those beings in the ultimate sense, (and so he asks himself:) who abuses or reviles me, who uses towards me mendacious or harsh words, or who gives me blows with clods, sticks, or swords? Like a magical illusion are all conditioned things, worthless, insignificant, void, fashioned like the firmament, devoid of self, etc. arisen from imagination. All these are discriminations (when you ask yourself:) who abuses or reviles me, etc. *to*: who gives me blows with clods, sticks, or swords? But I will not discriminate in such a way, basing myself on the emptiness of own-being and the emptiness of ultimate reality. This is called the patience which can look through to dharmas. When he considers thus he fulfils the perfection of patience and when he has done so, he acquires the patient acceptance of dharmas which fail to be produced.

Subhuti: What is this patient acceptance of dharmas which fail to be produced? What is its definition,[10] and what is its cognition?

The Lord: Even the least (*aṇu*) dharma is not produced, and that is why one speaks of what fails to be produced (*anutpattikam*). And here the cognition is called patient acceptance, and through that cognition he acquires the patient acceptance of dharmas which fail to be produced.

Subhuti: Is there any difference between the patient acceptance of dharmas which fail to be produced on the part of the Disciples and Pratyekabuddhas on the one side and on the part of the Bodhisattva on the other?

The Lord: What is the cognition and forsaking of the Streamwinner, etc. *to*: the Pratyekabuddha, that is (part of) the Patience of the Bodhisattva. And this is the difference between the Patience of all the Disciples and Pratyekabuddhas and that of the Bodhisattvas; that the Bodhisattva, who is endowed with this suchlike Patience, surpasses all the Disciples and Pratyekabuddhas, for, when he has stood in this Patience, in the patient acceptance of dharmas which fail to be produced, he courses in

[10]Lit. 'measure'. Its logical basis?

the path of a Bodhisattva and fulfils the knowledge of the modes of the path. Through this fulfilment he becomes one who is not lacking in the thirty-seven dharmas which act as wings to enlightenment, and in the concentrations on emptiness, the signless and the wishless. He becomes one who is not lacking in the five superknowledges, and so he can mature beings and purify the Buddha-field. As a result he reaches the knowledge of all modes through the wisdom which is conjoined with one single instant ((f. 274b)). It is thus that the Bodhisattva, who courses in perfect wisdom, fulfils the markless perfection of patience.

Moreover the Bodhisattva, having stood in the five grasping skandhas as like a dream, etc. *to* : like an apparition, and as without marks, exerts physical and mental vigour. He aspires for enlightenment with his physical vigour in that he travels to the world systems in all the ten directions, honours the Buddhas and Lords, and works the weal of beings. With the help of his physical vigour he matures beings, exhorts them to the triple vehicle and establishes them therein. It is thus that the Bodhisattva who courses in perfect wisdom fulfils the markless *perfection of vigour*. With a mental vigour which takes place on the path which is without outflows and which is included in that Path he fulfils the perfection of vigour in which all wholesome dharmas are included. When the Bodhisattva courses in them, he should fulfil the knowledge of all modes, and by fulfilling that he will forsake all the defilements together with their residues, and in consequence he will fulfil the full complement of the marks, accomplish the state of having a halo all round, and turn the wheel of Dharma, with its twelve aspects and its three revolutions. When he turns it, the great trichiliocosm will shake in six ways, etc. And this entire trichiliocosm will be irradiated with a sublime splendour. And he will induce the beings in that great trichiliocosm to listen to those sounds which issue from the Tathagata, and they will all become fixed on the three vehicles. It is thus that a Bodhisattva's perfection of vigour does much. When he has stood in the perfection of vigour the Bodhisattva should fulfil all the Buddhadharmas and reach the knowledge of all modes.

Furthermore the Bodhisattva, who courses in perfect wisdom, when he has stood in the five grasping skandhas as like a dream, etc. *to* : as like an apparition, fulfils the *perfection of meditation*. And how does he do so? Here ((f. 275 a)) the Bodhisattva dwells in the four trances, the four Unlimited, the four formless attainments, and he develops the concentrations on emptiness, the signless and the wishless,[11] the con-

[11] *AdT* seem to differ : With the exception of *(ma gtogs-pa)* the concentration of a Tathagata, the concentration which is like lightning, the right concentration, and the concentration which is like a thunderbolt, he enters on the concentrations suitable to *(ruṅ-ba, yogya)* the Disciples or Pratyekabuddhas, or any other classes of concentrations that may be suitable.

centration which is like lightning and the right concentration. When he has stood in the concentration which is like a thunderbolt, then, leaving aside the concentration of a Tathagata, he dwells as one who has entered on whichever concentrations are common to the Disciples and Pratyekabuddhas, as well as any other classes of concentrations and meditational achievements, after he has suffused them all with his body. But he does not relish those concentrations, nor the fruit of his meditational attainments. And why? Because he cognizes those concentrations as markless, and as having nonexistence for their own-being. How can a markless dharma relish a markless dharma? Not relishing them he will not gain a new rebirth through any of these concentrations, be it in the world of form or the formless world. And why? Because he does not apprehend those two worlds, nor him who enters (on concentration), or whereby he enters (on concentration). Not apprehending these he fulfils the markless perfection of meditation, and through that perfection of meditation he transcends the level of the Disciples and Pratyekabuddhas.

Subhuti: How does the Bodhisattva, who has fulfilled the perfection of meditation, transcend the level of the Disciples and Pratyekabuddhas?

The Lord: Here the Bodhisattva has been well trained in the various kinds of emptiness. But in all these emptinesses no dharma can be apprehended on which he could take his stand, be it the fruit of a Streamwinner, etc. *to* : the enlightenment of a Pratyekabuddha. And even that knowledge of all modes, that is empty through (those) emptinesses. When through these emptinesses the Bodhisattva has transcended the level of the Disciples and Pratyekabuddhas, then he enters on the certainty of a Bodhisattva's salvation.

Subhuti: What is the Bodhisattva's 'rawness' (*āma*) and what is his certainty[12] (*ny-āma*)?

The Lord: All the bases of a Bodhisattva are his 'rawness', all the baselessness is 'certainty'.

Subhuti: What is basis, what is baselessness?

The Lord: If form, etc. *to*: the knowledge of all modes is a basis for the Bodhisattva, that is his 'rawness'. The 'certainty', on the other hand, consists in that those dharmas—i.e. form, etc. *to* : the knowledge of all modes, are not apprehended as a subject of verbal communication. And why? Because the own-being of form, etc. is incommunicable by words. This is the Bodhisattva's 'certainty'. When he has entered on this 'certainty', the Bodhisattva fulfils all the concentrations, but he is not reborn as a result of them. How much less could he produce greed, hate or delusion, based on which he would bring about deeds which would make him fall into Samsāra! It is quite impossible that he should do so. On the

[12]Translated as "ripening" at *P* 120.

contrary, although he has stood in (the conviction that) dharmas are like a magical illusion, he works the weal of all beings. But he does not apprehend a being or a magical illusion. In spite of that he matures beings and acquires a Buddha-field. ((f. 275b)) It is thus that the Bodhisattva, having fulfilled the perfection of meditation, goes on until he turns the wheel of Dharma i.e. the wheel which is baseless and which is emptiness, signless, and wishless.

Moreover the Bodhisattva who courses in *the perfection of wisdom* comprehends all dharmas as like a dream, etc. *to*: like an apparition.

VII 4. The Single Instantaneous Reunion which Sees the Mark of Non-duality in All Dharmas.

Subhuti: And how does the Bodhisattva do that?

The Lord: Here the Bodhisattva, who courses in perfect wisdom, has not seen the dream or the one who sees the dream, etc. *to*: he has not seen the apparition or the one who sees the apparition. And why? Because a dream, etc. is a perverted view on the part of the foolish common people. But Arhats, Pratyekabuddhas, and Tathagatas do not see a dream or one who sees a dream, etc. *to*: they do not see an apparition or one who sees an apparition. And why? Because all dharmas have non-existence for their own-being, and they are the same as final Nirvana, because of their unreality. Not totally real are all dharmas, because they have not actually come into being. It is quite impossible that a Bodhisattva, who courses in perfect wisdom, should become one who has the notion of an existent, or of something totally real, or of something truly real. That would not be the perfection of wisdom if one were to apprehend the own-being of any dharma whatsoever, or its total reality, or its true reality. It is thus that the Bodhisattva, who courses in perfect wisdom, does not cling to form, etc. *to*: the five perfections. When he has stood in this perfection of wisdom, he fulfils the ten stages, without producing towards them passionate greed. And why? Because he does not apprehend those stages; how, then, can he produce passionate greed towards them? He courses in the perfection of wisdom, but does not apprehend it. Coursing in the baseless he sees all dharmas as contained in this perfection of wisdom, and yet he does not apprehend those dharmas. And why? Because these dharmas on the one hand and that perfection of wisdom on the other are not two nor divided. And why? Because there is no differentiation between these dharmas. All dharmas are undifferentiated because they have been identified with[13] the Dharma-element, with Suchness and ((f. 276a)) the Reality limit.

Subhuti: If all dharmas are undifferentiated, how can there be a distinctive definition[14] of dharmas as wholesome or unwholesome, as worldly

[13]*nirdeśena.*
[14]*nirdeśo*

or supramundane, as with or without outflows, as conditioned or unconditioned?

The Lord: What do you think, Subhuti; is there in that Dharmahood of dharmas any conventional utterance about any dharma, be it conditioned or unconditioned, or relating to the fruit of a Streamwinner, etc. *to*: to full enlightenment?

Subhuti: No, O Lord.

The Lord: By that method also you should know, Subhuti, that all dharmas are undifferentiated, unmarked, nonproduced and unmanifested. When I in the past have coursed in the course of a Bodhisattva I have not apprehended any dharma whatsoever. It is thus that the Bodhisattva courses in perfect wisdom from his first thought of enlightenment onwards up to the time when he awakes to full enlightenment, and that without taking anything as a basis. And he should become one who is skilful about the own-being of all dharmas, because then he can fulfil the path to enlightenment, mature beings, and acquire a Buddha-field. When he has established himself in that (Buddha-field) and has awoken to full enlightenment, he disciplines beings in such a way that they no longer appear in the three (inauspicious) places of becoming. It is thus that the Bodhisattva should course in the perfection of wisdom, through his devotion to[15] the absence of marks.

[15]or: by way of.

Chapter 73

THE PERFECTION OF THE IMPERISHABLE CONSUMMATION OF THE MARKS AND MINOR CHARACTERISTICS

VIII. THE RE-UNION WITH THE DHARMA-BODY.

VIII 1. The Substantial Body.
VIII 2. The Dharma-body.
VIII 3. The Enjoyment Body.
VIII 4. The Work of the Dharma-body by Means of the Transformation-body—in General.

Subhuti: How, O Lord, when all dharmas are like a dream, non-entities, with nonexistence for their own-being and empty of own-marks, can there be a definite distinction between them, to the effect that these dharmas are wholesome and those unwholesome, these worldly and those supramundane, these with and those without outflows, these conditioned and those unconditioned, these conducive to the fruit of a Streamwinner, etc. *to*: those conducive to the supreme enlightenment? And so with regard to those (dharmas) which are like an echo, a reflected image, a magical illusion, a mirage, a magical creation, which are nonentities, have nonexistence for own-being and are empty of own-marks—how can there be a definite distinction between them, to the effect that these dharmas are wholesome and those unwholesome, etc. *to*: those are conducive to the supreme enlightenment?

The Lord: Here, Subhuti, the foolish, untrained, common person apprehends the dream and apprehends him who sees it, etc. *to*: he apprehends the magical creation as well as him who sees it. As a result he brings about karma formations, by body, speech, or mind, which are wholesome, unwholesome, or immovable.[1] ((f. 276b)) In consequence the Bodhisattva who courses in perfect wisdom demonstrates Dharma to beings after he has stood in two kinds of emptiness, i.e. the absolute emptiness and the emptiness which is without beginning and end, (and he says that:) empty is all this that belongs to the triple world; therein there is no form, etc. *to*: no consciousness, no skandhas, elements or sense fields. A dream is all this, an echo, etc. *to*: a magical creation. Therein there are no skandhas, elements or sense fields, and also no dream or one who sees it, no echo or one who hears it, no reflected image,

[1]*aniñja*. Tranquil, because in a state of trance.

magical illusion, or mirage, and no one who sees them, no magical creation and no one who creates it. But all these dharmas are nonentities and have nonexistence for ownbeing. You therefore perceive skandhas, elements, and sense fields where there are none. In fact all these dharmas are due to conditioned coproduction, they have originated from the perverted views, they have been taken hold of as the result of karma. How, then, is it that you become perceivers of entities with regard to dharmas which are nonentities! It is thus that the Bodhisattva, who courses in perfect wisdom, by his skill in means turns niggardly beings away from their niggardliness, and exhorts them to the perfection of giving. And to them the giving of gifts becomes conducive to great wealth. Having moved them away from this,[2] he exhorts them to the perfection of morality, and their taking morality upon themselves becomes conducive to their being reborn in heaven. Having moved then away from this,[3] he exhorts them to transic concentration which in its turn is conducive to their rebirth in the Brahma-world. And so he exhorts them to the various trances, from the first trance to the attainment of the station of neither perception nor nonperception. He then dissuades them in various ways from those inferior things, like giving, morality, and concentration, and from their fruits, and encourages them to win the realm of Nirvana which leaves nothing behind, exhorts them to it and establishes them in it. He encourages and exhorts them to win the four applications of mindfulness, etc. *to*: the eighteen special Buddhadharmas, and he disciplines and establishes them in them. With the help of these dharmas without outflows, immaterial, undefinable, and nonreacting he establishes in the fruit of a Streamwinner those who strive for the fruit of a Streamwinner, etc. *to*: he describes the path of enlightenment to those who strive for the supreme enlightenment, points it out to them, fills them with enthusiasm for it, encourages it and establishes it. It is thus that a Bodhisattva, who courses in perfect wisdom, makes definite distinctions between dharmas ((f. 277a)), although they are all like a dream, nonentities, with nonexistence for their own-being and empty of own-marks.

Subhuti: It is wonderful and it is astonishing that the Bodhisattva, who courses in this deep perfection of wisdom, should when all dharmas have nonexistence for own-being, when they are absolutely empty and empty of both beginning and end, yet make a definite distinction between dharmas which are wholesome and unwholesome, etc. *to*: which are conditioned and unconditioned.

The Lord: So it is, Subhuti, so it is. It is indeed wonderful and astonishing of the Bodhisattvas that, when they course in this deep perfection of wisdom, they nevertheless make a definite distinction between

[2]niggardliness, or giving?
[3]immorality, or morality?

dharmas. And when, Subhuti, you consider this wonderful and astonishing dharma of a Bodhisattva, (you must admit that) it is not easy for all you Disciples and Pratyekabuddhas to repay the Bodhisattva (for his favours). All of you cannot possibly surpass this dharma of a Bodhisattva.

Subhuti: What, then, is this (wonderful and) astonishing dharma of a Bodhisattva which does not exist for all the Disciples and Pratyekabuddhas?

The Lord: Therefore, then, Subhuti, listen and attend well, I will explain this to you! Here the Bodhisattva, who courses in perfect wisdom, having stood in the six perfections born of karma result, in the five superknowledges, etc. *to*: in the eighteen special Buddhadharmas, and having travelled to the world systems in the ten directions, helps beings with what they require, whether it be gifts, morality, etc. *to*: the concentration on emptiness, the signless, the wishless.

Subhuti: How does the Bodhisattva help beings by giving?

The Lord: Here the Bodhisattva, who courses in perfect wisdom, gives gifts—food to those in need of food, etc. *to*: anything else that may be useful to human beings. And just as he gives to the Tathagata, so also to Pratyekabuddhas, Arhats, etc. *to*: Streamwinners, to those who are reborn in the right places of rebirth and to those who progress in the right direction, so he gives to humans and to those who are reborn as animals; to all he gives gifts after he has formed the notion of non-differentiation. And why? Because he has cognized all dharmas as being just one undifferentiatedness. Having given gifts without differentiating, he becomes the recipient of an undifferentiated dharma, i.e. the knowledge of all modes. But if a Bodhisattva, when faced with ((f. 277b)) a living being in the animal world who does not seem worthy of gifts, should produce a thought to the effect that 'a fully enlightened Buddha is worthy of my gifts, but not this animal', then he does not have the dharma of a Bodhisattva. And why? Because the Bodhisattva, who has raised his thought to enlightenment, has not set out for the supreme enlightenment with the reflection, 'these beings I should help with gifts, but not those'. Helped by gifts they will be reborn in good families, and in due course they will, by means of the three vehicles, enter into the realm of Nirvana which leaves nothing behind. If all people taken together should plan to kill the Bodhisattva, his thought should remain unaltered, he should not think 'should I give to them or should I not?', but with unshaken mind he should resolve to give gifts to just those people. And why? Because for the sake of those very people he has set out towards full enlightenment. And if he should so discriminate, he will become an object of reproach to those Buddhas, Bodhisattvas, Pratyekabuddhas, and Arhats, to those still in training and to the world with its gods, men and

Asuras, when he becomes at their request of all beings the shelter, the place of rest, the refuge, the final relief.[4]—Moreover, if humans and nonhumans come to the Bodhisattva and plan to cut him up limb by limb, then he should not produce a dual thought, to the effect that 'I will give, or I will not give'. And why? Because that Bodhisattva has taken hold of his bodily basis deliberately for the sake of beings, and with the intention that through his physical personality the welfare of beings should be worked. And he should produce a thought thus, 'may those people for whose sake I have appropriated this physical personality go away satisfied when they have received everything without having solicited for it!' And it is thus that the Bodhisattva should train in perfect wisdom.—Moreover, when the Bodhisattva is faced with a beggar, he should produce a thought thus : he who gives, he to whom he gives, what he gives, of all these dharmas the own-being cannot be apprehended. And why? Because these dharmas are empty through their absolute emptiness. And emptiness does not give anything or takes anything away. It is thus that the Bodhisattva should train in perfect wisdom, i.e. in the inward emptiness, etc. *to* : in the emptiness of own-marks. When he has stood in this emptiness, then, wherever he gives gifts, the perfection of giving will constantly and always be fulfilled in him. And when he has fulfilled this perfection of giving he will, when his inner and outer belongings are cut or broken off, produce the thought, 'there is nothing that cuts or breaks (me)'.

VIII 5. The Functions of the Dharma-body.

VIII 5,1. THE ACTIVITY WHICH APPEASES THE PLACES OF REBIRTH.

VIII 5,1a. THE ACTIVITY WHICH APPEASES THE HELLS.

Here, surveying the world with my Buddha-eye, I have seen in the Eastern direction, in world systems countless like the sands of the Ganges, Bodhisattvas who have deliberately hurled themselves into the great hells, and who, after they have appeased the sufferings (of beings) in these great hells, demonstrate Dharma to those beings in the hells by means of three kinds of miracles, i.e. their miraculous wonderworking power, the miraculous reading of their thoughts and their miraculous admonition. When they have first appeased the sufferings in those hells, they then demonstrate Dharma, with the help of their miraculous thought-reading ((f. 278a)) and their miraculous admonitions. And it is with their great lovingkindness, their great compassion, their great sympathetic joy, and their great impartiality that these Bodhisattvas demonstrate Dharma. Thereupon in the presence of these Bodhisattvas the thought

[4]This sentence is partly illegible in the Ms, and the translation is tentative.

of those beings in the hells becomes serene, and they emerge from those great hells. Thereafter they are reborn among gods and men, and will gradually, with the help of the three kinds of miracles,[5] make an end of ill. And so for the other directions.

VIII 5,1b. THE ACTIVITY WHICH APPEASES THE WORLD OF ANIMALS.

Here Subhuti, surveying the world with my Buddha-eye in all directions, in world systems countless like the sands of the Ganges, I have seen Bodhisattvas who serve upon the Buddhas and Lords with such an intense devotion that they are dear and not undear to them, that they please and do not displease them, and that they respect and do not disrespect them. And these Bodhisattvas learn the Dharma which those Buddhas and Lords teach, bear it in mind and never allow it to be forgotten again before they win the supreme enlightenment.—Moreover, Subhuti, surveying the world with my Buddha-eye, I have seen in all directions, in world systems countless like the sands of the Ganges, Bodhisattvas who, for the sake of animal beings, perform the surrender of themselves. Again and again all the limbs of these Bodhisattvas are torn to pieces and scattered in the ten directions, and then the animals eat their flesh. They (thus) acquire a feeling of friendliness for these Bodhisattvas, and through their acquisition of this friendliness they emerge from that animal world and are reborn among gods and men. On being reborn there they please the Buddhas and Lords, and serve upon them. They hear the Dharma from these Buddhas and Lords, and as a result they progress to Thusness. Gradually they are nirvanized in the realm of Nirvana which leaves nothing behind and that through the three vehicles, i.e. the Disciple-vehicle, the Pratyekabuddha-vehicle, or the great vehicle. It is thus that Bodhisattvas achieve much good when they raise their thought to the supreme enlightenment and progress to Thusness, etc. *to*: until they win final Nirvana in the realm of Nirvana which leaves nothing behind.

VIII 5,1c. THE ACTIVITY WHICH APPEASES THE WORLD OF YAMA.

Here, Subhuti, surveying the world with my Buddha-eye, I have seen in all directions in world systems countless like the sands of the Ganges Bodhisattvas who allay in the beings belonging to the realm of the hungry ghosts all the sufferings which they feel in that realm. Thereupon the hearts of those hungry ghosts become friendly towards these Bodhisattvas and as a result[6] they emerge from that world of hungry ghosts and are reborn in the world of gods and men. And they will never again be deprived of the Buddhas and Lords until they win final Nirvana in

[5] *P*, more likely: the three vehicles.

[6] *P* adds: of the merit produced by this friendly feeling.

the realm of Nirvana which leaves nothing behind. Thus, dwelling in the great compassion, the Bodhisattva is concerned with the welfare of beings, i.e. with leading them to final Nirvana.

VIII 5,1d. THE ACTIVITY WHICH APPEASES THE WORLD OF THE GODS.

Here, Subhuti, surveying the world with my Buddha-eye, I have seen ((f. 278b)) in all directions in world systems countless like the sands of the Ganges, Bodhisattvas who demonstrate Dharma to the gods of the Four Great Kings, etc. *to*: the Paranirmitavasavartin gods. And those gods who have heard the Dharma from these Bodhisattvas have, through the three vehicles, gradually won final Nirvana, do win final Nirvana, and will win final Nirvana. When they find that some gods have become intoxicated with the five kinds of the most excellent sense pleasures, they wait until their mansions are all ablaze and then demonstrate Dharma to them as follows: 'Surely, Sirs, impermanent are all conditioned things, ill, not your own,[7] unstable, unreliable, bound to deteriorate.[8] Who can trust in conditioned things!'—Here, Subhuti, surveying the world with my[9] Buddha-eye, I have seen in all directions in world systems countless like the sands of the Ganges Bodhisattvas who dissuade from views about Brahma those who have settled down in them. 'How, Sirs, can you produce such (false) views when all dharmas are empty, worthless, and insignificant!' It is thus that the Bodhisattvas, established in the great compassion, demonstrate Dharma to beings. Wonderful indeed is this astonishing dharma of the Bodhisattvas!

VIII 5,1e. THE ACTIVITY WHICH APPEASES THE WORLD OF MEN.

Here, Subhuti, surveying the world with my Buddha-eye, I have seen in all directions in world systems countless like the sands of the Ganges Bodhisattvas who help men with the four means of conversion. Which four? They are:

(I) Gifts,
(II) kind words,
(III) actions for their benefit,
(IV) consistency between words and deeds.

(I) And how does the Bodhisattva help beings with gifts? He helps them with two kinds of gifts, i.e. (Ia) material gifts and (Ib) the gift of Dharma.

(Ia) And how does he help beings with material gifts? Coursing in perfect wisdom he gives away gold, silver, etc. *to*: horses and elephants, and he says to them: 'Hey, you people come along! as I have not

[7]Lit. not the self.
[8]liable to reversal, or, liable to be overturned.
[9]*P* adds: unimpeded.

held on to these things, so also do you give them up!' Having given them this gift, he leads them on to take their refuge in the Buddha, Dharma, and Samgha. Some he makes take up the five precepts, others he makes observe the eight precepts on the sabbath, others he establishes in the ten wholesome ways of action, others he causes to enter on the first trance, etc. *to* : ((f. 279a)) others he establishes in Arhatship, or in the enlightenment of a Pratyekabuddha. It is thus that the Bodhisattva, who courses in perfect wisdom, gives material gifts to all beings and establishes them in a state of the highest security. This is the Bodhisattva's wonderful and astonishing Dharma.

(Ib) And how does the Bodhisattva who courses in perfect wisdom help beings with the gift of Dharma? There are two kinds of the gift of Dharma.—(Iba) the worldly and (Ibb) the supramundane.

(Iba) What then is the gift of the worldly Dharma? It is the teaching of (all) worldly dharmas, their demonstration and revelation, i.e. of the . . . ? . . . of the (9 kinds of) repulsiveness, the four trances, the four stations of Brahma, the four formless attainments, and of whatever other worldly dharma there may be that are shared by the foolish common people. And when the Bodhisattva has given this gift of worldly dharmas, he then by various methods turns them away from their cultivation and through his skill in means establishes them in holy dharmas and in their fruit. And which are the holy dharmas and which is their fruit? The holy dharmas are described as the 37 dharmas which act as wings to enlightenment and the three doors to deliverance. The fruit of the holy dharmas is the fruit of a Streamwinner, etc. *to* : Arhatship. Furthermore this is the holy dharma of a Bodhisattva that he has a cognition of the fruit of a Streamwinner, etc. *to*: Arhatship, of the enlightenment of a Pratyekabuddha, etc. *to* : of the 37 dharmas which act as wings to enlightenment, etc. *to* : of the ten powers of a Tathagata, etc. *to* : of the great friendliness, the great compassion, the great sympathetic joy and the great impartiality. And if there are (in addition to these) any other worldly and supramundane dharmas—with or without outflows, conditioned or unconditioned—their cognition up to the knowledge of all modes, these are called the holy dharmas of a Bodhisattva. And what again is for a Bodhisattva the fruit of the holy dharmas? (All the fruits) up to the forsaking of all defilements and their residues.

Subhuti : Does, then, the Bodhisattva reach the knowledge of all modes?

(*The Lord*: Yes, he does.)

Subhuti : In that case, what is the difference between him and a Tathagata?

The Lord: There is a difference between them.

Subhuti : What, then, is it?

The Lord: The Bodhisattva reaches the knowledge of all modes, but the Tathagata is called one who has attained to (its?) cognition. And why? For the thought in which he is established when he has reached the nonblindness for all dharmas cannot be apprehended as respectively different in the Bodhisattva and the Tathagata. So much about a Bodhisattva's gift of worldly dharma which becomes a basis for his gift of supramundane dharmas. It is thus that the Bodhisattva, when he has enjoined upon beings the gift of the worldly dharmas, goes on, through his skill in means, until he establishes them in the knowledge of all modes.

VIII 5,2. THE FOURFOLD MEANS OF CONVERSION.

(Ibb) And what is, on the part of the Bodhisattva, the gift of the supramundane dharmas, which are not shared with all the foolish common people? They are (1a) the four applications of mindfulness, (1b) the four right efforts ((f. 279b)), (lc) the four bases of psychic power, (1d) the five dominants, (1e) the five powers, (1f) the seven limbs of enlightenment, (1g) the holy eightfold path; (A) the three gateways to emancipation; (3) the eight deliverances, (4) the nine successive attainments, (13) the ten powers of a Tathagata, (14) the four grounds of selfconfidence, (10) the four analytical knowledges, (B) the great friendliness, (19) the great compassion, (20) the eighteen special dharmas of a Buddha, (C) the 32 marks of the superman, (D) the eighty accessory marks, (E) the five hundred dharani doors and (F) the hundreds of concentration doors.[10] This is the gift of Dharma which is supramundane and not worldly.

(VIII 5,2,1. THE 37 WINGS OF ENLIGHTENMENT).

(1a) And what, Subhuti, are the four applications of mindfulness? (i) With regard to the inward body he dwells as one who reviews the body, and so he dwells with regard to the outward body and to both the inward an outward body—ardent, clearly conscious, and mindful, after putting away all worldly covetousness and sadness. With regard to the body he dwells as one who reviews its origination, its disappearance, and both its origination and disappearance. He dwells as one who does not lean on anything, and as one who (does not) grasp at the world. And so with regard to (ii) feelings, (iii) thought and (iv) dharmas.

(1b) And what are the four right efforts? (i) He rouses his will to bring about the (future) nonproduction of evil and unwholesome dharmas, which have not yet been produced; (ii) he exerts himself to bring about the forsaking (of evil and unwholesome dharmas) which have been

[10]The Arabic numerals indicate those items which correspond to the twenty-one features of the Dharma-body in the list of *AA* VIII verses 2-6, as reproduced in *AA* VIII 5, 2, 1-21 of *P* (see pp. 654-656). A to F are additional items not mentioned in that list. Of these C and D appear in *AA* VIII verses 12-32 under the heading of "Enjoyment-Body".

produced; (iii) he rouses his will and puts forth vigour so as to bring about the production of wholesome dharmas which have not yet been produced; (iv) he rouses his will so as to bring about the growth of those (wholesome dharmas) which have been produced, their greater abundance and the fulfilment of their development.

(1c) And what are the four bases of psychic power? They are endowed with the formative forces of effort, and their concentration is caused, respectively, by desire-to-do, thought, vigour, or exploration.

(1d) And what are the five dominants? Faith, vigour, mindfulness, concentration, and wisdom. (1e) And what are the five powers? The same as (1d).

(1f) And which are the seven limbs of enlightenment? Mindfulness, investigation into dharma(s), vigour, joyous zest, tranquillity, concentration, and evenmindedness.

(1g) And what is the holy eightfold path? Right view, right intention, right speech, right conduct, right livelihood, right effort, right mindfulness, right concentration.

(VIII 5,2,2. THE FOUR UNLIMITED).

(A) And what are the three concentrations? The concentration on emptiness, on the signless, and on the wishless. And what is the concentration on emptiness? The onepointedness of thought which is achieved by the modes of the empty and the isolated. And what is the concentration on the signless? The onepointedness of thought which is achieved by the mode of calm quiet. And what is the concentration on the wishless? The onepointedness of thought which is achieved by the modes of impermanent and ill.

VIII 5,2,3. THE EIGHT DELIVERANCES.

(3) And what are the eight deliverances? (i) Having form he sees forms. (ii) Perceiving inward form he sees outward forms. (iii) He becomes resolved on loveliness. (iv) By completely overcoming all perceptions of form, by the going to rest of the perceptions of impact, by not attending to the perceptions of manifoldness, on thinking 'Endless Space', he dwells in the attainment of the station of endless space. (v) By completely overcoming the station of endless space, on thinking 'Infinite Consciousness', he dwells in the attainment of the station of infinite consciousness. (vi) By completely overcoming the station of infinite consciousness, on thinking that 'there is not anything', he dwells in the attainment of the station of nothing whatever. (vii) By completely overcoming the station of Nothing Whatever, he dwells in the attainment of the station of neither perception nor nonperception. (viii) By completely overcoming the station of neither perception nor nonperception, he dwells in the attainment of the cessation of perception and feeling.

VIII 5,2,4. THE NINE SUCCESSIVE ATTAINMENTS.

(4) And what are the nine successive attainments? Here (i) someone dwells, detached from sense desires, detached from evil and unwholesome dharmas, in the attainment of the first Trance, which is with thoughts applied and discursive, born of detachment, full of rapture and ease; etc. *to*: (viii) he dwells as one who has attained the station of neither perception nor nonperception; (ix) by completely overcoming the station of neither perception nor nonperception, he dwells in the attainment of the cessation of perception and feeling.

VIII 5,2,13. THE TEN POWERS.

(13) And what are the ten powers of a Tathagata? (i) Here a Tathagata wisely knows, as it really is, what can be as what can be, and what cannot be as what cannot be. (ii) He wisely knows, as they really are, the karmic results of past, future, and present actions and undertakings of actions, as to place and cause. (vii) He wisely knows, as they really are, (of other beings, other persons) the faculties and powers, as well as their limbs of enlightenment, trances, concentrations, and meditational attainments, and also their defilement and purification. (v) He wisely knows as they really are, the higher and lower faculties of other beings and persons, and also (iv) their various dispositions. (vi) He wisely knows, as it really is, the progressive Way that leads everywhere, and also (iii) the various elements in the world, its multifarious elements. (viii) He recollects his various past lives: (He recollects) one birth, etc. *to*: in all their modes and in detail. (ix) With his heavenly eye, pure and surpassing that of men, he sees beings, (as they die and arise again) etc. *to*: as they are reborn in a happy destiny, in heaven, amongst the gods. (x) He wisely knows, as it really is, that emancipation of his heart (effected through) wisdom which is without outflows and which results from the extinction of the outflows.

VIII 5,2,14. THE FOUR GROUNDS OF SELF-CONFIDENCE.

(14) And what are the four grounds of self-confidence? (i) That I who claim to be fully enlightened am not fully enlightened as to whose dharmas —I see nothing to indicate that anyone in this world with its gods, Maras, Brahma(n), brahmins, etc., can with justice make this charge. And, as I see nothing to indicate this, I dwell in the attainment of security and fearlessness. I claim my exalted place as the leader, rightly roar the lion's roar in the assembly, and set rolling the sacred wheel which cannot with justice be set rolling by any recluse, brahmin, god, Mara, or Brahman, or anyone else in the world. (ii) That I, who claim to have dried up the outflows, have not completely dried them up, (that charge is impossible), etc. *to*: (iii) that those dharmas which I have described as impediments

should have no power to impede him who pursues them, (that charge is impossible), etc. *to*: (iv) that he who cultivates the progressive path, which I have described as holy, conducive to going forth, and to penetration, and as bringing the doer of it to the right extinction of ill, should not go forth to the right extinction of ill, (that charge is impossible); etc. *to*: these are the four grounds of self-confidence.

VIII 5,2,10. THE FOUR ANALYTICAL KNOWLEDGES.

(10) What again are the four analytical knowledges? They are the analytical knowledge of the Meaning, of the Dharma, of Languages, of Inspired Speech. And which are they? They have meaning, dharma, languages, and inspired speech for their respective objective supports.

VIII 5,2,20. THE EIGHTEEN SPECIAL BUDDHADHARMAS.

(20) And what are ((f. 280b)) the eighteen special Buddhadharmas of a Tathagata? The Tathagata (i) does not trip up, (ii) is not rash or noisy in his speech, (iii) is never robbed of his mindfulness; (iv) his thought is never unconcentrated, (v) he has no perception of difference, (vi) his evenmindedness is not due to lack of consideration, he never fails in (vii) his zeal, (viii) vigour, (ix) mindfulness, (x) concentration, (xi) wisdom, or (xii) in his deliverance, or his vision and cognition of deliverance. All his deeds of (xiii) body, (xiv) voice and (xv) mind are preceded by cognition and continue to conform to cognition. His vision and cognition regarding the (xvi) past, (xvii) future, and (xviii) present period of time proceeds unobstructed and freely.

(*The Enjoyment-body*-AA VIII,3)

(C) And what are the Tathagata's thirty-two marks of a superman?[11] (1) The Lord's feet are well-placed, i.e. he places the entire soles of his feet evenly on the ground, just as a round basket which, when tipped up moves

[11] The meaning of the 32 marks is perfectly clear, except in the case of nos. 7 and 26, where the commentators have to resort to wild and confused guesswork. This text of *Ad* is very different from that of *P* which I have edited in the *Journal of the Oriental Institute (Baroda)*, XIV, 1965. 225-229, and it is clearly the earlier of the two. It has close affinities with the account of *Ta chih tu lun* (E. Lamotte, *Le traité*, etc. 1944, 271-281) and the *Daśasāhasrikā* (S. Konow, 1941, 48-51). To facilitate a comparison of *Ad* and *P* I list their respective numberings:

Ad	P	Ad	P	Ad	P	Ad	P	Ad	P
1	2	8	11	15	14	22	30	29	31
2	1	9	cf. 8	16	cf. 5	23	29	30	32
3	4	10	12	17	18	24	28	31	17
4	6	11	13	18	19	25	27	32	23
5	3	12	16	19	20	26	21		
6	7	13	10	20	22	27	cf. 24		
7	9	14	cf. 15	21	26	28	25		

down and when tipped down moves up.[12] (2) He has, stamped on the soles of his feet, lines depicting a wheel, i.e. on his two feet there grow wheels, with a thousand spokes, with rims and naves, complete in every respect. (3) The soles of his feet and the palms of his hands are tender and soft, i.e. his hands and feet are softer than those of others. (4) His toes and fingers are long, i.e. they are longer than those of others. (5) His hands and feet are joined by webs, i.e. as with the royal goose. (6) He has broad heels, i.e. his two heels are broader than those of others. (7) His feet have inconspicuous anklebones, i.e. his two anklebones grow high up. (8) His shanks are like those of the black antelope, i.e. because his shanks are gradually tapering away, like those of the black antelope, king of deer. (9) His bodily frame is well-grown, tall, and straight, i.e. it is not crooked, not bent, well-grown in all ways; its height is seven cubits, and everything is proportioned accordingly. (10) His arms reach to his knees, i.e. when he stands up, he can, without bending down, whenever he wants, touch and stroke his kneecaps with the two palms of his hands. (11) His male organ is hidden in a sheath, i.e. as in the case of a noble thoroughbred elephant or horse. (12) The hairs on his body stand separately, i.e. in each hairpore there grows only one single hair, which is soft, curls in rings and turns to the right. (13) The hairs on his body point upwards, i.e. the hairs of his head and body grow in such a way that they are turned unwards; they are blue-black, soft, curl in rings, and turn to the right. (14) His skin is smooth and delicate, i.e. water and dust do not cleave to his body. (15) (His skin) has a golden hue, (making him) handsome and attractive, i.e. his body shines brightly just like a bar of gold. (16) He has seven prominences, i.e. two below on the soles of his feet, two on his hands, ((f. 281a)) two on his shoulder blades and one behind on his neck—and they are all handsome, attractive, and beautiful to behold, with ample flesh and blood. (17) The upper part of his body is like that of a lion, i.e. it is large like that of the lion, king of beasts. (18) His shoulders are gently curved, i.e. because they are muscular his shoulders are everywhere amply developed. (19) The interval between his shoulders is well filled, i.e. his chest is wide and well elevated. (10) The circumference of his body is like that of the fig tree, i.e. as great as he is in height, so great is he in width; as great as he is in width, so great is he in height. (21) He has jaws like a lion, i.e. his jaws are well rounded, as those of the lion. (22) He has a total of forty teeth, i.e. twenty below and twenty above. (23) There are no gaps between his teeth, i.e. his teeth are all close together. (24) His teeth are equal in size, because not some teeth are higher and some lower. (25) His teeth are very white, i.e. they shine brilliantly.

[12]*Daśa*, S. Konow, p. 49 : 'he touches the ground with the entire soles; just as the bottom of a basket, when placed on an even base, touches the ground with the whole lower surface, because its bottom rests evenly'.

(26) He has (taste) conductors which give him the most excellent taste, i.e. the taste conductors in his throat are quite straight; those in his tongue are not twisted or bloodless; since his nerves[13] are so well endowed, his body is supremely fit. (27) His tongue is long, i.e. when he desires to do so he touches and strokes with this tongue the apertures of his two ears, and he covers with his tongue the apertures of his two eyes and his entire face up to the hairs. (28) His voice is like that of Brahmā, i.e. his voice can be heard as clearly in a large assembly as in the inside of a room, and his speech is as charming as the song of the Kalavinka bird.[14] (29) His eyes are intensely black, i.e. the black of his eyes is pure black, and the white pure white. (30) His eyelashes are like those of a magnificent heifer, i.e. his eye lashes are like those of a great bull; those below are just below and those above are just above; and they are in no way disarranged. (31) He has a tuft of hair between his eye-brows, i.e. a tuft of hair grows between his eye brows which is very white and soft, resembles a tuft of cotton, and is not in touch with his eyebrows—the hairs turning to the right and curling in rings. (32) There is a cowl on his head, i.e. his head is well rounded and through the large circumference of the cowl it looks exceedingly beautiful.

These are the thirty-two marks of a superman. With the help of them He irradiates the great trichiliocosm with His radiance and with His natural splendour He also irradiates the countless world systems, if He so wishes. And the Tathagata sustains beings with his halo out of pity for them. When, however, the Lord's halo no longer sustains them, then, overcome by His natural splendour, the light of sun and moon are no longer encountered, and the moon and the half moon, the days and the years cease to exist.[15] And with His natural voice he instructs the great trichiliocosm, as often as He wishes to do so and as far as His radiance reaches.

It is thus that ((f. 281b)) the Bodhisattva helps beings with the two kinds of gift, i.e. the worldly gift and the gift of Dharma. This is the Bodhisattva's wonderful and astonishing dharma.

[13]or : vein, artery.

[14]*Hobogirin*, p. 134. T 223 : *Que l'assemblée soit grande ou petite, chacun l'entend également; tantôt elle est tonitruante comme le tambour céleste, tantôt douce comme le murmure du kalavinka.*

[15]Petrus Damiani : *Non alternat luna vices, sol vel cursus siderum, Agnus est felicis urbis lumen inocciduum, Nox et tempus desunt, aevum diem fert continuum.*

'There the moon does not run through her changes, there is no sun, and no courses of the stars. The lamb is the neversetting light of that happy city. There is no night and no time : eternity brings endless day'. (F. Brittain). *Revelation* 21, 23 :

'And the city had no need of Sun or moon to shine upon it; for the glory of God gave it light, its lamp was the Lamb' (NEB). 'Nor had the city any need of Sun or moon to shine in it; the glory of God shone there, the Lamb gave it light'.

(II) And how does the Bodhisattva help[16a] beings with kind words? He helps them with the six perfections. And why? Because all wholesome dharmas are included[16a] in these perfections.

(III) And how does the Bodhisattva help beings with actions which benefit them? He has helped beings for a long time with these six perfections, i.e. with gifts, kind words, actions for their benefit and consistency between words and deeds.[17]

(D) And he demonstrates to beings the eighty accessory marks. Which are they? The nails of the Buddhas and Lords are 1. copper-coloured. 2. glossy[18] like a flower in full bloom[19] and 3. elevated. Their toes and fingers are 4. rounded, 5. elongated, 6. compact and 7. tapering. Their veins 8. do not bulge out, and 9. are free from knots. 10. Their anklebones do not bulge out, 11. their feet are not unequal in size; they walk with stride of 12. a lion, 13. an elephant, 14. the royal goose, and 15. of a lordly bull, and 16. they walk while turning to the right and 17 elegantly. Their limbs are 18. straight, 19. well rounded, 20. smooth and 21. slender. 22. Their knee-orbs are well formed. 23. Their genitals are fully developed. 24. Their bearing is always degnified. 25. . . . ? . . . 26. They walk at an even pace; 27. their limbs are salubrious, 28. soft and 29. clean. 30. They are worthy of being looked at. 31. Their face is not large, but 32. noble. 33. Their lips are red. 34. Their countenance is perfect. 35. Their . . . are deep. Their navels are 36. deep and 37. twisted to the right. Their bodies are 38. ever youthful and 39. unimpaired (by any defects), 40. they have prominences and 41. are firm and solid. 42. All their limbs are well proportioned. 43. Their hands and feet are well formed. Their bellies are 44. round, 45. smooth and 46. unmarked, and 47. do not hang down. 48. From all sides they are beautiful to behold, 49. their habits are clean. 50. they are free from black moles. 51. Their hands are soft like cotton wool, the lines on their hands are 52. deep, 53. extensive, 54. uncurtailed and 55. crimson. 56. Their countenance is serene. 57. Their face is like the moon. Their tongue is 58. slender and 59. copper-coloured. Their voices are 60. perfect in every way, 61. sweet and beautiful. Their eyeteeth are 62. round, 63. sharp and 64. very white. 65. Their noses are prominent. 66. Their eyes are very large, 67. their eyelashes shine beautifully, their eyebrows are 68. extensive ((f. 282a)), 69. smooth, 70. with hairs of equal length and 71. glossy. 72. Their ears

[16a], [16a] There is a play on words between *samgṛhṇāti* and *saṃgṛhīta*.

[17] After having said so much about the first of the four means of conversion, the Sutra is rather silent about the other three. The explanation of the third is perfunctory, and the fourth is omitted altogether. The above passage occurs verbally also in *AdT*, but after (D). Nothing corresponds to it in the Sanskrit Mss of *P*, but in the Tibetan translation of *P* (276b1-277a4) there is a slightly fuller description which I have given on pp. 664-665.

[18] smooth, resplendent.

[19] Or : having marks like flowers, *pushpita*, not in *P*.

are large and equal in size. Their foreheads are 73. well formed and 74. broad. The hair of their heads is 75. smooth, 76. not shaggy, 77. . . . 78. and not rough, 79.-80. They have the Srivatsa sign and the Svastika (on the palms of their hands and the soles of their feet). It is with these eighty accessory marks that the Tathagata's body is endowed.

VIII 5,3. THE COGNITION OF DEFILEMENT AND PURIFICATION.

(cf. E) Moreover, Subhuti, the Bodhisattva, who courses in perfect wisdom, admonishes the Bodhisattvas as follows: 'Sons of good family, may you become skilled in the consummation of the letters! May you become skilled in one letter, in two letters, etc. *to*: in forty-two letters! May you through these forty-two letters come to a state which has moved away from everything! May you meditate on the 42 letters as contained in one letter, and may you meditate on one single letter as contained in 42 letters!' And that Bodhisattva becomes skilled in the 42 letters, and in meditating on the 42 letters as (contained) in one letter, and in meditating on one letter as containing the 42 letters. When he has developed the skill in the consummation of the letters, he becomes one who is skilled in the consummation of the letters. Just as the Tathagata, skilled in dharma(s), skilled in letters demonstrates Dharma, and demonstrates with letters a Dharma which is without them. And yet that Dharma is not quite free from the mode(?) of letters!

Subhuti: If absolutely no being can be apprehended, no dharmas and no own-being of these dharmas, on account of absolute (emptiness and the) emptiness without beginning and end, how does the Bodhisattva who courses in the six perfections, etc. *to*: in the eighty accessory marks, demonstrate Dharma to beings after he has stood in the six superknowledges born of karma result? For therein he apprehends no being nor concept of a being. From the nonapprehension of a being there is the nonapprehension of form, etc. *to*: the eighteen special Buddhadharmas. And in the nonapprehension of a being one cannot conceive of the concept of a being. How can that Bodhisattva, who courses in perfect wisdom ((f. 282b)), demonstrate Dharma to beings? May that Bodhisattva not instigate beings to nonexistent dharmas, may he not enjoin perverted views upon them! And why? Because the Bodhisattva, who courses in perfect wisdom, does not even, to begin with, apprehend an enlightenment-being, how much less the dharmas which act as wings to enlightenment!

The Lord: So it is, Subhuti, so it is, as you say. From the nonapprehension of beings should be known the inward emptiness, etc. *to*: the emptiness of the nonexistence of own-being (?), the emptiness of the skandhas, etc. *to*: the emptiness of enlightenment and of the Buddha-field. But when the Bodhisattva, who courses in perfect wisdom, has seen all these dharmas to be empty, he demonstrates Dharma in such a way that he himself (?) does not enter into (?), (these?) emptinesses. When he has seen things in such a way, and has cognized all dharmas as without covering, he does not upset any dharma, or divide any one off. But he demonstrates (the Dharma) as it really is. It is just as when the magical creation of a Tathagata, after he has conjured up countless other magical creations, enjoins the perfection of giving on some, etc. *to*: enjoins enlightenment on others. What do you think, Subhuti, has then that magical creation effected the distinction (or separation) of any dharma whatsoever?

Subhuti: No, O Lord.

The Lord: By this method you should know, Subhuti, that it is thus that the Bodhisattva who courses in perfect wisdom demonstrates Dharma to beings, establishes them in true reality and frees them from the perverted views, by way of the fact that they are neither bound nor freed. And why? ((f. 283a)) Because form, etc. is neither bound nor freed. And the fact that form, etc. is neither bound nor freed, that is not form, etc. And why? Because form is absolutely pure; and so for all conditioned and unconditioned dharmas. It is thus surely that the Bodhisattva, who courses in perfect wisdom, demonstrates Dharma to beings, but without apprehending a being. It is in the nonapprehension of all dharmas that the Bodhisattva has stood, but without taking his stand on that. He has stood in the emptiness of form, etc. without taking his stand on that. For dharmas, whether conditioned or unconditioned, do not stand anywhere. And why? Because one cannot apprehend of them an own-being in which they could be established. For the nonexistent does not stand in the nonexistent, own-being does not stand in own-being, other-being does not stand in other-being. And why? Because they all cannot be apprehended, and an (object of) nonapprehension cannot stand anywhere. It is thus that the Bodhisattva, who courses in perfect wisdom, systematically meditates on these dharmas by way of all these emptinesses and it is thus that he becomes free from guilt with regard to the Buddhas, Bodhisattvas, Pratyekabuddhas, Disciples and all holy men. And why? Because the Buddhas, etc. *to*: all holy men have understood just this Dharmahood and, when they have done so, they demonstrate Dharma to all beings and they do not stray away from the Dharmahood of all dharmas. And why? Because Dharmahood does not stray away, nor Suchness, nor the Reality limit. And why? Because they have no own-being which could stray away.

Subhuti: If that is so, is then form one thing, and the realm of Dharma another, Suchness another, and the Reality limit another? *And so for all dharmas.*

The Lord: No, Subhuti. Form, etc. is not one thing, and the realm of

Dharma another, Suchness another and the Reality limit another.

Subhuti: If that is so, how, then, O Lord, does one make definite distinctions, such as: black dharmas lead to a black karma result, i.e. to the hells, the animal world, and the world of Yama; white dharmas lead to a white karma result, i.e. to (rebirth among) gods and men; black and white dharmas lead to a black and white karma result, i.e. the experience of both happiness and unhappiness; dharmas which are neither black nor white lead to a karma result which is neither black nor white, i.e. the fruit of a Streamwinner, etc. *to*: the supreme enlightenment.

The Lord: When conventional truth has been made into the standard, the definite determination of the fruits can be described, but not by way of ultimate truth. And why? Because that Dharma is undiscriminated and incommunicable, since name and form are nonproduction, nonstopping, nondefilement, nonpurification—this is the absolute emptiness,[20] the emptiness without beginning and end.

Subhuti: If the determination of the fruit takes places on account of conventional truth and not in ultimate reality, then all the foolish common people must already have the fruit of a Streamwinner, etc. *to*: ((f. 283b)) the supreme enlightenment?

The Lord: Do, then, the common people wisely know the conventional and the ultimate truth? If they do, they will also be able to determine the various fruits, i.e. the fruit of a Streamwinner etc. *to*: the supreme enlightenment. But the foolish common people do not have the path, nor its development nor a distinctive determination of (its stages)—so how can they have a distinctive determination of its fruits! It is the holy persons who have the path and its development, and it is therefore they who have a distinctive determination of its fruits.

Subhuti: Is there, then, an attainment of the fruit as a result of the development of the path and can a fruit be attained?

The Lord: No, Subhuti, there is no attainment of the fruit as a result of the development of the path, and no fruit can be attained. In fact there can be no attainment of the fruit without one's having developed the path, and at the same time no fruit can be attained through the path. It is thus that the Bodhisattva, who courses in perfect wisdom, distinctively defines the fruit of beings, but without having cut off the share of[21] either the conditioned or the unconditioned element.

Subhuti: If that is so, then the Lord has never said that: this is, the fruit of a Streamwinner, i.e. the forsaking of the threefold fetter; this the fruit of a Once-returner, i.e. the attenuation of greed for sense pleasures and of ill will; this the fruit of a Never-returner, i.e. the forsaking

[20]So *AdT*. But Ms and *PT*: since the truth about name, the truth about form, nonproduction etc. are the absolute emptiness, etc.

[21]*bhāgaccheda*, apportioning between?

of the five lower fetters; this is Arhatship i.e. the forsaking of the five higher fetters; this is the enlightenment of a Pratyekabuddha, i.e. that whatever was doomed to originate that is now invariably doomed to stop; this is the supreme enlightenment, i.e. the forsaking of all defilements together with their residues. How can we understand the meaning of the Lord's teaching, if the distinctive determination of the fruits does not take place through cutting off the share of either conditioned or unconditioned dharmas?

The Lord: Is, then, the fruit of a Streamwinner, etc. conditioned or unconditioned?

Subhuti: It is unconditioned, O Lord, not conditioned, O Well-Gone!

The Lord: Is there, then, such a thing as the cutting off of the share with regard to an unconditioned dharma?

Subhuti: No, O Lord.

The Lord: It is thus that the Bodhisattva, who courses in perfect wisdom, demonstrates Dharma to beings without cutting off the share, on account of the inward emptiness, etc. *to* : the emptiness of own-marks. He himself does not settle down in any dharma, and others also he does not settle down anywhere, in the perfection of giving, etc. *to* : in the knowledge of all modes. Not having settled down anywhere he does not get stuck anywhere. It is as with a magical creation of a Tathagata who, when he gives a gift, does not get stuck with the fruit of the gift, and does not experience the fruit of the gift, except in so far as it is conducive to leading all beings to final Nirvana. He does not stand anywhere, not in dharmas with or without outflows, worldly or supramundane, conditioned or unconditioned. It is thus that the Bodhisattva who courses in perfect wisdom, courses in all dharmas but does not stand in any dharma nor get stuck to one. And why? Because he has well penetrated the dharma-mark of dharmas.

Chapter 74

THE EXPOSITION OF THE SAMENESS OF ALL DHARMAS

Subhuti: When has the Bodhisattva well penetrated the dharma-mark of dharmas?

The Lord: As in the case of a fictitious magical creation there is the habitual absence[1] of greed, hate, and delusion; of the skandhas ((f. 284a)) of inner and outer dharmas, of the biases and prepossessions, of dharmas with or without outflows, worldly or supramundane, conditioned or unconditioned, and of both the path and its fruit. It is thus that the dharmic principle of dharmas has been well penetrated.

Subhuti: What is the path-development of a magical creation?

The Lord: It is that path-development thanks to which he is neither defiled nor purified, and does not (actually) appear in Samsara with its five places of rebirth.

Subhuti: How does the Bodhisattva penetrate to all dharmas if they are all nonentities?

The Lord: What do you think, Subhuti, does there exist for[2] the magical creation of a Tathagata some entity thanks to which he is defiled or purified, or (actually) appears in Samsara with its five places of rebirth?

Subhuti: No, O Lord, such an entity does not exist for[3] him.

The Lord: It is thus that the dharmic principle of dharmas has been well penetrated.

Subhuti: Are, then, all the skandhas like a Tathagata's magical creations?

The Lord: They are.

Subhuti: How, then, does a Bodhisattva's manly work take place, when[4] the skandhas are[4] like a magical creation. For a magical creation there are no skandhas, no defilement and purification, and no Samsara with its five places of rebirth from which he could liberate beings.

The Lord: What do you think, Subhuti, has the Bodhisattva, when he courses in a Bodhisattva's career, apprehended any being whom he could liberate from the hells, or the animal world, or the world of Yama, or life among the men or gods?

[1]nonproceeding.

[2]*AdT*: *gaṅ yaṅ dmigs-su (!) yod.*

[3]in?

[4,4]everything is, *AdT*.

Subhuti: No, O Lord.

The Lord: So it is, Subhuti, the Bodhisattva has not apprehended any being whom he could liberate from the triple world. Because he has cognized, seen, and known all dharmas as like magical illusions and magical creations.

Subhuti: If the Bodhisattva has cognized, seen, and known all dharmas as magical illusions and magical creations, for the sake of whom, then, does he course in the six perfections, etc. *to*: in the path to enlightenment; for the sake of whom does he purify the Buddha-field and mature beings?

The Lord: If beings on their own could cognize all dharmas as being like[5] magical creations, then the Bodhisattva would not for countless aeons course for the sake of beings in the career of a Bodhisattva. But because beings on their own do not cognize all beings as[6] magical creations, therefore the Bodhisattva courses for countless aeons in the six perfections, matures beings, and purifies the Buddha-field.

Subhuti: If all dharmas are like a dream, etc. *to*: like a magical creation, whereon are beings supported, and wherefrom does the Bodhisattva, when he courses in perfect wisdom, set them free?[7]

The Lord: Beings are supported on words and signs, based on imagining that which is not. It is from these words and signs that the Bodhisattva, when he courses in perfect wisdom, sets them free.

Subhuti: What are words and what are signs?

The Lord: An adventitious designation is this, something added on, i.e. 'words'[8] or 'signs'. They are artificial designations whether they refer to the skandhas, or to 'women' or 'men', 'sons', 'daughters', 'people in the hells', 'animals', 'beings in the world of Yama', 'gods' or 'men', 'conditioned dharmas' or 'unconditioned dharmas', 'the fruit of a Streamwinner', etc. *to*: ((f. 284b)) 'full enlightenment'. In fact, mere conceptual dharmas are all these words, because they are just words. Mere words are all these conditioned things to which the foolish common people have become attached. But the Bodhisattva, who courses in perfect wisdom and is endowed with skill in means, dissuades (those beings and says to them :) 'from false imagination has all this verbosity arisen. Do not get attached to a false imagination, to a nonexistent entity which is empty in its own-being.'[9] Since all dharmas are empty—well-informed people do not settle down in them'. It is thus that the Bodhisattva, coursing in perfect wisdom, demonstrates Dharma to beings with skill in means. And what is a sign? Twofold are the signs to which

[5]dreams or, *AdT*.

[6]as note #5.

[7]*uccālayati,* lit. 'divert from'.

[8]Lit. 'name'.

[9]empty of essential nature, *AdT*.

the foolish common people have become attached. Which two? The sign of form and the sign of the formless. And what is the sign of form? Whatever form there is—whether gross or fine, whether inferior or exalted—that one seizes on these momentary dharmas as the result of a false imagination, that is called the sign of form. And what is the sign of the formless? Whatever defilement may be generated in him who has imagined something about formless dharmas after seizing on their sign, that is called the sign of the formless. Therefore the Bodhisattva, who courses in perfect wisdom, by his skill in means turns people away from that sign, makes them enter into the signless realm and establishes them therein—and that in such a way that they do not fall into a duality, (distinguishing) the sign here from the signless there. It is thus that the Bodhisattva, when he courses in perfect wisdom, by his skill in means turns beings away from the sign and establishes them in the signless realm.

Subhuti: If all dharmas are no more than this, i.e. no more than words and signs, mere concepts, arisen from imaginations—how, then, does the Bodhisattva, when he courses in perfect wisdom, himself reach distinction in wholesome dharmas, and how does he establish others in the distinctive achievement of those wholesome dharmas by which they fulfil one stage after the other, and how does he enjoin the triple vehicle upon beings?

The Lord: If the sign were an entity and not a nonentity, then this Bodhisattva, who courses in perfect wisdom, could not reach distinction in wholesome dharmas, nor could he enjoin this distinction on others. But since the sign is a nonentity, and not an entity, the Bodhisattva, when he courses in perfect wisdom, fulfils all spiritual practices by way of the signless. Having fulfilled these wholesome dharmas, ((f. 285a)) he enjoins them also on others, but by way of the signless. If there existed in dharmas a sign of a dharma even as small as the fine point of the tip of a hair, then this Bodhisattva, who courses in perfect wisdom, could not fully awake to a dharma which is signless, unrememberable, and not a proper object of attention, and he could not establish beings in Thusness and in dharmas without outflows. For all dharmas without outflows are signless, unrememberable, and not a proper object of attention. It is thus that the Bodhisattva, who courses in perfect wisdom, works the weal of all beings through dharmas without outflows.

Subhuti: If all dharmas are signless, unrememberable, not a proper object of attention, how, then, can one enumerate as follows: these are dharmas with outflows, these dharmas without outflows, these are common dharmas, these uncommon dharmas, these are Discipledharmas, these Pratyekabuddhadharmas, these Bodhisattvadharmas and these Buddhadharmas?

The Lord: What do you think, Subhuti, is the signless one thing and are the Discipledharmas, etc. *to*: the Buddhadharmas another?

Subhuti: No, O Lord.

The Lord: Is, then, the signless the same as the fruit Streamwinner, etc. *to*: the dharmas of a Buddha?

Subhuti: So it is, O Lord, so it is, O Well-Gone.

The Lord: By this method also should one know that all dharmas are (the) signless. When the Bodhisattva trains in all dharmas as signless, then he grows in wholesome dharmas, i.e. the six perfections, etc. *to*: all Buddhadharmas. And why? Because the Bodhisattva should not train in any other way, i.e. other than in dharmas which are emptiness, signless, and wishless. And why? Because in these three doors to emancipation all wholesome dharmas are contained. And here the emptiness-door to emancipation means that which is empty of own-marks; the signless door to emancipation means the departure of signs; the wishless door to emancipation means that which has not been brought about.

When he trains in these three doors to emancipation the Bodhisattva trains in the five skandhas, the twelve sense fields, the eighteen elements, the four holy truths, conditioned coproduction with its twelve links, the emptinesses, etc. *to*: the eighteen special Buddhadharmas.

Subhuti: And how does the Bodhisattva, coursing in perfect wisdom, train himself with regard to the five grasping skandhas?

The Lord:[10] Here the Bodhisattva, who courses in perfect wisdom, wisely knows form, and how form is produced and stopped, and also what is the Suchness of form. How does he wisely know form? Since it is altogether full of cracks and holes, he wisely knows form to be as unsubstantial as a mass of foam. And how ((f. 285b)) does he wisely know the production of form? Since it is said that 'form does not come from anywhere nor does it go to anywhere', he wisely knows the production of form from the fact that 'form has not come from anywhere nor gone to anywhere'. It is thus that the Bodhisattva wisely knows the production and passing away of form. And how does he wisely know the Suchness of form? Suchness is not produced or stopped, does not come or go, is not defiled or purified, does not grow or diminish—thus he wisely knows Suchness. Suchness is never false to itself, that is why it is called Suchness. It is because it does not deviate from itself that it is called Suchness. It is thus that he wisely knows the Suchness of form. And how does he wisely know feeling, its production and passing away, and its Suchness? As (floating) water bubbles (swiftly) rise and (swiftly burst and) vanish, so he wisely knows feeling to be. He wisely knows that feeling does not come from anywhere and does not go to anywhere. He wisely knows Suchness as nonfalseness.

[10]The following passage has been translated by Arthur Waley from Hsüan-tsang's *Mahāprajñāpāramitā* in my *Buddhist Texts through the Ages*. 1954, pp. 154-158.

And the same for perception, with the difference that he wisely knows it as a mirage in which absolutely no water can be apprehended. And as to the impulses he wisely knows that they are like the plantain tree in that, when you strip off one leaf-sheath after another, you cannot apprehend any core (within). And as to consciousness he wisely knows it as a fourfold army conjured up by a magician.

And how does he wisely know the elements? The eye-element is empty of the own-being of the eye-element. And so for the other seventeen elements. And how does he wisely know the sense fields? Inward dharmas are empty of inward dharmas, and outward dharmas are empty of outward dharmas. And how does he wisely know the holy truths? He wisely knows ill, knows it as a truth, knows it as the truth of the holy men. He wisely knows the truth of the holy men to be released from duality, because it has been said that 'nondual is the truth of the holy ones'. And so for the other three truths. And how does he wisely know the Suchness of ill, and the other truths? He wisely knows the Suchness of ill as just Suchness. And so for the other three truths.

And how does he wisely know conditioned coproduction?[11] He wisely knows it as neither production nor stopping, neither cut off nor eternal, neither single nor manifold, neither coming nor going away, as the appeasement of all futile discoursings, and as bliss.

Subhuti: If the Bodhisattva, who courses in perfect wisdom, wisely knows the mutually separated dharmas in this manner, would not thereby the realm of Dharma be upset?

The Lord: The realm of Dharma could be upset if outside it there were any other dharma. But outside the realm of Dharma no other dharma can be apprehended. If one could be apprehended, then there would indeed be an upsetting of the realm of Dharma. And why? No Tathagata, Bodhisattva, Pratyekabuddha or Tathagata-disciple ((f. 286a)) has ever apprehended any dharma outside the realm of Dharma. Since none has been apprehended, one does not say that 'a dharma is apprehended outside the realm of Dharma'. It is thus that the Bodhisattva who courses in perfect wisdom should train in the realm of Dharma.

Subhuti: When a Bodhisattva trains in the realm of Dharma, wherein does he become trained?

The Lord: He becomes trained in all dharmas. And why? Because all dharmas are the realm of Dharma.

Subhuti: For what reason are all dharmas the realm of Dharma?

The Lord: Whether Tathagatas do, or do not, appear—this dharmic element is established in dharmas, because there is no discrimination about it. In other words, both the conditioned and the unconditioned

[11]This is very much like Nāgārjuna's famous verse, *Madhyamikakārikā* I 1-2, which is there said to be *deśayāmāsa saṃbuddhas*. It is perhaps derived from this passage.

realm are the realm of Dharma. It is thus that the Bodhisattva, when he trains in perfect wisdom, is trained in the realm of Dharma[12] and in all dharmas as well.[12]

Subhuti: If all dharmas are the realm of Dharma, how, then, should the Bodhisattva train in the perfections, etc. *to*: in ready speech? How should he train in the path to enlightenment wherein all dharmas should be cognized in all their modes? Since in the realm of Dharma these false discriminations do not exist, may the Bodhisattva avoid coursing in the perverted views, and may he not delay himself by something which is in fact no impediment! And why? Because these false discriminations are not in the realm of Dharma. For the realm of Dharma is not the skandhas, nor is it other than them, but the skandhas are just the realm of Dharma, and the realm of Dharma is just the skandhas. And so for all dharmas.

The Lord: So it is, Subhuti, so it is, as you say: the skandhas ((f. 286b)) are just the realm of Dharma and the realm of Dharma is just the skandhas. But if the Bodhisattva who courses in perfect wisdom would see any dharma outside the realm of Dharma, then he would not be one who has set out for the supreme enlightenment. But since all dharmas are the realm of Dharma, therefore the Bodhisattva who courses in perfect wisdom, after he has (correctly) cognized all dharmas as the realm of Dharma, demonstrates the nameless all-dharmas by way of name and conventional expression, as follows: 'this is form' etc. *to*: 'this is enlightenment'.

VIII 5,4. THE TRUE CHARACTER OF (THE WORK FOR) THE WEAL OF BEINGS.

It is as if some clever magician or magician's apprentice were, with the help of some suitable material preparations[13], to exhibit manifold kinds of shapes, i.e. figures of elephants, horses or bulls, of men, women, boys and girls, of delightful parks, mansions and pleasure groves, rivers and lotus ponds. In addition he would exhibit clothes, carpets and bedding, precious flowers and garlands, as well as food and drink, and he would delight people with songs and music. Whether he gives gifts, guards morality, perfects himself in patience, exerts vigour, plays with the concentrations or develops wisdom, he delights people in these ways. He exhibits the three kinds of good families, the various kinds of gods, and also[14] Streamwinners etc. *to*: Pratyekabuddhas. And he also exhibits those Bodhisattvas who, beginning with the first thought of enlightenment, course in the six perfections on the ten stages, enter on a Bodhisattva's special way of salvation, consummate the superknowledges and play with them, mature beings, purify the Buddha-field, play with the

[12,12] So Tib.

[13] see Jaeschke p. 468 s. v. *rdzas*.

[14] + (im)material?

trances, deliverances, concentrations, and meditational achievements, or give up all their limbs, or go on the difficult pilgrimage, or achieve the powers of a Tathagata, the grounds of self-confidence, the analytical knowledges, the great friendliness or the great compassion. Or he may also exhibit the figure of a Buddha, complete in body and limbs. In reaction to this, essentially foolish beings would think this to mean: 'Ah, how well-trained that man is, what a beautiful display he has made! How he delights all these people, how he exhibits so many kinds of shapes, even including the shape of a Buddha!' And if there are among them any men who are well-informed, judicious, clever, and endowed with the ability to make suchlike examinations, they will think to themselves: 'This is a wonderful and astonishing Dharma! And yet no dharma can therein be apprehended. For this man delights this crowd of people with nonexistent dharmas'. And they do not apprehend those perceptions of beings, on the ground that those beings do indeed perceive what is actually real in what is not actually real. It is thus that the Bodhisattva does not see any dharma as outside the Dharma-element. Coursing in perfect wisdom through skill in means, he yet does not apprehend a being and has no concept of a being.

VIII 5,5. THE SIX PERFECTIONS.

He himself gives gifts and he invites others also to giving, he speaks in praise of giving, and he also speaks in praise of those other beings who give gifts, one acquiescent; etc. *to*: ((f. 287a)) he himself develops wisdom, etc.

VIII 5,6. THE BUDDHA PATH.

He himself proceeds having taken the ten wholesome paths of action upon himself, and also others he establishes in the ten wholesome paths of action, and he speaks in praise of the ten wholesome paths of action and also of those other beings who proceed having taken the ten wholesome paths of action upon themselves, one acquiescent. And so for his observance of the sabbath maintaining the first eight precepts, for his undertaking of the five precepts, his entrance into the trances, etc. *to*: his development of the eighty accessory marks (of a superman).

VIII 5,7. THE EMPTINESS OF ESSENTIAL NATURE.

If there were no Dharma-element which is the same in the beginning, end, and middle, the Bodhisattva could not, with his skill in means, indicate the Dharma-element to beings and mature them. But because there is such a Dharma-element, the Bodhisattva, coursing in perfect wisdom, indicates through his skill in means the Dharma-element to beings, courses in the course of a Bodhisattva for the sake of beings and matures beings.

Chapter 75

THE EXPOSITION OF IMPERTURBABILITY

Subhuti: If absolutely no being is apprehended, nor the concept of a being, for the sake of whom does the Bodhisattva develop perfect wisdom?

The Lord: Having made the Reality limit into a standard, a Bodhisattva courses in perfect wisdom. If the Reality limit were one thing, and the beings limit another, a Bodhisattva would not course in perfect wisdom. But since the Reality limit is not one thing, and the beings limit another, therefore the Bodhisattva courses in perfect wisdom for the sake of beings. Coursing in perfect wisdom, the Bodhisattva, without upsetting the Reality limit, establishes beings in the Reality limit.

Subhuti: If the Reality limit is the beings limit, how, then, can one establish the Reality limit in the Reality limit? ((f. 287b)) If the Reality limit were (actually) established in the Reality limit, then own-being would be (actually) established in own-being. But own-being is not established in own-being. How then does the Bodhisattva, coursing in perfect wisdom, establish beings in the Reality limit?

The Lord: The Reality limit is not established in the Reality limit, nor own-being in own-being. Nevertheless the Bodhisattva through his skill in means establishes (the) beings (limit) in the Reality limit without upsetting the Reality limit. And yet, the Reality limit is not one thing and the beings limit another. In fact they are not two nor divided.

Subhuti: What is the skill in means of the Bodhisattva, endowed with which he establishes, coursing in perfect wisdom, beings in the Reality limit, but without upsetting the Reality limit?

The Lord: Here the Bodhisattva, coursing in perfect wisdom, from the first thought of enlightenment onwards establishes beings in giving. When he has done so he considers that gift at the beginning, end, and middle. Just as the gift is empty at the beginning, end, and middle, so is its fruit, and so are the donor and recipient. In this way all these objects do not really exist in the Reality limit. Do not imagine that the gift is one thing, its fruit another, the donor another, and the recipient another! If you do not imagine these things, then your gift will become deathless and terminate in the fruit of deathlessness. But do not through this gift take hold of any of the skandhas! And why? Because this gift is empty of a gift, its fruit is empty of a fruit, and also the donor is empty of a donor and the recipient empty of a recipient. For in emptiness no gift can be apprehended nor its fruit, no donor, and no recipient. And why? Because absolutely these dharmas are empty in their own-being.—Moreover the Bodhisattva, coursing in perfect wisdom, establishes beings through his skill in means in morality. Come here, son of good family, having forsaken the taking of life, do you become one who abstains from the taking of life! etc. *to*: having forsaken wrong views do you become one who abstains from wrong views! There exists in these dharmas no such own-being as you have imagined. Investigate therefore the dharmic facts when you rob living beings of life or (consider that) by which you rob them of their life![1] And this should be done up to wrong views. Endowed with this skill in means the Bodhisattva, who courses in perfect wisdom, matures beings. He describes the fruit of that gift or morality, (but he knows that) they are both empty in their own-being. Having known these fruits to be empty, he does not settle down in them and he produces first nondistraction and then wisdom. Through that wisdom he cuts of all unwholesome tendencies and all obsessions, and then enters the realm of Nirvana which leaves nothing behind—but by way of worldly convention and not in ultimate reality. And why? Because in emptiness no dharma can be apprehended which enters final Nirvana or which is made to enter it. For in fact absolute emptiness is his final Nirvana. ((f. 288a))—Moreover the Bodhisattva, on having seen other beings and persons who have angry and hostile thoughts, instructs and admonishes them as follows: 'Come here, son of good family, perfect yourself in patience, develop patience, and become a tolerant person! He who has ill will, that which makes you have ill will, that towards which you have ill will, all these dharmas are empty of an essential nature. Do therefore investigate him who has ill will, him towards whom he has ill will and that which causes him to have ill will, (and you will find that) all these dharmas are empty of an essential nature. But the emptiness of essential nature is never not emptiness. It has not been made by the Tathagatas, nor by the Pratyekabuddhas, or Disciples, or Bodhisattvas, or gods, Nagas etc. *to*: the gods of the station of neither perception nor non-perception. Do therefore investigate him who feels ill will, him toward whom you feel ill will, or that whereby you feel ill will, (and you will find that) all these dharmas are empty of an essential nature. For emptiness does not feel ill will toward anyone.' It is thus that a Bodhisattva, coursing in perfect wisdom, through his skill in means enjoins the emptiness of essential nature upon beings, both as regards the cause and as regards the fruit. As a result he encourages them to gradually win the supreme enlightenment and establishes them in it—and that again by way of worldly convention and not in ultimate reality. And why? Because in the emptiness of essential nature there is no one who could attain, nothing

[1]The construction of this sentence is not very clear.

through which he could attain, and not anything which he could attain. This is the Reality limit, the emptiness of essential nature, wherein the Bodhisattva courses in perfect wisdom for the sake of beings, although therein he apprehends no being or the concept of a being. And why? Because all dharmas have nothing to do with 'beings'.—Moreover the Bodhisattva who courses in perfect wisdom sees beings of inferior vigour and full of sloth, and with his skill in means he encourages them to physical and mental vigour: 'In the emptiness of essential nature, O son of good family, there exists no losing of heart on the part of any dharma. That about which he might lose heart, or whereby he would lose heart, or he who would lose heart, all these dharmas do not stray away from the emptiness of essential nature. Do generate mental and physical vigour, avoid indolence and exert yourself in wholesome dharmas, whether by way of giving, etc. *to* : by way of all Buddhadharmas! All those dharmas, O son of good family, you should see as unobstructed, because of their emptiness. For in unobstructed dharmas there exists no losing of heart on the part of any dharma. 'It is thus that the Bodhisattva, coursing in perfect wisdom, by his skill in means encourages beings to the emptiness of essential nature, settles, and establishes them in it. And he establishes them in such a way that no duality exists therein. And why? Because the emptiness of essential nature is not two nor divided. And a nondual dharma cannot lose heart anywhere. Moreover the Bodhisattva who courses in perfect wisdom instructs and admonishes beings in vigour by way of the emptiness of essential nature: 'Come here, son of good family, exert vigour, whether by way of giving, etc. *to* : by way of the eighteen special Buddhadharmas! But do not attend to these dharmas from duality or from nonduality! And why? ((f. 288b)) Because these dharmas are the emptiness of essential nature, and that should not be attended to from either duality or nonduality.' It is thus that the Bodhisattva, who courses in perfect wisdom, and who through his skill in means courses on the pilgrimage of a Bodhisattva, matures beings. Having done so, he gradually[2] establishes them in the fruit of a Streamwinner, etc. *to* : in the supreme enlightenment.—Moreover the Bodhisattva, who courses in perfect wisdom, through his skill in means instructs and admonishes beings whose thought is distracted: 'Come here, son of good family, and develop transic concentration! May you not become one who has notions about either distraction or concentration! And why? Because these dharmas are the emptiness of essential nature. And in the emptiness of essential nature no dharma can be apprehended which could either be distracted or become onepointed. When you have stood in this transic concentration, whatever wholesome root you may bring about, by body, voice, or mind, whether by your giving of gifts, etc. *to* :

[2]Successively; step by step.

by your purification of the Buddha-field, all these wholesome dharmas will become manifest in you with little trouble when you course in the emptiness of essential nature.' It is thus that the Bodhisattva, who courses in perfect wisdom, works the weal of beings through his skill in means ever after he has had his first thought of enlightenment. He always performs good works and constantly seeks for what is wholesome while working the weal of beings. He constantly passes on from Buddha-field to Buddha-field, and there honours the Buddhas and Lords. And the Dharma which he hears from those Buddhas and Lords, that he never forgets again until he has won the supreme enlightenment, even after he has passed beyond this present birth. He is constantly and always in possession of the dharanis, and his faculties are (always) complete,[3] whether they be physical, vocal, or mental. And why? Because he has constantly and always well developed the knowledge of all modes, and in consequence all the paths become well developed, i.e. the paths of the Disciples, Pratyekabuddhas, and Bodhisattvas. The superknowledges of that Bodhisattva will constantly and always be used to benefit others, because they are never lost. Having stood in these superknowledges which result from the maturation of deeds, he works the weal of beings, and does not avoid Samsara with its five places of rebirth. It is thus that the Bodhisattva, who courses in perfect wisdom, having stood in the emptiness of essential nature, works the weal of beings through his skill in means.—When he has well developed that perfection of wisdom, he instructs and admonishes beings as follows: 'Come here, son of good family, whatever deeds you may do, by body, voice, or mind, all that you should consider as empty of essential original nature, and then they will lead to a deathless fruit and terminate in the deathless. For in the emptiness of essential original nature one cannot apprehend any dharma which one could destroy or diminish. ((f. 289a)) And why? Because the emptiness of essential nature cannot be diminished, nor can any dharma be diminished in the emptiness of essential nature. And why? Because the emptiness of essential nature is neither an existent nor a nonexistent. How can anything be diminished if all dharmas have nonexistence for own-being?' It is thus that the Bodhisattva who courses in perfect wisdom instructs and admonishes beings through his skill in means. And when he instructs and admonishes them in such a manner, he never ceases to do good works. Constantly and always he himself observes the ten wholesome paths of action, and also others he encourages to observe them; etc. *to*: he himself produces the path to the supreme enlightenment, and also others he instructs in that path, admonishes them (to tread it), exhorts them to it, disciplines them, and establishes them in it. It is thus that the Bodhisattva, when he courses in perfect

[3]Lit. nondefective.

wisdom, through his skill in means is never one who does no deeds.

Subhuti: If all dharmas are empty of essential nature, and if in the emptiness of essential nature no being can be apprehended, no dharma and no non-dharma,[4] how does the Bodhisattva set out for[5] the knowledge of all modes?

The Lord: So it is, Subhuti, as you say: Empty of essential nature are all dharmas, and in the emptiness of essential nature no being can be apprehended, no dharma and no non-dharma.[6] If, however, all dharmas were not empty of essential nature, then the Bodhisattva could not be established[7] in the emptiness of essential nature. Nor could he, on having won full enlightenment, demonstrate dharmas as empty of essential nature. The skandhas are (actually) empty of essential nature. Therefore the Bodhisattva, when he courses in perfect wisdom, demonstrates Dharma to the effect that the five skandhas are empty of essential nature, etc. *to*: that the forsaking of all defilements together with their residues is empty of essential nature. ((f. 289b)) If again the inward emptiness[8] were not empty of essential nature, then the Bodhisattva would not demonstrate Dharma to the effect that all dharmas are empty of essential nature. And so for the other kinds of emptiness. Because if he did, the emptiness of essential nature would have been destroyed; but the emptiness of essential nature cannot be destroyed, nor does it overtower all change,[9] nor again does it depart (at some future time). And why? Because it does not stand in any spot or place; it does not come from anywhere nor does it go to anywhere. That is the stability of Dharma in which one can apprehend no accumulation or removal of any dharma, no diminution or growth, no production or stopping, no defilement or purification. And that is the essential nature of dharmas in which the Bodhisattvas have stood when they set out for the supreme enlightenment. And yet they do not review the setting out of any dharma, nor its not-setting-out. Because no dharma has set out or has stood (anywhere). This is the dharmic stability of dharmas. Therefore the Bodhisattva, who courses in perfect wisdom and who has seen all dharmas as empty of essential nature, does not turn back on the supreme enlightenment. And why? Because, reviewing no obstruction to any dharma, he reviews all dharmas as unobstructed. So how can he have doubts about the supreme enlightenment when in this emptiness of essential nature no being can be apprehended, etc. *to*: so one should consider (all) inward and outward dharmas, up to the eighty accessory marks.

[4]*Ti*: Path

[5]*saṃpratiṣthate*

[6]*Ti*: Path.

[7]*pratitiṣṭhet*

[8]or: emptiness of the subject, at *P* 195.

[9]*na kūṭastho bhavati* = 'unmoved' at *P* 195.

VIII 5,8. THE NONDUALITY OF DHARMAS.

Just as if the fictitious magical creation of a Tathagata were to demonstrate the Dharma to another fictitious magical creation—be it a monk or a nun, a layman or a laywoman—continuously for endless aeons—what do you think, Subhuti, would those fictitious magical creations be capable of attaining the fruit of a Streamwinner, etc. *to* : the supreme enlightenment?

Subhuti : No, O Lord. And why? Because they would have no objective basis (for that).

The Lord : So it is, Subhuti, so it is. When all dharmas have no objective basis,[10] what is that being whom the Bodhisattva could exhort to (win) the fruit of a Streamwinner, etc. *to* : the supreme enlightenment? So all that he actually does is to exhort people who are enveloped in perverted views and exhort them to nonperversion and establish them in it. And that perversion is in any case just a nonperversion, because it has issued from (nothing but) thought-constructions. For nonperversion is free from all discriminations. Where there is no perversion there is no self, no being, etc. *to* : no enlightenment. And where there is no form, etc. *to* : no enlightenment, that is the emptiness of essential nature, dwelling in which the Bodhisattva, coursing in perfect wisdom, frees beings subject to the perversions from the notion of a being, from notions about things with and without form, etc. *to* : from all dharmas with outflows. As to the ((f. 290) dharmas without outflows, i.e. the four applications of mindfulness, etc. *to* : the eighteen special Buddhadharmas, they also do not exist therein such as they are in ultimate reality. The Unconditioned, Nonproduction, Nonexistence, Nonmanifestation, that is the emptiness of essential nature, that is the enlightenment of the Buddhas and Lords, in which there is no being, etc. *to* : in which there are not the eighty accessory marks. For the Bodhisattva does not by means of the path set out for the supreme enlightenment except for the sake of the full comprehension of the emptiness of essential nature. And that emptiness of essential nature is an emptiness of essential nature at the beginning, at the end, and in the middle, and it is never not the emptiness of essential nature. Therefore the Bodhisattva, who courses in the perfections which are the emptiness of essential nature, courses in the knowledge of the modes of the path in order to free from all notions those beings who have formed the notion of a being. When he courses in the knowledge of the modes of the path he courses in all the paths, i.e. that of the Disciples, Pratyekabuddhas, and Bodhisattvas. And that Bodhisattva, after he has fulfilled all the paths, matured beings, purified the Buddha-field and sustained himself on the factors which make for a long lifespan, fully knows the supreme enlightenment. He does not cut short the guide of the

[10] =are nonentities.

Buddhas, i.e. the emptiness of essential nature. And this emptiness of essential nature is the Buddha-guide of the Buddhas and Lords who have been in the past period, of those who will be in the future period, and also of those who just at present in the world systems in the ten directions stand, hold, and maintain themselves. And apart from this emptiness of essential nature no manifestation in the world of the Buddhas and Lords takes place. It is in their presence that the Bodhisattva should course in the perfections which are the emptiness of essential nature, in such a way that he does not lose the knowledge of all modes.

Subhuti: It is wonderful, O Lord, that the Bodhisattvas should course in dharmas which are all empty of essential nature, and yet do not upset this emptiness of essential nature (by assuming that) form is one thing and the emptiness of essential nature another. And so up to enlightenment. Form is just the emptiness of essential nature, just the emptiness of essential nature is form. And so up to enlightenment.

The Lord: If form, etc. were one thing, and the emptiness of essential nature another, and if form etc. were not empty of essential nature, then the Bodhisattva could not know the supreme enlightenment. ((f. 290b)) But it is because form, etc. *to*: enlightenment are empty of essential nature that the Bodhisattva, having known all dharmas as without essential nature, knows the supreme enlightenment. And why? Because therein (i.e. in the emptiness of original nature) no dharma is destroyed, none overtowers all change, and none departs (at some future time), except for the fact that the world with its gods, Maras and Brahmas[11] deludes itself into thinking that 'this is form, I am form, mine is form, etc. *to*: this is consciousness, I am consciousness, mine is consciousness.[11]' Having settled down in form, etc. (these beings) course in I-making and Mine-making, and as a result they settle down in inward and outward entities. Having settled down in them they will, upon rebirth, grasp in the sense fields[12] at the five skandhas. They are not such as are set free from birth, old age, death, sorrow, lamentation, sadness, and despair, nor from Samsara with its five places of rebirth. Therefore the Bodhisattva, coursing in the perfections which are the emptiness of essential nature, does not upset form, etc. (by assuming that it is) empty or not empty. And why? Because the emptiness of form, etc. does not upset form, etc. (by assuming that) this is form, etc., this is the emptiness of form, etc. Just as space does not upset space, as inward space does not upset outward space and as outward space does not upset inward space, just so form, etc. does not upset emptiness, nor does emptiness upset form, etc. And why? Because they have no own-being which could (be)

[11]*P*, *AdT*: with its sramanas and brahmanas does not wisely know form, etc. as it really is, and in consequence the foolish common people settle down in form, etc.

[12]i.e. at the 5th stage of conditioned coproduction.

upset, (by assuming that) this is form, etc., and this is emptiness.

Subhuti: If all dharmas are (one vast) undifferentiatedness, how can the Bodhisattva, after he has set out for the supreme enlightenment, ever know that he fully knows it? For enlightenment causes no divisions, nor can anyone who causes divisions fully know the supreme enlightenment.

The Lord: So it is, Subhuti, so it is. No one who courses in duality can have enlightenment, nor does enlightenment cause divisions. For enlightenment is not two nor divided. The enlightenment of a Bodhisattva does not course in such divisive concepts as 'enlightenment' or 'enlightenment-being'. And that enlightenment of a Bodhisattva does not course in form, etc. *to*: enlightenment. And why? Enlightenment knows nothing of 'I' or 'mine', as in 'I shall course in form, mine is form', etc. *to*: 'I shall course in enlightenment, mine is enlightenment'. Nor does the enlightenment of a Bodhisattva course in taking up or in not taking up.

Subhuti: If a Bodhisattva's enlightenment does not course in taking up or in not taking up, wherein, then, does it course?

The Lord: What do you think, Subhuti, does the enlightenment of a Tathagata's magical creation course in taking up or in not taking up?

Subhuti: No, it does not, O Lord!

The Lord: What do you think, Subhuti, does the intellect of an Arhat, who is dreaming, course in taking up or in not taking up?

Subhuti: No, it does not, O Lord. On the other hand, since absolutely the Arhat is not asleep, how could his intellect during his sleep[13] course in taking up or in not taking up?

The Lord: It is just so that a Bodhisattva's enlightenment does not course in taking up or in not taking up.

Subhuti: If a Bodhisattva does not course in taking up or in not taking up, nor in form, etc. *to*: the knowledge of all modes, is it not so that ((f. 291a)) the Bodhisattva, having coursed in the ten stages and having stood in the six perfections, etc. *to*: the five superknowledges, purifies the Buddha-field, matures beings, and fully knows the knowledge of all modes? For it is not possible to fully know the supreme enlightenment without having stood on the ten stages, or in the six perfections, etc. *to*: in the five superknowledges, and without having entered a Bodhisattva's special way of salvation, having purified the Buddha-field, and having matured beings.

The Lord: So it is, Subhuti, so it is, as you say. It is not possible to fully know the knowledge of all modes without having fulfilled the ten stages, the six perfections, etc. *to*: the five superknowledges, and without having fulfilled the condition of being undeluded and of always dwelling

[13]dreams.

in evenmindedness. But when one has stood in the essential nature of form, etc. *to* : enlightenment, then one is able to attain the knowledge of all modes. And that essential nature is quite calm, and it does not effect with regard to any dharma an accumulation or removal, a production or stopping, a defilement or purification, an attainment or a reunion.

VIII 5,9. THE COGNITION (OF DHARMAS AS MERELY) CONVENTIONAL SYMBOLS.

It is therefore on account of what is dharmically a concept due to worldly convention that the Bodhisattva fully knows the supreme enlightenment. But in ultimate reality there is not anything that is form, etc. *to* : enlightenment, and there is no one who courses in enlightenment. All these dharmas have been conceived on account of convention, and not by way of ultimate reality. And in consequence that Bodhisattva who, from the first thought of enlightenment onwards, courses towards enlightenment does not apprehend those thoughts, as well as no beings or enlightenment, no Buddha or Bodhisattva. What do you think, Subhuti, at the time when Subhuti had forsaken the view of individuality, had acquired (the five cardinal) virtues, had attained the unimpeded concentration, or the fruit of a Streamwinner, etc. *to* : of Arhatship, had on that occasion a dream been apprehended, or a thought, or a path or a fruit?

Subhuti: No, O Lord.

The Lord: Had you, then, Subhuti, attained Arhatship when you announced that you had won the final saving gnosis?

Subhuti: Yes, by way of worldly convention.

The Lord: So it is, Subhuti. Through worldly convention has the Bodhisattva been conceived, and so has form, etc. *to* : the knowledge of all modes. But the Bodhisattva has not apprehended any dharma, of which he could effect an accumulation or removal, a benefit or harm—on account of the essential nature of dharma(s). And that dharmic nature of dharmas has not been apprehended, how much less could one apprehend the first thought of enlightenment, etc. *to*: the tenth stage, etc. *to* : the Buddhadharmas. That cannot possibly be. It is thus that the Bodhisattva works the weal of beings ((f. 291b)) after he has coursed in the supreme enlightenment and fully known it.

Chapter 76

THE ARMOUR (PUT ON) FOR THE SAKE OF MATURING BEINGS

VIII 5,10. The cognition which takes nothing as a basis.

Subhuti: If, O Lord, a Bodhisattva, coursing in the six perfections, etc. *to*: in the eighteen special Buddhadharmas, as well as in the fourteen kinds of emptiness, having fulfilled the enlightenment-path, is incapable of fully knowing the supreme enlightenment, how, then, does a Bodhisattva fully know the supreme enlightenment?

The Lord: When a Bodhisattva, coursing in perfect wisdom, courses through his skill in means in the perfection of giving, without apprehending a gift, donor, or recipient, and without coursing in any dharmas other than these, then he finds the path to enlightenment. It is thus that a Bodhisattva, who courses in perfect wisdom, will through his skill in means know the supreme enlightenment. And likewise the Bodhisattva will find the path to enlightenment if, coursing in perfect wisdom, he courses in the perfection of morality, but does not apprehend morality, or someone who observes morality, and also does not course in dharmas other than these. And likewise if he courses in the perfection of patience, but does not apprehend patience or someone who is patient, and also does not course in dharmas other than these. And so for the remaining three perfections, etc. *to*: up to the eighteen special Buddhadharmas.

Śāriputra: How does the Bodhisattva, when he courses in perfect wisdom, put forth an effort?

The Lord: Here the Bodhisattva, when he courses in perfect wisdom, through his skill in means ((f. 292a)) does not conjoin form, etc. nor disjoin it. And why? Because form, etc. has no own-being which he could conjoin or disjoin.

Śāriputra: If there exists no own-being of any dharma which one could conjoin or disjoin, how does the consummation of perfect wisdom take place, in which the Bodhisattva should train? For without having trained in perfect wisdom a Bodhisattva is unable to fully know the supreme enlightenment.

The Lord: So it is, Śāriputra, so it is, as you say. Without having trained in perfect wisdom a Bodhisattva is unable to fully know the supreme enlightenment. But it can be done through skill in means, though not without it. If the Bodhisattva, who courses in perfect wisdom, would apprehend the own-being of any dharma then he might grasp at it. Since, however, he does not apprehend it, how can he grasp at it as 'this is the perfection of wisdom', etc. *to* : even a Bodhisattva he does not apprehend, how can he grasp at him! Ungraspable are the perfection of wisdom, etc. *to* : the Buddhadharmas. This perfection is an ungraspable perfection, i.e. the perfection of wisdom. In it the Bodhisattva should train, and when he does so he will not apprehend even the training, how much less enlightenment, or the perfection of wisdom, or the dharmas of Bodhisattvas, Buddhas, Pratyekabuddhas, Disciples, or foolish common people. And why? Because there exists no own-being of any dharma whatsoever. When thus all dharmas have no own-being, what is a common person, what a Streamwinner, etc. *to*: what a Tathagata? When these persons cannot be apprehended, then wherefrom can these dharmas become manifest by which one could define that this is a common person, etc. *to* : this is a Tathagata?

Śāriputra: When all dharmas are nonentities, how should one interpret the canonical text which says that this is a common person, etc. *to* : this is a Tathagata?

The Lord: Is form, etc. an entity or something truly existent in the way in which the foolish common people have settled down in it?

Śāriputra: No, O Lord, except by way of perverted views. ((f. 292b)).

The Lord: So it is, Śāriputra, so it is. It is by way of perversion that beings imagine dharmas which are nonentities to be existents. It is because of this that a Bodhisattva, who courses in perfect wisdom and who sees, through this skill in means, all dharmas as nonentities, sets out for the supreme enlightenment.

VIII 5,11. THE MATURING OF BEINGS.

Śāriputra: What is the skill in means of the Bodhisattva by which, seeing all dharmas as nonentities, he sets out for the supreme enlightenment?

The Lord: Here the Bodhisattva, who courses in perfect wisdom, does not review any dharma as an entity by which he could be frustrated, with the result that he would crouch, lose heart, and become indolent. But because all dharmas are nonentities, without a living soul, devoid of a living soul, with nonexistence for their own-being, empty of essential nature and empty of own-marks, it is only through utter confusion that beings have adhered to what they call the 'skandhas', 'elements', or 'sense fields'. Therefore the Bodhisattva, who beholds all dharmas as having nonexistence for their own-being, as empty of essential nature, and as empty of own-marks, courses in perfect wisdom, sustains himself on a personality, which is like a magical illusion or like space, and demonstrates Dharma to beings. To stingy beings he preaches a sermon on giving, to the immoral a sermon on morality, etc. *to* : to the stupid he preaches a sermon on wisdom. And when those beings have become established in giving, etc. *to* : in the perfection of wisdom, then he finally preaches to them a sermon which is holy, leading to going forth and to penetration, and by which they attain the fruit of a Streamwinner, etc. *to* : the knowledge of all modes.

Śāriputra : How, then, does the Bodhisattva, who courses in perfect wisdom, become one who leans on a basis when he enjoins beings who are not and do not exist in giving, etc. *to* : in wisdom, and when he finally preaches a sermon which is holy and leads to going forth, by which they attain the fruit of a Streamwinner, etc. *to* : the knowledge of all modes?

The Lord: The Bodhisattva who courses in the perfection of wisdom has, of course, no basis at all. And why? Because he apprehends no beings whatsoever, except that he speaks of them by way of conventional language and agreed symbols. And thus the Bodhisattva demonstrates Dharma to beings after he has stood in the two truths, i.e. the conventional and the ultimate truth. For when he has considered both truths, he apprehends no being and has no concept of a being. It is, on the contrary, through his skill in means that the Bodhisattva, coursing in perfect wisdom, demonstrates Dharma to beings. In consequence, those beings in this very life do not apprehend a self, how much less that which they will attain, or that by which they will attain. It is thus that the Bodhisattva ((f. 293a)), who courses in perfect wisdom, demonstrates Dharma to beings through skill in means.

Śāriputra : A great product, indeed, O Lord, is the Bodhisattva, the great being! For he does not apprehend of any dharma whatsoever the singleness or manifoldness, or even the separateness. And he is armed with such an armour that he does not (actually) appear in the world of sense desire, the world of form, or the formless world, neither in the conditioned or the unconditioned world. He liberates beings from the triple world and yet he apprehends no beings or concept of a being. Where beings are not conceived they are neither bound nor freed, and they can undergo neither defilement nor purification, and no differentiation between the places of rebirth can therefore be conceived. In the absence of a differentiation between the places of rebirth there is also no karma and no defilement—how can there be a karma result by which selves and beings could (actually) appear in Samsara with its five places of rebirth?

The Lord: So it is, Subhuti, so it is, as you have said. If a being had existed in the past, and later on had not existed, that would be a fault. And it would likewise be a fault if the Bodhisattva or Tathagata had been an existent in the past and later on a nonexistent, and the same applies to Samsara with its five places of rebirth. But because, whether Tathagatas are produced or not, established is this Dharmahood of dharmas, their Suchness and Nonfalseness, wherein there is no self, being, living soul, person, doer, or agent;—how can there be the skandhas! And when those dharmas are not, how can there be that Samsara with its five places of rebirth from which beings should be liberated? But because these dharmas are empty of own-being, therefore the Bodhisattva, having listened to the Buddhas and Lords of the past, firmly sets out for the supreme enlightenment—though there is not therein any dharma which you could apprehend, or on which, after apprehending it, you could base your resolve, or in which beings have settled down—except by way of perversion. It is thus that the Bodhisattva is armed with the great armour which enables him not to turn back on the supreme enlightenment: 'Not should I not fully know the supreme enlightenment! In fact I should fully know it! Thereafter I shall work the weal of beings and thereby liberate them from the perversions!' It is as if a person who has been conjured up by a magician were to conjure up a vast number of living beings and refresh them with exquisite food and drinks, and would then cry out in triumph, 'Much merit have I begotten, much merit have I begotten!' What do you think, Sariputra, would in this case anybody have been fed or refreshed?

Śāriputra: No, O Lord.

The Lord: Just so the Bodhisattva, from the first thought of enlightenment onwards, coursing in the six perfections, etc. *to*: the eighteen special Buddhadharmas, ((f. 293b)) fulfils the path to enlightenment, purifies the Buddha-field and matures beings, and yet he does not apprehend any being[1] which he would discipline after having apprehended it.

VIII 5,12. THE PATH OF A BODHISATTVA.

Subhuti: What is the enlightenment-path of a Bodhisattva, coursing in which he should mature beings and purify the Buddha-field?

The Lord: Here the Bodhisattva, from the first thought of enlightenment onwards, courses in the six perfections, etc. *to*: in the eighteen special Buddhadharmas, and both matures beings and purifies the Buddha-field.

Subhuti: And how does he mature beings when he courses in the perfection of giving?

The Lord: Here the Bodhisattva gives gifts to beings, and thereupon instructs and admonishes them as follows: 'Here, son of good family, do not acquisitively grasp at the gift! May you not, seized by acquisitiveness with regard to the gift, reproduce your personality in such a way that in due course you will experience many ills! For here, in ultimate reality, there is no gift or its fruit, there is no donor or recipient. All these dharmas are empty of essential nature, and a dharma which is

[1]as a dharmic fact.

empty of essential nature cannot seize upon a dharma. For the emptiness of essential nature is ungraspable.' It is thus that a Bodhisattva, coursing in the perfection of giving, gives gifts to beings, but without apprehending a gift, donor, or recipient. A perfection without a basis is that, i.e. the perfection of giving. When he does not make a basis of these dharmas, he establishes beings in the fruit of a Streamwinner, etc. *to*: he enjoins the supreme enlightenment upon beings. It is thus that the Bodhisattva, coursing in perfect wisdom, matures beings. He himself gives gifts and others also he encourages to give gifts; he speaks in praise of giving, and of those others also who give gifts he speaks in praise, one acquiescent. In consequence the Bodhisattva, who has given great gifts in this manner, is reborn in good families, he becomes the king of a fort or a universal ruler, or he acquires universal kingship. He then wins over those beings by means of the four means of conversion. Which four? Namely, giving, kind words, helpfulness, and consistency between words and deeds. When he has won over beings by his gifts he gradually[2] establishes them in morality, etc., in the concentrations on emptiness, the signless, and the wishless, he enters on the certainty that he will win salvation by the methods appropriate to the Disciples, etc. *to*: he makes them attain Arhatship and the enlightenment of a Pratyekabuddha, and incites them to win the supreme enlightenment. 'Look here, you people, the supreme enlightenment is easy to know! In it no dharma exists by way of own-being, nor any beings except by way of the perverted views. Therefore cut yourselves off from seizing upon all the perverted views! ((f. 294a)) Free yourselves from Samsara, and free others as well! In this way you will work a great weal for yourselves, and also enjoin a great weal upon others!' It is thus that the Bodhisattva should course in the perfection of giving and as a result he will not, from the first thought of enlightenment onwards, ever fall again into a bad rebirth, nor will he ever fail to achieve universal kingship. And why? Just as the seed so is the fruit. When petitioners come again and again to that universal monarch, he thinks to himself: 'I have taken hold of universal kingship for no other reason than to benefit beings.' And he says: 'Whatever you may want, it will be given to you. It is yours and not mine. I have no desire even for this inward[3] body, how much less for anything else! I have laid hold of Samsara for no other reason than to benefit all beings.' Whereas he has no desire for Samsara he feels compassion and fulfils the great compassion, which enables him to work the weal of beings. And he does not apprehend those beings as fully real, but refers to them only as notions, agreed symbols, and conventional expressions. But this conventional expression is like an echo and should be known as incommuni-

[2]successively.

[3]This is Buddhist jargon for 'this, my own body'.

cable. It is thus that a Bodhisattva should course in the perfection of giving, i.e. in such a way that there is nothing that he has not abandoned to beings—not even his own flesh, how much less those outward services by which beings should be freed from Samsara.

Subhuti: And what are these services?

The Lord: The six perfections, etc. *to*: the eighteen special Buddhadharmas are the services which help beings to get free from Samsara.—Moreover the Bodhisattva who has stood in the perfection of giving and who gives gifts should then speak as follows: 'May you guard your morality! I will cause you to have an abundance of food, drinks, etc. *to*: anything else that may be useful to you. For it is through your deficiency in these things that you do immoral deeds. That is why I will cause you to have an abundance of food, drinks, etc. *to*: the seven treasures, and in consequence you will, having stood in moral restraint, gradually put an end to ill through the three vehicles, i.e. the vehicle of the Disciples, the vehicle of the Pratyekabuddhas, and the cognition of the knowledge of all modes'. It is thus that the Bodhisattva, who has stood in the perfection of giving, wins beings over through the perfection of morality.—Moreover the Bodhisattva when he has stood in the perfection of giving, speaks as follows to those beings who become enraged or who feel ill will: 'For what reason do you, sons of good family, feel ill will? If the lack of anything makes you feel ill will, then you can get it from me. I will bring about for you an abundance of food, drinks, etc. *to*: anything that might be useful to you, so that you may not become angry ((f. 294b)) or feel ill will'. In this way the Bodhisattva, who has stood in the perfection of giving, enjoins patience on beings: 'There is nowhere any existent or anything substantial from which your wrath is produced. An unreal fancy is this wrath. No real entity corresponds to it, nor is there a real entity which offends you, makes you feel anger or ill will, or which makes you belabour others with sticks or swords, or rob one another of life. When you have got angry as a result of an unfounded imagination, you will be hurled into the hells, the animal world, or the world of Yama, or any other place of bad rebirth where you will experience painful feelings—intense, harsh, and bitter. Do not, O you people, for the sake of dharmas which are nonentities acquire a karma which precludes the acquisition of a human rebirth, how much more so that of Buddhahood. In fact, hard to get, Sir, is Buddhahood, hard to get is the acquisition of a human birth. May you not be estranged from these timely rebirths, may you not be filled with doubts!' In consequence the Bodhisattva perfects himself in patience, and enjoins patience also on others; he speaks in praise of patience, and also of those others who develop patience, one acquiescent. Thereupon, having enjoined patience on those beings, having established them in patience, he leads them step by step to final

Nirvana through the three vehicles. It is thus that the Bodhisattva, when he has stood in the perfection of giving, wins beings over to the perfection of patience.—And how does the Bodhisattva, coursing in the perfection of giving, enjoin the perfection of vigour on beings? Here the Bodhisattva, who has known of beings who are indolent, will say to them: 'For what reason have you become so indolent?' And they will reply, 'because of the deficiency of the necessary conditions'. But the Bodhisattva, who courses in the perfection of giving, will say to them: 'I will surely provide you with all the necessary conditions, be they giving, or morality, or patience, or whatever else is necessary for you to exert vigour'. In consequence through the services of the Bodhisattva those beings exert vigour, physical or mental, and through that physical and mental vigour they fulfil all wholesome dharmas; through them again they develop the holy dharmas without outflows, and as a result they will attain the fruit of a Streamwinner, etc. *to*: they will fully know the supreme enlightenment. It is thus that the Bodhisattva, who has stood in the perfection of giving, wins beings over to the perfection of vigour.—And how does the Bodhisattva who courses in the perfection of giving enjoin the perfection of meditation on beings? Here the Bodhisattva, who has seen beings who are distracted in their thoughts, admonishes them as follows: 'How is it, O beings, that you do not enter on the trances?' And they reply to him, 'because of the deficiency in the necessary conditions'. But the Bodhisattva then says to them: 'I, my dear people, will provide you with the necessary conditions, which will enable you to have no discursive thoughts (concerning) either inward or outward'. Thereupon the Bodhisattva will provide these beings with the conditions which enable them to have no discursive thoughts. And these beings with their discursive thoughts cut off, will enter on the four trances and the four Unlimited. ((f. 295a)) Through those trances they will come to develop the eightfold path, and as a result will gradually reach final Nirvana through the three vehicles. And some of them will not lose the path of enlightenment until they win the supreme enlightenment. It is thus that the Bodhisattva, who has stood in the perfection of giving, wins beings over to the perfection of meditation.—And how does the Bodhisattva who courses in the perfection of giving win beings over to the perfection of wisdom? Here the Bodhisattva says to them: 'How is it, O beings, that you do not develop the perfection of wisdom?' And they will reply, 'because of the deficiency in the necessary conditions'. Thereupon the Bodhisattva who has stood in the perfection of giving admonishes those beings as follows: 'Avail yourselves of my services, and when you give gifts, etc. *to*: enter into trance, then, having fulfilled these modes, investigate as follows: is there any dharma which can be apprehended when the perfection of wisdom is being taught, i.e. a self, etc. *to*: the supreme enlightenment?' The Bodhisattva who courses in the perfection of wisdom thus does not apprehend any dharma; in consequence he does not settle down in one; and in consequence he does not review the production or stopping of any dharma whatsoever, nor its defilement or purification. As a result he does not discriminate as follows: this is someone in the hells, this is an animal, this is someone in the world of Yama, this one is an Asura, this one a god, this one a human being; this one a moral person, this one an immoral one; this one a Streamwinner, etc. *to*: this one a Tathagata, an Arhat, a fully enlighteed Buddha. It is thus that a Bodhisattva, who has stood in the perfection of wisdom, wins beings over to the perfection of wisdom.—And how does the Bodhisattva, when he has stood in the six perfections, go so far as to acquire the thirty-seven dharmas which act as wings to enlightenment? Here the Bodhisattva presents beings with services which help them to develop the four applications to mindfulness, etc. *to*: the holy eightfold path. And through acquiring that path they are freed from Samsara. It is thus that the Bodhisattva wins beings over to the holy dharmas without outflows.—Moreover the Bodhisattva, who courses in the perfection of giving, and who has seen beings who are helpless, suffering, and without food or shelter, matures them in this way: 'Come here, you sons of good family, take from me food, etc. *to*: the seven treasures, and let me thus help beings! And all that will contribute to your welfare, weal, and happiness for a long time. But do not think that this benefit is theirs and not ours! For it is just for the sake of beings that I have procured this benefit over a long time'. But he should give gifts after he has reflected that 'what is my very own that is yours'. In this way he enjoins (upon beings) that giving, morality, etc. *to*: the eighteen special Buddhadharmas (And he adds:) 'Do not be contented with these, but you must go further and establish those beings finally in the holy dharmas without outflows, in the fruit of a Streamwinner, etc. *to*: in the supreme enlightenment.' It is thus that a Bodhisattva, who courses in the perfection of wisdom, should mature beings in such a way that they are (gradually) liberated by the triple device, until in the end they are set free from Samsara.—Moreover the Bodhisattva, who has stood in the perfection of morality, should mature beings as follows: 'It is through the lack of the necessary conditions that you are immoral, but I will bestow those necessary conditions upon you, i.e. food, etc. *to*: anything that may be useful to you'. Having stood in the perfection of morality, he helps beings in this manner with the result that they conform to the ten wholesome ways of action. He has established them in moral restraint so that their morality becomes unimpaired, etc. *to*: untarnished.—And this should be worked out for all the six perfections.

Chapter 77

THE COGNITION OF THE PERFECT PURITY OF THE BUDDHA-FIELD

Subhuti: What is the Bodhisattva's path, having stood wherein he should put on this kind of armour?

The Lord: The six perfections, etc. *to*: the eighteen special Buddhadharmas. Moreover all dharmas are the Bodhisattva's path. What do you think, Subhuti, is there any dharma in which the Bodhisattva should not be trained, and yet win full enlightenment? There is no dharma in which he should not be trained, because untrained (in each and every dharma) a Bodhisattva is not capable of attaining the knowledge of all modes.

Subhuti: If all dharmas are empty, how can a Bodhisattva train in them? Does he not form discursive ideas about something which is without them if he thinks that: 'there are so many of these and not of those; these dharmas are worldly or supramundane, with or without outflows, conditioned or unconditioned, dharmas of the common people, etc. *to*: dharmas of Arhats, Pratyekabuddhas, or Buddhas'?

The Lord: So it is, Subhuti, so it is. All dharmas are empty. If again all dharmas were not empty, then, the Bodhisattva could not fully know the supreme enlightenment. But because all dharmas are empty, therefore the Bodhisattva does fully know the supreme enlightenment. Moreover, Subhuti, when you say, 'if all dharmas are empty, how does a Bodhisattva effect a differentiation of dharmas, to the effect that: there are so many of these and not of those; etc. *to*: there are the dharmas of the common people, etc. *to*: the dharmas of Arhats, Pratyekabuddhas, or Buddhas'. It is just possible that those beings might cognize that all dharmas are empty. If they did so, ((f. 269a)) that Bodhisattva would not reach the knowledge of all modes with regard to all dharmas. But because they do not cognize that 'all dharmas are empty', therefore the Bodhisattva, having fully known the supreme enlightenment, having noted the distinctive differentiation of all dharmas, demonstrates Dharma to beings.

VIII 5,13. The forsaking of all inclinations.

There the Bodhisattva who courses in the path to enlightenment should first of all[1] consider that there is therein not any dharma which could

[1] or: from the very beginning.

be apprehended in its own-being, except by way of the karma formations. And then he thus considers the own-being of all dharmas, he does not settle down in any dharma whatsoever, be it the perfections, etc. *to*: the supreme enlightenment. And why? Because through their own-being all dharmas are empty, and emptiness cannot settle down in emptiness. The very emptiness, to begin with, cannot be apprehended, how much less he who can settle down in emptiness! It is thus that the Bodhisattva dwells without having settled down in any dharma. Having stood in this training, he surveys all the practices in which beings course, asks himself wherein they do course and thinks to himself that they course in seizing on that which is not. And the Bodhisattva further reflects that 'well freed, surely, are those beings from seizing on that which is not!' Thereupon through skill in means, having stood in the perfection of wisdom, he admonishes them as follows: 'May you beings give gifts, and then you will have an abundance of all that you need. But do not put your minds to that which you need, because within it there is no core!' And so he admonishes them in morality: 'May you beings guard morality, but do not put your minds to that morality, for within it there is no core', and so for the other virtues, up to the dharmas of a Buddha. When he thus instructs and admonishes, he courses in the path to enlightenment, but does not settle down anywhere. And why? Because all dharmas are unfit to settle down in. For they have no own-being in which one could settle down, on account of the fact that their own-being consists of emptiness. In consequence the Bodhisattva who courses in the path to enlightenment does not abide anywhere. By way of abiding nowhere he courses in the six perfections, but does not abide in them. He enters on the trances, but does not abide in them. And why? Because the trance is empty of itself, and also he who enters on it is empty, and also the modes through which he enters are empty. ((f. 296b)) And so on, up to the enlightenment of a Pratyekabuddha.

Subhuti: For what reason does he not abide (therein?)

The Lord: For two reasons. Which two? The fruits in which he could abide have no own-being, nor has that by which he could abide, or he who could abide. Nor is he easily contented, (but he thinks to himself:) 'not should I not attain the fruit of a Streamwinner, but I should not stand still at that point'; etc. *to*: 'I should not rest until I have won the supreme enlightenment. And why? Because from the first thought of enlightenment onwards I have not acquired any thought which lies outside the supreme enlightenment. And why? Because I have not even from the first stage onwards produced any thought which lies outside the supreme enlightenment; and so up to the tenth stage; etc. *to*: when he has entered on a Bodhisattva's special mode of salvation, he has never produced any thought which lies outside the supreme enlightenment.'

As with an undistracted mind the Bodhisattva heroically advances by way of body, voice, and mind, he never does so without reference to this thought of enlightenment. It is thus that the Bodhisattva, having stood in the thought of enlightenment, produces the path to enlightenment with an undistracted mind.

Subhuti: If, O Lord, all dharmas are unproduced, how does the Bodhisattva produce the path to enlightenment?

The Lord: So it is, Subhuti, so it is. All dharmas are unproduced. For is it not so that all dharmas are unproduced for those who do not effect any karma formations?

Subhuti: Is it not so, O Lord, that whether Tathagatas are produced, or whether they are not produced, just established is this fixed dharmic order of dharmas?

The Lord: So it is, Subhuti, so it is. Whether Tathagatas are produced or not, just established is this fixed dharmic order of dharmas. But for the sake of those who do not cognize this fixed order of dharmas the Bodhisattva produces the path to enlightenment by which he frees beings from Samsara.

VIII 5,14. THE ATTAINMENT OF FULL ENLIGHTENMENT.

Subhuti: Is, then, enlightenment attained by a path which is produced?

The Lord: Not so, Subhuti.

Subhuti: Is it, then, attained by a path which is not produced?

The Lord: Not so, Subhuti.

Subhuti: Is it, then, attained by a path which is both produced and unproduced?

The Lord: Not so, Subhuti.

Subhuti: Is it, then, produced by a path which is neither produced nor not produced?

The Lord: Not so, Subhuti.

Subhuti: How, then, is enlightenment attained?

The Lord: Enlightenment is attained neither through a path nor through a nonpath. Just enlightenment is the path, just the path is enlightenment.

Subhuti: If just enlightenment is the path, and if just the path is enlightenment, then the Bodhisattva has already attained enlightenment. How, then, can a Tathagata be one who is recognised by the thirty-two marks of a superman, the ten powers of a Tathagata, the four grounds of self-confidence, the four analytical knowledges, etc. *to*: the eighteen special Buddhadharmas?

The Lord: ((f. 297a)) What do you think, Subhuti, does the Buddha attain enlightenment?

Subhuti: No, O Lord, he does not. Just the Buddha is enlightenment, just enlightenment is the Buddha.

The Lord: As to what Subhuti has said, 'then the Bodhisattva has already attained enlightenment'. Here a Bodhisattva, after he has fulfilled the six perfections, etc. *to* : the eighteen special Buddhadharmas, will, through the adamantine concentration, by a wisdom which is conjoined with one single thought-moment, fully know the supreme enlightenment. It is then that he is recognized as a Tathagata, as one who sees all and has full sovereignty over all dharmas.

VIII 5,15. THE PURITY OF THE BUDDHA-FIELD.

Subhuti: How does a Bodhisattva purify the Buddha-field?

The Lord: Here the Bodhisattva, from the first thought of enlightenment onward, cleanses away all wickedness of body, speech, and mind, on the part of himself and of others. Through their being perfectly pure he purifies the Buddha-field.

Subhuti: What is a Bodhisattva's wickedness of body, speech, and mind?

The Lord: Unwholesome bodily action, i.e. taking life, taking what is not given and sexual misconduct, that is his wickedness of body. Unwholesome verbal action, i.e. false speech, slander, harsh speech, and frivolous talk, that is his wickedness of speech. Unwholesome mental action, i.e. covetousness, ill will, and wrong views, that is his wickedness of mind. Moreover any thought of meanness is for a Bodhisattva wickedness of mind, and so is any thought of immorality, anger, indolence, distraction, unconcentratedness, or stupidity. Moreover any morality that is not perfectly pure, that is wickedness for a Bodhisattva. And so it is to be deprived of the four applications of mindfulness, etc. *to* : the wishless concentration; the realization of the fruit of a Streamwinner when accompanied by the longing for it, etc. *to* : the realisation of the enlightenment of a Pratyekabuddha when accompanied by the longing for it; the notion of the five skandhas, the twelve sense fields and the eighteen elements; ((f. 297b)) the notions of women and men, of the triple world, of wholesome and unwholesome, etc. *to* : the notion of the conditioned and of the unconditioned, that also is wickedness of body, speech, and mind. In consequence the Bodhisattva, who courses in perfect wisdom, abandons all those kinds of wickedness, and then he himself gives gifts and also encourages others to giving; he gives food to the hungry, etc. *to* : anything that may be useful, and also others he encourages to give anything that may be useful, and establishes them in giving these things. When he has made the resulting wholesome root common to all beings, he dedicates it to the purification of the Buddha-field. And so with morality, etc. *to* : wisdom. He himself perfects a great trichiliocosm which is made of the seven jewels, and then gives it as a gift to the Triple Jewel. And he thinks to himself: 'May I through that wholesome root have a Buddha-field made of the seven treasures!' Moreover the Bodhisattva plays heavenly musical instruments, in honour of the Buddhas or their shrines. And he thinks to himself that 'as a result of that wholesome root may I constantly and always have musical instruments which make heavenly and charming sounds!' Moreover the Bodhisattva fills the great trichiliocosm with heavenly perfumes and gives them to the Buddhas or their shrines. And he thinks to himself, 'through this wholesome root may my Buddha-field emit heavenly scents!' Moreover the Bodhisattva gives the most excellent foods to the Tathagatas or their disciples. And he thinks to himself, 'as a result of this wholesome root may there accrue the most excellent foods for the community of my disciples in my Buddha-field when I have known the supreme enlightenment!' Moreover the Bodhisattva gives heavenly ointments to the Tathagatas or to their shrines. And he thinks to himself, 'as a result of this wholesome root may there accrue in my Buddha-field, when I have known the supreme enlightenment, heavenly touchables to all beings!' Moreover the Bodhisattva thinks to himself, 'may I by my good intentions alone bestow upon the Buddhas and Lords, their disciples and all beings agreeable sense pleasures of the five kinds!' And when he has had this idea he thinks to himself, 'as a result of this wholesome root, when I have known the supreme enlightenment in that Buddha-field, the fivefold agreeable sense pleasures will be manifested to the whole community of the disciples and to all beings just as a result of their wishing for them'. Moreover the Bodhisattva gives the fivefold sense pleasures as a gift to the Buddhas and their disciples, together with all beings. Moreover the Bodhisattva who courses in the perfection of wisdom thinks as follows: 'Now that I have myself entered on the four trances, the four Unlimited, etc. may I also introduce other beings to them! When I have won the supreme enlightenment, may all beings not be deprived of the four trances, etc. *to*: the thirty-seven dharmas which act as wings to enlightenment!' It is thus that ((f. 298a)) the Bodhisattva purifies the Buddha-field. He does not know the supreme enlightenment until all those intentions are fulfilled. He himself becomes endowed with all wholesome roots, and he also causes all beings to be endowed with wholesome roots. His own body becomes handsome, and the bodies also of those beings whom he has matured become handsome, beautiful to behold, and graceful—with the help of his merit. It is thus that a Bodhisattva purifies the Buddha-field in such a way that there is no longer even the concept of the three states of woe, of the false views, of greed, hate, and delusion, of women and men, the two vehicles, impermanence, ill, and not-self, a recipient, I-making, and Mine-making, latent biases and obsessions, the perverted views or the differentiation between the various fruits. But there is a proclamation of the concentrations on emptiness, the signless, and the wishless. And when the wind stirs the branches of the trees, those beings hear an admonition to renounce both their inward and outward[2] properties. From all inward and outward dharmas there issues the message that 'this is emptiness, signless, and wishless', that it is nonproduction and nonstopping. Just as the own-being of these dharmas is, so the words express it, saying that all dharmas are empty of all dharmas. Whether Tathagatas are produced or not, all dharmas are empty of all dharmas. And what is empty, therein there is no sign and it is also wishless—this is the kind of demonstration of Dharma which will emerge. Night and day this kind of demonstration of Dharma will emerge in that Buddha-field when he has fully known the supreme enlightenment—to those who stand, sit, lie down, or walk along. And all the Buddhas and Lords in the world systems in the ten directions speak in praise of this Tathagata. And those who will hear His name, they will also be definitely destined for the supreme enlightenment. And none of the beings to whom the Tathagata, who has won the supreme enlightenment, teaches the Dharma has any uncertainty as to whether this is the Dharma and that is not the Dharma. And why? In the dharmic nature of all dharmas there is no non-dharma, and all of it is Dharma. But those beings who are possessed by unwholesome roots, who have not planted wholesome roots under the Buddhas or their disciples, or who have been taken hold of by bad spiritual teachers, they cling to the false view of a self, etc. *to* : they cling to all false views. They take their stand on the extremes, i.e. on annihilation or eternity. Seized by a wrong conception they form the notion of fully enlightened Buddhas with regard to those who are not fully enlightened Buddhas, and with regard to the fully enlightened Buddhas they form the notion that they are not fully enlightened Buddhas. They speak of what is not the Dharma as if it were the Dharma, and they speak of Dharma as if it were not the Dharma. They reject the Dharma, and in consequence when their body has broken up they will after their death fall into a state of woe and a bad destiny, and be reborn in the hells. And the Buddhas and Lords, after they have known the supreme enlightenment, will liberate those beings who are included in Samsara from both their evil places of rebirth and from their false views. Thereafter ((f. 298b)) they will establish them in the group of those whose destiny is not fixed either way; and after that they will again be reborn in the states of woe. It is thus that the Bodhisattva purifies the Buddha-field, with the result that beings will find no home in anything—worldly or supramundane dharmas, dharmas with or without outflows, conditioned or unconditioned dharmas—until they all become definitely destined for the supreme enlightenment.

[2]i.e. both their bodies and their other possessions.

Chapter 78

SKILL IN MEANS IN THE PURIFICATION OF THE BUDDHA-FIELD

VIII 5,16. Bound to win full enlightenment (soon).

Subhuti: Is again the Bodhisattva fixed (in his destiny), or is he not?

The Lord: He is fixed, and not not-fixed.

Subhuti: In which group, then, is he fixed—that of the Disciples, that of the Pratyekabuddhas or that of the Buddhas?

The Lord: The Bodhisattva is not fixed on the level of the Disciples or Pratyekabuddhas, but he is fixed on the level of a Buddha.

Subhuti: Is, then, the Bodhisattva fixed when he has had his first thought of enlightenment, or when he has become irreversible, or when he is in his last becoming?

The Lord: They are all equally fixed.

Shubuti: Is, then, the Bodhisattva who is fixed (in his destiny) reborn in the states of woe?

The Lord: No, he is not. What do you think, Subhuti, are the eighth-lowest, the Streamwinner, etc. *to*: the Pratyekabuddha reborn in the states of woe?

Subhuti: No, O Lord.

The Lord: So it is quite impossible that a Bodhisattva could be reborn in the states of woe if, beginning with the first thought of enlightenment, he gives gifts, etc. *to*: develops wisdom, develops friendliness, compassion, sympathetic joy, and impartiality towards all beings, and has established himself in such a way as to forsake all unwholesome dharmas. It is likewise impossible that he should be reborn among the long-lived gods; or in regions inhabited by stupid people among whom wholesome dharmas are not current; or among the impious barbarians of the border regions where the four assemblies[1] are unknown; or in families which hold wrong views; or in places where one does not hear of the Buddha, Dharma, or Samgha. It is likewise impossible that he should fall into the false view that there is no karma or retribution. And it is also quite impossible that a Bodhisattva who, from the first thought of enlightenment onwards has resolutely set out for the supreme enlightenment, should commit himself to the ten unwholesome paths of action.

Subhuti: If the Bodhisattva, thus endowed with wholesome roots,

[1] i.e. monks, nuns, laymen, and laywomen.

is no longer reborn in the odious places of rebirth, how is it that the Tathagata has told about himself those Jataka stories in which he appears as an animal? Whereto had those wholesome roots gone on those occasions?

The Lord: It is not as a result of insalubrious karma that the Bodhisattva is reborn as an animal. But he acquires, for the sake of beings, deliberately, of his own free will, any kind of body through which he can work the weal of beings. Do Arhats or Pratyekabuddhas have that skill in means ((f. 299a)) which would enable them to be reborn as animals?

Subhuti: No, O Lord.

The Lord: The Tathagata, however, has the skill in means which enables him to be reborn there. And when confronted with those who struggle to kill him, the Bodhisattva renounces himself with supreme patience for the sake of those very beings and does them no harm. In this way, Subhuti, you should know that the Bodhisattva, when for the sake of beings he fulfils the great compassion, is even on the way to his supreme enlightenment reborn as an animal, but is not stained by the faults of animal life.

Subhuti: Having stood in which wholesome dharmas do Bodhisattvas acquire these kinds of bodies?

The Lord: Which is the wholesome dharma that the Bodhisattva should not fulfil? The supreme enlightenment is the fulfilment of all wholesome dharmas. Therefore there is not any wholesome dharma which the Bodhisattva should not fulfil—from the first thought of enlightenment onward until he is seated on the terrace of enlightenment. For it is impossible for him to know the supreme enlightenment while even one single wholesome dharma has remained unfulfilled. Therefore, then, the Bodhisattva should, from the first thought of enlightenment onward train in the fulfilment of all wholesome dharmas and, having trained therein, he reaches the knowledge of all modes and will forsake the last residues of the defilements.

Subhuti: How again is it that the Bodhisattva, when he is endowed with such pure dharmas, with the holy dharma(s) without outflows, is reborn in the states of woe or among animals?

The Lord: Is, then, the Tathagata holy and without outflows?

Subhuti: He is, O Lord.

The Lord: Can, then, the Tathagata conjure up an animal which does his Buddha-work (for him)?

Subhuti: He can, O Lord.

The Lord: Does, then, the Tathagata become an animal?

Subhuti: No, O Lord!

The Lord: Does he, then, experience an animal's sufferings?

Subhuti: No, O Lord!

The Lord: It is thus that the Bodhisattva, endowed with the holy Dharma without outflows, deliberately and of his own free will acquires a body which enables him to mature beings suitably in accordance with their deserts.

Subhuti: Can, then, an Arhat conjure up a fictitious magical creation who can do the work of an Arhat, which generates joyous zest in others?

The Lord: He can, Subhuti, he can. It is thus that a Bodhisattva. endowed with the Dharma which is holy and without outflows, acquires deliberately and of his own free will a body which allows him to do a Buddha's work for living beings. But through this body he does not become subject to suffering, nor does he experience painful feelings. What do you think, Subhuti, if a magician exhibits illusory beings, in the shape of elephants, horses, bulls, or any other illusory beings, do they then become actual elephants, horses, bulls, or any other animals?

Subhuti: No, O Lord.

The Lord: It is thus that the Bodhisattva becomes endowed with the Dharma which is holy and without outflows, and acquires deliberately and of his own free will a body which enables him to work the weal of beings, but he does not experience the feelings which normally go with it.

Subhuti: Greatly skilled in means, O Lord, is the Bodhisattva who, even when endowed with the holy cognition, acquires any body which enables him to work the weal of beings.

VIII 5,17. THE WEAL OF COUNTLESS BEINGS.

In which pure dharmas has the Bodhisattva stood when ((f. 299b)) he performed these kinds of skill in means, and yet was not stained by his activities?

The Lord: It is when he has stood in perfect wisdom that the Bodhisattva performs these kinds of skill in means, with the result that in all the directions and subdirections in countless world systems he does the work of beings. But he is not affected by anything anywhere. And why? Because the Bodhisattva nowhere apprehends a dharma which could affect him, or whereby or wherein he could be affected. And why? Because all these three dharmas are empty of own-being. For emptiness does not affect emptiness, nor can any dharma affect emptiness, nor can emptiness he affected at all. And why? Because emptiness, being empty in its own-being, cannot be apprehended in emptiness. This is the emptiness without basis in which the Bodhisattva has stood before he knows full enlightenment.

Subhuti: Has he just stood in perfect wisdom and not in other dharmas?

The Lord: Is there, then, any dharma which is not included in the perfection of wisdom?

Subhuti: If perfect wisdom is through its own-being empty, how, then, are all dharmas included in it? For in emptiness no dharma is included or nonincluded.

The Lord: Are, then, all dharmas empty of all dharmas?

Subhuti: They are, O Lord.

The Lord: If all dharmas are empty of all dharmas, are, then, not all dharmas included in emptiness?

Subhuti: So it is, O Lord.

The Lord: By this method also you should know that, when he has stood in perfect wisdom, the Bodhisattva performs this kind of skill in means.

VIII 5,18. THE VIRTUOUS ACTS WHICH CONSIST IN APPROACHING, TENDING, ETC. THE BUDDHAS.

Subhuti: How does the Bodhisattva, who courses in perfect wisdom and has stood in the emptiness of all dharmas, conjure up the perfection of superknowledges, which enables him to travel in the East, etc. *to*: countless world systems, to honour the Buddhas and Lords who stand, hold and maintain themselves in those world systems, and demonstrate the Dharma there, to hear the Dharma from them, and to plant wholesome roots in the presence of those Buddhas and Lords?

The Lord: Here, Subhuti, the Bodhisattva who courses in perfect wisdom sees all the countless world systems in the East, etc. as empty. And the Buddhas and Lords who are in them are empty of own-being, and they can be described only by way of names and conventional expressions which rely on concepts. All these concepts, however, are empty of own-being. If those world systems were not empty of own-being, as well as those Buddhas and Lords and the habitual conceptions, then that emptiness would be only a limited one; but because emptiness is not limited, therefore all dharmas are empty of all dharmas. In consequence the Bodhisattva who through his skill in means courses in the perfection of wisdom consummates the perfection of the superknowledges. Having stood in the superknowledges, he consummates the heavenly eye, the heavenly ear, the magical powers, the cognition of others' thoughts and the knowledge of the decease and rebirth of beings. And it is not without the superknowledges that a Bodhisattva can know the supreme enlightenment. ((f. 301a)) Since therefore the enlightenment of a Bodhisattva and the perfection of the superknowledges are mutually included within each other, one should strive to attain enlightenment through just those superknowledges.

In the process of doing so (the Bodhisattva) with his heavenly eye sees for himself those wholesome dharmas, and he enjoins them also on others. But he does not settle down in these wholesome dharmas. And why? Because they are all empty in their own-being. But on account of emptiness one cannot settle down anywhere, or relish that in which one has settled down. For emptiness cannot be relished. Therefore the Bodhisattva, who courses in perfect wisdom, consummates the heavenly eye which enables him to see all dharmas as empty. Thereupon the Bodhisattva, aware of the true dharmic situation, voluntarily performs those deeds which enable him to demonstrate Dharma to beings, but without apprehending a being or the concept of a being. It is thus by way of basing himself on nothing at all that the Bodhisattva conjures up the perfection of the superknowledges, and brings about all the dharmas which should be achieved through these superknowledges. And here the Bodhisattva, with his heavenly eye, purified, and surpassing that of men, sees the world systems in all the directions, and with the help of his wonderworking powers he travels there and works the weal of beings, whether by giving or morality, etc. *to* : by the Buddhadharmas he does the work of those beings. And to beings who are stingy he demonstrates Dharma as follows : 'Do give gifts! For poverty is a painful thing. One is unable, when poor, to accomplish one's own welfare, much less that of others! In consequence you yourselves will suffer, and you will also make others suffer. May it not be that overpowered by poverty you will be unable to free from the places of woe those who feed on each other's flesh!' And to those who are immoral he demonstrates the Dharma as follows : 'Immorality, O you people, leads to suffering. For through immorality one cannot accomplish one's own welfare, how much less that of others! The immoral will find their punishment in the hells, or in the world of animals, or in the world of Yama. Once you have been hurled into the three states of woe, you will be unable to accomplish your own welfare, how much less that of others! Therefore may you not give an opportunity to even one single thought of immorality, so that later on you may have no reason to repent!' And to those beings who feel ill will for one another he demonstrates Dharma as follows : 'May you not feel ill will towards one another! For to those that have angry thoughts not one single wholesome dharma can manifest itself. It is therefore quite certain that you who are angry towards one another will be reborn in the hells, or the world of animals, or the world of Yama. May you not feel even one angry thought, how much less should you give an opportunity to other unwholesome thoughts!' He encourages the indolent to vigour, etc. *to* : he encourages those who have distracted thoughts to the practice of trance, and the stupid to wisdom, and those who course in greed he encourages to meditate on the Unlovely, those who course in hate to the practice of friendliness, and ((f. 301b)) those who course in delusion to meditate on conditioned coproduction. Those who have set out on the wrong path he encourages to the (right) path, whether it be that of the Disciples or the Pratyekabuddhas. And he demonstrates Dharma to them as follows: 'Those dharmas in which you have settled down, they are empty in their own-being. One cannot possibly settle down in dharmas which are empty of own-being. For emptiness is something in which one cannot settle down'. It is thus that the Bodhisattva who courses in perfect wisdom and who has stood in the superknowledges works the weal of beings. No Bodhisattva can demonstrate Dharma to beings without having first stood in the superknowledges. And it is quite impossible that those who have strayed on to a wrong path can make others enter the (true) path. Just as a bird without wings cannot soar into space, just so the Bodhisattva cannot demonstrate Dharma without resorting to the superknowledges. Therefore, then, a Bodhisattva who courses in perfect wisdom should consummate the superknowledges. When he has done so, he makes those beings happy whose weal he desires to work. With his heavenly eye he will see countless world systems, and also the beings who are reborn in them. With the help of his wonder-working powers he travels to them, wisely knows their thought with his own thought, and in his wisdom he demonstrates the Dharma just as it is—be it a sermon on giving, etc. *to*: a sermon on release. With his heavenly ear-element he hears both kinds of sound, heavenly and human. He hears the dharmas which the Buddhas and Lords demonstrate in countless world systems, learns them as they are, and demonstrates them without introducing any falsehood into them—whether they be a sermon on giving, etc. *to*: a sermon on release. His knowledge of others' mental make-up becomes quite pure. Through it he wisely knows the hearts of beings, and demonstrates to them Dharma as it is—whether it be a sermon on giving,etc. *to*: a sermon on release. He remembers his own former rebirths and those of others. As a result he cognizes that these were the names of the Tathagatas of the past, who had their own communities of disciples; and to those beings who will be resolved on the recollection of their past lives he will demonstrate Dharma just as it is—whether it be a sermon on giving or a sermon on release. With his wonderworking powers he travels to many world systems, honours the Buddhas and Lords that are in them, and through his superknowledge demonstrates Dharma to beings—whether it be a sermon on giving or a sermon on release. With his cognition of the extinction of the outflows, well understood, he demonstrates Dharma to beings—whether it be a sermon on giving or a sermon on release. It is thus that the Bodhisattva, who courses in perfect wisdom, should consummate the superknowledges. When he has become quite familiar with these superknowledges, he takes upon himself any body that he wishes to take upon himself, though thereby he does not become one who is at ease or ill, who is glad or sad, or who feels affection or aversion.

Just as a person who is ((f. 302a)) a magical creation of the Tathagata does all the work demanded of him, and yet is not stained by ease or ill. Just so the Bodhisattva, who courses in perfect wisdom, should become one who plays with the superknowledges and by playing with them he will purify the Buddha-field and mature beings. For a Bodhisattva cannot know the supreme enlightenment without having purified his Buddha-field and without having matured beings. And why? A Bodhisattva who is deficient in the limbs of the path cannot win the supreme enlightenment.

VIII 5,19. THE LIMBS OF ENLIGHTENMENT.

Subhuti: Which are the limbs of the path[2] which a Bodhisattva fulfils before he knows the supreme enlightenment?

The Lord: All the wholesome dharmas are the limbs of the path[2] of the Bodhisattva.

Subhuti: What, then, are they?

The Lord: From the first thought of enlightenment onwards the perfection of giving is such a wholesome dharma, when it is carried out without false imaginations, and when one does not discriminate with regard to the act of giving that 'this is the gift, to him I give, it is I who gives'. In fact one does not imagine any of these three, on account of the emptiness of own-being. Through this perfection he saves himself and rescues also others from the flood of Samsara. These are the wholesome dharmas which are a Bodhisattva's path to the supreme enlightenment, and it is by this path that the past, future, and present Bodhisattvas have been saved, are being saved, and will be saved from the flood of Samsara, after they have taken with them countless other beings. And so for the other perfections, etc. *to* : the eighteen special Buddhadharmas. Whichever paths to enlightenment there may be, these are the wholesome dharmas which a Bodhisattva should fulfil so as to reach the knowledge of all modes and thereafter turn the wheel of Dharma.

[2]*P, AdT*: limbs of enlightenment.

CHAPTER 79

THE EXPOSITION OF THE NONEXISTENCE OF OWN-BEING

VIII 5,20. THE FRUITS WHICH RESULT FROM HIS DEEDS ARE NEVER LOST.

Subhuti: If these are the dharmas of a Bodhisattva, which, then, are the dharmas of a Buddha?

The Lord:[1] Just these are the dharmas of a Buddha when he fully knows them in all their modes; he then attains the knowledge of all modes and forsakes all the defilements together with their residues. The Bodhisattva fully knows these things, but the Tathagata is one who has fully known all dharmas through a wisdom which is conjoined with one single mark.[2] This is the difference between the Bodhisattva on the one side and the Tathagata on the other. Just as the candidate is one thing and the one who is established in the fruit is another, and yet they are not both of them not holy persons, just so the Bodhisattva stands in the place of a candidate to the unimpeded path, ((f. 302b)) whereas the Tathagata has attained a state of nonblindness[3] for all dharmas. This is the difference between the Bodhisattva on the one side and the Tathagata on the other.

Subhuti: If, however, these dharmas are empty of own-marks, how can with regard to dharmas which are empty of own-marks a difference or distinction be apprehended (to the effect that one says) 'this one is a being in the hells, this one an animal, this one someone in the world of Yama, this one a god, this one a human, this one is on the stage where he becomes one of the clan, etc. *to*: this one is a Tathagata.' And as these persons cannot be apprehended, so likewise their karma or its karma result.

The Lord: So it is, Subhuti, so it is, as you say. In respect of dharmas which are empty of own-marks no karma or karma result can be apprehended. But when those too ignorant to cognize dharmas as empty of own-marks manufacture a karma—be it badly done or well done, with or without outflows—then, through badly done karma they are hurled into the three states of woe, through what is well done they are reborn among gods and men, and through flawless karma they are reborn in the world of form and the formless world. Therefore the Bodhisattva, who

[1] *AdT* adds: The dharmas of a Bodhisattva are also those of a Buddha.

[2] *AdT*: moment.

[3] *P, AdT*: unobstructed cognition.

courses in the perfection of giving, etc. *to* : in the eighteen special Buddha-dharmas, as a flawless practitioner produces these dharmas of a Bodhisattva; when he has produced them he enters into the adamantine concentration which is attended by the retinue of the limbs of enlightenment, and then he fully knows the supreme enlightenment; after that he works the weal of beings. When that weal has been worked, he never again forgets (what he has learned) and in consequence he cannot be hurled again into the Samsara with its five places of rebirth.

Subhuti: Has, then, the Lord, when he has fully known the supreme enlightenment, apprehended Samsara with its five places of rebith?

The Lord: Certainly not!

Subhuti: Has, then, the Lord apprehended the dharmas which are black, white, or both black and white?

The Lord: Certainly not!

Subhuti: If they have not been apprehended, how could he conceive of the hells, the world of animals, etc. *to*: the Streamwinner, etc. *to*: the Tathagata?

The Lord: Do, then, those beings cognize all dharmas as empty of own-marks?

Subhuti: Certainly not!

The Lord: If those beings were to cognize that 'all dharmas are empty of own-marks', then the Bodhisattva would not set out for the supreme enlightenment and in consequence he would not set beings free from the three states of woe, etc. *to* : from Samsara with its (five) places of rebirth. But because beings do not cognize dharmas as empty of own marks they are not set free from Samsara with its five places of rebirth. Therefore the Bodhisattva who has heard from the Buddhas and Lords that dharmas are empty of own-marks sets out for the supreme enlightenment for the sake of beings. These dharmas do not exist in such a way as the foolish common people have settled down in them. It is thus that these beings imagine and apprehend dharmas as existing in their own right when in fact they are not and do not exist, and then form the notion of a living being with regard to what is not a living being, the notion of form with regard to what is not form, etc. *to*: ((f. 303a)) the notion of unconditioned dharmas with regard to what are not unconditioned dharmas. Their throughts perverted by the perverted views they bring about karma by body, voice, and mind. Such people are not liberated from Samsara with its five places of rebirth. Therefore the Bodhisattva, coursing in the perfection of wisdom, performs all the wholesome dharmas included in it, and courses in the course of a Bodhisattva with the result that he fully knows the supreme enlightenment.

VIII 5,21. THE VISION OF THE (HOLY) TRUTHS.

Having fully known them he proclaims ill, its origination, its stopping and the progressive path which leads to the stopping of ill; he demonstrates and illuminates them, reveals, explains, and expounds them, and establishes others in them. In these four holy truths are included all wholesome dharmas as well as those dharmas which act as wings to enlightenment and through which the respective determination of the three Treasures takes place. Which three? The treasure of Buddha, Dharma, and Samgha. Through the manifestation of these three treasures beings are liberated from Samsara with its five places of rebirth.

Subhuti: Does, then, Parinirvana take place through the cognition of ill or through ill, through the cognition of origination or through origination, through the cognition of the stopping of ill or through the stopping of ill, through the cognition of the path or through the path?

The Lord: Parinirvana does not take place through any of these. But it is the sameness of the four holy Truths which I have taught as Parinirvana.

Subhuti: What, then, is the sameness of the four holy truths?

The Lord: It is where there is no ill nor cognition of ill, no origination nor cognition of origination, no stopping nor cognition of stopping, no path nor cognition of the path—the Suchness of those holy truths, their nonfalseness, their Dharmahood, (i.e.) the Dharma-element, fixed sequence of Dharma, stability of Dharma. It is the element, i.e. the Dharma-element which is firmly established whether Tathagatas are produced or not, and conduces to the (dharmic state which is) undeluded and never fails. Thus it is that a Bodhisattva who courses in perfect wisdom courses towards the understanding of the truths. And yet the truths are not something that should be understood.

Subhuti: And how again does the Bodhisattva who courses in perfect wisdom course towards the understanding of the truths? As he courses so he understands the truths, and when he has fully known them he penetrates to (their) Thusness, with the result that he does not fall on the level of a Disciple or Pratyekabuddha, but enters on a Bodhisattva's special way of salvation.

The Lord: Here the Bodhisattva, who courses in perfect wisdom, does not see those dharmas in such a way that, when seeing them, he apprehends any dharma whatever. Not apprehending them he sees that 'all dharmas are empty'. He sees that they are all empty, whether they are included in the truths or not included in them. When he views things in this way, the Bodhisattva who enters on a Bodhisattva's special way of salvation becomes established on the stage of those who have become one of the Bodhisattva-clan, and as a result he cannot fall from the Summits ((f. 303b)) unto the level of a Disciple or Pratyekabuddha. Having stood on the level of the Bodhisattva-clan, he produces the four trances, the four Unlimited, and the four formless attainments. Having stood on this level of quiescence he carefully examines all dharmas and thoroughly understands the four holy truths. He comprehends ill, but does not produce a thought which has ill for its objective support. He forsakes origination, but does not have a thought which has origination for its objective support. He realises cessation, but does not produce a thought which has cessation for its objective support. He develops the path, but does not produce a thought which has the path for its objective support. But what he does is to see with a thought inclined to enlightenment all dharmas such as they really are.

Subhuti: What is the real truth about dharmas such as they are?

The Lord: Emptiness.

Subhuti: What emptiness?

The Lord: The emptiness of own-marks. Through this kind of insight he discerns that 'all dharmas are empty'. Not of any dharma does he see an own-being which would provide him with an existent on which he has stood when fully knowing enlightenment.

Subhuti: Is, then, enlightenment nonexistent?

The Lord: So it is, Subhuti, so it is, as you say. Enlightenment also is a nonexistent. It has not been made by Buddhas, Pratyekabuddhas, or Arhats, nor by those Bodhisattvas who here course towards enlightenment. It is only because beings do not cognize or see what things really are that the Bodhisattva, coursing in perfect wisdom, demonstrates Dharma to beings through his skill in means.[4]

[4] *P* 578-584 are reproduced here on pages 644 to 652.

Chapter 80

THE ABSENCE OF (ALL) DEFILEMENT AND PURIFICATION

VIII 5,22. The four perverted views.

Subhuti: If all dharmas in their own-being are nonexistent, and if they have not been made by the Buddhas, Pratyekabuddhas, or Arhats, etc. *to*: by the Streamwinners, by the candidates (to the fruits), or by the Bodhisattvas who course towards enlightenment—how can one conceive of any distinction between these dharmas, and how can one respectively determine them as denizens of the hells, as animals, etc. *to*: as humans? How can one say that from this karma there result the hells, the animal world, etc. *to*: the Tathagata? For the nonexistent performs no actions through which it could go to hell, the animal world, etc. *to*: through which it could be reborn among the various kinds of gods, etc. *to*: through which it could attain the fruit of a Streamwinner etc. *to*: or through which the Bodhisattva could course in the path to enlightenment, or through which the Tathagata could attain to the knowledge of all modes, thereafter setting beings free from Samsara.

The Lord: So it is, Subhuti, so it is, as you say. The nonexistent can have no karma, no activity, and no fruit. But a foolish untutored common person, who is not conversant with the holy dharmas, does not wisely know that dharmas in their own-being are nonexistent. With thoughts which have arisen from perverted views he brings about various deeds and he gets the kind of personality which corresponds to them, whether in the hells, etc. *to*: ((f. 304a)) among the gods of the station of neither perception nor nonperception. So the nonexistent has no karma, activity, or fruit. And what is nonexistent, that is just nonexistent. As to what Subhuti has further said about the fruit of a Streamwinner, etc. *to*: the Tathagata's knowledge of all modes—is not the path nonexistent, and so also the fruit of a Streamwinner, etc. *to*: the knowledge of all modes?

Subhuti: Yes, they are all nonexistent.

The Lord: Can then a nonexistent dharma reach a nonexistent dharma?

Subhuti: No, O Lord.

The Lord: It is thus that both the nonexistent and the Path are dharmas which are neither conjoined nor disjoined, which are immaterial, undefinable, nonresisting, with one mark only, i.e. no mark. But the

Bodhisattva, who courses in perfect wisdom, dissuades through his skill in means those beings who are inclined to the four perverted views, and who, with regard to the five skandhas perceive permanence in the impermanent, ease in what is ill, a self in that which has no self, a loveliness in that which is unlovely, and he also dissuades those who have settled down in a belief in existents from that belief.

VIII 5,23. THE COGNITION THAT THE PERVERTED VIEWS ARE UNFOUNDED IN ENTITIES.

Subhuti: Is there perhaps an entity which is a truly real existent, which is such as it is and not false, on which the foolish common people have taken their stand with the result that they have settled down in it as being a truly real entity, an existent, which is such as it is and not false? For if there is none such, how do they bring about the deeds which prevent them from being liberated from Samsara with its five places of rebirth?

The Lord: There is no entity even as fine as the fine point of the tip of a hair on which the foolish common people could base themselves to bring about deeds—except by way of the perverted views. I will give you a simile which will make this point clearer so that intelligent people can understand it. What do you think, Subhuti, when someone sees something in a dream does he see an entity on which he could base his enjoyment of the five sense pleasures?

Subhuti: The dream, to begin with, is not—how much less that on which the dreamer could base his enjoyment of the five sense pleasures!

The Lord: What do you think, Subhuti, is there a dharma—conditioned or unconditioned, with or without outflows—which is not like a dream?

Subhuti: No, there is not.

The Lord: Does Samsara with its five places of rebirth exist in a dream?

Subhuti: No, O Lord.

The Lord: What do you think, Subhuti, does there take place in a dream the development of the path, thanks to which one would be neither defiled nor purified?

Subhuti: No, O Lord. That dharma (seen in a dream?) is a nonentity outside all conceptions and it cannot be conceived by any words or verbal expressions.

The Lord: When a reflected image is seen in a mirror, is there, then, an entity which could bring about deeds with the result that it would go to one of the five places of rebirth?

Subhuti: No, O Lord. A nonentity is that reflected image, except for the foolish common people being deceived. How, then, could it ((f. 304b)) perform the deeds through which it would go to one of the five places of rebirth?

The Lord: Does it, then, have a development of the path thanks to which it would be neither defiled nor purified?

Subhuti: No, it does not. Because that reflected image is a nonentity.

The Lord: When an echo emerges from a wood, a cave, a mountain, a glen, or a steep slope,—is, then, that echo an entity which performs deeds by which it goes to the various places of rebirth?

Subhuti: It does not, O Lord, because that echo is a nonentity.

The Lord: Does that echo have a development of the path thanks to which it would be neither defiled nor purified?

Subhuti: It does not, because absolutely that echo does not exist.

The Lord: Since with regard to a mirage there is the perception of water, a river, a city, and of parks where there are none of these things, can then that perception of a mirage perform deeds through which it could go to the various places of rebirth?

Subhuti: No, it cannot, because absolutely there is in that mirage no water, river, city, or park, except for a perversion of perception and a delusion of the eye.

The Lord: Does there take place in this perverted perception a development of the path thanks to which it would be neither defiled nor purified?

Subhuti: No, O Lord.

The Lord: If a magician had conjured up various illusions, such as the body of an elephant, a horse, or a bull, an army division or a chariot, a woman or a man, would then that illusion be an entity which performs deeds through which it would go to the various places of rebirth?

Subhuti: No, O Lord. No entity corresponds to that illusion, not even one as tiny as the fine point of the tip of a hair. So there is nothing on which these deeds could be based.

The Lord: Could it, then, have a development of the path thanks to which it would be neither defiled nor purified?

Subhuti: No, O Lord. On the part of a dharma which is a nonentity ((f. 305a)), how could there be a development of the path, or a defilement of purification!

The Lord: Is an illusory magical creation, conjured up by the Tathagata, an entity which performs deeds through which it would go to the various places of rebirth?

Subhuti: No, O Lord. That magical creation is a nonentity.

The Lord: Could, then, that illusory magical creation have a development of the path, thanks to which it would be neither defiled nor purified?

Subhuti: No, O Lord.

The Lord: What do you think, Subhuti, is anyone therein defiled or purified?

Subhuti: No, O Lord.

The Lord: Just because there is no one who is defiled or purified, so there is no defilement or purification. And why? It is because they have stood in I-making and Mine-making that beings are defiled or purified. But since one who sees true reality is neither defiled nor purified, there is (in fact) no defilement or purification.

CHAPTER 81

BEING JOINED TO ULTIMATE REALITY

VIII 5,24. PURIFICATION.

Subhuti: One who sees what is real is not defiled or purified; one who does not see what is real is also not defiled or purified. For all dharmas have nonexistence for own-being. The nonexistent cannot be defiled or purified, nor can the existent, nor the self-existent[1], nor that which in its self-existence[2] is nonexistent. What then is that which the Lord has expounded as purification?

The Lord: It is the sameness of all dharmas.

Subhuti: And what is that sameness of all dharmas?

The Lord: It is Suchness, nonfalseness, unaltered Suchness, the nature of Dharma, the realm of Dharma, the established order of Dharma, the fixed sequence of Dharma, the Reality limit. That which, whether Tathagatas are or are not produced, is just established as the established order of Dharma, as the realm of Dharma, that is purification. And although that is conventionally spoken about by means of worldly conventional terms, it is in fact inexpressible, incommunicable, quite beyond the paths of language, speech, and sound.

VIII 5,25. THE EQUIPMENT (WHICH RESULTS) FROM PURIFICATION.

Subhuti: If all dharmas are like a dream, an echo, a reflected image, a mirage, a magical illusion, or a magical creation, how does the Bodhisattva in the face of dharmas which are thus nonentities and not actually real raise his thought to the supreme enlightenment, (and accordingly resolve to) fulfil the six perfections, etc. *to*: the eighty subsidiary marks? How does he achieve the great halo with which he illuminates countless world systems, or a voice like that of Brahmā, which enables him to demonstrate Dharma with one single sound ((f. 305b)) to beings in the world systems in the ten directions, after he has read their thoughts and understood their intentions?

The Lord: These dharmas of which you have spoken, are they not like a dream, etc. *to*: like a magical creation?

Subhuti: How, then, if all dharmas are like a dream, etc. can the Bodhisattva course in the perfection of wisdom? For a dream is not

[1]usually = own-being.

[2]same as n. 1.

actually real, etc. *to*: a magical creation is not actually real. And by means of what is not actually real one cannot fully know the supreme enlightenment after one has coursed in the six perfections, etc. *to*: in the eighteen special dharmas of a Buddha.

The Lord: So it is, Subhuti, so it is. All these dharmas are contrived activities, planned and willed, and through them the knowledge of all modes cannot be reached. All these dharmas serve to bring near the path and to produce it, but do not lead to the obtainment of the fruit. For the nonproduction and nonmanifestation of these dharmas means that they are without marks. Therefore from the first thought of enlightenment onwards the Bodhisattva continues to exert himself in wholesome dharmas, be it the perfection of giving, etc. *to*: the special Buddhadharmas. And he cognizes all this as a magical illusion. Without having fulfilled those dharmas one cannot mature beings. Therefore the Bodhisattva, who courses in perfect wisdom, cognizes as like a dream, etc. *to*: as like a magical creation each and every wholesome dharma in which he exerts himself. When he courses in perfect wisdom he cognizes everything up to the knowledge of all modes as like a dream, etc. He cognizes that all these beings are moving about in a dream, etc. Therefore the Bodhisattva who courses in perfect wisdom does not seize on dreamlike dharmas, etc. *to*: on dharmas which are like magical creations, as either existent or nonexistent, and when he has done so he reaches the knowledge of all modes. For unseizable is the perfection of wisdom and so is everything up to the eighteen special Buddhadharmas. Therefore the Bodhisattva, having known all dharmas as unseizable, strives after the supreme enlightenment. And why? Because all dharmas are unseizble, nonentities, like a dream, etc. *to*: like a magical creation. ((f. 306a)) But one cannot reach an unseizable dharma through an unseizable dharma, except for beings who do not cognize or see these dharmas. Therefore the Bodhisattva sets out for the supreme enlightenment for the sake of all beings. From the first thought of enlightenment onwards, whatever gift he gives, etc. *to*: whatever wisdom he develops, he does so for the sake of all beings and not for the sake of his own self. It is exclusively for the sake of all beings that he sets out for the supreme enlightenment. When he courses in perfect wisdom he dissuades from their perverted views those who have perceived a being in what is not a being, a self in what is not the self, etc. *to*: a viewer in what is not a viewer, and thereafter he establishes them in the deathless element where these habitual concepts, such as the notion of self, etc. no longer proceed. When he has given up all these tendencies to make affirmations and negations about objects, and all these restless tremulations of intellectual multiplicity, he dwells with a heart which does not mind anything as one who has achieved much. It is by this device that the Bodhisattva, when he courses in perfect wisdom, does not himself settle down in any dharma whatever and establishes also all beings in the avoidance of settling down —by way of worldly convention, and not by way of ultimate reality.

Subhuti: That Dharma which has been fully known by the Tathagata, has that been fully known by way of worldly convention, or by way of ultimate reality?

The Lord: By way of worldly convention one says that 'this Dharma has been fully known by the Tathagata'. But when one says that 'this dharma has been fully known by that dharma' one really gets hold of nothing. And why? It would be a basis if one were to say that 'through this dharma has that dharma been fully known'. And through duality there can be no attainment or reunion.

Subhuti: If through duality there is no attainment and no reunion, is there, then, an attainment and reunion through nonduality?

The Lord: There is no attainment or reunion through either duality or nonduality; there can be attainment and reunion only where there is neither duality nor nonduality. And why? Because they would otherwise imply an intellectual multiplicity. But in the sameness of Dharma there is no intellectual multiplicity, for the nature of Dharma is without intellectual multiplicity.

Subhuti: What is the sameness of Dharma in respect of dharmas which all have nonexistence for own-being?

The Lord: The sameness of Dharma is where there is no existent, no nonexistent, no own-being, and no doctrinal statement. For about the sameness of Dharma no doctrinal statement is possible. Since outside the sameness of Dharma no dharma can be apprehended, the sameness of Dharma has transcended all dharmas. The sameness of Dharma is inaccessible to anyone, be they fools or holy men, and it lies outside their range.

Subhuti: Does, then, the sameness of Dharma lie outside the range also of the Tathagata?

The Lord: It lies outside the range of all holy men, ((f. 306b)) including the Tathagatas.

Subhuti: Does, then, the Tathagata not have sovereignty over the range of all dharmas?

The Lord: The Tathagata would be a sovereign over the range of all dharmas if the sameness of Dharma were one thing and the Tathagata another. But the dharmic sameness of the common people, and that of the Streamwinners, etc. *to*: of the Tathagatas, that is just one single sameness, and in this sameness there is not any difference. Since the sameness of the common people and that of all holy men is just one single sameness, there is no duality in it, (so that one could say that) 'this is a common person', etc. *to*: 'this is a Tathagata'. All these dharmas are not apprehended in sameness.

Subhuti: If in the sameness of all dharmas all these dharmas are not apprehended, i.e. that 'this is a common person', etc. *to*: 'this is a Tathagata', then there will be no difference between the common people, etc. *to*: the Tathagatas.

The Lord: So it is, Subhuti, so it is. In the sameness of all dharmas there is no difference between these various kinds of persons.

Subhuti: If that is so, wherefrom, then, is there the manifestation in the world of the three Treasures, i.e. the Buddha, Dharma, and Samgha?

The Lord: Is the treasure of the Buddha one thing, the treasure of the Dharma another, the treasure of the Samgha another, and the sameness of Dharma again another?

Subhuti: As I understand the meaning of the Lord's teaching, the treasure of the Buddha is not one thing, the treasure of the Dharma another, the treasure of the Samgha another, and the sameness of Dharma another. But the three Treasures are just the sameness of Dharma. All these dharmas are not conjoined or disjoined, they are immaterial, undefinable, nonresisting, with one mark only, i.e. no mark. How, then, can the Lord bring about[3] with regard to these markless dharmas a distinctive determination between common persons, Streamwinners, etc. *to*: Tathagatas?

The Lord: So it is, Subhuti, so it is. It is within the range of the Tathagata's power, it is the work of the Tathagata's manly competence, that he brings about a distinctive determination of markless dharmas. What do you think, Subhuti, if the Tathagata had not, after fully knowing the supreme enlightenment,[4] effected a distinctive determination of dharmas, could one then conceive of the hells, etc. *to*: of the various kinds of gods, of the applications of mindfulness, etc. *to*: of the eighteen special Buddhadharmas?

Subhuti: No, one could not, O Lord. ((f. 307a))

The Lord: Therefore, then, this is the work of the Tathagata's manly competence that, although he does not swerve from the sameness of Dharma, he nevertheless brings about a distinctive determination of dharmas.

Subhuti: Is it not so, O Lord, that, as the Tathagata does not swerve from the sameness of Dharma, so also the common people do not swerve from it, and likewise the Streamwinners, etc. *to*: the Bodhisattvas?

The Lord: So it is, Subhuti, so it is. All dharmas do not swerve from the sameness of Dharma, nor do they turn away from it. And why?

[3]So *P*.—*Ad* perhaps: how can it be within the range of the Lord's power to bring about, etc.

[4]So *P*.—*AdT*: had not fully known the supreme enlightenment and in consequence had not effected, etc.

What is the Suchness of the Tathagatas, their nonfalseness, etc. that is also the Suchness, etc. of the foolish common people, the faith-followers, etc. *to* : the Bodhisattvas, the great beings. All these dharmas do not transgress against the sameness of Dharma. And why? Because this is just their Suchness, etc. and that is no other than the sameness of Dharma.

Subhuti : If, O Lord, the sameness of Dharma is the same whether it is that of the common people, of the Streamwinners, etc. *to* : of the Tathagatas, how is it that these dharmas with distinguishing marks,[5] which differ from one another in their dharmic nature, i.e. form, feeling, etc. *to* : the conditioned element and the unconditioned element, have a Dharmahood which has one mark only? And how can there be a distinctive determination of dharmas? Whereupon does the Bodhisattva base his distinctive determination when, coursing in perfect wisdom, he effects a differentiation between dharmas? For without having effected a differentiation of dharmas a Bodhisattva is not able to course in the perfection of wisdom. How, then, does the Bodhisattva, coursing in perfect wisdom, pass on from stage to stage and enter on a Bodhisattva's special mode of salvation, which enables him to surpass the level of the Disciples and Pratyekabuddhas, and, as a result of that, to fulfil the superknowledges? When he plays with these superknowledges, his perfection of giving, etc. *to* : his perfection of meditation becomes fulfilled, he passes on from Buddha-field to Buddha-field, honours the Buddhas and Lords, and in their presence plants wholesome roots which allow him to mature beings and to acquire a Buddha-field.

The Lord : As Subhuti has just said, 'if the sameness of all dharmas is the same for the common people, etc. *to* : the Tathagatas, it does not seem logical to describe the dharmic sameness of dharmas which have distinguishing marks as having one mark only'. What do you think, Subhuti, is ((307b)) the dharmic nature of anything just emptiness—be it form, etc. *to* : the Tathagatas?

Subhuti : It is just emptiness, O Lord!

The Lord : What do you think, Subhuti, can one in emptiness apprehend dharmas with distinguishing marks, and thus distinguish between the marks of form, etc. *to* : the Tathagata?

Subhuti : No, one cannot, O Lord.

The Lord : By this method also one should know that in the dharmic nature of dharmas there are no common people, nor anyone other than a common person, etc. *to* : no Tathagata nor anyone other than the Tathagata.

[5]*vilakṣaṇa*. Here both the context and the Tibetan *(mtshan ñid tha-dad-pa)* requires the above translation. In my Dictionary under *P* 518 as 'having no distinguishing marks', cr. to Gilgit f. 273b, 'without distinguishing marks'. Both contradictory meanings also in Monier Williams 952a, cf. 984c.

VIII 5,26. THE COMPREHENSION OF THE NONDISTINCTION BETWEEN THE CONDITIONED AND THE UNCONDITIONED.

Subhuti: Is, then, that Dharmahood conditioned or unconditioned?

The Lord: It is neither conditioned nor unconditioned. For the unconditioned cannot be got hold of by the exclusion of the conditioned, nor can the conditioned be got hold of by the exclusion of the unconditioned. Both the conditioned element and the unconditioned element are in this way dharmas which are neither conjoined nor disjoined, immaterial, undefinable, nonresisting, with one mark only, i.e. no mark. And when the Tathagata speaks about this he does so by way of worldly convention and not by way of ultimate reality. For in ultimate reality there is not anything which results from the formative influence of body, voice, or mind, nor can ultimate reality be apprehended as otherwise than the formative influence of body, voice, and mind. The sameness of these conditioned and unconditioned dharmas, that is ultimate reality. It is thus that the Bodhisattva, who courses in perfect wisdom, does not swerve from ultimate reality and nevertheless does a Bodhisattva's work.

Chapter 82

THE EXPOSITION OF THE UNALTERABLE NATURE OF DHARMA

Subhuti: If the sameness of all dharmas is empty of essential nature, then no dharma does anything to any other. When dharmas have nothing whatever and are nothing whatever, how, then, is it that the Bodhisattva on the one side does not swerve from ultimate reality, and on the other does the work of beings, through the four means of conversion?

The Lord: So it is, Subhuti, so it is, as you say. Emptiness does not do anything whatever to anything, nor does it do not anything[1]. If beings on their own could cognize emptiness, then there would be no need for the Tathagata's manly effort when he does not swerve from emptiness and yet dissuades beings from the notion of a self, etc. and then through emptiness liberates them from Samsara and establishes them in the unconditioned element. And also that unconditioned element is empty.

VIII 5,27. Nirvana.

Subhuti: Of what is it empty?

The Lord: It is empty of all notions. On the other hand, Subhuti, if a magical creation magically creates another magical creation, is there, then, perhaps in connection with that an entity which is not emptiness?

Subhuti: No, O Lord. Both these dharmas—the emptiness and the magical creation—are not conjoined or disjoined, they are both empty through emptiness.

[2]*The Lord*: What do you think, Subhuti, is then the difference between emptiness and magical creation mysteriously concealed?

Subhuti: It is not. And why? Because they both are not apprehended in emptiness, i.e. 'this is emptiness' and 'this is a magical creation'.

The Lord: There is nothing about the five skandhas which is not a magical creation.[2]

Subhuti: If these worldly dharmas are magical creations, are, then, also the supramundane dharmas magical creations, i.e. the four applications of mindfulness, etc. *to*: ((f. 308a)) their fruits by which the holy men are conceived, i.e. the Streamwinners, etc. *to*: the Tathagata?

The Lord: Since all dharmas are magical creations, each Disciple

[1]P adds: 'It does no work or no-work'.

[2]The text here is corrupt and the original reading can no longer be restored with certainty.

must be a magical creation, each Pratyekabuddha, each Bodhisattva, each Tathagata, each defilement, and each deed. By this method all dharmas are like magical creations.

Subhuti: And again, O Lord, as to this forsaking—as to the fruit of a Streamwinner, etc. *to*: Arhatship, or as to the level of a Pratyekabuddha, or that of a Buddha, or the forsaking of all defilements with their residues—are these dharmas also magical creations?

The Lord: Any dharmas that there are, as long as they have been produced or stopped, are all magical creations.

Subhuti: What is the dharma which is not a magical creation?

The Lord: The dharma of which there is no production or stopping.

Subhuti: What, then, is that?

The Lord: Nirvana which by its dharmic nature is undeluded.[3]

Subhuti: But the Lord has said that he does not swerve away from emptiness, that it is not apprehended through duality, and that there is no dharma which is not emptiness. Therefore the Nirvana which by its dharmic nature is undeluded must be a magical creation.

The Lord: So it is, Subhuti, so it is. All dharmas are empty through their own-being. They have not been made by the Disciples, or by the Pratyekabuddhas, or by the Bodhisattvas, or the Tathagatas. But Nirvana is the emptiness of own-marks.

Subhuti: How should a person who is a beginner be instructed, how admonished, so that he can cognize the emptiness of own-being?

The Lord: 'How is it possible that something was an existent in the past and later on becomes a nonexistent!' There is in it no existent, no nonexistent, no own-being and no other-being. How can there be an emptiness of own-being?

[3]The Gilgit Ms, but not P or *AdT*, adds the word *samaya* which I do not know how to interpret. *Samaya-vimukta* means "released temporarily, occassionally, from time to time" (*E* 565b), and *asamaya-vimutta* "definitely released" (*CPD* 500a). The word *samaya* itself has many meanings in *MW* 1164a, and becomes very important in Tantric terminology.

Chapter 83

THE MANIFESTATION OF A BODHISATTVA'S TRAINING[1]

(I. *Problems of Training.*)

Thereupon the Bodhisattva *Maitreya,* the great being, said this to the Lord: If, O Lord, all dharmas have nonexistence for own-being, how then should the Bodhisattva, who courses in the perfection of wisdom and who wants to train in the training of a Bodhisattva, train in the five skandhas, the twelve sense fields, the eighteen elements; in the sense fields of eye contact, etc. *to*: mind contact; in ignorance, etc. *to*: decay and earth; in the truths of suffering, origination, stopping, and the path? How should he train in dharmas which are with or without form, definable or undefinable, resisting or nonresisting, conditioned or unconditioned, with or without outflows, with or without blemish, mean of exalted, inward or outward, seen, heard, known, or discerned, past, future, or present, wholesome or unwholesome, determined or undetermined, associated with the world of sence desire, the world of form or the formless world, belonging to those in training, to the adepts or those who are neither in training nor adepts? How should he train in greed, aversion, pride, ignorance, wrong view, or doubt? How should he train in stinginess or giving, immorality or morality, ill will or patience, indolence or vigour, distraction or concentration, stupidity or wisdom? How should he train in discrimination or emptiness, in the sign or the signless, in wrong wishes or right wishes, in lovely or repulsive dharmas? How should he train in the defilements or their forsaking, in defiling or purification, in birth-and-death or the realm of Nirvana? How should he train in the Buddhadharmas?

(II. *All things are mere words*)

The Lord: A Bodhisattva, Maitreya, a great being who courses in perfect wisdom, and who wants to train in the training of a Bodhisattva, should train in that 'form, etc. *to*: the Buddhadharmas are mere names'.[2]

[1]Or: "The distinctive features" *(rab-tu phye (dbye)-ba, prabhāvanā)* of a Bodhisattva's training". In the Tibetan tradition this is known as "The chapter preached at the request of Maitreya" *(Byams shus-kyi le'u)*. For a discussion of the significance of this chapter see my edition of the Sanskrit text in *Mélanges d'Indianisme à la mémoire de Louis Renou,* 1968, on pages 230-233.

[2]This refers back to an earlier passage of the *Prajñāpāramitā* which was a great favourite

Maitreya: If, O Lord, this designation, i.e. 'this is form', etc. were apprehended as though it were an entity, on account of its being taken for the sign of something conditioned, how, then, could a Bodhisattva train in that 'form, etc. are mere names'? But since it is without a corresponding entity, is it not improper to say of this name even that it is a mere name, or to say of 'this is form, etc.' that it is a mere name?

The Lord: As something adventitious has that designation been added on[3] to that entity which is the sign of something conditioned, i.e. when one says that 'this is form', etc. And since through that entity which is the sign of something conditioned that name, i.e. 'form', etc. is followed by[4] the conviction, the assignment, the recognition[5] that 'it is form', therefore one should know also by this method that as adventitious has that designation been added on to that entity which is the sign of something conditioned, i.e. 'this is form', etc. What do you think, Maitreya, does someone perhaps have with regard to this entity which is the sign of something conditioned a notion, concept, name, conventional expression, or (false) belief?

Maitreya: So it is.

The Lord: By this method also, Maitreya, you should know that as adventitious has that designation been added on to this entity which is the sign of something conditioned, i.e. 'this is form', etc.

(III. *The actual reality of named things*)

Maitreya: If this is so, is then form, etc. actually apprehended by way of own-being (as a result of taking hold of) that entity which is the sign of something conditioned and on account of which there takes place the name, notion, concept and conventional expression, 'this is form', etc.

The Lord: 'Form', etc. is a name, notion, concept, and conventional expression with regard to an entity which is the sign of something conditioned. What do you think, Maitreya, is also the own-being of that form, etc. merely conceptual?

with the Yogācārins, and of which five different versions have been printed in E. Conze, *The Prajñāpāramitā Literature*, 1960, pp. 98-100.

[3]This refers back to *A* ii 47 (≐*P* 219a, p. 219 above): "The word 'being' denotes no dharma or non-dharma. It is a term that has been added on (to what is really there), as something adventitious, groundless, nothing in itself, unfounded in objective fact." Haribhadra p. 179 comments: 'added on' means superimposed, merely conventional.

[4]This is a possible meaning for the locative.

[5]These three terms are not very well attested in the dictionaries. Our translation of the first follows Monier Williams. But since the *Mahāvyutpatti* gives *sampratipatti* as an equivalent of *yaṅ-dag-par rtogs-pa*, the meaning might also be "affirmation". For the second, Monier Williams does not fit, and since in the *Lankāvatāra Sūtra suprativibhāga* renders *rab-tu rtogs-pa*, one might also translate as "apportioning", or "distinctive attribution". For the third, the usual rendering "experience" seems unsuitable here, and we follow Edgerton s. v. *apratisaṃvedanā*.

Maitreya: It is merely conceptual, merely conceptual.

The Lord: In that case you can surely not assume that the real own-being of form, etc. has actually been apprehended when one takes up that entity which is the sign of something conditioned on account of[6] which there takes place the name, notion, concept, and conventional expression that 'this is form', etc.?

Maitreya: If form, etc. are nothing but mere names, notions, social agreements, concepts and conventional expressions, is it not so that their own-being is then actually apprehended in the sense that they are nothing but mere names, notions, social agreements, concepts, and conventional expressions?

The Lord: What do you think, Maitreya, when 'form', etc. are nothing but mere names, notions, social agreements, concepts, and conventional expressions, can one then conceive of their production or passing away, of their defiling or purification?

Maitreya: No, O Lord.

The Lord: In that case, Maitreya, you can surely not assume that the real own-being of form, etc. has actually been apprehended?

Maitreya: Do then form, etc. altogether not exist by way of their own-marks?

The Lord: That I do not teach!

Maitreya: How, then, do form, etc. exist?

The Lord: Form, etc. exist by way of worldly social agreements and conventional expressions, but not in ultimate reality.

Maitreya: As I, O Lord, understand of meaning of the Lord's teaching, the inexpressible realm[7] exists by way of ultimate reality. But if that is so, how is it that that entity which is the sign of something conditioned and to which 'form', etc. has been added on as an adventitious designation, does not exist by way of ultimate reality? If that[8] does not exist by way of ultimate reality,[9] how, then, does the inexpressible realm exist? For is it not logical to equate the entity which is the sign of something conditioned with the inexpressible realm?

The Lord: I will therefore, Maitreya, question you on this, and you may answer as best you can. What do you think, Maitreya, when your wisdom becomes united with the inexpressible realm, do you then on that occasion apprehend the entity which is the sign of something conditioned and to which is added on the adventitious designation that 'this is form', etc.?

[6]*upādāya, ñe-bar bzuṅ-nas*. DR: by taking up which

[7]i.e. the *dharmadhātu* (DR)

[8] =all dharmas (DR)

[9]If no dharmas exist, you cannot talk of nonexisting, and also not of a *dharmadhātu* (DR).

Maitreya: No, O Lord.

The Lord: In this way, also, Maitreya, you should know that that entity which is the sign of something conditioned is neither other than the inexpressible realm, nor not other.[10] And why is this so?[11] If the inexpressible realm were not other than the entity which is the sign of something condition and to which an adventitious designation, i.e. 'this is form', etc. has been added on, then even just now all the foolish common people would enter Parinirvana and would fully know the supreme enlightenment. But if the inexpressible realm were other than the entity which is the sign of something conditioned, then even just now that sign could not be apprehended through which there would be penetration into this inexpressible realm.[12] In this way also, Maitreya, you should know that the inexpressible realm is neither other nor not other than that entity which is the sign of something conditioned and to which an adventitious designation has been added on, i.e. 'this is form', etc.

Maitreya: If, O Lord, the Bodhisattva, the great being, when he proceeds in the wise observation which is in direct contact with the inexpressible realm, does not apprehend that entity which is the sign of something conditioned to which has been added on an adventitious designation, i.e. 'this is form', etc., is it not so that he apprehends neither something which exists nor something which does not exist?

The Lord: Neither existence nor nonexistence apply to that entity which is the sign of something conditioned. And why? On the occasion that you discriminate that entity which is the sign of something conditioned, on that occasion it is grasped by way of discrimination. But on the occasion that, when proceeding in the wise observation which is in direct contact with the inexpressible realm, you do not discriminate it, is it on that occasion grasped by way of nondiscrimination?

Maitreya: So it is, O Lord.

The Lord: But if that is so, is this then not mere discrimination, i.e. the entity which is the sign of something conditioned to which an adventitious designation has been added, i.e. 'this is form', etc.? When, however, somebody proceeds (in the idea) that this is mere discrimination, or in the indiscriminate realm, then, since his discriminations have departed, how can he apprehend the existence or nonexistence of that to which this adventitious designation, i.e. 'this is form', etc., has been added on?

[10]*Ta,b* have: 'it is not it. . .it is not other than it'.

[11]This addition is, I think, required by the context.

[12]This statement may, or may not, be connected with what Proclus (*The Elements of Theology*, ed. E.R. Dodds, 1933, pp. 109-111, prop. 123) says, i.e. 'All that is divine is itself ineffable and unknowable by any secondary being because of its supraexistential unity, but it may be apprehended and known from the existents which participate in it'.

(IV. The three aspects)

Maitreya: When the Bodhisattva who courses in the perfection of wisdom proceeds in the skill in the subdivision of dharmas,[13] by which modes should he follow up the conceptual subdivisions of form, etc.?

The Lord: By three modes, i.e. 'this is the imagined form', 'this is the discerned[14] form', 'this is the dharmic nature of form'; etc.

Maitreya: Which are they?

The Lord: Imagined form, etc. is the false imagination which has the own-beingness of form, etc. for its object,[15] and which is based on the name, notion, social agreement, concept, and conventional expression 'form', etc. with regard to that entity which is the sign of something conditioned. Discerned form, etc. is the definition[16] of that entity which is the sign of something conditioned as in its dharmic nature mere discernment, as a verbal expression which is conditioned by discernment and to which refers this name, notion, social agreement, concept, and conventional expression, i.e. 'this is form', etc. The dharmic nature of form, etc. is that dharmic nature of dharmas which is established whether Tathagatas are produced or not, the established order of dharmas, the realm of Dharma, the absence of own-being which is characteristic eternally and through all eternity, constantly and through all time, of that discerned form because of that imagined form,[17] the absence of self in dharmas, Suchness, the Reality limit.

Maitreya: Of these three kinds of form, etc. which one should be viewed as unsubstantial,[18] which one as substantial, and which one as neither substantial nor unsubstantial, but as derived from[19] ultimate reality?

The Lord: Imagined form, etc. should be seen as unsubstantial. Discerned form, etc. should, because of its substantiality,[20] be viewed as substantial, although it never occurs as an independent reality. The dharmic nature of form, etc. should be viewed as neither unsubstantial

[13]into the five skandhas, eighteen elements, etc.

[14]This is an attempt to find a word which covers the two meanings of *vikalpita* intended here, i.e. (1) discriminated, (2) examined, compared, looked through to.

[15]Lit. Through the own-beingness; *instrumentalis*; *Tab*:*-du*. DR: Because the own-beingness of form is its object, and to be an object is one of the four kinds of cause. There is difference here between 'of' and 'by'

[16]A more literal translation would be 'standing' *(gnas-pa)*, in the sense of 'established repute or position'.

[17]Lamotte II 1. p. 91 translates: En raison de cette matière imaginaire *(parikalpitarūpa)*. la matière pensée *(vikalparūpa)* est éternelle et constante: c 'est la vraie nature *(tathatā)*, etc.—We have not understood this phrase.

[18]or: nonsubstantial.

[19]*prabhāvita*; *rab-tu phye-ba*. Five possible meanings of this term have been enumerated in E. Conze's edition of the *Vajracchedikā*, 1957, pp. 98-99.

[20]*Tab*: 'because of the substantiality of the discernment'!

nor substantial, but as derived from ultimate reality.

Maitreya: The Lord has proclaimed that to speak of 'form', etc. is to make a count of what is not-two;[21] but since there is[22] this conceptual subdivision of form, etc., with what hidden intent has the Lord then taught that 'to speak of 'form', etc. is to make a count of what is not-two'?

The Lord: What do you think, Maitreya, is form, etc. the nonsubstantiality of form, etc. or is it not?

Maitreya: It is not, O Lord.

The Lord: Is form, etc. then the fact that 'form', etc. is mere name, notion, concept, and conventional expression?

Maitreya: It is not, O Lord.

The Lord: By this method, Maitreya, you should know that what is imagined form, that is neither form nor no-form; and what is neither form nor no-form, that is nondual. It is with this hidden intent that I have taught that to speak of 'this is form', etc. is to make a count of what is not-two. What do you think, Maitreya, is the substantiality of discerned form that form on account of which there occurs the name, notion, concept, and conventional expression 'form'?

Maitreya: It is not, O Lord.

The Lord: What do you think, Maitreya, is form the own-beingness as well as the own-marks of the discerned[23] form which results from the sign of form being imagined?

Maitreya: It is not, O Lord.

The Lord: By this method, Maitreya, you should know that also what is discerned form is neither form nor no-form; and what is neither form nor no-form, that is nondual. It is with this hidden intent that I have taught that to speak of 'this is form', etc. is to make a count of what is not two. What do you think, Maitreya, is form the recognition[24] of form in its dharmic nature by the fact that it is devoid of a self?

Maitreya: It is not, O Lord.

The Lord: Is, then, form the dharmic nature of form as it is thus in its dharmic nature?

Maitreya: It is not, O Lord.

The Lord: By this method, Maitreya, you should know that also form in its dharmic nature is neither form nor no-form; and what is neither form nor no-form, that is nondual. It is with this hidden intent that I have taught that to speak of 'form', etc. is to make a count of what is not-two.

[21]e.g. at *A* i 27.

[22]*Ta,b*: 'is not'.

[23]*S*: 'imagined'. *Tab* differs and the passage is corrupt.

[24]*prabhāvitatā, rab-tu phye-ba'i.* DR: The dharmic nature of form has the meaning of not-self. It means the state of being separate, that it is put or set apart *(sur-du bshag-pa)* from the other two by the fact that it is not (=that it is devoid of a self?). It is similar to *(ṅos 'dzin-pa)*; and one recognizes that they are separate.

(V. *Comprehension, etc.*)

Maitreya: In a Bodhisattva, who courses in the perfection of wisdom, who is thus skilled in the nondual mark of form, etc. who has avoided the two extremes and who progresses on the middle way, how should the mark of his comprehension[25] be viewed, how that of his forsaking, realisation, and development?

The Lord: For the Bodhisattva who courses in the perfection of wisdom, who has avoided the two extremes and who progresses on the middle way, the noncomprehension as well as the non-noncomprehension of form, etc. that is his comprehension. The nonforsaking as well as the non-nonforsaking of form, etc. that is his forsaking. The nonrealisation of the forsaking of form, etc. as well as its non-nonrealization, that is his realization. The nondevelopment of the path as well as its non-nondevelopment which he carries out for the forsaking of form, etc. that is his development.

(VI. *Nirvana*)

Maitreya: What is the Nirvana of the Bodhisattva who courses in the perfection of wisdom and it thus endowed with this kind of comprehension, forsaking, realisation and development?

The Lord: Deep, Maitreya, exceedingly deep is the Nirvana of the Bodhisattvas, the great beings!

Maitreya: For what reason is it so deep, so exceedingly deep?

The Lord: It is because the Nirvana of the Bodhisattvas, the great beings, is both not Nirvana and not no-Nirvana.

Maitreya: How is that?

The Lord: The nonrenunciation of Samsara in the interest of others is not Nirvana. The nonrenunciation of Nirvana in one's own interest is not no-Nirvana.

Maitreya: If, O Lord, the Bodhisattva in the interest of others does not renounce Samsara, how is it that through his nonrenunciation of Samsara he has not also renounced Nirvana? If the Bodhisattva has in his own interest not (completely)[26] renounced Nirvana, how is it that as a result of his nonrenunciation of Nirvana he has not also[27] renounced Samsara?

The Lord: Here, Maitreya, the Bodhisattva, the great being who courses in perfect wisdom, neither discriminates[28] Samsara as Samsara, nor Nirvana as Nirvana. When he thus does not discriminate, they, i.e. Samsara and Nirvana, become exactly the same.[29] And why? Because,

[25]Or: 'has comprehension of the marks'?

[26]So the DR.

[27]*dis*, by the same token, i.e. out of self-interest (DR).

[28]discriminatingly considers as; thinks, by way of discrimination, of S. as S.

[29]So DR explains *mñam-pas mñam-pa*. The repetition makes it emphatic.—this is the Sakyapa doctrine: *'khor 'das dbye* (separate) *med*.

when he does not discriminate Samsara as Samsara, he does not become alarmed by Samsara; and so, when he does not discriminate Nirvana as Nirvana, he does not fall away from[30] Nirvana. Thus one should know that for one who is established in the indiscriminate realm there can for this reason be no renunciation of Samsara and no renunciation of Nirvana.

Maitreya: Since for the Bodhisattva, the great being who courses in perfect wisdom and who is established in the indiscriminate realm, Samsara, just as it has not been renounced, so it has not been appropriated —how is it then, O Lord, that it is something which has not been renounced? And likewise Nirvana, as it has not been renounced, so it has not been appropriated—how is it then that it is something which has not been renounced?

The Lord: It is not thus, Maitreya, that I teach liberation from[31] Samsara or its nonappropriation, or that I teach the appropriation or nonappropriation of Nirvana. But when Bodhisattvas, great beings who course in perfect wisdom, obtain the sovereignty of thought through a cognition which has the indiscriminate realm for its object—then, on account of their exhibiting (themselves in) Samsara through skill in means in countless world systems in the world with its ten directions, I teach the nonrenunciation of Samsara on the part of the Bodhisattvas, the great beings who have reached (the Mahayanistic) Nirvana; and on account of their being established in the baseless realm of emptiness I teach their nonrenunciation of Nirvana.

Maitreya: How should one view the inherent mark of discrimination?

The Lord: The nonduality of existence and nonexistence, as well as the absence of intellectual multiplicity with regard to dharmas, such as form, etc. and also with regard to the emptiness of form, etc. that should be viewed as the inherent mark of nondiscrimination.

*(*VII. *The three lineages.)*

Maitreya: Do, then, all the disciples have an absolute assurance of their establishment in Nirvana?

The Lord: No, they have not. And why? Because this world has beings of various dispositions, of manifold dispositions.[32] And among sentient beings with these various dispositions one can apprehend a variety of patterns[33] with regard to their lineage.[34] Some beings belong

[30] *Tab*: 'does not fall away from Nirvana; and likewise he does not fall away from (=fall into?) Samsara'. *Tc* has 'does not settle down in' *(na-abhiniviśate)* in both cases. The Sanskrit, 'does not become alarmed' gives little sense, and seems to be a scribal error.

[31] *Tab*: 'the appropriation off'.

[32] or 'lineages'; *dhātu=kula=gotra.*

[33] So *Tab. S*: 'beginnings'.

[34] The three 'families' *(gdul-bya rigs can)* are: Mahāyāna, Hīnayāna, *aniyata* and therefore adaptable to either Hīnayāna or Mahāyāna.

to a lineage in which from the beginning they strive for an exalted goal, and they also reach that exalted goal. Others belong to a lineage where from the beginning they strive for a low goal, they reach just that low goal, and are quite contented with that. Others again belong to a lineage where at the beginning they strive for a low goal and reach that low goal; not contented with that, however, they further on strive for an exalted goal and reach just that exalted goal.

Maitreya: If a person who belongs to the third kind of lineage, on having attained Arhatship, wants thereafter to eagerly strive after the supreme enlightenment, how can he (possibly) attain that without ever being reborn again? The Lord has not said anything about his rebirth which would (be necessary to) enable him to make further progress.

The Lord: I do not proclaim for him the kind of rebirth which is the effect of karmic defilements, but proclaim for the Arhat an unthinkable rebirth which allows him to advance to the beyond of Nirvana.[35]

Maitreya: It is wonderful, O Lord, how sublime are the intentions of the Bodhisattvas, the great beings, how magnanimous are their resolutions, in that even just now they strive from the very beginning after an exalted goal, and in that they reach just that exalted goal! What, O Lord, is the state of mind of the Bodhisattvas, the great beings, which gives them their sublime intentions and their magnanimous resolutions?

The Lord: Without caring for the position of Sakra, or Brahma, of that of a world guardian, or that of a universal monarch, or any other kind of worldly achievement the Bodhisattva, the great being, because of his nonattachment to them and his complete freedom from them, dedicates his store of merit to the supreme enlightenment (of all beings); such are the Bodhisattva's sublime intentions. But that the Bodhisattva wishes to make that ease of nonattachment, that ease of freedom, that ease of the Blessed Rest common to all beings, and therefore dedicates his store of merit to the supreme enlightenment (of all beings), i.e. by his nonrenunciation of Samsara, that should be seen as his magnanimous resolution.

Maitreya: Wonderful and astonishing, O Lord, are the dharmas of a Bodhisattva! Wonderful and astonishing. O Lord, is the training of a Bodhisattva! The son or daughter of good family who wants to obtain[36] the wonderful and astonishing dharmas of a Bodhisattva should raise his thought to the supreme enlightenment.

[35]The phrase can mean, "to Nirvana which is the Beyond", or "to the beyond of the (Hinayanistic) Nirvana".—Whereas ordinary people take birth as a result of their *kleśas*, Bodhisattvas appear in Samsara by virtue of their Vow. A Bodhisattva's body emanates from his spiritual cognition, and is sometimes called *jñāna-śarīra* (e.g. *Lankāvatāra Sūtra* 20, 3). For some useful remarks about the rebirth of Arhats see also Ruegg, JAOS 82, 1962, 327-8.

[36]*Tab*: 'train in'.

Appendix I[1]

VIII. THE REUNION WITH THE DHARMA-BODY

VIII 1. The Substantial Body.

Again, Subhuti, of those all-dharmas, which are like a dream, which are nonentities, which have nonexistence for own-being, which are empty of own-marks, which are perfectly pure through the knowledge of all modes, which are without outflows, the essential original nature, which has one mark only, i.e. no mark, should be known as the Tathagata, the Arhat, the fully Enlightened One. It is thus that the Bodhisattva, the great being, should train in perfect wisdom.

Subhuti: What again, O Lord, are those all-dharmas without outflows?

The Lord: The 37 wings of enlightenment, the holy Unlimited, the eight emancipations,. . . the four perfect purities, the ten perfections, the ten powers, the four grounds of self-confidence, the three ways in which (the Tathagata) has nothing to hide, the threefold mindful equanimity, the nature which is never bewildered, the knowledge of all modes, the knowledge of the paths, all-knowledge—these, Subhuti, are the all-dharmas without outflows. It is thus, Subhuti, that the Bodhisattva, the great being, should train in the perfection of wisdom.

VIII 2. The Enjoyment Body.

Moreover, Subhuti, when he has trained in perfect wisdom, when by the full attainment of just these dharmas he has known full enlightenment, his body always and everywhere adorned with the 32 marks of the superman and his 80 accessory characteristics, the Tathagata, the Arhat, the fully Enlightened One, demonstrates to the Bodhisattvas, the great beings, the supreme dharma of the Mahayana which brings them unsurpassed delight and joy, happiness and ease. It is thus that the Bodhisattva, the great being, should train in perfect wisdom.

VIII 3. The Transformation Body.

Moreover, having trained in perfect wisdom, having, through the full attainment of just these dharmas, known full enlightenment, the Tathagata, etc. in the ten directions, in endless and boundless world systems, during the whole of time, works the weal of all beings by means of a multi-form cloud of transformation bodies. It is thus that the Bodhi-

[1]Sections of *AA* omitted in *Ad*.

sattva, the great being, should train in perfect wisdom.

....

VIII 5,2,5. THE TEN ALL-BASES ('DEVICES' IN AA).

And what, Subhuti, are the ten All-Bases? The earth-device, the water-device, the fire-device, the wind-device, the blue-device, the yellow-device, the red-device, the white-device, the consciousness-device, the space-device. These are called the ten All-Bases. (D no. 42: resolutely intent on all elements as the earth-element, everything becomes just one element, becomes earth-element. And so with the other nine. They are called 'All-Bases' because they pervade everywhere, and each single 'base' becomes everything).

VIII 5,2,6. THE EIGHT BASES OF OVERCOMING.

And what, Subhuti, are the eight bases of overcoming? (1) A percipient of inward form, he sees outward forms, which are finite, of good or bad colour, and having overcome just these forms, he cognizes and sees. (2) Not being a percipient of inward form, he sees outward forms which are large, of good or bad colour, and, having overcome just these forms, he cognizes and sees. (3) Not being a percipient of inward form, he sees outward forms, blue, blue in colour, blue in appearance, blue in reflection, (4) Yellow, yellow in colour, etc. (5) red, red in colour, etc., (6) white, white in colour, etc.—such as (3) a flax blossom or a perfect cloth from Benares, (4) a blossom of Pterospermum acerifolium or a perfect cloth from Benares, (6) the colour of the morning star, or a perfect cloth of Benares. (7) = the first formless attainment, (8) = the second formless attainment. These are called the eight Bases of Overcoming.

VIII 5,2,7. THE APPEASEMENT. (The meditative trance which appeases the defilements in others).

And what, Subhuti, is Appeasement? The concentration and wisdom by which, relying on trance, he protects other people from the arising of the defilements, together with the dharmas of thought and its constituents which are associated with that—that is called 'the Appeasement'.

VIII 5,2,8. THE COGNITION WHICH RESULTS FROM RESOLVE.

And what, Subhuti, is the cognition which results from resolve? The concentration by which he succeeds in his resolve, 'relying on trance I shall cognize whatever I may wish to cognize in the three periods of time', together with the dharmas of thought and its constituents which are associated with that—that is called 'the cognition which results from resolve'.

VIII 5,2,9. THE SIX SUPERKNOWLEDGES.

And what, Subhuti, are the six superknowledges? The ability to work wonders, the heavenly eye, the heavenly ear, the cognition of others' thoughts, the recollection of former lives, the cognition of the extinction of the ourflows, and the superknowledge of realization—these are called the six superknowledges.

VIII 5,2,11. THE FOUR KINDS OF PERFECT AND ALL-ROUND PURITY.

And what, Subhuti, are the four perfect and all-round purities? The perfect purity of the physical basis, the perfect purity of the objective support, the perfect purity of thought, the perfect purity of cognition, these are called the four perfect purities in every respect.

VIII 5,2,12. THE TEN SOVEREIGNTIES.

And what, Subhuti, are the ten sovereignties? The sovereignty over the lifespan, over thought, over the requisites of life, over karma, over rebirth, over determination, over resolve, over the miraculous powers, over cognition, over dharma—these are called the 'ten sovereignties'.

VIII 5,2,15. THE THREE WAYS IN WHICH (THE TATHAGATA) HAS NOTHING TO HIDE.

And which, Subhuti, are the three ways in which the Tathagata has nothing to hide? Perfectly pure are his deeds of body, perfectly pure are his deeds of speech, perfectly pure are his deeds of mind.

VIII 5,2,16. THE TRIPLE MINDFUL EQUANIMITY.

And what, Subhuti, is the triple mindful equanimity? Whether people want to listen, whether they do not want to listen, whether they want both (to listen and not to listen), the Tathagata, the Arhat, the fully Enlightened One, free from both affection and aversion, dwells just evenmindedly in mindful self-possession.

VIII 5,2,17. A NATURE WHICH IS NEVER BEWILDERED.

And what, Subhuti, is the nature which is never bewildered? His mindfulness is always fixed in all his actions,. . . , all his devices, and at all times.

VIII 5,2,18. THE UPROOTING OF THE RESIDUES.

And what, Subhuti, is the uprooting of the residues? In each and every way the notion of the defilements or anything like them is habitually absent.

VIII 5,2,19. THE GREAT COMPASSION.

And what, Subhuti, is the great compassion? The unsurpassed resolute intention to further the well-being and welfare of all beings at all times.

VIII 5,2,21. THE KNOWLEDGE OF ALL MODES.

(The explanation is missing in all the Mss of *P*).

Appendix II.

Each of the large Tibetan versions of the Sutra contains a passage dealing with the thirty-two marks.[1] *Only three recensions of the Sanskrit text have survived. the first is the Gilgit Ms of the version in* 18,000 *lines (ff.* 280*b*14-281*a*12; *see pages* 583-585). *The second occurs in the* 63*rd chapter of the version in* 100,000 *lines. The third, which is translated below, can be found in the version in* 25,000 *lines, revised to conform with the Abhisamayālaṅkāra.*

This text first emumerates the thirty-two marks, then explains them, and thirdly outlines both their cause and their consequence.[2] *As for the third part, it is of special interest as this section of the Prajñāpāramitā is probably the only surviving Sanskrit document which deals with this aspect of the doctrine in some detail. It shows many similarities with the Lakkhaṇa-suttanta of Dīgha Nikāya (no. XXX)*[3] *where it is said that "seers not of our communion (bahiraka isayo) are acquainted with (dhārenti) these marks, but they know (jānanti) not for what deeds done any of the marks is acquired."*[4] *The traditions on these matters must go back rather far because they are shared also by the Sarvāstivādins.*[5]

And what, Subhuti, are the Tathagata's *thirty-two marks of a superman?* 1. He has, stamped on his hands and feet, lines dipicting a wheel, 2. his hands and feet are well-placed, 3. his hands and feet have webs, 4. his hands and feet are tender and soft, 5. his body has seven protuberances, 6. his (toes and) fingers are long, 7. he has broad heels, 8. his bodily frame is tall and straight, 9. his feet have inconspicuous ankle joints, 10. the hairs on his body point upwards, 11. his shanks are like those of

[1]Sten Konow has restored the Sanskrit text of the *Daśasahasrikā* in 1941 on pp. 108-110 of his *The first two chapters of the Daśasāhasrikā Prajñāpāramitā.*

[2]The first two parts correspond to *Abhisamayālaṅkāra* VIII, vv. 13 to 17, and the third to vv. 18 to 20.

[3]The two sources agree at 4-8, 13-14, 29-32; they agree in part at 1-3, 11, 18-19, 21, 24-28; they disagree at 9-10, 12, 15-17, 20, 22-23.

[4]p. 145.

[5]E.g. we read in *Abhidharmakośa,* trad. L. de la Vallée Poussin, I, 1923. p. 69 that the *Prajñaptiśāstra* says that the mark of *brahmasvaratā* "résulte de la pratique parfaite de l'abstinence du langage injurieux" (IV 76c). (See our no. 25).—The *Kāraṇaprajñapti* begins in Narthang mdo 62, 107 and ends at 127b2. For the second mark see de la Vallée Poussin, *Cosmologie*, pp. 326-328.

the black antelope, 12. his arms are long and powerful, 13. his male organ is hidden in a sheath, 14. his skin has a golden hue, 15. his skin is quite smooth, 16. the hairs on his body stand separately by themselves and curl to the right, 17. his face is adorned with a hairtuft, 18. the upper part of his body is like that of a lion, 19. his shoulders are gently curved, 20. the flesh between his shoulder blades is quite compact, 21. he possesses a most excellent taste, 22. the circumference of his figure is like that of the fig tree, 23. there is a cowl on his head, 24. his tongue is long and slender, 25. he has a divine voice, 26. he has jaws like a lion, 27. his teeth are very white. 28. his teeth are equal in size, 29. there are no gaps between his teeth, 30. he has a total of 40 equal teeth, 31. his eyes are intensely black, 32. his eye-lashes are like those of a mganificent heifer.

1. 'He has, stamped on his hands and feet, lines depicting a wheel'—on the soles of the Tathagata's feet and on the palms of his hands there grow wheels, with a thousand spokes, with rims and naves, complete in every respect; as though beautifully engraved on bone or ivory. 2. Because he places the soles of his feet evenly on the earth, and his feet are not arched—'his hands and feet are well-placed'. 3. Because, as with the royal goose, the fingers of his hands and the toes on his feet are joined by webs—'his hands and feet are joined by webs'. 4. Because the soles of his feet and the palms of his hands are very soft like a ball of cotton wool, and exceedingly tender—'his hands and feet are tender and soft'. 5. Because he has protuberances in seven regions—on his two hands, his two feet, his two shoulders, and above his neck—'his body has seven protuberances'. 6. Because the toes of his feet and the fingers of his hands extend far—'his toes and fingers are long'. 7. Because his heels are extensive—'he has broad heels'. 8. Because his body is seven cubits tall and upright—'his bodily frame is tall and straight'. 9. Because his knees and ankles are well concealed above—'his feet have inconspicuous anklebones'. 10. Because the hairs of his body curl upwards, turning to the right, curling in rings—'the hairs of his body point upwards'. 11. Because his shanks are like those of some deer, are safe and sound, and are regularly built up and rounded—'his shanks are like those of the black antelope'. 12. When he stands up with his thighs straight and without bending the body, he can touch his kneecaps with the two palms of his hands—therefore 'his arms are long and powerful'. 13. Because his male organ is concealed within a beautifully formed sheath, and is like that of a thoroughbred elephant or stallion—'his male organ is hidden in a sheath'. 14. Because his skin has the hue of the finest burnished gold—'his skin has a golden hue'. 15. Because his skin is smooth like well-worked gold and silver, and because dust cannot soil his limbs—'his skin is quite smooth'. 16. Because the hairs of his body are well separated, grow each one singly, without a second by the side—'the hairs of his

body stand separately'. 17. Because his face is adorned with a hairtuft between his eyebrows, which is a hundred times more brilliant than the moon and sun, and which is white in colour, like a jasmine flower, the moon, cow's milk, or a hoarfrost blossom—'his face is adorned with a hairtuft'. 18. Because the upper part of his body is large—'the upper part of his body is like that of a lion'. 19. Because the nape of his neck is well rounded and tightly knit—'his shoulders are gently curved'. 20. Because his shoulders and chest are solid and well-smoothed like a golden slab—'the flesh in between his shoulder blades is quite compact'. 21. Because his taste is unimpaired by wind, bile, or phlegm, because he perceives each individual taste as it occurs, and because his consciousness conforms to it—'he possesses a most excellent taste'. 22. Because his body measures a fathom, both in height and width—'the circumference of his figure is like that of the fig tree'. 23. Because he has on the top of his head something like a cowl, which is well-rounded and turns to the right, which is well-formed and beautiful to behold—'there is a cowl on his head'. 24. Because it is the colour of the petals of the red Utpala flower, and when extended is exceedingly extensive—'his tongue is long and slender'. 25. Because his voice is like that of Hiranyagarbha or of the Kalavinka bird—'he has a divine voice'. 26. Because his jaw is like a circular mirror, well-finished, powerful, pleasant to behold, and fascinating—'he has jaws like a lion'. 27. Because his teeth are exceedingly white, like the jasmine flower, the moon, or a fragment of conch shell—'his teeth are very white'. 28. Because not some teeth are higher, and some lower—'his teeth are equal in size'. 29. Because there are no intervals between them—'there are no gaps between his teeth'. 30. Because they are neither more nor less (than 40), and because they are neither bent nor crooked—'he has a total of 40 equal teeth'. 31. Because both the black and the white parts of his eyes are unstained and quite pure (in their colour), and because they never become bloodshot—'his eyes are intensely black'. 32. Because his eye-lashes, above or below, are just at the right angle, and because they are very neat—'the Tathagata's eyelashes are like those of a magnificent heifer'.

(1) Because he has followed the spiritual teachers and gone to meet them, has listened to the Dharma and praised it, has honoured the monasteries, shrines, and so on—he has, stamped on his hand and feet, lines depicting a wheel; and this is furthermore a (prophetic) sign indicating that he will have a great retinue. (2) Because he has had a firm sense of obligation (as a result of his Vow)—his hands and feet are well-placed; and that is a sign indicating that he will be unshakeable. (3) Because of his cultivation of the four means of conversion, i.e. gifts, kind words, beneficial actions, consistency between words and deeds—his hands

and feet have webs; and that is a sign indicating that he will have the ability to convert beings quickly, (as a net draws them in). (4), (5) Because he has given away fine food and drink—his hands and feet are tender and soft, and his body has seven protuberances; and both these are signs indicating that he himself also will receive fine food and drink. (6), (7), (8) Because he has freed prisoners who had been condemned to death, has helped living beings, and scrupulously abstained from taking life—his toes and fingers are long, he has broad heels, and his bodily frame is tall and straight; and these are signs indicating that he will have a long life. (9), (10) Because he has cultivated wholesome dharmas and taken hold of them, and because they continue to grow, and never diminish—his feet have inconspicuous ankle joints, and the hairs of his body point upwards; these being signs that he will be endowed with a Dharma and Vinaya which he will never lose again. (11) Because he has honoured others by bestowing upon them (the knowledge of) crafts, sciences, actions (etc.), after he has first learned them himself—his shanks are like those of the black antelope; and this is a sign indicating that he will quickly learn them again. (12) Because he had given all the wealth which was his to those who asked for it, and never refused anyone—his arms and legs are long and powerful; and that is a sign that he will have sovereignty over the donations and the discipline. (13) Because he did not separate those friends, relatives, and kinsmen who were united in amity, urged those beings who lived apart (from their families) to lead a chaste life, and because he has guarded the secret mantras—his male organ is hidden in a sheath; and this signifies that he will have a great many (spiritual) sons. (14), (15) Because he has given away fine coverlets, cloaks, and undergarments, as well as palatial buildings and stately houses—his skin has a golden hue, and is quite smooth; both these signify that he will be the recipient of such fine coverlets, cloaks, and undergarments, palatial buildings, mansions, and stately houses. (16), (17) Because he has avoided society, and because he has suitably served upon his spiritual superiors, such as his preceptors, teachers, parents, and so on, has shown respect to them, and has not scorned their advice—the hairs on his body stand separately by themselves, curling to the right, and his face is adorned with a hairtuft; these being signs indicating that he is without an equal. (18), (19) Because his speech has not been scurrilous or deprecatory, but kind and helpful, and because his well-spoken words conformed (to the needs of his listeners)—the upper half of his body is like that of a lion, and his shoulders are gently curved; and these are signs which indicate that he cannot be obstructed. (20), (21) Because he has freely bestowed upon the sick drugs, help, and medical treatment, as well as suitable foods, and has attended to their needs—the flesh in between his shoulder blades is quite compact, and he possesses a most excellent taste; this signifies that he will be rarely oppressed by sickness. (22), (23) Because in the past he has encouraged others to construct pleasure groves, assembly halls, parks, ponds, bridges leading to inaccessible places, refectories, pavilions, dams, monasteries, etc. and because he has himself also given away all these things to an extraordinary extent—the circumference of his figure is like that of the fig-tree, and there is a cowl on his head; and this indicates that he will win overlordship. (24), (25) Because he has for a long time spoken with a soft, kind, and sweet voice—his tongue is long and slender, and he has a divine voice; and these two presage the acquisition of a voice which has five qualities, i.e. it is intelligible and distinct, delightful and nonrepugnant when being heard, deep and resonant, clear and pleasant to the ear, skilful and unconfused. (26) Because for a long time he has refrained from idle talk, and has spoken in due season—he has jaws like a lion; and that is a sign indicating that his words will always be acceptable. (27), (28) Because he has respected others and felt no undue sense of pride, and because his mode of livelihood has been perfectly pure—his teeth are very white, and equal in size; and that is a sign that he has built up his retinue in the past. (29), (30) Because for a long time he has habitually spoken the truth and never slandered anyone—there are no gaps between his teeth, and he has a total of 40 equal teeth; and this indicates that he will have a retinue which cannot be broken up. (31), (32) Because, as one whose mind was mature and who never rejected anyone, he has viewed people with an eye free from passion, hate, and delusion—he now has eyes which are intensely black, and his eyelashes are like those of a magnificent heifer, and that presages the fact that he will in every way be lovely to behold.

These are the 32 marks of the superman. The Tathagata's body, Subhuti, is endowed with these 32 marks of a superman.

The Eighty Accessory Marks

And what, Subhuti, are the eighty accessory marks of a Tathagata? (1) The Buddhas, the Lords, have copper-coloured nails because their minds are free from passion *(virakta)* with regard to all conditioned things. (2) The Buddhas, the Lords, have glossy *(snigdha)* nails because their minds are intent on the happiness and welfare of all beings, as if they were their own beloved *(snigdha)* relatives. (3) The Buddhas, the Lords, have elevated *(tuṅga)* nails because they are the offspring of a lineage marked by superior *(tuṅga)* merit. (4) Their toes and fingers are rounded *(vṛtta)* because their conduct *(vṛttam)* is faultless. (5) Their toes and fingers are compact because they have accumulated (535a) extensive wholesome roots. (6) Their toes and fingers are tapering because they have gradually stored up their wholesome roots. (7) Their veins do not bulge out (*gūḍha*) because their work and life—by body, voice, and mind—has been well hidden *(su-nigūḍha)*, (by their living apart in solitude). (8) Their veins are free from knots because they have broken up the knots of the defilements. (9) Their anklebones do not bulge out because they have understood the well-hidden Dharma. (10) Their feet are not unequal *(avishama)* in size because they have finished with all difficulties *(vishama)*. (11) They walk with the stride of lions because they are lions among men. (12) They walk with the stride of elephants because they are elephants among men. (13) They move in the manner of geese because, like the royal goose, they can fly through the air. (14) They walk with the stride of a lordly bull because they are bulls among men. (15) They walk while turning to the right because their path is worthy of respect. (16) They walk elegantly *(cāru)* because they are beautiful *(cāru)* to behold. (17) Their bodies are upright because their minds are constantly straight. (18) Their limbs are well-rounded because they proclaim the virtues of pure conduct. (19) Their limbs are smooth *(mṛṣṭa)* because they have polished away *(pramṛṣṭa)* all evil. (20) Their limbs are slender *(anupūrva)* because they demonstrate dharma gradually *(anupūrva)*. (21) Their limbs are clean because they are endowed with cleanliness of body, voice, and mind. (22) Their limbs are soft because their minds are in their own-being soft. (23) Their limbs are pure because their minds are in their own-being pure. (24) Their genitals are fully developed because they have well fulfilled the Dharma and Vinaya. (25) Their knee-orbs are large and beautiful because they have proclaimed the virtues which are large and beautiful. (26) They walk at an even pace because they have even thoughts toward all beings. (27) Their eyes are pure because they are most pure to behold. (28) Their bodies are ever youthful because they demonstrate the ever youthful dharma (29) Their bodies are unimpaired (by any defects), *(adīna)*, because their minds are constantly undejected *(adīna)*. (30) His body has prominences *(utsada)* because his unwholesome roots have completely vanished *(utsanna)*. (31) Their bodies are firm and solid because the extinction of their rebirth is assured. (32) All their limbs are well-proportioned because they have well shown all the limbs of conditioned coproduction. (33) The pure light (which emanates from their bodies) dispels the darkness, because they are most pure to behold. (34) Their bellies are round, because they have pupils whose conduct is perfect. (35) Their bellies are smooth, because they have emerged from the faults of Samsara. (36) Their bellies are unmarked, because their horns are broken off. (37) Their bellies do not hang down, because they have caused people to turn back on the extinction of Dharma. (38) Their navels are deep, because they have penetrated the foremost deep dharmas. (39) Their navels are twisted to the right, because their pupils learn in the right way. (40) From all sides they are beautiful to behold, because they have a community consisting of pupils who are beautiful to behold. (41) Their habits are clean, because their minds are supremely clean. (42) Their bodies are free from black moles, because their Dharma and Vinaya are free from black doctrines. (43) Their hands are soft like cotton wool, because with a body light as cotton wool they demonstrate the Dharma. (44) The lines on their hands are fresh, because by their love for their own people and for people in general they gladden the great Disciples. (45) The lines on their hands are deep, because they are firmly established in what is foremost and deep. (46) The lines on their hands are extensive, because they have proclaimed a Dharma of vast patience. (47) Their faces are not too long, because they have drawn up a code of moral training which is not excessive. (48) Their lips are (red) like the Bimba berry, because they have got rid of all the worlds as if they were a reflected image *(pratibimba)*. (49) Their tongues are supple, because they have been gentle leaders in the past. (50) Their tongues are slender, because they have been reborn with abundant virtues. (51) Their tongues are red *(rakta)*, because they have disciplined passionate *(rakta)* common people in the Dharma which is hard to fathom. (52) Their voices are deep, like thunder, because they have remained unafraid when they have heard the rumblings of thunder. (53) The sound of their voices is sweet, beautiful and soft, because they have pupils who discourse in sweet, beautiful and soft voices. (54) Their eye-teeth are round, because they have transcended the fetters of becoming. (55) Their eye-teeth are sharp, because they are skilled in disciplining people of keen intelligence. (56) Their eye-teeth are very white, because their Dharma and Vinaya are extremely pure. (57) Their eye-teeth are equal (in size), because they are established in an equal share of the Stages. (58) Their eye-teeth are regular *(anupūrva)*, because they have demonstrated the gradual *(anupūrva)* re-union. (59) Their noses are prominent, because they stand on the prominent mountain of wisdom. (60) Their noses are clean, because they give rise to purity in the persons to be disciplined. (61) Their eyes are very large, because the Buddhadharmas are extremely large. (62) Their eyelashes are well-developed, because the hosts of beings around them are exceedingly numerous. (63) Their eyes are (white and dark-blue) like the petals of the (blue) lotus, because, like the petals of the blue lotus, they are welcomed by gods and Asuras, by men and by beautiful young women. (64) Their eyebrows are extensive, because they always appear to be stately and dignified. (65) Their eyebrows are smooth, because they are skilled in the unsullied Vinaya. (66) Their eyebrows have hairs of equal *(sama)* length, because they have known all faults from every side *(samantā)*. (67) Their eyebrows are glossy, because they have lovingly disciplined beings...(68) Their arms are long and muscular, because they possess the Dharma which is extensive and full of meaning.

(69) Their two ears are equal in size, because they have won all their battles. (70) Their ability to hear is not impaired in any way, because their disciplining of beings is not impaired in any way. (71) Their foreheads are unwrinkled, because they are no longer subject to anything that leads to false views. (72) Their foreheads are broad, because they have crushed all the false teachers, be they Shramanas or Brahmins. (73) Their heads are large, because they have well fulfilled their supreme vows. (74) The hair of their heads is (as dark) as a black bee, because they have turned away from the delight in the humming of the sense-objects. (75) The hair of their heads is thick, because they have laid aside the latent tendencies which should be forsaken with regard to vision and development. (76) The hair of their heads is smooth, because with their smooth intellects they have cognized the core of the religion. (77) The hair of their heads is not shaggy, because their minds are never disarranged. (78) The hair of their heads is not rough, because they never speak harshly. (79) The hair of their heads has a fragrant smell (which captivates of hearts of men), because they are men who have turned to the wings of enlightenment, which are like fragrant flowers. (80) They have the Srivatsa sign and the Svastika on the palms of their hands and the soles of their feet, because their hands and feet are adorned with them.

These are called the 80 accessory marks. With these 80 accessory marks does the Tathagata become endowed. It is thus, Subhuti, that one should know the Dharma-gift of the Bodhisattva, the great being. (T only:) Subhuti, to teach these modes of dharma to others, to demonstrate them, to reveal them, that is called the 'gift of the supramundane dharma'. Subhuti, it is thus that the Bodhisattva, the great being, gives both the material gifts and the gift of the Dharma. This, Subhuti, is the wonderful and astonishing dharma of the Bodhisattvas, the great beings. (II) And how does the Bodhisattva, the great being, help beings with kind words? There, Subhuti, the Bodhisattva, the great being, establishes beings in the six perfections, i.e. the perfection of giving, etc. Speaking kind words the Bodhisattva, the great being, establishes beings in the six perfections. And why? Because in these six perfections all wholesome dharmas are contained. It is thus that the Bodhisattva, the great being, helps beings by speaking kind words to them. (III) And how does the Bodhisattva, the great being, help beings by acting for their benefit? Here the Bodhisattva, the great being, helps beings by acting for their benefit through the six perfections. And why? Because in these six perfections all wholesome dharmas are contained. It is thus that the Bodhisattva, the great being, helps beings by acting for their benefit. (IV) And how, Subhuti, does the Bodhisattva, the great being, help beings by consistency between words and deeds? Here, Subhuti, the Bodhisattva, the great being, has first himself conformed to the meaning of the six perfections, and then he establishes beings in them. And why? Because in these six perfections all the wholesome dharmas are contained. It is thus, Subhuti, that the Bodhisattva, the great being, helps beings by the consistency between his words and deeds. This also, Subhuti, is the wonderful and astonishing dharma of the Bodhisattvas, the great beings.

Numerical Lists

3 jewels *(ratna)*: Buddha, Dharma, Samgha.

3 dominants *(indriya)*, supramundane: "I shall come to understand the not yet understood", understanding, "one who has understood".

3 doors to deliverance *(vimoksha-dvāra)*; emptiness, signlessness, wishlessness.

3 kinds of knowledge (lore) *(vidyā)* = last three of 6 superknowledges.

3 roots of evil: greed, hate, delusion.

3 worlds (planes): sense desire, form, formlessness.

4 Aids to Penetration *(nirvedha-bhāgiya)*: Heat, Summits, Steadfastness, Supreme worldly dharmas.

4 Analytical knowledges *(pratisamvid)*: of meaning, dharmas, languages, ready speech.

4 Applications of Mindfulness *(smṛty-upasthāna)*: to body, feelings, thought, dharmas. See *P* 203-207.

4 bases of psychic power *(ṛddhi-pāda)*, see *P* 207.

4 bonds *(grantha)*: covetousness, ill will, contagion of mere rule and ritual, religious fanaticism. (So *V.M.* 683).

4 floods *(ogha)*: greed for sense objects, greed for becoming, wrong views, ignorance.

4 formless attainments *(ārūpya-samāpatti)*: endless space, infinite consciousness, nothing whatever, neither perception nor nonperception.

4 graspings *(upādāna)*: at sense objects, wrong views, mere rule and ritual, the word "self".

4 grounds of self-confidence *(vaiśāradya)*. see *P* 211.

4 holy truths *(ārya-satya)*: suffering, origination of suffering, stopping of suffering, path that leads to the stopping of suffering.

4 means of conversion *(saṃgraha-vastu)*: giving, kind words, helpfulness, consistency between words and deeds.

4 outflows *(āsrava)*: sense desire, becoming, ignorance, views.

4 pairs of men: = 8 holy persons.

4 Paths *(mārga)*: Streamwinner, Once-returner, Never-returner. Arhat.

4 perverted views *(viparyāsa)*: one mistakes the impermanent for the permanent, ill for ease, the not-self for the self, the repulsive for the lovely.

4 right efforts *(saṃyak-prahāṇa)*, see *P* 207.

4 stations of Brahman: = 4 Unlimited.

4 trances *(dhyāna)*: first, second, third, fourth. See *P* 210.

4 Unlimited *(apramāṇa)*: friendliness, compassion, sympathetic joy, even-mindedness.

5 Aids to salvation *(moksha-bhāgīya)* = 5 dominants.

5 destinies *(gati)*: gods, men, animals, ghosts, beings in the hells.

5 dominants *(indriya)*, or cardinal virtues: faith, vigour, mindfulness, concentration, wisdom.

5 eyes: fleshly, heavenly, wisdom—, Dharma—, Buddha—. See *P* 77-83.

5 hindrances *(nīvaraṇa)*: sense desire, ill will, sloth and torpor, excitedness and sense of guilt, doubt.

5 limbs of trance *(dhyānāngāni)*: thoughts adjusted, thoughts discoursing, zest, ease, one-pointedness of thought.

The 5 main divisions of the Path :

Disciples and Pratyeka-buddhas	The Path	Bodhisattvas
Worldly Dominated by faith 1. Stage of bright insight	A. The Path of Equipment with merit 5 Aids to salvation	Stage of beginner. Production of thought of enlightenment
Dominated by resolve 2. Stage of becoming one of the clan	B. The Path of methodical training. 4 Aids to Penetration Unimpeded concentration.	
Supramundane 3. Eighth-lowest stage. 1st Path 4. Stage of Vision. Ist Fruit.	C. The Path of Vision 16 moments	1st stage
5. Stage of refinement. 2nd Fruit. 6. Stage of dispassion. 3rd Fruit.	D. The Path of Development Adamantine concentration.	2nd stage. 3rd-9th stage. Instantaneous re-union.
	The Fruit.	
All-knowledge. 7. The stage of one who has done. Arhatship. 4th fruit. Cognition of extinction and of nonproduction.	E. The Path of the Adept (The Path of Deliverance).	The knowledge of all modes. 10th stage. A Buddha with his fourfold body.

5 powers *(bala)* = 5 dominants.

5 precepts : do not take life; do not take what is not given; no sexual misconduct; no false speech; no intoxicants.

5 skandhas : form, feelings, perceptions, impulses, consciousness.

6 destinies : as 5 destinies + Asuras.

6 elements *(dhātu)*, physical : earth, water, fire, air (wind), space (ether), consciousness.

6 perfections *(pāramitā)* : giving, morality, patience, vigour, concentration, wisdom.

6 superknowledges *(abhijñā)* : psychic power, heavenly ear, cognition of others' thoughts, recollection of past lives, heavenly eye, cognition of the extinction of the outflows. See *P* 83-89.

7 limbs of enlightenment *(bodhyaṅga)* : mindfulness, investigation into dharmas, vigour, joyous zest, tranquillity, concentration, evenmindedness.

7 prizes *(dhana)* : faith, morality, sense of shame, dread of blame, learning, renunciation, wisdom.

8 deliverances *(vimoksha)* : See *P* 210.

8 discoursings (reasonings, *vitarka*) of the Superman : see Sten Konow p. 84.

8 great personages := 8 holy persons.

8 holy persons *(ārya-pudgala)* : see the Roman numerals at the 20 kinds of Saints.

8 -fold Path *(mārga)* : right views, intentions, speech, conduct, livelihood, effort, mindfulness, concentration.

8 precepts on the Sabbath: 5 precepts plus not eating at wrong times, avoiding wordly amusements, using neither unguents nor ornaments. See *A.N.* IV 248 sq. about the *aṭṭangasamannāgata uposatha.*

8 Stations of Mastery (Bases of Overcoming), *(abhibhv-āyatana)* : see Sten Konow no. 41. Mhvy. 1520-27.

9 attainments of successive stations *(anupūrva-vihāra-samāpatti)* : 4 trances+4 formless attainments+trance of cessation of perception and feeling.

9 kinds of repulsiveness := 9 unlovely perceptions.

9 unlovely perceptions *(aśubha-samjñā)*; see *P* 19-20, 165.

10 All-Bases *(kṛtsnāyatana)* : earth device, water, fire, wind, space, blue, yellow, red, white, consciousness.

10 fetters *(saṃyojana)* : view of individuality, contagion of mere rule and ritual, doubts, greed for sensuous passions, greed for the form world, greed for the formless world, ill will, excitedness, conceit, ignorance.

10 perfections: The 6 perfections+skill in means, vow, power, cognition.

10 powers *(bala)* of a Tathagata: see *P* 210.

10 recollections *(anusmṛti)* : Buddha, Dharma, Samgha, morality, renunciation, gods, breathing, agitation, death, concerning the body; see *P* 505-7.

10 stages *(bhūmi)* : see *P* 214-225.

10 unwholesome karma-paths (ways of action) *(akuśala-karma-patha)* : taking life, taking what is not given, sexual misconduct, false speech, slander, harsh speech, frivolous talk, covetousness, ill will, wrong views.

10 wholesome karma-paths (ways of action): Abstention from the 10 unwholesome ways of action.

11 cognitious *(jñāna)* : see *P* 208-9.

12 ascetic practices *(dhutaguṇa)* : forest dweller, begs his food from door to door, wears clothes made of rags from dust heaps, never eats after mid-day, eats his meal in one sitting, lives on alms-food, lives in cemeteries, lives in an open unsheltered place, dwells at the foot of a tree, even in his sleep he remains in a sitting posture, sleeps at night wherever he may happen to be, possesses no more than three robes.

12 links of conditioned coproduction: ignorance, karma formations, consciousness, name and form, six (inner and outer) sense fields, contact, feelings, craving, grasping, becoming, birth, decay and death.

12 sense fields *(āyatana)* : eye, sight objects; ear, sounds; nose, smells; tongue, tastes; body, touchables; mind, mind objects.

16 aspects *(ākāra)* of the four holy Truths: impermanent, ill, empty, impersonal; cause, origination, product, condition; stopping, calm quietude, sublime, definite escape; the path, correct method, progress, factor of release.

16 moments *(kshaṇa)* of the Path of Vision: 1. Acceptance of cognition of dharma in suffering; 2. cognition of dharma in suffering; 3. Acceptance of subsequent cognition in suffering; 4. subsequent cognition in suffering. The same: 5-8 with "origination", 9-12 with "stopping", 13-16 with "the path".

18 elements *(dhātu)* :

sight organ.	sight object.	sight consciousness.
ear.	sounds.	ear consciousness.
nose.	smells.	nose consciousness.
tongue.	tastes.	tongue consciousness.

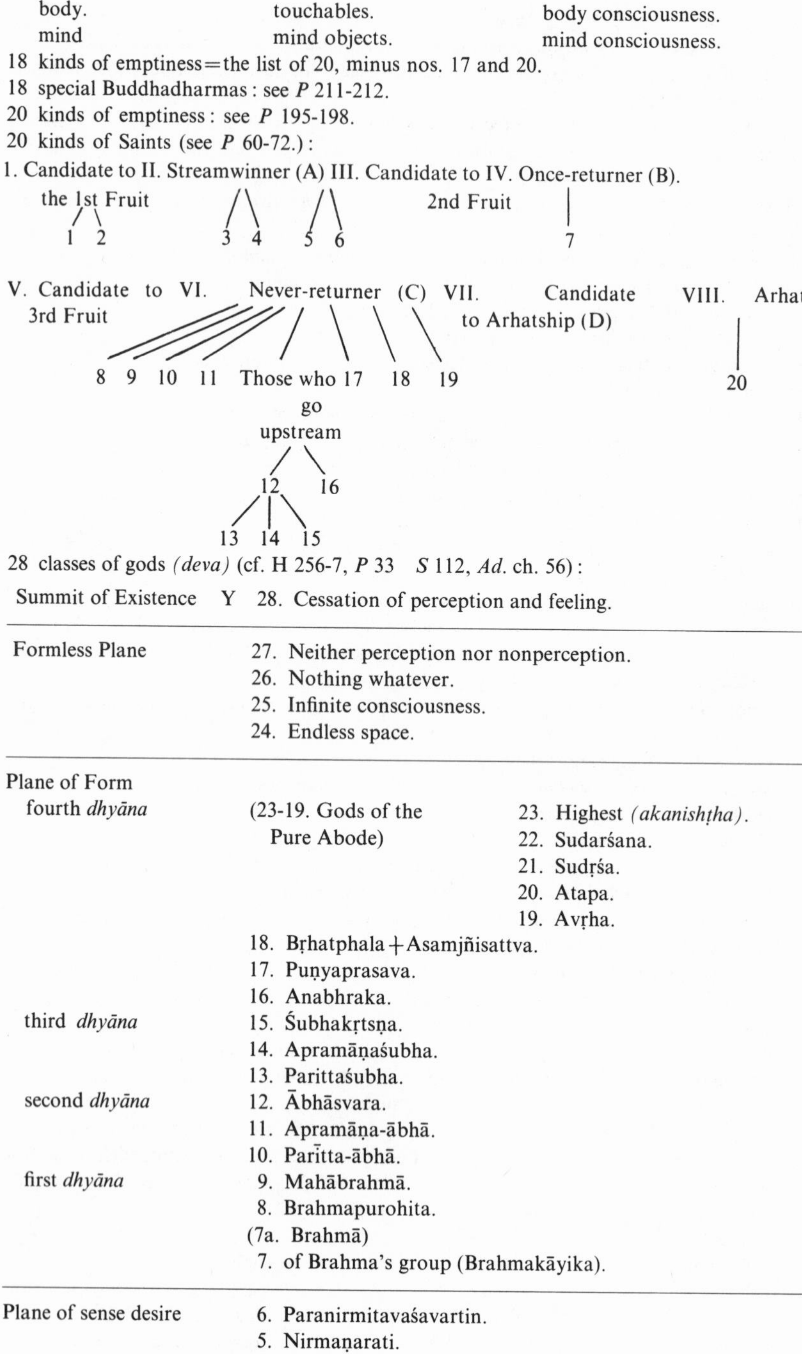

body.	touchables.	body consciousness.
mind	mind objects.	mind consciousness.

18 kinds of emptiness = the list of 20, minus nos. 17 and 20.

18 special Buddhadharmas: see *P* 211-212.

20 kinds of emptiness: see *P* 195-198.

20 kinds of Saints (see *P* 60-72.):

1. Candidate to the 1st Fruit → 1, 2; II. Streamwinner (A) → 3, 4; III. Candidate to 2nd Fruit → 5, 6; IV. Once-returner (B) → 7.

V. Candidate to 3rd Fruit; VI. Never-returner (C) → 8, 9, 10, 11, Those who go upstream, 17, 18, 19; VII. Candidate to Arhatship (D); VIII. Arhat → 20.

Those who go upstream → 12, 16; 12 → 13, 14, 15.

28 classes of gods *(deva)* (cf. H 256-7, *P* 33 *S* 112, *Ad.* ch. 56):

Summit of Existence Y 28. Cessation of perception and feeling.

Formless Plane

27. Neither perception nor nonperception.
26. Nothing whatever.
25. Infinite consciousness.
24. Endless space.

Plane of Form

fourth *dhyāna*

(23-19. Gods of the Pure Abode)

23. Highest *(akanishṭha)*.
22. Sudarśana.
21. Sudṛśa.
20. Atapa.
19. Avṛha.

18. Bṛhatphala + Asamjñisattva.
17. Puṇyaprasava.
16. Anabhraka.

third *dhyāna*

15. Śubhakṛtsṇa.
14. Apramāṇaśubha.
13. Parittaśubha.

second *dhyāna*

12. Ābhāsvara.
11. Apramāṇa-ābhā.
10. Paritta-ābhā.

first *dhyāna*

9. Mahābrahmā.
8. Brahmapurohita.

(7a. Brahmā)

7. of Brahma's group (Brahmakāyika).

Plane of sense desire

6. Paranirmitavaśavartin.
5. Nirmaṇarati.

4. Tushita.
3. Yāma.
2. The Gods of the Thirty-three.
1. The four Great Kings.

32 marks of a superman *(mahāpurusha-lakshaṇa)*: see *P* 533-534.

37 wings of enlightenment *(bodhi-paksha)*: 4 applications of mindfulness, 4 right efforts, 4 bases of psychic power, 5 dominants, 5 powers, 7 limbs of enlightenment, 8 limbs of the Path.

80 minor (accessory) characteristics *(anuvyañjana)* of a superman: see *P* 535-536.

INDEX